# Communications
# in Computer and Information Science    1826

## Editorial Board Members

### Rationale

The CCIS series is devoted to the publication of proceedings of computer science conferences. Its aim is to efficiently disseminate original research results in informatics in printed and electronic form. While the focus is on publication of peer-reviewed full papers presenting mature work, inclusion of reviewed short papers reporting on work in progress is welcome, too. Besides globally relevant meetings with internationally representative program committees guaranteeing a strict peer-reviewing and paper selection process, conferences run by societies or of high regional or national relevance are also considered for publication.

### Topics

The topical scope of CCIS spans the entire spectrum of informatics ranging from foundational topics in the theory of computing to information and communications science and technology and a broad variety of interdisciplinary application fields.

### Information for Volume Editors and Authors

Publication in CCIS is free of charge. No royalties are paid, however, we offer registered conference participants temporary free access to the online version of the conference proceedings on SpringerLink (http://link.springer.com) by means of an http referrer from the conference website and/or a number of complimentary printed copies, as specified in the official acceptance email of the event.

CCIS proceedings can be published in time for distribution at conferences or as post-proceedings, and delivered in the form of printed books and/or electronically as USBs and/or e-content licenses for accessing proceedings at SpringerLink. Furthermore, CCIS proceedings are included in the CCIS electronic book series hosted in the SpringerLink digital library at http://link.springer.com/bookseries/7899. Conferences publishing in CCIS are allowed to use Online Conference Service (OCS) for managing the whole proceedings lifecycle (from submission and reviewing to preparing for publication) free of charge.

### Publication process

The language of publication is exclusively English. Authors publishing in CCIS have to sign the Springer CCIS copyright transfer form, however, they are free to use their material published in CCIS for substantially changed, more elaborate subsequent publications elsewhere. For the preparation of the camera-ready papers/files, authors have to strictly adhere to the Springer CCIS Authors' Instructions and are strongly encouraged to use the CCIS LaTeX style files or templates.

### Abstracting/Indexing

CCIS is abstracted/indexed in DBLP, Google Scholar, EI-Compendex, Mathematical Reviews, SCImago, Scopus. CCIS volumes are also submitted for the inclusion in ISI Proceedings.

### How to start

To start the evaluation of your proposal for inclusion in the CCIS series, please send an e-mail to ccis@springer.com.

Lazaros Iliadis · Ilias Maglogiannis ·
Serafin Alonso · Chrisina Jayne · Elias Pimenidis
Editors

# Engineering Applications of Neural Networks

24th International Conference, EAAAI/EANN 2023
León, Spain, June 14–17, 2023
Proceedings

 Springer

*Editors*
Lazaros Iliadis ⓘ
Democritus University of Thrace
Xanthi, Greece

Serafin Alonso ⓘ
University of Leon
León, Spain

Elias Pimenidis ⓘ
University of the West of England
Bristol, UK

Ilias Maglogiannis ⓘ
University of Piraeus
Piraeus, Greece

Chrisina Jayne ⓘ
Teesside University
Middlesbrough, UK

ISSN 1865-0929        ISSN 1865-0937 (electronic)
Communications in Computer and Information Science
ISBN 978-3-031-34203-5        ISBN 978-3-031-34204-2 (eBook)
https://doi.org/10.1007/978-3-031-34204-2

This Springer imprint is published by the registered company Springer Nature Switzerland AG
The registered company address is: Gewerbestrasse 11, 6330 Cham, Switzerland

# Preface

In the 21st century, Neural Network (NN) algorithms are still offering robust models, as they constitute the real core of Deep Learning. They have been employed by Machine Learning Engineers for decades, trying to model real-world problems in various domains, such as Image and Speech Recognition, Natural Language Processing, and many more. *ChatGPT* uses a Deep Learning architecture called the *Transformer* to generate human-like text. It is a typical case of how NNs' applications can have a deep impact on our post-modern societies. There are numerous architectures of neural networks employing specific Learning algorithms trying to solve real-life problems. Recent advances such as *Generative Adversarial* Neural Networks try to fuse "imagination" to Artificial Intelligence (AI), and *Convolutional Neural Networks* significantly contribute to the enhancement of pattern recognition, machine translation, anomaly-detection, and machine vision. *Generative Neural Networks* are capable of generating image datasets, realistic photographs of human faces, cartoon characters, Image to Image Translation, Face Aging, Photos to Emojis, Photo Blending, and Super Resolution, and they can even calculate the distance between different objects.

*The Engineering Applications of Neural Networks conference is a historical one, having a life of more than 2 decades in the literature. Following the cataclysmic technological revolution, it is gradually evolving and becoming broader, in order to embrace all AI aspects and achievements. In the next 2 years it is going to become the EAAAI (Engineering Applications and Advances in Artificial Intelligence/ex-EANN).* In this sense, the conference Steering Committee aims to bring together scientists from all AI domains and to give them the chance to exchange ideas and to announce their achievements.

Since the first conference in 1995, EANN has provided a great discussion forum on engineering applications of all Artificial Intelligence technologies, focusing on Artificial Neural Networks. More specifically, EANN promotes the use of modeling techniques from all subdomains of AI in diverse application areas, where significant benefits can be derived. The conference also reports advances in theoretical AI aspects. Thus, both innovative applications and methods are particularly appreciated.

EAAAI/EANN is a mature and well-established international scientific conference held in Europe. Its history is long and very successful, following and spreading the evolution of Intelligent Systems.

The first EANN event was organized in Otaniemi, Finland, in 1995. Since then, it has had a continuous and dynamic presence as a major global, but mainly European, scientific event. More specifically, it has been organized in Finland, UK, Sweden, Gibraltar, Poland, Italy, Spain, France, Bulgaria, Greece, and Spain. It has been technically supported by the International Neural Networks Society (INNS) and more specifically by the EANN/EAAAI Special Interest Group.

This is the Proceedings volume, and it belongs to Springer's CCIS (Communications in Computer and Information Science) Series. It contains the papers that were accepted to be presented orally at the 24th EANN conference in León, Spain. The diverse nature of the papers presented demonstrates the vitality of Artificial Intelligence algorithms and approaches. The conference is not only related to Neural Networks, but it certainly provides a very wide forum for AI applications as well.

The event was held in a hybrid mode (both physically and remotely attended via Webex) from the 14th to the 17th of June, 2023.

In total, 125 papers were initially submitted. All papers were peer reviewed by at least two independent academic referees. Where needed, a third referee was consulted to resolve any potential conflicts. A total of 39% of the submitted manuscripts (49 papers) have been accepted to be published in the Springer proceedings.

**Algorithms and Areas of Research:**

The accepted papers of the 24th EANN conference are related to the following thematic topics:

Learning
Reinforcement Learning
Federated Learning
Adversarial Learning Neural Networks
Machine Learning
Transfer Learning
Natural Language
Recommendation Systems
Classification
Filtering
Genetic Algorithms
Computational Methods
Ethology
Complex Dynamic Networks
Optimization – Genetic Algorithms
Graph Neural Networks
Convolutional Neural Networks
Spiking Neural Networks
Deep Learning
Learning in Engineering Applications

The following scientific workshop on a hot AI-related subject was organized under the framework of the 24th EANN.

WORKSHOPS ORGANIZATION

- The 3rd Workshop on AI and Ethics (AIETH 2023)

   Coordinator: Professor John Macintyre
   The 3rd AIETH workshop was coordinated and organized by Professor John Macintyre (University of Sunderland, UK). It included short presentations from the panel members and an open Q&A session where the audience members were able to ask, and answer, important questions about the current and future development of Generative

AI models. It aimed to emphasize the need for responsible global AI. The respective scientific community must be preparing to act preemptively and ensure that our societies will avoid negative effects of AI and of the 4th Industrial Revolution in general.

The authors of submitted papers came from **19** different countries from all over the globe (from 3 continents: Europe, Asia, Americas) namely: Austria, Brazil, Canada, China, Germany, Greece, Honduras, Italy, Japan, Sweden, Kuwait, Lebanon, The Netherlands, Pakistan, Poland, Portugal, Saudi Arabia, Spain, the UK, and the USA.

June 2023

Lazaros Iliadis
Ilias Maglogiannis
Serafin Alonso
Chrisina Jayne
Elias Pimenidis

# Organization

## General Co-chairs

John Macintyre — University of Sunderland, UK
Manuel Domínguez — Universidad de León, Spain
Ilias Maglogiannis — University of Piraeus, Greece

## Program Co-chairs

Lazaros Iliadis — Democritus University of Thrace, Greece
Serafin Alonso — Universidad de León, Spain
Chrisina Jayne — Teesside University, UK
Nikolaos Passalis — Aristotle University of Thessaloniki, Greece

## Steering Committee

Lazaros Iliadis — Democritus University of Thrace, Greece
Elias Pimenidis — University of the West of England, UK
Chrisina Jayne — Teesside University, UK

## Honorary Chairs

Nikola Kasabov — Auckland University of Technology, New Zealand
Vera Kurkova — Czech Academy of Sciences, Czech Republic

## Organizing Co-chairs

Antonios Papaleonidas — Democritus University of Thrace, Greece
Antonio Moran — University of León, Spain

## Advisory Co-chairs

George Magoulas                       Birkbeck, University of London, UK
Elias Pimenidis                           University of the West of England, UK
Paulo Cortez                              University of Minho, Portugal
Plamen Angelov                         Lancaster University, UK

## Doctoral Consortium Co-chairs

Valerio Bellandi                         Università degli Studi di Milano, Italy
Ioannis Anagnostopoulos         University of Thessaly, Greece

## Publication and Publicity Co-chairs

Antonios Papaleonidas            Democritus University of Thrace, Greece
Anastasios Panagiotis Psathas   Democritus University of Thrace, Greece

## Liaison Chair

Ioannis Chochliouros              Hellenic Telecommunications Organisation,
                                       Greece

## Workshops Co-chairs

Peter Hajek                               University of Pardubice, Czech Republic
Spyros Sioutas                         University of Patras, Greece

## Special Sessions and Tutorials Co-chairs

Luca Magri                               Politecnico di Milano, Italy

## Local Organizing/Hybrid Facilitation Committee

Anastasios Panagiotis Psathas   Democritus University of Thrace, Greece
Athanasios Kallipolitis            University of Piraeus, Greece

| | |
|---|---|
| Dionysios Koulouris | University of Piraeus, Greece |
| Guzmán González Mateos | Universidad de León, Spain |
| Héctor Alaiz Moretón | Universidad de León, Spain |
| Ioanna-Maria Erentzi | Democritus University of Thrace, Greece |
| Ioannis Skopelitis | Democritus University of Thrace, Greece |
| José Ramón Rodriguez Ossorio | Universidad de León, Spain |
| Lambros Kazelis | Democritus University of Thrace, Greece |
| Leandros Tsatsaronis | Democritus University of Thrace, Greece |
| María del Carmen Benavides Cuéllar | Universidad de León, Spain |
| Maria Teresa García Ordás | Universidad de León, Spain |
| Natalia Prieto Fernández | Universidad de León, Spain |
| Nikiforos Mpotzoris | Democritus University of Thrace, Greece |
| Nikos Zervis | Democritus University of Thrace, Greece |
| Panagiotis Restos | Democritus University of Thrace, Greece |
| Raúl González Herbón | Universidad de León, Spain |
| Tassos Giannakopoulos | Democritus University of Thrace, Greece |

## Program Committee

| | |
|---|---|
| Alexander Ryjov | Lomonosov Moscow State University, Russia |
| Aliki Stefanopoulou | CERTH, Greece |
| Anastasios Panagiotis Psathas | Democritus University of Thrace, Greece |
| Andreas Kanavos | Ionian University, Greece |
| Andreas Menychtas | University of Piraeus, Greece |
| Ángel Lareo | Universidad Autónoma de Madrid, Spain |
| Antonino Staiano | University of Naples Parthenope, Italy |
| Antonio José Serrano-López | University of Valencia, Spain |
| Antonio Morán | University of Leon, Spain |
| Antonios Kalampakas | AUM, Kuwait |
| Antonios Papaleonidas | Democritus University of Thrace, Greece |
| Aristidis Likas | University of Ioannina, Greece |
| Asimina Dimara | CERTH, Greece |
| Athanasios Alexiou | NGCEF, Australia |
| Athanasios Kallipolitis | University of Piraeus, Greece |
| Athanasios Koutras | University of the Peloponnese, Greece |
| Athanasios Tsadiras | Aristotle University of Thessaloniki, Greece |
| Boudjelal Meftah | University Mustapha Stambouli, Mascara, Algeria |
| Catalin Stoean | University of Craiova, Romania |
| Cen Wan | Birkbeck, University of London, UK |
| Christos Diou | Harokopio University of Athens, Greece |

| | |
|---|---|
| Christos Makris | University of Patras, Greece |
| Christos Timplalexis | CERTH/ITI, Greece |
| Claudio Gallicchio | University of Pisa, Italy |
| Daniel Pérez | University of Leon, Spain |
| Daniel Stamate | Goldsmiths, University of London, UK |
| Denise Gorse | University College London, UK |
| Doina Logofatu | Frankfurt University of Applied Sciences, Germany |
| Duc-Hong Pham | Vietnam National University, Hanoi, Vietnam |
| Efstratios Georgopoulos | University of the Peloponnese, Greece |
| Elias Pimenidis | University of the West of England, UK |
| Emilio Soria Olivas | University of Valencia, Spain |
| Evaggelos Spyrou | University of Thessaly, Greece |
| Fabio Pereira | Universidade Nove de Julho, Brazil |
| Florin Leon | Technical University of Iasi, Romania |
| Francesco Marcelloni | University of Pisa, Italy |
| Francisco Zamora-Martinez | Veridas Digital Authentication Solutions S.L., Spain |
| George Anastassopoulos | Democritus University of Thrace, Greece |
| George Magoulas | Birkbeck, University of London, UK |
| Georgios Alexandridis | University of the Aegean, Greece |
| Georgios Drakopoulos | Ionian University, Greece |
| Gerasimos Vonitsanos | Hellenic Open University, Greece |
| Gul Muhammad Khan | UET Peshawar, Pakistan |
| Haigen Hu | Zhejiang University of Technology, China |
| Hakan Haberdar | University of Houston, USA |
| Hassan Kazemian | London Metropolitan University, UK |
| Ignacio Díaz | University of Oviedo, Spain |
| Ioannis Chamodrakas | National and Kapodistrian University of Athens, Greece |
| Ioannis Hatzilygeroudis | University of Patras, Greece |
| Ioannis Livieris | University of Patras, Greece |
| Isidoros Perikos | University of Patras, Greece |
| Ivo Bukovsky | University of South Bohemia in České Budějovice, Czech Republic |
| Jielin Qiu | Shanghai Jiao Tong University, China |
| Jivitesh Sharma | University of Agder, Norway |
| Joan Vila-Francés | University of Valencia, Spain |
| Jose Maria Enguita | University of Oviedo, Spain |
| Juan Jose Fuertes | University of Leon, Spain |
| Katia Lida Kermanidis | Ionian University, Greece |
| Kazuyuki Hara | Nihon University, Japan |

| | |
|---|---|
| Kleanthis Malialis | University of Cyprus, Cyprus |
| Konstantinos Demertzis | Democritus University of Thrace, Greece |
| Konstantinos Moutselos | University of Piraeus, Greece |
| Kostas Karatzas | Aristotle University of Thessaloniki, Greece |
| Kostas Karpouzis | ICCS-NTUA, Greece |
| Kostas Votis | CERTH, Greece |
| Lazaros Iliadis | Democritus University of Thrace, Greece |
| Lei Shi | Durham University, UK |
| Leon Bobrowski | Bialystok University of Technology, Poland |
| Lluís Belanche | Univ. Politècnica de Catalunya, Spain |
| Luca Oneto | University of Genoa, Italy |
| Manuel Domínguez Gonzalez | Universidad de León, Spain |
| Mario Malcangi | Università degli Studi di Milano, Italy |
| Michel Aldanondo | IMT Mines Albi, France |
| Miguel Ángel Prada | Universidad de León, Spain |
| Mikko Kolehmainen | University of Eastern Finland, Finland |
| Mirjana Ivanovic | University of Novi Sad, Serbia |
| Neslihan Serap Sengor | Istanbul Technical University, Turkey |
| Nikolaos Mitianoudis | Democritus University of Thrace, Greece |
| Nikolaos Passalis | Aristotle University of Thessaloniki, Greece |
| Nikolaos Polatidis | University of Brighton, UK |
| Nikos Kanakaris | University of Patras, Greece |
| Nikos Karacapilidis | University of Patras, Greece |
| Panagiotis Pintelas | University of Patras, Greece |
| Paraskevas Koukaras | Centre for Research and Technology Hellas, Greece |
| Paulo Cortez | University of Minho, Portugal |
| Paulo Vitor Campos Souza | CEFET-MG, Brazil |
| Petia Koprinkova-Hristova | Bulgarian Academy of Sciences, Bulgaria |
| Petr Hajek | University of Pardubice, Czech Republic |
| Petra Vidnerová | Czech Academy of Sciences, Czech Republic |
| Petros Kefalas | University of Sheffield International Faculty, Greece |
| Phivos Mylonas | National Technical University of Athens, Greece |
| Raffaele Giancarlo | University of Palermo, Italy |
| Riccardo Rizzo | National Research Council of Italy, Italy |
| Ruggero Labati | Università degli Studi di Milano, Italy |
| Salvatore Aiello | Politecnico di Torino, Italy |
| Samira Maghool | University of Milan, Italy |
| Sebastian Otte | University of Tübingen, Germany |
| Serafin Alonso | University of Leon, Spain |

| | |
|---|---|
| Sergey Dolenko | D.V. Skobeltsyn Institute of Nuclear Physics, M.V. Lomonosov Moscow State University, Russia |
| Shareeful Islam | Anglia Ruskin University, UK |
| Simone Bonechi | University of Siena, Italy |
| Sotiris Kotsiantis | University of Patras, Greece |
| Sotiris Koussouris | Suite5 Data Intelligence Solutions Ltd., Cyprus |
| Spiros Likothanassis | University of Patras, Greece |
| Spyros Sioutas | University of Patras, Greece |
| Stefanos Kollias | University of Lincoln, UK |
| Stefanos Nikiforos | Ionian University, Greece |
| Stelios Krinidis | International Hellenic University (IHU), Greece |
| Vaios Papaioannou | University of Patras, Greece |
| Vasileios Mezaris | CERTH, Greece |
| Vilson Luiz Dalle Mole | UTFPR, Brazil |
| Will Serrano | University College London, UK |
| Wilmuth Müller | Fraunhofer IOSB, Germany |
| Xin-She Yang | Middlesex University London, UK |
| Ziad Doughan | Beirut Arab University, Lebanon |

# Abstracts of Invited Talks

# Evolutionary Neural Architecture Search: Computational Efficiency, Privacy Preservation and Robustness Enhancement

Yaochu Jin

Bielefeld University, Germany and Distinguished Chair,
University of Surrey

**Abstract:** Evolutionary neural architecture search has received considerable attention in deep learning. This talk begins with a presentation of computationally efficient evolutionary neural architecture search algorithms by means of sampled training and partial weight sharing. Then, we introduce communication-efficient deep neural architecture search in a federated learning environment. Finally, a surrogate-assisted evolutionary search algorithm for neural architectures that are robust to adversarial attacks is described. The talk is concluded with a brief discussion of open questions for future research.

# Interpretable-by-Design Prototype-Based Deep Learning

Plamen Angelov

Lancaster University, UK

**Abstract:** Deep Learning justifiably attracted the attention and interest of the scientific community and industry as well as of the wider society and even policy makers. However, the predominant architectures (from Convolutional Neural Networks to Transformers) are hyper-parametric models with weights/parameters being detached from the physical meaning of the object of modelling. They are, essentially, embedded functions of functions which do provide the power of deep learning; however, they are also the main reason of diminished transparency and difficulties in explaining and interpreting the decisions made by deep neural network classifiers. Some dub this "black box" approach. This makes problematic the use of such algorithms in high stake complex problems such as aviation, health, bailing from jail, etc. where the clear rationale for a particular decision is very important and the errors are very costly. This motivated researchers and regulators to focus efforts on the quest for "explainable" yet highly efficient models. Most of the solutions proposed in this direction so far are, however, post-hoc and only partially addressing the problem. At the same time, it is remarkable that humans learn in a principally different manner (by examples, using similarities) and not by fitting (hyper-) parametric models, and can easily perform the so-called "zero-shot learning". Current deep learning is focused primarily on accuracy and overlooks explainability, the semantic meaning of the internal model representation, reasoning and decision making, and its link with the specific problem domain. Once trained, such models are inflexible to new knowledge. They cannot dynamically evolve their internal structure to start recognising new classes. They are good only for what they were originally trained for. The empirical results achieved by these types of methods according to Terry Sejnowski "should not be possible according to sample complexity in statistics and nonconvex optimization theory" [1]. The challenge is to bring together the high levels of accuracy with the semantically meaningful and theoretically sound and provable solutions.

All these challenges and identified gaps require a dramatic paradigm shift and a radical new approach. In this talk, the speaker will present such a new approach towards the next generation of explainable-by-design deep learning [2–5]. It is based on prototypes and uses kernel-like functions making it interpretable-by-design. It is dramatically easier to train and adapt without the need for complete re-training, can start learning from few training data samples, explore the data space, detect and learn from unseen data patterns [6]. Indeed, the ability to detect the unseen and unexpected and start learning this new class/es in real time with no or very little supervision is critically important and is something that no currently existing classifier can offer. This method was applied to a range of applications including but not limited to remote sensing [7–8], autonomous driving [2, 6], health and others.

# References

1. Sejnowski, T.J.: The unreasonable effectiveness of deep learning in AI. PNAS **117**(48), 30033–30038 (January 2020)
2. Soares, E.A., Angelov, P.: Towards explainable deep neural networks (xDNN). Neural Networks **130**, 185–194 (October 2020)
3. Angelov, P.P., Gu, X.: Toward anthropomorphic machine learning. IEEE Comput. **51**(9), 18–27 (2018)
4. Angelov, P., Gu, X.: Empirical Approach to Machine Learning. Springer, Cham (2019). https://doi.org/10.1007/978-3-030-02384-3
5. Angelov, P., Gu, X., Principe, J.: A generalized methodology for data analysis. IEEE Trans. Cybern. **48**(10), 2981–2993 (October 2018)
6. Soares, E.A., Angelov, P.: Detecting and Learning from Unknown by Extremely Weak Supervision: eXploratory Classifier (xClass), Neural Computing and Applications (2021). https://arxiv.org/pdf/1911.00616.pdf
7. Gu, X., Angelov, P.P., Zhang, C., Atkinson, P.M.: A semi-supervised deep rule-based approach for complex satellite sensor image analysis. IEEE Trans. Pattern Anal. Mach. Intell. (TPAMI) **44**(5), 2281–2292 (May 2022). https://doi.org/10.1109/TPAMI.2020.3048268
8. Gu, X., Zhang, C., Shen, Q., Han, J., Angelov, P.P., Atkinson, P.M.: A self-training hierarchical prototype-based ensemble framework for remote sensing scene classification. Inf. Fusion **80**, 179–204 (April 2022)
9. Jiang, Z., Rahmani, H., Angelov, P., Black, S., Williams, B.: Graph-context attention networks for size-varied deep graph matching. In: IEEE/CVF Conference on Computer Vision and Pattern Recognition (CVPR 2022), New Orleans, USA, pp. 2343–2352 (June 2022)

# Intelligent Mobile Sensing for Understanding Human Behaviour

Oresti Baños Legrán

Tenured Professor of Computational Behaviour Modelling,
Department of Computer Engineering, Automation and Robotics,
Research Centre for Information and Communications Technology,
University of Granada, Spain

**Abstract:** Understanding people's behaviour is essential to characterise patient progress, make treatment decisions and elicit effective and relevant coaching actions. Hence, a great deal of research has been devoted in recent years to the automatic sensing and intelligent analysis of human behaviour. Among all sensing options, smartphones stand out as they enable the unobtrusive observation and detection of a wide variety of behaviours as we go about our physical and virtual interactions with the world. This talk aims at giving the audience a taste of the unparalleled potential that mobile sensing in combination with artificial intelligence offers for the study of human individual and collective behaviour.

# Secure, Efficient and High-Performance Computing: A Computer Architecture Perspective

Tamara Silbergleit Lehman

Assistant Professor at the University of Colorado Boulder

**Abstract:** Distributed systems and new architectures introduce new sets of security risks. Microarchitectural attacks have presented many challenges in the computer architecture community and this talk will present a few of the methods that the Boulder Computer Architecture Lab (BCAL) has been studying in order to address these vulnerabilities. The talk will first introduce physical and microarchitectural attacks and why they are hard to mitigate. Then, the talk will introduce an efficient implementation of speculative integrity verification, Poisonivy, to construct an efficient and high performance secure memory system. Finally, the talk will show how we can leverage emerging memory technologies such as near memory processing to defend and identify microarchitectural side-channel attacks. The talk will end by briefly introducing a new research direction that is investigating the Rowhammer attack impact on neural network accuracy running on GPUs and how we can leverage secure memory to protect the accuracy of the models.

# How AI/Machine Learning has the Power of Revolutionizing (for Good?) Cybersecurity?

Javier Alonso Lopez

Principal Machine Learning Applied Scientist Microsoft
AI Platform – Microsoft OpenAI

**Abstract:** As we already know, Machine Learning is already used in various cybersecurity tasks such as malware identification/classification, intrusion detection, botnet identification, phishing, predicting cyberattacks like denial of service, fraud detection, etc. However, during the last years there has been a revolution of machine learning, specifically, deep learning that creates not only an unbelievable opportunity to develop more effective solutions but also represents a new threat and a new tool to be used to attack and gain control over systems, organizations and even countries.

In this talk, we will overview the major applications of Machine Learning in the field of cybersecurity both to prevent attacks but also how Machine learning can be used to pose a threat. We will review the main advances of Deep Learning in the last 5 years and their application into Cybersecurity. Finally, we will discuss the possible future trends we can expect (I do not expect a high accuracy, but high recall :D) in the intersection of Deep Learning and Cybersecurity.

# Contents

## Complex Dynamic Networks' Optimization/Graph Neural Networks

## Convolutional Neural Networks/Spiking Neural Networks

**Deep Learning Modeling**

**Deep/Machine Learning in Engineering**

## Learning (Reinforcemet - Federated - Adversarial - Transfer)

## Natural Language - Recommendation Systems

# Artificial Intelligence - Computational Methods - Ethology

# A Machine Learning Approach for Seismic Vulnerability Ranking

Ioannis Karampinis[✉] and Lazaros Iliadis

Department of Civil Engineering-Lab of Mathematics and Informatics (ISCE),
Democritus University of Thrace, 67100 Xanthi, Greece
{ioankara25,liliadis}@civil.duth.gr

**Abstract.** Structures often suffer damages as a result of earthquakes, potentially threatening human lives, disrupting the economy and requiring large amounts of monetary reparations. Thus, it is essential for governments to be able to rank a given population of structures according to their expected degree of damage in an earthquake, in order for them to properly allocate the available resources for prevention. In this paper, the authors present a ranking approach, based on Machine Learning (ML) algorithms for pairwise comparisons, coupled with *ad hoc* ranking rules. The degree of damage of several structures from the Athens 1999 earthquake, along with collected attributes of the building, were used as input. The performance of the ML classification algorithms was evaluated using the respective metrics of Precision, Recall, F1-score, Accuracy and Area Under Curve (AUC). The overall performance was evaluated using Kendall's tau distance and by viewing the problem as a classification into bins. The obtained results were promising, outperforming currently employed engineering practices. They have shown the capabilities and potential of these models in mitigating the effects of earthquakes on society.

**Keywords:** Machine Learning · Ranking · Seismic Vulnerability

## 1 Introduction and Literature Review

Following the recent 7.8R and 7.5R seismic events in Turkey on 6th of February 2023 along the Southeastern Anatolian rift, we witnessed one of the largest global seismic disasters with extremely severe consequences. Reports so far mention more than 45,000 human lives lost and over 130,000 injured. More than 15,000 structures have fully or partially collapsed during the earthquake, disrupting the lives of the survivors, the economy and causing the need for monetary reparations in the magnitude of tenths of billions of dollars. Such events accentuate the need for a reliable seismic vulnerability assessment, especially in large urban areas with great population density.

The term "seismic vulnerability" of a building refers to its potential to suffer a certain degree of damage, when subjected to an earthquake of predefined inten-

L. Iliadis et al. (Eds.): EANN 2023, CCIS 1826, pp. 3–16, 2023.
https://doi.org/10.1007/978-3-031-34204-2_1

sity [19,37]. Extending this to a regional level can allow authorities to identify the most vulnerable buildings in the population. In turn, this can allow them to efficiently allocate their limited resources on those, thus preventing the loss of human lives, mitigating the disruption of economic activities and reduce the future need of reparations [2,35]. Thus, there is a clear need for a tool capable of ranking a given population of structures with respect to their seismic vulnerability to aid them in their decisions.

There are many comprehensive reviews on the subject, collecting and summarizing currently accepted engineering practices for this task [2,3,25]. As is evident from the plethora of related literature, there is no universally accepted solution to the problem, which often leads to different countries and organizations each employing their own methods. However, all the above methods are based on calculating a vulnerability index for each building. Initially, each structure is assigned a base scoring, based on its structural type and age. Then, a series of modifying factors are applied, which either increase or reduce this initial scoring to produce the final index. The structures are then ranked in descending order of vulnerability and the most vulnerable ones are usually subject to further steps of evaluation. These steps are referred to as Rapid Visual Screening (RVS) [25,27]. The modifying factors applied come from a variety of attributes observed for each structure. These include the design codes used on the structure, the type of soil, the presence o vertical or horizontal irregularities in the shape of the structure, the number of storeys, the current condition of the structure and others [1,6,22].

On the other hand, Machine Learning algorithms have been previously employed for the task of seismic vulnerability assessment. Ghasemi et al. [11] employed a Decision Tree algorithm using two features to classify reinforced concrete (RC) frames in distinct damage states. Rosti et al. [30] used clustering techniques, later assigning vulnerability classes to the clusters. Closer to current engineering practices, Ruggieri et al. [31] employed the RVS procedure described above by using a Convolutional Neural Network (CNN) on photographs to automatically find the attributes of the buildings. Luo and German [23] used an ML algorithm to predict drift capacity, the value of which they used as a seismic vulnerability assessment index. These two methods approach the problem indirectly, using ML algorithms to predict a vulnerability index which they can then be used to rank the structures.

To the best of our knowledge, no methodology has employed ML algorithms to address the ranking problem explicitly. This research attempts to provide a methodology that directly ranks a given set of structures according to their seismic vulnerability, without the need to compute a vulnerability index. The methodology is based on reducing the ranking to a binary classification problem, from which the ranking is obtained by pairwise comparisons and ranking rules [20]. As an input to our models, we have used data from 404 structures of the Athens 1999 earthquake [14]. These pertained to the degree of damage the structured suffered as well as their attributes, obtained via RVS.

# 2   Dataset

As was already mentioned, we drew our dataset from a set of measurements in structures obtained after the Athens 1999 earthquake [14]. This consisted of 404 structures with various degrees of damage drawn from different municipalities of Athens. To isolate potential local effects from the study, the authors in [14] drew samples from every damage category in nearby building blocks per municipality. The degree of damage was classified into 4 categories, namely:

1. "Black", with total or partial collapse of the structure,
2. "Red", with significant damage to the load bearing structural system,
3. "Yellow", with medium damages to the structural system and/or extended damages to non bearing walls
4. "Green", with very minor, if any at all, damages.

**Table 1.** Number of buildings in the dataset in each damage category.

| Damage Category | Number of Structures |
| --- | --- |
| Black | 93 |
| Red | 201 |
| Yellow | 69 |
| Green | 41 |

The distribution of the dataset in these categories is shown in Table 1. For each of these structures, 12 attributes were observed, namely:

1. *Pilotis and/or short columns:* This indicated whether the structure had a storey with significantly lower structural rigidity than the rest.
2. *Regularity of walls:* This indicated whether the non bearing walls were of sufficient thickness (the length of a brick) and with few openings.
3. *Lack of modern seismic codes:* This was applied to buildings that were not designed with the most modern seismic codes of the time and thus, was mainly attributed to pre-1985 and especially pre-1960 buildings.
4. *Poor condition:* This pertained to a variety of reasons, e.g. buildings with aggregates segregation in the concrete, eroded concrete, or very high and/or non uniform ground sinking.
5. *Previous damages:* This only applied in cases where any previous damages on the structural system had not been adequately repaired.
6. *Significant height:* This applied in cases where the structure had more than 5 storeys.
7. *Irregularity in-height:* This applies to structures where there are discontinuities in the vertical path of the loads. Such discontinuities can appear, for example, where the surface area of a storey is significantly less than the rest.
8. *Irregularity in-plan:* This applies to buildings with an irregular floor plan, e.g. buildings with highly acute angles in their outer walls, E, Z, H or similarly shaped floor plans.

9. *Torsion:* This applied to buildings with significant structural eccentricity.
10. *Pounding with neighboring buildings:* This applies to buildings with lack of sufficient gaps from their neighbors, especially in the case where the storeys of the two buildings are on different heights. This is because, during the earthquake, the slabs of one building can ram the columns of the other.
11. *Heavy non structural elements:* Falling of such elements during the earthquake, aside from the threat human lives, leads to eccentricities and thus torsion.
12. *Underlying soil:* This pertains to the classification of the underlying soil according to the Greek Code for Seismic Resistant Structures - EAK 2000 [1]. In particular, EAK classifies soils into categories A, B, C, D and X. Class A refers to rock or semi-rock formations extending in wide area and large depth. Class B refers to strongly weathered rocks or soils, mechanically equivalent to granular materials. Classes C and D refer to granular materials and soft clay respectively, while class X refers to to loose fine-grained silt [1]. In [14] and in the present study, soils in EAK category A are classified as S1, category B is classified as S2 and categories C and D are classified as S3. Soils in EAK category X were not encountered.

Each of the above attributes was given as a binary feature and the soil category was one-hot-encoded. However, it is clear that this binary approach does not always reflect the full picture for a given structure, as, for example, "poor condition" or "previous damages" can be exhibited at different degrees, while in the present dataset all structures either did or did not exhibit this attribute.

Finally, even though it wasn't categorized as an attribute, in 399/404 structures of the dataset the researchers noted the exact number of storeys, not just whether or not this was greater than 5. Given this, we opted to use this feature instead in our study, removing the 5 structures that lacked this from the dataset.

## 3    Data Preprocessing - Pairwise Ranking Transformation

As a first step in the preprocessing, note that the classes are heavily imbalanced, with Red structures comprising 50% of the total. To alleviate this, we undersampled this class randomly by a factor of 0.5.

In order to rank a given set of structures, our proposed algorithm is based on learning a Machine Learning model that, given a single pair of structures, predicts which of the two should rank higher, *i.e.* is predicted to have a higher degree of damage severity. This reduces the problem of ranking to a binary classification problem, which, through pairwise comparisons and an application rule will yield the final ranking [20].

To this end, we first transform the given labels into ordinal ranks [12], *i.e.* Green, Yellow, Red, Black$\rightarrow \{1, 2, 3, 4\}$. Given our dataset consisting of $m = 290$ structures (after undersampling Red), each having $n = 12$ features, a pair of structures $(s_i, s_j)$ will correspond to the feature vectors $\mathbf{x}_i, \mathbf{x}_j \in \mathbb{R}^n$ respectively. Then, our binary classifier will predict $\hat{y} = sign(y_j - y_i)$, where *sign* denotes the sign function. Therefore, $\hat{y}$ will be $+1$ if $s_j$ should rank higher than $s_i$ and $-1$ if

$s_i$ should rank higher than $s_j$. To represent the pair $(\mathbf{x}_i, \mathbf{x}_j)$ using a single feature vector, any transformation $\mathbb{R}^n \times \mathbb{R}^n \to \mathbb{R}^n$ can be used. This so called "pairwise transformation" has been implemented before, e.g. [13, 21]. In the present study, we will simply take their difference, $i.e.$ $\mathbf{x}_{i,j}^{new} = \mathbf{x}_j - \mathbf{x}_j$. Similarly, for a given pair $(y_i, y_j) \in \{1, 2, 3, 4\}^2$ of the target variables belonging to different damage categories, the transformed target will be $y^{new} = sign(y_j - y_i)$. Note that the number of such pairs is given by $p = (m^2 - \sum_{c_i=1}^{c} m_{c_i}^2)/2$, where $c$ is the number of classes/ranks and $m_{c_i}$ is the number of instances in each class [21]. In our case, this leads to $p = 30,339$ pairs and $\mathbf{X}^{new} \in \mathbb{R}^{30339} \times \mathbb{R}^{12}$, $\mathbf{y}^{new} \in \mathbb{R}^{30339}$. In the transformed dataset, $17,017$ instances are in class $-1$ while the other $13,322$ are in class $+1$, $i.e.$ a $55:45$ ratio, which is not deemed a significantly imbalanced dataset.

Furthermore, note that in the original dataset, even prior to the undersampling, we had 399 samples and 12 features. Thus, the so-called "curse of dimensionality" [15] hinders the ability of any model to learn from such small data, unless many features were to be removed from the model. However, the pairwise approach introduced in [21] and implemented here directly addresses this issue since, as was mentioned, the transformed dataset has now $30,339$ instances.

## 4 Description of the Algorithm

### 4.1 General Overview

After training the introduced binary classifier, the ranking algorithm proceeded as follows:

1. For each structure $\mathbf{x}_i$, $i \in \{1, 2, ..., m\}$ in our test set, consider all the pairs $(\mathbf{x}_i, \mathbf{x}_j)$, $j \in \{1, 2, ..., m\} - \{i\}$.
2. Using the pairwise transform, compute $\mathbf{x}_{i,j}^{new}$ and use it to make a prediction $y_{pred} \in \{+1, -1\}$.
3. If $y_{pred} = +1$, assign a "win" to $s_j$. Otherwise, assign a "win" to $s_i$.
4. Keep track of the "wins" of every structure and as a secondary metric, keep track of the probabilities of the prediction. So, for example, suppose for a given pair of structures $(s_i, s_j)$ our classifier yields the class probabilities $[0.3, 0.7]$ and thus, $y_{pred} = +1$. Then, not only will we assign a "win" to $s_j$ as in 3 above, but for structure $s_j$ we will add the "win" probability 0.7 to a running sum of probabilities for each structure.
5. The ranking step is simply sorting the structures in the test set based on the number of "wins", using the sum of probabilities as a tie breaker, $i.e.$ if two structures have the same number of wins, then the one with the highest sum of probabilities should rank higher. This results in a permutation of the structures, denoted by $\{i_1, i_2, ...i_m\}$, where, for $k \in \{1, 2, ..., m\}$, $i_k$ denotes the index of the structure in the original dataset that was ranked in position $m$.

As a secondary ranking step, we can select the top $k$ structures of the initial ranking obtained as above and re-run part of the above process to obtain better results. The process can be described as follows:

6. For a given $k < m$, split the original ranking obtained above as $r_{top} = \{i_1, i_2, ...i_k\}$, $r_{bottom} = \{i_{k+1}, i_{k+2}, ...i_m\}$. Retain $r_{bottom}$.
7. For the structures in $r_{top}$, repeat 1-5 above, using a binary classifier trained only with the subset of the original dataset, for which $y_i \in \{3, 4\}$. This will result in a new ranking, call it $r'_{top} = \{i'_1, i'_2, ...i'_k\}$.
8. The final ranking is obtained as $r_{final} = \{i'_1, i'_2, ...i'_k, i_{k+1}, i_{k+2}, ...i_m\}$, *i.e.* by appending $r'_{top}$ and $r_{bottom}$.

In order to reduce the variance induced by the train/test splitting and make use of our full dataset, we employed a 5-fold cross validation scheme, executing steps 1-8 from the above, on the transformed sets $\mathbf{X}^{new}, \mathbf{y}^{new}$.

## 4.2  Employed Machine Learning Modelling Algorithms

As is evident from the above, the very core of our proposed algorithm lies in learning a binary classifier $f : \mathbb{R}^n \times \mathbb{R}^n \rightarrow \{-1, +1\}$ that, given a pair $\mathbf{x}_i$, $\mathbf{x}_j$, predicts whether $s_j$ should rank higher than $s_i$ or vice versa. There are many reviews on classification problems in general and binary classification in particular, for example [17,18,34]. Here we present an overview of the most commonly used classifiers that were also employed in the present study.

1. **Decision Tree Classifier:** This is a tree-based method where, at each step, the algorithm uses a predefined criterion, e.g. Gini Impurity [40], to split the dataset into subsets, assigning a class to each end (leaf) node [16].
2. **Random Forest Classifier:** This is an ensemble method [29] where the results from many individual Decision Trees, trained on bootstrapped samples of the original dataset and with a random subset of features at each split, are combined in the final prediction. This both improves the accuracy of using any individual tree and reduces overfitting [8].
3. **Extra Trees Classifier:** It is a shorthand for Extremely Randomized Trees. In many ways a similar classifier to Random Forest, as it is also an ensemble of Decision Trees. It differs, however, in that it uses the whole set in training and not a bootstrapped sample and that it introduces randomness in the splitting criterion of each tree [10].
4. **k-Nearset Neighbors classifier:** This is a classifier that for each instance identifies the $k$ most similar-based on some similarity metric-instances in the training set and makes a prediction based on voting [7].
5. **Logistic Regression:** Logistic regression is a binary classification algorithm. Given two classes "+1" and "-1" and $p$ denoting the probability that an instance belongs to "+1", the classifier predicts the so-called logit, *i.e.* $\log \frac{p}{1-p}$ via a linear combination of the features. Then, if the predicted $p$ is above a threshold, the classifier predicts "+1", otherwise "-1' [33].
6. **Ridge Classifier:** In a binary classification setting, this model predicts a target $y$ that, if positive, assigns the instance to class "+1", otherwise to "-1". It uses a penalty on the $\mathcal{L}_2$ norm of the trained parameters to reduce overfitting [32].

7. **Gradient Boosting Classifier:** This is a meta classifier [36]. It iteratively builds the model, starting from a "weak" classifier and trains the next iteration using the current predictions and an arbitrary differentiable loss function [26].

The implementation of the above algorithms was carried out in `Python` programming language using the machine learning library `scikit-learn` [28]. The best performing algorithm was Gradient Boosting, which is what we will be using in the sequel. In the present study, the default `scikit-learn` hyperparameters were employed for each classifier. An extensive fine-tuning of these can be done in future research.

## 5 Results

In the sequel, "primary classifier" will refer to the classifier trained on structures across the damage spectrum, *i.e.* with $y_i \in \{1, 2, 3, 4\}$, and used for steps 1-5 described in 4.1. Likewise, "secondary classifier" will refer to the classifier trained on structures with $y_i \in \{3, 4\}$ and used for steps 6-8.

In our numerical experiments, we obtained an average fold accuracy of the primary classifier of 0.75743, with a standard deviation of 0.04347. The secondary classifier had an average fold accuracy of 0.84994, with a standard deviation of 0.02509. To obtain a result calibrated on the whole dataset, we perform a cross validation scheme, as described above. The classification metrics results obtained this way are shown in Table 2, while the corresponding Receiver Operating Characteristic (ROC) curves are shown in Fig. 1.

As explained in detail in Sect. 4.1, the result of our algorithm is a ranking of the given set of structures. In order to assess the performance of this ranking, we compare it with the actual ranking obtained by the known damage these structures suffered during the earthquake, along with a baseline ranking, as described below.

Given our dataset consisting of $m = 290$ structures and their respective known responses $y_i \in \{1, 2, 3, 4\}$, $i = 1, 2, ..., m$, recall that we had 90 structures in the "Black" category, 101 structures in the "Red", 60 in the "Yellow" and 39 in the "Green". Thus, if we were to rank them in order of descending damage, we would expect the 90 "Black" structures to be in the top 90 positions, followed by the 101 "Red" and so on, as shown in Fig. 2a. Our algorithm ranked them

**Table 2.** Classification metrics for the primary and secondary binary classifiers, cross validated on the whole dataset.

| | -1 | +1 | | | -1 | +1 |
|---|---|---|---|---|---|---|
| Precision | 0.76585 | 0.74488 | | Precision | 0.85980 | 0.83734 |
| Recall | 0.81747 | 0.68075 | | Recall | 0.87107 | 0.82371 |
| F1-score | 0.79082 | 0.71137 | | F1-score | 0.86540 | 0.83047 |
| Accuracy | 0.75744 | | | Accuracy | 0.84994 | |
| AUC | 0.83195 | | | AUC | 0.92789 | |

(a) Classification metrics of the primary classifier.     (b) Classification metrics of the secondary classifier.

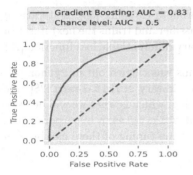
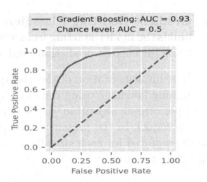

(a) ROC curve for the best performing primary classifier using all the available labels.

(b) ROC curve for the best performing secondary binary classifier using only Red/Black labels.

**Fig. 1.** ROC curves for the best performing binary classifiers.

as shown in 2b where, in general we have $i_k^{true} \neq i_k^{pred}$. Using this binning, however, we can define a metric of accuracy for the ranking as follows. For each damage index $d \in \{Black, Red, Yellow, Green\}$, let $bin_d^{true}$ denote the subset of structures that belong to this category and similarly, let $bin_d^{pred}$ denote the subset of structures that were predicted to fall in that bin. Then we can define a metric of bin accuracy (BAC) for each bin as

$$\text{BAC}_d = \frac{|bin_d^{pred} \cap bin_d^{true}|}{|bin_d^{true}|}. \tag{1}$$

Using the definition of accuracy as defined in (1), we have performed two runs of our proposed algorithm. In the first run, only steps 1-5 or the algorithm were employed, *i.e.* the secondary sorting was not implemented. In the second run, we added the steps 6-8 of the algorithm, iteratively for $k = 10, 20, .., 180, 191$, which was the total number of "Black" and "Red" structures. For each run, we measured the accuracy of each bin, as defined in (1).

For comparison of the results of our proposed ranking, we used as baseline an ordering obtained by calculating a vulnerability index. This approach has been used, for example in [14,31]. What the methods in these references have in common is that the computed vulnerability index is of the form

$$V_I = V_I^b + \sum \Delta V_m, \tag{2}$$

where $V_I^b$ is a basic vulnerability index which depends on the structural type of the building as well as the year the structure was designed and built. Similarly, $\Delta V_m$ are modification coefficients [14,31], which either increase or decrease $V_I^b$ to yield $V_I$. In the present study, we used the coefficients of [14] for the comparisons. The results are shown in Table 3.

Finally, we can view each bin as a label in a classification problem. For example, as shown in Fig. 2, structures $1 - 90$ in the ranking correspond to the black structures. Similarly, structures $91 - 191$ in the ranking correspond to red. Thus, besides from the bin accuracy defined in (1), it is important to know the correct bin of wrongly ranked instances. To demonstrate this, consider the reduced example of a "Black" bin consisting of 10 structures (*i.e.* ideally we would expect $y_i = 4 \; \forall i \in \{1, 2, ..., 10\}$) and consider the following two rankings:

$$\text{ranking}_1 = [4, 4, 4, 4, 4, 4, 4, 3, 3, 3], \tag{3a}$$

$$\text{ranking}_2 = [4, 4, 4, 4, 4, 4, 4, 1, 1, 1]. \tag{3b}$$

Then, even though both rankings have $BAC_4 = 0.7$, the ranking in (3a) is clearly to be preferred. To visualize this, we can construct the corresponding confusion matrices [24,38] for each run of our algorithm, as well as the baseline. This is shown in Table 4.

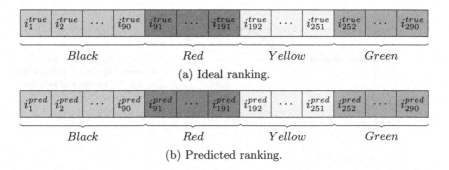

**Fig. 2.** Expected ideal and predicted ranking of the given structures in decreasing damage severity.

**Table 3.** Comparison of the results of the ranking of our algorithm with and without the secondary step against the two baselines.

|  | Bin accuracy (%) | | | |
| --- | --- | --- | --- | --- |
|  | Black | Red | Yellow | Green |
| Primary ranking only | 61.11 | 38.61 | 25 | 33.33 |
| Ranking with secondary step ($k = 190$) | 71.11 | 54.45 | 25 | 33.33 |
| Ranking using the $V_I$ of [14] | 54.44 | 38.61 | 36.66 | 25.64 |

**Table 4.** Confusion matrices for the 3 different approaches presented.

|  |  | Predicted bin | | | |
|---|---|---|---|---|---|
|  |  | Green | Yellow | Red | Black |
| True bin | Green | 13 | 14 | 12 | 0 |
|  | Yellow | 14 | 15 | 23 | 8 |
|  | Red | 9 | 26 | 39 | 27 |
|  | Black | 3 | 5 | 27 | 55 |

(a) Primary ranking only.

|  |  | Predicted bin | | | |
|---|---|---|---|---|---|
|  |  | Green | Yellow | Red | Black |
| True bin | Green | 13 | 14 | 7 | 5 |
|  | Yellow | 14 | 15 | 21 | 10 |
|  | Red | 9 | 26 | 55 | 11 |
|  | Black | 3 | 5 | 18 | 64 |

(b) Secondary ranking, with $k = 190$.

|  |  | Predicted bin | | | |
|---|---|---|---|---|---|
|  |  | Green | Yellow | Red | Black |
| True bin | Green | 10 | 14 | 12 | 3 |
|  | Yellow | 4 | 22 | 21 | 13 |
|  | Red | 21 | 16 | 39 | 25 |
|  | Black | 4 | 8 | 29 | 49 |

(c) Ranking using the $V_I$ of [14].

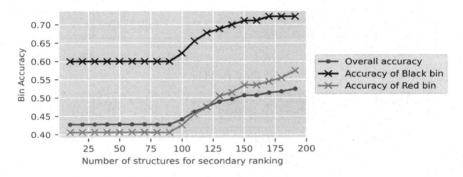

**Fig. 3.** Bin accuracy for the Black and Red bins and overall accuracy of the algorithm with secondary ranking, for $k = 10, 20, ..., 180, 191$. (Color figure online)

The accuracy metric defined in (1) only shows how many structures lie in the expected bin after ranking, but it provides no information on how the correct instances of the bin are distributed inside the bin itself. To demonstrate this, consider the reduced example of a "Black" bin consisting of 10 structures (*i.e.* ideally we would expect $y_i = 4 \; \forall i \in \{1, 2, ..., 10\}$) and consider the following two rankings produced by the algorithm:

$$\text{ranking}_1 = [4, 4, 4, 4, 4, 4, 4, 3, 2, 1], \tag{4a}$$

$$\text{ranking}_2 = [4, 4, 4, 1, 4, 2, 4, 3, 4, 4]. \tag{4b}$$

Even though both rankings have bin accuracy 70%, it is clear that the ranking in (4a) is to be preferred over the one in (4b), because the correct instances in the bin rank higher than the wrong ones. To quantify this, we will use a slight modification of the so-called Kendall tau distance [5,39]. To this end, a pair $(s_i, s_j)$ is called discordant if $i > y$ and $y_i < y_j$. Then, for a given set consisting of $n$ ranked elements, Kendall's tau distance is defined as

$$K = \frac{2|D|}{n(n-1)}, \tag{5}$$

where $|D|$ is the total number of discordant pairs. Note that $K$ is normalized in the range $[0,1]$, since $|D| \geq 0$ and $|D| \leq \binom{n}{2} = \frac{n(n-1)}{2}$. We will slightly modify (5) and define the pairwise accuracy (PAC) as:

$$PAC = 1 - \frac{2|D|}{n(n-1)}, \tag{6}$$

where the difference is that in (6) $|D| = 0 \Rightarrow PAC = 1$ while in (5) $|D| = 0 \Rightarrow K = 0$. Similarly to Fig. 3, we present in Fig. 4 below the results for $k = 10, 20, ..., 191$ for the pairwise accuracy defined in (6).

Finally, as a way to combine these two metrics into a single number, we propose the use of the harmonic mean of the two metrics, similar to how the well-known $F1$-score is defined as the harmonic mean of precision and recall in a classification problem [4,9]. Thus given a predefined bin, which can be the whole set of structures, we define

$$\text{combined accuracy} = \frac{2}{\frac{1}{\text{bin accuracy}} + \frac{1}{\text{pairwise accuracy}}}. \tag{7}$$

Similar to Fig. 3 and Fig. 4, we present in Fig. 5 the results of this combined accuracy for $k = 10, 20, ..., 180, 191$ for the Black and Red bins, as well as over the whole dataset.

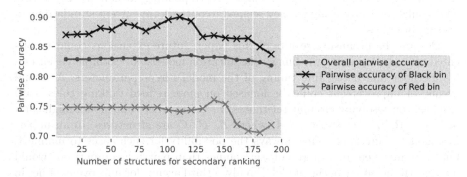

**Fig. 4.** Pairwise accuracy for the Black and Red bins and overall pairwise accuracy of the algorithm with secondary ranking, for $k = 10, 20, ..., 180, 191$. (Color figure online)

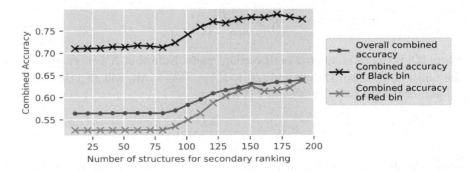

**Fig. 5.** Combined accuracy for the Black and Red bins and overall combined accuracy of the algorithm with secondary ranking, for $k = 10, 20, ..., 180, 191$. (Color figure online)

## 6    Conclusions and Future Work

This paper deals with the problem of ranking a given set of structures according to their seismic vulnerability. It uses a Machine Learning to perform pairwise comparisons with binary classification and *ad hoc* rules to obtain the final ranking. Attributes obtained during Rapid Visual Screening of the structures were used as input for the models. Precision, recall, F1-score, overall accuracy and Area Under Curve were used as evaluation metrics for the binary classifiers. Kendall's tau was used to evaluate the performance of the overall ranking. We also used confusion matrices, which we implemented by binning the obtained ranking and labelling the bins as classes corresponding to damage categories. The results were promising as they seemed to outperform current standard engineering practices.

Despite the promising results of this paper, future extensions could be oriented towards improving the binary classification models, for example via ensemble methods and better fine tuning of the model's hyperparameters. A second avenue of improvement could be focused on more refined ranking rules, with emphasis on resolving circular references, *i.e.* cases where our model might predict $A > B$, $B > C$ and $C > A$, where $A$, $B$, $C$ are structures. In an imperfect model, there is of course always the possibility for such cases to manifest, but resolving them in a more holistic manner than pairwise comparisons would increase the accuracy of the model. Finally, a third avenue for improvement lies in improving the data quality itself. On the one hand, this can be done by exploring other potential attributes that affect seismic vulnerability and not taken into consideration here. On the other hand, there were attributes in the available dataset that were reported as binary, even though a continuous grading could be used. Such were, for example,"Poor Condition" and "Previous Damages". Obtaining a continuous grading for such features would improve the binary classification performance and thus the overall ranking.

# References

1. Greek code for seismic resistant structures - EAK (2000). https://iisee.kenken.go.jp/worldlist/23_Greece/23_Greece_Code.pdf
2. Alam, N., Alam, M.S., Tesfamariam, S.: Buildings' seismic vulnerability assessment methods: a comparative study. Nat. Hazards **62**, 405–424 (2012)
3. Barbat, A.H., Carreño, M.L., Pujades, L.G., Lantada, N., Cardona, O.D., Marulanda, M.C.: Seismic vulnerability and risk evaluation methods for urban areas a review with application to a pilot area. Struct Infrastructure Eng. **6**(1–2), 17–38 (2010)
4. Buckland, M., Gey, F.: The relationship between recall and precision. J. Am. Society Inf. Sci. **45**(1), 12–19 (1994)
5. Cicirello, V.A.: Kendall tau sequence distance: Extending Kendall tau from ranks to sequences. arXiv preprint arXiv:1905.02752 (2019)
6. Code, P.: Eurocode 8: Design of structures for earthquake resistance-part 1: general rules, seismic actions and rules for buildings. European Committee for Standardization, Brussels (2005)
7. Cunningham, P., Delany, S.J.: k-nearest neighbour classifiers-A tutorial. ACM Comput. Surv. (CSUR) **54**(6), 1–25 (2021)
8. Fawagreh, K., Gaber, M.M., Elyan, E.: Random forests: from early developments to recent advancements. Syst. Sci. Control Eng. An Open Access J. **2**(1), 602–609 (2014)
9. Flach, P., Kull, M.: Precision-recall-gain curves: PR analysis done right. In: Advances in Neural Information Processing Systems 28 (2015)
10. Geurts, P., Ernst, D., Wehenkel, L.: Extremely randomized trees. Mach. Learn. **63**, 3–42 (2006)
11. Ghasemi, S.H., Bahrami, H., Akbari, M.: Classification of seismic vulnerability based on machine learning techniques for RC frames. J. Soft Comput. Civil Eng. (2020)
12. Gutiérrez, P.A., Perez-Ortiz, M., Sanchez-Monedero, J., Fernandez-Navarro, F., Hervas-Martinez, C.: Ordinal regression methods: survey and experimental study. IEEE Trans. Knowl. Data Eng. **28**(1), 127–146 (2015)
13. Herbrich, R.: Support vector learning for ordinal regression. In: Proceedings of 9th International Conference on Neural Networks 1999, pp. 97–102 (1999)
14. Karabinis, A.: Calibration of Rapid Visual Screening in Reinforced Concrete Structures based on data after a near field earthquake (7.9.1999 Athens - Greece) (2004). https://www.oasp.gr/assigned_program/2385
15. Köppen, M.: The curse of dimensionality. In: 5th Online World Conference on Soft Computing in Industrial Applications (WSC5), vol. 1, pp. 4–8 (2000)
16. Kotsiantis, S.B.: Decision trees: a recent overview. Artif. Intell. Rev. **39**, 261–283 (2013)
17. Kotsiantis, S.B., Zaharakis, I., Pintelas, P., et al.: Supervised machine learning: A review of classification techniques. Emerging Artifi. Intell. Appli. Comput. Eng. **160**(1), 3–24 (2007)
18. Kumari, R., Srivastava, S.K.: Machine learning: A review on binary classification. Int. J. Comput. Appli. **160**(7) (2017)
19. Lang, K., Bachmann, H.: On the seismic vulnerability of existing unreinforced masonry buildings. J. Earthquake Eng. **7**(03), 407–426 (2003)
20. Li, L., Lin, H.T.: Ordinal regression by extended binary classification. In: Advances in Neural Information Processing Systems 19 (2006)

21. Liu, Y., Li, X., Kong, A.W.K., Goh, C.K.: Learning from small data: A pairwise approach for ordinal regression. In: 2016 IEEE Symposium Series on Computational Intelligence (SSCI), pp. 1–6. IEEE (2016)
22. Lizundia, B., et al.: Update of fema p-154: Rapid visual screening for potential seismic hazards. In: Improving the Seismic Performance of Existing Buildings and Other Structures 2015, pp. 775–786 (2015)
23. Luo, H., Paal, S.G.: A locally weighted machine learning model for generalized prediction of drift capacity in seismic vulnerability assessments. Comput. Aided Civil Infrastructure Eng. **34**(11), 935–950 (2019)
24. Marom, N.D., Rokach, L., Shmilovici, A.: Using the confusion matrix for improving ensemble classifiers. In: 2010 IEEE 26-th Convention of Electrical and Electronics Engineers in Israel, pp. 000555–000559. IEEE (2010)
25. Nanda, R., Majhi, D.: Review on rapid seismic vulnerability assessment for bulk of buildings. J. Institution of Eng. (India): Series A **94**, 187–197 (2013)
26. Natekin, A., Knoll, A.: Gradient boosting machines, a tutorial. Front. Neurorobot. **7**, 21 (2013)
27. Ningthoujam, M., Nanda, R.P.: Rapid visual screening procedure of existing building based on statistical analysis. In. J. Disaster Risk Reduct. **28**, 720–730 (2018)
28. Pedregosa, F., et al.: Scikit-learn: Machine learning in Python. J. Mach. Learn. Res. **12**, 2825–2830 (2011)
29. Rahman, A., Tasnim, S.: Ensemble classifiers and their applications: a review. arXiv preprint arXiv:1404.4088 (2014)
30. Rosti, A., Rota, M., Penna, A.: An empirical seismic vulnerability model. Bull. Earthquake Eng., 1–27 (2022). https://doi.org/10.1007/s10518-022-01374-3
31. Ruggieri, S., Cardellicchio, A., Leggieri, V., Uva, G.: Machine-learning based vulnerability analysis of existing buildings. Autom. Constr. **132**, 103936 (2021)
32. Singh, A., Prakash, B.S., Chandrasekaran, K.: A comparison of linear discriminant analysis and ridge classifier on Twitter data. In: 2016 International Conference on Computing, Communication and Automation (ICCCA), pp. 133–138. IEEE (2016)
33. So, Y.: A tutorial on logistic regression. SAS White Papers (1995)
34. Soofi, A.A., Awan, A.: Classification techniques in machine learning: applications and issues. J. Basic Appl. Sci **13**, 459–465 (2017)
35. Tesfamariam, S., Saatcioglu, M.: Risk-based seismic evaluation of reinforced concrete buildings. Earthq. Spectra **24**(3), 795–821 (2008)
36. Vanschoren, J.: Meta-learning: A survey. arXiv preprint arXiv:1810.03548 (2018)
37. Vicente, R., Parodi, S., Lagomarsino, S., Varum, H., Silva, J.M.: Seismic vulnerability and risk assessment: case study of the historic city centre of Coimbra, Portugal. Bull. Earthq. Eng. **9**, 1067–1096 (2011)
38. Visa, S., Ramsay, B., Ralescu, A.L., Van Der Knaap, E.: Confusion matrix-based feature selection. Maics **710**(1), 120–127 (2011)
39. Wauthier, F., Jordan, M., Jojic, N.: Efficient ranking from pairwise comparisons. In: International Conference on Machine Learning, pp. 109–117. PMLR (2013)
40. Yuan, Y., Wu, L., Zhang, X.: Gini-impurity index analysis. IEEE Trans. Inf. Forensics Secur. **16**, 3154–3169 (2021)

# Computational Ethology: Short Review of Current Sensors and Artificial Intelligence Based Methods

Marina Aguilar-Moreno[✉] and Manuel Graña

Computational Intelligence Group, University of the Basque Country (UPV/EHU),
San Sebastian, Spain
marina.aguilar@ehu.eus

**Abstract.** Computational Ethology provides automated and precise measurement of animal behavior. Artificial Intelligence (AI) techniques have also introduced the enhanced capabilities to interpret experimental data in order to extract accurate ethograms allowing the comparison of animal models with high discriminative power. In this short review we introduce the most recent software tools that employ AI tools for this endeavor, including the popular deep learning approaches.

**Keywords:** Computational Ethology · Animal Behavior · Sensors · Tracking · Machine Learning · Deep Learning

## 1 Introduction

Ethology is defined as the discipline that studies the animal behavior in terms of its phenomenological, causal, ontogenetic and evolutionary aspects, in order to provide answers to the causes and development that animal behavior undergoes, as well as to understand how it is performed [5], bearing in mind that behavior is understood as the set of muscular responses of a living being as a consequence of an external stimulus [30] and internal motivation.

Early ethology studies were conducted visually, describing qualitatively what researchers saw in each experiment. Later on, they began to evaluate certain behaviors on the basis of some predefined criteria, thus beginning a quantitative approach. However, this new methodology had many drawbacks:

- Time-consuming: The time needed to pre-process an experiment can require up to three times its actual duration.
- Humdrum: Behavior observation and annotation is a very repetitive task that must be performed for hours during several weeks. At a certain point, the observer is tired and performs the task mechanically losing ability to notice new patterns.
- Difficult to transfer knowledge: When it is not possible to express it in plain words, different team members may make different annotations for the same experiment. This makes the process strongly subject to the scientist's judgment, difficult to standardise, and to reproduce in other laboratories with different equipment.

L. Iliadis et al. (Eds.): EANN 2023, CCIS 1826, pp. 17–27, 2023.
https://doi.org/10.1007/978-3-031-34204-2_2

- Limited to the visual acuity of the observer: If there are several animals, it is difficult to pay attention to the behavior of all of them at the same time.
- Low-dimensional. Through human observation it is not possible to annotate a large number of variables for each behavior.

To address all these issues, a new discipline called computational ethology emerged. It allows the incorporation of advances in computer vision and artificial intelligence (AI) in the study of animal behavior, providing the following advantages:

- Decrease the processing time of experiments, because it is now possible to implement algorithms that automatically extract relevant information from experimental records.
- Eliminate the limitations of the observer, allowing the processing of several animals at the same time with increased accuracy.
- Increasing the dimensionality of behavior measurements. By being able to extract more characteristics from the same behavior it is possible to increase the information and therefore improve its analysis.
- Standardise the characteristics of behaviors, since it is possible to describe behaviors quantitatively thanks to the increase in information, and the standardization of the capture instruments.

This paper covers some recent tools and advances that have been introduced by the growing application of artificial intelligence techniques to ethological experimental data analysis. Section 2 comments on current sensors employed in ethology experiments. Section 3 goes into detail of current AI based data analysis techniques and supporting software packages that can be used. Finally, Sect. 4 provides some conclusions of this short review.

## 2   Sensors

This section will describe the most commonly used physical devices in computational ethology, i.e. sensors, which are of very different types such as video, infrared and depth cameras, microphones, RFID antennas, pressure sensors, accelerometers, magnetometers and gyroscopes. Currently, RGB video cameras are the most used sensors to record experiments in open field arenas [55,80], operant conditioning chambers [17], and in animal natural environment [24]. The systems can be composed of a single RGB camera [14] or a multi-camera system [7,28,71]. Low cost configurations with video cameras use a Raspberry Pi to carry out the recording system and store the data for further processing [49]. Recent systems featured depth cameras providing 3D measurements of the kinematics of the animals [56]. This type of camera can be used both to track animals and for behavioral detection and classification [29,65]. Infrared cameras allow to monitor the behavior of animals during the day and during the darkness of the night [13], and as a non-invasive system in group-housed animals [54]. Specific examples of their application are the study of monkeys hunting fish

[73], and the study of Japanese eels to understand the environmental conditions that must be met for them to climb a low-height vertical weir [45]. In addition, infrared cameras have been used to obtain high-resolution images allowing precision tracking of certain parts of a rat's body [62]. Infrared sensors are also used to track an animal's movements to see when it is approaching a certain object [10].

Other sensors also widely used in computational ethology are inertial sensors and accelerometers, which can be placed on the heads of animals to study sensorimotor responses in pigeons [4], mice [75] and fox squirrels [27].

Though they have reduced precision, RFID antennas are also used to track animals because they are robust against visual occlusions and allow a greater space of free movements. They have been applied on rodents, to track each animal while moving freely in the study of the "Individuality Paradigm" [43], and on broilers, to identify, describe and quantify a wide range of behaviors in combination of video recording [22].

Pressure sensors are emerging for behavioral studies because they are non-invasive and allow animals to move without restriction. One example is pressure sensors based on piezoelectric materials, which can be used to detect animal movements for further processing and analysis. This platform also offers a high sensitivity for detecting pressure changes, which has even made it possible to detect freezing episodes, breathing and heartbeats in mice [11,12]. Another example is the use wearable pressure sensors to study pressure changes in the jaw movements of cattle [15].

In addition to movements, audio signals captured by microphones allow the study of the vocalizations that certain animals emit to communicate with each other [58,76]. This can be used to measure the response to stress [19], or how they communicate during mating [34], or while performing a task [68]. There exist specific software applications for detecting and classifying ultrasonic vocalizations such as DeepSqueak [18] or BootSnap [1].

## 3   Methods

In computational ethology, techniques developed in the field of computer vision and AI are used to process the data collected in the experiments. To study the trajectory and locomotion of an animal, tracking algorithms segment the animal with respect to the background obtaining the center of mass and orientation, among others properties, automatically. To study other behaviors such as grooming, resting or rearing, it is necessary to label these behaviors firstly. This task can be performed using a supervised approach, where the behaviors to be studied are indicated in the algorithm that extracts the time segments in which they occur, and an unsupervised approach, where the data is fed into an algorithm to extract patterns, which is very interesting for highlighting behaviors that were not previously foreseen by the scientist or that escape the human eye. These algorithms study temporal dynamics in the time or frequency domain, where the former studies how data vary as a function of time and the latter how cyclic movements vary as a function of their frequency [20]. In the following we discuss current approaches and tools for the two fundamental tasks of tracking and behavior classification.

## 3.1 Tracking

DeepLabCut [57] is a markerless motion tracking system based on transfer learning that can be easily tailored to the specific experimental setting. Recently, it has been used for measuring monocular ability of mice to assess distances [6,61], the behavioral risk assessment of mice [78], study of novelty induced behavioral dynamics in threat prediction [3], the management of fish passage in rivers [53], kinematics of time-varying lumbar flexion-extension [31], behavioral profiling of rodent stroke recovery [79], X-ray video analysis of rodent locomotion [44], cardiac physiology assessment in zebra fish [72], multianimal pose estimation and tracking [47], pose estimation of speech articulators [81], gait analysis in stroke survivors [50]. DeepLabCut can be also used as the basis for the development of dedicated systems, such as the Anipose system for estimation of 3D pose [42]. In addition to estimating the 3D pose, it enables the camera calibration, the filtering of the trajectories and allows the visualisation of the tracked data. Some independent comparative evaluations found that markerless tracking systems are still requiring improvements in order to achieve the same tracking accuracy as current marker based systems [59], while others found good agreement between markerless system and marker based gold standard motion tracking in specific tasks [23,70,77].

Bonsai is a programming framework for neuroscience experimentation that allows data acquisition, experiment control, data processing, and pose tracking [51]. Also, Bonsai allows the integration of one or more sensors such as cameras and local field potential (LFP) recording thanks to its Open Ephys acquisition system [74]. This open-source software has given rise to several products in the field of neuroscience, such as the GoFish platform, which uses Bonsai to experiment with fish [2], rodents [16] and flies [33]. It has been used to study the impact of feeding on the organism neural systems [66], how chronic stress affects the body [67], the frailty associated with Alzheimer's disease [46], and mice torpor [35].

Another popular system is LEAP, which also provides a pose estimation and tracking system based on deep neural networks. It follows 3 steps: i) registration and alignment of centroid to improve the efficiency and accuracy, ii) labeling and training of images to create the ground truth to train the neural network and helps the system to find the body parts, iii) pose estimation itself [64]. However, LEAP has been superseded by SLEAP (Social LEAP) that is able to track groups of animals in order to study social interactions between individuals. SLEAP provides animal poses in a multi-animal system experimentation [63] using a type of convolutional neural network called DenseNet, where all layers are connected directly to each other [37]. DeepPoseKit [32] is another recent toolkit for animal pose estimation based on Stacked DenseNe, which is a variant of DenseNet.

## 3.2    Behavioral Classification

There are many open-source applications to annotate animal behaviors automatically based on AI methods, which can either be supervised or unsupervised. In the former type, the user has to tag some frames to train the models, whereas in the latter type there is no need for prior labeling, reducing user bias.

A classic software resource for behavior classification is JAABA [41], which is an open-source application based on a semi-supervised machine learning algorithm, where the user tags the behaviors of a small series of frames and then the algorithm is able to classify the rest of the dataset. Moreover, this system is used as support for human annotators in the manual process to obtain the ground truth that will be used to train other behavior classifiers. Events that occur during experiments with more than one animal can also be labeled [60]. Allowing free interaction among animals is a desirable trait. The Mouse Action Recognition System (MARS) [69] is an automated method for pose estimation and behavior quantification in couples of mice that can interact freely. MotionMapper [8] is another classical system for mapping animal actions from raw images. Once the images are segmented and aligned, a Morlet wavelet is applied to obtain the spectrogram for each postural mode. After a normalization, a watershed transform is applied to isolate the peaks. As a result they obtain behavioral regions where can be differentiate several movements such as fast leg movements, slow movements, wing movements, posterior movements, locomotion gits and anterior movements. This way, they can compare the behavior between males and females.

Deep learning techniques area also extensively used for behavior recognition. DeepEthogram[9] classifies behaviors applying deep supervised learning from raw pixels. Its is composed of two convolutional neural networks extracting spatial and dynamic flow features. This classifier is widely used, for instance to extract walking or grooming events [25], or small-scale movements such as rat liking after having eaten tasty food [38]. In addition, transfer learning is very useful for building models from previously trained networks as it requires less computational time and less data [40].

There are unsupervised methods such as B-SOiD [36], which identifies behaviors without user interaction. It first extracts pose relationships to identify patterns and find the optimal number of cluster groups. Then a random forest model is trained to predict categories of behaviors. This algorithm has been referenced in several works, to classify repetitive behaviors using data from tracking beads, where the system is fed with data on distances, angles and velocities [48].

Unsupervised deep learning approaches have also found application in behavior categorization. The Selfee [39] method for self-supervised feature extraction can also be used as input to the B-SOiD algorithm. Selfee uses a convolutional neural network to extract features from raw video recordings to feed other classification algorithms. VAME [52] is another unsupervised deep learning framework that identifies behavioral motifs from bottom-up images. This algorithm uses DeepLabCut to estimate the pose of the animal and once the trajectory is obtained, a recurrent neural network is fed to obtain the motifs. Finally, VAME results can be clustered with the k-means algorithm [67] in order to extract the relevant behavioral motifs. PyRAT [21] is an open-source python library to analise animal behavior by estimating traveled distance, speed and area occupancy. The unsupervised algorithms used in this library are hierarchical agglomerative clustering and t-distributed stochastic neighbor embedding (t-SNE) for classification and clustering.

Apart from this, there are different tools to detect behaviors based on heuristic algorithms such as BehaviorDEPOT, a tool that uses statistics based on animal dynamics and posture [26].

## 4   Conclusion and Future Perspective

This short review includes an overview of the sensors currently used in experimentation, the best known of which are RGB video and depth cameras, pressure sensors, RFID antennas, accelerometers and microphones for recording mice vocalizations. In this short review we have aimed to make a compilation of the most widely used and known methods and algorithms in computational ethology for both tracking and classification of behaviors. Based on machine learning and deep learning, these methods can follow two basic learning approaches: supervised or unsupervised. In the first one, the data is previously labeled and the rest of the data is searched for known information. The second approach is the unsupervised approach, in which the data is not labeled in order to look for common patterns of behavior and even discover unforeseen ones. While supervised methods may achieve greater precision in tracking, unsupervised methods have the advantage of not requiring labeled inputs in order to obtain relevant behavior categories.

Although the levels of precise measurement of behaviors achieved with current methods is very high, there are still limitations to overcome, such as the extension of the methods to large experimental arenas, which resemble natural spaces more closely.

**Acknowledgments.** This work has been partially supported by FEDER funds through MINECO project TIN2017-85827-P, and grant IT1284-19 as university research group of excellence from the Basque Government.

## References

1. Abbasi, R., Balazs, P., Marconi, M.A., Nicolakis, D., Zala, S.M., Penn, D.J.: Capturing the songs of mice with an improved detection and classification method for ultrasonic vocalizations (bootsnap). PLoS Comput. Biol. **18**(5), e1010049 (2022). https://doi.org/10.1371/journal.pcbi.1010049

2. Ajuwon, V., Cruz, B.F., Carriço, P., et al.: GoFish: a low-cost, open-source platform for closed-loop behavioural experiments on fish. Behav. Res. (2023). https://doi.org/10.3758/s13428-022-02049-2

3. Akiti, K., et al.: Striatal dopamine explains novelty-induced behavioral dynamics and individual variability in threat prediction. Neuron **110**(22), 3789–3804 (2022). https://doi.org/10.1016/j.neuron.2022.08.022

4. Aldoumani, N., Meydan, T., Dillingham, C.M., Erichsen, J.T.: Enhanced tracking system based on micro inertial measurements unit to measure sensorimotor responses in pigeons. IEEE Sens. J. **16**(24), 8847–8853 (2016). https://doi.org/10.1109/JSEN.2016.2586540

5. Anderson, D., Perona, P.: Toward a science of computational ethology. Neuron **84**(1), 18–31 (2014). https://doi.org/10.1016/j.neuron.2014.09.005

6. Arvin, S., Rasmussen, R.N., Yonehara, K.: Eyeloop: An open-source system for high-speed, closed-loop eye-tracking. Front. Cell. Neurosci. **15**, 779628 (2021). https://doi.org/10.3389/fncel.2021.779628

7. Bala, P.C., Eisenreich, B.R., Yoo, S.B.M., Hayden, B.Y., Park, H.S., Zimmermann, J.: Automated markerless pose estimation in freely moving macaques with open-monkeystudio. Nat. Commun. **11**(1), 4560 (2020). https://doi.org/10.1038/s41467-020-18441-5

8. Berman, G., Choi, D., Bialek, W., Shaevitz, J.: Mapping the stereotyped behaviour of freely moving fruit flies. J. Royal Soc. Interface **11**(99) (2014). https://doi.org/10.1098/rsif.2014.0672

9. Bohnslav, J., et al.: Deepethogram, a machine learning pipeline for supervised behavior classification from raw pixels. eLife **10** (2021). https://doi.org/10.7554/eLife.63377

10. Bova, A., Kernodle, K., Mulligan, K., Leventhal, D.: Automated rat single-pellet reaching with 3-dimensional reconstruction of paw and digit trajectories. J. Vis. Exp. 2019(149) (2019). https://doi.org/10.3791/59979

11. Carreño-Munoz, M., et al.: Potential involvement of impaired bk ca channel function in sensory defensiveness and some behavioral disturbances induced by unfamiliar environment in a mouse model of fragile x syndrome. Neuropsychopharmacology **43**(3), 492–502 (2018). https://doi.org/10.1038/npp.2017.149

12. Carreño-Muñoz, M., et al.: Detecting fine and elaborate movements with piezo sensors provides non-invasive access to overlooked behavioral components. Neuropsychopharmacology **47**(4), 933–943 (2022). https://doi.org/10.1038/s41386-021-01217-w

13. Chaput, S.L., Burggren, W.W., Hurd, P.L., Hamilton, T.J.: Zebrafish (danio rerio) shoaling in light and dark conditions involves a complex interplay between vision and lateral line. Behav. Brain Res. **439**, 114228 (2023)

14. Chen, C.P.J., Morota, G., Lee, K., Zhang, Z., Cheng, H.: Vtag: a semi-supervised pipeline for tracking pig activity with a single top-view camera. J. Animal Sci. **100** (2022)

15. Chen, G., Li, C., Guo, Y., Shu, H., Cao, Z., Xu, B.: Recognition of cattle's feeding behaviors using noseband pressure sensor with machine learning. Front. Veterinary Sci. **9**, 822621 (2022)

16. Choi, S., et al.: Parallel ascending spinal pathways for affective touch and pain. Nature **587**(7833), 258–263 (2020). https://doi.org/10.1038/s41586-020-2860-1

17. Clemensson, E.K.H., Abbaszadeh, M., Fanni, S., Espa, E., Cenci, M.A.: Tracking rats in operant conditioning chambers using a versatile homemade video camera and deeplabcut. J. Vis. Exp. (160) (2020). https://doi.org/10.3791/61409

18. Coffey, K., Marx, R., Neumaier, J.: Deepsqueak: a deep learning-based system for detection and analysis of ultrasonic vocalizations. Neuropsychopharmacology **44**(5), 859–868 (2019). https://doi.org/10.1038/s41386-018-0303-6

19. Cristancho, A.G., Tulina, N., Brown, A.G., Anton, L., Barila, G., Elovitz, M.A.: Intrauterine inflammation leads to select sex- and age-specific behavior and molecular differences in mice. Int. J. Molec. Sci. **24** (2022)

20. Datta, S., Anderson, D., Branson, K., Perona, P., Leifer, A.: Computational neuroethology: A call to action. Neuron **104**(1), 11–24 (2019). https://doi.org/10.1016/j.neuron.2019.09.038

21. De Almeida, T., Spinelli, B., Hypolito Lima, R., Gonzalez, M., Rodrigues, A.: Pyrat: An open-source python library for animal behavior analysis. Front. Neurosci. **16** (2022). https://doi.org/10.3389/fnins.2022.779106

22. Doornweerd, J.E., et al.: Passive radio frequency identification and video tracking for the determination of location and movement of broilers. Poult. Sci. **102**, 102412 (2022)

23. Drazan, J.F., Phillips, W.T., Seethapathi, N., Hullfish, T.J., Baxter, J.R.: Moving outside the lab: Markerless motion capture accurately quantifies sagittal plane kinematics during the vertical jump. J. Biomech. **125**, 110547 (2021). https://doi.org/10.1016/j.jbiomech.2021.110547

24. Feng, J., Xiao, X.: Multiobject tracking of wildlife in videos using few-shot learning. Animals: Open Access J. MDPI **12** (2022)

25. Fujiwara, T., Brotas, M., Chiappe, M.: Walking strides direct rapid and flexible recruitment of visual circuits for course control in drosophila. Neuron **110**(13), 2124-2138.e8 (2022). https://doi.org/10.1016/j.neuron.2022.04.008

26. Gabriel, C.J., et al.: Behaviordepot is a simple, flexible tool for automated behavioral detection based on markerless pose tracking. Elife **11** (2022). https://doi.org/10.7554/eLife.74314

27. Gaidica, M., Dantzer, B.: An implantable neurophysiology platform: Broadening research capabilities in free-living and non-traditional animals. Front. Neural Circ. **16**, 940989 (2022)

28. Geelen, J.E., Branco, M.P., Ramsey, N.F., van der Helm, F.C.T., Mugge, W., Schouten, A.C.: Markerless motion capture: Ml-mocap, a low-cost modular multi-camera setup. Annu. Int. Conf. IEEE. Eng. Med. Biol. Soc. **2021**, 4859–4862 (2021). https://doi.org/10.1109/EMBC46164.2021.9629749

29. Gerós, A., Magalhães, A., Aguiar, P.: Improved 3d tracking and automated classification of rodents' behavioral activity using depth-sensing cameras. Behav. Res. Methods **52**(5), 2156–2167 (2020). https://doi.org/10.3758/s13428-020-01381-9

30. Gomez-Marin, A.: A clash of umwelts: Anthropomorphism in behavioral neuroscience. Behav. Brain Sci. **42**, e229 (2019). https://doi.org/10.1017/S0140525X19001237

31. Goncharow, P.N., Beaudette, S.M.: Assessing time-varying lumbar flexion-extension kinematics using automated pose estimation. J. Appl. Biomech. **38**(5), 355–360 (2022). https://doi.org/10.1123/jab.2022-0041

32. Graving, J., et al.: Deepposekit, a software toolkit for fast and robust animal pose estimation using deep learning. eLife **8** (2019). https://doi.org/10.7554/eLife.47994

33. Henriques, S., et al.: Metabolic cross-feeding in imbalanced diets allows gut microbes to improve reproduction and alter host behaviour. Nat. Commun. **11**(1) (2020). https://doi.org/10.1038/s41467-020-18049-9

34. Hood, K.E., Long, E., Navarro, E., Hurley, L.M.: Playback of broadband vocalizations of female mice suppresses male ultrasonic calls. PLoS ONE **18**, e0273742 (2023)

35. Hrvatin, S., et al.: Neurons that regulate mouse torpor. Nature **583**(7814), 115–121 (2020). https://doi.org/10.1038/s41586-020-2387-5
36. Hsu, A., Yttri, E.: B-soid, an open-source unsupervised algorithm for identification and fast prediction of behaviors. Nat. Commun. **12**(1) (2021). https://doi.org/10.1038/s41467-021-25420-x
37. Huang, G., Liu, Z., Van Der Maaten, L., Weinberger, K.: Densely connected convolutional networks, pp. 2261–2269 (January 2017). https://doi.org/10.1109/CVPR.2017.243
38. Hurley, M., et al.: Adolescent female rats recovered from the activity-based anorexia display blunted hedonic responding. Int. J. Eating Disorders **55**(8), 1042–1053 (2022). https://doi.org/10.1002/eat.23752
39. Jia, Y., et al.: Selfee, self-supervised features extraction of animal behaviors. eLife **11** (2022). https://doi.org/10.7554/eLife.76218
40. Jin, T., Duan, F.: Rat behavior observation system based on transfer learning. IEEE Access **7**, 62152–62162 (2019). https://doi.org/10.1109/ACCESS.2019.2916339
41. Kabra, M., Robie, A., Rivera-Alba, M., Branson, S., Branson, K.: Jaaba: Interactive machine learning for automatic annotation of animal behavior. Nat. Methods **10**(1), 64–67 (2013). https://doi.org/10.1038/nmeth.2281
42. Karashchuk, P., et al.: Anipose: A toolkit for robust markerless 3d pose estimation. Cell Rep. **36**(13), 109730 (2021). https://doi.org/10.1016/j.celrep.2021.109730
43. Kempermann, G., et al.: The individuality paradigm: Automated longitudinal activity tracking of large cohorts of genetically identical mice in an enriched environment. Neurobiol. Dis. **175**, 105916 (2022)
44. Kirkpatrick, N.J., Butera, R.J., Chang, Y.H.: Deeplabcut increases markerless tracking efficiency in x-ray video analysis of rodent locomotion. J. Exp. Biol. **225**(16) (2022). https://doi.org/10.1242/jeb.244540
45. Kume, M., Yoshikawa, Y., Tanaka, T., Watanabe, S., Mitamura, H., Yamashita, Y.: Water temperature and precipitation stimulate small-sized japanese eels to climb a low-height vertical weir. PLoS ONE **17**, e0279617 (2022)
46. Kuramoto, E., et al.: Development of a system to analyze oral frailty associated with alzheimer's disease using a mouse model. Front. Aging Neurosci. **14** (2022). https://doi.org/10.3389/fnagi.2022.935033
47. Lauer, J., et al.: Multi-animal pose estimation, identification and tracking with deeplabcut. Nat. Methods **19**(4), 496–504 (2022). https://doi.org/10.1038/s41592-022-01443-0
48. Li, J., Kells, P., Osgood, A., Gautam, S., Shew, W.: Collapse of complexity of brain and body activity due to excessive inhibition and mecp2 disruption. Proc. National Acad. Sci. United States Am. **118**(43) (2021). https://doi.org/10.1073/pnas.2106378118
49. Li, Y., et al.: A novel open-source raspberry pi-based behavioral testing in zebrafish. PLoS ONE **17**, e0279550 (2022)
50. Lonini, L., et al.: Video-based pose estimation for gait analysis in stroke survivors during clinical assessments: A proof-of-concept study. Digit Biomark **6**(1), 9–18 (2022). https://doi.org/10.1159/000520732
51. Lopes, G., Monteiro, P.: New open-source tools: Using bonsai for behavioral tracking and closed-loop experiments. Front. Behav. Neurosci. **15** (2021). https://doi.org/10.3389/fnbeh.2021.647640
52. Luxem, K., et al.: Identifying behavioral structure from deep variational embeddings of animal motion. Communications Biology **5**(1) (2022). https://doi.org/10.1038/s42003-022-04080-7

53. Magaju, D., Montgomery, J., Franklin, P., Baker, C., Friedrich, H.: Machine learning based assessment of small-bodied fish tracking to evaluate spoiler baffle fish passage design. J. Environ. Manage. **325**(Pt A), 116507 (2023). https://doi.org/10.1016/j.jenvman.2022.116507

54. Marcus, A.D., Achanta, S., Jordt, S.E.: Protocol for non-invasive assessment of spontaneous movements of group-housed animals using remote video monitoring. STAR Protocols **3**, 101326 (2022)

55. Marks, M., et al.: Deep-learning based identification, tracking, pose estimation, and behavior classification of interacting primates and mice in complex environments. Nat. Mach. Intell. **4**, 331–340 (2022)

56. Marshall, J.D., Li, T., Wu, J.H., Dunn, T.W.: Leaving flatland: Advances in 3d behavioral measurement. Curr. Opin. Neurobiol. **73**, 102522 (2022)

57. Mathis, A., et al.: Deeplabcut: markerless pose estimation of user-defined body parts with deep learning. Nat. Neurosci. **21**(9), 1281–1289 (2018). https://doi.org/10.1038/s41593-018-0209-y

58. Narayanan, D.Z., Takahashi, D.Y., Kelly, L.M., Hlavaty, S.I., Huang, J., Ghazanfar, A.A.: Prenatal development of neonatal vocalizations. eLife **11** (2022)

59. Needham, L., et al.: The accuracy of several pose estimation methods for 3d joint centre localisation. Sci. Rep. **11**(1), 20673 (2021). https://doi.org/10.1038/s41598-021-00212-x

60. Neunuebel, J., Taylor, A., Arthur, B., Roian Egnor, S.: Female mice ultrasonically interact with males during courtship displays. eLife 4, 1–24 (2015). https://doi.org/10.7554/eLife.06203

61. Parker, P.R.L., et al.: Distance estimation from monocular cues in an ethological visuomotor task. Elife **11** (2022). https://doi.org/10.7554/eLife.74708,https://doi.org/10.7554%2Felife.74708

62. Parmiani, P., Lucchetti, C., Bonifazzi, C., Franchi, G.: A kinematic study of skilled reaching movement in rat. J. Neurosci. Methods **328**, 108404 (2019). https://doi.org/10.1016/j.jneumeth.2019.108404

63. Pereira, T.D., et al.: Sleap: A deep learning system for multi-animal pose tracking. Nat. Methods **19**, 486–495 (2022)

64. Pereira, T., et al.: Fast animal pose estimation using deep neural networks. Nature Methods **16**(1), 117–125 (2019). https://doi.org/10.1038/s41592-018-0234-5

65. Pons, P., Jaen, J., Catala, A.: Assessing machine learning classifiers for the detection of animals' behavior using depth-based tracking. Expert Systems with Applications **86**, 235–246 (2017). https://doi.org/10.1016/j.eswa.2017.05.063, https://www.sciencedirect.com/science/article/pii/S0957417417303913

66. Popov, A., et al.: A high-fat diet changes astrocytic metabolism to promote synaptic plasticity and behavior. Acta Physiologica **236**(1) (2022). https://doi.org/10.1111/apha.13847

67. Rodrigues, D., et al.: Chronic stress causes striatal disinhibition mediated by sominterneurons in male mice. Nat. Commun. **13**(1) (2022). https://doi.org/10.1038/s41467-022-35028-4

68. Sangarapillai, N., Wöhr, M., Schwarting, R.K.W.: Appetitive 50 khz calls in a pavlovian conditioned approach task in cacna1c haploinsufficient rats. Phys. Behav. **250**, 113795 (2022)

69. Segalin, C., et al.: The mouse action recognition system (mars) software pipeline for automated analysis of social behaviors in mice. eLife **10** (2021). https://doi.org/10.7554/eLife.63720

70. Sturman, O., et al.: Deep learning-based behavioral analysis reaches human accuracy and is capable of outperforming commercial solutions. Neuropsychopharmacology **45**(11), 1942–1952 (2020). https://doi.org/10.1038/s41386-020-0776-y

71. Su, F., et al.: Noninvasive tracking of every individual in unmarked mouse groups using multi-camera fusion and deep learning. Neurosci. Bull. (2022)

72. Suryanto, M.E., et al.: Using deeplabcut as a real-time and markerless tool for cardiac physiology assessment in zebrafish. Biology (Basel) **11**(8) (2022). https://doi.org/10.3390/biology11081243

73. Takenaka, M., et al.: Behavior of snow monkeys hunting fish to survive winter. Sci. Rep. **12**, 20324 (2022)

74. Tarcsay, G., Boublil, B., Ewell, L.: Low-cost platform for multianimal chronic local field potential video monitoring with graphical user interface (gui) for seizure detection and behavioral scoring. eNeuro **9**(5) (2022). https://doi.org/10.1523/ENEURO.0283-22.2022

75. Venkatraman, S., Jin, X., Costa, R., Carmena, J.: Investigating neural correlates of behavior in freely behaving rodents using inertial sensors. Journal of Neurophysiology **104**(1), 569–575 (2010). https://doi.org/10.1152/jn.00121.2010

76. Vester, H., Hammerschmidt, K., Timme, M., Hallerberg, S.: Quantifying group specificity of animal vocalizations without specific sender information. Phys. Rev. E **93**(2), 022138 (2016). https://doi.org/10.1103/PhysRevE.93.022138

77. Vonstad, E.K., Su, X., Vereijken, B., Bach, K., Nilsen, J.H.: Comparison of a deep learning-based pose estimation system to marker-based and kinect systems in exergaming for balance training. Sensors (Basel) **20**(23) (2020). https://doi.org/10.3390/s20236940

78. Wang, J., Karbasi, P., Wang, L., Meeks, J.P.: A layered, hybrid machine learning analytic workflow for mouse risk assessment behavior. eNeuro (2022). https://doi.org/10.1523/ENEURO.0335-22.2022

79. Weber, R.Z., Mulders, G., Kaiser, J., Tackenberg, C., Rust, R.: Deep learning-based behavioral profiling of rodent stroke recovery. BMC Biol. **20**(1), 232 (2022). https://doi.org/10.1186/s12915-022-01434-9

80. Whiteway, M.R.: Partitioning variability in animal behavioral videos using semi-supervised variational autoencoders. PLoS Comput. Biol. **17**(9), e1009439 (2021). https://doi.org/10.1371/journal.pcbi.1009439

81. Wrench, A., Balch-Tomes, J.: Beyond the edge: Markerless pose estimation of speech articulators from ultrasound and camera images using deeplabcut. Sensors (Basel) **22**(3) (2022). https://doi.org/10.3390/s22031133

# Toward an Epidermal Patch for Voice Prosthesis and Diseases Prediction by a Fuzzy-Neuro Paradigm

Mario Malcangi[1]([⊠]), Giovanni Felisati[2], Alberto Saibene[2], Enrico Alfonsi[3],
Mauro Fresia[3], and Pasquale Cambiaghi[4]

[1] Computer Science Department, Università Degli Studi Di Milano, Milano, Italy
malcangi@di.unimi.it
[2] Department of Heath Science, Università Degli Studi Di Milano, Milano, Italy
{giovanni.felisati,alberto.saibene}@unimi.it
[3] IRCCS Mondino Foundation, Pavia, Italy
enrico.alfonsi@mondino.it
[4] MRS srl Cazzaniga, Bergamo, Italy
p.cambiaghi@acmrs.com

**Abstract.** Voice rehabilitation and diseases prediction is required today because neural degeneration or neurological injury alters the motor component of the speech system in the phonation area of the brain. A novel approach to voice rehabilitation consists in predicting the phonetic control by the EMG. In a previous work we demonstrated that the voice-production apparatus (tongue muscle) generates a specific EMG signal that identify the phoneme emitted. The inference paradigm is EFuNN (Evolving Fuzzy Neural Network) trained by the sampled EMG (Electro Myo Gram) signal at phonation-. Time. A phoneme-to-speech non-invasive epidermal patch is to be designed with energy harvestimg and MEMS loudspeakers.

**Keywords:** EFuNN · Evolving Fuzzy Neural Network · voice dysarthria · Voice rehabilitation · Myoelectric signal · Patch

## 1 Introduction

In a previous investigation work [1] we demonstrate that voice prosthesis is feasible if an Evolving Fuzzy Neural Network (EFuNN) is trained by the Electromyogram EMG (Electro Myo Gram) generated by the voice signal, but the standard electronics is too invasive.

For these reasons we design an epidermal patch (Fig. 1) to be non-invasive. Several Investigations concerns epidermal patch, The most advanced is the one of Samsung [2] South Korea were some investigators develop stretchable heart rate monitoring skin patch. This was possible because Samsung detects the technology of flexible displays, so a skin patch has valuable performances in integrating stretchable oled technology

© The Author(s), under exclusive license to Springer Nature Switzerland AG 2023
L. Iliadis et al. (Eds.): EANN 2023, CCIS 1826, pp. 28–32, 2023.
https://doi.org/10.1007/978-3-031-34204-2_3

to display HR (Heart Rate) in real-time and no-invasiveness. But Samsung's patch is intended to displayn only HR, not vital signs like our patch.

Another investigation concerns epidermal patch for monitoring metabolism [3]. InThis investigation with non-invasive approach try to predicts degenerations due to daily activities.

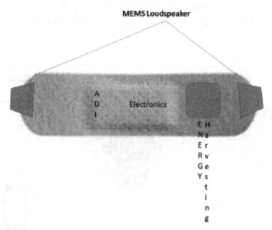

**Fig. 1.** The patch has two MEMS loudspeakers to reproduce aloud the synthesized voice and an harvesting system to provide electrical energy to the electronic vircuits. (Analog Devices sensors).

Several trials and research and development efforts were engaged in the time, but the mayor difficulty is to have the approvals by the FDA (Food nd drug Administration).

## 2 Energy Harvesting

Energy harvesting is a common practice in body devices because it is the only way to provide electrical energy wirelessly and without recharge. The Japanese company Seiko has developed an harvesting technology named Kinetik [4] that harvest electrical energy from movement, charging a supercapacitor (SUPERCAP) to provide electric power to a microstep motor that moves the watch's parts.

Several harwesting modes have been implemented in the e-health field named body harvesting, like body thermal harvesting or photovoltaic harvesting, but none of them capable to solve adequately the electronics powering.

Prof. Thibado University of Arkansas (USA) has defined a method and the electronics to harvest electrical energy by graphene.

This method is independent from time and position, so it is the best option for patch's energy requirements.

At ambient temperature, micro sized-sheets of freestanding graphene are is in contant motion even in the presence of an applied bias voltage. Thibado and his investigation team quantify out-of-plane movement by collecting the displacement current [5].

## 3  Flexible PCB

AnalogDevices INCorporate (ADI) have integrated on a SoP (System-on-Package) all the needed electronics for vital signs measurements: the AFE (Analog-Front-End), the LEDs (Ligth-Emitted-Diodes), the mixed signal electronics, the MCU (MicroController Unit) (ARM-architecture-based) and BLE (Blue Tooth Low Energy) to wirelessly connect to the APPs (Fig. 2) of a smartphone. If flexible PCB is available to integrate the SoP electronics for vital signs detection, so a patch-like could be designed.

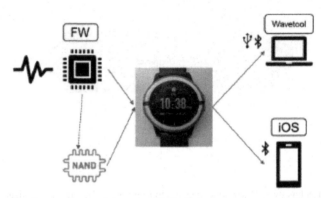

**Fig. 2.** The analog Devices's watch has on a SoP all the resources to acquire vital signs from human being and visualize in apps android/IOS OR ADI like wavetool. (courtesy of Analog Devices).

## 4  Ng and Processing the Myoelectric Signal

The ADI's (Analog Devices Inc) SoP integrated all the electronic to detect the myoelectric signal by means of two stainless-steel surface electrodes available at bottom of the watch and placed on the neck sublingual muscles during swallowing and speech. A third electrode (reference) was also placed. The three-electrode set detects in differential mode the electric potential that controls the muscle during utterance of each phoneme of the word. The electrodes are connected to a smartphone. (Fig. 2). The recorded myoelectric patterns have been displayed on the smartphone as EMG and microcontroller running the EFuNN application converts it into the uttered phoneme (Fig. 3).

/a/

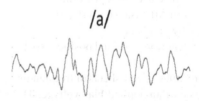

**Fig. 3.**  Each EMG pattern is generated by a speech phoneme.

## 5 Electro Myo GRAM and Phonemes

Each phoneme generates an Electro Myo Gram (EMG) pattern (Fig. 3), so a neural network (NN)can be trained to infer about the intention to speech a specific word by the subject tested.

The EMG is collected by the two metal electrodes on the bottom of the watch applied to the neck of the subject that swallow the phonem. The pattern, captured and digitalized is labeled and used to train the EFuNN (Fig. 3.).

The training dataset consisted of the raw sampled data from the myoelectric signal and one label that classify the pattern as generated by a specific phoneme. Thousands of patterns need to be collected and classified to proceed to supervised learning of the predicting paradigm. After learning the paradigm will be able to predict from a myoelectric pattern the phoneme that the subject is to utter.

## 6 He EFuNN Paradigm

EFuNN (Fig. 4) is a particular implementation of the ECOS [7] (Evolving COnnectionist System). ECOS IS a biologically inspired framework. IEFuNN Synthesize the rules by a BPNN (Back Propagation Neural Netwok), otherwise fuzzy systems need of an expert (human). I t is a paradigm that evolves through incremental, on-line learning, both supervised and unsupervised. EFuNN [7, 8] is fasterfaster than multilayer perceptrons and fuzzy networks.

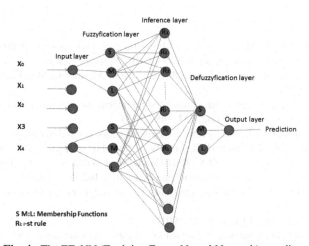

**Fig. 4.** The EFuNN (Evolving Fuzzy Neural Network) paradigm.

## 7 Daftaset, Training and Test

To trainThe E FuNN [9] from the myoelectric patterns a dataset has been built. The dataset consists as follows:

$V_1 \; V_2 \; V_3 \; V_4 \; V_5 \; V_6 V_7 \; V_8 \; V_9 \; V_{10} \; V_{11} \; V \ldots \; V_j \; \ldots \; V_N \; L_n.$

$V_j$: j-th amplitude of the j-th sample of the n-th myoelectric pattern.

$L_n$: n-th label associated to the n-th sequence.

To test the EFuNN [9] we apply the same dataset used to train. Tthe wovels used are the five from Italian langue /a/, /e/, //i/, /o/, /u/, and the word /aiuole/ that inludes all the wovels.

## 8    Conclusion and Future Developments

To develop a real patch we have to design a fexible PCB to host all the needed electronics, included the energy harvesting and MEMS loudspeakers. Fraunhofer IPMS investigators [13] develop all silicon MEMS speaker for mobile audio. This is a novel audio trsducer technology that we intend to test and integrate on the patch because it is enegy efficient and specifically optimized for transduction.

We intend also to investigate how to port efficiently the EFuNN paradigm on an ARM M4-M3 architecture or like NXP CSP (Chip Scale Package) ARM Cortex M0 + processor MCU. It is interesting because it is ultra-low power and optimized for low-leakage applications.

A third step in future investigation concerns the harvesting mode. Thibado graphene-based is interesting but covered by a patent and need to be investigated about his feasibllity .

## References

1. Malcangi, M., et al.: Myo-to-speech-evolving fuzzy neural network predicion of speech utterances from myoelectric signal, vol. 893. CCIS. Springer ( 2018)
2. Samsung Researchers Develop Stretchable Heart Rate Monitoring Skin Patch: MobiHealt-News.htm (2022)
3. Sempionatto, J.R. : An epidermal patch for simulltaneus monitoring of haemodynamic and metabolic markers. Nat. Med. Eng. **737**, 748 (2021)
4. https://www.seiko+kinetic+harvesting&tbm=isch&chips=q:seiko+kinetic+harvesting, online_chips:energy+harvester:sNEtyCmbPVc%3D,online_chips:wearable+devices.
5. Thibado M.N., Kumar p., Singh S., Ruiz-Garcia M., Lasanta A., Bonilla L.L.: Fluctation-Induced current from freestanding graphene, Phys. Rev. **102**, 042101(2020)
6. Kasabov, N.: Evolving Connectionist Systems: The knoledge engineering approach. Springer, Heidelberg (2007)
7. Kasabov, N.: EFuNN, IEEE Tr SMC (2001)
8. Kasabov, N.: Evolving fuzzy neural networks – algorithms, applications and biological moti-vation, In: Yamakawa, Matsumoto (eds.) Methodologies for the Conception, Design and Application of the Soft Computing, World Computing, pp. 271–274 (1998)
9. http://www.kedri.aut.ac.nz/areas-of-expertise/data-mining-and-decision-support-systems/neucom,
10. Conrad, H., et al.: A small gap Electrostatic micro Actuator for large Deflections. Nat. Commun. **6**, 10078 (2015)

# Towards Improved User Experience
# for Artificial Intelligence Systems

Lisa Brand[1] , Bernhard G. Humm[2]([✉]) , Andrea Krajewski[1] ,
and Alexander Zender[2] 

[1] Department of Media, Darmstadt University of Applied Sciences, Schöfferstr. 3, 64295
Darmstadt, Germany
{lisa.brand,andrea.krajewski}@h-da.de
[2] Department of Computer Science, Darmstadt University of Applied Sciences, Schöfferstr. 3,
64295 Darmstadt, Germany
{bernhard.humm,alexander.zender}@h-da.de

**Abstract.** In this paper, the factors of positive user experiences when using AI
systems are investigated. For this purpose, a two-stage qualitative usability study
was conducted for the OMA-ML platform as an example. OMA-ML is an AutoML
platform that automates complex tasks in machine learning (ML) and generates
ML pipelines. The usability of OMA-ML was measured against the ISO 9241-
110:2020 standard in an expert evaluation. The vulnerabilities with the greatest
impact on the application were prioritised and tested in a qualitative usability
test. The results of the usability test are presented along with recommendations
in a usability evaluation. This study aims to contribute to the understanding of
the usability of AI systems and their impact on the experience of the different
user groups. It found that special attention needs to be paid to those interaction
principles that serve to build user trust towards the AI system. For this purpose,
the interaction principles with the main design dimensions for interaction with AI
systems were derived.

**Keywords:** Artificial Intelligence Systems · Automated Machine Learning ·
User Experience · Usability

## 1 Introduction

*Artificial intelligence (AI) systems*, in particular ones using machine learning (ML), are
in everyday use (Russell and Norvig 2020)[1]. *User Experience (UX)* is important when
assessing the relationship between AI and users, as it is necessary to comprehend users'

This work was partially funded by the German federal ministry of education and research (BMBF)
in the program Zukunft der Wertschöpfung (funding code 02L19C157), supported by Projektträger
Karlsruhe (PTKA), and by hessian.AI Connectom for project "Innovative UX für User-Centered
AI Systeme". The responsibility for the content of this publication lies with the authors.

[1] In this paper, we use the term *AI systems* as a general term for AI-based IT systems, including
AI applications for end users (e.g., medical doctors) as well as AI platforms for AI specialists
(e.g., ML experts developing end-user AI applications).

L. Iliadis et al. (Eds.): EANN 2023, CCIS 1826, pp. 33–44, 2023.
https://doi.org/10.1007/978-3-031-34204-2_4

needs and behaviours (Chapman et al. 2016). *Usability* is an important element of UX that emphasizes on a product's ease of use and learnability. It can have a significant influence on user satisfaction and task performance (Lazar et al. 2017). Unfortunately, the discussion of UX issues in the scientific AI community is limited (see related work). This paper aims to raise awareness for this issue by presenting a case study and providing and discussing respective guidelines. Our underlying goal is to make AI systems better accessible to people.

The case study focuses on *OMA-ML (Ontology-based Meta AutoML)* (Humm and Zender 2021; Zender and Humm 2022), an AI platform for *automated machine learning (AutoML)*. OMA-ML with its claim "effective machine learning made easy" serves the goal of making AI applications better accessible to end-users in two ways: directly and indirectly. By allowing domain experts (e.g., in biomedicine) with limited programming and ML expertise to generate ML models, this *directly* broadens the access of AI technology to science and industry. ML models that have been generated using OMA-ML may be integrated in end-user AI applications, e.g., for medical doctors. Via ML model explainability features (see e.g. (Lundberg and Lee 2017), OMA-ML *indirectly* supports accessibility of end-user AI applications by providing the background information for explanations of predictions to end users like medical doctors.

The remainder of this paper is structured as follows. Section 2 presents related work, in particular criteria for UX in AI systems. Section 3 introduces the user interaction concept of OMA-ML. We then describe the methodology and main findings of a UX survey of OMA-ML in Sect. 4. In this survey, users were interviewed regarding their UX requirements and the implementation of those requirements in OMA-ML was evaluated. The survey results were used for improving the UX of the OMA-ML platform. They have also been used as a basis for a set of UX recommendations for AI systems which is the main contribution of this paper (Sect. 5). Section 6 concludes the paper and indicates future work.

## 2   Related Work

AI systems which use ML have gained increasing importance in recent years, with applications ranging from image and speech recognition to natural language processing and prediction systems (Alcácer and Cruz-Machado 2019; Bonaccorso 2017; Lu 2017). However, the success of these systems depends not only on their underlying algorithms and data, but also on how they are presented to human users and how they interact with them (Moustakis and Herrmann 1997). UX is a collection of techniques for understanding users' needs and behaviours to create useful, usable systems and services (Chapman et al. 2016). To encourage improved UX for AI systems, the human-computer interface (HCI) community is calling for multidisciplinary collaboration and a user-centred approach (Abdul et al. 2018; Wang et al. 2019).

Unfortunately, the role of UX in AI systems has received little academic attention in the past years (Chromik et al. 2020). Nonetheless, the number of pertinent papers has been slowly rising and has continued to do so as AI is becoming more and more prominent in a variety of settings. For example, Fucs et al. (2020) present findings from a case study of the use of a storytelling method to design and validate the UX of AI assistants for the oil and gas industry by using animated sketch-based video. Li and Lu (2021) investigate how non-AI-expert end users can be engaged in the design process of an AI-enabled application by using a framework called Smart Service Blueprint Scape (SSBS). Kurdziolek (2022) states that in the realm of ML, usability is also a crucial factor. If users do not understand how ML-based technologies work, they will be less likely to trust and adopt them. The term *usability* refers to techniques used to make a product more user-friendly during the design process (Nielsen 2012). In addition, usability also measures satisfaction, which involves UX (ISO 2019a). The audiences for ML model explanations come from varied backgrounds and have different levels of experience with statistics and mathematical reasoning, making it challenging to communicate and explain ML models effectively. Additionally, cognitive biases can affect how users interpret and understand explanations. Ensuring transparent and understandable explanations is important for increasing trust and adoption of ML-based technologies (Kurdziolek 2022).

Another important part of usability is *user expectations*. According to the expectancy disconfirmation theory (Oliver 1977), user expectations can significantly impact their perception of usability. When the quality of the usability experience falls below expectations, it can lead to dissatisfaction. On the other hand, if the quality exceeds expectations, it can result in satisfaction. Venkatesh et al. (2003) also state that it has been proven through empirical evidence that an employee's expectations of usability can predict the likelihood of adoption, particularly in the context of information system usability. The key is knowing the users' expectations towards controllability versus the technically possible high-level automation of the system and the real need for control (Shneiderman 2020).

## 3   OMA-ML User Interaction Concept

OMA-ML is an AI platform with two target user groups: *domain experts* (experts in an application domain like biomedicine who may not have programming expertise) and *AI experts* (users with programming and AI/ML expertise). OMA-ML allows both user groups to automatically generate ML pipelines containing ML models trained on datasets. Domain experts may use the automatically deployed ML pipelines for making predictions for new data on the platform, e.g. predicting diseases based on medical conditions. AI experts may download the source code for ML pipelines to include them in newly developed AI applications for end-users. A major benefit of OMA-ML compared to existing AI platforms like Rapidminer is the diversity of automatically generated ML pipelines. To the best of our knowledge, OMA-ML is the only AI platform that generates ML pipelines for a large variety of ML libraries, avoiding vendor lock-in common in commercial AI platforms.

We will use OMA-ML as a sample AI system for the UX study presented in the next section. In this section, we briefly present the user interaction concept for OMA-ML. See Fig. 1 with a screenshot of the model dashboard page.

Users may upload datasets in various formats to the platform, including tabular data, images, texts, and time series. In the example shown in Fig. 1, a CSV file (tabular data) has been uploaded containing medical conditions of diabetes patients. The uploaded dataset can be used for training ML models. For this, various AutoML solutions can generate ML

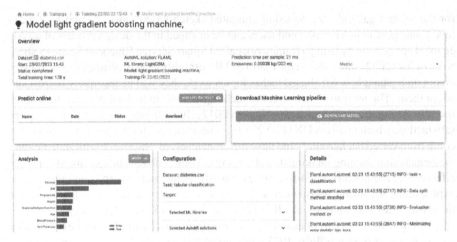

**Fig. 1.** OMA-ML model dashboard.

pipelines for various ML libraries in parallel (for details see Zender and Humm 2022). Domain experts may use a wizard for starting ML training in a simple and intuitive way; AI experts may configure the training session in a sophisticated and detailed way. After training has completed (which may take a few minutes or several days, depending on the complexity of the dataset and the time limit configured by the user), a leaderboard is displayed. The leaderboard allows comparing all generated ML models regarding their performance: prediction quality, prediction time and environmental impact. The user may select an ML model depending on his or her preferences. When selecting a model, the model dashboard shown in Fig. 1 is opened. In this example, a LightGBM (light gradient boosting machine) model was generated by the AutoML solution FLAML, as is indicated in the overview card of the dashboard (top). Other cards of the dashboard show details about the configuration or the training process which may be relevant for AI experts (bottom right). The explainable AI module is shown in the analysis card (bottom left) which may be interesting for domain experts and AI experts alike. It indicates the importance of various features of the dataset (here: Glucose, BMI, Pregnancies etc.) on the prediction of diabetes disease in this ML model. Domain experts may check the validity of the ML model with their medical domain knowledge. Both cards in the centre of the dashboard allow using the ML model. Medical doctors may upload a file with new patient data and use the OMA-ML platform for predicting the likelihood of those patients suffering from diabetes (predict online card centre left). AI experts may download the generated ML pipeline as a set of Python source code files (download ML pipeline card centre right). They may be included in a new AI application for medical doctors working with diabetes patients.

# 4   UX Evaluation of OMA-ML

## 4.1   Methodology

In 2022 an *expert review* in the field of usability was conducted to detect usability weak points and to increase the overall user experience of OMA-ML. A *use case model* (Bittner and Spence 2003) was created beforehand to set the scope for the research. The usability weak points were identified using the interaction principles of (ISO 9241-110 2020). An *actual-versus-target analysis* was built to show a direct comparison in order to highlight the usability weak points. In total, eight usability tests were carried out in order to reveal potential areas of confusion and uncover opportunities for improving the overall UX. Both target user groups of OMA-ML were included in the usability tests in equal parts. The ages of participants ranged from 24 to 44 years. Participants were from Brazil (1), Dubai (1), and Germany (6)[2]. Each usability test lasted between 1.5 and 2 h on average. A usability evaluation was performed for all usability test findings.

**Methods Used.** For this study, qualitative research techniques were selected to enable comprehending what users value most in their experiences (Merriam 1998). Qualitative methods in usability research are used to identify possible usage barriers and their reasons among users. The question is not whether a problem is statistically frequent, but rather to identify the possible problems and to understand the mental models behind them. Mental models are experience-dependent, excerpt-based, conceptual notions of users of how to deal with an application and what consequences and meanings result from it, established prior to its use (Dutke 1994). Knowledge about mental models of the specific user group of an application is especially important for the introduction of novel technologies for users' acceptance and positive usage experience.

To gain insight into how to improve the usability of OMA-ML, the *phenomenological method* was used. Phenomenology is a useful approach for examining the experiences of a small group of people and uncovering the essential elements of those experiences. This method can be used to identify patterns and relationships that contribute to a deeper understanding of the phenomenon being studied (Creswell and Creswell 2017; Moustakas 1994). A *Use-Case Model* was created to define the scope of this research paper. It was used to identify the processes that the target groups will later experience with the system. Use-Cases characterize the functionality of a system and, by extension, its external behaviour. A significant advantage of Use-Cases is that they break down the variety of functions from the user's perspective into logical units and define them in more detail step by step (Bittner and Spence 2003; Richter and Flückiger 2010).

Well-known challenges with qualitative methods, in addition to small sample size and sample selection (Oppong 2013), include the *Hawthorne effect*, which accounts for the influence of unnatural interview situations (Sedgwick and Greenwood 2015). For this reason, it is important to understand the analysis not in terms of a quantitative evaluation, but as a basis for discussion of alternative mental models of users. Furthermore, the interviews were conducted online, allowing subjects to engage with the test subject

---

[2] The participants were required to sign a declaration of consent to have their data collected. The signed consent forms can be obtained on request. All participants were given the right to revoke the consent form and withdraw from the data collection.

in a familiar environment. To minimize the known *risk of observer bias* (Nagappan 2001), pre-planning and repeated consensus-seeking through peer debriefing was used to reduce the risk (Stiles 1993). The main aspects of the usability test were discussed with the OMA-ML development team and two other UX specialists to formulate a plan that minimized observer bias. The usability test itself was practiced and optimized several times before the actual test began.

An expert review (usability inspection method) was conducted to identify potential usability problems within the scope of the research. This type of review involves examining a system, like a website or an app, for any potential issues with usability. While there may be some overlap between expert reviews and heuristic evaluations, it is acceptable to consider an expert review as a more comprehensive version of a heuristic evaluation (Harley 2018). Heuristic evaluation is a common way to check for usability issues, and it is relatively simple, inexpensive, and effective at identifying both major and minor problems. However, it may not catch domain-specific issues, which is why it is important to use the appropriate heuristics (Nielsen 1994, 2005). One of the most important and current sets of guidelines, rules, and best practices is the ISO Standard 9241, with part ISO 9241-110:2020 specifically outlining interaction principles. The expert review in this study was conducted using these interaction principles.

The usability issues identified in an expert review may differ from those found in a usability test, which is why using both methods together leads to the most effective overall design (Harley 2018).

To present the usability issues, a *radar chart* was used to create a comparison between the intended function of the system and its current performance. This analysis, called an *actual-versus-target analysis*, allows for the presentation of any discrepancies between the actual and desired system state. The findings of the usability test were collected and organised in a *usability evaluation*.

**Usability Heuristic Used.** The variables of the actual-versus-target analysis were the interaction principles by (ISO 9241-110 2020) are as followed: *suitability for the user's tasks, self-descriptiveness, conformity with user expectations, learnability, controllability, user error robustness* and *user engagement*.

The order in which the principles are presented here does not imply any priority (ISO 9241-110 2020, p. 11). The German version of (ISO 9241-110 2020) provides a checklist which was used for the expert review to determine whether the interaction requirements have been met (ISO 9241-110 2020, pp. 34–45).

**Measurements.** The variables were measured by a scale of 1 to 5. The target state numbers indicate the extent to which the AI platform interface needs to meet the specified values within the use case model, while the numbers of the actual state represent the current state of the usability in OMA-ML. To differentiate the numbers from one another, each number was given a unique formulation for the desired target-state: (01) expectation does not need to be met, (02) expectation needs to be met very rarely, (03) occasionally, (04) very frequently, (05) fully.

If the actual state of the interface did not meet the desired target state, this would indicate that the interaction variable required further refinement, as it was considered a weak point. The findings of the expert review can be seen in Sect. 4.2.

**Usability Test.** *Pretesting questions* were conducted to collect precise information about the participants' demographics, motives, beliefs, expectations, existing approaches, and prior experience with AI platforms. In the next phase, participants were guided to OMA-ML to engage with the interface, identify any pain points in their experience and perform their work tasks, within the use cases. During the observations, *follow-up questions* were asked to reveal hidden motivations and expectations behind user behaviour. The task was moderated, and participants were guided through the instances. The moment the participants were prompted to share their screen, the moderator invited the participants to think aloud while interacting with OMA-ML. The participants were also frequently encouraged to share their thoughts. After the task completion, the participants moved to the *post testing questions* to gather feedback on the overall user experience. The objective was to analyse the end-to-end user experience, which gives insight into any necessary workflow modifications within the experience of the AI platform. The participants were asked about their overall impression of the experience. Content analysis was used to analyse the usability test data that had been collected.

**Usability Evaluation.** The findings were then collected, structured and ranked in order to prioritise the issues that needed to be addressed following the five severity levels by Nielsen Norman Group (1994): (0) Not a usability problem at all; (1) Cosmetic problem only: need not be fixed unless extra time is available on project; (2) Minor usability problem: fixing this should be given low priority; (3) Major usability problem: important to fix, so should be given high priority; (4) Usability catastrophe: imperative to fix this before product can be released.

## 4.2  Main Results

**Results of the Expert Review in the Field of Usability.** The expert review in the field of usability uncovered a total of four interaction principles with weak points. The weak points identified were *suitability for the User's tasks, self-descriptiveness, conformity with user expectations,* and *user engagement.* The data was then used to create a radar chart to highlight the usability weaknesses of OMA-ML (Fig. 2). The measurements shown are explained in Sect. 4.1.

**Results of the Usability Test Evaluation.** The usability test evaluation counted 73 usability problems in total. Each usability problem was assigned one or more interaction principles: conformity with user expectations (35), self-descriptiveness (30), controllability (16), suitability for the User's tasks (13), user engagement (11), use error robustness (5), and learnability (1). Major usability flaws were collected, some of the most notable ones were:

- **Correlation matrix:** Based on the uploaded data, a correlation matrix is displayed in a dataset overview. Most participants had difficulty viewing and understanding

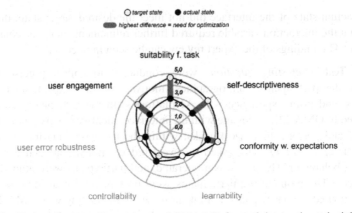

**Fig. 2.** Actual state and target state of OMA-ML for each interaction principle.

the interface element "analysis" in which the correlation matrix was located. Most issues were the viewing experience in the context of the size and white space, the lack of information about the source, as well as the missing purpose and type of the illustrated correlation matrix. This usability problem addressed the interaction weak points: Self-descriptiveness, conformity with user expectations, and user engagement.

- **Predict Online:** OMA-ML offers a powerful feature to make predictions online based on the ML model trained. The participants felt confused in the final stages of the usability test and did not grasp the context of "predict online" and therefore did not understand what to do next. This feature is a major advantage of OMA-ML, but by not providing sufficient information about how to use it, OMA-ML missed an opportunity to showcase its capabilities. This usability problem addressed the interaction weak points: Self-descriptiveness, suitability for the user's tasks, conformity with user expectations, and user engagement.

## 5   Recommendations for UX in AI Systems

As described, the interaction principles formulated in (ISO 9241-110 2020) provide a basis for eliciting usage requirements that lead to a positive UX via satisfactory usability. UX is defined in (ISO 9241-210 2019) as "perception and reaction of a person resulting from the actual and/or expected use of a system, product or service". In this sense, it is important to pay attention *to what users perceive AI-based systems as,* or what expectations and requirements they derive. Their perceptions are formed from their experiences and their accompanying mental states and mental models. This can vary from user group to user group, which is why intensive user experience research is essential.

The interaction principles have been developed to ensure smooth human-computer interaction. The human involved was considered as the *user* of an application or system, who should be enabled to operate, or control it, by observing the criteria of dialog design. With the integration of AI into systems, the roles of humans and machines may change. The user who controls a tool is transformed by the service of AI into a *beneficiary* who benefits from the decisions of the system. This new role must be worked out for the particular AI system – also depending on process situations. According to Shneiderman (2020), one is moving here in a decision space (HCAI framework) in which the degree of control and automation must be situationally relevant and dynamically adapted. If the new role of the user no longer requires constant control of the application by the user but, on the contrary, its at least temporary abandonment, the requirements for the design of user interfaces of such applications change. Instead of the experience of control, the *experience of trust* must be brought more to the fore (Botsman 2017).

This requirement could be traced in the usability study of OMA-ML. Those interaction principles that aim at the users' autonomy and ensure their control over the system took a back seat in the users' requirements. These are: *controllability, learnability,* and *error robustness.* In contrast, those principles were considered more significant and critical that strengthened the cooperation between human and AI system and, thus, the trust in the decisions of the system. These are: *suitability for the user's tasks, self-descriptiveness,* and *user engagement.* Furthermore, the divergence between the look, interaction offer and behaviour of the application and the expectations of the users (*expectation conformity*) must be considered (Fig. 2).

Based on this study the following measures are recommended to ensure a good UX for AI systems:

### (a) User Engagement:

- **The system motivates the user to use it.** It demonstrates attractively and respectfully, that it addresses the users' needs.
- **The system demonstrates its trustworthiness to the user.** It assists with user decisions, clarifies processes, explains risks and consequences, and how to eliminate them if necessary. The information provided gives orientation at all times about location in navigation, process stage and possible actions.
- **The system involves the user.** It allows the user to object where appropriate, or to set their own preferences within the given framework. Furthermore, it offers the user the opportunity to submit improving suggestions for changes and system enhancements.

### (b) Self Descriptiveness:

**The system provides understandable information.** The (and only this) information is given to the user exactly when it is needed, transparently and formulated in such a way that the user can understand it.

**The system clearly shows its system state.** Necessary user input, progress in the process and changes in the system state are clearly displayed.

**The system is role-transparent.** Depending on the situation, the roles between the user and the system are addressed and information is provided about them.

**The system provides information about AI processes.** It offers meaningful information about the logic involved and the scope and intended effects of such processing. It explains how decisions have been made and provides the user with opportunities to give feedback or ask questions.

### (c) Suitability for the User's Task:

**The system informs about its task suitability.** It provides the users with enough information to enable them to determine for themselves whether the system is suitable for the results they are seeking.

**The system enables effort optimization in the execution of tasks.** It provides tools exactly when they should be used. The process to be performed by the user can be reasoned in terms of task and not technology.

### (d) Conformity with User Expectations:

**The system behaves appropriately from the user's point of view.** It provides steps for completing the task that are consistent with the users' understanding of the task. It does not require steps that users do not consider appropriate based on their understanding.
**The system behaves and communicates consistently.** It uses cultural, professional, and linguistic conventions for representation, input, and control that are familiar to users. It behaves consistently within the interactive system and across other interactive systems with which the user is expected to interact.
**The system is able to respond to changes in the context of use.** It is able to respond to the different needs of individual users, to changes regarding the physical environment, as well as to changes of connected resources.

To ensure a positive UX when using AI systems, a participatory development process is necessary. The following *recommendations* help addressing the criteria in the development of AI systems:

- **Early interdisciplinary collaboration:** UX designers also need to understand the technical concept, goals, opportunities, and risks of the application being developed in order to properly set up tests, for example.
- **Deep understanding of the user group:** This includes knowledge of the users' domain-related processes, the context of use, and also the mental models and perceptions with which the AI system will be encountered.
- **Early user involvement:** Users should already be involved in the concept phase to ensure trust in the AI system through a positive UX. Today, the development of AI systems is still often technically motivated. The technical perspective ("What works?") should be abandoned in favour of the user perspective ("What helps?").
- **Multiple iterations:** Several iterations with user participation should be included in the development process. Tests should be conducted at early stages (expectation determination, context analysis, concept test, flow test, wireframe test, prototype test) and not only at the end of the development phase.

## 6   Conclusions and Future Work

The role of UX in the development and design of applications is critical. UX focuses on creating a positive and meaningful experience for users when interacting with a product or service. In addition to influencing user happiness and productivity, the design of AI systems may also promote technological uptake and utilisation. Nevertheless, UX does not yet play a major role in the field of AI. In this context, the interaction between humans and AI systems represents a paradigm shift in human-computer interaction: the transformation of the user from operator to beneficiary of an application.

In order to better understand how to improve the usability and, therefore, the user experience of an ML-based AI system like OMA-ML, this research took a qualitative and user-centric approach. The usability study comprised two test groups (domain experts and AI experts). The evaluation was based on the seven interaction principles (ISO 9241-110, 2020). Subsequently, the results from the tests were re-examined and evaluated on the basis of the changing user role. The study suggests a focus on those interaction principles that serve to build trust between humans and the system to ensure a good UX for AI systems.

The interaction principles formulated in (ISO 9241-110, 2020) were developed to standardise human-machine interaction. This study suggests that the focus is different for human-AI system interaction. The study elaborated the interaction principles relevant here. In the future studies, the recommendation of interaction principles specifically focused on AI systems shall be analysed and reformulated if necessary.

# References

Russell, S.J., Norvig, P.: Artificial Intelligence: A Modern Approach, 4th edn. Pearson Series in Artificial Intelligence. Pearson, Upper Saddle River (2021). ISBN 9780134610993

Chapman, S., Fry, A., Deschenes, A., McDonald, C.G.: Strategies to improve the user experience. Serials Review (2016). https://doi.org/10.1080/00987913.2016.1140614. Accessed 8 Mar 2023

Lazar, J., Feng, J.H., Hochheiser, H.: Research Methods in Human-Computer Interaction. Morgan Kaufmann, Burlington (2017)

Humm, B.G., Zender, A.: An ontology-based concept for meta AutoML. In: Maglogiannis, I., Macintyre, J., Iliadis, L. (eds.) Artificial Intelligence Applications and Innovations, ser. Springer eBook Collection, vol. 627, pp. 117–128. Springer, Cham (2021). https://doi.org/10.1007/978-3-030-79150-6_10

Zender, A., Humm, B.G.: Ontology-based Meta AutoML. Integr. Comput. Aided Eng. **29**(4), 351–366 (2022)

Lundberg, S., Lee, S.: A unified approach to interpreting model predictions. In: Advances in Neural Information Processing Systems, vol. 30, pp. 4765–4774. Curran Associates, Inc. (2017)

Alcácer, V., Cruz-Machado, V.: Scanning the Industry 4.0: a literature review on technologies for manufacturing systems. Eng. Sci. Technol. Int. J. **22**(3), 899–919 (2019). https://doi.org/10.1016/j.jestch.2019.01.006

Bonaccorso, G.: Machine Learning Algorithms. Packt Publishing Ltd., Berkeley (2017)

Lu, Y.: Industry 4.0: a survey on technologies, applications and open research issues. J. Ind. Inf. Integr. **6**, 1–10 (2017). https://doi.org/10.1016/j.jii.2017.04.005

Moustakis, V.S., Herrmann, J.: Where do machine learning and human-computer interaction meet? Appl. Artif. Intell. **11**(7–8), 595–609 (1997). https://doi.org/10.1080/088395197117948

Chapman, S., Fry, A., Deschenes, A., McDonald, C.G.: Strategies to improve the user experience. Serials Review (2016). https://doi.org/10.1080/00987913.2016.1140614

Abdul, A., Vermeulen, J., Wang, D., Lim, B.Y., Kankanhalli, M.: Trends and trajectories for explainable, accountable and intelligible systems: an HCI research agenda. In: Conference on Human Factors in Computing Systems - Proceedings (2018). https://doi.org/10.1145/3173574.3174156

Wang, D., Yang, Q., Abdul, A., Lim, B.Y.: Designing theory-driven user-centric explainable AI. In: Conference on Human Factors in Computing Systems – Proceedings (2019). https://doi.org/10.1145/3290605.3300831

Chromik, M., Lachner, F., Butz, A.: Ml for UX? An inventory and predictions on the use of machine learning techniques for UX research. In: Proceedings of the 11th Nordic Conference on Human-Computer Interaction: Shaping Experiences, Shaping Society, pp. 1–11 (2020)

Fucs, A., Ferreira, J.J., Segura, V., De Paulo, B., de Paula, R., Cerqueira, R.: Sketch-based video; Storytelling for UX validation in AI design for applied research. In: Extended Abstracts of the 2020 CHI Conference on Human Factors in Computing Systems, pp. 1–8 (2020)

Li, F., Lu, Y.: Engaging end users in an AI-enabled smart service design-the application of the smart service blueprint scape (SSBS) framework. Proc. Des. Soc. **1**, 1363–1372 (2021)

Kurdziolek, M.: Explaining the Unexplainable: Explainable AI (XAI) for UX. User Experience - The Magazine of the User Experience Professionals Association. https://uxpamagazine.org/explaining-the-unexplainable-explainable-ai-xai-for-ux. Accessed 8 Mar 2023

Nielsen, J.: Usability 101: Introduction to usability. Nielsen Norman Group (2012). https://www.nngroup.com/articles/usability-101-introduction-to-usability/. Accessed 2022

International Organization for Standardization (ISO): ISO 9241-210: Ergonomics of Human–System Interaction - Human-Centred Design for Interactive Systems. International Organization for Standardization, Geneva (2019)

Oliver, R.L.: Effect of expectation and disconfirmation on postexposure product evaluations: an alternative interpretation. J. Appl. Psychol. **62**, 480–486 (1977). https://doi.org/10.1037/0021-9010.62.4.480

Venkatesh, V., Morris, M.G., Davis, G.B., Davis, F.D.: User acceptance of information technology: toward a unified view. MIS Q. **27**(3), 425–478 (2003). https://doi.org/10.2307/30036540

Shneiderman, B.: Human-centered artificial intelligence: reliable, safe and trustworthy. Int. J. Hum.-Comput. Interact. **36**(6), 495–504 (2020). https://doi.org/10.1080/10447318.2020.1741118

Bittner, K., Spence, I.: Use Case Modeling. Addison-Wesley Professional, Boston (2003)

International Organization for Standardization (ISO) (2020). ISO 9241-110:2020 Ergonomics of human-system interaction — Part 110: Interaction principles. https://www.iso.org/obp/ui/#iso:std:iso:9241:-110:ed-2:v1:en

Merriam, S.B.: Qualitative Research and Case Study Applications in Education. Revised and Expanded from "Case Study Research in Education", p. 94104. Jossey-Bass Publishers, San Francisco (1998)

Dutke, S.: Mentale Modelle - Konstrukte des Wissens und Verstehens: Kognitionspschologische Grundlagen für die Software-Ergonomie (1994)

Creswell, J.W., Creswell, J.D.: Research Design: Qualitative, Quantitative, and Mixed Methods Approaches. Sage Publications, New York (2017)

Moustakas, C.: Phenomenological Research Methods. Sage Publications, New York (1994)

Richter, M., Flückiger, M.D., Richter, M., Flückiger, M.D.: Die 7 ± 2 wichtigsten usability-methoden. Usability Engineering kompakt: Benutzbare Software gezielt entwickeln, pp. 21–76 (2010)

Oppong, S.H.: The problem of sampling in qualitative research. Asian J. Manage. Sci. Educ. **2**(2), 202–210 (2013)

Sedgwick, P., Greenwood, N.: Understanding the Hawthorne effect. BMJ **351**, h4672 (2015)

Nagappan, R.: Dealing with biases in qualitative research: a balancing act for researchers (2001)

Stiles, W.B.: Quality control in qualitative research. Clin. Psychol. Rev. **13**(6), 593–618 (1993)

Harley. UX Expert Reviews. Nielsen Norman Group (2018). https://www.nngroup.com/articles/ux-expert-reviews/

Nielsen, J.: Usability Engineering. Morgan Kaufmann, New York (1994)

Nielsen, J.: Ten usability heuristics (2005). http://www.nngroup.com/articles/ten-usability-heuristics/

Nielsen, J.: Severity Ratings for Usability Problems: Article by Jakob Nielsen. Nielsen Norman Group (1994). https://www.nngroup.com/articles/ten-usability-heuristics

Botsman, R.: Who Can You Trust? How Technology Brought Us Together - and Why It Could Drive Us Apart, p. 179. Penguin Books Ltd. Kindle Version (2017)

# Classification - Filtering - Genetic Algorithms

# A Critical Analysis of Classifier Selection in Learned Bloom Filters: The Essentials

Dario Malchiodi[1]([✉]) [ID], Davide Raimondi[1] [ID], Giacomo Fumagalli[1] [ID], Raffaele Giancarlo[2] [ID], and Marco Frasca[1] [ID]

[1] Department of Computer Science, University of Milan, Via Celoria 18, 20133 Milan, Italy
{malchiodi,frasca}@di.unimi.it,
{davide.raimondi2,giacomo.fumagalli1}@studenti.unimi.it
[2] Department of Mathematics and CS, University of Palermo, Palermo, Italy
raffaele.giancarlo@unipa.it

**Abstract.** It is well known that Bloom Filters have a performance essentially independent of the data used to query the filters themselves, but this is no more true when considering Learned Bloom Filters. In this work we analyze how the performance of such learned data structures is impacted by the classifier chosen to build the filter and by the complexity of the dataset used in the training phase. Such analysis, which has not been proposed so far in the literature, involves the key performance indicators of space efficiency, false positive rate, and reject time. By screening various implementations of Learned Bloom Filters, our experimental study highlights that only one of these implementations exhibits higher robustness to classifier performance and to noisy data, and that only two families of classifiers have desirable properties in relation to the previous performance indicators.

**Keywords:** Learned Bloom filters · Data complexity · Learned data structures

## 1 Introduction

Recent studies have highlighted how the impact of machine learning has the potential to change the way we design and analyze data structures. Indeed, the resulting research area of Learned Data Structures has had a well documented impact on a broad and strategic domain such as that of Data Bases, and an analogous impact can be expected for Network Management [25] and Computational Biology [13]. More in general, as well argued in [14], this novel way to use machine learning has the potential to change how Data Systems are designed. The common theme to this new approach is that of training a Classifier [10] or a Regression Model [11] on the input data. Then such a learned model is used as an "oracle" that a given "classical" data structure can use in order to answer queries with improved performance (usually w.r.t. time). In this work, we focus

L. Iliadis et al. (Eds.): EANN 2023, CCIS 1826, pp. 47–61, 2023.
https://doi.org/10.1007/978-3-031-34204-2_5

on Bloom Filters (BFs) [1] which have also received attention in the realm of Learned Data Structures. Such an attention is quite natural, due to the fundamental nature and pervasive use of BFs. Indeed, many variants and alternatives for these filters have been already proposed, prior to the Learned versions [2].

*Problem Statement, Performance of a Bloom Filter and a Learned Version.* Bloom Filters (BF) solve the *Approximate Set Membership* problem, defined as follows: having fixed a *universe* $U$ and a set of *keys* $S \subset U$, for any given $x \in U$, find out whether or not $x \in S$. *False negatives*, that is negative answers when $x \in S$, are not allowed. On the other hand, we can have *false positives* (i.e., elements in $U \backslash S$ wrongly decreed as keys), albeit their fraction (termed henceforth *false positive rate*, FPR for short) should be bounded by a given $\epsilon$. The key parameters of any data structure solving the approximate set membership problem are: (i) the FPR $\epsilon$; (ii) the total space needed by the data structure; and (iii) the *reject time*, defined as the expected time for rejecting a non-key.

Kraska et al. [15] have proposed a Learned version of Bloom Filters (LBF) in which a suitably trained binary classifier is introduced with the aim of reducing space occupancy w.r.t. a classical BF, having fixed the FPR. Such classifier is initially queried to predict the set membership, with a fallback to a standard BF in order to avoid false negatives. Mitzenmacher [20] has provided a mathematical analysis for those filters and novel LBF variants, together with a discussion of their pros/cons. Additional models have been introduced recently [7,23].

*The Central Role of Classifier Selection.* Apart from an initial investigation [8,12], the problem of suitably choosing the classifier to be used to build a specific LBF has not been fully addressed so far. Moreover, the role that the *complexity* of a dataset plays in guiding the practical choice of a Learned Data Structure for that dataset has been considered to some extent for Learned Indexes only [18].

*Paper Contribution.* Given the above State of the Art, our aim is to provide a methodology and the associated software to guide the design, analysis and deployment of Learned Boom Filters with respect to given constraints about their space efficiency, false positive rate, and reject time. In order to achieve these goals, our contributions are the following.

(1) **We revisit BFs** in their original and learned versions (Sect. 2), detailing the hyperparameters to be tuned within the related training procedures.
(2) **We propose a methodology**, which can guide both developers and users of LBFs in their design choices (Sect. 3), to study the interplay among: (a) the parameters indicating how a filter, learned or classic, performs on an input dataset; (b) the classifier used to build the LBF; (c) the classification complexity of the dataset.
(3) **Software platform and findings**: we provide a software platform implementing the above-mentioned methodology, along with important insights about the overall applicability of LBF, as detailed next.

(a) We address the problem of choosing the most appropriate classifier in order to design a LBF having as only prior knowledge the total space budget, the data complexity, the list of available classifiers, and their inference time. A related problem has been considered in [20] with two important differences: the filter is fixed, and the obtained results supply only partial answers, leading to the suggestion of an experimental methodology, which has not been validated and it is not supported by software. Our experiments (Sect. 4) shows that among the many classifiers used in this research, only two classifiers are worth of attention. Remarkably, none of the two has been considered before for LBFs (Sect. 5).

(b) As a further contribution, we assess how the performance of State-of-the-Art BFs is affected by datasets of increasing complexity (Sect. 5). In particular, we identify a variant of Learned Bloom Filters more robust to variations of data complexity and classifier performance.

(c) We also provide user guidelines on how to use State-of-the-Art LBF solutions (Sect. 6).

## 2   Bloom Filters and Learned Bloom Filters

A Bloom Filter [1] is a data structure solving the Approximate Set Membership problem defined in the Introduction, based on a boolean array $v$ of $m$ entries and on $k$ hash functions $h_1, \ldots, h_k$ mapping $U$ to $\{1, \ldots, m\}$. These functions are usually assumed to be *k-wise independent* [3,24], although much less demanding schemes work well in practice [1]. A BF is built by initializing all the entries of $v$ to zero, subsequently considering all keys $x \in S$ and setting $v_{h_j(x)} \leftarrow 1$ for each $j \in \{1, \ldots k\}$; a location can be set to 1 several times, but only the first change has an effect. Once the filter has been built, any $x \in U$ is tested against membership in $S$ by evaluating the entry $v_{h_j(x)}$, for each hash function $h_j$: $x$ is classified as a key if all tested entries are equal to 1, and rejected (a shorthand for saying that it is classified as a non-key) otherwise. False positives might arise because of hash collisions, and the corresponding rate $\epsilon$ is inversely bound to the array size $m$. More precisely, Eq. (21) in [1] connects reject time, space occupancy and FPR, so that one can choose the configuration of the filter: for instance, given the available space, one can derive the reject time that minimizes the FPR. Analogous trade-offs [2,20] can be used to tune the hyperparameters of a BF (namely, $m$ and $k$) in order to drive the inference process towards the most space-conscious solution. In particular, fixed an FPR $\epsilon$ and a number $n = |S|$ of keys, a BF ensuring optimal reject time requires an array of

$$m = 1.44n \log(1/\epsilon) \text{ bits.} \tag{1}$$

A Learned Bloom Filter [15] is a data structure simulating a BF to reduce its resource demand or its FPR by leveraging a classifier. The main components of a LBF are a classifier $C : U \rightarrow [0,1]$ and a BF $F$, defined as it follows.

1. Using supervised machine learning techniques, $C$ is induced from a labeled dataset $D$ made of items $(x, y_x)$, where $y_x$ equals 1 if $x \in S$ and 0 otherwise. In other words, $C$ is trained to classify keys in $S$ so that the higher is $C(x)$, the more likely $x \in S$. A binary prediction is ensured by thresholding using $\tau \in [0, 1]$, i.e. classifying $x \in U$ as a key if and only if $C(x) > \tau$.
2. Of course, nothing prevents us from having a set of false negatives $\{x \in S \mid C(x) \leq \tau\} \neq \emptyset$, thus a *backup* (classical) Bloom Filter $F$ for this set is built. Summing up, $x \in U$ is predicted to be a key if $C(x) > \tau$, or $C(x) \leq \tau$ and $F$ does not reject $x$. In all other cases, $x$ is rejected.

It is important to underline that the FPR of a classical BF is essentially independent of the distribution of data used to query it. This is no more true for a LBF [20], in which such rate should be estimated from a query set $\overline{S} \subset U \backslash S$. To remark such difference, one commonly refers to the *empirical FPR* of a learned filter, which is computed as $\epsilon = \epsilon_\tau + (1 - \epsilon_\tau)\epsilon_F$, where:

1. $\epsilon_\tau = |\{x \in \overline{S} \mid C(x) > \tau\}|/|\overline{S}|$ is the analogous empirical FPR of the classifier $C$ on $\overline{S}$, and
2. $\epsilon_F$ is the false positive rate of the backup BF.

Hence, having fixed a target value for $\epsilon$, the backup filter can be built setting $\epsilon_F = (\epsilon - \epsilon_\tau)/(1 - \epsilon_\tau)$, under the obvious constraint $\epsilon_\tau < \epsilon$. Within the learned setting, the three key factors of the filter are connected (and influenced) by the choice of $\tau$. However, due to the dependency on the query set distribution, reliably estimating the FPR of a LBFs is no longer immediate, as pointed out in [20], that also suggests an experimental methodology to assess it. The latter is part of the evaluation setting proposed in this paper.

Here below we outline the main features of the LBF variants which we have considered. With the exception of the one in [23], for which the software is neither public nor available from the authors, our selection is State of the Art.

*Sandwiched LBFs* [20]. The Sandwiched variant of LBFs (SLBF for brevity) is based on the idea that space efficiency can be optimized by filtering out non-keys *before* querying the classifier $C$, requiring as consequence a smaller backup filter $F$. More in detail, a BF $I$ for $S$ is initially built and used as a first processing step. All the elements of $S$ that are not rejected by $I$ are then used to build a LBF as described earlier. The SLBF immediately rejects an element $x \in U$ if $I$ rejects it, otherwise the answer for $x$ of the subsequent LBF is returned. The empirical FPR of the SLBF is $\epsilon = \epsilon_I(\epsilon_\tau + (1 - \epsilon_\tau)\epsilon_F)$, where $\epsilon_I$ is the FPR of $I$. Here, fixed the desired $\epsilon$, the corresponding FPR to construct $I$ is $\epsilon_I = (\epsilon/\epsilon_\tau)(1 - \text{FN}/n)$, where FN is the number of false negatives of $C$. Also in this case, the classifier accuracy affects the FPR, space and reject time, with the constraint $\epsilon(1 - \text{FN}/n) \leq \epsilon_\tau \leq 1 - \text{FN}/n$.

*Adaptive LBFs* [7]. Adaptive LBFs (ADA-BF) represent an extension of LBF, partioning the training instances $x$ into $g$ groups, according to their classification score $C(x)$. Then, the same number of hash functions the backup filter of an LBF would use are partitioned across groups, and the membership for the instances belonging to a given group is tested only using the hash functions assigned to it. Even for ADA-BF the expected FPR can only be estimated empirically, but in this case the formula is rather complicated: the interested reader can refer to [7]. We retained here the best performing variant of ADA-BF.

*Hyperparameters.* The Learned Bloom Filters described above have some parameters to be tuned. Namely, the threshold $\tau$ for LBF and SLBF, and two parameters $g$ and $\bar{c}$ for ADA-BF, representing the number of groups in which the classifier score interval is divided into, and the proportion of non-keys scores falling in two consecutive groups. The details on the tuning of these hyperparameters are discussed in Sect. 4.2.

## 3   Experimental Methodology

In this section we present the methodology which we adopt in order to design and analyse LBFs with regard to the inherent complexity of input data to be classified, subsumed as follows. The starting point is a dataset, either real-world or generated through a procedure suitable for synthesize data in function of some classification complexity metrics. Overall, the pipeline adopted is the following: collect/generate data; induce a classifier from data and estimate its empirical FPR; construct a Learned Bloom Filter exploiting the learnt classifier, and in turn estimate its empirical FPR. The following sections review the considered classifier families and describe in depth the adopted data generation procedure.

### 3.1   A Representative Set of Binary Classifiers

Starting from an initial list of classifiers—without presuming to be exhaustive— we performed a set of preliminary experiments, from which we received indications about the families of classifiers to be further analyzed, based on their time performance/space requirements trade-off[1]. Namely, from the initial list, we have removed the following classifiers: Logistic Regression [5], Naive Bayes [9] and Recurrent Neural Networks [4], due to their poor trade-off performance, confirming the results of a preliminary study [12]. The remaining ones are briefly described in the following paragraphs. Since our evaluation considers both balanced and unbalanced classification problems, we also detail how their inference is managed in an unbalanced context. The hyperparameters of the corresponding learning algorithms are distinguished between *regular* and *key* hyperparameters, the latter affecting the space occupancy of the classifier. The model selection phase only involves non-key hyperparameters, while different configurations for key hyperparameters are analysed in dedicated experiments aiming at studying the interplay among FPR, space occupancy and reject time of Learned Bloom Filters.

---

[1] The experiments and data about this preliminary part are available upon request.

## 3.2 Measures of Classification Complexity and a Related Data Generation Procedure

In order to evaluate dataset complexity, several measures are available (see [16] for a survey). We specifically focus on measures suitable for binary classification tasks, and hereafter we use the notation "class $i$", $i = 1, 2$, to refer to one of the two classes. A preliminary analysis highlighted that some of the measures in [16] were insensitive across a variety of synthetic data, as happened, e.g., with the *F1*, *T2*, or *T3* measures, or needed an excessive amount of RAM (such as network- or neighborhood-based measures, like *LSC* and *N1*). As a consequence, we selected the *feature-based* measure *F1v* and the *class-imbalance* measure *C2*, Both measures are in $\in [0, 1]$, and the higher the value, the higher the complexity.

*Data Generation Procedure.* In order to generate a binary classification dataset of size $N$ with a given level of complexity, $n_1$ positive and $n_2 = \lceil \rho n_1 \rceil$ negative instances (with $N = n_1 + n_2$), we proceed as follows. Let $D = \{x_1, \ldots x_N\} \subset \mathbb{R}^q$ be the set of samples, with each sample $x_i$ having $q$ features $x_{i1}, \ldots, x_{iq}$, and a binary label $y_i \in \{0, 1\}$. The $N$ samples are drawn from a multivariate normal distribution $\mathcal{N}(0, \Sigma)$, with $\Sigma = \gamma I_q$ (where $\gamma > 0$ and $I_q$ denotes the $q \times q$ identity matrix). In our experiments we set $\gamma = 5$ so as to have enough data spread, reminding that this value however does not affect the data complexity. Without loss of generality, we consider the case $q = 2$. To determine the classes of positive and negative samples, the parabola $x_2 - ax_1^2 = 0$ is considered, with $a > 0$: a point $x_i = (x_{i1}, x_{i2})$ is positive ($y_i = 1$) if $x_{i2} - ax_{i1}^2 > 0$, negative otherwise ($y_i = 0$). This choice allows us to control the linear separability of positive and negative classes by varying the parameter $a$: the closer $a$ to 0, the more linear the separation boundary. As a consequence, $a$ controls the problem complexity for a linear classifier, and $\rho$, instead, controls the data imbalance. Further, to vary the data complexity even for nonlinear classifiers, labels are permuted with different levels of noise: we flip the label of a fraction $r$ of positive samples, selected uniformly and at random, with an equal number on randomly selected negatives.

# 4 Experiments

## 4.1 Data

*Domain-Specific Data.* We use a URL dataset and a DNA dictionary. The first has been already studied as a benchmark for Learned Bloom Filters [7], and the authors of this research kindly provided us the dataset. It contains 485730 URLs described by 17 lexical features: 80002 URLs are *malicious* (and they constitute our key set), while the remaining ones are *benign*. The DNA dictionary regards the storage and retrieval of $k$-mers (i.e., strings of length $k$ appearing in a given genome, whose spectrum is the dictionary of $k$-mers) [21], and was directly generated by us. More precisely, it refers to the human chromosome 14, containing

$n = 49906253$ 14-mers [21] constituting the set of our keys. As non-keys, we uniformly generate other $n$ 14-mers from the $4^{14}$ possible strings on the alphabet $\{A, T, C, G\}$. We point out that no sensible information is contained in these datasets. We study them because they represent two extreme cases of classification complexity: the URL dataset is *easy* ($F1v = 0.08172$, $C2 = 0.62040$), the DNA data is *hard* ($F1v = 0.99972$, $C2 = 0$).

*Synthetic Data.* Using the technique described in Sect. 3.2 we generate two categories of synthetic data, each attempting to reproduce the complexity of one of the domain-specific data. The first category has nearly the same $C2$ complexity of the URL dataset, i.e., it is *unbalanced*, with $n_1 = 10^5$ and $\rho = 5$. The second one has the same $C2$ complexity of the DNA dataset, i.e., it is *balanced*, with $n_1 = 10^5$ and $\rho = 1$. The choice of $n_1$ allows to have a number of keys similar to that in the URL data, and at the same time to reduce the number of experiments planned. Indeed, both balanced and unbalanced categories contain nine datasets, exhibiting increasing levels of $F1v$ complexity (see Table 1). Specifically, all possible combinations of parameters $a \in \{0.01, 0.1, 1\}$ and $r \in \{0, 0.1, 0.25\}$ are used. The corresponding complexity estimations are consistent, as $F1v$ increases with $a$ and $r$ and $C2$ reflects the complexities of the URL and DNA datasets respectively in the unbalanced and balanced case.

**Table 1.** $F1v$ complexity measure of the synthetic data. The $C2$ index is equal to 0.0 and 0.615, respectively, in the balanced and unbalanced case.

| $a$ | 0.01 | 0.1 | 1 | 0.01 | 0.1 | 1 | 0.01 | 0.1 | 1 |
|---|---|---|---|---|---|---|---|---|---|
| $r$ | 0 | 0 | 0 | 0.1 | 0.1 | 0.1 | 0.25 | 0.25 | 0.25 |
| **Balanced** | 0.127 | 0.181 | 0.306 | 0.268 | 0.327 | 0.459 | 0.571 | 0.619 | 0.718 |
| **Unbalanced** | 0.129 | 0.202 | 0.360 | 0.187 | 0.269 | 0.433 | 0.308 | 0.399 | 0.563 |

## 4.2 Model Selection

*Classifiers.* The classifier generalization ability is assessed independently of the filter employing it, via a 3-fold cross validation (CV) procedure; performance is measured in terms of the area under (i) the ROC curve (AUC), and of (ii) the precision-recall curve (AUPRC), averaged across folds. However, for synthetic data, we report only the AUPRC results, since AUC results showed very similar trends and no enough room is available. The key hyperparameters for a given classifier are set in order not to exhaust all available space budget, while non-key hyperparameters are selected through a grid search using an inner 3-fold CV on the current training set, retaining the best configuration. When possible, for each classifier, we selected different hyperparameter configurations yielding models of different complexity, from simpler to more complex ones. Finally, for a fair comparison, the key hyperparameters for NNs are selected so as to yield

**Table 2.** Space budget in Mbits adopted on the various datasets. $\epsilon$ is the false positive rate, $n$ is the number of keys in the dataset.

| Data | $\epsilon$ | Budget (Mbits) | $n$ |
|---|---|---|---|
| Synth | $0.05, 0.01$ | $0.62, 0.96$ | $10^5$ |
| URL | $0.01, 0.005, 0.001, 0.0005, 0.0001$ | $0.76, 0.88, 1.15, 1.26, 1.53$ | $8 \cdot 10^4$ |
| DNA | $0.01, 0.005, 0.001, 0.0005, 0.0001$ | $477.46, 549.32, 716.19, 788.06, 954.92$ | $4.99 \cdot 10^7$ |

three models nearly having the same size of the SVM and of the two RFs models. Summarizing: i) SVM has no key hyperparameters; ii) for RF, we used $t = 10, 20$ (URL, synthetic) and $t = 10, 100$ (DNA); iii) for NNs, we considered NN-25, NN-150, 50 and NN-200, 75 (synthetic dataset); NN-7, NN-150, 35 and NN-175, 70 (URL dataset); NN-7, NN-125, 50, NN-500, 150 (DNA dataset).

*Learned Bloom Filters.* The Bloom Filter variants under study are evaluated under the setting proposed in [7], that is: 1) train the classifiers on all keys and 30% of non-keys, and query the filter using remaining 70% of non-keys to compute the empirical FPR; 2) fix an overall memory budget of $m$ bits for each filter, and compare them in terms of their empirical FPR $\epsilon$. Each filter variant is trained leveraging in turn each of the considered classifiers. The budget $m$ is related to the desired (expected) $\epsilon$ of a classical Bloom Filter, according to (1). Being the space budget directly influenced by the key set size $n$, we adopt a setting tailored on each dataset. Concerning synthetic data, as we generate numerous datasets, for each of them we only test two different choices for the space budget $m$: namely, those yielding $\epsilon \in \{0.05, 0.01\}$ for the classical Bloom Filter. On real datasets, we test five space budgets corresponding to $\epsilon \in \{0.01, 0.005, 0.001, 0.0005, 0.0001\}$. Table 2 contains the resulting budget configurations for all the considered datasets. To build the learned Bloom Filters variants, the hyperparameters have been selected via grid search on the training data, optimizing with respect to the FPR, according to the following setting: (a) 15 different values for threshold $\tau$, and (b) the ranges $[3, 15]$, and $[1, 5]$ for hyperparameters $g$ and $\bar{c}$, respectively (cfr. Sect. 2). Importantly, the latter choice includes and extends the configurations suggested in the original paper [6], namely, $[8, 12]$ for $g$ and $[1.6, 2.5]$ for $\bar{c}$.

## 5   Results and Discussion

As evident from Sect. 2, the classifier can be interpreted as an oracle for a learned BF, where the better the oracle, the better the related filter, i.e., its FPR once fixed the space budget. Accordingly, it is of interest to evaluate the performance of classifiers. All classifiers described in Sect. 3.1 have been tested on the datasets described in Sect. 4.1, with the configuration described in Sect. 4.2. Figure 1 depicts the performance of classifiers on synthetic and real data. However, it is central here to emphasize that the interpretation of such results is somewhat different than what one would do in a standard machine learning setting. Indeed, we have a space budget for the entire filter, and the classifier must discriminate well keys and non-keys, while being substantially succinct with regard to the space budget of the data structure. Such a scenario implicitly imposes a performance/space trade-off: hypothetically, we might have a perfect classifier using less space than the budget, and on the other extreme, a poor classifier exceeding the space budget. Surprisingly, from the behaviour of classifiers it emerges a crisp separation of the data in terms of complexity (cfr. Table 1), that corresponds to datasets *easy* to classify (roughly $F1v \leq 0.35$) and *hard* ($F1v > 0.35$) to classify. Here we address the question of how to choose a classifier to build the filter upon, based only on the knowledge of space budget and data classification complexity/classifier performance. On synthetic and URL data (cfr. Fig. 1), more complex classifiers perform just slightly better than the simpler ones, likely due to the low data complexity in these cases. At the same time, they require a sensibly higher fraction of the space budget (cfr. Table 2), and it is thereby natural to retain in those cases only the smallest/simplest variants, namely: RF-10 and NN-25 (synthetic) and NN-7 (URL), in addition to SVM. Conversely, in DNA experiments, more complex classifiers substantially outperform the simpler counterparts, coherently with the fact that this classification problem is much harder. Since the available space budget is higher in this case, all classifiers have been retained in the subsequent filter evaluation.

**Learned Filters Performance w.r.t. Data Classification Complexity**

*Easy Datasets.* Figure 2 reports the FPR results of learned Bloom Filters on balanced and unbalanced synthetic data, respectively, whereas Fig. 3 depicts the results on URL and DNA data. According to the definition provided above ($F1v$ around 0.35 or smaller), easy data can be associated to the three/four leftmost configurations on the $x$-axis in Fig. 2 of synthetic and to URL data. In these cases, we observe results coherent with the literature, where ADA-BF slightly outperforms the other competitors [7], and when using RF-10 as classifier lower FPRs are obtained with regard to the classical BF. Notwithstanding, it clearly emerges that such a classifier is not the best choice, underlining all the doubts

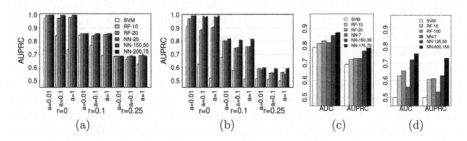

**Fig. 1.** Performance averaged across folds of compared classifiers on synthetic (a-balanced, b-unbalanced), URL (c) and DNA data (d). On synthetic data, bars are grouped by dataset, in turn denoted by a couple $(a, r)$.

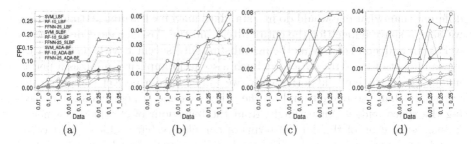

**Fig. 2.** False positive rates of learned filters attained on balanced (a, b) and unbalanced (c, d) synthetic datasets. On the horizontal axis, labels $X\_Y$ denote the dataset obtained when using $a = X$ and $r = Y$. The blue dotted line corresponds to the empirical false positive rate of the classical BF in that setting. Two space budgets $m$ are tested, ensuring that $\epsilon = 0.05$ ((a), (c)) and $\epsilon = 0.01$ ((b), (d)) for the classical BF. (Color figure online)

about a selection not motivated in the original studies. For instance, on URL data there are at least two classifiers yielding a lower FPR in most cases and for all filter variants (SVM and NN-7). In addition, SVMs are much faster. NN-7 (or NN-25 for synthetic data) remains the best choice even when the separation boundary becomes less linear ($a > 0.01$), and filters induced by SVMs become less effective or even worse than the baseline BF.

*Hard Datasets.* Our experiments show a novel scenario with the increase of data complexity, i.e., when moving towards right on the horizontal axis in Fig. 2, or when considering DNA data. We observe that the performance of the filters drops more and more, in line with the performance decay of the corresponding classifiers, and unexpectedly the drop is faster in ADA-BF (and LBF) w.r.t. SLBF. This happens for instance on all synthetic data having $r > 0$ (noise injection). We say unexpectedly since we have an inversion of the trend also reported in the literature, where usually ADA-BF outperforms SLBF (which in turn improves LBF). Indeed, SLBFs here exhibit behaviours more robust to noise, which are likely due to a reduced dependency on the classifier for SLBF, yielded by the usage of the initial Bloom Filter. Such a filter allows the classifier to be queried only on a subset of the data. Noteworthy is the behavior of filters when using RFs in this setting: their FPR strongly increases, and potential explanations are the excessive score discretization (having 10 trees we have only 11 distinct scores for all queries), and the space occupancy is larger (limiting the space that can be assigned to initial/backup filters). These results find a particularly relevant confirmation on the very hard, real-world, large, and novel DNA dataset. Here, surprisingly, the LBF cannot attain any improvement with regard to the baseline BF, differently from SLBF and ADA-BF. A potential cause can reside in the worse performance achieved by classifiers on this hard dataset, compared to those obtained on synthetic and URL data, and in a too marked dependency of LBF on the classifier performance, mitigated instead in the other two filter variants by the usage of the initial BF (SLBF) and by the fine-grained

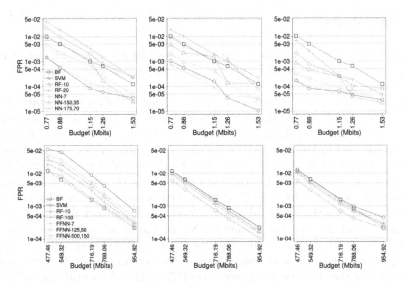

**Fig. 3.** Empirical false positive rate of LBF (left), SLFB (central), and ADA-BF (right) filters on URL data (first row) and DNA data (second row). On the horizontal axis the different budgets configurations. Dotted blue line represents the baseline Bloom Filter. (Color figure online)

classifier score partition (ADA-BF). SLBF outperforms both LBF and baseline of one order of magnitude in FPR with the same space amount, and ADA-BF when using weaker classifiers and when a higher budget is available. This is likely due to overfitting of ADA-BF in partitioning the classifier codomain when the classifier performance is not excellent (or similarly when the data complexity is high), as with DNA data. Differently from hard synthetic data, where the key set was smaller (as consequently was the space budget), here the classifiers leading to the best FPR are the most complex, in particular NN-500,150 and NN-125,50 (which are also the top performing ones—they could be even further compressed [19]). In other words, on hard datasets simple classifiers are useless or even deleterious (SVM never improve the baseline, and in some cases they are even worse).

**Reject Time.** The results concerning reject time analysis are provided in full in [17]. Here we bring to light that learned BF are sometimes faster than the baseline, which in principle is not expected, since they have to query a classifier in addition to a classical BF. Our interpretation is that it can happen for two main reasons: 1) the classifier is very fast and effective, allowing in most cases to skip querying the backup filter; 2) the key set is very large and it requires a large baseline BF, whereas a good classifier sensibly drops the dimension of backup filters, making their invocation much faster. See for instance the case of DNA data, where most learned filters are faster than the baseline, with most classifiers.

# 6    Guidelines

We summarize here our findings about the configuration of learned Bloom Filters exploiting the prior knowledge of data complexity and available space budget.

*Dataset Complexity and Classifier Choice.* We have roughly distinguished two main categories of data based on their complexity and the related behaviour of filters: easy dataset, having $F1v \leq 0.35$, and hard dataset, having $F1v > 0.35$. The dataset complexity emerged as a central discriminant for the filter setup. Indeed, when dealing with easy datasets, the choice of the classifier becomes quite easy, and, independently of the space budget, it is always more convenient to select simple classifiers. Specifically, our experiments designate linear SVMs as best choice for the easiest datasets (those having almost linear separation boundary), and the smallest/simplest NNs for the more complex data in this category. In addition, the classifier inference time plays an important role for this data category: although a fastest classifier does not necessarily implies a lower reject time of the corresponding filter (see [17]), when the average performance of two classifiers is close, then the inference time can be a discriminant feature for the classifier selection. But only in this case: see for instance the URL results, where the RF-10 performed just slightly better than SVMs, but although having an inference time one order of magnitude higher, the induced LBF has a lower reject time (see [17] for the relative discussion.) Surprisingly, this analysis has been overlooked in the literature. For instance, benchmark URL data falls in this category, but all previous experimental studies regarding learned BF on this data do not consider neither SVMs, nor NNs.

For hard datasets instead, the space budget is central for the classifier choice. Indeed, within the budget given by (1), on synthetic datasets, having a relative small key set and accordingly a lower budget, the choice is almost forced towards small although inaccurate classifiers, being the larger ones too demanding for the available budget. In particular, SVM is to be excluded due to the increased difficulty w.r.t. that of URL data, and for the remaining classifiers, we note that they behave very similarly (Fig. 1). Thus the most succinct ones, namely the smallest NN, are to be preferred. As opposite, when the space budget increases, as it happens for DNA data, our findings suggest to learn more accurate classifiers, even if this requires the usage of a considerable budget fraction. Indeed, the gain induced by higher classification abilities allows to save space when constructing the backup filter, to have consequently a smaller reject time, as well as an overall more efficient structure (cfr. Sect. 5). This is also motivated by the fact that to accurately train complex classifiers the sample size must be large enough [22].

*Learned Bloom Filters Choice.* Our experiments reveal three main trends: 1) on benchmark data, that is those used also in the literature so far (URL data), ADA-BF is confirmed as more effective variant in terms of FPR, having fixed the budget; 2) however, its reject time is always and largely the highest one (see [17]), thus suggesting to exclude its usage in applications where fast responses are necessary (e.g., real-time applications). This subject includes also the classifier choice, since the most effective filters are in most cases induced by NNs, but they are also slower in terms of reject time of the counterparts induced by faster classifiers, and accordingly a trade-off FPR/reject time must be carefully investigated; 3) SLBF is the filter most robust to data noise, and the only one able to benefit more even from classifier with poor performance (cfr. synthetic noisy and DNA results). As a consequence, SBLF is clearly the filter to choose in presence of very complex data. In particular, the point 3) is a new and quite unforeseen behaviour, emerged only thanks to the study of data complexity and relative noise injection procedure designed in this study, and which to some extent changes the ranking of most effective learned BF in practice, since most real datasets are typically characterized by noise.

## 7    Conclusions and Future Developments

We have proposed an experimental methodology that can guide in the design and validation of learned Bloom Filters. The key point is to base the choice of the used classifier on the space budget of the entire data structure as well as the classification complexity of the input dataset. We empirically detected two class of problems, *easy* and *hard*, and confirmed (to some extent) the results on the former one, which is the only scenario considered so far in the Literature, while the unexplored *hard* scenario revealed novel trends, and almost inverted the ranking of LBFs emerged in the easy case. A potential limitation of such results is that they might be dependent on the considered data; nonetheless, this is somehow inevitable due to the nature of Learned Data Structures. In addition, Learned Bloom Filters can be quite sensitive to the input query distribution. Yet, no study is available to quantify this aspect, and our methodology can be easily extended in this sense.

**Acknowledgements.** This work has been supported by the Italian MUR PRIN project 2017WR7SHH "Multicriteria data structures and algorithms: from compressed to learned indexes, and beyond". Additional support to R.G. has been granted by Project INdAM - GNCS "Analysis and Processing of Big Data based on Graph Models".

## References

1. Bloom, B.H.: Space/time trade-offs in hash coding with allowable errors. Commun. ACM **13**(7), 422–426 (1970)
2. Broder, A., Mitzenmacher, M.: Network applications of bloom filters, a survey. Internet Math. **1**, 636–646 (2002)
3. Carter, J., Wegman, M.N.: Universal classes of hash functions. J. Comput. Syst. Sci. **18**(2), 143–154 (1979)

4. Cho, K., van Merriënboer, B., Bahdanau, D., Bengio, Y.: On the properties of neural machine translation: Encoder-decoder approaches. In: Proceedings of SSST-8, Eighth Workshop on Syntax, Semantics and Structure in Statistical Translation, pp. 103–111. Association for Computational Linguistics, Doha, Qatar, October 2014

5. Cox, D.R.: The regression analysis of binary sequences. J. Roy. Stat. Soc.: Ser. B (Methodol.) **20**(2), 215–232 (1958)

6. Dai, Z.: Adaptive learned bloom filter (ADA-BF): efficient utilization of the classifier (2022). https://github.com/DAIZHENWEI/Ada-BF. Checked 8 Nov 2022

7. Dai, Z., Shrivastava, A.: Adaptive Learned Bloom Filter (Ada-BF): efficient utilization of the classifier with application to real-time information filtering on the web. In: Advances in Neural Information Processing Systems, vol. 33, pp. 11700–11710. Curran Associates, Inc. (2020)

8. Dai, Z., Shrivastava, A., Reviriego, P., Hernández, J.A.: Optimizing learned bloom filters: how much should be learned? IEEE Embed. Syst. Lett. **14**(3), 123–126 (2022). https://doi.org/10.1109/LES.2022.3156019

9. Duda, R.O., Hart, P.E.: Pattern Classification and Scene Analysis. Willey, New York (1973)

10. Duda, R.O., Hart, P.E., Stork, D.G.: Pattern Classification. Wiley, New York (2000)

11. Freedman, D.: Statistical Models: Theory and Practice. Cambridge University Press, Cambridge (2005)

12. Fumagalli, G., Raimondi, D., Giancarlo, R., Malchiodi, D., Frasca, M.: On the choice of general purpose classifiers in learned bloom filters: an initial analysis within basic filters. In: Proceedings of the 11th International Conference on Pattern Recognition Applications and Methods (ICPRAM), pp. 675–682 (2022)

13. Kirsche, M., Das, A., Schatz, M.C.: Sapling: accelerating suffix array queries with learned data models. Bioinformatics **37**(6), 744–749 (2020)

14. Kraska, T.: Towards instance-optimized data systems. Proc. VLDB Endow. **14**(12), 3222–3232 (2021)

15. Kraska, T., Beutel, A., Chi, E.H., Dean, J., Polyzotis, N.: The case for learned index structures. In: Proceedings of the 2018 International Conference on Management of Data, SIGMOD 2018, pp. 489–504. Association for Computing Machinery, New York, NY, USA (2018)

16. Lorena, A.C., Garcia, L.P.F., Lehmann, J., Souto, M.C.P., Ho, T.K.: How complex is your classification problem? A survey on measuring classification complexity. ACM Comput. Surv. **52**(5), 1–34 (2019)

17. Malchiodi, D., Raimondi, D., Fumagalli, G., Giancarlo, R., Frasca, M.: A critical analysis of classifier selection in learned bloom filters (2022). https://doi.org/10.48550/ARXIV.2211.15565, https://arxiv.org/abs/2211.15565

18. Maltry, M., Dittrich, J.: A critical analysis of recursive model indexes. CoRR abs/2106.16166 (2021). https://arxiv.org/abs/2106.16166

19. Marinò, G.C., Petrini, A., Malchiodi, D., Frasca, M.: Deep neural networks compression: a comparative survey and choice recommendations. Neurocomputing **520**, 152–170 (2023)

20. Mitzenmacher, M.: A model for learned bloom filters and optimizing by sandwiching. In: Advances in Neural Information Processing Systems, vol. 31 (2018)

21. Rahman, A., Medevedev, P.: Representation of k-Mer sets using spectrum-preserving string sets. J. Comput. Biol. **28**(4), 381–394 (2021)

22. Raudys, S.: On the problems of sample size in pattern recognition. In: Detection, Pattern Recognition and Experiment Design. Proceedings of the 2nd All-Union Conference Statistical Methods in Control Theory. Publ. House "Nauka" (1970)
23. Vaidya, K., Knorr, E., Kraska, T., Mitzenmacher, M.: Partitioned learned bloom filters. In: International Conference on Learning Representations (2021)
24. Wegman, M.N., Carter, J.: New hash functions and their use in authentication and set equality. J. Comput. Syst. Sci. **22**(3), 265–279 (1981)
25. Wu, Q., Wang, Q., Zhang, M., Zheng, R., Zhu, J., Hu, J.: Learned bloom-filter for the efficient name lookup in information-centric networking. J. Netw. Comput. Appl. **186**, 103077 (2021)

# Balancing High-Dimensional Datasets with Complex Layers

Leon Bobrowski[1,2]([✉]) [ID]

[1] Faculty of Computer Science, Bialystok University of Technology, Wiejska 45A,
Bialystok, Poland
l.bobrowski@pb.edu.pl
[2] Institute of Biocybernetics and Biomedical Engineering, PAS, Warsaw, Poland

**Abstract.** Unbalanced datasets generate difficulties in designing good classification models because those classes that are represented by the most numerous training sets are harmfully preferred. For this reason, learning sets are often balanced by adding some synthetic feature vectors or by reducing the most numerous learning sets.

High-dimensional learning sets give possibility to design complex layer of linear classifiers. Such layers can also be used for balancing purposes. In this approach, averaging of a small number of feature vectors is partially complemented by averaging vertices based on balanced feature subsets.

**Keywords:** High-dimensional Data · Unbalanced Learning Sets · Multiple Feature Selection

## 1 Introduction

Learning sets consisting of labelled feature vectors representing individual classes are unbalanced when the numbers of feature vectors representing various classes are very different [1]. Unbalanced learning sets can hamper the accuracy of the designed classification models [2].

Learning sets can be balanced be adding some synthetic feature vectors or by reducing the most numerous learning sets [3]. The currently used methods of reducing the effects of unbalanced data sets do not always bring satisfactory results in practice.

A new concept of using complex layers in reducing the effects of unbalanced learning sets is described in this article. Complex layers of linear classifiers are designed on the basis of datasets consisting of a small number of multidimensional feature vectors [4].

## 2 High-Dimensional Learning Sets

Consider $m$ objects (cases, patients) $O_j$ $(j = 1, \ldots, m)$ represented in the high-dimensional feature space $F[n]$ as feature vectors $\mathbf{x}_j$ $(\mathbf{x}_j \in F[n])$. The component $x_{j,i}$ of the vector $\mathbf{x}_j = [x_{j,1}, \ldots, x_{j,n}]^T$ can be numerical result of the measurement of the $i$-th

© The Author(s), under exclusive license to Springer Nature Switzerland AG 2023
L. Iliadis et al. (Eds.): EANN 2023, CCIS 1826, pp. 62–70, 2023.
https://doi.org/10.1007/978-3-031-34204-2_6

feature $X_i (i = 1, \ldots, n)$ on the $j$-th object $O_j (x_{j,i} \in \{0, 1\}$ or $x_{j,i} \in R)$ The feature space $F[n]$ is formed on the set $F(n)$ of a large number $n$ of features $X_i (i = 1, \ldots, n)$:

$$F(n) = \{X_1, \ldots, X_n\}. \tag{1}$$

Let us assume that objects $O_j (j = 1, \ldots, m)$ have been divided according to some a priori knowledge into $K$ classes $\omega_k (k = 1, \ldots, K)$. As a consequence, feature vectors $x_j$ can be labelled and associated with particular categories $\omega_k$. The $k$-th learning set $C_k$ contains $m_k$ examples of feature vectors $\mathbf{x}_j(k) = [x_{j,1}, \ldots, x_{j,n}]^T$ assigned to the $k$-th category $\omega_k$:

$$(\forall k \in \{1, \ldots, K\}) \quad C_k = \{\mathbf{x}_j(k) : j \in J_k\} \tag{2}$$

where $J_k$ is the set of indices $j$ of $m_k$ feature vectors $\mathbf{x}_j(k)$ assigned to the $k$-th class (category) $\omega_k$.

Learning sets $C_k$ (2) are *high-dimensional* if the numbers $m_k$ of feature vectors $\mathbf{x}_j(k)$ are much smaller than the dimension $n$ of these vectors ($m_k << n$). Datasets $C_k$ (2) are *unbalanced* if the numbers $m_k$ of vectors $\mathbf{x}_j(k)$ are very different in these sets [3]. The possibility of separating datasets $C_k$ (2) with hyperplanes $H(\mathbf{w}_k, \theta_k)$ in the feature space $F[n]$ is investigated in pattern recognition methods [5]:defined as the sum o

$$H(\mathbf{w}_k, \theta_k) = \left\{ \mathbf{x} : \mathbf{w}_k^T \mathbf{x} = \theta_k \right\} \tag{3}$$

where $\mathbf{w}_k = [w_{k,1}, \ldots, w_{k,n}]^T \in R^n$ is the $k$-th weight vector, $\theta_k \in R^1$ is the threshold, and $\mathbf{w}_k^T \mathbf{x} = \Sigma_i W_{k,i} x_i$ is the inner product.

*Definition* 1: The datasets $C_k$ (2) are *linearly separable* in the $n$-dimen- sional feature space $F[n]$ if each of the sets $C_k$ can be fully separated from the sum of the remaining sets $C_i$ by some hyperplane $H(\mathbf{w}_k, \theta_k)$:

$$(\exists k \in \{1, \ldots, K\}) \ (\exists \mathbf{w}_k, \theta_k) \ (\forall \mathbf{x}_j(k) \in C_k) \quad \mathbf{w}_k^T \mathbf{x}_j \geq \theta_k + 1,$$
$$and \ (\forall \mathbf{x}_j(k') \in C_{k'}, k' \neq k) \quad \mathbf{w}_k^T \mathbf{x}_j \leq \theta_k - 1 \tag{4}$$

Inequalities (4) describe the linear separation of the learning sets $C_k$ (2) with the margin $\delta(\mathbf{w}_k) = 2/\|\mathbf{w}_k\|$ determined as follows in the case of the Euclidean ($L_2$) norm [1]:

$$\delta(\mathbf{w}_k)_{L2} = 2/\left(\mathbf{w}_k^T \mathbf{w}_k\right)^{1/2} = 2/\left(\Sigma_i w_{k,i}^2\right)^{1/2} \tag{5}$$

The margins $\delta(\mathbf{w}_k)_{L2}$ (5) are used in support vector machines (*SVM*), the basic method of machine learning [6].The SVM classifier design algorithms are based on quadratic programming The margins $\delta(\mathbf{w}_k)_{L1}$ based on the $L_1$ norm were determined similarly [4]:

$$\delta(\mathbf{w}_k)_{L1} = 2/\left(\sum_i |W_{k,i}|\right) \tag{6}$$

Maximized margins $\delta(\mathbf{w}_k)_{L1}$ (6) are obtained by minimizing the perceptron criterion function, which is a convex and piecewise linear function (*CPL*) [5]. In this case, the design algorithms are related to linear programming and vertex calculations [7].

Increasing the margins $\delta(\mathbf{w}_k)_{L2}$ (5) or $\delta(\mathbf{w}_k)_{L1}$ (6) serves to increase the generalization power of the classification rules [2]. The generalization power of a given classification rule is characterized by the frequency of misclassified feature vectors $\mathbf{x}_{j'}$ not belonging to the learning sets $\mathbf{C}_k$ (2). The generalization power is high when a large number of new vectors $\mathbf{x}_{j'} (\mathbf{x}_{j'} \notin \cup_k \mathbf{C}_k)$ are correctly classified.

## 3   Linear Separability Resulting from Linear Independence

The augmented feature vectors $\mathbf{y}_j(k)$ are defined as follows based on the $k$-th learning dataset $\mathbf{C}_k$ (2) [1]:

$$(\forall k \in \{1, \dots, K\}) (\forall j \in \{1, \dots, m\})$$

$$\mathbf{y}_j(k) = \left[\mathbf{x}_j^T, 1\right]^T if \ \mathbf{x}_j \in \mathbf{C}_k(2) \ and \ \mathbf{y}_j(k) = -\left[\mathbf{x}_j^T, 1\right]^T if \ \mathbf{x}_j \in \cup_{k' \neq k} \mathbf{C}_{k'} \quad (7)$$

Consider the learning subsets $\mathbf{G}_{k(l)}^+ \subset \mathbf{C}_k$ (2) and $\mathbf{G}_{k(l)}^- \subset \cup_{k' \neq k} \mathbf{C}_{k'}$ of the vectors $\mathbf{y}_j(k)$ (7) which can be defined multiple times $l$ ($l = 1, \dots, L$):

$$\mathbf{G}_{k(l)}^+ = \left\{\mathbf{y}_j(k) : j \in J_{k(l)}^+\right\} and \ \mathbf{G}_{k(l)}^- = \left\{\mathbf{y}_j(k) : j \in J_{k(l)}^-\right\} \quad (8)$$

where $J_{k(l)}^+$ is a subset of the indices $j$ of some feature vectors $\mathbf{x}_j$ from the $k(l)$-th learning subsets $\mathbf{G}_{k(l)}^+$ and $J_{k(l)}^-$ is a subset of the indices $j$ of some feature vectors $\mathbf{x}_j$ from the subset $\mathbf{G}_{k(l)^-}$.

The learning subsets $\mathbf{G}_{k(l)}^+$ and $\mathbf{G}_{k(l)}^-$ (8) are linearly separable (4) by the parameters vector $\mathbf{v}_k = [\mathbf{w}_k, -\theta_k]^T$ if the following inequalities are met:

$$\left(\forall \mathbf{y}_j(k) \in \mathbf{G}_{k(l)}^+ \cup \mathbf{G}_{k(l)}^-\right) \quad \mathbf{v}_k^T \mathbf{y}_j(k) \geq 1 \quad (9)$$

where $\mathbf{v}_k = \left[\mathbf{w}_{k,1}, \dots, \mathbf{w}_{k,n}, -\theta_k\right]^T \in \mathbf{R}^{n+1}$ is the vector of parameters [1].

Linear separability (9) of the sets $\mathbf{G}_{k(l)}^+$ and $\mathbf{G}_{k(l)}^-$ (8) can be related to linear independence of feature vectors $\mathbf{x}_j$ (1) and can be checked by minimizing the perceptron criterion function [5].

*Lemma 1:* The learning sets $\mathbf{G}_{k(l)}^+$ and $\mathbf{G}_{k(l)}^-$ (8) composed of $m_{k(l)} = m_{k(l)}^+ + m_{k(l)}^-$ linearly independent feature vectors $\mathbf{y}_j(k)$ ($\mathbf{y}_j(k) \in \mathbf{F}[n+1]$ (7)) are linearly separable (15).

Feature vectors $\mathbf{y}_j(k)$ (7) making up the learning sets $\mathbf{G}_{k(l)}^+$ and $\mathbf{G}_{k(l)}^-$ (8) are linearly independent if neither of these vectors can be expressed as a linear combination of $l$ ($l \in \{1, \dots, m - 1\}$) other vectors. The number of linearly independent vectors $\mathbf{y}_j(k)$ can be no larger that the dimension $n + 1$ of the feature space $\mathbf{F}[n + 1]$. The learning sets $\mathbf{G}_{k(l)}^+$ and $\mathbf{G}_{k(l)}^-$ (8) are usually linearly separable (9) if the number $n$ of features $X_i$ is much larger than the number $m_{k(l)}$ of vectors $\mathbf{y}_j(k)$ because such vectors are typically linearly independent. The linear independence of the vectors $\mathbf{y}_j(k)$ (7) may disappear as a result of ineractions between features $X_i$.

## 4 Perceptron Criterion Function

Perceptron penalty functions $\varphi_j(\mathbf{v})$ are related to inequalities (9) and are defined for each element $\mathbf{y}_j(k)$ of the learning sets $\mathbf{G}^+_{k(l)}$ and $\mathbf{G}^-_{k(l)}$ (8) as:

$$\left(\forall \mathbf{y}_j(k) \in \mathbf{G}^+_{k(l)} \cup \mathbf{G}^-_{k(l)}\right)$$
$$\varphi_j(\mathbf{v}) = 1 - \mathbf{y}_j(k)^T\mathbf{v} \; if \; \mathbf{y}_j(k)^T\mathbf{v} < 1 \; and \; \varphi_j(\mathbf{v}) = 0 \; if \; \mathbf{y}_j(k)^T\mathbf{v} \geq 1 \tag{10}$$

The *perceptron* criterion function $\Phi_{k(l)}(\mathbf{v})$ is defined as the sum of the penalty functions $\varphi_j(\mathbf{v})$ (16) defined on elements $\mathbf{y}_j(k)$ of the learning sets $\mathbf{G}^+_{k(l)}$ and $\mathbf{G}^-_{k(l)}$ (8) [5]:

$$\Phi_{k(l)}(\mathbf{v}) = \sum_j \varphi_j(\mathbf{v}) \tag{11}$$

The following theorem can be proved [1]:

*Theorem* 1: The minimum value $\Phi_{k(l)}\left(\mathbf{v}^p_{k(l)}\right)$ of the perceptron criterion function $\Phi_{k(l)}(\mathbf{v})$ (11) is equal to zero $\left(\Phi_{k(l)}\left(\mathbf{v}^p_{k(l)}\right) = 0\right)$ if and only if the learning sets $\mathbf{G}^+_{k(l)}$ and $\mathbf{G}^-_{k(l)}$ (8) are linearly separable (9).

The proof of Lemma 1 and Theorem 1 can be based on the vertexical linear equations defined in the work [5], and also is described later in this text. In this approach, the optimal vertex $\mathbf{v}^p_{k(l)}$ is calculated as a solution of a well-defined system of $m_k$ linear equations, where $m_k$ is the number of feature vectors $\mathbf{y}_j(k(l))$ of dimension $n$ in the learning sets $\mathbf{G}^+_{k(l)}$ and $\mathbf{G}^-_{k(l)}$ (14) ($m_{k(l)} << n$).

The regularized criterion function $\Psi_{k(l)}(\mathbf{v})$ is defined as the weighted sum of the perceptron criterion function $\Phi_{k(l)}(\mathbf{v})$ (11) and the absolute values $|w_i|$ of weighs $w_i$, where $\mathbf{v} = [w_1, ..., w_n, -\theta_k]^T$ []:

$$\Psi_{k(l)}(\mathbf{v}) = \Phi_{k(l)}(\mathbf{v}) + \sum_{i \in \{1,...,n\}} |w_i| \tag{12}$$

The optimal vector $\mathbf{v}^*_{k(l)}$ constitutes the global minimum $\Psi_{k(l)}\left(\mathbf{v}^*_{k(l)}\right)$ of the *CPL* criterion function $\Psi_{k(l)}(\mathbf{v})$ (12) defined on elements $\mathbf{y}_j(k)$ of the learning sets $\mathbf{G}^+_{k(l)}$ and $\mathbf{G}^-_{k(l)}$ (8). The minimum value $\Psi_{k(l)}(\mathbf{v}^*_{k(l)})$ of the criterion function $\Psi_k(\mathbf{v})$ (12) is used, among others, in the *relaxed linear separability* (*RLS*) method of selection optimal subsets of genes $X_i$ [8]. It has been shown that the minimization of the regularized criterion function $\Psi_k(\mathbf{v})$ (12) leads to the maximization of the margin $\delta(\mathbf{v}_k)_{L1}$ (6).

## 5 Vertices in Parameter Space

The perceptron criterion function $\Phi_k(\mathbf{v})$ (11) is convex and piecewise-linear (*CPL*). As a result, the global minimum $\Phi_k\left(\mathbf{v}^p_k\right)$ of the function $\Phi_k(\mathbf{v})$ (11) can be determined in the optimal vertex $\mathbf{v}^p_k = [\mathbf{w}^p_k, -\theta^p_k]^T$ of a certain convex polyhedron in the parameter space [7].

To simplify the notation, consider the vertices $\mathbf{w}_k$ in the parameter (weight) space $R^n (\mathbf{w}_k \in R^n)$ associated with the perceptron criterion function $\Phi_k(\mathbf{w})$ (18) with a fixed threshold $\theta_k$ equal to zero ($\theta_k = 0$). In this case, the vertices $\mathbf{w}_k$ are defined by dual hyperplanes $h_j^1$ and $h_i^0$ [5]:

$$
\begin{aligned}
\left(\forall \mathbf{y}_j(k) \in G_k^+ (14)\right) h_j^1 &= \left\{ \mathbf{w} \in R^n : (\mathbf{x}_j)^T \mathbf{w} = 1 \right\} \text{ and} \\
\left(\forall \mathbf{y}_j(k) \in G_k^- (14)\right) h_j^1 &= \left\{ \mathbf{w} \in R^n : (-\mathbf{x}_j)^T \mathbf{w} = 1 \right\}
\end{aligned}
\tag{13}
$$

The dual hyperplanes $h_j^0$ are defined by unit vectors $\mathbf{e}_i$ [10]:

$$
\left(\forall i \in (1, \ldots, n)\right) h_i^0 = \left\{ \mathbf{w} \in R^n : \mathbf{e}_i^T \mathbf{w} = 0 \right\} = \left\{ \mathbf{w} \in R^n : w_i = 0 \right\}
\tag{14}
$$

*Definition 2*: The vertex $\mathbf{w}_k$ of the *rank* $r_k$ ($r_k \leq n$) in the weight space $R^n(\mathbf{w}_k \in R^n)$ is the intersection of hyperplanes $h_j^1$ (13) defined by $r_k$ linearly indepenedent feature vectors $\mathbf{x}_j (j \in J_k)$ from the data set $C_k$ (1) and hyperplanes $h_i^0$ defined by $n - r_k$ unit vectors $\mathbf{e}_i (i \in I_k)$ (14) [7].

The vertex $\mathbf{w}_k$ can be defined by the following set of $n$ linear equations:

$$
(\forall j \in J_k) \quad \mathbf{w}_k^T \mathbf{x}_j = 1 \text{ and } (\forall i \in I_k) \quad \mathbf{w}_k^T \mathbf{e}_i = 0
\tag{15}
$$

or in matrix form:

$$
\mathbf{B}_k \mathbf{w}_k = \mathbf{1}_{rk}
\tag{16}
$$

where $\mathbf{1}_{rk} = [1, \ldots, 1, 0, \ldots, 0]^T$ is the vector with the first $r_k$ components equal to one and the remaining $n - r_k$ components are equal to zero.

The square matrix $\mathbf{B}_k$ (17) consists of $r_k$ feature vectors $\mathbf{x}_j (j \in J_k)$ (15)) and $n - k$ unit vectors $\mathbf{e}_i (i \in I_k)$ (15)) [7]:

$$
\mathbf{B}_k = \left[ \mathbf{x}_{j(1),\ldots,}, \mathbf{x}_{j(r(k))}, \mathbf{e}_{i(r(k)+1)}, \ldots, \mathbf{e}_{i(n)} \right]^T
\tag{17}
$$

where the symbol $\mathbf{e}_{i(l)}$ denotes such unit vector, which is the $l$-th row of the matrix $\mathbf{B}_k$ (17).

If feature vectors $\mathbf{x}_j (j \in J_k$ (15)) making up $r_k$ rows of the matrix $\mathbf{B}_k$ (17) are linearly independent, then the basis exchange algorithm allows to find the inverse matrix $\mathbf{B}_k^{-1}$ step by step, starting from the unit matrix $I = [\mathbf{e}_1, \ldots, \mathbf{e}_n]^T$ []. The non-singular matrix $\mathbf{B}_k$ (17) is the *basis* of the feature space $F[n]$ related to the vertex $\mathbf{w}_k = [w_{k,1}, \ldots, w_{k,n}]^T$:

$$
\mathbf{w}_k = \mathbf{B}_k^{-1} \mathbf{1}_{rk} = \mathbf{r}_1 + \ldots + \mathbf{r}_{rk}
\tag{18}
$$

Since the last $n - r_k$ components of the vector $\mathbf{1}_{rk}$ (16) are equal to zero, the last $n - r_k$ components $w_{k,i}$ of the vector $\mathbf{w}_k = [w_{k,1}, \ldots, w_{k,n}]^T$ (18) are also equal to zero ($\forall i \in \{r_k + 1, \ldots, n\}$ $w_{k,i} = 0$) [7].

## 6  Optimal Subsets of Features

Minimization of the *CPL*-type criterion functons $\Phi_{k(l)}(\mathbf{w})$ (11) and $\Psi_{k(l)}(\mathbf{w})$ (12) defined on the learning sets $G_{k(l)}^+$ and $G_{k(l)}^-$ (8) allows to determine the optimal subsets $F_l(n_l)$ of $n_l$ features $X_i$ ($F_l(n_l) \subset F(n)$ (1)).

Assume that both learning sets $G_{k(l)}^+$ and $G_{k(l)}^-$ (8) contain the same numbers $m_{k(l)}$ $\left( m_{k(l)}^+ = m_{k(l)}^- \right)$ of vectors $\mathbf{y}_j(k)$ (7). In this case, the minimization of the perceptron criterion functon $\Phi_{k(l)}(\mathbf{w})$ (11) determines the optimal vertex $\mathbf{w}_{k(l)}^p = [w_{k,1}^p, \ldots, w_{k,nl}^p]^T$ and the subset $R_l(n_l)^p$ ($R_l(n_l)^p \subset F(n)$ (1)) containing $n_l = 2m_{k(l)}$ acitive features $X_i$ with weights $w_{k,i}^p$ different from zero ($w_{k,i}^p \neq 0$):

$$R_l(n_l)^p = \left\{ X_{i(1)}, \ldots, X_{i(nl)} \right\}. \tag{19}$$

In accordance with the previous remarks, we can assume that the minimum value $\Phi_{k(l)}(\mathbf{w}_{k(l)}^p)$ of the perceptron criterion function $\Phi_{k(l)}(\mathbf{w})$ (11) is equal to zero in the case of high-dimensional sets $C_k$ (2):

$$\Phi_{k(l)}\left( \mathbf{w}_{k(l)}^p \right) = \Phi_{k(l)}^p = 0 \tag{20}$$

The constrained minimization of criterion functons $\Psi_{k(l)}(\mathbf{w})$ (12) under the condition $\Phi_{k(l)}(\mathbf{w}) = 0$ (20) can be repesented as follows:

$$\Psi_{k(l)}\left( \mathbf{w}_{k(l)}^* \right) = \min\left\{ \Psi_{k(l)}(\mathbf{w}) : \Phi_k(\mathbf{w}) = 0 \right\} \tag{21}$$

Solving the above mininimization problem allows to obtain the optimal vertex $\mathbf{w}_{k(l)}^* = [w_{k,1}^*, \ldots, w_{k,nl}^*]^T$ (21) and the optimal subset $R_l(n_l)^*$ of $n_l = 2m_{k(l)}$ features $X_i(R_l(n_l)^* \subset F(n)$ (1)). The number $n_l$ of features $X_i$ in the subset $R_l(n_l)^*$ is the same as in the subset $R_l(n_l)^p$ (19).

*Lemma* 2: The optimal vertex $\mathbf{w}_{k(l)}^*$ (21) is characterized by the largest margin $\delta(\mathbf{w}_{k(l)}^*)_{L1}$ (7) among all vertices $\mathbf{w}_{k(l)}$ (18) of the rank $n_l = 2m_{k(l)}$, where $m_{k(l)} = m_{k(l)}^+ = m_{k(l)}^-$.

## 7  Balanced Complex Layers

The learning sets $C_k$ (2) contain $m_k$ feature vectors $\mathbf{x}_j$ assigned to particular categories $\omega_k$ ($k = 1, \ldots, K$). The complex layer can be designed separately for each category $\omega_k$ based on the high-dimensional learning sets $C_k$ (2). In this case, the number $m_k$ of feature vectors $\mathbf{x}_j$ in each learning set $C_k$ (2) is much smaller than the dimension $n$ of the vectors $\mathbf{x}_j$ ($m_k << n$). If the numbers $m_k$ of elements $\mathbf{x}_j$ are very different in the learning sets $C_k$ (2) then these sets are unbalanced [3]. The unbalance of the learning sets $C_k$ (2) can significantly deteriorate the quality of classifiers designed on the basis of such sets [2].

The unbalance of learning sets $C_k$ (2) can be reduced by procesing with complex layers. For this purpose, it is proposed here that each category $\omega_k$ be represented by a complex layer with the same number of $L$ of the optimal vertices $\mathbf{w}_{k(l)}^* = [w_{k,1}^*, \ldots, w_{k,nl}^*]^T$ (21) ($l = 1, \ldots, L$).

Moreover, each optimal vertex $\mathbf{w}^*_{k(l)}$ (21) of the complex layer can be designed in a balanced way on the learning subsets $G^+_{k(l)}$ and $G^-_{k(l)}$ (8) containing the same numbers $m_{k(l)}$ $\left(m^+_{k(l)} = m^+_{k(l)}\right)$ of vectors $\mathbf{y}_j(k)$ (7). The learning subsets $G^+_{k(l)}$ and $G^-_{k(l)}$ (8) with the same number $m_r$ of elements $\mathbf{y}_j(k)$ (7) cen be used to design all complex layers:

$$(\forall k \in \{1, \dots, K\}) \ (\forall l \in \{1, \dots, L\}) \ m_{k(l)} = m_r \tag{22}$$

The reduced number $m_r$ of vectors $\mathbf{y}_j(k)$ (7) may be equal to the smallest number $m_k$ of feature vectors $\mathbf{x}_j$ in the learning sets $C_k$ (2).

$$m_r = min\{m_1, \dots, m_K\} \tag{23}$$

Such a choice of the reduced number $m_r$ aims to balance the representation of all categories $\omega_k (k = 1, \dots, K)$.

## 8   Classifiers Based on Complex Layers

The feature vectors $\mathbf{x}_j$ forming the learning sets $C_k$ (2) represent $K$ categories $\omega_k (k = 1, \dots, K)$ in the feature space $F[n]$ ($\mathbf{x}_j \in F[n]$). For each category $\omega_k$, its balanced complex layer can be designed based on the dataset $C_k$ (2). The complex layer associated with the $k$-th category $\omega_k$ is based on $L$ optimal vertices $\mathbf{w}^*_{k(l)}$ (21) ($l = 1, \dots, L$).

Each optimal vertex $\mathbf{w}^*_{k(l)} = [w^*_{k(l),1}, \dots, w^*_{k(l),n}]^T$ (21) of the $k$-th complex layer is based on its own subset $R_{k(l)}(n_l)^* = \{X_{i(1)}, \dots, X_{i(nl)}\}^*$ (19) of $n_l$ active features $X_i$ (21) associated with non-zero weigths $w^*_{k(l),i} (w^*_{k(l),i} \neq 0)$. It was assumed that the optimal subsets $R_{k(l)}(n_l)^*$ associated with different vertices $\mathbf{w}^*_{k(l)}$ (21) are disjoint:

$$(l' \neq l) \Rightarrow R_{k(l')}(n_l)^* \cap R_{k(l)}(n_l)^* = \emptyset \tag{24}$$

The optimal vertex $\mathbf{w}^*_{k(l)} = [w^*_{k(l),1}, \dots, w^*_{k(l),n}]^T$ (21) of the $k$-th complex layer defines the following linear classifier (formal neuron) [7]:

$$(\forall \mathbf{x} \in F[n])$$

$$r_{k(l)} = r\left(\mathbf{w}^*_{k(l)}; \mathbf{x}\right) = \begin{cases} 1 \ if \ \left(\mathbf{w}^*_{k(l)}\right)^T \mathbf{x} > 0 \\ \\ 0 \ if \ \left(\mathbf{w}^*_{k(t)}\right)^T \mathbf{x} \leq 0 \end{cases} \tag{25}$$

It can be seen that the complex layer associated with the $k$-th category $\omega_k$ transforms feature vectors $\mathbf{x}_j$ from the learning sets $C_k$ (2) into vectors $\mathbf{z}(\mathbf{x}_j) = [z_1, \dots, z_n]^T$ with components $z_{j,i}$ equal to zero or to one:

$$(\forall k \in \{1, \dots, K\}) \ (\forall \mathbf{x}_j \in C_k) \ \mathbf{z}_k(\mathbf{x}_j) = \left[\mathbf{0}^T_1, \dots, \mathbf{1}^T_k, \dots, \mathbf{0}^T_L\right]^T \tag{26}$$

where $\mathbf{1}_k = [1, \ldots, 1]^T$ and $\mathbf{0}_i = [0, \ldots, 0]^T$ are vectors with $L$ components. The following decision rule was based on $K$ complex layers (26):

$$(\forall \mathbf{x} \in F[n])\,(\forall k \in \{1, \ldots, K\})$$
$$\textit{if } \|\mathbf{z}_{k'}(\mathbf{x})\| \geq \|\mathbf{z}_k(\mathbf{x})\|, \textit{ then } \mathbf{x} \in C_{k'}\,(2) \tag{27}$$

where $\|\mathbf{z}_k(\mathbf{x})\|$ is the norm of the vector $\mathbf{z}_k(\mathbf{x})$ (26).

According to the classification rule (27), the object $O$ represented by the feature vectors $\mathbf{x}$ is assigned to the $k'$ - th category $\omega_{k'}$.

*Lemma* 3: If the feature vectors $\mathbf{x}_j$ forming the learning sets $C_k$ (2) are based on a sufficiently large number of linearly independent features $X_i$ ($X_i \in F(n)$ (1)), then the classification rule (27) can correctly assigns all these vectors $\mathbf{x}_j$.

This lemma results from the designing of optimal vertices $\mathbf{w}^*_{k(l)}$ (21).

## 9 Concluding Remarks

Unbalanced learning sets $C_k$ (2) can cause serious problems in the design of classification models. The paper proposes a new concept of balancing datasets by transforming them with complex layers. Each learning set $C_k$ (2) is transformed by its own complex layer.

The general assumption about the high-dimensionality of the learning sets $C_k$ (2) allows for the design of balanced, complex layers. Consequently, each category $\omega_k$ can be similarly represented in a balanced way by its own complex layer ($k = 1, \ldots, K$).

Each balanced complex layer is made up of the same number $L$ of linear classifiers (36) based on the optimal vertices $\mathbf{w}^*_{k(l)}$ (21), where $l = 1 \ldots, L$. Each optimal vertex $\mathbf{w}^*_{k(l)}$ (21) is determined by $m_r$ feature vectors $\mathbf{x}_j$ from the $k$-th learning set $C_k$ (2) and by the same number $m_r$ of vectors $\mathbf{x}'_j$ from the remaining sets $C_{k'}(\mathbf{x}_{j'} \in \cup_{k' \neq k} C_{k'}(2))$.

The vertex $\mathbf{w}^*_{k(l)}$ (21) is associated with the optimal subset $R_l(n_l)^*$ of $n_l = 2m_r$ features $X_i$. It was assumed that the optimal subsets $R_l(n_l)^*$ of features $X_i$ are disjoined (24). This assumption can be satisfied when the learning sets $C_k$ (2) are high-dimensional ($m_k << n$).

The aggregated classification rule (27) allocates correctly all feature vectors $\mathbf{x}_j$ from the learning sets $C_k$ (2). The generalization power of the aggregated classification rule (27) is expected to be high. The first results of experiments with classification based on complex layers are encouraging [9].

**Acknowledgments.** The presented study was supported by the grant WZ/WI-IIT/4/2023 from the Bialystok University of Technology and funded from the resources for research by the Polish Ministry of Science and Higher Education.

## References

1. Duda, O.R., Hart, P.E., Stork, D.G.: Pattern Classification. J. Wiley, New York (2001)
2. Bishop, C.M.: Pattern Recognition and Machine Learning. Springer, Heidelberg (2006)

3. Chawla, N.V., et al.: SMOTE: synthetic minority over-sampling technique. J. Artif. Intell. Res. **16**, 321–357 (2002)
4. Bobrowski, L.: complex layers of formal neurons. In: Engineering Applications of Neural Networks - EAAAI/EANN 2022, EANN 2022, pp. 81–89. Springer, Heidelberg (2022)
5. Bobrowski, L.: Data Exploration and Linear Separability, pp. 1–172. Lambert Academic Publishing, Saarbrücken 2019
6. Boser, B.E., Guyon, I., Vapnik, V.N.: A training algorithm for optimal margin classifiers. In: Proceedings of the Fifth Annual Workshop of Computational Learning Theory, vol. 5, pp. 144–152. ACM, Pittsburgh (1992)
7. Bobrowski, L.: Computing on vertices in data mining, pp. 1–19. Data mining, Intech Open (2021)
8. Bobrowski, L., Łukaszuk, T.: Relaxed linear separability (RLS) approach to feature (gene) subset selection. In: Xia, X (ed.) Selected Works in Bioinformatics, INTECH, pp. 103–118 (2011)
9. Bobrowski, L., Zabielski, P.: Classification model with collinear grouping of features. J. Inf. Telecommun. **7**(1), 73–88 (2023)

# BotDroid: Permission-Based Android Botnet Detection Using Neural Networks

Saeed Seraj[1], Elias Pimenidis[2], Michalis Pavlidis[1], Stelios Kapetanakis[3], Marcello Trovati[4], and Nikolaos Polatidis[1(✉)]

[1] School of Architecture, Technology and Engineering, University of Brighton, BN2 4GJ Brighton, UK
{S.Seraj,M.Pavlidis,N.Polatidis}@Brighton.ac.uk
[2] Department of Computer Science and Creative Technologies, University of the West of England, BS16 1QY Bristol, UK
Elias.Pimenidis@uwe.ac.uk
[3] Distributed Analytics Solutions, 17 Fawe Street, London 14 6FD, UK
Stelios@distributedanalytics.co.uk
[4] Department of Computer Science, Edge Hill University, Ormskirk L39 4QP, UK
Marcello.Trovati@edgehill.ac.uk

**Abstract.** Android devices can now offer a wide range of services. They support a variety of applications, including those for banking, business, health, and entertainment. The popularity and functionality of Android devices, along with the open-source nature of the Android operating system, have made them a prime target for attackers. One of the most dangerous malwares is an Android botnet, which an attacker known as a botmaster can remotely control to launch destructive attacks. This paper investigates Android botnets by using static analysis to extract features from reverse-engineered applications. Furthermore, this article delivers a new dataset of Android apps, including botnet or benign, and an optimized multi-layer perceptron neural network (MLP) for detecting botnets infected by malware based on the permissions of the apps. Experimental results show that the proposed methodology is both practical and effective while outperforming other standard classifiers in various evaluation metrics.

**Keywords:** Android Malware detection · Botnets · Neural Networks · New dataset

## 1 Introduction

Today, Android is one of the most well-known operating systems. It has millions of applications that are distributed through accredited or unofficial distributors. As a result, it is one of the most common targets for malicious cyber-attacks. The Play Store on Android is not very restrictive, making it simple to install malicious apps. Botnet applications are classified as malware because they can be distributed through these stores and downloaded by unlucky users onto their smartphones. Botnets are among the most dangerous hacking techniques used on the internet today. Botnet developers frequently

L. Iliadis et al. (Eds.): EANN 2023, CCIS 1826, pp. 71–84, 2023.
https://doi.org/10.1007/978-3-031-34204-2_7

target smartphone users to install malicious tools and target a larger number of devices. This is frequently done to gain access to sensitive data such as credit card numbers or to cause damage to individual hosts or organisational resources through denial of service (DDoS) attacks. [1, 2].

Botnet attacks have become a threat and risk to network and internet security in recent years. They include several malicious activities in network traffic. A botnet is made up of separate robot and network components. The botmaster programmes and builds the bot for specific purposes using computers known as zombies. In the network, these computers are clearly breaking the law. Botnets are extremely widespread and can affect millions of computers. Botnets are networks made up of personal computers and smart devices known as bots. One or more attackers, known as botmasters, oversee these bots, and their goal is to carry out malicious activities. In other words, bots contain harmful software that runs on host computers and enables the botmaster to remotely command and control the system [3]. Moreover, the popularity and adoption of Android smartphones have attracted malware authors to spread the malware to smartphone users. Malware on smartphones can take the form of Trojans, viruses, worms, or mobile botnets. Mobile botnets, also known as Android botnets, are more dangerous because they pose serious threats by stealing user credentials, sending spam, and launching distributed denial of service (DDoS) attacks. A mobile botnet is defined as a collection of compromised mobile smartphones that are controlled by a botmaster via a command and control (C&C) channel and used to carry out malicious activities [4].

Although numerous studies have been conducted to detect Android botnet attacks, classification accuracy can still be improved. Insufficient or smaller data in the experiments results in lower accuracy. Machine learning is incapable of handling large amounts of unstructured data because it typically requires structured data and uses traditional algorithms. The small size of the dataset is also to blame for Android botnet detection's poor performance. Because the size of the sample data collection is limited, the confidence in the estimate decreases and the uncertainty increases, resulting in lower precision. More data is always a good idea when it comes to achieving the high efficacy of Android botnet detection. Furthermore, the use of untrained data affects an effect on the detection of Android botnets. Trained data is the most important and primary data that machines use to learn and predict. Increased training data provides more information and assist in better user fit [5].

As a result, according to the explanation provided, there is an urgent need to develop new methods for defeating mobile botnets. Because of the popularity of Android mobile devices, the goal of this paper is to propose an innovative method for detecting botnets in Android-based devices. This paper aims to produce a new mobile botnet classification/detection based on permissions. For this purpose, we have created and introduced a new dataset based on permissions that are described in detail in Sect. 3. Moreover, the botnet dataset is a classification dataset that only includes legitimate Android apps and botnets. We have created an optimised multilayer perceptron neural network (MLP) that is highly accurate at detecting botnets.

The contributions of the paper are as follows:

- We deliver a novel dataset with 453 permissions as features to discover Botnets through the Android operating system.

- We propose an optimized multilayer perceptron neural network (MLP) to detect Android Botnets which can detect botnets with very high accuracy.

The rest of the paper is organized as follows: Sect. 2 is the research background, Sect. 3 is the related work, Sect. 4 describes the dataset, Sect. 5 explains the proposed method, Sect. 6 delivers the experimental evaluation and Sect. 7 contains the conclusions.

## 2  Background

### 2.1  Overview of Android Botnet

Botnets are a type of malware that enables an attacker to gain control of a victim's computer. The botmaster, C&C server, and bot-infected machines are common botnet components. The botnet is designed to infect mobile phones or computers and make them under the control of botnet owners or the "Botmaster". Botmasters are those who operate the command and control of botnets to attack the target via a communication channel, such as HTTP, Internet Relay Chat (IRC), or peer-to-peer (P2P). The botmaster will use a botnet to attack the victim in a variety of ways, including denial of service (DDoS) attacks, spamming, malware and advertisement distribution, espionage, hosting malicious applications, and other activities. The overview of a Botnet is demonstrated in Fig. 1.

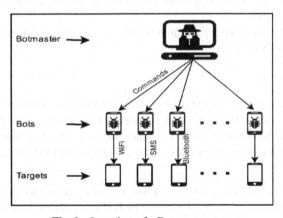

**Fig. 1.**  Overview of a Botnet structure

### 2.2  Types of Botnets

A botnet includes three types of programmes:

A. Server programmes: These programmes are located on the command-and-control server and are used to control infected computers or bots.
B. Client programme: These are programmes installed on infected computers while they wait for control instructions.

C. Malicious programme: These are the software or programmes, also known as malware, which is used over the Internet to infect or compromise vulnerable computers.

Communication is the most important aspect of a botnet. The command-and-control server continues to communicate with bots, instructing them to engage in malicious behaviour. The bots, in turn, continue to wait for instructions, perform the tasks assigned to them, and send the collected data to the command-and-control server [25].

## 2.3  Botnet lifecycle

In general, botnets have four main phases in their lifecycle:

A. Phase Of Spread and Infection: Botmasters will employ various methods and techniques to infect new targets and transform them into new bots. After infecting the target, it will run a script or shell code and install itself on the victim machine.
B. Phase Of Command & Control: The command and control (C&C) mechanism create a communication interface between bot-bot, C&C servers-bots, and C&C servers-bot master. Command and control mechanisms are classified into three types: centralised, decentralised, and unstructured.
C. Phase Of Attack: The botnet is a collection of malicious activities that spread throughout computer networks. DDoS attacks, spamming, spreading malware and advertisements, espionage, and hosting malicious applications and activities are just a few examples of attacks.
D. Phase Of Destruction: After performing malicious activities, botmasters may destruct a portion of the botnet [15].

## 2.4  Botnet Attacks

Botnet attacks are typically carried out by a group of hackers, and the owner has no idea that he or she is on the victim list. Botnets are currently classified into five types based on the Command and Control (C&C) channel. Because the programme is developed by the methods and techniques employed, the botnets are divided into these categories. They are as follows:

A. IRC Botnet (Internet Relay Chat): An IRC botnet is created by using a centralised system to monitor the victim to perform malicious activities, and the targeted bots are controlled by the main C&C channel.
B. P2P Botnet (Peer to Peer): It is accomplished using P2P protocols and a decentralised system with a network of nodes that keeps it alive, containing the attacked bots as well as all relevant data transmission.
C. HTTP Botnet: An HTTP Botnet is a centralised system-based structure that conducts attacks via the HTTP protocol. The bots use a specific URL and IP address specified by the main botmaster as the C&C server. These hacking attempts are carried out for financial theft.
D. Mobile Botnet: This attack makes use of mobile phone sharing, Bluetooth technology, and text messaging. The botmaster can easily access the data using this method via the C&C Channel.

E. Botnet Cloud: This is a very difficult task, so the botmaster creates and manages the bots using the cloud service, putting the bots at significant risk of being discovered.

## 3 Related works

This section describes various machine learning-based Android malware analysis techniques that have been proposed in the literature. To identify android malware, three approaches have been proposed: static, dynamic, and hybrid.

### 3.1 Static Techniques

Static techniques use few resources and are quick and secure. However, they are unable to decipher malware that has been encrypted or obfuscated. Most static methods frequently produce false positives and are unable to deal with unidentified malware. Therefore, static analysis may need to be combined with other security models for effective malware detection.

In this proposed research work, a security application is developed which scans all applications installed and identifies probable harmful applications on the user's smartphone. It organises all permissions on each application into predefined categories. The risk factor of the respective application is calculated based on the permission category. If the risk factor/score exceeds the predetermined threshold, the user is notified of the application's risk. This will inform users about applications that can exploit personal information stored on their devices in real-time [6]. Another permission-based research presents the Android botnet attack detection using deep learning algorithms, Convolutional Neural Networks (CNN) and Artificial Neural Networks (ANN) using different categories of permission features [5]. In another work, Android Botnets are investigated using static analysis to extract potential features from the source code of the applications after they have been reverse-engineered. To identify such malicious applications, efficient machine-learning models are then developed using the features. The study also suggests a new set of features for using the target mobile to access resources [1]. Another similar work to the previous paper introduces an approach to detect botnet Android mobile apps by using source code mining. Several examples of malicious and non-malicious apps analyse the source code using reverse engineering and data mining techniques. To build datasets, they employ two methods. In the first, they build several datasets by text mining the source code, and in the second, they create one dataset by extracting source code metrics using an open-source tool [2]. This study uses similar features to the previous one. They propose a system for detecting Android botnets using automated text mining of manifest files obtained from apps in this paper. The proposed method extracts the features from manifest files using NLP techniques, and a deep learning-based classification model is used to detect botnet applications [26]. This paper introduces a new classification for mobile botnets based on smartphone permissions and Application Programming Interface (API) calls. The Drebin dataset [24] is utilised as the training dataset for this classification, which is created using static analysis in a controlled lab setting [7]. In this study, they suggest a static method for detecting mobile botnets. Using a machine learning algorithm and a combination of MD5, permissions, broadcast receivers, and background services, this technique can identify applications that can be used to create mobile botnets. In this method, android application features are extracted and used to create a machine-learning classifier for identifying mobile botnet attacks [8]. In another one, they present a novel approach for identifying Android botnet applications that rely on Android permissions and convolutional neural networks (CNNs). They also proposed a novel way to represent each application as an image that is constructed based on the co-occurrence of permissions given to that application, being the first developed method that applies CNNs for this purpose. A binary classifier that is trained using these images is the proposed CNN [9]. This paper suggests a new method for identifying mobile botnets based on features taken from images and a manifest file. The method uses a Histogram of Oriented Gradients and byte histograms obtained from images representing the app executable and combines these with features obtained from the manifest files. Then feature selection is used to choose the best features for classification using machine learning algorithms [10]. In a research work with similar features, they present Bot- IMG, a framework for machine learning-based image-based visualisation and Android botnet detection. Additionally, they used the ISCX botnet dataset [23] to assess the Bot-IMG framework's effectiveness. They specifically use Autoencoders in with traditional machine learning classifiers to implement an image-based detection method using a Histogram of Oriented Gradients (HOG) as feature descriptors within the framework [11]. The new risk assessment method that focuses on GPS exploitation for Android botnet detection is proposed to assess the level of risk connected to each app in terms of privacy, financial, and smartphone system risk. Static analysis using feature set permission and API calls served as the foundation for the evaluation. Using a quantitative calculation model, it was possible to distinguish between benign and botnet apps [12]. And finally, A comparison of deep learning techniques for Android botnet detection using 6802 Android applications made up of 1929 botnet applications from the ISCX botnet dataset is presented in this paper. Using 342 static features derived from the applications, they assess the performance of several deep learning techniques, including CNN, DNN, LSTM, GRU, CNN-LSTM, and CNN-GRU models [13].

### 3.2 Dynamic Techniques

The application is executed on an Android platform in dynamic approaches, and all related system calls and network traffics are monitored. Malware is detected based on its runtime behaviour and interactions with the system. Dynamic methods can deal with malware that has been obfuscated or encrypted. They outperform static analysis in detecting both known and unknown malware. However, they are slow, resource-intensive, and vulnerable due to the limitation of code reachability. As a result, they may be dangerous at times.

To discover specific trends and characteristics relating to botnet behaviour, this paper analyses Android malware. A thorough literature review of well-known Android malware apps helps identify the trends and characteristics of botnets. The Android Botnet Discovery Process and the Android Botnet Development Model are then used to further examine the identified characteristics. The frequently recognised trends and characteristics help in both the understanding of Android botnet operations and the potential identification of an Android bot [14]. In this research work, to identify potential malware in Android applications, they created a system called ABIS (Android Botnet Identification System). Their system learns the characteristics of each Android botnet family from the dataset offered by the University of New Brunswick to identify the Android botnets [15]. In another one, to accurately identify Android botnets, they suggest using an approach called Smart Self-Adaptive Learning Based Particle Swarm Optimization Support Vector Machine (SSLPSO-SVM). The SSLPSO algorithm, which is based on the PSO algorithm, simultaneously employs five different search-space scanning techniques [16]. They present an anomaly-based and host-based method for identifying mobile botnets. In the suggested method, statistical features extracted from system calls are used to identify anomalous behaviours. They were able to test the effectiveness of their method in a situation that was like reality using a self-generated dataset made up of 13 families of mobile botnets and legitimate applications [17]. "Logdog," suggests an improved log-based botnet detection method for mobile devices. Their method relies on looking through mobile device logs to find signs of botnet activity [18]. This paper introduces a novel method for botnet detection in networks. The IRC, HTTP, DNS, and P2P attacks that botnets use is compared using the proposed detection model. This model also rates the precision of botnet detection. To identify botnets, they employ network nerves, correlation, and NSA (negative selection algorithm), which is based on an artificial immune system [18]. However, their model differs from one that was previously proposed, which concentrated on 81 attributes gathered from features of network traffic. They used Weka machine learning to test ten families of Android botnets. They have 32762 instances that fall under the attack and non-attack categories [19]. At last, the research focuses on creating a cloud-based malware detection system for Android botnets. The proposed system's prototype, which offers an Android malware analysis in real-time, has been deployed. Using a botnet detection learning dataset and a multi-layered algorithm used to predict the botnet family of a specific application, the paper explains the architectural implementation of the developed system [20].

### 3.3 Hybrid Techniques

For greater accuracy, hybrid techniques combine static and dynamic approaches. They use static analysis to analyse an application first and then use dynamic analysis to overcome both static and dynamic limitations [21]. In general, the hybrid technique usually produces the best results. Nonetheless, due to their complexity, they require a lot of resources and time. This paper aims to use machine learning methods to categorise Android applications (apps) as benign or botnet. System calls, permission requests, and API calls were analysed and classified using machine learning techniques and hybrid analysis, which combines static and dynamic analyses [4]. Also, another research focuses on developing a functional prototype of a system that uses artificial intelligence to analyse various Android application behavioural parameters. Signature-based detection techniques were also incorporated into the prototype during implementation. [22].

## 4 Dataset

We deliver a new dataset for Botnet detection in Android platforms. As a result, we created an Android Botnet dataset with 2713 entries. The dataset contains 454 columns, including 453 specific features and the label, which is the last column. The first row of the dataset describes column titles, and the remaining rows contain features from 2712 Android Botnets and benign applications. To do this, we downloaded 1483 benign applications from Google Play and different categories and 1229 Android Botnets. All values are in binary format, which means they are either 0 or 1. Figure 2 presents a small portion of the dataset. The entire dataset is available on Kaggle [28].

| | INTERNET | CLEAR APP CACHE | GET TASKS | CHANGE WIFI STATE | READ PHONE STATE | SYSTEM ALERT WINDOW | WRITE EXTERNAL STORAGE | CALL_ PHONE | CAMERA | READ CALL LOG | USES POLICY FORCE LOCK | WAKE UP STOKER | Risk score |
|---|---|---|---|---|---|---|---|---|---|---|---|---|---|
| 2 | 1 | 1 | 0 | 1 | 0 | 1 | 1 | 0 | 0 | 0 | 0 | 0 | 0 |
| 3 | 1 | 1 | 1 | 1 | 1 | 1 | 1 | 0 | 1 | 0 | 0 | 0 | 0 |
| 4 | 1 | 0 | 0 | 0 | 0 | 0 | 0 | 0 | 0 | 0 | 0 | 0 | 1 |
| 5 | 1 | 1 | 1 | 1 | 1 | 1 | 1 | 0 | 0 | 0 | 0 | 0 | 0 |
| 6 | 1 | 1 | 1 | 1 | 1 | 1 | 1 | 0 | 1 | 0 | 0 | 0 | 0 |

**Fig. 2.** A representation of a small portion of the proposed dataset

### 4.1 Feature Selection

Feature selection is critical in detecting mobile malware and botnets. Feature selection can help machine learning algorithms produce more accurate results by removing noise and irrelevant data from datasets. It can also reduce the runtime of machine learning algorithms during training. In this research, permissions are our features. Permissions are used to validate the system's requirements. The developer must declare permissions for use in their applications. Declared permissions are useful and effective in revealing the potential risks of installing Apps. According to [5], the protection level of the permission feature consists of three categories: Dangerous permission feature, Normal permission feature and Signature permission feature as shown in Table 1.

**Table 1.** The protection level of a permission feature

| Protection Level | Description |
|---|---|
| Dangerous | A higher-risk permission provides access to specific application-level features to the requesting applications while posing little risk to other applications, the system, or the user |
| Normal | A lower-risk permission would grant the requesting app access to sensitive user information or device control, both of which could be harmful to the user |
| Signature | The system will only grant this permission if the requesting application is registered with the same certificate as the one that declared on the permission |

## 4.2 Feature Extraction

VirusTotal [27] was used to decompress our botnet dataset and benign applications'.apk files. By uploading the apk file to VirusTotal, it decompiles the files to source code folders that provide detailed information about each dataset file, allowing the features to be extracted. Basic properties, permissions, activities, receivers, intent filters by action, intent filters by category, interesting strings, warnings, contents metadata, contained files by type, and contained files by extension are among the useful information. In addition, VirusTotal declares the files of the benign application to be virus-free and identifies the malware percentage of the botnet dataset files. We classified the apk files using over 70 trusted anti-malware detection engines. The android Botnet dataset includes several families, including Anserverbot, Botmaster, DroidDream, Sandroid, Wroba and Zitmo. We put all the information in a file to make the dataset usable. CSV file format, which is simple to open and process. When an app requires permission, the value in the corresponding dataset entry is 1, and when an app does not require permission, the value is 0. Based on VirusTotal's report, an Android app recognised as malware by most antivirus companies is considered risky, and the value in the label column is set to 1, indicating a Botnet. The list of Android mobile botnet families and the number of samples are listed in Table 2.

**Table 2.** Botnet Families

| Botnet Family | Year of Discovery | Number of Samples | Type of C&C | Motivation |
|---|---|---|---|---|
| Anserverbot | 2011 | 244 | HTPP | Propagation of possible Malware |
| Bmaster | 2012 | 6 | HTPP | Financial, SMS Stealing |
| DroidDream | 2011 | 362 | HTPP | Data Stealing |
| Gemini | 2010 | 262 | HTTP | Data Stealing |
| Sandroid | 2014 | 61 | HTTP | Financial, Mobile Banking Attack |
| Wroba | 2014 | 152 | HTTP | Financial, Mobile Banking Attack |
| Zitmo | 2012 | 142 | SMS | Financial, SMS mobile Transaction, Authentication Number, (mTAN) stealing |

# 5  Proposed Method

We have used an MLP neural network to detect malware Botnets in our dataset. A multilayer perceptron is a good estimator in our case due to the immense flexibility of the math performed in the overall function. It is a purely mathematical system that gradually approximates complex input-output relationships with large amounts of data.

The number of input nodes must match the number of permissions in the dataset which is exactly 453. Besides, only one output node is needed even for so many input nodes since the classification here is a yes/no decision maker. For extremely powerful classification, one hidden layer is enough. The number of nodes within the hidden layer can be variable and we have found 454 as the optimum number through trial and error with extensive attempts. According to the neural network structure, data entries are multiplied by weights and subjected to an activation function. As shown in Eq. 1. We used a differentiable activation function called standard logistic sigmoid for both hidden and output nodes in the MLP structure ($K = 1, L = 1$) because a gradient tells us how to modify weights. This activation function promotes successful system training while also contributing to the neural network's learning process stability. Each computational node's input is calculated using Eq. 2, where N denotes the output of the preceding layer's nodes, w is the weight vector, and n denotes the number of nodes in the preceding layer. In Eq. 3, the weights of a node are modified in proportion to the slope of the error function, where the target is the expected output, the learning rate, and f′ is the logistic activation function's derivative. It would be unnecessary to use the logistic function's derivative expression for a given input value if we had already calculated the function's output, as shown in Eq. 4.

$$f(x) = \frac{L}{1 + e^{-kx}} \quad \xrightarrow{L = 1, K = 1} \quad f(x) = \frac{1}{1 + e^{-x}} \tag{1}$$

$$preN_i = w.N = w_1 N_1 + w_2 N_2 + \ldots + w_n N_n \tag{2}$$

$$weight_{new} = weight_{old} + ax(target - output)xf'(input) \tag{3}$$

$$f'(x) = \frac{e^x}{(1 + e^x)^2} = f(x)(1 - f(x)) \tag{4}$$

# 6  Experimental Evaluation

We have developed an optimised Multilayer Perceptron (MLP) using Python and the Scikit-learn library, as described in Sect. 5. Moreover, 5-fold cross-validation has been used throughout all experiments. Using the proposed Botnet dataset, we trained and validated our MLP neural network classifier using the Python programming language. The Numpy and Pandas libraries are required for array operations and reading data from files. The simulation is divided into four stages: defining the network's parameters, such as node numbers and learning rate, reading the Botnet dataset, training the MLP neural network with a portion of the dataset, and finally verifying the neural network with the rest of the dataset.

## 6.1 Evaluation Metrics

We used the Python programming language with the sci-kit-learn library for the experimental analysis. We have used Accuracy, Precision, Recall, and F1 as evaluation metrics; these metrics are described in Eqs. 5, 6, 7, and 8 respectively. True positive, true negative, false positive, and false negative are all abbreviated as TP, TN, FP, and FN, respectively.

$$Accuracy = \frac{TP + TN}{TP + TN + FP + FN} \tag{5}$$

$$Precision = \frac{TP}{TP + FP} \tag{6}$$

$$Recall = \frac{TP}{TP + FN} \tag{7}$$

$$F1 = 2 * \frac{Precision * Recall}{Precision + Recall} \tag{8}$$

## 6.2 Results

This section describes the experiments and compares the proposed method to other well-known classifiers as well as the most relevant previous research in this field. For evaluating the proposed method, we used our hand-crafted dataset and selected 1229 Android botnet samples from 7 different families. All the benign samples were scanned with the VirusTotal to make sure that the benign class does not include any malware samples. The dataset consists of 2713 samples, and 5-fold cross-validation was used to evaluate the proposed method using this dataset. All experiments were performed on 64-bit Microsoft Windows 11 pro–operating system and using hardware with intel(R) Core (TM) i5-8365U @ 1.60GHz 1.90GHz CPU, 16.00GB RAM, and an Intel UHD Graphics 620 GPU.

## 6.3 Comparisons with other Classifiers

The following algorithms were used in the comparisons, with the default settings from the sci-kit learn library: Decision Tree, Random Forest, KNN, SVM, and Naive Bayes. The results are shown in Table 3, which compares the proposed method to other well-known classifiers based on Accuracy, Precision, Recall, F-1, and AUC using 5-fold cross-validation. To highlight the significance of this research result, a comparison is made with previous similar research. Table 4 indicates the comparison between [5, 9, 10], and [26], respectively. These comparative results show that the research method in this paper surpasses previous similar efforts.

**Table 3.** Comparisons with other classifiers

| Algorithm | Accuracy% | Precision% | Recall% | F-1% | AUC% |
| --- | --- | --- | --- | --- | --- |
| Decision Tree | 96.50 | 98.36 | 94.14 | 96.20 | 96.37 |
| Random Forest | 98.15 | 97.63 | 98.41 | 98.02 | 98.17 |
| K-NN | 98.34 | 99.52 | 96.31 | 97.89 | 98.00 |
| SVM | 97.60 | 98.39 | 96.45 | 97.41 | 97.53 |
| Naïve Bayes | 79.18 | 68.53 | 99.59 | 81.19 | 81.00 |
| **BotDroid** | **98.88** | **99.99** | **98.46** | **98.88** | **98.80** |

### 6.4 Comparisons with the Most Recent Botnet Detection Studies

Table 4 shows the obtained results from the proposed method compared to other best researchers that have used traditional Machine Learning approaches (in terms of the used dataset, number of samples, and performance). The table indicates that the proposed method is completely successful in classifying benign and botnet applications.

Moreover, we distinguished botnet and benign applications just by utilizing given permissions, while some of the mentioned works employed more features alongside given permissions such as API calls or permissions protection level. Our promising results with high accuracy indicate that our method can effectively detect Android botnets based on only given permissions as features.

**Table 4.** Comparison with other related botnet detection studies

| Reference | Type | Method | Accuracy% | Precision% | Recall% | F-1% |
| --- | --- | --- | --- | --- | --- | --- |
| [9], 2020 | Permissions | CNN | 97.2 | 95.5 | 96 | 95.7 |
| [10], 2022 | Images and a manifest file | HOG | 97.5 | 98.0 | 98.0 | 98.0 |
| [5], 2022 | Permissions | CNN-SVM | 96.9 | - | - | 96.9 |
| [26], 2022 | Manifest file texts | CNN | 95.44 | 95.4 | 95.4 | 95.4 |
| | | ANN | 96.35 | 96.4 | 96.4 | 96.3 |
| **BotDroid** | **Permissions** | **MLP** | **98.88** | **99.99** | **98.46** | **98.80** |

## 7    Conclusions

In this paper, we employed Android permissions and an optimised multilayer perceptron (MLP) to propose a novel method to detect Android botnets. To the best of our knowledge, this is the first Android botnet detection method that applies a dataset with 453 permissions as a feature. Initially, we downloaded 2713 apk files from various categories from the Google play store and other third-party websites to create our intended dataset based on permissions. Then, reverse engineering was applied on 1483 benign and 1229 botnet applications from our hand-crafted dataset to extract the AndroidManifest.xml files that provided access to the permissions given to each application. Finally, we trained and tested a proposed MLP model using the employed dataset in a 5-fold cross-validation experiment. Based on our experiments, the proposed method outperforms several conventional ML methods in this field by achieving 98.88% accuracy and 99.99% precision. These promising results indicate that the proposed method can effectively detect Android botnets by employing the given permissions.

In the future we plan to investigate how to use permissions to detect other types of malwares such as Adware. Moreover, we aim to use Android API calls alongside the permissions to detect sophisticated various Android malwares.

# References

1. Alqatawna, J.F., Ala'M, A. Z., Hassonah, M. A., & Faris, H.: Android botnet detection using machine learning models based on a comprehensive static analysis approach. Journal of Information Security and Applications **58**, 102735 (2021)
2. Alothman, B., Rattadilok, P.: Android botnet detection: An integrated source code mining approach. In: 2017 12th International Conference for Internet Technology and Secured Transactions (ICITST), (pp. 111–115) (2017, December). IEEE
3. Hosseini, S., Nezhad, A.E., Seilani, H.: Botnet detection using negative selection algorithm, convolution neural network and classification methods. Evol. Syst. **13**, 1–15 (2021). https://doi.org/10.1007/s12530-020-09362-1
4. Yusof, M., Saudi, M. M., Ridzuan, F.: Mobile botnet classification by using hybrid analysis. In: International Journal of Engineering and Technology (UAE) (2018)
5. Balasunthar, S., Abdullah, Z.: Comparison of Convolutional Neural Network and Artificial Neural Network for Android Botnet Attack Detection. Applied Information Technology And Computer Science **3**(2), 32–49 (2022)
6. Kothari, S., Joshi, S.: Analysis of Android Applications to Detect Botnet Attacks. In: 2020 International Conference on Smart Innovations in Design, Environment, Management, Planning and Computing (ICSIDEMPC) (pp. 144–150) (2020, October). IEEE
7. Yusof, M., Saudi, M.M., Ridzuan, F.: A new mobile botnet classification based on permission and API calls. In: 2017 Seventh International Conference on Emerging Security Technologies (EST) (pp. 122–127) (2017, September). IEEE
8. Anwar, S., Zain, J.M., Inayat, Z., Haq, R. U., Karim, A., Jabir, A.N.: A static approach towards mobile botnet detection. In: 2016 3rd International Conference on Electronic Design (ICED), (pp. 563–567) (2016, August). IEEE
9. Hojjatinia, S., Hamzenejadi, S., Mohseni, H.: Android botnet detection using convolutional neural networks. In: 2020 28th Iranian Conference on Electrical Engineering (ICEE), (pp. 1–6) (2020, August). IEEE
10. Yerima, S.Y., Bashar, A.: A novel Android botnet detection system using image-based and manifest file features. Electronics **11**(3), 486 (2022)
11. Yerima, S.Y., Bashar, A.: Bot-IMG: A framework for image-based detection of Android botnets using machine learning. In: 2021 IEEE/ACS 18th International Conference on Computer Systems and Applications (AICCSA), (pp. 1–7), (2021, November). IEEE
12. Yusof, M., Saudi, M.M., Ridzuan, F.: Android Botnet Detection Using Risk Assessment
13. Yerima, S.Y., Alzaylaee, M.K., Shajan, A.: Deep learning techniques for android botnet detection. Electronics **10**(4), 519 (2021)

14. Pieterse, H., Olivier, M.S.: Android botnets on the rise: Trends and characteristics. In: 2012 information security for South Africa (pp. 1–5) (2012, August).. IEEE
15. Tansettanakorn, C., Thongprasit, S., Thamkongka, S., & Visoottiviseth, V. (2016, May). ABIS: a prototype of android botnet identification system. In: 2016 Fifth ICT International Student Project Conference (ICT-ISPC), (pp. 1–5). IEEE
16. Moodi, M., Ghazvini, M., Moodi, H.: A hybrid intelligent approach to detect android botnet using smart self-adaptive learning-based PSO-SVM. Knowl.-Based Syst. **222**, 106988 (2021)
17. da Costa, V.G., Barbon, S., Miani, R.S., Rodrigues, J.J., Zarpelão, B.B.: Detecting mobile botnets through machine learning and system calls analysis. In: 2017 IEEE International Conference on Communications (ICC) (pp. 1–6) (2017, May). IEEE
18. Girei, D.A., Shah, M.A., Shahid, M.B.: An enhanced botnet detection technique for mobile devices using log analysis. In: 2016 22nd International Conference on Automation and Computing (ICAC) (pp. 450–455) (2016, September). IEEE
19. Rasheed, M.M., Faieq, A.K., Hashim, A.A.: Android Botnet Detection Using Machine Learning. Ingénierie des Systèmes d Inf. **25**(1), 127–130 (2020)
20. Jadhav, S., Dutia, S., Calangutkar, K., Oh, T., Kim, Y. H., & Kim, J. N. (2015, July). Cloud-based android botnet malware detection system. In: 2015 17th International Conference on Advanced Communication Technology (ICACT), (pp. 347–352). IEEE
21. Seraj, S., Khodambashi, S., Pavlidis, M., Polatidis, N.: HamDroid: permission-based harmful android anti-malware detection using neural networks. Neural Comput. Appl. **34**, 1 (2021). https://doi.org/10.1007/s00521-021-06755-4
22. Oh, T., Jadhav, S., Kim, Y.H.: Android botnet categorization and family detection based on behavioural and signature data. In: 2015 International Conference on Information and Communication Technology Convergence (ICTC) (pp. 647–652) (2015, October). IEEE
23. Abdul Kadir, A.F., Stakhanova, N., &Ghorbani, A.A.: Android botnets: What urls are telling us. In: International Conference on Network and System Security (pp. 78–91), (2015, November). Springer, Cham
24. Arp, D., Spreitzenbarth, M., Hubner, M., Gascon, H., Rieck, K., Siemens, C.E.R.T.: Drebin: Effective and explainable detection of android malware in your pocket. In: Ndss (Vol. 14, pp. 23–26), (2014, February).
25. Baruah, S. : Botnet detection: analysis of various techniques. In: International Journal of Computational Intelligence & IoT 2(2)
26. Yerima, S.Y., To, Y.: A deep learning-enhanced botnet detection system based on Android manifest text mining
27. VirusTotal. Free online virus, malware and URL scanner https://www.virustotal.com/
28. https://www.kaggle.com/datasets/saeedseraj/botdroid-android-botnet-detection/

# Classification of Time Signals Using Machine Learning Techniques

Ishfaq Ahmad Jadoon, Doina Logofătu[(✉)], and Mohammad Nahin Islam

Frankfurt University of Applied Sciences, Frankfurt am Main, Germany
logofatu@fb2.fra-uas.de

**Abstract.** This study presents a comprehensive overview of the classification of time signals over a variety of objects. Signals were initially processed using the Hilbert-Huang transform, followed by supervised machine learning and deep learning to classify objects. Multilayer Perceptron (MLP) and Support Vector Machines (SVM) were used for sound discrimination. The result is a program that effectively detects and classifies time signals as "Object 1" or "Not Object 1" (i.e., Object #2 and Object 3).

**Keywords:** Machine Learning · Deep Learning · Supervised Learning · Neural Network · Multi-Layer Perceptron (MLP) · Hilbert-Huang Transform (HHT) · Empirical Mode Decomposition (EMD) · Object Classification

## 1 Introduction

The paper contains five sections. In the Sect. 1 the main tasks of the work have been discussed and then a general flow diagram has been provided in Fig. 1. Section 2 contains theoretical research insights on topics such as Machine Learning (ML), Multilayer Perceptron (MLP), and Hilbert Huang Transform (HHT). Section 3 describes in detail the implementation of the project and Sect. 4 discusses the results. The reference to related papers is provided in last section.

This work aims to classify sampled time signals after the HHT is applied to the data, and then a machine learning model is designed using multilayer perceptron and SVM. To determine whether the signal belongs to the correct class or the signal is misclassified, we analyze how the signals are classified into multiple classes and perform the accuracy check of the classification. Later, it is determined which machine learning model gives the highest accuracy, between Multilayer Perceptron (MLP) and Support Vector Machine (SVM). After inputting the data, the HHT is first applied using the Empirical Mode Decomposition (EMD) technique to compute additional features such as the Instantaneous Frequency (IF) and the energy at that IF or the Instantaneous Amplitude (IA) of the sampled time signal. This results in obtaining the Hilbert spectrum using IF and IA [1]. Then, the HHT spectrum data is used to train machine learning models, MLPs, and SVMs, which will be employed to perform classification

© The Author(s), under exclusive license to Springer Nature Switzerland AG 2023
L. Iliadis et al. (Eds.): EANN 2023, CCIS 1826, pp. 85–96, 2023.
https://doi.org/10.1007/978-3-031-34204-2_8

tasks for Object 1, Object 2, and Object 3. The data under consideration are humans, detected by a sensor, walking around at different heights and clothing. More details about MLP, SVM, and HHT can be found in Sect. 2.

In this experiment, different data sources were used, consisting of 315, 200, and 400 rows of time signals for Object 1, Object 2, and Object 3, respectively. For model training and validation purposes, the data was split in an 80:20 ratio. Details of the training, testing, and classifier evaluation procedures are described in Sect. 3. Furthermore, from a predetermined starting column in the data source, the software program was programmed to extract only relevant data, namely the actual time signal length with 3400 scan points of each sample. Both the "scan point" length and the "starting column" are dynamic variables that can be changed if necessary.

## 2    Background

### 2.1    Hilbert Transform

The Hilbert transform is a method that extracts important features from a given time series data and makes it more meaningful for analysis. The Hilbert Transform, Y(t), can be obtained for any given time series, X(t), using the following equation:

$$Y(t) = \frac{1}{\pi} P \int \frac{X(t')}{t - t'} dt' \tag{1}$$

Here, $P$ denotes the Cauchy principal value. This transformation exists for all Lp functions [12]. Using this definition, X(t) and Y(t) becomes a complex conjugate pair which allows us to obtain an analytic signal, Z(t).

$$Z(t) = X(t) + iY(t) = a(t)e^{i\theta(t)} \tag{2}$$

$i$ is the imaginary unit, $a(t)$ is the amplitude of the complex analytic signal and $\theta(t)$ is the instantaneous phase of the complex analytic signal, which is the angle formed by $Z(t)$. Now, a(t) and $\theta(t)$ can be obtained:

$$a(t) = \sqrt{X^2(t) + Y^2(t)} \tag{3}$$

$$\theta(t) = arctg\left(\frac{Y(t)}{X(t)}\right) \tag{4}$$

## 3    Methodology

This section provides a comprehensive guide to the discrimination of time signals belonging to different objects using the SVM and MLP models. The Hilbert transform is used for data preprocessing before classification. Additionally, model accuracy is evaluated using a confusion matrix to compare results.

## 3.1 Data Reading

The experiment consists of three objects, and for each object a corresponding dataset is available in the form of Excel files called Data Object1, Data Object2, and Data Object3. Each file is further divided into "Train Data" and "Test Data" sets.

The rows of each dataset represent the number of samples. The columns represent the number of features or sample points for each time signal. Each sample in the datasets contains 3400 samples depicted in Fig. 1. This is done by defining three different classes. The length of the feature vector or the number of sample points is also defined. They are labeled 0, 1, and 2, respectively, to distinguish the objects.

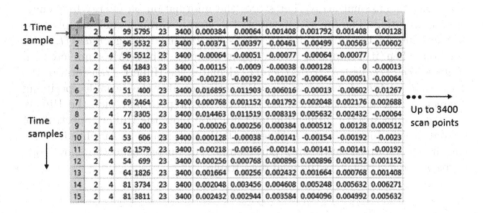

Fig. 1. Time Signals of an Object

## 3.2 Applying Hilbert Transform

On the completion of reading the Excel files the data is processed using the Hilbert Huang Transform (HHT) algorithm.

In the first step of the HHT algorithm, Intrinsic Mode Functions (IMFs) are created for each sample input. In the next step, the IMFs are applied to Hilbert Transform. As a result, Hilbert Spectrum is obtained. Using this Hilbert Spectrum, new features are obtained such as Instantaneous Frequency (IF), Instantaneous Amplitude (IA) etc., which will be later fed into the MLP model.

The code snippet, Fig. 2, indicates the python code used to calculate Hilbert Huang Transform.

```
hht1 = np.empty([0, f_div, 3400])
for i in range(trainData1.shape[0]):
    imf = emd.sift.sift(trainData1[i])
    IP, IF, IA = emd.spectra.frequency_transform(imf, sample_rate, 'hilbert')
    freq_edges, freq_bins = emd.spectra.define_hist_bins(0, 100, f_div)
    temp_hht = emd.spectra.hilberthuang(IF, IA, freq_edges)
    temp_hht3d = temp_hht[np.newaxis, :]
    hht1 = np.append(hht1, temp_hht3d, axis=0)
```

**Fig. 2.** Algorithm for Hilbert Huang Transform

Here, the variable hht1 is created to store the Hilbert spectrum. Variable hht1 is a three-dimensional array that stores the information on energy-frequency-time distribution. The for loop is created to iterate through each sample (row of Excel file) of the provided data. IMFs are obtained using $emd.sift.sift()$ function when it is applied to an input sample. When IMFs are created, $emd.spectra.\,frequency\_\,transform()$ calculates the Hilbert Transform of the data. $emd.spectra.\,define\_hist\_bins()$ function creates the variable specifying 'frequency divisions' which will be required to prepare and plot the Hilbert Spectrum. $emd.spectra.\,hilberthuang()$ function plots the Hilbert Spectrum of the data using 'Instantaneous Frequency (IF)', 'Instantaneous Amplitude (IA)', and 'frequency divisions (f_ div)' parameters. The output from the above code is given in Fig. 3. which is the final data frame.

```
Final DataFrame
     Hilber Huang Transform(min)  Hilber Huang Transform(max)  Object
0                      -0.086009                     0.089721       1
1                      -0.114679                     0.111479       1
2                      -0.134261                     0.131829       1
3                      -0.053628                     0.049916       1
4                      -0.071674                     0.068986       1
..                           ...                          ...     ...
910                    -0.080761                     0.077178       3
911                    -0.089209                     0.089721       3
912                    -0.081273                     0.077306       3
913                    -0.102392                     0.100472       3
914                    -0.133237                     0.131189       3

[915 rows x 3 columns]
```

**Fig. 3.** Final Data Frame

## 3.3 Support Vector Machine (SVM) Implemention

The next step is to develop an SVM algorithm using different libraries like NumPy, Pandas and scikit-learn after processing the data with HHT. In order to evaluate the accuracy of the model, a confusion matrix is generated at the end of the process. We use the "train-test-split" feature to split the data, with 80% of the data to train the ML model and the remaining 20% to test it.

**Hyper-parameter Tuning.** Hyperparameter tuning is a critical step in the optimization of SVM algorithms to achieve higher accuracy and better learning rates. Hyperparameters are model arguments whose values are set before the training process begins. We have tuned three hyperparameters i.e., *kernel*, *Cparameter*, and *degree* of SVM using the "GridSearchCV" feature of sci-kit learn.

**Hyperparameter Tuning Results.** Using the GridSearchCV different values of hyperparameters are tested which can be seen in Fig. 4(a). The results of the best values of the hyperparameters can be seen in Fig. 4(b).

```
#Hyper-Tuning Parameters using GridSearchCV
param_grid={'C':[0.1,1,100,1000],'kernel':['linear','poly','rbf','sigmoid'],'degree':[1,2,3,4,5,6]}
grid=GridSearchCV(SVC(),param_grid)
grid.fit(X_train,y_train)
```

(a) Hyperparameter Tuning

```
{'C': 1000, 'degree': 1, 'kernel': 'rbf'}
0.6830601092896175
```

```
{'C': 1000, 'degree': 1, 'kernel': 'rbf'}
0.6830601092896175
```

(b) Hyperparameter Tuning Result  (c) Accuracy & F1 Score.

**Fig. 4.** SVM: Hyperparameters

**Kernel** is considered to be the most significant hyperparameter of the SVM. Functionally, the focus of *kernel* is to take low-dimensional input space and transform it into a higher-dimensional space. It must be either one of the types - *linear* (used for linearly separable data), *poly* (maps non-linear data into a higher-dimensional space using a polynomial function.), *rbf* (maps the data into an infinite-dimensional space by using Gaussian functions), *sigmoid* (used for non-linear data and maps the data into a higher-dimensional space using a hyperbolic tangent function), *precomputed* (uses a user-defined kernel matrix instead of computing the kernel function on the data), or *callable* (defined by the user that takes two inputs and returns the kernel value). If no kernel is provided as an attribute, 'rbf' will be used as the default kernel.

**C (Regularization).** C is the SVM penalty parameter that determines the cost of misclassification. The algorithm allows more misclassifications but produces a limit with a wider range. Conversely, a large C value results in fewer misclassifications but a smaller margin.

**Degree.** The degree hyperparameter determines the degree of polynomials in the polynomial kernel function and is exclusive to the polynomial kernel, unlike the other kernels.

**Predicting New Signal Data.** The trained SVM model is used to predict the object from new signal data. This is completely new data for our model, which has to predict which object the test data belongs to. The predicted data was from object 2 and our model has correctly predicted that the data belongs to object 2 (Fig. 5).

```
pred = poly.predict(final_test_frame.iloc[[5]])
print("Predicted Object :", pred)

Predicted Object : [2]
```

**Fig. 5.** Predicting new signal data

**Confusion Matrix.** The performance of the SVM classifier was evaluated using the confusion matrix method. The confusion matrix indicates how accurately the classifier can classify new data. The confusion matrix of the SVM classifier is shown in Fig. 6.

Labels 1, 2, and 3 correspond to Object 1, Object 2, and Object 3, respectively. The true positive values for object 1, object 2, and object 3 are 0, 40, and 85, respectively.

### 3.4   Implementing Multi-Layer Perceptron (MLP)

The second test of algorithm compilation for MLP is also made following the same procedure that has already been discussed in the earlier subsection to evaluate the model accuracy.

Firstly, the model is loaded with the train data as well as test data (now already processed with HHT) which is taken from one of the available data sources.

All data are merged and stacked vertically after loading and labeling. The train data is subjected to this reshaping action. This is a good practice in machine learning algorithms to feed data to the model.

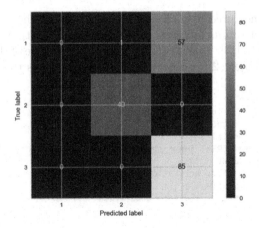

**Fig. 6.** Confusion Matrix

```
# Combining the Hilbert Huang transformed data and their labels vertically
X_train = np.vstack((hht1, hht2, hht3))
Y_train = np.vstack((trainLabel1, trainLabel2, trainLabel3))
```

**Fig. 7.** Reshape Train Data

The following shows the matrix that has been generated after the operation that has been done in Fig. 7.

$$\text{X\_Train} = \begin{bmatrix} trainData1(Object1) \\ trainData2(Object2) \\ trainData3(Object3) \end{bmatrix}, \text{Y\_Train} = \begin{bmatrix} trainLabel1(0) \\ trainLabel2(1) \\ trainLabel3(0) \end{bmatrix}$$

This function divides the labeled data into a binary diagonal matrix to achieve output. Hence it will label "1" for each of the target classes. If the data is for 'object 1' it will place "1" for it and "0" for 'object 2'. Y Train shows the general matrix after converting the class to categorial ones.

$$\text{Y\_Train} = \begin{bmatrix} 1 & 0 & 0 \\ 0 & 1 & 0 \\ 0 & 0 & 1 \end{bmatrix}$$

The MLP model has a simple three-layer architecture consisting of an "Input Layer", a "Hidden Layer", and an "Output Layer". The input layer receives the raw data, and it has 34000 nodes designed for this purpose (the number of scan points x the frequency divisions = $3400 \times 10$). The first hidden layer contains 1000 nodes and the second hidden layer contains 50 nodes. The ReLU function is used to activate the hidden layers. The output layer has three nodes.

These represent the three defined objects. In addition, the output layer uses the *"softmax"* activation function, ensuring that the output is a probability distribution function [13]. Since the final output must be one of the three objects, namely object 1, object 2, or object 3. Figure 8 illustrates the code snippet of the model.

```
# Create the model
model = Sequential()
model.add(Dense(950, input_shape=input_shape, activation='tanh'))
model.add(Dropout(0.2))
model.add(Dense(30, activation='tanh'))
model.add(Dropout(0.2))
model.add(Dense(num_classes, activation='softmax'))
```

**Fig. 8.** Algorithm for MLP Model

*Drop Out* is another important parameter used in the model, set to 0.2. Its primary purpose is to prevent the model from overfitting, which occurs when the model describes the random error in the data instead of the relationships among the variables. Overfitting typically occurs when the model is too complex to explain [14]. Dropping out is therefore used to overcome this problem.

Once the model has been prepared, the next step is to train the model using a loss function called "categorical entropy". In order to identify a single final output from a set of possible outcomes, this function is applied to the PDF output. The MLP uses stochastic gradient descent optimization, and we use the "Adam" optimizer in our algorithm, as mentioned earlier.

```
# Configure the model and start training
model.compile(loss='categorical_crossentropy', optimizer='adam', metrics=['accuracy'])
model.summary()
model.fit(X_train, Y_train, epochs=5, batch_size=40 , verbose=1, validation_split=0.2) # (X_test, Y_test)
```

**Fig. 9.** MLP Model Paramters

Figure 9 shows the model's 5 epochs and batch size of 40, taking 19 iterations to complete 1 epoch. Increasing the number of time samples may increase the iterations per epoch. Figure 10 demonstrates the validation of the trained model using the test dataset.

**Using Classifier to Discriminate New Data.** A classification function is added to Python code using the NumPy and TensorFlow Keras libraries for object detection and prediction. The pre-trained MLP model is loaded into the object classification algorithm as a first step. Figure 11 indicates loading the trained model in Python code.

```
# Test the model after training
test_results = model.evaluate(X_train, Y_train, verbose=1)  # (X_test, Y_test)
print(f'Test results - Loss: {test_results[0]} - Accuracy: {test_results[1]}%')

# Predict using the model after training
Y_pred = model.predict(X_train) # (X_test)
Y_pred = np.argmax(Y_pred, axis=1)
Y_actual = np.argmax(Y_train, axis=1) # (Y_train)
```

**Fig. 10.** Model Saving & Evaluation

```
model = load_model("mlp_hht_tanh.h5")
```

**Fig. 11.** Model load for Object Classification

To perform classification, we provide new data to our machine learning model. We have a test file in which we have data of 50 rows with 3400 scan points and the data can belong to any object e.g. object 1, 2, or 3.

Figure 12 shows that our program performs the classification after we have specified the starting column and the total number of scan points in the Python program, using three objects: "Object 1", "Object 2", and "Object 3". The model accurately predicted that the data in the test file belongs to "Object 2".

```
# Predict using the model after training
Y_pred = model.predict(X_test)
Y_pred = np.argmax(Y_pred, axis=1)

i = 0
while ( i < len(Y_pred) ):

    if Y_pred[i] == 0:
        print(f'row {i+1} Predicted: Object 1')

    if Y_pred[i] == 1:
        print(f'row {i+1} Predicted: Object 2')

    if Y_pred[i] == 2:
        print(f'row {i+1} Predicted: Object 3')

    i += 1
```

**Fig. 12.** Prediction Algorithm

**Results of MLP Model.** Figure 13 illustrates a sample time signal along with its Intrinsic Mode Functions and finally calculated Hilbert Spectrum. The same operation has been done on each time sample before the application of machine learning.

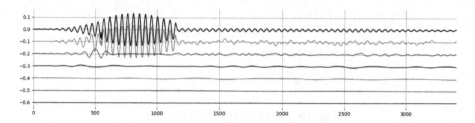

**Fig. 13.** Time Signal and its calculated IMFs for HHT

Using the IMFs from all time samples, Hilbert Spectrum is calculated which indicates the amplitude-frequency-time distribution for the given time sample. Hilbert Spectrum of the signal is shown in Fig. 14. The MLP model has been tested with different settings to achieve the optimum results.

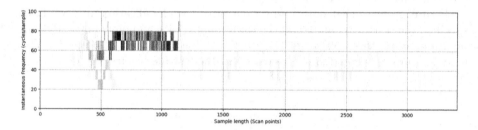

**Fig. 14.** Hilbert Spectrum of a sample Time signal

**Confusion Matrix for MLP Model.** The Confusion matrix of the trained model illustrated in Fig. 15 shows labels 0, 1, and 2 which indicate object 1, object 2, and object 3, respectively. True Positive for Object 1 is 287, for Object 2 it is 199 and for Object 3 it is 316.

## 4    Final Results of SVM and MLP Model

We have observed a significant accuracy increase in MLP model (85%) as compared to SVM model (68%), illustrated in Fig. 16. Additionally, The MLP model surpasses the SVM model in the classification task, as demonstrated by their confusion matrices compared in earlier chapters. Notably, the MLP model achieves a substantially higher true positive rate than the SVM model. Hence, it can be inferred that the **Multilayer Perceptron (MLP)** model is the best fit for our dataset's training and prediction.

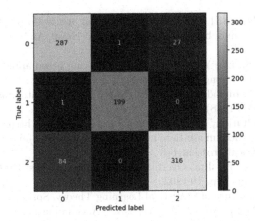

**Fig. 15.** Generated Confusion Matrix of best ML Model for classification of 3 Objects

```
Test results - Loss: 0.5270921587944031 - Accuracy: 0.8469945192337036%
29/29 [==============================] - 1s 17ms/step
```

**Fig. 16.** Accuracy Output for best ML model

# References

1. Huang, N.E., et al.: The empirical mode decomposition and the Hilbert spectrum for nonlinear and non-stationary time series analysis. Proc. Roy. Soc. A Math. Phys. Eng. Sci. **454**(1971), 903–995 (1998)
2. Samuel, A.L.: Some studies in machine learning using the game of checkers. IBM J. Res. Dev. **3**(3), 210–229 (1959)
3. Schmidhuber, J.: Deep learning in neural networks: an overview. Neural Netw. **61**, 85–117 (2015)
4. Artificial Intelligence (AI) in IBM Cloud Learn Hub, IBM. https://www.ibm.com/cloud/learn/artificial-intelligence. Accessed 8 Aug 2021
5. Aery, M.K.: Research Gate, A Review on Machine Learning: Trends and Future Prospects, November 2017. https://www.researchgate.net/publication/323377718_A_REVIEW_ON_MACHINE_LEARNING_TRENDS_AND_FUTURE_PROSPECTS
6. Goyal, K.: upGrad blog, 6 Types of Activation Function in Neural Networks You Need to Know, 13 February 2020. https://www.upgrad.com/blog/types-of-activation-function-in-neural-networks/
7. Nicholson, C.: A Beginner's Guide to Multilayer Perceptrons (MLP), Pathmind. https://wiki.pathmind.com/multilayer-perceptron
8. Toprak, M.: Medium, Activation Functions for Deep Learning, 14 June 2020. https://medium.com/@toprak.mhmt/activation-functions-for-deep-learning-13d8b9b20e
9. Leite, T.M.: Medium, Neural Networks, Multilayer Perceptron and the Backpropagation Algorithm, 10 May 2018

10. Chen, Z.-S., Rhee, S.H., Liu, G.-L.: Empirical mode decomposition based on Fourier transform and band-pass filter. Int. J. Naval Arch. Ocean Eng. **11**(2), 939–951 (2019)
11. Huang, N., Lin, S., Lei, Y., Yang, J.: Hilbert-Huang based approach for structural damage detection. J. Eng. Mech. (2004)
12. Titchmarsh, E.C.: Introduction to the Theory of Fourier Integrals. Oxford University Press, Oxford (1948)
13. Peltarion, "Peltarion," Categorical crossentropy. https://peltarion.com/knowledge-center/documentation/modeling-view/build-an-ai-model/loss-functions/categorical-crossentropy
14. Frost, J.: Statistics By Jim. Overfitting Regression Models: Problems, Detection, and Avoidance, vol. 1, p. 10 (2020)
15. Vapnik, V.: The Nature of Statistical Learning Theory. Springer, New York (2000)
16. Shen, Q., Shi, W.M., Kong, W., Ye, B.X.: A combination of modified particle swarm optimization algorithm and support vector machine for gene selection and tumor classification. Talanta **71**, 1679–1683 (2007)
17. Subasi, A.: Classification of EMG signals using PSO optimized SVM for diagnosis of neuromuscular disorders. Comput. Biol. Med. **43**(5), 576–586 (2013)
18. Abe, S.: Support Vector Machines for Pattern Classification. Springer, London (2005). https://doi.org/10.1007/978-1-84996-098-4

# Conductivity Classification Using Machine Learning Algorithms in the "Bramianon" Dam

Kiourt Nichat[(⊠)], Lazaros Iliadis, and Antonios Papaleonidas

School of Engineering, Department of Civil Engineering, Democritus University of Thrace,
Xanthi, Greece
{nkiourt,liliadis}@civil.duth.gr

**Abstract.** During the "water cycle" process, inorganic as well as organic substances are dissolved, which is completely normal. Organic substances can originate from decaying tree leaves that fall into rivers and lakes, from sewage from living organisms that live in water (e.g. fish) and human waste. Inorganic substances can come from lead and copper in water pipes, from pesticides and generally from various human activities. All these elements contribute to increase of water conductivity. The higher the conductivity in water, the more dangerous it becomes for humans [4]. The purpose of this research is to evaluate and classify water conductivity levels at the "Bramianon" dam of Crete, with the development of powerful Machine Learning models capable of successfully assigning three labels "Low", "Medium", "High".

**Keywords:** Machine Learning · Classification · Water Conductivity

## 1 Introduction

### 1.1 Defining the Problem

The natural quality of water has undergone serious degradation in recent decades, due to various sources of pollution (e.g., municipal sewage, industrial liquid waste, detergents, agricultural liquid waste, livestock liquid waste and seawater intrusion. This has resulted to resolved oxygen reduction, eutrophication of water, and to the pollution of groundwater and drinking water [5]. Drinking water must be clean from a physical, biological and microbiological perspective, as its consumption must not endanger human health. Moreover, the water must be colorless, odorless, with a pleasant taste. It must not have high level of hardness, organic substances, heavy metals or pathogenic parasites or microbes [5]. When water conductivity becomes high enough, things start to get dangerous. That is why it is important to know the level of conductivity in the water we are consuming. The conductivity limit in the US for drinking water is 500 ppm (parts per million). The following Table 1 presents the existing classification values, related to water hardness as they appear in the literature [4].

The following Table 2 presents the typical water classes, related to Water Conductivity (WA_CO) in Greece, as they appear in the literature [4].

© The Author(s), under exclusive license to Springer Nature Switzerland AG 2023
L. Iliadis et al. (Eds.): EANN 2023, CCIS 1826, pp. 97–109, 2023.
https://doi.org/10.1007/978-3-031-34204-2_9

**Table 1.** Water classification based on its hardness.

| Hardness in ppm | Class of Water |
| --- | --- |
| 0–70 | Very Soft |
| 70–150 | Soft |
| 150–250 | Soft to Hard |
| 250–320 | Hard Enough |
| 320–420 | Hard |
| Over 420 | Very Hard |

**Table 2.** Water classes based on WA_CO in Greece

| WA_CO in ppm | Description |
| --- | --- |
| 0–20 | Deionized water |
| Close to 180 | Water of Attica area |
| 180–200 | Bottled Water |
| Up to 5,000 | In network waters throughout Greece |
| More than 5,000 | In brackish drilling water |
| 25,000–35,000 | Sea water |

Measuring the conductivity or hardness of water, a Total Dissolved Solids device (TDS) is required. This instrument measures the concentration of salts, anions, cations, metals and organic matter which are dissolved in water. The TDS does not consider only the suspended particles that are not dissolved. Conductivity measurement is an alternative way to find out how hard our water is, as salts make up a significant percentage of water [4].

## 1.2  Aim of This Machine Learning Modeling Effort

Learning is one of the fundamental properties of intelligent human behavior. Despite years of studies and research by cognitive psychologists and philosophers, the concept of learning has not been fully understood. The goal of Artificial Intelligence is the development of computer systems capable of learning through Machine Learning (ML) patterns in order to continuously improve their performance without the need to be reprogrammed [1]. The main objective of this research is the development of robust ML models for the rational and effective classification of water conductivity levels of the "Bramianon" Dam which is located in Crete, Greece. More specifically, this modeling effort will employ three WA_CO classes, namely, "Low", "Medium" and "High". This will enable not only the local authorities but also the public to be aware of the potability of the available water resources in the specific area under study.

### 1.3 Literature Review

This section performs a comprehensive literature review on the application of ML towards water quality modeling. P. Sharma et al. 2020, have used five ML Regression algorithms namely: Neural Networks, Gradient Boost, Support Vector Machines(SVM), Decision Trees and Random Forest in an effort to model the actual Water Conductivity values [11]. N. Radhakrishnan and A. S. Pillai 2020, introduced various water quality classification models (SVM, Decision Trees, and Naïve Bayes) [10]. H. Lu, X. Ma 2020, introduced two hybrid decision tree-based models (based on Gradient Boosting and Random Forest) to obtain short-term water quality prediction results for the Gales Creek site in Tualatin River (one of the most polluted rivers in the world) [13]. S. N. Araya, and T. A. Ghezzehei 2019, attempted to maximize information extraction from a large WA_CO database of 18,000 records, using ML modeling [12]. Elias Dritsas, Maria Triga 2023, used the supervised learning approach in order to design as accurate as possible predictive models from a labeled training data set to determine the suitability of water, either for consumption or other uses, with the help of various machine learning algorithms (such as Naive Bayes – Note Logistic Regression–LR, k Nearest Neighbors–kNN, tree-based classifiers and ensemble techniques) [20]. Hamza et al.2023, proposed an automated water quality prediction system that effectively deals with missing values in the dataset and achieves good accuracy for water quality prediction, while the performance of the proposed system is compared with that of seven machine learning algorithms [21].

To the best of our knowledge, this paper presents one of the first research attempts globally, towards Machine Learning Water Conductivity classification, in a closed aquatic system, such as the important "Bramianon" dam located in the island of Crete Greece.

## 2   Area of Research – Data

It is well expected that the water conductivity values at the Bramianon dam are always quite high, as it is an artificial dam and not a spring of natural running water, intended for drinking consumption. The data was collected from the website of the Decentralized Administration of Crete (DC_C), Greece [6]. The publicly available data is stored in a respective website that serves as the central repository of the DC_C [16].

The "Bramianon" Dam has a capacity of 16,000,000 m3 and a surface area of 1,050,000 square meters (1,050 acres). The annual water evaporation amounts to approximately 500,000 m3 of water.

The retaining wall is 560 m long, its height is 43 m, it has a depth of 32 m and there is an average annual rainfall of 300 mm. The dam is the third largest wetland in Southern Greece, after the "Amario" Rivers and the "Aposelemi" Dams. About 30,000 acres of greenhouse crops are irrigated from this lake. The map below (Map 1) shows the area of the "Ierapetra" basin as well as the dam lake of "Bramianon" [7].

The wider area of "Ierapetra" in Crete faced a three-year drought period from 2016 to 2018. Due to the sharp decrease in average rainfall in these three years, the level of the 16,000,000 m3 capacity dams, reached marginally low, with water reserves measured below than 1,000,000 m3 [7]. However, during the last three years, 2019, 2020 and 2021,

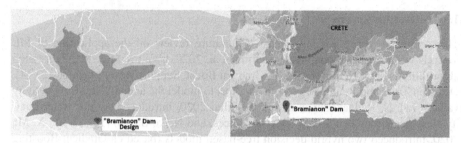

**Map 1.** The basin of "Bramianon" dam and its location in the south-eastern part of Crete.

the satisfactory rainfall level and the snowfall in the western highlands of "Ierapetra", contributed towards filling the "Bramianon" reservoir again. Thus, in the next few years it is capable to address the needs of the area's farmers in irrigation water. Table 3 below, categorizes the water reserves' level according to its adequacy.

**Table 3.** Classification of the water reserves of Bramianon dam

| Reserves in m³ | Label |
| --- | --- |
| More than 13 million | Adequacy |
| Between 10 and 13 million | Mild Deficit |
| Between 6 and 10 million | Deficit |
| Between 2 and 6 million | Seriously Deficit |
| Below 2 million | Extremely Deficit |

The data set considered in this research, contains 1,752 daily measurements from 2015 to date (collected at the same time of the day). It comprises of the following features: water conductivity, water volume, water temperature, precipitation and water depth. It is worth mentioning that only in two cases the conductivity value was less than 500 ppm (the limit of water potability). Moreover, in 198 data records the conductivity values fall in the interval [501, 1000] ppm and in 1,552 records they are higher than 1,001 ppm. Obviously in the last two cases, the water was considered as unsuitable for human consumption due to the increased WA_CO values.

## 3 Machine Learning Modeling

Machine Learning (ML) is a subfield of artificial intelligence, which is broadly defined as the capability of a machine to imitate intelligent human behavior. Artificial intelligence systems are used to perform complex tasks in a way that is similar to how humans solve problems [17]. In machine learning, algorithms are trained to find patterns and correlations in large data sets and make the best decisions and predictions based on that analysis. ML applications improve with use and become more accurate the more data they access [1]. There are three types of ML namely, *Supervised Learning (SUP_L), Unsupervised Learning, Semi Supervised Learning and Reinforcement Learning.*

This research involves SUP_L which comprises of the following subprocesses:

– Data collection
– Data Preprocessing: Converting the actual numerical values of the depended feature (DF) to the respective notation of each class. In other words, adding labels corresponding to the numerical values of the DF.
– Feature selection and feature engineering.
– Selection of each ML algorithm and training-evaluating each model.
– Determination of the optimal model.

## 3.1 Water Conductivity Modeling

### 3.1.1 Data Preprocessing

The first stage of this research was data pre-processing that was performed under the MS-Excel environment. This stage was divided in two parts, namely: Data Normalization and Development of classes.

A. **Data Normalization:** Since the range of values of raw data varies widely, in some machine learning algorithms, objective functions will not work properly without normalization. For example, many classifiers calculate the distance between two points by the Euclidean distance. If one of the features has a broad range of values, the distance will be governed by this particular feature. Therefore, the range of all features should be normalized so that each feature contributes approximately proportionately to the final distance. Another reason why feature scaling is applied is that gradient descent converges much faster with feature scaling than without it [18, 19]. Thus, the first step of the modeling effort was the normalization of data based on the following scaling function 1. By doing so, all features will be transformed into the range [0,1] meaning that the minimum and maximum value of a feature/variable is going to be 0 and 1, respectively.

$$x' = \frac{x - \min(x)}{\max(x) - \min(x)} \tag{1}$$

**Function 1.** Scale Normalization function.

This was done so that the variables with the largest magnitude, do not dominate over those with the smallest. Moreover, this process ensured that these values will be compatible to the Definition Range of the employed Transfer functions. Microsoft Excel was used to calculate the maximum, the minimum value, and the standard deviation of the water conductivity. The standard deviation is used to correct the normal distribution across the entire data set. In a normal distribution, almost all data fall into three standard deviations of the average.

B. **Development of classes:** In the second part of data Preprocessing, the numerical values of WA_CO were converted to class labels following a deterministic approach [3]. More specifically, Fuzzy Algebraic Functions (FAF) were used in the stage of labels' assignment, related to the *conductivity* values. Through this process, the dataset gained an additional feature, which comprises of the respective labels (Linguistics), determined by applying proper fuzzy algebraic membership functions on the existing conductivity values. More specifically, the following mathematical operations were performed:

A Triangular FMF (Function 2) was employed to determine the boundaries of the "Low WA_CO" Fuzzy Set (class) and to process the Fuzzy Membership Value (FMV) of each record to this class (Fig. 1).

The respective MATLAB command is *"low = fismf("trimf", [500 800 1200],"Name", "low");"*. As it is clearly shown from the above MATLAB command, the vector of the boundary hyperparameters' values was equal to [500, 800, 1200].

$$\mu_A(x) = \begin{cases} 0 & \text{if } x \leq a \\ \frac{x-a}{b-a} & \text{if } a \leq x \leq b \\ \frac{c-x}{c-b} & \text{if } b \leq x \leq c \\ 0 & \text{if } x \geq c \end{cases} \tag{2}$$

**Function 2.** Triangular Fuzzy Algebraic Membership function.

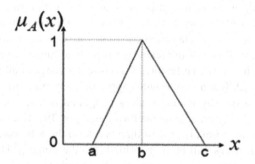

**Fig. 1.** Triangular Fuzzy Algebraic Membership function

Moreover, a Trapezoidal FMF (Fig. 2, function 3) was used to determine the boundaries of the "Medium WA_CO" Fuzzy Set (class) and to determine the FMV of each record to the "Medium" class. The respective MATLAB command is: *"medium = fismf("trapmf", [1000 1200 1600 1800], "Name", "medium");"*

As it is clearly shown by the above command the values of the hyperparameters' boundaries were 1,000, 1,200, 1,600, 1,800. They were determined by considering the lowest and highest value of the available data and by following a symmetrical distribution of the respective data intervals.

$$\text{Trapezoidal}(x; a, b, c, d) = \begin{cases} 0 & x < a \\ \frac{x-a}{b-a} & a \leq x \leq b \\ 1 & b \leq x \leq c \\ \frac{d-x}{d-c} & c \leq x \leq d \\ 0 & d \leq x \end{cases} \tag{3}$$

**Function 3.** Trapezoidal Fuzzy Algebraic Membership function.

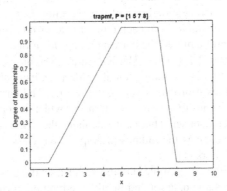

**Fig. 2.** Trapezoidal Fuzzy Algebraic Membership function

The class labeled as "High" was the one with the extreme conductivity values. The following MATLAB command was used in order to model the fuzzy set "High" via a Triangular FAF "high = fismf ("trimf", [1,200 2,000 2,500], "Name", "high");"

The 2$^{nd}$ stage was the development of Machine Learning algorithms used for training, validation and testing under the MATLAB platform for the optimization of the classification process.

## 3.2  Development of ML Models

The data from the "*Bramianon*" Dam come from the Decentralized Administration of Crete. After pre-processing, they were imported into MATLAB and an attempt was made to classify the conductivity according to the limits of danger for the human organism, with the help of various Machine Learning algorithms. The following classifiers were used: *Decision Trees, Naïve Bayes, Support Vector Machines, k-Nearest Neighbors, and Ensembles of Classifiers.*

- Decision Trees: Decision Trees (DETR) is the most well-known supervised Inductive Learning algorithm and has been successfully applied in many domains where classification is required. The DETR algorithm leads to the creation of a tree form whose leaves are the corresponding classes. This tree-like form can also be read as a set of rules called classification rules [1].

  - Naïve Bayes Classifiers: The Simple Bayes classifier is based on the Bayes theorem and further assumes that the features are independent of each other. Thus, a simpler but quite effective classifier is obtained. Let X be an instance described by the attributes: $\{X_1, X_2, X_3, \ldots, X_n\}$ and we search for the class it belongs to. The categories of the class are denoted by $\{k_1, k_2, \ldots, k_m\}$. Thus, based on Bayes' theorem, it suffices to calculate for each category K the probability that an instance X belongs to this category [14].

- Support Vector Machines: The purpose of Support Vector Machines (SVMs) is to find one or more hyper-levels in the multidimensional feature space that separate two classes of samples with the largest possible margin (margin) between them, minimizing the generalization error of the classifier. Depending on whether the data are linearly separable from each other, linear or non-linear kernels are used to transform the problem into the corresponding linear one [15].
- K-Nearest Neighbor Classifiers: The K-Nearest Neighbors (KNN) algorithm is one of the most popular classification algorithms as its operation is very simple but in specific cases it produces very good results. The basic logic of the KNN algorithm is that it tries to classify a pattern, for which it does not know its class, based on the given data set. That is, it calculates the distance from the K closest templates to it and gives the unknown template the class that dominates the K surrounding neighbors [1].
- Ensembles Classifiers: Ensemble classifiers train a set of classifiers from the above categories for the same data set and finally combine the results of each one. The most common methods of constructing set classifiers are as follows [15]:

i. Bagging: The training set is resampled to create a set of smaller datasets, and then a classifier is trained with each of these sets. When an unknown sample needs to be classified, it is first categorized by all the classifiers and the final decision is made by voting among them.

ii. Boosting: Here, a set of classifiers is trained again, with the difference that each sample carries a weight (according to its "importance" in the set it belongs to. This weight is renewed iteratively. Each sample misclassified by the classifier increases its weight for the next classifier, otherwise it decreases it. Each classifier is asked to give more weight to samples that have so far eluded correct categorization. The final decision is made by voting, possibly weighted by some evaluation metric.

### 3.3 Models' Assessment Indices

*Precision quantifies the* number of positive class predictions that actually belong to the positive class. *Recall* (also known as *Sensitivity*) quantifies the number of positive class predictions made from all positive examples in the dataset. *F-Measure* provides a single score that balances both the concerns of precision and recall in one number. While *Recall* identifies the rate at which observations from the positive class are correctly predicted, Precision indicates the rate at which positive predictions are correct. Recall is a measure of how well a machine learning model can detect positive instances [2]. It is used to evaluate model performance because it allows us to see how many positive instances the model was able to correctly identify. This research effort is using three classes, namely: *Low_Conductivity, Medium_Conductivity* and *High_Conductivity*. Thus, it is a case of *Multiclass classification.* Following the **Macro Averaging** approach, (one versus the rest) in Multiclass classification we must estimate one Precision and one Recall index for each class separately. In this research we have three classes and a 3X3 Confusion Matrix A, so we have to calculate three values of Precision and three of Recall (one for each class). The *Precision* for class i is obtained by dividing the respective element of the main diagonal $A_{ii}$ by the sum of all the elements of line i. In this research for the *first class A, Precision is equal to* $A_{11}/(A_{11}+A_{12} + A_{13})$, *for class B it is equal to* $B_{22}/(B_{21}+B_{21} + B_{23})$, *and for class C it is equal to* $C_{33}/(C_{31} + C_{32}+ C_{33})$. Respectively *Recall* for class i is estimated by dividing the respective element of the main diagonal Aii by the sum of all elements of column i. In this research for the *first class A, Recall is equal to* $A_{11}/(A_{11}+A_{21} + A_{31})$, *for class B it is equal to* $B_{22}/(B_{12} + B_{22} + B_{32})$, *and for class C it is equal to* $C_{33}/(A_{13} + B_{23} + C_{33})$ (Fig. 3).

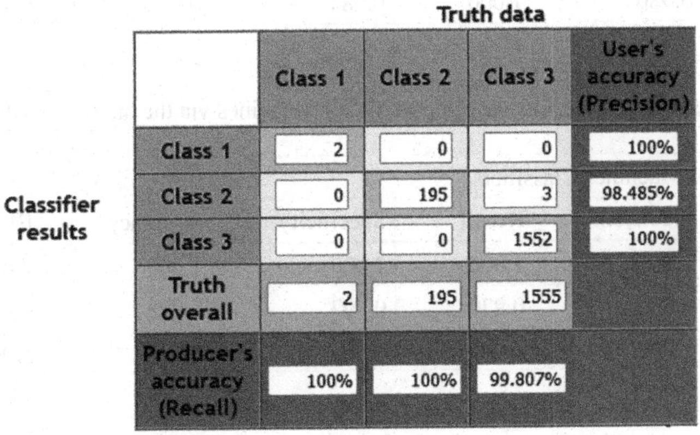

| | | Truth data | | | |
|---|---|---|---|---|---|
| | | Class 1 | Class 2 | Class 3 | User's accuracy (Precision) |
| **Classifier results** | Class 1 | 2 | 0 | 0 | 100% |
| | Class 2 | 0 | 195 | 3 | 98.485% |
| | Class 3 | 0 | 0 | 1552 | 100% |
| | Truth overall | 2 | 195 | 1555 | |
| | Producer's accuracy (Recall) | 100% | 100% | 99.807% | |

**Fig. 3.** Example of Metrics' estimation for all three classes in Multiclass classification

For a multi-class classification problem, we don't calculate an overall F-1 score Instead, we calculate the F-1 score per class in a one-vs-rest manner. In this approach, we rate each class's success separately, as if there are distinct classifiers for each class. F-1 score is the harmonic mean between the Precision and the Recall for each class. F1 Score$_i$ for class i is: F1 Score$_i$ = 2*(Recall$_i$ * Precision$_i$)/(Recall$_i$ + Precision$_i$).

## 4  Performance Results

The following chapter 4 presents the performance evaluation of the classification effort as it is summarised in Tables 4, 5, 6, 7 and 8 below.

**Table 4.** Classification results for Decision Trees via the one versus all approach

| Decision Trees Classifier | | | | | |
|---|---|---|---|---|---|
| | Precision | Recall | Specificity | Accuracy | F1-Score |
| Class 1 | 1.000 | 0.670 | 1.000 | 0,999 | 0.800 |
| Class 2 | 0.980 | 1.000 | 0.998 | 0,978 | 0.990 |
| Class 3 | 1.000 | 0.998 | 1.000 | 0,998 | 1.000 |

**Table 5.** Classification results for Naïve Bayes via the one versus all approach

| Naïve Bayes Classifiers | | | | | |
| --- | --- | --- | --- | --- | --- |
| | Precision | Recall | Specificity | Accuracy | F1-Score |
| Class 1 | 1.000 | 1.000 | 1.000 | 1.000 | 1.000 |
| Class 2 | 1.000 | 0.880 | 1.000 | 0.984 | 0.940 |
| Class 3 | 0.980 | 1.000 | 0.984 | 0.984 | 0.990 |

**Table 6.** Classification results for Support Vector Machines via the one versus all approach

| Support Vector Machines Classifiers | | | | | |
| --- | --- | --- | --- | --- | --- |
| | Precision | Recall | Specificity | Accuracy | F1-Score |
| Class 1 | 1.000 | 1.000 | 1.000 | 1.000 | 1.000 |
| Class 2 | 0.980 | 0.970 | 0.997 | 0.993 | 0.970 |
| Class 3 | 1.000 | 1.000 | 0.996 | 0.993 | 1.000 |

**Table 7.** Classification results for K-Nearest Neighbor via the one versus all approach

| K-Nearest Neighbor Classifiers | | | | | |
| --- | --- | --- | --- | --- | --- |
| | Precision | Recall | Specificity | Accuracy | F1-Score |
| Class 1 | 1.000 | 1.000 | 1.000 | 1.000 | 1.000 |
| Class 2 | 0.960 | 0.990 | 0.996 | 0.994 | 0.980 |
| Class 3 | 1.000 | 1.000 | 0.998 | 0.994 | 1.000 |

**Table 8.** Classification results for Ensembles Classifiers via the one versus all approach

| Ensembles Classifiers | | | | | |
| --- | --- | --- | --- | --- | --- |
| | Precision | Recall | Specificity | Accuracy | F1-Score |
| Class 1 | 1.000 | 1.000 | 1.000 | 1.000 | 1.000 |
| Class 2 | 0.984 | 1.000 | 0.998 | 0.998 | 0.992 |
| Class 3 | 1.000 | 0.998 | 1.000 | 0.998 | 1.000 |

The best classification algorithm for our problem turned out to be the *Bagged trees of Ensembles Classifiers* algorithm [9] with an accuracy of 99.8%. It is worth mentioning that the other algorithms had equally good results but with a longer execution time, which is why you choose the fastest algorithm (2.7279 s.) of Bagged trees of Ensembles

Classifiers. In Fig. 4 we see the Confusion Matrix and the actual behavior for each class for the Bagged trees of Ensembles Classifier.

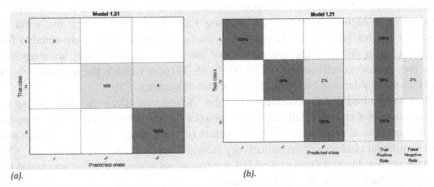

(a).                                                              (b).

**Fig. 4.** Modeling with Bagged trees of Ensembles Classifiers. Confusion Matrix with the classification of the data records in the 3 classes (a. with the number of records b. with percentages of records).

In the above figure we observe that in all three classes the algorithm could and correctly identified all cases correctly with the exception of only 3 cases in class 2, which it considered to belong to class 3 when in fact they belong to class 2. The remarkable thing is that, even though in class 1 we have only 2 measurements (Minority), the algorithm was able to detect both measurements correctly.

For all classes the ROC curves [8] have an AUC equal to 1 (Fig. 5).

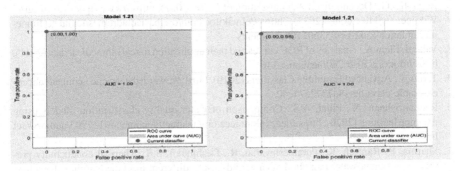

**Fig. 5.** ROC Curve for classes 1 and 2

## 5  Discussion-Conclusion

In the present research, an attempt was made to classify the water conductivity in the Bramian Dam with the help of various machine learning algorithms. The performance of each algorithm was examined and retrieved from the confusion matrix the partial indices used in Multi class classification and the ROC curve. The extracted results showed us a slightly better performance in the Bagged trees method of the Ensembles Classifiers classification algorithms compared to the corresponding classification algorithms, with an accuracy (Accuracy) reaching as high as 99.8%. According to the processed data of our measurements, we find that the levels of conductivity in the water of the *"Bramianon"* dam are quite high with an average reaching 1,268 ppm. We find that the water is definitely not for human consumption, we can say that these waters are suitable for irrigation use in the fields and greenhouses of the study area, where they are intended, since they do not exceed the limits of 25,000 to 35,000 ppm which is the seawater, which could create problems in the primary production of the area.

Finally, we find that the conductivity in the *"Bramianon"* Dam waters according to our data does not change at all when the amount of water volume in the dam changes. So, no matter how much water in cubic meters $(m^3)$ the reservoir stores, we will not have significant changes in the conductivity values. Thus, we conclude that the WA_CO changes are not due to natural causes, but due to various sources of pollution caused by human activities as have already we mentioned.

# References

1. Georgouli, A.: Machine Learning (chapter 4). Artificial Intelligence. Kallipos (open academic publishing) (2015). https://repository.kallipos.gr/handle/11419/3382
2. Iliadis, L.: Artificial Intelligence & Intelligent Agents. Tziola (2017)
3. Kulkarni, A.: Foundations of data imbalance and solutions for a data democracy (2020)
4. Margiolos, G.: Filtranerou (2018). https://www.filtra.nerou.gr/ti-einai-i-agogimotita-kai-pos-na-ti-metriso/
5. Modern Analytics (2022). https://modernanalytics.gr/water-quality/
6. Republic, G.: Decentralized Administration of Crete (2022). https://www.apdkritis.gov.gr/el
7. Wikiloc: wikiloc.com (2022). https://el.wikiloc.com/oreibasiadiadromes/tekhnete-limne-mpramianon-kuklike-93360110#comments
8. Valanti, Eleni A.: Analysis of ROC curves and their application to real biomedical data (2011). https://doi.org/10.26240/heal.ntua.246
9. Tarun A.: Advanced Ensemble Classifiers (2019). https://towardsdatascience.com/advanced-ensemble-classifiers8d7372e74e40
10. Radhakrishnan, N., Pillai, A.S.: Comparison of water quality classification models using machine learning (2020). https://ieeexplore.ieee.org/abstract/document/9137903/authors#authors
11. Sharma, P., Ramesh, K., Parameshwaran, R., Deshmukh, S.S.: Thermal conductivity prediction of titania-water nanofluid: a case study using different machine learning algorithms (2022). https://www.sciencedirect.com/science/article/pii/S2214157X21008212
12. Araya, S.N., Ghezzehei, T.A.: Using machine learning for prediction of saturated hydraulic conductivity and its sensitivity to soil structural perturbations (2019). https://doi.org/10.1029/2018WR024357
13. Lu, H., Ma, X.: Hybrid decision tree-based machine learning models for short-term water quality prediction (2020). https://www.sciencedirect.com/science/article/abs/pii/S00456535 20303623?casatoken=i6XAYel24IkAAAAA:C4MoJJXCEQKif2Egqa2IZSydMixWpVzMb ZGzSPWa7Pion2NF4oW7NF%20Cuxe%20C8rw%20ZYMz4%20S4Q
14. Katsantonis, A.: Data analysis and categorization (2020). https://dione.lib. upi.gr/xmlui/bitstream/handle/unipi/12983/Katsantonis_1608.pdf?sequence=1&isAllowed=y

15. Filotheou. A.X.: Multi-category Sorting with Brainstorming Classifier Systems (2013). http://ikee.lib.auth.gr/record/291560/files/philotheou-Thesis-AUTh-2013.pdf
16. Hydrological Data of "Bramianon Dam" Hydrological Station (2022). https://data.apdkritis.gov.gr/el/dataset/%CF%85%CE%B4%CF%81%CE%BF%CE%BB%CE%BF%CE%B3%CE%B9%CE%BA%CE%AC%CE%B4%CE%B5%CE%B4%CE%BF%CE%BC%CE%AD%CE%BD%CE%B1%CF%85%CE%B4%CF%81%CE%BF%CE%BB%CE%BF%CE%B3%CE%B9%CE%BA%CE%BF%CF%8D%CF%83%CF%84%CE%B1%CE%B8%CE%BC%CE%BF%CF%8D%CF%86%CF%81%CE%AC%CE%B3%CE%BC%CE%B1%CE%BC%CF%80%CF%81%CE%B1%CE%BC%CE%B9%CE%B1%CE%BD%CF%8E%CE%BD
17. Brown, B.: Machine learning, explained (2021). https://mitsloan.mit.edu/ideas-made-to-matter/machine-learning-explained
18. Feature scaling (2022). https://en.wikipedia.org/wiki/feature_scaling#cite_note-2
19. Gupta, S.: Machine Learning Concepts (2021). https://ml-concepts.com/2021/10/08/min-max-normalization/
20. Dritsas, E., Trigka, M.: Efficient Data-Driven Machine Learning Models for Water Quality Prediction (2023). https://doi.org/10.3390/computation11020016
21. Hamza, A.M., et al.: Water-Quality Prediction Based on H$_2$O AutoML and Explainable AI Techniques (2023). https://www.mdpi.com/2073-4441/15/3/475

# Generation of Bases for Classification in the Bio-inspired Layered Networks

Naohiro Ishii[1]([✉]), Kazunori Iwata[2], and Tokuro Matsuo[1]

[1] Advanced Institute of Industrial Technology, Tokyo 140-0011, Japan
nishii@acm.org, matsuo@aiit.ac.jp
[2] Aichi University, Nagoya 453-8777, Japan
kazunori@aichi-u.ac.jp

**Abstract.** Machine learning, deep learning and neural networks are extensively developed in many fields. As the function of cortical neural model, a sparse coding has been studied which is based on the bases functions of input stimulus. In this paper, it is shown that the bio-inspired networks are useful for the explanation of network functions. First, the asymmetric network with nonlinear functions is created based on the bio-inspired retinal network. They have orthogonal properties useful for features classification and processing. Second, it is shown that the asymmetric network is superior to the conventional symmetric network in the classification performance. Further, the asymmetric network is extended to the layered networks, which are also generated on the bio-inspired model of brain cortex. In the extended asymmetric layered networks, the higher dimensional orthogonal bases are created. To improve the classification performance, the bases replacements are performed in the layered networks. It is shown the bases replacements in the layered networks improve classification performance in both asymmetric and symmetric networks.

**Keywords:** asymmetric and symmetric networks · generation of orthogonal bases · classification performance of networks · replacement of bases · extended layered networks

## 1 Introduction

Recently, there has been a great deal of excitement and interesting in deep neural networks, because they have achieved breakthrough results in areas as machine learning, computer vision, neural computations and artificial intelligence [1–3]. Their networks are expected to be transparent, understandable and explainable in their successive processing in the multilayered structures [3]. In their developments, orthogonality is a fundamental topic in learning and neural networks. Pseudo orthogonal bases perform generalization capability in neural network learning [4]. The task specific information is represented along orthogonal axes, which minimizes interference and shows robustness to noise [5]. In this paper, it is shown that the bio-inspired network generates useful bases for the explanation of features classification. First, the asymmetric network with nonlinear

© The Author(s), under exclusive license to Springer Nature Switzerland AG 2023
L. Iliadis et al. (Eds.): EANN 2023, CCIS 1826, pp. 110–120, 2023.
https://doi.org/10.1007/978-3-031-34204-2_10

functions is created based on the bio-inspired retinal network. They have orthogonal properties useful for the classification of features [12, 13], which are based on characteristic bases. Second the extended layered asymmetric networks are derived, which are also based on the model of the brain cortex network. Then, the higher dimensional orthogonal bases are generated in the layered networks. To improve the classification performance in the extended layered networks, the replacement of bases are proposed in their networks. Their replacements show the improvement of the classification performance in the extended layered networks. Thus, the orthogonal bases are expected to perform features synthesis and integration in the deep layered networks.

## 2  Bio-inspired Neural Networks

### 2.1  Background of Asymmetric Neural Networks Based on the Bio-inspired Network

In the biological neural networks, the structure of the network, is closely related to the functions of the network. Naka et al. [10] presented a simplified, but essential networks of catfish inner retina as shown in Fig. 1. Visual perception is carried out firstly in the retinal neural network as the special processing between neurons.

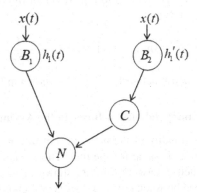

**Fig. 1.** Asymmetric network with linear and squaring nonlinear pathways

Visual perception is carried out firstly in the retinal neural network as the special processing between neurons. The following asymmetric neural network is extracted from the catfish retinal network [10]. The asymmetric structure network with a quadratic nonlinearity is shown in Fig. 1, which composes of the pathway from the bipolar cell B to the amacrine cell N and that from the bipolar cell, B, via the amacrine cell C to the N [10, 11]. Figure 1 shows a network which plays an important role in the movement perception as the fundamental network. It is shown that N cell response is realized by a linear filter, which is composed of a differentiation filter followed by a low-pass filter. Thus, the asymmetric network in Fig. 1 is composed of a linear pathway and a nonlinear pathway with the cell C, which works as a squaring function.

## 2.2  Model of Asymmetric Networks

Models of the asymmetric and symmetric networks are shown in Fig. 2(a) and (b), respectively, in which impulse response functions of cells are shown in $h_1(t)$ and $h'_1(t)$. The $(\ )^2$ shows a squared operation in the pathway. The symmetric model called energy model is proposed in the bio-inspired network [8].

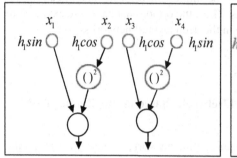 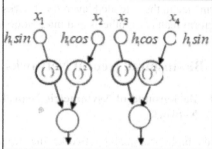

(a) Asymmetric network unit                    (b) Symmetric network unit

**Fig. 2.** Asymmetric unit and symmetric unit in the 1$^{st}$ layer of the network

As the impulse functions $h_1(t)$, $h'_1(t)$ in Fig. 1, Gabor filters are well known in the visual system [8] as shown in Eq. (1).

$$G_s(t') = \frac{1}{\sqrt{2\pi}\sigma}e^{-\frac{t'^2}{2\sigma^2\xi^2}}sin(t') \quad and \quad G_c(t') = \frac{1}{\sqrt{2\pi}\sigma}e^{-\frac{t'^2}{2\sigma^2\xi^2}}cos(t') \qquad (1)$$

Basic unit of the asymmetric network in Fig. 1 is shown in Fig. 2.

## 2.3  Orthogonality and Independence of Bases in the Asymmetric Network Unit

We can compute the orthogonality of the network unit in Fig. 2. We assume here the input $\{x\}(x = x_i, i = 1 \sim 4)$ is same for the unit. Then, relation of the orthogonality of the bases of the asymmetric network unit are shown in the arc in Fig. 3. Only the orthogonality is not satisfied between $cos^2x$ and $sin^2x$, which is indicated in $\times$ with the arc. Independence is also an important characteristic for classification and integration of features [13]. We compare the asymmetric networks and the symmetric ones from the independence. Then, the following theorems are derived.

**Theorem 1.** The bases set $\{sin\,x, cos^2x, cos\,x, sin^2x\}$ in the asymmetric network unit in Fig. 3, is independent.

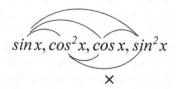

**Fig. 3.** Relations of orthogonality in the asymmetrical unit

This is proved using the following Eq. (3), where all the constant coefficients

$$\alpha_1 sin^2 x + \alpha_2 cos^2 x + \alpha_3 cos^2 x + \alpha_4 sin^2 x = 0 \qquad (3)$$

$\alpha_i = 0, i = 1 \sim 4$ hold by setting $x = 0, x = (\pi/6), x = (\pi/3)$ and $x = (\pi/2)$ in Eq. (3). Then, the solution $\alpha_i = 0, \ i = 1 \sim 4, \ x \neq x', x \neq x'', \ x' \neq x''$ satisfy Eq. (3). Thus, the bases are independent in the asymmetric unit, while bases set in the symmetric network unit, is dependent in the following equation.

$$\alpha_1 sin^2 x + \alpha_2 cos^2 x + \alpha_3 cos^2 x' + \alpha_4 sin^2 x'' = 0 \qquad (4)$$

By setting the same value of $x$ in Eq. (4), $\alpha_i = 0, i = 1 \sim 4$ does not obtained. This shows the dependence of the bases set in the symmetric network. Under the variable conditions, the independence is realized in the symmetric network unit as follows.

**Corollary 2.** Under the variable conditions, $x \neq x', x \neq x''$ and $x' \neq x''$, Eq. (5)

$$\alpha_1 sin^2 x + \alpha_2 cos^2 x + \alpha_3 cos^2 x' + \alpha_4 sin^2 x'' = 0 \qquad (5)$$

is satisfied, when only at $\alpha_i = 0, i = 1 \sim 4$.

This is proved by setting $x = 0, x' = (\pi/2), x'' = \pi; x = (\pi/2), x' = \pi, x'' = 0;$ $x = \pi, x' = 0, x'' = (\pi/2)$ and $x = (3\pi/2), x' = (\pi/2), x'' = 0$.

Thus, the independence is changed to the variable conditions.

## 3  Classification Evaluation in the Asymmetric Network

Independence plays an important role for the classification scheme. The independence of the network outputs is measured by their determinant of the matrix [7]. We compare the classification performance between asymmetric networks in Fig. 2(a) and the symmetric networks in Fig. 2(b). We assume the first 4-dimensional input as the $X_1 = (x_{11} x_{12} x_{13} x_{14})$, which is a component of the total input $X = [X_1 X_2 X_3 X_4]$. The $X$ is described in 4-dimensional input matrix as Eq. 6. Further, we assume a simple 4-dimensional restricted input example with components value $\{x_{ij}\} = \{0, 1\}$ as the third term in Eq. (6). The output of the network in Fig. 3 becomes $\{sin(x_1), \ cos^2(x_2), \ cos(x_3), \ sin^2(x_4)\}$ for the input $\{x_1, x_2, x_3, x_4\}$, in which $h_1$ to be 1 for the simplicity. We assume $a = sin(x_i)$ and $b = cos(x_j)$.

$$X = \begin{bmatrix} x_{11} & \cdots & x_{14} \\ \vdots & \ddots & \vdots \\ x_{41} & \cdots & x_{44} \end{bmatrix} \left( \equiv \begin{bmatrix} 1 & 0 & 0 & 1 \\ 0 & 1 & 1 & 0 \\ 0 & 0 & 1 & 1 \\ 1 & 1 & 0 & 0 \end{bmatrix} \right) \qquad (6)$$

The determinant of the outputs of asymmetric networks for Eq. (6) is shown in Eq. (7).

$$\|Asym.\| \, for \, Eq. \, (6) = \begin{Vmatrix} a & 1 & 1 & a^2 \\ 0 & b^2 & b & 0 \\ a & 1 & b & a^2 \\ 0 & b^2 & 1 & 0 \end{Vmatrix} \qquad (7)$$

The determinant of the outputs of networks including Eq. (7) is represented as

$$\|Asym.\| = \left(a^3\right)\{(\pm b)[Z_1] + (\pm 1)[Z_2]\} \tag{8}$$

where $[Z_1]$ shows the summed determinants of matrices by the cofactor, variable $\pm b$ expansion across the $3^{rd}$ column in Eq. (7) and $[Z_2]$ shows those by the cofactor $\pm 1$ expansion. Similarly, the determinant of symmetric networks in Eq. (6) is in Eq. 9.

$$\|Sym.\| \, for \, Eq. \, (6) = \begin{vmatrix} a^2 & 1 & 1 & a^2 \\ 0 & b^2 & b^2 & 0 \\ a^2 & 1 & b^2 & a^2 \\ 0 & b^2 & 1 & 0 \end{vmatrix} \tag{9}$$

The determinant of the output of symmetrical networks including Eq. (9) is represented as

$$\|Sym.\| = \left(a^4\right)\left\{\left(\pm b^2\right)[Z_1] + (\pm 1)[Z_2]\right\} \tag{10}$$

Note here the determinant $\{[Z_1] + (\pm 1)[Z_2]\}$ is same in both Eqs. (9) and (10).

### 3.1 Conditions of independence of ‖Asym.‖ and ‖Sym.‖

Independence of data plays an important role for the classification of their data. The independence in the asymmetric networks and the symmetric ones are evaluated based on the $\|Asym.\|$ and $\|Sym.\|$ In Eqs. (8) and (10). The $\|Asym.\|$ and $\|Sym.\|$ are simply classified as shown in Fig. 4.

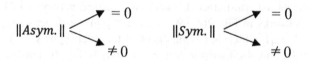

**Fig. 4.** Classification of $\|Asym.\|$ and $\|Sym.\|$

Conditions of independence of $\|Asym.\|$ and $\|Sym.\|$ in Fig. 4 are characterized in the following theorems in terms of the determinants $[Z_1]$ and $[Z_2]$.

**Theorem 3.** Under the condition $[Z_1] \neq 0$, the determinant of asymmetric networks, $\|Asym.\| \neq 0$ holds.

This is proved as follows. The first term, $(\pm b)[Z_1]$ in the determinant of asymmetric networks in Eq. (8), have the odd order exponentiation of the variable b, while the second term $(\pm 1)[Z_2]$ have the even order exponentiation of the variable b. Thus, these terms do not generate the summation to be zero.

**Corollary 4.** Under the condition $[Z_1] \neq 0$, if the determinant of symmetric networks, $\|Sym.\| = 0$, then that of asymmetric networks, $\|Asym.\| \neq 0$.

This is proved as follows. If $\|Sym.\| = 0$, then from Eq. (10) the equality equation $(\pm b^2)[Z_1] = -[Z_2]$ holds. This equation is substituted in Eq. (8). Thus, Eq. (11) holds.

$$\left\{\left(\pm b^2\right) - (\pm b)\right\}[Z_1] \tag{11}$$

Since Eq. (11) $\neq 0$ holds under the condition $[Z_1] \neq 0$, the determinant of asymmetric networks, $Asym. \neq 0$.

**Lemma 5.** The determinants $[Z_1]$ and $[Z_2]$ in the asymmetric and symmetric network are described in a quadratic polynomial of variable b in the following.

$$[Z_1] = mb^2 + l \text{ and } [Z_2] = kb^2 + n \tag{12}$$

where $m, l, k$ and $n$ are numerical coefficients.

This is proved from the definition of the matrix. Since $[Z_1]$ and $[Z_2]$ are computed by the cofactor of expansion across the $3^{rd}$ column in the 4-demensional matrix, variable $b^2$ exists only in the $2^{nd}$ column of the matrix.

**Theorem 6.** A necessary and sufficient condition for $\|Asym.\| = 0$ is $m = 0$, $(l+k) = 0$ and $n = 0$. Similarly, this condition holds for $\|Sym.\| = 0$.

**Theorem 7.** When $\|Sym.\| = 0$ holds, the parameters $l = -k \neq 0$ holds. Then, if $l = -k \neq 0$ holds, $\|Asym.\| \neq 0$ is satisfied.

**Theorem 8.** When $\|Sym.\| \neq 0$ holds, $\|Asym.\| \neq 0$ is also satisfied.

This is by the contradiction of the statement; if $\|Asym.\| = 0$ holds, then $\|Sym.\| = 0$ holds. From Theorems 6, 7 and 8, the performances are compared in the next theorem. We define here the performance of the classification to be the number of the determinant, which is not zero.

**Theorem 9.** The performance of the classification of $|Asym.|$ include that of $|Sym.|$. This shows $|Asym.|$ is superior to $|Sym.|$ in the classification ability.

## 3.2   Patterns Design for Independence in Asymmetric and Symmetric Networks

To compare the classification ability experimentally between the asymmetric and symmetric networks, the 4-dimensional input matrices $\{X\}$ in Eq. (6) are generated with components $\{0,1\}$. We define the symmetrical input patterns in the following.

**Definition 10.** Symmetric patterns $X$ is defined to have the following rows (1) or (2) in the 4-dimensional matrix.

(1) $X_i = (x_{i1} \, x_{i2} \, x_{i3} \, x_{i4})$ and $X_j = (x_{j1} \, x_{j2} \, x_{j3} \, x_{j4})$, in which $x_{j1} = x_{i4}$, $x_{j2} = x_{i3}$,

$$x_{j3} = x_{i2} \text{ and } x_{j4} = x_{i1} \text{ are satisfied} \tag{13}$$

$$(2) \quad X_k = (x_{k1} \, x_{k2} \, x_{k3} \, x_{k4}) = (x_{k4} \, x_{k3} \, x_{k2} \, x_{k1}) \tag{14}$$

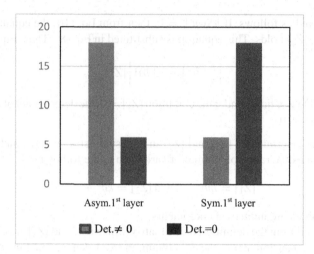

**Fig. 5.** Experimental results of independent and dependent ratio for symmetric patterns

Asymmetric patterns $X$ is defined not to have the rows (1) or (2) in Eqs. (13) and (14), respectively (Fig. 5).

(Example: the matrix with {0.1} in Eq. (6) is a symmetric pattern) The $1^{st}$ and $2^{nd}$ rows show from (2) in Definition 10, while the $3^{rd}$ and $4^{th}$ rows show from (1) in Definition 10. Total 24 symmetric patterns are generated, in which classification independence performance is evaluated between asymmetric and symmetric networks using the determinants of the respective networks, in Eqs. (8) and (10), respectively. Generation of Orthogonality in Layered Asymmetric Networks.

### 3.3   Generation of Combined Bases for Orthogonality

The orthogonality is generated based on the orthogonality bases. To generate orthogonal bases, the combined generation is considered in the layered asymmetric networks. Realization of the asymmetric layered networks Fig. 6 shows a model of the V1 followed by the MT area in the cortex [9] after the retinal network, which is proposed as the unit of the asymmetric neural networks are shown in Fig. 2(a).

Rectification in the visual system [9] plays an important role for the generation of the orthogonality. Then, the half-wave rectification [9] is approximated in the following equation (Fig. 6).

$$f(x) = \frac{1}{1 + e^{-\eta(x-\theta)}} \tag{15}$$

By Taylor expansion of Eq. (15) at $x = \theta$, the Eq. (3) is derived as follows,

$$f(x)_{x=\theta} = f(\theta) + f'(\theta)(x-\theta) + \frac{1}{2!}f''(\theta)(x-\theta)^2 + \cdots$$

$$= \frac{1}{2} + \frac{\eta}{4}(x-\theta) + \frac{1}{2!}(-\frac{\eta^2}{4} + \frac{\eta^2 e^{-\eta\theta}}{2})(x-\theta)^2 + \cdots \tag{16}$$

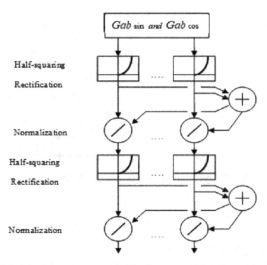

**Fig. 6.** Model of neural network of brain cortex V1 followed by MT [9]

The nonlinear terms, $x^2, x^3, x^4, \ldots$ are generated in Eq. (16). The inputs in the 2nd layer is from responses of the 1st layer in Fig. 3, which are wavelets of the product of Gaussian and trigonometric functions of Eq. (1) as follows,

$$Ae^{-\frac{t^2}{2\sigma^2\xi^2}}\sin(t),\ A^2(e^{-\frac{t^2}{2\sigma^2\xi^2}})^2\sin^2(t),\ A^3(e^{-\frac{t^2}{2\sigma^2\xi^2}})^3\sin^3(t)\ldots \tag{17}$$

$$Ae^{-\frac{t^2}{2\sigma^2\xi^2}}\cos(t),\ A^2(e^{-\frac{t^2}{2\sigma^2\xi^2}})^2\cos^2(t),\ A^3(e^{-\frac{t^2}{2\sigma^2\xi^2}})^3\cos^3(t)\ldots \tag{18}$$

By applying the power reducing formula in the trigonometric functions, the orthogonality is computed. When n and m are odd,

$$\int_{-\pi}^{\pi} \sin((n-2k)t) \cdot \cos((m-2k')t)dt$$
$$= \frac{1}{2}\int_{-\pi}^{\pi}\{\sin((n-m)-2(k-k'))t + \sin((n-m)+2(k-k'))t\}dt = 0 \tag{19}$$

Thus, the pair $\{(sin^n t),(cos^m t)\}$ becomes to be orthogonal. Similarly, the pair $\{(sin^n t), (cos^m t)\}$ becomes orthogonal in case of n to be odd and m to be even, and in case of n to be even and m to be odd. Only the pair $\{(sin^n t), (cos^m t)\}$ is not orthogonal in case of n to be even and m to be even. Thus, much orthogonal wavelets with the product of Gaussian and trigonometric function are generated in the 2nd and 3rd layers.

### 3.4 Generation of the Higher Dimensional Bases in the Layered Networks

The output of cell $G$ in Fig. 7 is assumed to be $(G)$, which is described in Eq. (20).

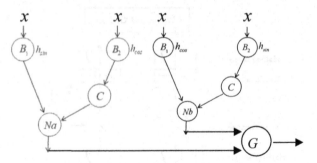

**Fig. 7.** $1^{st}$ layer unit of the asymmetric layered networks

$$(G) = sinx + cos^2x + cos\ x + sin^2x$$
$$= sinx + k \cdot cos^2x + (1-k) \cdot cos^2x + cos\ x + k \cdot sin^2x + (1-k) \cdot sin^2x \qquad (20)$$
$$= k + sinx + (1-k) \cdot cos^2x + cos\ x + (1-k) \cdot sin^2x$$

The output of the cell $H$ is assumed to be $(H)$, which is described in Eq. (21)

$$(H) = (G) + (G)^2$$
$$= k + sinx + cos\ x + k_1sin^2x + k_1cos^2x + k_2sinx \cdot cosx + k_3cos^2x \cdot cosx \cdots \qquad (21)$$

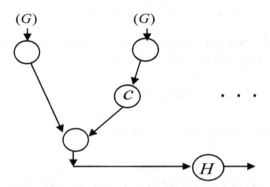

**Fig. 8.** $2^{nd}$ layer of the asymmetric networks followed by $1^{st}$ one

Further, the output of the $3^{rd}$ layer becomes

$$(H) + (H)^2 = (G) + (G)^2 + k_i(G)^3 + (G)^4 \qquad (22)$$

## 3.5  Replacement of the Orthogonal Bases in the 2$^{nd}$ Layered Network

The 1$^{st}$ layer network in Fig. 7 has the bases set $\{sin\,x_1, cos^2x_2, cos\,x_3, sin^2x_4\}$, which is also shown in $\{sin\,x_1, (1 + cos2x_2)/2, cos\,x_3, (1 - cos\,2x_4)/2\}$. Then, we call the components of the bases set to be $\{sin\,x, cos\,2x, cos\,x, cos\,2x\}$. As shown in Eq. (2), the base $sin^2x_1$ and $cos^2x_2$ are not orthogonal, since they consist of the same $cos\,2x$ component. To improve the orthogonality bases set, the base $sin^2x$ is replaced with $sin^2x_4 \cdot cos^2x_2 (= (1 - cos\,4x)/8)$. Then, the orthogonal components of new bases set become $\{sin\,x, cos\,2x, cos\,x, sin\,4x\}$. Since the new basis $sin^2x \cdot cos^2x$ is made in the 2$^{nd}$ layer of the network in Fig. 8, these replaces of the bases are new operation realized in the network. Using these operation of replaces of bases, the independence of the classification is expected. These replace operations are performed step by step in the following experiments, which are processed in the 2$^{nd}$ layer in Fig. 8. In the 1$^{st}$ step, the replace operation is performed for in the asymmetric 2nd layer network in Fig. 8. In the 2nd step, the basis is replaced with in the asymmetric 2nd layer network. As the 3rd step, two bases, $cos^2x_2$ and $sin^2x_4$ are replaced with $\{cos^2x_2 \cdot sin^2x_4\}$ and $\{sin^2x_4 \cdot sin\,x_1\}$, respectively. Similar 3rd operation is performed in the symmetric 2$^{nd}$ layer network. Thus, all the determinants of patterns are non-zero, which implies that the independence of all cases is realized in the 1$^{st}$ and 2$^{nd}$ layers networks (Fig. 9).

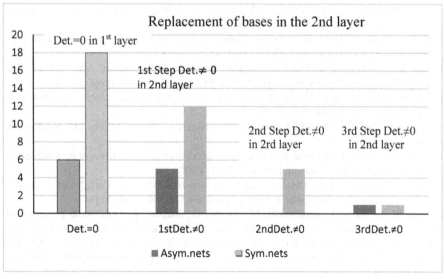

**Fig. 9.** Generation of independence by bases replacements in the 2$^{nd}$ layer

## 4  Conclusion

Studies of machine learning, artificial intelligence and neural networks have been developed greatly. In this paper, it is shown that the asymmetrical network with nonlinear functions in the bio-inspired networks have characteristics of orthogonal basis, which play an important role for the classification. It is shown that the asymmetric network is superior to the conventional symmetric network in the classification performance. To improve the classification performance, the extended layered networks are developed based on the brain cortex model. The replacement of their higher dimensional bases is proposed, which improves greatly the classification performance of the asymmetric and symmetric networks. These higher dimensional orthogonal bases are expected to create the synthetic features and to generate the integrated features in the higher layered networks.

## References

1. LeCun, Y., Bengio, Y., Hinton, G.: Deep learning. Nature **521**, 436–444 (2015)
2. Samek, W., Lapusckn, S., Anders, C.J., Muller, K.-R.: Explaining deep neural networks and beyond: a review of methods and applications. Proc. IEEE **103**(3), 247–278 (2021)
3. Peng, X., Li, Y., Tsang, I.W., Zhu, H., Lv, J., Zhou, J.T.: XAI beyond classification: interpretable neural clustering. J. Mach. Learn. Res. **23**, 1–28 (2022)
4. Sugiyama, M., Ogawa, H.: Active learning for optimal generalization in trigonometric polynomial models. IEICE Trans. Fundam. Electron. Commun. Comput. Sci. **E84-A**(9), 2319–2329 (2001)
5. Flesch, T., Juechems, K., Dumbalska, T., Saxe, A., Summerfield, C.: Orthogonal representations for robust context dependent task performance in brains and neural networks, Neuron **11**, 1258–1270 (2022)
6. Olshausen, B.A., Field, D.J.: Sparse coding with an overcomplete basis set: a strategy employed by V1? Vision. Res. **37**(23), 3311–3325 (1997)
7. Fan, K.: On systems of linear inequalities. In: Kuhn, H.W., Tucker, A.W. (eds.) Linear Inequalities and Related Systems, pp. 99–156. Princeton University Press (1966)
8. Adelson, E.H., Bergen, J.R.: Spatiotemporal energy models for the perception of motion. J. Optical Soc. Am. A, 284–298 (1985)
9. Simonceli, E.P., Heeger, D.J.: A model of neuronal responses in visual area MT. Vis. Res. **38**, 743–761 (1996)
10. Naka, K-I., Sakai, H.M., Ishii, N.: Generation of transformation of second order nonlinearity in Catfish retina. Ann. Biomed. Eng. **16**, 53–64 (1988)
11. Sakai, H.M., Naka, K-I.: Dissection of the neuron network in the Catfish inner retina. I. Transmission to Ganglion cells. J. Neurophysiol. **60**(5), 1549–1567 (1988)
12. Ishii, N., Deguchi, T., Kawaguchi, M., Sasaki, H., Matsuo, T.: Orthogonal properties of asymmetric neural networks with Gabor filters. In: Pérez García, H., Sánchez González, L., Castejón Limas, M., Quintián Pardo, H., Corchado Rodríguez, E. (eds.) HAIS 2019. LNCS (LNAI), vol. 11734, pp. 589–601. Springer, Cham (2019). https://doi.org/10.1007/978-3-030-29859-3_50
13. Ishii, N., Iwata, K., Mukai, N., Odagiri, K., Matsuo, T.: Features spaces with reduced variables based on nearest neighbor relations and their inheritances. In: Rojas, I., Joya, G., Català, A. (eds.) IWANN 2021. LNCS, vol. 12861, pp. 77–88. Springer, Cham (2021). https://doi.org/10.1007/978-3-030-85030-2_7

# Load-Shedding Management in a Smart Grid Architecture Through Smart Metering

Muhammad Faizan Khan[✉] and Gul Muhammad Khan

University of Engineering and Technology, Peshawar, Pakistan
faizankhaan@gmail.com, gk502@uetpeshawar.edu.pk
https://uetpeshawar.edu.pk

**Abstract.** This research focuses on load-forecasting using Cartesian Genetic Programming evolved Artificial Neural Networks (CGPANN) and load-balancing using Genetic Algorithm in an electrical system. An unbalanced load in a distribution feeder has adverse effects on the system. All the transformer units connected to the feeder have different operating loads, and the system's overall behaviour depends on them. Even if the transformers are not overloaded, any feeder phase can become overloaded due to excessive load contributed by individual transformers on that phase which results in a system-wide blackout. A custom-built monitoring device is installed on each transformer to monitor real-time electrical load data. A switching mechanism introduced at the transformer level can interchange the load between phases. This combination helps eliminate excessive load conditions and minimize unbalanced load conditions. Considering the involved parameters, i.e. transformers, phases, switching possibilities, and operating load, this constitutes a search problem within an available solution set. An optimum solution could be searched for and identified by interchanging the loads. This study aims to develop a feasible algorithm for such a search problem. The developed Genetic Algorithm can arrive at an optimum solution in minimum iterations. The load-forecasting model is used to predict load and identify system anomalies while the load-balancing model can re-adjust the system by shifting loads on individual transformers so as to balance the feeder's overall load with no excessive load condition.

**Keywords:** Cartesian Genetic Programming · Artificial Neural Networks · CGPANN · Genetic Algorithm · Load-forecasting · Load-balancing

## 1 Introduction

The term 'load shedding' refers to intentionally cutting the electricity supply for a specified interval of an area or multiple areas connected to a power distribution system to avoid a total blackout of the entire power system. Theoretically,

Supported by National Centre of Artificial Intelligence, UET Peshawar.

this is the last resort measure taken by any electric utility company to overcome the possibility of a complete failure of the national grid system. Load shedding occurs when the electricity demand exceeds the supply. Another reason can be inadequate resources or infrastructure. The overall process of scheduling load-shedding, or load-shedding management, is generally called rolling blackout or feeder rotation. It is a common phenomenon in developing countries where electricity infrastructure management is inadequate, and the generation capacity is always less than that of electricity demand. However, in developed countries, such roll-outs rarely occur and are appropriately scheduled. Technically, these blackouts can even occur without warning as the frequency falls below the safe threshold of the system. The most common method for load-shedding management is the "round robin" approach, where an entire feeder is disconnected from the system, resulting in either under-shedding or over-shedding. It is nearly impossible to shed the exact amount of load using the round-robin approach, which constitutes an untapped area for exploration where the load-shedding management techniques can be dramatically improved using modern techniques.

## 1.1    Smart Grid Architecture and Smart Meter

The smart grid architecture was introduced in the early 2000s. The primary focus is to equip the conventional grid system with novel technologies and introduce bidirectional communication support. The smart grid concept taps into every electrical power system stage, including generation, transmission, and distribution which requires complete remodelling of the conventional grid system. The bidirectional communication infrastructure is made possible through wired and wireless communication technologies. At the user end, technologies such as smart metering solutions are introduced, which can effectively outperform traditional energy meters with their advanced features and capabilities. Since the smart grid architecture digitizes the conventional grid system, it also imposes security challenges on the grid system. Thus, it becomes essential to standardize the smart grid concept at every level and devise regulations for implementation. This study primarily focuses on the smart metering component within a smart grid architecture for the experimental setup.

The term smart meter refers to an energy meter or electric load-measuring device; however, the definition can extend to other domains, such as water or natural gas metering. In contrast to the traditional automated meter reading (AMR) concept, smart meters use sensors to monitor electrical load in real-time or near real-time with a pre-defined frequency, i.e. every minute, every half an hour, every hour. This consumption data is communicated to a central server (owned by the electric utility company) which is processed for billing and monitoring with advanced features such as notifications related to power outages, load imbalance, voltage and current monitoring, system load monitoring and data-driven smart switching mechanisms. This study focuses on a custom-built smart metering solution, known as the TransfoCure, which is a successful product based on years of research and development.

## 2    Previous Work

Different methods have been proposed in the literature for effective load-shedding management. The conventional methods previously devised [1] include the Breaker Interlock Scheme in which a source breaker would be interlocked via hardwired or remote signals to a set of load breakers pre-selected to trip. Under Frequency Load Shedding (UFLS) and Under Voltage Load Shedding (UVLS) are attracting more attention [2], as large disturbances occur more frequently now than in the past. In another study, a centralized, adaptive load-shedding algorithm has been developed [2], which considers reactive power. A novel grading scheme for loads is proposed in [12] to minimize the impact of load shedding by considering revenue loss and social factors. An intelligent Load shedding Scheme is introduced in [13] to provide an optimal solution for load relief based on time priority assigned to various loads. Another solution for load forecasting, load shedding and load control has been proposed in [14] based on Autoregressive Integrated Moving Average (ARIMA) prediction model in which a hundred consumers were considered for analysis. This study focuses on the fact that outages are not primarily caused only by insufficient power generation but also due to utilization and consumption patterns of the end consumers. The system tends to introduce a Demand Response (DS) mechanism and assumes that all customers are equipped with Advance Metering Infrastructure (AMI) and smart meters with Energy Consumption Scheduling (ECS). The results show up to a 30% reduction in peak load. Using the Design Science Methodology, the current design of smart meters can be improved to introduce micro-load shedding smart metering technology [15]. This study shows that micro-load management can improve the overall impact on peak load by turning off specific loads during peak load intervals. To manage load at the consumer level, another term Demand Side Management (DSM) was introduced in the 1973 energy crisis. The main aim of the DSM is to encourage a reduction in energy consumption during peak hours or by shifting the excessive load to off-peak timing. A research study uses the Load Curve Technique to shift the load to an off-peak interval [16] based on statistics collected from twenty different consumers and MATLAB-based simulations. It concludes that DSM is useful in short-term load-shedding management.

## 3    Methodology

A solution is presented for the optimal management of load across the three phases of the power distribution network. To ensure the feasibility of the solution, it has been practically implemented and deployed over a production power distribution network in the locality. First, the load is monitored and redistributed to make it balanced immediately after the system's initial deployment. Then the seasonal effects on load distribution are monitored, and the optimal load distribution for the year is calculated. Future load distribution is predicted after gathering data for several months. Since the system collects statistics about the health of transformers and power lines, it was also used for faults detection, up-time monitoring and system health reporting. Cartesian genetic programming and neural network models are used for load-forecasting. Similarly, these models can forecast the peak load in any given interval [17]. Genetic Algorithm is used for load-balancing by utilizing the deployed switching mechanism at transformer level based on the anomalies detected in the forecasted load data by CGPANN.

## 3.1 Experimental Setup

**Hardware Design and Measurements.** The module used for recording and collecting field data, TransfoCure, is a single board circuit for monitoring electrical load thus serving as a stand-alone metering solution. To qualify primarily as an energy meter, the module should be able to measure the electrical load of an end-user accurately for energy unit calculation. All other features are secondary in nature and required by the module for essential services, i.e. interface with peripherals, communication with a central server, and data exchange. The voltage and current of individual phase of a transformer unit serves as the input to the module and is interfaced to a dedicated Analog to Digital Converter (ADC) channel for measurement. The module has multiple analog channels and thus capable of measuring multiple inputs simultaneously. The ADC channel is configured to record 1000 samples per power cycle 50 Hz. The positive cycle is recorded which represents 50% of the cycle. The Root Mean Square (RMS) value of the voltage and current is calculated along with the power factor. This cycle is repeated 100 times and then averaged to obtain more accurate values of RMS that are crucial to energy units calculation.

**Data Exchange and Central Server.** The consumed units are constantly recorded, calculated, and stored on the module during operation which is then communicated to a central server for further processing. Any module deployed in the field continuously shares its data with the central server where it is accumulated. The central server is based on a web-based application which acts as a central hub for all field-deployed modules and follows a distributed model for stand-alone deployment. The storage capacity on the server is scalable and thus virtually unlimited for storing data recorded by the modules.

## 3.2 Computational Intelligence

**Load Forecasting.** An Artificial Neural Network (ANN) is a simulation program that comprises individual processing units (or nodes) called neurons. The interconnected network formation of neurons constitutes an ANN used to calculate unknown functions with many inputs. Cartesian Genetic Programming (CGP) is a popular form of genetic programming that uses a two-dimensional grid of nodes. CGP is used to evolve ANN, resulting in the CGPANN model, which is used for forecasting purposes in many scientific regimes. Based on the advantages of the CGPANN, it is used for accurate load prediction and to devise an effective model for load shedding management.

**Load Balancing.** A feeder system consists of multiple transformers whose individual load contributes to the overall load. There are three individual phases in a feeder system for load distribution. Hence, all three phases of each transformer unit contribute independently to the respective phase of the feeder. For the load to be balanced, the load on individual phases of the feeder need to be distributed equally. An unbalanced system can cause problems like excessive neutral current, excessive power loss, voltage or current shift. The load on any phase should not exceed the individual maximum phase load capacity for the given feeder. For any unbalanced and excessive load condition, many possible solutions exist in the form of different switching arrangements of the phases. An optimum solution will have *no excessive load, a fairly balanced load,* and *minimum switching*. Genetic Algorithm (GA), a search heuristic based on the natural evolution process, is used to search for and find such solutions.

### 3.3 Data Collection, Presentation and Intervals

The TransfoCure modules were installed on each transformer connected to a single feeder for monitoring real-time data i.e., phase voltage (volt), phase current (ampere), and power factor which is communicated to the central server at a pre-defined one-minute interval. Complete data was recorded for a period of three months. The collected raw data of electrical load is first converted into kilo-volt-ampere or KVA, which is the standard unit for apparent power so that it can be easily processed to determine current operating load on each phase at any given instance. The data is further segmented into fifteen, thirty, and sixty minute intervals to examine and test the algorithms in different scenarios and determine their performance. The peak load value within these intervals is selected which represents the maximum operating load during that specific interval. The Table 1 represents collected data converted into KVA and segregated into 15-minutes interval for further processing.

**Table 1.** Sample Data: 15-minutes interval

| Interval Start | Interval End | $KVA1_{MAX}$ | $KVA2_{MAX}$ | $KVA3_{MAX}$ |
|---|---|---|---|---|
| 01/10/2019 0:30 | 01/10/2019 0:45 | 2.1977 | 3.9358 | 4.5758 |
| 01/10/2019 0:45 | 01/10/2019 1:00 | 2.2367 | 4.1586 | 4.6243 |
| 01/10/2019 1:00 | 01/10/2019 1:15 | 2.2443 | 4.1761 | 4.6274 |
| 01/10/2019 1:15 | 01/10/2019 1:30 | 2.2317 | 4.1557 | 4.5948 |
| 01/10/2019 1:30 | 01/10/2019 1:45 | 2.2419 | 5.9634 | 4.6158 |

The ideal load on each phase is represented by $L_i$ which can be theoretically determined by the ratio of total operating load of the feeder to the number of phases. A control parameter, Load-balancing Range ($L_{BR}$) is introduced to determine how close the load value is to $L_i$ and is preferred to be as close as possible to $L_i$. Another control parameter, Load-switching Range ($L_{SR}$) is also introduced to determine the amount of switching or interchanging phases and is preferred to be minimum as switching is a physical process that involves mechanical work and causes system transients.

### 3.4    Data Normalization and Processing

To feed the data into the load forecasting algorithms, the data is normalized using the below Eq. 1, where X represents the KVA value to be normalized. The minimum value refers to the minimum KVA in the dataset, while the maximum value refers to the total capacity of the transformer.

$$X_{normalized} = \frac{(X - X_{minimum})}{(X_{maximum} - X_{minimum})} \tag{1}$$

Table 2 represents normalized data for the same 15-minutes interval (Table 1) to be provided as input to the load-forecasting model for load prediction.

**Table 2.** Sample Data (Normalized): 15-minutes interval

| Interval Start | Interval End | $KVA1_{MAX}$ | $KVA2_{MAX}$ | $KVA3_{MAX}$ |
|---|---|---|---|---|
| 01/10/2019 0:30 | 01/10/2019 0:45 | 0.0258 | 0.0441 | 0.0515 |
| 01/10/2019 0:45 | 01/10/2019 1:00 | 0.0262 | 0.0466 | 0.0520 |
| 01/10/2019 1:00 | 01/10/2019 1:15 | 0.0263 | 0.0468 | 0.0521 |
| 01/10/2019 1:15 | 01/10/2019 1:30 | 0.0262 | 0.0465 | 0.0517 |
| 01/10/2019 1:30 | 01/10/2019 1:45 | 0.0263 | 0.0668 | 0.0519 |

## 4    Results

### 4.1    Load-Forecasting Algorithm

The normalized and zero-adjusted data is fed into the CGPANN for load-forecasting. The data is divided into two segments i.e., training and testing. The training data set is used to train the algorithm and then load is predicted for the next intervals. This predicted load is compared with the testing data for accuracy. After running the experiments, an average percentage error of 3.9% for 15-minutes, 4.55% for 30-minutes, and 11.6% for 60-minutes interval was observed which results in an overall average percentage error of 6.68% for the load-forecasting model. Table 3 represents the percentage error between the actual load and the forecasted load of individual transformers for 15, 30, and 60 min intervals.

### 4.2    Load-Balancing Algorithm

The algorithm analyses data to identify excessive and unbalanced load conditions and then uses Genetic Algorithm, as defined in Table 4, to find the optimum solution for eliminating excessive load and balancing the load.

**Table 3.** Percentage Error: Actual Load vs. Forecasted Load

| Interval | Phase | TF1 | TF2 | TF3 | TF4 | TF5 | TF6 | TF7 | TF8 | TF9 | TF10 |
|---|---|---|---|---|---|---|---|---|---|---|---|
| 15 min | KVA1 | 1.48 | 2.93 | 5.54 | 3.37 | 5.14 | 10.16 | 1.83 | 2.26 | 6.56 | 1.91 |
| | KVA2 | 1.49 | 3.93 | 2.14 | 6.94 | 11.19 | 6.53 | 1.56 | 4.96 | 2.50 | 1.33 |
| | KVA3 | 1.07 | 4.89 | 9.15 | 1.68 | 6.07 | 3.38 | 0.33 | 4.50 | 0.99 | 1.08 |
| 30 min | KVA1 | 1.60 | 5.78 | 14.82 | 3.12 | 6.57 | 10.79 | 15.33 | 5.42 | 11.11 | 8.89 |
| | KVA2 | 0.11 | 3.82 | 3.44 | 2.77 | 1.06 | 2.07 | 3.95 | 1.80 | 2.41 | 3.97 |
| | KVA3 | 1.05 | 6.02 | 6.71 | 1.88 | 1.14 | 6.31 | 0.76 | 0.33 | 1.31 | 2.31 |
| 60 min | KVA1 | 14.85 | 4.83 | 8.47 | 2.42 | 45.43 | 45.95 | 11.04 | 6.93 | 7.05 | 25.42 |
| | KVA2 | 1.08 | 3.67 | 26.52 | 0.92 | 19.04 | 1.74 | 18.78 | 4.71 | 0.42 | 1.11 |
| | KVA3 | 0.42 | 10.29 | 13.08 | 3.56 | 8.05 | 30.36 | 1.69 | 10.55 | 11.17 | 8.34 |

**Table 4.** Pseudo-code: Genetic Algorithm

| |
|---|
| Start Program |
| Generate the first population (random) |
| Calculate Fitness |
| Loop |
| Selection |
| Crossover |
| Mutation |
| Calculate Fitness |
| Check if fitness achieved |
| End program |

The genetic algorithm arrives at an optimum solution (if available) based on the provided control parameters through natural selection. This search continues unless and until the algorithm arrives at the required solution or the maximum number of iterations is exceeded. The number of iterations is another control parameter to stop the algorithm from running indefinitely. The total number of iterations processed by a genetic algorithm to arrive at a solution is considered its performance indicator. An algorithm that can arrive at the solution in minimum iterations is suitable for implementation to minimize processing time and resource usage.

### 4.3   Performance of the Genetic Algorithm

For the available dataset, a total of 290 anomalies were detected. To assess the performance of the genetic algorithm, these detected anomalies were fed as inputs to find the optimum solution. The Table 5 is the result of simulating multiple experiments with varying $L_{SR}$ while keeping $L_{BR}$ constant at a suitable value.

Unsolved cases refer to situations where the algorithm cannot find an optimum solution. One possibility of such an occurrence is that the control parameters are too strict. Another possibility is that the system was so overloaded that it wasn't possible to eliminate exceeding load conditions, or the individual load distribution was such that load balancing was impossible. The mean iterations reflect the algorithm's performance, which tends to improve as we allow more switching (which is not desirable). The mean iterations are exclusive of unsolved cases.

**Table 5.** Performance of Genetic Algorithm

| S. No. | $L_{SR}(\%)$ | $L_{BR}(\%)$ | Unsolved | Mean Iterations |
|--------|--------------|--------------|----------|-----------------|
| 1 | 10 | 10 | 81 | 6609 |
| 2 | 20 | 10 | 22 | 1525 |
| 3 | 30 | 10 | 8 | 384 |
| 4 | 40 | 10 | 5 | 177 |
| 5 | 50 | 10 | 4 | 114 |
| 6 | 60 | 10 | 4 | 279 |
| 7 | 70 | 10 | 4 | 293 |
| 8 | 80 | 10 | 4 | 74 |
| 9 | 90 | 10 | 4 | 84 |
| 10 | 100 | 10 | 4 | 84 |

In terms of $L_{BR}$ and $L_{SR}$, there are different possible scenarios to assess the performance of the Genetic Algorithm.

**Minimum $L_{BR}$ and Maximum $L_{SR}$.** The load was balanced within ±2% of $L_i$ with a standard deviation of 2.81 at the expense of high $L_{SR}$ which is undesirable.

**Maximum $L_{BR}$ and Minimum $L_{SR}$.** The load was balanced within ±8% of $L_i$ with a standard deviation of 7.77 along-with minimum $L_{SR}$ which eliminated excessive load condition but is not well balanced.

**Variable $L_{BR}$ and Minimum $L_{SR}$.** The load was balanced within ±5% of $L_i$ with a standard deviation of 7.77 along-with $L_{SR}$ similar to the previous scenario which eliminated excessive load condition but is still not well balanced.

**Minimum $L_{BR}$ and Variable $L_{SR}$.** The load was balanced within ±2% of $L_i$ with a standard deviation of 2.21 along-with reduced $L_{SR}$ as compared to previous scenarios.

**Variable $L_{BR}$ and Variable $L_{SR}$.** The load was balanced within ±4% of $L_i$ with a standard deviation of 4.61 along-with reduced $L_{SR}$ having the least number of switching as compared to other scenarios. This has great practical value as there is minimum switching involved and the load is also well balanced across all phases.

# 5  Discussion

The above discussion sheds light on how different controlling parameters can impact the search process of the genetic algorithm. Since the algorithm follows the natural evolution process, tweaking and tuning these parameters will result in a completely different solution set. The selection of parameters and their corresponding values is crucial to finding the optimum solution.

Every problem has a different set of parameters; thus, it is impossible to devise a single criterion that could be applied universally. Based on the scenario, the controlling parameters could vary in nature and values. In this study, parameters such as $L_{BR}$ and $L_{SR}$ are introduced to determine the fitness of a solution. By tweaking these parameters carefully, a well-balanced system can be achieved through minimum switching.

Setting the parameters too close to ideal conditions will force the algorithm to keep looking for a solution that may not exist, and the search will continue for a long time. Such configurations are resource extensive and will exhaust the computation engine. On the other hand, setting the parameters too far away from ideal conditions will force the algorithm to conclude the search with a solution that might not be optimum. The search will end quickly, but the results will not be desirable.

However, as demonstrated through different scenarios in the previous section, there is a delicate balance between achieving a perfectly balanced load and minimum switching. It is not always possible to achieve the two simultaneously.

# 6  Conclusion and Way Forward

This research embodies an array of novel approaches, such as neural networks for load-forecasting, a genetic algorithm for load-balancing, and a mechanism for load-switching at the feeder level. Each approach poses a unique challenge for achieving the goal, i.e. a balanced system. The forecasting model was trained on a dataset recorded for a few months in real-world conditions. The results were thoroughly analysed to ensure their reliability and accuracy. Similarly, the load-balancing algorithm was tested intensively to minimize iterations and overload on the processing engine. The switching mechanisms are also being tested in a laboratory environment for safe switching during load transitions between the phases. This study introduces a novel approach for load-balancing in an electrical system. The use of TransfoCure modules enables us to monitor the load constantly and in real-time. This accumulated load data was utilized to develop a forecasting model that could accurately forecast the load. Based on this forecasted load, the load-balancing model was developed that can help eliminate unbalanced and excessive load conditions in the system. Further research in tweaking the load-forecasting model, load-balancing model and switching mechanism can improve the involved processes and reduce the overhead of the processing engine. Such improvements will enhance the response time as well as ensure the system's reliability.

**Acknowledgements.** This research became possible with the support of National Centre of Artificial Intelligence, UET Peshawar which provided all the resources and equipment to collect data for this study and conclude with results that have practical value and could be deployed as a solution.

# References

1. Shokooh, F., Dail, J.: An intelligent load shedding (ILS) system application in a large industrial facility. In: IEEE IAS (2005)
2. Tang, J., Liu, J.: Adaptive load shedding based on combined frequency and voltage stability assessment using synchrophasor measurements. IEEE Trans. Power Syst. **28** (2013)
3. Xu, Y., Tolbert, L., Kueck, J., Rizy, D.: Voltage and current unbalance compensation using a static VAR compensator. IEEE Trans. Power Electron. **3**, 977–988 (2010)
4. Sahito, A., Memon, Z., Shaikh, P., Raj, A.: Unbalanced loading: an overlooked contributor to power losses in HESCO. Sindh Univ. Res. J. (Sci. Ser.) **47**, 779–782 (2015)
5. Hatziargyriou, N., Asano, H., Iravani, R., Marnay, C.: Microgrids. Energy Power Mag. **5**, 78–94 (2007)
6. Kim, G., Hwang, C., Jeon, J., Ahn, J., Kim, E.: A novel three-phase four-leg inverter based load unbalance compensator for stand-alone microgrid. Int. J. Electr. Power Energy Syst. **65**, 70–75 (2015)
7. Shahnia, F., Majumder, R., Ghosh, A., Ledwich, G., Zare, F.: Operation and control of a hybrid microgrid containing unbalanced and nonlinear loads. Electr. Power Syst. Res. **80**, 954–965 (2010)
8. Li, Y., Vilathgamuwa, D., Loh, P.: Microgrid power quality enhancement using a three-phase four-wire grid interfacing compensator. IEEE Trans. Ind. Appl. **41**, 1707–1719 (2005)
9. Gyugyi, L.: Power electronics in electric utilities: static VAR compensators. Proc. IEEE **76**, 483–494 (2002)
10. Kern, A., Schroder, G.: A novel approach to power factor control and balancing problems. Ind. Electron. Control Instrum. (1994)
11. El-Sadek, M.: Balancing of unbalanced loads using static VAR compensators. Electric Power Syst. Res. **12**, 137–148 (1987)
12. Rao, K., Bhat, H.: A novel grading scheme for loads to optimize load shedding using genetic algorithm in a smart grid environment. In: IEEE ISGT Asia (2013)
13. Shokooh, S., Khandelwal, T., Shokooh, F., Tastet, J., Dai, J.: Intelligent load shedding need for a fast and optimal solution. In: IEEE PCIC Europe (2005)
14. Mortaji, H., Ow, S., Moghavvemi, M., Almurib, H.: Smart grid demand response management using Internet of Things for load shedding and smart-direct load control. IEEE Trans. Ind. Appl. **53**, 7 (2017)
15. Azasoo, J., Boateng, K.: Optimizing the effects of load-shedding through micro-load management in generation. In: 2nd IEEE International Conference on Computer and Communication, Chengdu (2016)
16. Ali, M., Yousaf, A., Usman, F.: Designing and simulation of load control & monitoring system through demand side management technique. In: The 8th International Renewable Energy Congress (IREC 2017), Jordan (2017)
17. Miller, J.: Cartesian genetic programming. In: Miller, J. (eds.) Genetic Programming, Natural Computing Series. Springer, Cham (2011). https://doi.org/10.1007/978-3-642-17310-3_2

# MiniAnDE: A Reduced AnDE Ensemble to Deal with Microarray Data

Pablo Torrijos[1,2]($\boxtimes$) (ID), José A. Gámez[1,2] (ID), and José M. Puerta[1,2] (ID)

[1] Instituto de Investigación en Informática de Albacete (I3A), Universidad de Castilla-La Mancha, Albacete 02071, Spain
{Pablo.Torrijos,Jose.Gamez,Jose.Puerta}@uclm.es
[2] Departamento de Sistemas Informáticos, Universidad de Castilla-La Mancha, Albacete 02071, Spain

**Abstract.** This article focuses on the supervised classification of datasets with a large number of variables and a small number of instances. This is the case, for example, for microarray data sets commonly used in bioinformatics. Complex classifiers that require estimating statistics over many variables are not suitable for this type of data. Probabilistic classifiers with low-order probability tables, e.g., Naive Bayes (NB) and Averaged One-Dependence Estimators (AODE), are good alternatives for dealing with this data type. AODE usually improves NB in accuracy but suffers from high spatial complexity since $k$ models, each with $n + 1$ variables, are included in the AODE ensemble. In this paper, we propose MiniAnDE, an algorithm that includes only a small number of heterogeneous base classifiers in the ensemble, i.e., each model only includes a different subset of the $k$ predictive variables. Experimental evaluation shows that using MiniAnDE classifiers on microarray data is feasible and outperforms NB and other ensembles such as bagging and random forest.

**Keywords:** Bayesian network classifiers · Averaged $n$-Dependence Estimators · Microarray data · High dimensionality

## 1 Introduction

Supervised classification, i.e., predicting the category $c \in dom(C) = \{c_1, \ldots, c_r\}$ for an object $\mathbf{x}$ defined over a set of attributes $\mathbf{X} = \{X_1, \ldots, X_k\}$, is one of the most profusely tackled tasks in machine learning. The objective is to learn a classifier $\mathcal{C} : X_1 \times \cdots \times X_k \to C$, from a data set $\mathbf{D} = \{(\mathbf{x}^{(i)}, c^{(i)})\}_{i=1}^{m}$, such that $\mathcal{C}$ generalises well to new data.

This paper focuses on a niche of supervised classification problems: data defined over many features/attributes and with scarce instances. Such data sets, where $k \gg m$, are common in microarray data problems [1], where the expression level of thousands of genes is analyzed simultaneously. Still, due to sampling costs, only a few dozen or a few hundred cases are available. This scarcity of

© The Author(s), under exclusive license to Springer Nature Switzerland AG 2023
L. Iliadis et al. (Eds.): EANN 2023, CCIS 1826, pp. 131–143, 2023.
https://doi.org/10.1007/978-3-031-34204-2_12

cases means that models that need to estimate complex statistics, e.g., higher-order statistics, or measures subject to a particular context (e.g., a deep branch in a decision tree) cannot be reliably learned. A common solution to combat this dimensionality curse is performing a prior feature selection process [5]. However, this paper focuses on a different solution: using models that, while complex overall, only require estimating statistics on a very small number of variables.

The Naive Bayes (NB) classifier [19] is the simplest Bayesian network model used for classification. It is based on the hypothesis (assumption) that all the predictive attributes are independent of each other given the value of the class variable (Fig. 1). This independence hypothesis gives rise to the following factorization:

$$P(c, x_1, \ldots, x_k) = P(c) \prod_{i=1}^{k} P(x_i|c), \tag{1}$$

which enables: (1) NB does not require structural learning; (2) parametric learning is very efficient (a single pass through the BD); and (3) it is only necessary to estimate bi-variate statistics, so a small number of cases is enough.

Among the different improvements made to NB trying to circumvent the independence hypothesis, one of the most outstanding for its exceptional performance is Averaged One-Dependence Estimators (AODE) [20]. AODE can be seen as an ensemble formed by $n$ Super Parent One-Dependence Estimator (SPODE) classifiers, i.e., a NB extended with one attribute also being the parent of the other features (Fig. 2). Thus, in a SPODE, each variable depends on another variable apart from the class. Combined with the fact that AODE includes all the $n$ possible SPODEs, allows AODE to consider a large number of possible dependencies between attributes. Despite the strong relaxation of the NB independence assumption that AODE implies, parametric learning is still very efficient and only requires estimating three-variate statistics, so the number of cases needed remains moderate. More dependencies are considered in Averaged $n$-Dependence Estimators (AnDE) [21], where $n$ features play the role of super-parents in each member (SPnDE) of the ensemble. AnDE ($n \geq 2$) can manage more complex dependency relations than AODE (A1DE). However, more cases are necessary to obtain reliable estimations for $(n + 1) - ary$ statistics.

The motivation for this work comes from the fact that when dealing with microarray data, the main problem related to AnDE, even with $n = 1$ (AODE), is the size of the ensemble, which can easily run out of memory. For example, let us consider a problem with $k = 10000$ attributes, each taking 5 different values, as well as the class. In this case, A1DE has to store 10000 SPODEs, each with 10000 probability tables of size $5^3$, assuming 32 bits per float value, which means 50 GB. Of course, things are worse if we increase $n$, giving rise to the problem of dealing with *big models* [3].

This work proposes *Mini Averaged n-Dependence Estimators (MiniAnDE)*, an algorithm that tries to build small AnDE models in which only a subset of SPnDEs are included in the ensemble, also limiting to a subset of **X** the features included in each SPnDE. We introduce a structural learning stage in which relevant feature-class and feature-feature relations are identified, constructing the SPnDEs based on the identified relevant relations. Experiments over nineteen microarray datasets confirm the competitiveness of our approach.

This paper is organized as follows. Section 2 revises our baseline algorithm, Averaged n-Dependence Estimators (AnDE) [21]. Section 3 introduces the MiniAnDE classifier proposed in this paper. Section 4 presents the experimental evaluation. Finally, Sect. 5 concludes the paper and outlines potential avenues for future research.

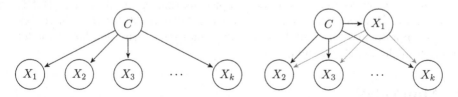

**Fig. 1.** Graphical structure of NB          **Fig. 2.** Graphical structure of SPODE

## 2    Averaged $n$-Dependence Estimators (AnDE)

Averaged n-Dependence Estimators (AnDE) [21] extend the AODE (A1DE) algorithm by allowing $n$ super-parent variables in each model (SPnDE). As $n$ grows, the classifier estimates probability distributions of higher dimension, thus reducing its bias but probably increasing its variance, which, however, will be reduced when the ensemble aggregates all the predictions of the base models.

The class label $c^*$ of an instance $\mathbf{x}$ is obtained by:

$$c^* = \arg \max_{c_i \in dom(C)} P(c_i, \mathbf{x}) = \sum_{S \in \binom{\mathbf{x}}{n}} P(c_i, \mathbf{x}_S) \prod_{X_j \in \mathbf{X}-S} P(x_j | c_i, \mathbf{x}_S), \qquad (2)$$

where $\binom{\mathbf{x}}{n}$ represents the subsets of $\mathbf{X}$ having exactly $n$ variables; $\mathbf{x}_S$ is the projection of $\mathbf{x}$ over $S$; the expression inside the summation is the factorization of the joint probability carried out by the SPnDE; and the summation stands for the aggregation carried out in the AnDE ensemble.

In particular, for A1DE, the previous expression reduces to:

$$c^* = \arg \max_{c_i \in dom(C)} P(c_i, \mathbf{x}) = \sum_{l=1}^{k} P(c_i, \mathbf{x}_l) \prod_{j \neq l} P(x_j | c_i, \mathbf{x}_l). \qquad (3)$$

The main problem in AnDE is its spatial complexity and the increase in the number of samples needed to make reliable estimates of increasingly larger statistics. Thus, A1DE requires $n$ models, each with $k-1$ distributions of order 3; A2DE requires $O(n^2)$ models each with $k-2$ distributions of order 4; A3DE requires $O(n^3)$ models, each with $k-3$ distributions of order 5; etc. This means that in practice, AnDE can only be used with $n = 1$ for moderate/large domains and with $n = 2$ for small domains.

In literature, we can find different approaches to make AnDE usable when $n$ and/or $k$ grows. In [15], the A1DE ensemble is replaced by a single model whose super-parent is a latent variable estimated using the EM algorithm. SAnDE [10] and SASAnDE [9] follow a model selection-based approach, which relies on the assumption that the conditional mutual information of the super parent set of attributes given the class is a good approximation of the resulting SPnDE performance. However, the study conducted in [4] over 43 datasets challenges this assumption and the usefulness of using mutual information-based model selection in the AnDE ensemble.

## 3   MiniAnDE

The main objective of the *Mini Averaged n-Dependence Estimators (MiniAnDE)* classifier is to reduce the enormous spatial complexity of AnDE which, in practice, impedes their use in databases with thousands of variables ($k$) in the case of A1DE and hundreds in the case of A2DE. The aim is to reduce both the number of SPnDEs generated ($s$) and the number of variables included in each SPnDE ($r_i$) so that $s \ll k$ and $r_i \ll k$. Thus, we create much smaller and faster models that can handle high-dimensional datasets.

As in [10], we need to select the variable(s) that will act as super-parent(s) and thus give rise to the SPnDEs included in the AnDE model. In addition, we also have to select the *child* features to be included in each SPnDE. Unlike previous work, instead of calculating information-based measures, we propose to use a different machine learning model, a decision tree, from which the relationships between features can be borrowed for our MiniAnDE model.

The use of decision trees (DTs) to select the relevant variables for a classification problem is quite old [8]. From a probabilistic point of view, the subset of variables appearing in the tree could be seen to constitute the Markov blanket of the class variable, i.e., the set of variables that makes the rest irrelevant for classification purposes. Later, ensemble-based methods, particularly random forests, have also been used to obtain the importance of predictive variables in the classification process, using so-called out-of-bag estimation [7]. This technique has become very popular and can be found in almost any ML software, e.g., Scikit-Learn or WEKA.

In this paper, we propose to use an ensemble of DTs to identify the SPnDEs to be included in our MiniAnDE model. In addition to the ability of the DTs to select the relevant variables for the class, we will also exploit the location in which these variables are placed in the tree. Thus, it is well known that one of the advantages of DTs is their context-based analysis of the data, where by context we mean a (partial) branch of the three. Therefore, we traverse the tree to identify all paths of length $n$ and create an SPnDE for each of them by setting the variables in the path as super-parents. Then, all variables in the tree that are adjacent to the super-parent variables are included as children in that SPnDE. To obtain a more robust MiniAnDE model we consider a set of diverse DTs, that is, an ensemble.

---

**Algorithm 1.** MiniAnDE

---

**Require:** Dataset $\mathbf{D}$ defined over $\mathbf{X} \cup \{C\}$; $n$; $t$
1: $SP \leftarrow \emptyset$
2: $\mathcal{T} \leftarrow \emptyset$
3: **for** $i \leftarrow 1$ to $t$ **do**
4:     $T \leftarrow$ learn a DT from a sample of $\mathbf{D}$
5:     $\mathcal{T} \leftarrow \mathcal{T} \cup \{T\}$
6:     $SP^t \leftarrow \{$sets of $n$ consecutive variables in $T\}$
7:     $SP \leftarrow SP \cup SP^t$
8: **end for**
9: $\forall sp \in SP$, children$(sp) \leftarrow \bigcup_{T \in \mathcal{T} \wedge sp \in T} \left\{ \bigcup_{X \in sp} \text{adjacent}(X, T) \right\}$
10: $\mathcal{M} \leftarrow \emptyset$
11: **for** each $sp \in SP$ do **do**
12:     Create an SPnDE $m$ with $sp$ as super-parent and children$(sp)$ as features
13:     $\mathcal{M} \leftarrow \mathcal{M} \cup \{m\}$
14: **end for**
15: **return** $\mathcal{M}$

---

Algorithm 1 provides a scheme of the previous idea. Let us illustrate its working process with an example taking $n = 1$ and $t = 2$. Let us also assume that Fig. 3a shows two DTs learned from two different samples of $\mathbf{D}$. The algorithm starts with $T_1$ and identify $SP^1 = \{\{X_1\}, \{X_2\}, \{X_3\}\}$. Now $SP \leftarrow SP^1$ and $T_2$ are considered. The algorithm computes $SP^2 = \{\{X_1\}, \{X_2\}, \{X_3\}, \{X_4\}\}$, and so $SP = \{\{X_1\}, \{X_2\}, \{X_3\}, \{X_4\}\}$. Next, children sets are computed as: children$(\{X_1\}) = \{X_2, X_3\}$, children$(\{X_2\}) = \{X_1, X_3, X_4\}$, children$(\{X_3\}) = \{X_1, X_2\}$ and children$(\{X_4\}) = \{X_2\}$. Therefore, the SP1DEs included in the resulting MiniA1DE are those shown in Fig. 3b. If the same process is applied with $n = 2$, $SP^1 = \{\{X_1, X_2\}, \{X_1, X_3\}, \{\{X_2, X_3\}\}$, $SP^2 = \{\{X_1, X_2\}, \{X_1, X_3\}, \{\{X_2, X_3\}, \{\{X_2, X_4\}\}$ and $SP = \{\{X_1, X_2\}, \{X_1, X_3\}, \{X_2, X_3\}, \{X_2, X_4\}\}$. Next, children sets are computed as: children$(\{X_1, X_2\}) = \{X_3, X_4\}$, children$(\{X_1, X_3\}) = \{X_2\}$, children$(\{X_2, X_3\}) = \{X_1, X_4\}$ and children$(\{X_2, X_4\}) = \{X_1, X_3\}$. Figure 4 shows the resulting MiniA2DE.

Like the original AnDE algorithm, MiniAnDE only works with discrete variables, so if numerical predictive attributes are included in the dataset, they must first be discretized. Once the SPnDEs have been determined, only parametric learning is required, which can be performed in a single pass through the dataset. Therefore, the complexity of learning a MiniAnDE model is dominated by the learning process of the set of decision trees. In this sense, it is worth noting that due to the small number of instances in the microarray data, the obtained tree will be shallow, which, coupled with the use of only discrete (discretized) variables, results in a fast learning process. On the other hand, the inference

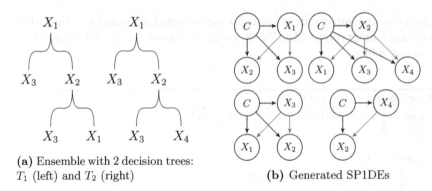

(a) Ensemble with 2 decision trees: $T_1$ (left) and $T_2$ (right)

(b) Generated SP1DEs

**Fig. 3.** MiniA1DE obtained from the ensemble $\{T_1, T_2\}$

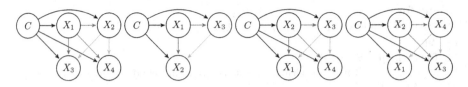

**Fig. 4.** MiniA2DE obtained from the ensemble $\{T_1, T_2\}$ in Fig. 3a

is also faster than in the original AnDE models since only a few SPnDEs are aggregated instead of $k$.

The MiniAnDE algorithm can be instantiated with any decision tree and ensemble learning algorithm, e.g., bagging [6] or random forest [7]. This fact, together with the DT/ensemble learning hyperparameters (pruning or no-pruning, max depth, number of trees, etc.), provides a wide range of combinations to generate the MiniAnDE classifier, making it possible to fine-tune it for a given dataset.

To conclude this section, we present a possible extension of the MiniAnDE algorithm. As with AnDE, MiniAnDE is expected to be a better estimator than NB for posterior class label probabilities. However, in some cases, some attribute configurations and class values may be missing or underrepresented in the learning dataset, resulting in a nearly uniform posterior probability distribution for the class given the input instance. To alleviate this drawback, we produce the output as a convex combination of MiniAnDE and NB, adding it to the ensemble according to a parameter $\alpha \in [0,1]$: $p(c|\mathbf{x}) = \alpha\, p_{NB}(c|\mathbf{x}) + (1 - \alpha)\, p_{MiniAnDE}(c|\mathbf{x})$. We compare the MiniAnDE algorithm with $\alpha = 0$ and $\alpha \neq 0$ in the experiments performed in Sect. 4.

## 4    Experimental Evaluation

In the next sections, we describe the datasets utilized, the algorithms evaluated, the methodology employed, and analyze the results obtained.

## 4.1 Data Sets

Table 1 describes the 19 microarray data sets used to evaluate the proposed algorithms, commonly used in the literature [1, 5, 12, 22].

**Table 1.** Data sets used in the experimental evaluation. I is the number of instances, N the number of predictible variables and K the number of classes.

| Data Set | Features | | | Data Set | Features | | |
|---|---|---|---|---|---|---|---|
| | I | N | K | | I | N | K |
| 9 Tumors | 60 | 5 726 | 9 | Lung | 203 | 12 600 | 5 |
| 11 Tumors | 174 | 12 533 | 11 | Lymphoma 3 | 66 | 4 026 | 3 |
| Breast | 97 | 24 481 | 2 | Lymphoma 9 | 96 | 4 026 | 9 |
| CNS | 60 | 7 130 | 2 | Lymphoma 11 | 96 | 4 026 | 11 |
| Colon | 62 | 2 000 | 2 | MLL | 72 | 12 582 | 3 |
| DLBCL | 77 | 5 469 | 2 | Ovarian | 253 | 15 154 | 2 |
| GLI | 85 | 22 283 | 2 | Prostate | 102 | 12 600 | 2 |
| Leukemia | 72 | 7 129 | 2 | SMK | 187 | 19 993 | 2 |
| Leukemia 3 | 72 | 7 129 | 3 | SRBCT | 83 | 2 308 | 4 |
| Leukemia 4 | 72 | 7 129 | 4 | | | | |

## 4.2 Reproducibility

The entire MiniAnDE algorithm's family has been programmed from scratch and tested using Java (OpenJDK 8) and the library WEKA 3.9.6[1]. All experiments were conducted on machines running the CentOS 7 operating system with an Intel Xeon E5-2650 8-Core Processor limited to 8 threads and 32 GB of RAM per execution.

To reproduce the experiments, all of the code and the execution scripts are provided at GitHub[2]. Regarding the data, for convenience, we provide in OpenML[3] a common source repository for the 19 datasets, with reference to their original articles.

## 4.3 Algorithms

In this study, the following algorithms have been evaluated:

- The MiniAnDE algorithm introduced in Sect. 3, with $n = 1$ and $n = 2$. The following parameters have been fine-tuned by using grid-search for each dataset:

---

[1] https://www.cs.waikato.ac.nz/ml/weka/.

[2] https://github.com/ptorrijos99/mAnDE.

[3] https://www.openml.org/search?type=data&uploader_id=%3D_33148.

- Bagging is considered to generate the ensemble of trees used to learn the structure of those SPnDEs included in the MiniAnDE model. The number of trees is taken from the set $\{50, 100, 150, 200\}$.
- The     weight     of     NB     is     chosen     from     the set $\alpha = 0.02, 0.05, 0.1, 0.15, 0.2, 0.25, 0.3, 0.35, 0.4\}$. The case of $\alpha = 0$ is always reported, corresponding to the canonical MiniAnDE introduced in Algorithm 1.

- The Naive Bayes algorithm [19].
- The Bagging ensemble algorithm [6]. The number of trees (50, 100, 150, and 200) is selected for each dataset using a grid-search.
- The Random Forest algorithm [7]. Default value $\sqrt{k}$ is used to select the random subset of variables evaluated at each split. The number of trees (50, 100, 150, and 200) is selected for each dataset using a grid-search.

Please, note that the original AnDE algorithm [21] is not included because of its spatial complexity. In fact, under the resources described in the previous section, the A1DE algorithm only can cope with 1 out of the 19 datasets (colon), obtaining an accuracy of 80.64.

## 4.4   Methodology

We have taken the following design decisions:

- Each algorithm has been evaluated employing a double cross-validation. Leave-one-out cross-validation has been used for external validation, and stratified 5-fold cross-validation has been used for the internal validation in which the best hyperparameter(s) value(s) are selected by using grid-search. This approach ensured that the results were robust and not influenced by the specific partitioning of the data, especially given the small number of instances in microarray data.
- Numerical variables are discretized. Discretization intervals are learned from the training partition and then applied over the validation/test one. We used the following procedure: (1) supervised entropy-based discretization following Fayyad and Irani algorithm [13] was applied; and (2) those variables left in a single interval are then discretized into 2 intervals (bins) by using unsupervised equal frequency. Note that variables discretized in a single bin by Fayyad and Irani algorithm are those *marginally* independent to the class, but can be relevant when used in conjunction with other attributes (e.g., as in an X-OR dataset).
- The study's results have been analyzed using the methodology specified in [11,17], and the analysis has been conducted using the exreport R package [2]. The analysis begins by performing a Friedman test [16] with the null hypothesis that all algorithms have equal performance. If the null hypothesis is rejected, a posthoc test using Holm's procedure [18] is carried out to compare all algorithms against the one ranked first by the Friedman test. Both assessments are conducted at a significance level of 5%.

## 4.5  Results

The summary of the accuracy results is shown in Table 2, including the result of each algorithm[4] for each database as well as the total average of each algorithm. The algorithm(s) with the highest accuracy are highlighted in bold. In accordance with the procedure described in Sect. 4.4, we analyzed the results of our experiments. We found evidence to reject the null hypothesis of equal performance across all algorithms with a computed p-value of $1.490 \times 10^{-2}$. The detailed results of the posthoc test are presented in Table 3, which shows the ranking generated by the Friedman test and the p-value adjusted using Holm's procedure (non-rejected null hypotheses are boldfaced), along with the number of wins, ties, and losses for each algorithm versus the algorithm that ranked first. Based on the statistical analysis, we draw the following conclusions:

**Table 2.** Accuracy of each algorithm.

| Data Set | Algorithm | | | | | | |
|---|---|---|---|---|---|---|---|
| | mA1DE | mA2DE | mA1DE $\alpha > 0$ | mA2DE $\alpha > 0$ | NB | Bagging | RF |
| 11 Tumors | 83.91 | 85.06 | **89.66** | 88.51 | 84.48 | 87.36 | 85.06 |
| 9 Tumors | 33.33 | 35.00 | 50.00 | 48.33 | **53.33** | 36.67 | 36.67 |
| Breast | 67.01 | 67.01 | 64.95 | 68.04 | **69.07** | 67.01 | 62.89 |
| CNS | 60.00 | 65.00 | 63.33 | 71.67 | 60.00 | **73.33** | 65.00 |
| Colon | 85.48 | **87.10** | **87.10** | **87.10** | **87.10** | 85.48 | **87.10** |
| DLBCL | **89.61** | 84.42 | 84.42 | 81.82 | 80.52 | 87.01 | 88.31 |
| GLI | **87.06** | 85.88 | 85.88 | 84.71 | 82.35 | 85.88 | 85.88 |
| Leukemia | 95.83 | 95.83 | **97.22** | 94.44 | 87.50 | 91.67 | 94.44 |
| Leukemia 3 | 94.44 | 94.44 | **95.83** | 94.44 | 83.33 | 94.44 | 87.50 |
| Leukemia 4 | **91.67** | 90.28 | 90.28 | 90.28 | 79.17 | 88.89 | 77.78 |
| Lung | 90.64 | 91.13 | 92.61 | 94.09 | 72.91 | **96.55** | 89.16 |
| Lymphoma 11 | 77.08 | 81.25 | 90.62 | **91.67** | **91.67** | 81.25 | 84.38 |
| Lymphoma 3 | 95.45 | 93.94 | 98.48 | 98.48 | **100.00** | 93.94 | 93.94 |
| Lymphoma 9 | 78.12 | 76.04 | 89.58 | 91.67 | **95.83** | 81.25 | 81.25 |
| MLL | 94.44 | 95.83 | **97.22** | 95.83 | 90.28 | 93.06 | 94.44 |
| Ovarian | 97.63 | **98.42** | 97.63 | 98.02 | 92.49 | 98.02 | 95.26 |
| Prostate | **93.14** | 91.18 | 91.18 | 88.24 | 65.69 | 91.18 | 86.27 |
| SMK | 70.05 | 70.05 | **71.66** | **71.66** | 65.24 | 70.59 | 65.24 |
| SRBCT | 98.80 | 97.59 | 98.80 | 97.59 | 92.77 | 95.18 | **100.00** |
| Mean | 83.35 | 83.44 | 86.13 | **86.14** | 80.72 | 84.15 | 82.14 |

---

[4] mANDE denotes the canonical MiniAnDE algorithm ($\alpha = 0$) and mANDE $\alpha > 0$ denotes its combination with NB using $\alpha > 0$. The parameter $\alpha$ is set using a grid search and CV, as noted above.

**Table 3.** Post-hoc test results for the accuracy of each algorithm.

| ALGORITHM | $p$-VALUE | RANK | WIN | TIE | LOSS |
|---|---|---|---|---|---|
| MINIA1DE ($\alpha > 0$) | – | 2.84 | – | – | – |
| MINIA2DE ($\alpha > 0$) | $\mathbf{7.073 \times 10^{-1}}$ | 3.11 | 9 | 4 | 6 |
| MINIA2DE ($\alpha = 0$) | $\mathbf{2.419 \times 10^{-1}}$ | 4.00 | 11 | 5 | 3 |
| BAGGING | $\mathbf{2.419 \times 10^{-1}}$ | 4.08 | 12 | 2 | 5 |
| MINIA1DE ($\alpha = 0$) | $\mathbf{2.419 \times 10^{-1}}$ | 4.16 | 12 | 2 | 5 |
| RANDOM FOREST | $3.432 \times 10^{-2}$ | 4.74 | 14 | 2 | 3 |
| NAIVE BAYES | $8.492 \times 10^{-3}$ | 5.08 | 13 | 1 | 5 |

- The MiniA1DE algorithm with $\alpha > 0$ is ranked in the first place, although there is no significant difference (confidence level 0.05) with respect to the other three MiniAnDE algorithms and bagging. A significant difference is observed with respect to NB and random forest.
- Both MiniAnDE algorithms with $\alpha > 0$ rank ahead, although without significant difference among them, of their counterpart canonical versions without incorporating NB. This corroborated the fact that in some cases, due to the small sample size in microarray datasets, it is good to incorporate the prediction of a simple low-bias classifier.
- Regarding the use of $n = 1$ or $n = 2$, there do not seem to be major differences in either MiniAnDE ($\alpha = 0$) or MiniAnDE ($\alpha > 0$), with either option working better depending on the data set, resulting in an almost identical average accuracy.
- NB is ranked in the last position, which is not unexpected due to the fact that it is by far the simpler model tried. However, it is interesting to observe the bad results obtained by RF, which is ranked behind bagging. It seems that the use of pseudorandom DTs does not match with the large number of variables and small data size of microarray data.

As for computational efficiency, the CPU time is shown in Table 4. As expected, NB is the fastest algorithm (linear in the number of variables and instances). On the other hand, the MiniAnDE algorithms require an affordable amount of CPU time, almost identical to bagging, the classifier it uses to train the trees. Furthermore, the effect of using MiniAnDE with $\alpha > 0$ is practically insignificant. In general, we can say that the MiniAnDE approach is the best choice among the tested hypotheses when dealing with microarray data.

**Table 4.** Execution time per L.O.O. iteration (seconds) of each algorithm.

| DATA SET | ALGORITHM | | | | | | |
|---|---|---|---|---|---|---|---|
| | MA1DE | MA2DE | MA1DE $\alpha > 0$ | MA2DE $\alpha > 0$ | NB | BAGGING | RF |
| 11 TUMORS | 4.05 | 4.94 | 5.31 | 5.23 | **0.83** | 4.50 | 1.50 |
| 9 TUMORS | 0.96 | 0.92 | 0.95 | 1.05 | **0.20** | 0.95 | 0.37 |
| BREAST | 3.23 | 3.27 | 3.49 | 3.58 | **0.83** | 3.44 | 1.41 |
| CNS | 0.59 | 0.66 | 0.66 | 0.68 | **0.18** | 0.61 | 0.42 |
| COLON | 0.72 | 0.74 | 0.74 | 0.77 | **0.18** | 0.66 | **0.18** |
| DLBCL | 0.40 | 0.43 | 0.54 | 0.42 | **0.14** | 0.37 | 0.28 |
| GLI | 2.08 | 2.07 | 1.94 | 2.12 | **0.66** | 1.58 | 1.03 |
| LEUKEMIA | 0.46 | 0.48 | 0.44 | 0.45 | **0.19** | 0.47 | 0.34 |
| LEUKEMIA 3 | 0.60 | 0.53 | 0.52 | 0.52 | **0.17** | 0.53 | 0.37 |
| LEUKEMIA 4 | 0.73 | 0.60 | 0.69 | 0.66 | **0.19** | 0.57 | 0.36 |
| LUNG | 3.69 | 3.81 | 3.80 | 4.03 | **0.95** | 4.00 | 1.36 |
| LYMPHOMA 11 | 0.96 | 1.06 | 1.02 | 0.90 | **0.18** | 0.87 | 0.42 |
| LYMPHOMA 3 | 0.37 | 0.35 | 0.32 | 0.33 | **0.12** | 0.28 | 0.24 |
| LYMPHOMA 9 | 0.81 | 0.86 | 0.88 | 0.86 | **0.21** | 0.80 | 0.29 |
| MLL | 0.92 | 0.81 | 0.89 | 0.85 | **0.29** | 0.70 | 0.55 |
| OVARIAN | 3.00 | 3.03 | 3.07 | 2.98 | **1.23** | 2.94 | 1.50 |
| PROSTATE | 1.38 | 1.27 | 1.38 | 1.46 | **0.41** | 1.37 | 0.71 |
| SMK | 7.42 | 8.98 | 7.69 | 7.98 | **1.22** | 7.46 | 2.07 |
| SRBCT | 0.28 | 0.29 | 0.29 | 0.29 | **0.09** | 0.30 | 0.18 |
| **MEAN** | 1.72 | 1.85 | 1.82 | 1.85 | **0.44** | 1.70 | 0.72 |

## 5 Conclusions

A new algorithm for learning AnDE-like classifiers has been proposed. The method is tailored to the special case of microarray data, where few data instances are available but the number of variables is so large (thousands) that standard AnDE classifiers do not fit in memory. The proposed algorithm incorporates a structural learning stage, which based on the use of shallow decision trees, allows the selection of a few SPnDEs in the resulting MiniAnDE ensemble. Furthermore, a small subset of variables is included in each SPnDE, leading to a very light model regarding spatial needs and providing fast inference. The experiments' results over 19 microarray datasets show the competitivity of our proposal regarding decision tree-based ensembles, both in accuracy and efficiency.

As future works, we plan to study our proposal without the need of discretizing numerical variables, by considering AnDE models based on the use of conditional Gaussian networks [14].

**Acknowledgements.** This work has been funded by the Government of Castilla-La Mancha and "ERDF A way of making Europe" under project SBPLY/21/180225/000062. It is also partially funded by MCIN/AEI/10.13039/501100011033 and "ESF Investing your future" through the projects PID2019–106758GB–C33 and FPU21/01074.

# References

1. Abd-Elnaby, M., Alfonse, M., Roushdy, M.: Classification of breast cancer using microarray gene expression data: a survey. J. Biomed. Inform. **117**, 103764 (2021)
2. Arias, J., Cozar, J.: exreport: Fast, Reliable and Elegant Reproducible Research (2016). https://CRAN.R-project.org/package=exreport. R package version 0.4.1
3. Arias, J., Gámez, J.A., Puerta, J.M.: Learning distributed discrete Bayesian network classifiers under Mapreduce with apache spark. Knowl. Based Syst. **117**, 16–26 (2017)
4. Arias, J., Gámez, J.A., Puerta, J.M.: Bayesian network classifiers under the ensemble perspective. In: Studený, M., Kratochvíl, V. (eds.) International Conference on Probabilistic Graphical Models, PGM 2018, 11–14 September 2018, Prague, Czech Republic. Proceedings of Machine Learning Research, vol. 72, pp. 1–12 (2018)
5. Bolón-Canedo, V., Sánchez-Maroño, N., Alonso-Betanzos, A., Benítez, J., Herrera, F.: A review of microarray datasets and applied feature selection methods. Inf. Sci. **282**, 111–135 (2014)
6. Breiman, L.: Bagging predictors. Mach. Learn. **24**(2), 123–140 (1996)
7. Breiman, L.: Random forests. Mach. Learn. **45**(1), 5–32 (2001)
8. Cardie, C.: Using decision trees to improve case-based learning. In: Proceedings of the Tenth International Conference on Machine Learning (ICML-93), pp. 25–32 (1993)
9. Chen, S., Martínez, A.M., Webb, G.I., Wang, L.: Sample-based attribute selective AnDE for large data. IEEE Trans. Knowl. Data Eng. **29**(1), 172–185 (2017)
10. Chen, S., Martínez, A.M., Webb, G.I., Wang, L.: Selective AnDE for large data learning: a low-bias memory constrained approach. Knowl. Inf. Syst. **50**(2), 475–503 (2017)
11. Demsar, J.: Statistical comparisons of classifiers over multiple data sets. J. Mach. Learn. Res. **7**, 1–30 (2006)
12. Díaz-Uriarte, R., de Andrés, S.A.: Gene selection and classification of microarray data using random forest. BMC Biol. **7**(1), 3 (2006)
13. Fayyad, U.M., Irani, K.B.: Multi-interval discretization of continuous-valued attributes for classification learning. In: International Joint Conference on Artificial Intelligence (1993)
14. Flores, M.J., Gámez, J.A., Martínez, A.M., Puerta, J.M.: GAODE and HAODE: two proposals based on AODE to deal with continuous variables. In: Proceedings of the 26th Annual International Conference on Machine Learning, ICML 2009, Montreal, Quebec, Canada, 14–18 June 2009. vol. 382, pp. 313–320. ACM (2009)
15. Flores, M.J., Gámez, J.A., Martínez, A.M., Puerta, J.M.: HODE: hidden one-dependence estimator. In: Sossai, C., Chemello, G. (eds.) ECSQARU 2009. LNCS (LNAI), vol. 5590, pp. 481–492. Springer, Heidelberg (2009). https://doi.org/10.1007/978-3-642-02906-6_42
16. Friedman, M.: A comparison of alternative tests of significance for the problem of $m$ rankings. Ann. Math. Stat. **11**(1), 86–92 (1940)

17. García, S., Herrera, F.: An extension on "statistical comparisons of classifiers over multiple data sets" for all pairwise comparisons. J. Mach. Learn. Res. **9**, 2677–2694 (2008)
18. Holm, S.: A simple sequentially rejective multiple test procedure. Scand. J. Stat. **6**, 65–70 (1979)
19. Webb, G.I.: Naïve Bayes. In: Encyclopedia of Machine Learning, pp. 713–714. Springer Science+Business Media (2010)
20. Webb, G.I., Boughton, J.R., Wang, Z.: Not so Naive Bayes: aggregating one-dependence estimators. Mach. Learn. **58**(1), 5–24 (2005)
21. Webb, G.I., Boughton, J.R., Zheng, F., Ting, K.M., Salem, H.: Learning by extrapolation from marginal to full-multivariate probability distributions: decreasingly naive bayesian classification. Mach. Learn. **86**(2), 233–272 (2011)
22. Zhu, Z., Ong, Y.S., Dash, M.: Markov blanket-embedded genetic algorithm for gene selection. Pattern Recog. **40**(11), 3236–3248 (2007)

# Multi-view Semi-supervised Learning Using Privileged Information

Evgueni Smirnov[1(✉)], Richard Delava[1], Ron Diris[2], and Nikolay Nikolaev[3]

[1] Department of Advanced Computing Sciences, Maastricht University, Maastricht, The Netherlands
{smirnov,r.delava}@maastrichtuniversity.nl
[2] Institute of Tax Law and Economics, Leiden University, Leiden, The Netherlands
r.e.m.diris@law.leidenuniv.nl
[3] Department of Computing, Goldsmiths College, University of London, London, UK
n.nikolaev@gold.ac.uk

**Abstract.** In this paper we propose to combine the paradigm of multi-view semi-supervised learning with that of learning using privileged information. The combination is realized by a new method that we introduce in detail. A distinctive feature of the method is that it is classifier agnostic which contracts with most of the methods for learning using privileged information. An experimental study on a real-life problem shows that using privileged information is capable of improving multi-view semi-supervised learning.

## 1 Introduction

The task of supervised multi-view learning assumes that training data $L$ is given in multiple views $\mathcal{X}_m$[1] while labeled by a common output variable $Y$ [11]. To solve the task, we first train prediction models $h_m : \mathcal{X}_m \to Y$ for all the views and, then, aggregate their predictions to estimate the values of $Y$ for new query instances. Successful examples include applications in web, drug discovery, part-of-speech tagging etc. for tasks that involve collecting data based on different measurement processes.

Recently, Vapnik proposed a new paradigm of learning using privileged information (LUPI) [10] that is closely related to multi-view learning. Given non-empty views $\mathcal{X}_i \subset \mathcal{X}_j$ and output variable $Y$ LUPI seeks to find a prediction model $h : \mathcal{X}_i \to Y$ from labeled training data given in $\mathcal{X}_j$. According to his definition, to implement LUPI we need first to train prediction models $h$ on data given in bigger view $\mathcal{X}_j$ and then to estimate the values of $Y$ for query instances given in smaller view $\mathcal{X}_i$. This means that view $\mathcal{X}_j \setminus \mathcal{X}_i$ is a privileged view that is available only during the training phase.

Vapnik and Izmailov proposed in [9] the first prediction model for LUPI, SVM+. The key idea is to use the information from the privileged view to estimate the values of the slack variables in the optimization process of SVM. Pasunuri et al. proposed in [5] a LUPI model for decision trees: the data is first

---

[1] A view is a subset of available input variables.

© The Author(s), under exclusive license to Springer Nature Switzerland AG 2023
L. Iliadis et al. (Eds.): EANN 2023, CCIS 1826, pp. 144–152, 2023.
https://doi.org/10.1007/978-3-031-34204-2_13

clustered in privileged view $\mathcal{X}_j \setminus \mathcal{X}_i$ to identify "privileged" labels and then a decision tree is built by selecting input variables using supervised information from the initial output variable $Y$ and privileged labels. Fouad et al. proposed in [4] to adapt the distance metric in non-privileged view $\mathcal{X}_i$ using information from privileged view $\mathcal{X}_j \setminus \mathcal{X}_i$ and then to employ simple $k$-nearest neighbor in view $\mathcal{X}_i$ for instance prediction.

Recently, LUPI was extended for semi-supervised learning when plenty of unlabeled training data $U$ is available in addition to labeled training data $L$. The main extensions involve intrinsically semi-supervised maximum-margin classifiers [8] based on SVM+ [2,6].

In this paper we make one step further: we propose to combine the paradigm of multi-view semi-supervised learning with that of LUPI. We develop a method that implements this combination. A distinctive feature of the method is that it is classifier agnostic which contracts with most of the methods for learning using privileged information (see above). The model is experimented on a prediction task of formulating final advices for secondary education of students in the Netherlands. The experiments show that using privileged information is capable of improving multi-view semi-supervised learning.

The rest of the paper is organized as follows. The specific task of multi-view semi-supervised learning that we study in this paper is introduced in Sect. 2. We consider two methods for this task in Sect. 3. We show experimentally in Sect. 4 that the method that employs LUPI outperforms the one that does not. Section 5 concludes the paper.

## 2   Task of Multi-View Semi-Supervised Learning

We assume the presence of $K$ input variables $X_k$ and one output class variable $Y$. The input variables are divided into $M$ number of views $\mathcal{X}_m$ such that $\emptyset \subset \mathcal{X}_1 \subset \mathcal{X}_2 \subset, \ldots, \subset \mathcal{X}_M = \{X_1, X_2, \ldots, X_K\}$. We assume an unknown joint probability distribution $P(\mathcal{X}_m, Y)$ defined over $\mathcal{X}_m \times Y$ for all $m \in \{1, 2, \ldots, M\}^2$. Marginal probability distribution $P(\mathcal{X}_m)$ i.i.d. generates unlabeled data $U_m$ and probability distribution $P(\mathcal{X}_m, Y)$ i.i.d. generates labeled data $L_m$. Given training data unlabeled data $U_m$ and labeled data $L_m$ for all $m \in \{1, \ldots, M\}$, the task of multi-view semi-supervised learning is to provide an estimate $\hat{y}$ of the class variable $Y$ for a query instance $x_m$ in view $\mathcal{X}_m$ for some $m \in \{1, \ldots, M\}$. The task is illustrated in Fig. 1.

To estimate the class value for the test instance $x_m$ in view $\mathcal{X}_m$ we need a classifier $h_m : \mathcal{X}_m \to Y$ for that view. In the next section we will consider two possible ways how to learn classifiers $h_m$ for all $m \in \{1, 2, \ldots, M\}$.

## 3   Multiple Self Training with Privileged Information

We consider two model-agnostic methods for the task of multi-view semi-supervised learning defined in the previous Section. The first method is a stan-

---

[2] By construction for each $m$ with $1 < m \leq M$ probability distribution $P(\mathcal{X}_{m-1}, Y)$ is a marginal distribution of probability distribution $P(\mathcal{X}_m, Y)$.

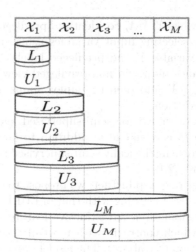

**Fig. 1.** Task of multi-view semi-supervised learning

dard multi-view self-training method (MVSTM). It does not employ privileged information and is used as a baseline in the rest of the paper. The method operates uniformly for each view $\mathcal{X}_m$ with $m \in \{1, 2, \ldots, M\}$. It first trains classifier $h_m$ on labeled training data $L_m$. Classifier $h_m$ is used to pseudo-label all the instances in the unlabeled training data $U$. Those pseudo-labeled instances that received labels with high confidences are added to data $L_m$[3] and removed from data $U_m$. The steps are repeated until convergence is established when no change in data $L_m$ and, thus, in data $U_m$ is observed. The pseudocode of the proposed method is provided in Algorithm 1.

---

**Algorithm 1.** Multi-View Self Training Method

---

**Input:**    Unlabeled data $U_m$ for $m \in \{1, 2, \ldots, M\}$,
            Labeled data $L_m$ for $m \in \{1, 2, \ldots, M\}$.
**Output:** Index set of classifiers $\{h_m\}_{m \in \{1,2,\ldots,M\}}$ .
  **for** $m := M$ to 1 **do**
    **repeat**
    */\* Self Training \*/*
    Train classifier $h_m$ on $L_m$;
    **for** each unlabeled instance $x \in U_m$ **do**
      $y = h_m(x)$;
      **if** confidence value for label $y$ is high **then**
        $L_m = L_m \cup \{(x, y)\}$;
        $U_m = U_m \setminus \{x\}$;
    **until** No change in set $L_m$;
  **output** $\{h_m\}_{m \in \{1,2,\ldots,M\}}$.

---

[3] For example, if the prediction model is a probabilistic classifier, then the confidence value is the posterior probability of the label for an unlabeled instance.

The MVSTM method trains classifiers $h_m$ independently from each other. Thus, it does not exploit the fact that probability distributions $P(\mathcal{X}_{m-1})$ and $P(\mathcal{X}_{m-1}, Y)$ for any $m$ are marginal to probability distributions $P(\mathcal{X}_m)$ and $P(\mathcal{X}_m, Y)$ for $m \in \{2, \ldots, M\}$. This issue is addressed during the prediction phase. Given a query instance $x$ in view $\mathcal{X}_{m_q}$, the predictions for $x$ from classifiers $h_m$ for $m \le m_q$ are received and aggregated using a majority voting rule. In this way the variance of the final predictions is reduced [11].

To exploit the relationship between probability distributions $P(\mathcal{X}_m)$ and $P(\mathcal{X}_m, Y)$ for $m \in \{2, \ldots, M\}$ we propose to train classifiers $h_m$ by transferring unsupervised and supervised information between the data in different views. The unsupervised information transfer is employed for unlabeled data while the supervised information transfer for labeled data. Both types of transfers are realized in the direction from big views $\mathcal{X}_{m+1}$ to small views $\mathcal{X}_m$ using two procedures described below.

For the case of unlabeled data, given views $\mathcal{X}_m$ and $\mathcal{X}_{m+1}$, we observe that any instance $x$ in $\mathcal{X}_{m+1}$ has a unique projection $p_m(x)$ in $\mathcal{X}_m$. Hence, the procedure for the unsupervised information transfer from view $\mathcal{X}_{m+1}$ to view $\mathcal{X}_m$ is straightforward: the projections $p_m(x)$ in $\mathcal{X}_m$ of all the instances $x$ in the unlabeled data set $U_{m+1}$ are added to the unlabeled data set $U_m$. In this way the unlabeled data set $U_m$ can be substantially expanded with unlabeled projections of the instances from $U_{m+1}$ which in turn can improve self training in view $\mathcal{X}_m$.

For the case of labeled data, given views $\mathcal{X}_m$ and $\mathcal{X}_{m+1}$, we observe that if we have an instance $(x, y)$ in $\mathcal{X}_{m+1} \times Y$ then its projection $p_m(x)$ in $\mathcal{X}_m$ is likely to receive the same value $y$ for the output class variable $Y$ (with probability greater than zero). We employ this observation in a classifier-guided procedure for the supervised information transfer from view $\mathcal{X}_{m+1}$ to view $\mathcal{X}_m$. The procedure first projects all the labeled instances in $L_{m+1}$ to view $\mathcal{X}_m$ and adds them to labeled data $L_m$. Then, it trains a classifier $h_m : \mathcal{X}_m \to Y$ on $L_m$. Finally, the procedure uses classifier $h_m$ to output a label $y$ for each unlabeled instance $x \in U_{m+1}$ and adds labeled instance $(x, y)$ to $L_m$ if classifier $h_m$ is confident in label $y$. In this way the labeled data sets $L_m$ can be substantially expanded which in turn can improve self training in each view.

The procedures for the unsupervised and supervised information transfer implicitly implement learning with privileged information. This is due to the fact that both rules realize information transfer in the direction from big views $\mathcal{X}_{m+1}$ to small views $\mathcal{X}_m$ for $m \in \{1, \ldots, M - 1\}$. In this way the unlabeled data set $U_m$ and labeled data set $L_m$ are enriched by unlabeled and labeled projections of instances from the unlabeled data set $U_{m+1}$ and labeled data set $L_{m+1}$, respectively. Thus, whenever we train a classifier $h_m : \mathcal{X}_m \to Y$ using a self-training algorithm on $U_m$ and $L_m$ we employ information from the privileged view $\mathcal{X}_{m+1} \setminus \mathcal{X}_m$ that is not explicitly present. This implies that whenever we classify with $h_m$ we also employ information from that privileged view.

The method that employs both procedures for the unsupervised and supervised information transfer is the main method that we propose for the task of multi-view semi-supervised learning. It is called multi-view self-training method

---

**Algorithm 2.** Multi-View Self Training Method with Privileged Information

---

**Input:**    Unlabeled data $U_m$ for $m \in \{1, 2, \ldots, M\}$,
                Labeled data $L_m$ for $m \in \{1, 2, \ldots, M\}$.
**Output:** Index set of classifiers $\{h_m\}_{m \in \{1,2,\ldots,M\}}$ .

   **for** $m := M$ **to** 1 **do**
      **repeat**
         **if** $m \neq M$ **then**
            /* *Unsupervised Information Transfer* */
            **for** each unlabeled instance $x \in U_{m+1}$ **do**
               Compute projection $p_m(x)$ of $x$ in $\mathcal{X}_m$;
               $U_m = U_m \cup \{p_m(x)\}$;
            /* *Supervised Information Transfer* */
            **for** each labeled instance $(x, y) \in L_{m+1}$ **do**
               Compute projection $p_m(x)$ of $x$ in $\mathcal{X}_m$;
               $L_m = L_m \cup \{(p_m(x), y)\}$;
         /* *Supervised Information Transfer and Self Training* */
         Train classifier $h_m$ on $L_m$;
         **for** each unlabeled instance $x \in U_m$ **do**
            $y = h_m(x)$;
            **if** confidence value for label $y$ is high **then**
               $L_m = L_m \cup \{(x, y)\}$;
               $U_m = U_m \setminus \{x\}$;
      **until** No change in set $L_m$;
      **output** $\{h_m\}_{m \in \{1,2,\ldots,M\}}$.

---

with privileged information (MVSTMPI). Its pseudocode is given in Algorithm 2. Given unlabeled data set $U_m$ and labeled data set $L_m$ for all the views $\mathcal{X}_m$ with $m \in \{1, 2, \ldots, M\}$, the method outputs an index set of classifiers $\{h_m\}_{m \in \{1,2,\ldots,M\}}$ for those views. This is realized iteratively from big views $\mathcal{X}_{m+1}$ to small views $\mathcal{X}_m$. That is why, in the very first iteration when $m = M$, the method does not perform any information transfer. It just learns classifier $h_M$ with self training on unlabeled data and labeled data sets $U_M$ and $L_M$, and then updates these sets if there are any changes caused by self training. In the next iteration for $m < M$ the method enriches first the unlabeled data set $U_m$ and labeled data set $L_m$ by unsupervised and supervised information transfer from the unlabeled data and labeled data sets $U_{m+1}$ and $L_{m+1}$. Once the sets $U_m$ and $L_m$ are complete, the method trains classifier $h_m$ using self training on those sets. Then, it updates these sets if there are any changes caused by self training.

The MVSTMPI method is a semi-supervised method. Its main differences w.r.t. other semi-supervised methods are as follows:

- the unlabeled data in each view can be enriched with data from bigger views, and
- the labeled data in each view can be enriched by labeling unlabeled data using information from bigger views.

Since data enrichment is realized prior of actual process of self training, it can improve the process of semi-supervised learning.

The prediction procedure related to the MVSTMPI method is similar to that of the MVSTM method. Given a query instance $x$ in view $\mathcal{X}_{m_q}$, the predictions for $x$ from classifiers $h_m$ for $m \leq m_q$ are received and aggregated using a majority voting rule. As before we aim at reducing the variance of the final predictions.

## 4   Experimental Study

The MVSTMPI method was designed on request to develop classifiers capable of predicting advices for secondary education for Dutch primary-education students. Below we first describe the task, then the experimental setting, and, finally, the results.

### 4.1   Task of Predicting Student Advice for Secondary Education

Any student in the Netherlands receives a final advice for secondary education by the end of her/his primary school. There exist four possible advises: profession-oriented education, technical education, higher general continued education, and preparatory scientific education. The task of formulating the advises is a task of teachers that follow the students: they take into account 51 nationally standardized student tests for language and math over the last six years of the primary school. The accuracy of the advises is important because they determine the optimality of the educational environment for further development of the students. That is why, we were asked to develop a decision-support system for teachers. The system includes a classifier that predicts the advice for a student given the student tests grades.

We formalized the task of predicting advice for secondary education as follows. Every student is represented by 51 input variables $X_k$ that correspond to 51 nationally standardized student tests. The variables are organized in 6 views, $\mathcal{X}_1 \subset \mathcal{X}_2 \subset \mathcal{X}_3 \subset \mathcal{X}_4 \subset \mathcal{X}_5 \subset \mathcal{X}_6$, so that variables $X_k$ that correspond to the tests prior to year $m$ or in year $m$ belong to view $\mathcal{X}_m$. This means that a student in year $m$ is given by view $\mathcal{X}_m$.

Since the advices for secondary education are given in the last year, only students in year 6 have received actual advice. This means that the output variable $Y$, that stands for the type of advice, has value only for students in year 6. Thus, the data of students for year $m < 6$ is not labeled and the data of students for year $m = 6$ is labeled. This makes the task for predicting advice for secondary education as a specific instantiation of the task for multi-view semi-supervised learning when unlabeled data $U_m$ is non-empty and labeled data $L_m$ is empty for $m < 6$ and unlabeled data $U_m$ is empty and labeled data $L_m$ is non-empty for $m = 6$ (see Fig. 1).

The data we received consists of records of 30 000 students collected over 11 years. We selected further these records in such a way that we could estimate the accuracy rate of every classifier $h_m$ for $m \in \{1, \ldots, 6\}$. For this purpose we recorded the final advices (labels) of the students in every year $m < 6$ noting that they had actually received these advices after $6 - m$ years. This supervised information was used only for estimating the accuracy rate of classifiers $h_m$, not for their training.

## 4.2  Experimental Setup

We experimented with the two methods proposed in the previous section: the MVSTM and MVSTMPI methods in order to decide whether privileged information improves the generalization performance. In this context, we note that the MVSTM method is not directly applicable to our task of predicting advice for secondary education since for $m < 6$ we have only unlabeled data $U_m$. Thus, we created a special version of the data for the MVSTM method. We artificially created labeled data $L_m$ for any $m < 6$ by projecting labeled data $L_6$ in view $\mathcal{X}_m$.

The base classifier for the MVSTM and MVSTMPI methods was the XGBoost classifier [1] with default settings. The methods were left till self-training convergence that was established after 2 self-training iterations for both methods.

The method of validation was 5-fold cross validation. The generalization performance of the classifiers was measured using the accuracy rate.

## 4.3  Results

**Table 1.** The accuracy rates of classifiers $f_1$ to $f_6$ in the MVSTM and MVSTMPI methods on the student advise data. The accuracy rates are given for the case of no self training (No-ST), the first self-training iteration, and the second self-training iteration. The accuracy rates classifiers $f_1$ to $f_6$ of MVSTM and MVSTMPI are compared for each iteration using a paired t-test on 5% significance level and statistically better classifiers are given in bold.

| MVSTM | No-ST | iter.1 | iter.2 | MVSTMPI | No-ST | iter.1 | iter.2 |
|-------|-------|--------|--------|---------|-------|--------|--------|
| $h_1$ | 0.46 | 0.47 | 0.47 | $h_1$ | 0.46 | **0.49** | **0.49** |
| $h_2$ | 0.54 | 0.54 | 0.54 | $h_2$ | 0.54 | **0.56** | **0.57** |
| $h_3$ | 0.58 | 0.59 | 0.59 | $h_3$ | 0.58 | **0.60** | **0.60** |
| $h_4$ | 0.61 | 0.62 | 0.63 | $h_4$ | 0.61 | **0.64** | **0.64** |
| $h_5$ | 0.67 | 0.67 | 0.67 | $h_5$ | 0.67 | 0.68 | 0.68 |
| $h_6$ | 0.72 | 0.72 | 0.72 | $h_6$ | 0.72 | 0.72 | 0.72 |

The results are provided in Table 1. They show that the MVSTM and MVSTMPI methods produce the same results when no self training takes place (due to the specific design of the data for the MVSTM method). They also produce the same results for classifier $h_6$ since the data of the year-6 students is fully labeled. In all other cases when self training is on, the MVSTMPI method outperforms the MVSTM method. We compared the classifiers of both methods for each iteration using a paired t-test on 5% significance level. The test revealed that classifiers $h_1$, $h_2$, $h_3$, and $h_4$ in the MVSTMPI method have significantly higher accuracy rates than those of their counter parts from the MVSTM method. The biggest gain we received for classifiers $h_1$ and $h_2$. This is due to the fact that the unsupervised and supervised information transfer is maximized for views $\mathcal{X}_1$ and $\mathcal{X}_2$; i.e. learning with privileged information is best presented for these views.

## 5  Conclusion

In this paper we proposed a novel method for multi-view semi-supervised learning using privileged information. The method is classifier agnostic in contract to most of the methods for learning using privileged information. The method was tested on the task of predicting student advice for secondary education. The experiments show that privileged information improves the predicted advises and this improvement depends on semi-supervised learning. Therefore, future research will focus on advanced semi-supervised learning algorithms that add newly labeled data only if it statistically complies with the initial data [7] or it directly leads to a better performance [3].

## References

1. Chen, T., Guestrin, C.: Xgboost: a scalable tree boosting system. In: Proceedings of the 22nd ACM SIGKDD International Conference on Knowledge Discovery and Data Mining, San Francisco, CA, USA, pp. 785–794 (2016)
2. Chen, X., Gong, C., Ma, C., Huang, X., Yang, J:. Privileged semi-supervised learning. In: 2018 IEEE International Conference on Image Processing, ICIP 2018, Athens, Greece, 7–10 October 2018, pp. 2999–3003. IEEE (2018)
3. Courtnage, C., Smirnov, E.: Shapley-value data valuation for semi-supervised learning. In: Soares, C., Torgo, L. (eds.) DS 2021. LNCS (LNAI), vol. 12986, pp. 94–108. Springer, Cham (2021). https://doi.org/10.1007/978-3-030-88942-5_8
4. Fouad, S., Tiño, P., Raychaudhury, S., Schneider, P.: Incorporating privileged information through metric learning. IEEE Trans. Neural Netw. Learn. Syst. **24**(7), 1086–1098 (2013)
5. Pasunuri, R., Odom, P., Khot, T., Kersting, K., Natarajan, S.: Learning with privileged information: decision-trees and boosting. http://users.sussex.ac.uk/~nq28/beyondlabeler/PasOdoKhoKeretal16.pdf. Accessed 16 Apr 2023
6. Qi, Z., Tian, Y., Niu, L., Wang, B.: Semi-supervised classification with privileged information. Int. J. Mach. Learn. Cybern. **6**(4), 667–676 (2015)
7. Smirnov, E.N., Vanderlooy, S., Sprinkhuizen-Kuyper, I.G.: Meta-typicalness approach to reliable classification. In: Proceedings of the 17th European Conference on Artificial Intelligence, ECAI 2006, vol. 141 of Frontiers in Artificial Intelligence and Applications, pp. 811–812. IOS Press (2006)
8. van Engelen, J.E., Hoos, H.H.: A survey on semi-supervised learning. Mach. Learn. **109**(2), 373–440 (2020)

 9. Vapnik, V., Izmailov, R.: Learning using privileged information: similarity control and knowledge transfer. J. Mach. Learn. Res. **16**, 2023–2049 (2015)
10. Vapnik, V., Vashist, A.: A new learning paradigm: learning using privileged information. Neural Netw. **22**(5–6), 544–557 (2009)
11. Zhao, J., Xie, X., Xin, X., Sun, S.: Multi-view learning overview: recent progress and new challenges. Inf. Fusion **38**, 43–54 (2017)

# Complex Dynamic Networks' Optimization/Graph Neural Networks

# A Multi-relationship Language Acquisition Model for Predicting Child Vocabulary Growth

Andrew Roxburgh[✉], Floriana Grasso, and Terry R. Payne

Department of Computer Science, University of Liverpool, Liverpool L69 3BX, UK
a.roxburgh@liverpool.ac.uk

**Abstract.** If we can predict the words a child is likely to learn next, it may lay the foundations for developing a tool to assist child language acquisition, especially for children experiencing language delay. Previous studies have demonstrated vocabulary predictions using neural network techniques and graph models; however, individually these models do not fully capture the complexities of language learning in infants. In this paper, we describe a multi-relationship-layer predictive model, based on a graph neural network. Our model combines vocabulary development over time with quantified connections between words calculated from fifteen different norms, incorporating an ensemble output stage to combine the predictions from each layer. We present results from each relationship layer and the most effective ensemble arrangement.

**Keywords:** graph neural networks · language acquisition

## 1 Introduction

The acquisition of language and communication skills during early years plays a crucial role in the overall cognitive and social growth of children, such that any interruption or delay can have far reaching consequences to language development and educational attainment in later years. Language impairment, where a child's language abilities are insufficient for their next stage of cognitive, educational, and social development, has been demonstrated to impede the child's development from an early age, and without proper support they can fall behind and fail to catch up with their peers [1]. *Developmental Language Disorder* (DLD), which is a condition whereby a child's language development is delayed or disordered for no clear reason, affects 6.44% of all UK children [2], and is the most prevalent childhood disability, requiring specialist support in order for affected children to learn and communicate to the very best of their ability [3]. DLD has been linked with lower academic achievement, lower employment and poor mental health [4]. Even in neurologically 'typical' children, factors such as their communication environment and family circumstances can have an effect on their language development, and research has shown that delayed communication skills can lead to adverse learning outcomes several years later [5].

© The Author(s), under exclusive license to Springer Nature Switzerland AG 2023
L. Iliadis et al. (Eds.): EANN 2023, CCIS 1826, pp. 155–167, 2023.
https://doi.org/10.1007/978-3-031-34204-2_14

To establish whether a child's language is developing normally, standardised tools are used such as the MacArthur-Bates Communicative Development Inventory (CDI) [6,7]. The CDI consists of a series of questions and checklists designed to assess vocabulary comprehension, production, gesture use, and early grammar. It is usually accompanied by a Family Questionnaire that is compiled by the child's primary carer or by a researcher. By comparing the answers against national norms, it is possible to establish whether the child is developing normally or could be delayed.

Originally designed as a paper instrument, online web or mobile platform versions offer novel research prospects such as the capability to offer recommendations and direction to parents regarding the words they should teach their child next.

A simple but naive way of achieving this would be by referencing the *Age-of-Acquisition* norms [8] that identify words that typical children would acquire at a similar age. However, children tend not to learn the same words at the same rate or age, and thus a more tailored approach is required, based on the child's current knowledge. This predictive technique could be used to inform the child's primary carer of 'candidate' words to emphasise when teaching language [9], and form the basis of a novel language intervention tool. In this paper we present a novel approach for predicting a child's language acquisition by utilizing Spatio-Temporal Graph Neural Networks (STGCN), which aims to improve upon the existing literature in terms of accuracy. We evaluate the viability and efficacy of using such a network, utilising published lexical datasets; and illustrate how this approach is worthy of further investigation.

## 2 Existing Work

A seminal work on the prediction of word acquisition by young children based on their current vocabulary, Beckage, Mozer & Colunga [10] explored the use of conditional probabilities by examining the CDI questionnaire data of 77 subjects over a 1-year period at monthly intervals. By using a network growth technique, they built three different models based on calculating the conditional probability of a word being learnt within the next month using different approaches, given words that had been learnt overall and in the previous month. They found that the accuracy of predictions could be enhanced by increasing the temporal resolution of the data (e.g. more frequent than monthly intervals) or by including more meaningful connections between words in the predictive model.

Other work has looked at the use of Artificial Neural Network (ANN) models for predicting the probabilities of word acquisition over a subsequent month [11]. ANNs have a long history of use in early learning research including language modelling, and have proven themselves to be excellent statistical learning tools. A number of different neural-network based predictive models were investigated using various qualitatively different sources of information as inputs [10]. All of these models augmented an initial set of 6 inputs representing demographic information about the child. One model used a representation of the child's current vocabulary, as indicated by the answers provided by their parents to the

CDI questionnaire, consisting of an additional 677 inputs. A different model utilised a representation of the semantic features of words in the child's vocabulary, based on the McRae feature norms [12], through 30 additional inputs. Other models considered the phonological composition of the child's productive vocabulary (represented by 37 additional inputs), or representations that captured the production of words within specific categories of the CDI questionnaire (22 additional inputs). Other studies exploited a Word2Vec [13] based representation of the child's productive vocabulary that combined vectors in a high-dimensional linguistic space and comprising 200 inputs.

Beckage et. al. [11] also explored the use of ensemble models to determine if some language representations were unnecessary or if the combination of multiple representations could improve the model's predictability. From these studies, they observe that: (i) a child's existing vocabulary and demographic information significantly affect their future vocabulary development; (ii) the specific words a child knows are valuable in forecasting their future vocabulary growth; (iii) the model that considered a child's current vocabulary performed better than one relying solely on demographic data; and (iv) the words in a child's vocabulary contain valuable information besides their age and current vocabulary size. They also noted that models based on semantic features and phonology were less effective than those models based on child demographics and current vocabulary, as they don't meaningfully combine the child's existing vocabulary knowledge.

## 3  Child Vocabulary as a Multi-relationship Graph

Child vocabulary growth has been modelled in the literature using a variety of network-based methods. Graphs have been used when modelling vocabulary growth over time [14], whereas neural networks were used when attempting to model the way that a brain acquires language [15]. These models exploit the fact that a typical vocabulary consists of a collection of words that are inherently connected with each other, and as such can be easily represented as a network. Typically, words are represented as nodes, with edges representing some inter-word relationship (e.g. Fig. 1 shows a semantic network that focuses on the word *water*). In this model, each node of the graph represents a word and incorporates a feature vector, which contains information about the state or features of the word. Each node is also associated with a state representation of the child's level of knowledge regarding that node:

1. a child may understand a word without production;
2. a child may produce a word without meaning,
3. a child may both understand and produce a word, or
4. a child may have no knowledge of a word.

While cognitive nuances of word knowledge extend beyond these four discrete states, for the purpose of analyzing a child's vocabulary, they serve as easily observable and universally understood indicators.

In our study, we enhanced the model by integrating multiple relationships that are effectively superimposed upon each other as in layers. In our structure, the nodes, representing words, are shared across all layers, while each layer exhibits distinct edge configurations (see Fig. 2 for a visualisation). To incorporate a new observation into the model, the nodes' feature vectors are suitably adjusted to capture word knowledge at the respective time period.

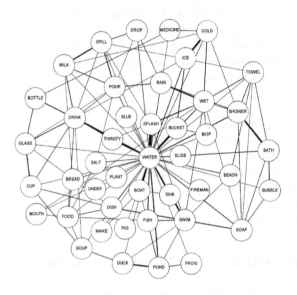

**Fig. 1.** Simplified example of a vocabulary graph: word-association graph focused on *water*. Edge and node features not shown.

As to which relationships to include in the model, we excluded those focusing on words from an exclusively adult viewpoint, and we concentrated on those more aligned with an infant's cognitive perspective, and grounded in the literature. Relationships commonly used in language research include *Semantic Feature norms* (ratings of the attributes or characteristics of words that provide information about their meaning in context), *Word Association data* (for a given cue word, the target word that a person immediately thinks of next), *Phonological Similarity data* (the degree to which words sound similar when spoken), and Psycholinguistic norms such as: *Imageability* (the ease with which a word can be mentally visualised); *Concreteness* (the tangibility of a word as opposed to an abstract concept, e.g. 'chair' is more concrete than 'time'); *Familiarity* (rating a word based on how commonly it is used in everyday speech); and *Word Length* (a measure of how difficult a word is to remember or say). From a cognitive research perspective, *Sensorimotor Norms* allow to compare words from the conceptual point of view of children at the earliest development stage, when they learn to use their senses to build an understanding of the world and use motor movements (grasping, sucking, touching) to interact with it.

Specifically, for our model, we chose: Nelson *et al.* association norms [16], which are utilised to construct a layer that accounts for the associative relationships between words in human memory; the semantic feature production norms by McRae *et al.* [12] and those by Buchanan *et al.* [17] to measure the similarity of meaning between two given words. We also incorporate a measure of Phonological Similarity, based on IPA phonemes, which are extracted from the BEEP phonetic dictionary [18]. Finally, we use the Lancaster Sensorimotor Norms [19] which evaluate English words based on six perceptual modalities: touch, hearing, smell, taste, vision, and interoception), and five action effectors: mouth/throat, hand/arm, foot/leg, (head excluding mouth/throat), and torso.

**Fig. 2.** A Multi-relationship vocabulary graph structure.

Both McRae *et al.* and Buchanan *et al.* data is published along with cosine similarity matrices, allowing for direct representation of connection strengths between words. To similarly adapt the Lancaster norms to our model's structure, a weighted adjacency matrix was created for all possible word pairs within each category. This weight was calculated by normalizing the product of each pair's scores, resulting in a strong connection between words with high scores in the same category and weak connections between dissimilar words. Self-loops are given a weight of 1.0. The Phonological Similarity model was constructed by decomposing each word into its constituent IPA phonemes, derived from the BEEP, and computing, for every pair of words, similarity scores based on the Jaccard similarity metric, allowing us to create an adjacency matrix.

For all models, we used the adjacency matrices to define graph edges, and created a list of nodes by de-duplicating the edges list. The nodes' feature vectors represent the level of knowledge that a child has of the word. This resulted in a collection of graphs $G_n = (V_n, E_n)$ for each category, where V represents the vertices (i.e. nodes) and E represents the edges. A node list was created for every observation in the data and was populated with the corresponding observed data. These node lists were then combined to form a time series. The edge lists were processed by combining each edge list with each node list in the time series, resulting in the creation of a time series of graphs for each of the 15 models. This was used as an input to our model, as explained in the following Section.

## 4   Model Selection

Our aim is to predict a child's future vocabulary based on the child's past and existing knowledge. Given our series of graphs representing different relationships between words in a vocabulary, we can embed the nodes with feature vectors representing the child's current knowledge of the word (Fig. 3). Given that each node has been classified as being 'understood', 'understood and spoken', 'spoken but not understood', or 'unknown', a classifier is required that can re-classify the nodes based on their features, connections and history.

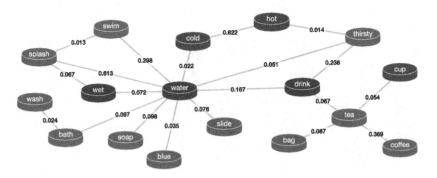

**Fig. 3.** Example graph portion representing words and semantic connections between them. Edges show strength of connection (in this case semantic relatedness). Node colours represent word's feature vectors: *wet*, *water* and *drink* are known and understood by the child; *cold*, *hot*, and *cup* are either known or understood but not both, and the remaining nodes represent words that are completely unknown to the child.

*Graph Neural Networks* (GNN) efficiently apply machine learning to graph-structured data [20]. GNNs process the input graph by taking each node in turn and aggregating information from its neighboring nodes and edges, updating the representations of the nodes in each iteration, until a final representation for each node is obtained. These node embeddings encode the structural and feature data of themselves, their neighbours, and ultimately of all other nodes in the graph, and can then be used in further operations such as edge prediction, classification, labelling, feature prediction and more. In our application we classify the nodes to determine the probability that the words that they represent are 'known'. *Graph Convolutional Networks* [21] are a variety of GNN that attempt to apply a convolution operation to graphs, in a similar manner to traditional Convolutional Neural Networks (CNNs). The type of GCN is determined by the convolution filtering method and is either Spectral (where the convolutions take place in the Fourier domain) or Spatial (in the spatial domain). Following Kipf & Welling [22], we use a technique that bridges the two methods - it uses spectral graph convolutions, but with some simplifications to reduce the processing overhead that comes with computing a Fourier transform of a graph.

An extension of the GCN model is the *Spatio-Temporal Graph Convolutional Network* (STGCN), which considers features of a GCN as a function of both space and time. They have been shown to work well in problems of traffic prediction [23] where the aim is to predict the traffic speeds, given information from sensors on other roads. The data from a road network with traffic sensors can be described as a graph, with the sensors serving as nodes, direct routes between sensors as edges, and the distance between sensors as edge weights. Each node may have features such as vehicle speed or number of passing vehicles. By taking the history of the sensor data into account as well as the relationship of the nodes to each other, features of particular sensors can be predicted accurately and efficiently [24]. This scenario is analogous to our word prediction problem - nodes representing words rather than sensors, edges representing inter-word relationship strength rather than distance between sensors, and features representing the probability of increased word knowledge rather than vehicle speed. By combining graph convolutional operations with temporal convolutional operations, STGCNs are able to model the dependencies between nodes in a dynamic graph structure over time, making it suitable for forecasting the relationships between nodes at a future point in time, based on recent history as well as current state. This makes it suitable for forecasting the future state of a child's vocabulary, given current and past states of the vocabulary and the relationships between words.

## 5 Methodology

We have developed a STGCN-based model using Python and *Stellargraph* [25], a software library built on *Tensorflow* [26] which facilitates the construction of graph-based machine learning models. Our full model consists of 15 relationship layers, each of which is a separate STGCN model that has been individually trained and executed. Some nodes in these relationship layers may not have connections as they have no meaningful associations with other words. When a new prediction is required, a vector representing the child's current vocabulary is used to populate the feature vectors of each node on each relationship layer - indicating that certain new words have been learned. The GCN classifier, in conjunction with the STGCN's spatial-temporal block, is then applied to these input graphs to re-classify the 'unknown' nodes, from which we can determine the words that are likely to be influenced the most by its neighbours, and so may be learned next. This produces a list of candidate words from each relationship layer, from which the most likely ones can be determined.

### 5.1   Assumptions and Data Preparation

**Observational Data.** Our observational dataset consists of item-level CDI Survey responses extracted from all available forms in English downloaded from Wordbank [27], combined with additional data collected via volunteers through our website. We have chosen only data for which there are longitudinal sequences, to enable the STGCN algorithm's spatial-temporal block to train on temporal data. Words were converted to our standardised vocabulary to allow for dialect differences. The overall data consisted of 718 observations (i.e. vocabulary inventories), with 150 test subjects, each providing between four and six consecutive observations.

Due to the nature of human-collected data about human behaviour, inevitably there will be errors present. For instance, a child may be observed at one time period as understanding, but not producing, a particular word, e.g. the child may appear to understand 'bath' by going to the bathroom when a parent says it. On a subsequent observation the child may use the word 'bath', but use it incorrectly to refer to, say, a bath toy kept in the bathroom. Or, the parent may not be aware that a child knows a particular word. The child may have used the word at a grandparents' home for instance. Parents can change their mind if they believe that a child has said and/or understood a word, but then they realise it is not so. Finally there is the added complication of correctly understanding words produced by a toddler, which can often be far from clear. Such data presents challenges, especially in a smaller dataset, where errors can have a bigger negative effect on the model. Given that errors involving words dropping out of the observed vocabulary could adversely affect the ability to accurately train a classifier on the data, we remove contradictory data by generating two datasets: an **optimistic dataset**, in which we assume that children have continued to understand the word in subsequent observation periods, and a **pessimistic dataset** where we assume that they are false observations and that the children did not in fact understand the word during the first observation.

**Relationship Datasets.** Arguably, standardizing data is one of the biggest challenges when combining multiple independent sources of language data into one model accounting for synonyms ('rabbit' and 'bunny'), multiple dialects ('mommy', 'mummy', 'mom', 'mum', 'ma', 'mama') and international spelling variations ('colour' and 'color'). In these cases we renamed the words to match our own standardised vocabulary. To address the issue of homographs (words with multiple meanings, like 'back' or 'drink'), we maintain standardization by appending a label to ambiguous words (e.g. 'drink' becomes 'drink(beverage)' and 'drink(verb)'). For a child, certain words may hold different meanings compared to adults. As an example, the idea of 'fish' being a food and 'fish' being an animal are typically treated as distinct concepts for children, whereas for adults 'fish' is understood as both a food and an animal at the same time. Again these words are appended with a context-appropriate label. We created a Python script to simplify the labelling and transforming process, necessary for handling all 15 relationship datasets and all observational data.

After finishing the pre-processing of the input data, the data representing the structure of input graphs was generated. For each relationship model, this included Edge data, represented by an adjacency matrix, and a time-series of Node lists, each depicting the state of nodes at a particular observation and featuring a feature vector indicating the child's understanding of the word at that time. This comprehension attribute was assigned a starting value from one of four levels, reflecting the child's knowledge of that word at the given observation. (0.0 representing no comprehension, 0.3 representing production without understanding, 0.6 representing understanding but no production, and 1.0 representing full comprehension and production).

## 5.2  Training and Validation

The training stage of our STGCN involves presenting the model with a time series of observations of childrens' vocabulary changing over time. The hyperparameters of our STGCN were: Epoch size 1000, Batch size 6, optimiser ADAM, the loss function was Mean Absolute Error (MAE), and the metric function was Mean Squared Error. Our Feedforward Neural Network model, trained only on vocabulary data with no relationship element, had hyperparameters: Two hidden layers, Epoch size 1000, Learning Rate 0.8, Batch size 6, Momentum 0.7, Alpha Decay 200, Loss Function Mean Squared Error (MSE).

**Table 1.** Example prediction made on the same data sample by all models. The Ground Truth column shows new words that have been learned by the child since the previous observation. The dots represent correct prediction of increased knowledge.

| Ground Truth | Head | Torso | Vis | Mouth | Foot | Olf | Gust | Inter | Haptic | Aud | Hand | Nels | Mcrae | Phon | Buch |
|---|---|---|---|---|---|---|---|---|---|---|---|---|---|---|---|
| BAA BAA |  | • |  | • |  | • | • |  |  |  |  | • |  | • | • |
| BABY | • |  | • |  |  |  | • |  |  |  |  | • |  |  | • |
| BATH | • | • | • |  | • | • |  | • |  |  |  | • | • | • | • |
| BUBBLES | • |  | • |  |  | • |  |  |  |  |  | • |  |  |  |
| CHOO CHOO |  |  | • |  |  |  |  |  |  |  |  |  |  |  |  |
| DADDY | • | • | • | • | • | • | • | • | • | • | • | • | • | • | • |
| GRANDMA | • | • | • | • | • | • | • | • |  | • | • |  | • | • | • |
| GRANDPA | • | • | • | • |  | • | • |  |  |  |  | • | • | • |  |
| MEOW |  | • | • |  |  |  |  |  |  |  |  |  |  |  | • |
| MILK | • | • | • | • | • | • | • |  |  | • | • | • | • | • | • |
| MOO |  |  | • |  |  |  |  |  |  |  |  |  |  |  |  |
| MORE | • |  | • |  |  |  | • |  |  |  |  | • | • |  | • |
| MUMMY | • |  | • | • | • | • | • | • |  | • | • | • | • |  | • |
| QUACK | • | • | • |  |  | • |  |  |  |  |  |  | • |  |  |
| WOOF | • | • | • |  |  | • |  |  |  |  | • | • | • | • | • |
| YES | • | • | • |  |  | • |  | • |  |  |  | • | • | • | • |
| YUM | • | • | • |  |  | • |  | • |  |  |  | • | • | • | • |

## 5.3  Ensemble Models

Given that we were utilising multiple predictive models for comparison in our experiment, an ensemble algorithm was used in order to combine the outputs of the individual models, and potentially improve predictability. There are many approaches to model ensembles [28] and we evaluated the following techniques:

*Simple Average, Weighted Average, Majority Voting, OR Classifier* and *AND Classifier*. For each of these techniques, the predictive models' outputs were evaluated to determine an increased level of knowledge, whereby a positive result was obtained when the model predicted productive or receptive knowledge of a word when the most recent observation showed that the child did not possess such knowledge. The *Simple Average* ensemble takes the mean of all individual models to arrive at a final output. The *Weighted Average* obtains the combined output by averaging the individual models with different weights [28], assigning more importance to some models compared to others. We chose to build fifteen Weighted Average ensembles, each giving more weight to a different model, and include the best two performers in the results table. *Majority Voting* obtains a positive result only if more than half of the models have produced a positive prediction. The *OR Classifier* operates in a similar fashion to the OR logic gate, whereby a positive output is obtained if any of the models indicate a positive prediction. Similarly the *AND Classifier* functions like an AND logic gate, producing a positive outcome only when all input models agree on a prediction.

**Table 2.** Results scores of all individual models and ensembles.

| Model | Precision | Recall | F1 | Accuracy |
|---|---|---|---|---|
| **Semantic Relationships:** | | | | |
| McRae *et al.* | 0.32 | 0.48 | 0.38 | 0.58 |
| Buchanan *et al.* | 0.37 | 0.41 | 0.39 | 0.58 |
| **Word Association Relationships:** | | | | |
| Nelson *et al.* | 0.33 | 0.41 | 0.37 | 0.57 |
| **Phonological Relationships:** | | | | |
| BEEP (Jaccard) | 0.34 | 0.53 | 0.41 | 0.55 |
| **Sensorimotor Relationships:** | | | | |
| Lancaster (Head) | 0.30 | 0.46 | 0.36 | 0.53 |
| Lancaster (Gustatory) | 0.35 | 0.35 | 0.40 | 0.57 |
| Lancaster (Mouth) | 0.32 | 0.46 | 0.38 | 0.59 |
| Lancaster (Olfactory) | 0.37 | 0.47 | 0.41 | 0.58 |
| Lancaster (Torso) | 0.36 | 0.42 | 0.39 | 0.58 |
| Lancaster (FootLeg) | 0.33 | 0.47 | 0.38 | 0.56 |
| Lancaster (Visual) | 0.34 | 0.53 | 0.41 | 0.56 |
| Lancaster (Interoceptive) | 0.34 | 0.40 | 0.37 | 0.56 |
| Lancaster (Auditory) | 0.36 | 0.46 | 0.40 | 0.58 |
| Lancaster (Haptic) | 0.39 | 0.43 | 0.41 | 0.59 |
| Lancaster (HandArm) | 0.32 | 0.41 | 0.36 | 0.56 |
| **Ensembles:** | | | | |
| Simple Average | 0.22 | 0.24 | 0.23 | 0.26 |
| Weighted Average (Buch. Semantic) | 0.38 | 0.52 | 0.42 | 0.73 |
| Weighted Average (Lanc Haptic) | 0.37 | 0.52 | 0.43 | 0.72 |
| 'OR' Classifier | 0.23 | 0.81 | 0.37 | 0.43 |
| 'AND' Classifier | 0.06 | 0.07 | 0.06 | 0.36 |
| Majority Vote | 0.13 | 0.36 | 0.20 | 0.40 |
| 2-Layer Feedforward Neural Network | 0.79 | 0.60 | 0.68 | 0.64 |

## 5.4   Evaluation

By way of illustration of a typical result, Table 1 displays a randomly selected output from the test dataset for each individual model. Despite similarities in some regions (e.g. all models accurately predicting the appearance of the word 'Daddy' on this observation), it does show some stark differences in predictive accuracy, at least on a per-observation level, as one may expect considering the differences in word relationships.

The 'optimistic' version of the observational data, in which we corrected contradictions in observations by assuming the child did in fact know words that appeared to be 'forgotten', outperformed the 'pessimistic' version, which assumed an observational error by the carer and that the child did not know the word.

Table 2 shows the preliminary results of the fifteen models and six ensembles, plus the output from a Feedforward Neural Network for comparison. In our experiments, the standard Neural Network model displayed the highest accuracy of 0.64, rendering it the best performing individual model. However the Weighted Average ensembles all outperformed the Neural Network, with the Buchanan-emphasised variant performing the best, showing an accuracy of 0.73. The other ensemble algorithms generally showed a decrease in performance.

# 6   Conclusions and Future Work

We have presented a multi-relationship model that can be used to make predictions about a child's upcoming vocabulary, and the process of constructing it. It has built upon ideas from existing research into infant language acquisition prediction using Neural Networks and graph models, and we have expanded this by considering the current and past vocabularies of a given child combined with multiple relationships between the words. Our findings have shown increased performance of this technique over a standard Neural Network based predictor. Consequently, this technique could serve as a viable foundation for a prospective tool for parents and clinicians, by providing suggestions regarding the most effective words to teach a given child at a particular time for optimal results.

We have identified a number priorities for future development. First, training on more observational data should increase the predictive power of the models. Second, we plan to expand the number of models used to inform the input graphs, including additional psycholinguistic and phonological relationships. This in itself may open up new avenues of research. Third, there may be validity in attempting to optimise the weights used to bias the Weighted Average ensemble. Finally, there are parameters chosen during the process of transforming data from norms into graphs that are worth examining for opportunities to optimise.

# References

1. Feinstein, L., Duckworth, K.: Development in the early years: its importance for school performance and adult outcomes. Centre for Research on the Wider Benefits of Learning, London (2006)
2. Scerri, T.S., et al.: DCDC2, KIAA0319 and CMIP are associated with reading-related traits. Biol Psychiatry **70**(3), 237–245 (2011)
3. Lindsay, G., et al.: Educational provision for children with specific speech and language difficulties in England and Wales. In: IoE and CEDAR (2002)
4. Clegg, J., et al.: Developmental language disorders - a follow-up in later adult life. cognitive, language and psychosocial outcomes. J. Child Psychol. Psychiat. **46**, 128–149 (2005)
5. Roulstone, S., et al.: Investigating the role of language in children's early educational outcomes. Technical Report DFE-RR134, Department of Education, UK (2011)
6. Fenson, L., et al.: MacArthur-Bates Communicative Development Inventories. Paul H. Brookes Publishing Company, Baltimore (2007)
7. Alcock, K.J., et al.: Construction and standardisation of the UK communicative development inventory (UK-CDI), words and gestures. In: International Conference on Infant Studies (2016)
8. Stadthagen-Gonzalez, H., Davis, C.J.: The Bristol norms for age of acquisition, imageability, and familiarity. Behav. Res. Methods **38**(4), 598–605 (2006)
9. Johnson, E.K., Jusczyk, P.W.: Word segmentation by 8-month-olds: when speech cues count more than statistics. J. Mem. Lang. **44**, 548–567 (2001)
10. Beckage, N., Mozer, M., Colunga, E.: Predicting a child's trajectory of lexical acquisition. In: Noelle, D.C., et al. (eds.) 37th Annual Meeting of the Cognitive Science Society, CogSci. cognitivesciencesociety.org (2015)
11. Beckage, N.M., Mozer, M.C., Colunga, E.: Quantifying the role of vocabulary knowledge in predicting future word learning. IEEE Trans. Cogn. Dev. Syst. **12**, 148–159 (2020)
12. McRae, K., et al.: Semantic feature production norms for a large set of living and nonliving things. Behav. Res. Methods **37**, 547–559 (2005)
13. Mikolov, T., Chen, K., Corrado, G., Dean, J.: Efficient estimation of word representations in vector space. In: Bengio, Y., LeCun, Y. (eds.) 1st International Conference on Learning Representations, ICLR 2013, Workshop Track Proceedings (2013)
14. Ke, J., Yao, Y.: Analysing language development from a network approach. J. Quant. Linguist. **15**(1), 70–99 (2008)
15. Sims, C., Schilling, S., Colunga, E.: Exploring the developmental feedback loop: word learning in neural networks and toddlers. In: Knauff, M., Pauen, M., Sebanz, N., Wachsmuth, I. (eds.) Proceedings of the Annual Meeting of the Cognitive Science Society, CogSci 2013, vol. 35, pp. 3408–3413 (2013)
16. Nelson, D.L., et al.: The university of South Florida free association, rhyme, and word fragment norms. Behav. Res. Methods Inst. Comput. **36**, 402–407 (2004)
17. Buchanan, L., Westbury, C., Burgess, C.: Characterizing semantic space: neighborhood effects in word recognition. Psychon. Bull. Rev. **8**, 531–544 (2001)
18. Robinson, T.: British English Example Pronunciation (BEEP) dictionary (1996). http://svr-www.eng.cam.ac.uk/comp.speech/Section1/Lexical/beep.html
19. Lynott, D., et al.: The Lancaster Sensorimotor Norms: multidimensional measures of perceptual and action strength for 40,000 English words. Behav. Res. Methods **52**(3), 1271–1291 (2020)

20. Gori, M., Monfardini, G., Scarselli, F.: A new model for learning in graph domains. In: Proceedings. 2005 IEEE International Joint Conference on Neural Networks, 2005, Montreal, Que, Canada, vol. 2, pp. 729–734. IEEE (2005)

21. Bruna, J., et al.: Spectral networks and locally connected networks on graphs. arXiv:1312.6203 [cs] (2014)

22. Kipf, T., Welling, M.: Semi-supervised classification with graph convolutional networks. In: 5th International Conference on Learning Representations, ICLR 2017, Toulon, France, 24–26 April 2017, Conference Track Proceedings (2017)

23. Zhao, L., et al.: T-GCN: a temporal graph convolutional network for traffic prediction. IEEE Trans. Intell. Transp. Syst. **21**(9), 3848–3858 (2020)

24. Jiang, W., Luo, J.: Graph neural network for traffic forecasting: a survey. Expert Syst. Appl., 117921 (2022)

25. CSIRO's Data61. Stellargraph machine learning library (2018). https://github.com/stellargraph/stellargraph

26. Abadi, M., et al.: Tensorflow: large-scale machine learning on heterogeneous systems (2015). https://www.tensorflow.org/

27. Frank, M.C., Braginsky, M., Yurovsky, D., et al.: Wordbank: an open repository for developmental vocabulary data. J. Child Lang. **44**, 677–694 (2017)

28. Zhang, C., Ma, Y. (eds.): Ensemble Machine Learning. Springer, Heidelberg (2012). https://doi.org/10.1007/978-1-4419-9326-7

# Knowledge Graph of Urban Firefighting with Rule-Based Entity Extraction

Xudong Wang[1], Slam Nady[2]([✉]), Zixiang Zhang[1,2], Mingtong Zhang[1,2], and Jingrong Wang[1,2]

[1] National Languages Information Technology, Northwest Minzu University, Lanzhou 730030, China
[2] Key Laboratory of China's Ethnic Languages and Information Technology of Ministry of Education, Lanzhou, China
nady128@xbmu.edu.cn

**Abstract.** There is little research on entity extraction in constructing the knowledge graphs for urban firefighting. In this paper, we propose a rule-based entity extraction method for this field. The Precision of the experiment is 85.25%, while the Recall is 83.58%. In addition, we establish the relationships between entities in urban firefighting in advance with the experience of domain experts. Through the above two steps, we have initially established a knowledge graph in the field of urban firefighting, which including 13 types of entities and 12 types of relationships. This study will provide reference for the construction of knowledge graphs in the field of urban firefighting.

**Keywords:** Urban Firefighting · Ontology · Knowledge Graph · Rule-based Entity Extraction

## 1 Introduction

With the development of the "smart city", the traditional urban firefighting has gradually evolved into intelligent firefighting. Applying the technology of the knowledge graphs in urban firefighting can help the intelligence of urban firefighting emergency management. The application of knowledge graphs technology can improve the efficiency of urban firefighting emergency decision-making.

However, there are relatively few related studies on the construction of knowledge graphs in the field of urban firefighting, and most of them only focus on building the firefighting ontology. Additionally, most of the researches focus on some espects of building such a knowledge graph, and lack of a relatively complete knowledge graphs for urban firefighting. To solve this problem, in this paper, we first complete the construction of urban firefighting domain ontology by consulting domain knowledge. Then we extract entities from text with rule-based entity extraction method, and define the relationships between different

This work was supported by the Northwest Minzu University Project for Introduced Talents under Grant No. Z20062 and Fundamental scientific research expenses for central colleges and universities under Grant No.31920210133.

entities. Through these tasks, the construction of a knowledge graph for urban firefighting domain is completed systematically.

The Sect. 2 presents related research on the construction of a knowledge graph in the field of urban firefighting. The Sect. 3 talks about the construction of a knowledge graph in the field of urban firefighting, including ontology construction, entity extraction, fire level reasoning, fire event name establishment, entity relationship establishment, and so on. The Sect. 4 includes the data collection and preprocessing, the characteristics of the network structure of the urban firefighting knowledge graph, and the analysis of the experimental results. The Sect. 5 is the conclusion.

## 2    Related Work

### 2.1    Urban Firefighting Ontology

Ontology is the conceptual template of a structured knowledge base, which is used to define the types of things in the domain and the attributes used to describe them; it is a generalized data model. In recent years, people have carried out the work on the ontology construction of firefighting. Wang Fang et al. constructed an ontology for fire emergency management, in this study, the effectiveness and integrity of the constructed fire emergency ontology were verified by qualitative evaluation and OntoQA quantitative evaluation [1]. On the basis of the ontology construction method, Zhang Botao et al. realized the comprehensive integration of firefighting domain knowledge and laid the foundation for the reasoning of industrial firefighting ontology [2]. Both methods construct an ontology for the firefighting domain, but not specifically for the urban firefighting domain.

### 2.2    Urban Firefighting Knowledge Graph

A knowledge graph is a semantic network that reveals the relationships between entities, which can formally describe things in the real world and their interrelationships.

Al-Moslmi et al. summarized the related methods of entity extraction, which applied natural language processing technology to entity extraction [3]. Rei M et al. proposed a new architecture for combining alternative word representations. Evaluating different architectures on a range of sequence labeling datasets shows that scaling at the character level improves performance on each benchmark [4].

Nguyen et al. used convolutional neural networks for relation extraction, and experimental results demonstrate the effectiveness of the proposed CNN [5]. Ji G et al. propose a sentence-level attention model to select valid instances, which fully utilizes the supervised information from the knowledge base, and the experimental results show that the method significantly outperforms all baseline systems [6].

For the disambiguation of knowledge graphs, Zhang Y et al. proposed a novel representation learning method that combines global and local information and an end-to-end cluster size estimation method that significantly outperforms traditional BIC-based methods [7].

In link prediction of knowledge graphs, Guo S et al. embedded the knowledge graph based on the iterative guidance of soft rules, combined embedded learning and logical reasoning, and made significant and consistent improvements on the most advanced baseline [8]. Dettmers et al. used a multi-layer convolutional network model for link prediction with high parameter efficiency [9].

In the research on the knowledge graphs in the fire domain, there is ontology-based forest fire emergency modeling and reasoning, which defines a rule-based framework to identify information in the domain [10]. Ge X et al. proposed a forest fire prediction method that combines spatiotemporal knowledge graphs and machine learning models. This method is conducive to the fusion of multi-source spatiotemporal data and greatly improves the prediction performance in real forest fire prediction scenarios [11].

Open public knowledge graphs include FreeBase, DBpedia, Schema.org, Wikidata, OpenKG.CN[1], and so on.Among them, OpenKG.CN has gathered a large amount of open Chinese knowledge graphs data, and the CEC data set contains 75 pieces of fire data, including information such as the time of the fire, the location of the fire, the number of firefighters, the number of fire trucks, casualties, and so on.

## 3   A Knowledge Graph for Urban Firefighting

### 3.1   The Framework for Building the Urban Firefighting Knowledge Graph

The research content of this study includes the construction of an urban firefighting ontology, rule-based entity extraction, abstract node reasoning and the construction of urban firefighting knowledge graph. First, the study determines the hierarchical structure of ontology, according to the collected domain information, then determines the basic hierarchical structure of ontology, and gradually refines it. Entity extraction rules are made according to the collected unstructured text information, and then the fire level is deduced according to the extracted nodes, after which the entity nodes are obtained. Finally, the knowledge graph is constructed by using Neo4j software, and the extracted entity nodes are stored in csv files according to the corresponding categories, and then imported into Neo4j in batches by using Cypher statements. The framework for building the urban firefighting knowledge graph is shown in Fig. 1.

### 3.2   Construction of Urban Firefighting Ontology

The ontology contains 15 classes and 3 levels, of which the parent class is a fire event. The following are 9 subcategories: fire name, fire level, geographical location, cause of fire, number of firefighters, number of firefighting vehicles, fire loss,

---

[1] Website of OpenKG : http://www.openkg.cn/home
Website of CEC data set: https://github.com/daselab/CEC-Corpus/tree/master/CEC/%E7%81%AB%E7%81%BE

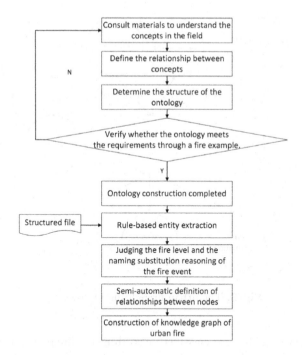

**Fig. 1.** The framework for building the urban firefighting knowledge graph

command, and time information. Among them, there are three subcategories of fire loss: the number of injuries, the number of deaths, and property losses. The time information contains three subcategories: date, quarter, and time of day. The ontology structure diagram of Fig. 2 shows the relationships between different entity concepts, in which the circle represents different entities, the solid line represents the relationship between the two kinds of concepts, and the dotted line represents the information that can be derived from existing concepts.

### 3.3   Building the Urban Firefighting Knowledge Graph

The ontology in the previous section represents the relationships between different entity concepts, firstly extracting the entity information that can be obtained directly, then analyzing the fire level information according to the existing information and naming the fire event. After the entity extraction is completed, the relationships between different nodes in the knowledge graph is determined manually according to the conceptual relationships of the ontology graph.

**Rule-Based Urban Firefighting Entity Extraction and Abstract Node Reasoning.** For conventional entity nodes, entity extraction rules are defined by manually consulting the relevant data in the field. The entity information contained in the text is extracted according to the defined regular expression,

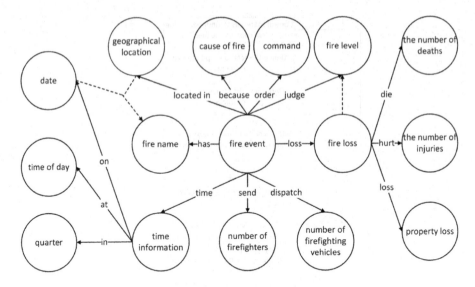

**Fig. 2.** The urban firefighting Ontology

then the extracted nodes are classified according to different extraction rules. Finally, the classified nodes are stored in a csv file through the Python statement, and a column is a type of node. Then the csv files are placed in the import folder of Neo4j, and the batch import of entity nodes is completed through the Cypher statement. Cypher is the query language for Neo4j graph data. The extraction rules for some entity nodes are shown in Table 1.

**Table 1.** Extraction Rule

| Node name | Extraction rule | Example |
|---|---|---|
| Data | \d{4}-\d{1,2}-\d{1,2} | 2022-12-5 |
| Time of day | \d{1,2}:\d{1,2}:\d{1,2} | 5:39:15 |
| Geographical location | .*?Province | Gansu Province |

Some information is not intuitively explained in the text, so the information contained in the text must be synthesized in order to make an accurate judgment. Generally, there is no fire name, and the knowledge graph needs the fire name to connect the fire information, but using the place name or time alone as the name will cause confusion because there are too many fires in the same place or date. Therefore, the combination of geographical location and occurrence date is used as the fire name.

There are three indicators to judge the fire level: the number injured, the number of deaths, and property loss. According to these three indicators, the fire can be divided into particularly major fire, major fire, large fire, and general fire. In this study, we first extract these three indicators, then judge according to the extracted results. In order to facilitate the judgment of the fire grade, the fire grade is coded in this study, which is shown in Table 2.

**Table 2.** Fire level coding and judgment standard

| Fire level | Coding | Deaths | Injured | Property loss |
|---|---|---|---|---|
| General fire | 1 | <3 | <30 | <10 million yuan |
| Large fire | 2 | [3,10) | [10,50) | [10 million, 50 million) |
| Major fire | 3 | [10,30) | [50,100) | [50 million, 100 million) |
| Particularly major fire | 4 | >30 | >100 | >100 million |

For the missing information in the fire text, the common method is to use the average to replace the missing value, and when there is more missing data, using the average to replace the missing value may cause overall data distortion due to some larger values. Considering the correlation between the number of casualties and property losses, the missing data value is set to 0 and the remaining indicators are used to judge. The flow chart of the judgment algorithm is shown in Fig. 3.

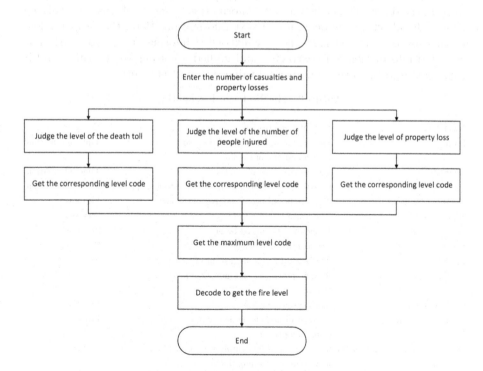

**Fig. 3.** The fire level judgment rule

**Construction of the Relationship in the Knowledge Graph of Urban Firefighting.** The knowledge graph in the field of urban firefighting belongs to the vertical field, and the data in the field of firefighting need to be used, so the relationships between entities can be determined by experience. After extracting the entity nodes, the nodes are classified according to the extraction rules, and the node information is stored in the csv file, then imported into Neo4j in batches. Then manually define the relationships between nodes, through Cypher statements to establish the relationships between different types of nodes.

## 4   Verification of the Proposed Method

### 4.1   Data Acquisition and Preprocessing

The data set we use is obtained by our team from the firefighting official website and is related to the field of emergency management. The knowledge graph we constructed includes 569 nodes and 827 edges. The data is stored in a unstructured way. Data preprocessing of the collected data includes the unification of the format and loss property preprocessing. For example, to facilitate the extraction of time format, we first unify the format of time and money.

There are also many ways of expression and units of lossed property, and the reasoning of fire level needs to use lossed property, so it is necessary to unify its units. In the direct replacement of text information, some words may be replaced incorrectly, affecting the accuracy of text information. Here, the property loss information is extracted first, then the extracted information is processed. The extracted information is re-extracted and unified according to the rules, and it is changed into the form of numerical value (the unit is yuan).

**Table 3.** The Nodes of Firefighting

| Node name | Semantic description | Category |
|---|---|---|
| Data | Specific information about the year month and day of the fire | Time information |
| Time of day | The specific time of the fire | Time information |
| Quarter | Quarterly fire information, divided into four quarters | Time information |
| Number of injuries | The number of people injured in the fire | Fire loss |
| Number of deaths | The death toll in a fire | Fire loss |
| Property losses | Economic loss caused by fire | Fire loss |
| Command | Fire fighting deployment | Fire event |
| Fire level | The level of fire is divided into four levels | Fire event |
| Geographical location | Specific provincial and municipal location information of the fire | Fire event |
| Cause of fire | The cause of the fire | Fire event |
| Number of firefighters | Number of firefighters deployed as a result of rescuing the fire | Fire event |
| Number of firefighting vehicles | The number of firefighting vehicles deployed as a result of rescuing the fire | Fire event |
| Fire name | It is expressed by the combination of geographical location and date of the fire | Fire event |

## 4.2   The Knowledge Graph of Urban Firefighting

There are 13 kinds of entity nodes in the knowledge graph, and the types of nodes are obtained according to the ontology. The meaning of its representation and the category to which it belongs are shown in Table 3.

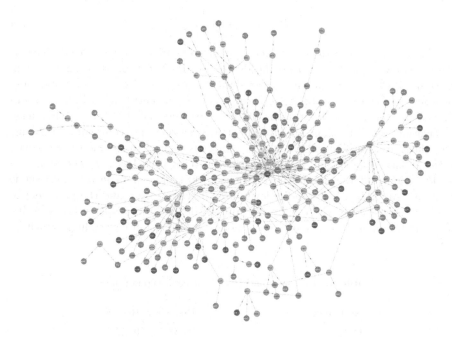

**Fig. 4.** The knowledge graph of urban firefighting

## 4.3   Result and Discussion

The experimental results show the effectiveness of this research. This research has successfully completed the construction of urban firefighting domain from ontology to a knowledge graph. The constructed knowledge graph contains 36 fire cases. In this study, the precision and recall rate are used to evaluate the experimental results. Through calculation, the average precision of this study reached 85.25%, and the average recall rate reached 83.58%. There are two main reasons for the low recall rate. Firstly, there was not enough data to study, which led to some sentence patterns not being considered when making rules. Secondly, due to the characteristics of the rules, the constantly updated rules easily conflict with the existing rules.

The Precision is the proportion of those which are correctly predicted as positive class to the total forecast as positive class. The Recall is the proportion of those which are really positive among all the predicted positive classes.The formulas for calculating accuracy and recall are shown in (1) and (2).

$$Precision = \frac{TP}{TP + FP} \tag{1}$$

$$Recall = \frac{TP}{TP + FN} \tag{2}$$

The Precision and Recall of each type of node are given in Table 4. Because there are few ways to describe the death toll, its Precision is relatively high, reaching 100%. There are few clear data on property loss in our data, only two pieces of data describe it, so there is a big gap between its Precision and Precision. Due to the limitations of the rules and the flexibility of language description, the Precision and Recall of fire reasons and command situations are relatively low. The judgment of a quarter is related to the month, and even if the month appears multiple times in the text, it is basically the same, so its Precision and Recall rate have reached 100%. The data in our data set is relatively small, in which the fire levels are all general fires, and the judgment of fire level is related to the number of injuries, deaths and property losses. With the constraints of these three types of nodes, its Precision is very high, reaching 100%.

**Table 4.** Precision and Recall for each type of node

| Node name | Precision | Recall |
|---|---|---|
| Data | 95.33% | 95.33% |
| Time of day | 81.31% | 81.31% |
| Quarter | 100% | 100% |
| Number of injuries | 97.14% | 91.89% |
| Number of deaths | 100% | 94.44% |
| Property losses | 100% | 50% |
| Command | 73.12% | 67.33% |
| Fire level | 100% | 94.44% |
| Geographical location | 69.16% | 69.16% |
| Cause of fire | 63.41% | 57.78% |
| Number of firefighters | 92.68% | 90.48% |
| Number of firefighting vehicles | 87.50% | 85.37% |

The knowledge graph is constructed by Neo4j software, and the extracted nodes information is stored in the csv file. Then these nodes will be imported in batches to get these nodes information. The nodes relationships are defined manually according to the corresponding rules. After the nodes information are imported, the relationships are imported in batches through the defined relationships between different nodes. The result of the knowledge graph is shown in Fig. 4.

## 5   Conclusion

This study is a preliminary attempt to establish a knowledge graph in the field of urban firefighting. An ontology for urban firefighting is established firstly, and then, a rule-based method is used to extract firefighting entities from the unstructured text. In addition, the relationships between nodes in the firefighting knowledge graph are obtained by domain experts according to their experience. The experimental results show that the proposed method is effective and reasonable. At present, there are only 13 nodes and 12 relationships in the proposed knowledge graph.

In the future, we will continue to increase the precision and recall of the rule-based entity extraction method, and carry out relationships extraction experiment. In this way, we will further improve the scale of the proposed urban firefighting knowledge graphs. Besids, we will try to apply this research to the intelligent decision-making system for urban fire protection.

## References

1. Fang, W., Jing, Y., Lulu, X.: Ontology construction for fire emergency management. J. China Soc. Sci. Tech. Inf. **39**(9), 914–925 (2020). (Chinese)
2. Botao, Z., Yan, D., Jinguang, G.: Ontology construction oriented towards industrial firefighting decision-making. Comput. Appl. Softw. **31**(3), 5 (2014). (Chinese)
3. Al-Moslmi, T., et al.: Named entity extraction for knowledge graphs: a literature overview. IEEE Access **8**, 32862–32881 (2020)
4. Rei, M., Crichton, G.K.O., Pyysalo, S.: Attending to characters in neural sequence labeling models. arXiv preprint arXiv:1611.04361 (2016)
5. Nguyen, T.H., Grishman, R.: Relation extraction: perspective from convolutional neural networks. In: Proceedings of the 1st Workshop on Vector Space Modeling for Natural Language Processing (2015)
6. Ji, G., et al.: Distant supervision for relation extraction with sentence-level attention and entity descriptions. In: Proceedings of the AAAI Conference on Artificial Intelligence, vol. 31. no. 1 (2017)
7. Zhang, Y., et al.: Name disambiguation in AMiner: clustering, maintenance, and human in the loop. In: Proceedings of the 24th ACM SIGKDD International Conference on Knowledge Discovery & Data Mining (2018)
8. Guo, S., et al.: Knowledge graph embedding with iterative guidance from soft rules. In: Proceedings of the AAAI Conference on Artificial Intelligence, vol. 32, no. 1 (2018)
9. Dettmers, T., et al.: Convolutional 2d knowledge graph embeddings. In: Proceedings of the AAAI Conference on Artificial Intelligence, vol. 32, no. 1 (2018)
10. Masa, P., et al.: Ontology-based modelling and reasoning for forest fire emergencies in resilient societies. In: Proceedings of the 12th Hellenic Conference on Artificial Intelligence (2022)
11. Ge, X., et al.: Spatio-temporal knowledge graph based forest fire prediction with multi source heterogeneous data. Remote Sens. **14**(14), 3496 (2022)

# Optimal Traffic Flow Distributions on Dynamic Networks

Armen Bagdasaryan[1]([✉]), Antonios Kalampakas[1], Mansoor Saburov[1], and Stefanos Spartalis[2,3]

[1] College of Engineering and Technology, American University of the Middle East, 54200 Egaila, Kuwait
{armen.bagdasaryan,antonios.kalampakas,mansur.saburov}@aum.edu.kw
[2] Department of Production and Management Engineering, Laboratory of Computational Mathematics, School of Engineering, Democritus University of Thrace, V. Sofias 12, Prokat, Building A1, 67132 Xanthi, Greece
sspart@pme.duth.gr
[3] School of Science and Technology, Studies in Physics, Hellenic Open University, 18 Aristoteles Street, 26335 Patra, Greece
spartalis.stefanos@ac.eap.gr

**Abstract.** In a parallel network, the Wardrop equilibrium is the optimal distribution of the given total one unit flow across alternative parallel links that minimizes the effective costs of the links which are defined as the sum of the latency at the given flow and the price of the link. Meanwhile, the system optimum is the optimal distribution of the given total one unit flow for which the average effective cost is minimal. In this paper, we study the so-called *Wardrop optimal flow* that is the Wardrop equilibrium as well as the system optimum of the network. We propose a discrete-time replicator equation on a *Wardrop optimal network* for which the Nash equilibrium, the Wardrop equilibrium and the system optimum are the same flow distribution in the dynamic network. We also describe the conceptual and functional model of intelligent information system for dynamic traffic flow assignment in transportation networks.

**Keywords:** Dynamic network · Optimal flow distribution · Traffic flow · Wardrop optimal flow · Wardrop optimal network · Replicator equation · Dynamical model · Intelligent information system · Algorithmic scheme

## 1 Introduction

The optimal traffic flow allocation is one of the most important problems with both theoretical and practical aspects not only in transportation networks, but also in economics and communication. In 1952 John Glen Wardrop formulated two principles of optimality of flows in networks that describe the situations of the *user* (or *Wardrop*) *equilibrium* and the *system optimum*. The first Wardrop principle describes an optimal flow distribution across alternative parallel links in the network, namely, it states that the effective costs of all utilized links are equal and less than the effective costs of those unutilized links for every fixed source-destination pair, while the system optimum is the optimal distribution of the flow for which the average effective cost for all used links is minimal. A flow satisfying the Wardrop's second principle is obviously optimal from a network owner point of view. The problems of finding a Wardrop equilibrium and system optimum are the topics of active research both in theory and practice. In general, for a given network the flows that satisfy Wardrop's first and second prinicples do not coincide, but there are networks that have identical Wardrop equilibrium and system optimum.

We study the *Wardrop optimal flows* that satisfy both principles that is the Wardrop equlibrium as well as the system optimum. A network that has a Wardrop optimal flow is called a *Wardrop optimal network*. We investigate dynamic properties of the Wardrop optimal networks and examine the Wardrop optimal flows on networks of parallel links [1]. In this setup, the traffic traveling from the origin to the destination can use any of the alternative parallel links, and the flow passing through each link of the network creates a congestion externality that causes an increase in the time needed for the journey, which is captured by an increasing link-specific latency function. We would like to stress that a great amount of works related to the study of optimization problems in networks from one side and of Wardrop equilibrium in networks from the other side mostly focus on static networks, in which temporal factors are not taken into account. However, many application fields require consideration of *dynamic networks*, among which, for example, are transportation [2,3], evacuation planning [4], electronic communication [5], job scheduling [6], network routing [7], and parallel computing [8]. This necessity has led to the dynamic network flow model, often called network flow over time [9–11].

Our approach to dynamic networks slightly differs from the known ones and also brings some new properties to dynamic networks. The difference is that in addition to free-flow transition time (or cost) and link capacity, usually associated with dynamic networks in the literature, in which the actual travel time of the flow on a link depends on both the free-flow time and the capacity, we consider the networks in which link latency functions change over time, more exactly at each next time instant (iteration, observation) the functions may differ from the functions at the previous step. We can see that, using this approach, the dynamic networks become more suitable and powerful for modeling networks with congestion effects, such as transportation networks and communication networks, and include the situations of sudden road incidents, weather conditions, or the season. To this end, we present a new dynamical model of optimal flow distribution by proposing a discrete-time replicator equation on the Wardrop optimal network, using the ideas of evolutionary game theory.

Evolutionary game theory, unlike the classical game theory, focuses on the dynamics of strategy change. *The Nash equilibrium*, which was invented by Nash [12,13], is the solution concept in classical non-cooperative game theory in which each strategy in the Nash equilibrium is the best response to all other strategies in that equilibrium. In other words, it is a strategy profile in which no player can do better by unilaterally changing their strategy to another strategy. It should be noted that the primary way to study the evolutionary dynamics in games is through replicator equations that are used to describe the evolutionary dynamics of an entity called replicator which has means of making more or less accurate copies of itself. The replicator equation, which is the cornerstone of evolutionary game dynamics [14–17], shows the growth rate of the proportion of players using a certain strategy and that rate is equal to the difference between the average payoff of that strategy and the average payoff of the population as a whole. The general idea is that replicators whose fitness is larger (smaller) than the average fitness of population will increase (decrease) in numbers [18, 19].

In this regard, we also provide a geometric description of the optimal flow and describe the equilibrium and stability conditions of the replicator equation dynamics. For the proposed replicator equation on the Wardrop optimal network, the Nash equilibrium, the Wardrop equilibrium, and the system optimum are the same flow distribution of the dynamic network. We also present an algorithm for simulation of dynamic flow distribution in networks, and discuss conceptual and functional structure of intelligent information system for dynamic traffic flow assignment in transportation networks.

## 2    The Model of a Network

We consider a network of $m$ parallel links between two nodes as a single origin-destination pair. We let $\mathbf{I}_m = \{1, 2, \ldots, m\}$ denote the set of links in the network. We denote by $x_k \geq 0$, $k \in \mathbf{I}_m$, the total flow passing through the link $k$ and $\mathbf{x} = (x_1, x_2, \ldots, x_m)$ denote a flow vector of the network. We are interested in the problem of routing total one unit of flow across $m$ alternative parallel links. Assuming all traffic is routed, we obviously have $\sum_{i=1}^m x_i \leq 1$. In the routing problem, a journey time is the main component of a travel cost. The link journey times increase when the load of flow becomes heavier that may lead to congestion. Since the flow in each link causes congestion externality which increases the delay while traversing the link, each link has a *flow-dependent latency* function

$$\ell_k : [0, \infty) \to [0, \infty), \ k \in \mathbf{I}_m$$

which measures the journey time as a function of the total flow $x_k$ on the link $k$. Throughout this paper, for each $k \in \mathbf{I}_m$ the latency function $\ell_k$ will be assumed to be a convex, strictly increasing, continuously differentiable function.

Let $L(\mathbf{x}) = (\ell_1(x_1), \ldots, \ell_m(x_m))$ denote a latency vector function at a flow vector $\mathbf{x} = (x_1, \ldots, x_m)$. Hence a network $\mathbf{L_m}$ of $m$ parallel links between two nodes can be identified with the latency vector function $\mathbf{L_m} = (\ell_1(\cdot), \cdots, \ell_m(\cdot))$. A network $\mathbf{L_m} = (\ell_1(\cdot), \ldots, \ell_m(\cdot))$ is called *differentiable network* (resp. *convex network*) if all the latency functions $\ell_k$ are differentiable (resp. convex). In this paper, we will interchangeably use a latency vector function and a network.

We denote by $\mathbb{S}^{m-1} = \{\mathbf{x} \in \mathbb{R}_+^m : \sum_{i=1}^m x_i = 1\}$ the standard simplex. Define $\mathbf{supp(x)} := \{i \in \mathbf{I}_m : x_i \neq 0\}$ and set $\mathrm{int}\mathbb{S}^{m-1} = \{x \in \mathbb{S}^{m-1} : \mathbf{supp(x)} = \mathbf{I}_m\}$.

In order to characterize an optimal flow distribution in the network, *Wardrop's first principle*, the Wardrop equilibrium, is adopted: *the effective costs of all utilized links are equal and less than the effective costs of those unutilized links.* It is worth mentioning that a *Wardrop equilibrium* is well-known and frequently applied in transportation and communication networks [1, 20–23]. It is intuitively very appealing and has had successful applications in a wide variety of social sciences. For a thorough review of the *Wardrop equilibrium*, one can refer to [20].

A *Wardrop equilibrium* of a network $\mathbf{L_m} = (\ell_1(\cdot), \ldots, \ell_m(\cdot))$ is a flow vector $\mathbf{x} = (x_1, \ldots, x_m) \in \mathbb{S}^{m-1}$ such that

$$\ell_k(x_k) = \min_{i \in \mathbf{I}_m} \{\ell_i(x_i)\}, \quad \text{for all } k \in \mathbf{I}_m \text{ with } x_k > 0,$$

i.e., the latency is the same across all links with nonzero flow and smaller than the zero flow latency of the rest of the links. The *average delay* of a network $\mathbf{L_m} = (\ell_1(\cdot), \ldots, \ell_m(\cdot))$ at flow $\mathbf{x} = (x_1, \ldots, x_m) \in \mathbb{S}^{m-1}$ is given by the sum $\sum_{i=1}^{m} x_i \ell_i(x_i)$. A *system optimum* of a network $\mathbf{L_m} = (\ell_1(\cdot), \ldots, \ell_m(\cdot))$ is a flow $\mathbf{x} = (x_1, \ldots, x_m) \in \mathbb{S}^{m-1}$ that minimizes the average delay.

Further, we assume that each link $k$ in the network is owned by a service provider who sets a link price of $q_k$. Let $\mathbf{q} = (q_1, \ldots, q_m)$ denote a price vector of the network. In order to choose the amount of flow and the routing pattern optimally, we define an *effective cost* of using link $k$ to be the sum of the latency $\ell_k(x_k)$ and the link price $q_k$ when the total flow on the link $k$ is $x_k$, i.e., $\ell_k(x_k) + q_k$. Let $\tilde{L}(\mathbf{x}) := L(\mathbf{x}) + \mathbf{q}$ denote an effective cost vector at the flow vector $\mathbf{x} = (x_1, \ldots, x_m)$. We also assume that a *reservation utility (link capacity)* is $R$ and a flow is not being sent when the effective cost of the link exceeds the reservation utility $R$. Let $\mathbf{R} = (R, \ldots, R)$ denote a reservation utility vector (see Fig. 1). It should be mentioned [1, 21] that for any $\mathbf{q} \in \mathbb{R}_+^m$ with $\mathbf{q} \leq \mathbf{R}$ there always exists a unique Wardrop equilibrium $\mathbf{x}^{(\mathbf{q})} = (x_1^{(\mathbf{q})}, x_2^{(\mathbf{q})}, \ldots, x_m^{(\mathbf{q})}) \in \mathbb{R}_+^m$ with either of the following properties (we denote $\|\mathbf{x}\|_1 := \sum_{k=1}^{m} |x_k|$):

$$\ell_i(x_i^{(\mathbf{q})}) + q_i = \min_{k \in \mathbf{I}_m} \left\{\ell_k(x_k^{(\mathbf{q})}) + q_k\right\} < R, \quad \forall\, i \in \text{supp}\left(\mathbf{x}^{(\mathbf{q})}\right), \quad \|\mathbf{x}^{(\mathbf{q})}\|_1 = 1,$$

$$\ell_i(x_i^{(\mathbf{q})}) + q_i = \min_{k \in \mathbf{I}_m} \left\{\ell_k(x_k^{(\mathbf{q})}) + q_k\right\} = R, \quad \forall\, i \in \text{supp}\left(\mathbf{x}^{(\mathbf{q})}\right), \quad \|\mathbf{x}^{(\mathbf{q})}\|_1 \leq 1.$$

**Definition 1.** *A flow vector* $\mathbf{x}^{(\mathbf{we})} = \left(x_1^{(\mathbf{we})}, \cdots, x_m^{(\mathbf{we})}\right)$ *is a **Wardrop equilibrium** if it is a solution to the following optimization problem*

$$\mathbf{x}^{(\mathbf{we})} \in \underset{\substack{\mathbf{y} \geq 0 \\ \|\mathbf{y}\|_1 \leq 1}}{\mathbf{Argmax}} \left\{\sum_{k=1}^{m} \left(R - \ell_k(x_k^{(\mathbf{we})}) - q_k\right) y_k\right\}.$$

**Definition 2.** *A flow vector* $\mathbf{x}^{(\mathbf{so})} = \left(x_1^{(\mathbf{so})}, \cdots, x_m^{(\mathbf{so})}\right)$ *is called a **system optimum** if it is a solution to the following optimization problem*

$$\mathbf{x}^{(\mathbf{so})} \in \underset{\substack{\mathbf{y} \geq 0 \\ \|\mathbf{y}\|_1 \leq 1}}{\mathbf{Argmax}} \left\{\sum_{k=1}^{m} \left(R - \ell_k(y_k) - q_k\right) y_k\right\}.$$

For the definitions of a Wardrop equilibrium and the system optimum see also [1,24,25]. In the next definition we introduce the notions of a *Wardrop optimal flow* and a *Wardrop optimal network*.

**Definition 3.** *A flow vector* $\mathbf{x}^{(\mathbf{wof})} = \left(x_1^{(\mathbf{wof})}, \cdots, x_m^{(\mathbf{wof})}\right)$ *is called a* **Wardrop optimal flow** *if it is simultaneously a Wardrop equilibrium and a system optimum of the network. A network that has a Wardrop optimal flow is called a* **Wardrop optimal network.**

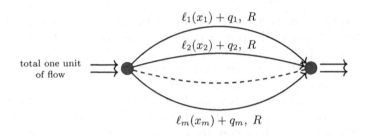

**Fig. 1.** Model of a parallel network with $m$ links

Given a network $\mathbf{L_m}$ $(\widetilde{\mathbf{L}}_m)$, a flow $\mathbf{x} = (x_1, \ldots, x_m) \in \mathbb{S}^{m-1}$ is called a *Wardrop optimal flow* if it is Wardrop equilibrium and system optimum of $\mathbf{L_m}$ $(\widetilde{\mathbf{L}}_m)$. A network that has a Wardrop optimal flow is referred to as a *Wardrop optimal network*. We denote by **WOF** the class of all Wardrop optimal networks.

## 3  The Main Results

All the definitions that we use in this section are summarized in the Appendix. In this section we present our results on Wardrop Optimal Flows and propose the replicator model of optimal flow distribution on dynamic networks. We also study the stability and dynamics of the replicator equation.

### 3.1  Wardrop Optimal Flows

We begin with statements regarding the existence and uniqueness of a Wardrop equilibrium and system optimum (optimal flow) of a network.

**Proposition 1.** *Every network (latency vector function)* $\mathbf{L_m} = (\ell_1(\cdot), \cdots, \ell_m(\cdot))$ *has a unique Wardrop equilibrium in the simplex* $\mathbb{S}^{m-1}$.

From Proposition 1 we obtain the following statement regarding the uniqueness of an optimal flow.

**Proposition 2.** *There exists a unique system optimum for a differentiable and convex network* $\mathbf{L_m} = (\ell_1(\cdot), \cdots, \ell_m(\cdot))$.

The following result provides some sufficient condition which ensures an existence of Wardrop equilibrium inside the simplex $\mathbb{S}^{m-1} = \{\mathbf{x} \in \mathbb{R}^m : \|\mathbf{x}\|_1 = 1, \mathbf{x} \geq 0\}$ and in fact describes the capacity of Wardrop's equilibrium.

**Proposition 3.** *Let $\ell_k^{-1}$ be the inverse function of the latency function $\ell_k$ for all $k \in \mathbf{I}_m$ and assume $(q_1, \ldots, q_m) = \mathbf{q} < \mathbf{R} = (R, R, \ldots, R)$. Then the following statements are true:*

**(i)** *If $\sum_{k=1}^m \ell_k^{-1}(R - q_k) < 1$ then $\|\mathbf{x}^{(we)}\|_1 < 1$;*
**(ii)** *If $\sum_{k=1}^m \ell_k^{-1}(R - q_k) \geq 1$ the $\|\mathbf{x}^{(we)}\|_1 = 1$.*

We consider a Wardrop equilibrium $\mathbf{x}^{(we)}$ (a Wardrop optimal flow $\mathbf{x}^{(wof)}$) with full capacity 1, i.e., $\|\mathbf{x}^{(we)}\|_1 = 1$ ($\|\mathbf{x}^{(wof)}\|_1 = 1$). Let $\mathbb{S}^{m-1} := \{\mathbf{x} \in \mathbb{R}_+^m : \|\mathbf{x}\|_1 = 1\}$ be the simplex. Let $\widetilde{L}(\mathbf{x}) = (\tilde{\ell}_1(x_1), \cdots, \tilde{\ell}_m(x_m))$ be an effective cost vector at the flow $\mathbf{x} = (x_1, \ldots, x_m)$, where $\tilde{\ell}_k(x_k) = \ell_k(x_k) + q_k$ is an *effective cost* of the link $k \in \mathbf{I}_m$.

We now provide a characterization of a Wardrop optimal flow $\mathbf{x}^{(wof)}$ with full capacity 1, i.e. $\mathbf{x}^{(wof)} \in \mathbb{S}^{m-1}$, in the following theorem.

**Theorem 1.** *Given a differentiable and convex network $\widetilde{\mathbf{L}}_m = (\tilde{\ell}_1(\cdot), \ldots, \tilde{\ell}_m(\cdot))$, a flow vector $\mathbf{x} = (x_1, \ldots, x_m) \in \mathbb{S}^{m-1}$ is a Wardrop optimal flow if and only if the following conditions are satisfied:*

**(i)** $\tilde{\ell}_i(x_i) = \tilde{\ell}_j(x_j)$ *for all $i, j \in \mathbf{I}_m$ with $x_i > 0$ and $x_j > 0$;*
**(ii)** $x_i \tilde{\ell}_i'(x_i) = x_j \tilde{\ell}_j'(x_j)$ *for all $i, j \in \mathbf{I}_m$ with $x_i > 0$ and $x_j > 0$;*
**(iii)** $\tilde{\ell}_i(0) \geq \tilde{\ell}_j(x_j) + x_j \tilde{\ell}_j'(x_j)$ *for all $i, j \in \mathbf{I}_m$ with $x_i = 0$ and $x_j > 0$.*

In case of interior flows, $\mathbf{x} \in \text{Int} \mathbb{S}^{m-1}$, the condition (iii) can be omitted.

Given any flow vector $\mathbf{p} = (p_1, \ldots, p_m) \in \mathbb{S}^{m-1}$ with $\mathbf{p} > 0$, let $\frac{\mathbf{x}}{\mathbf{p}} := \left(\frac{x_1}{p_1}, \ldots, \frac{x_m}{p_m}\right)$ for any $\mathbf{x} \in \mathbb{S}^{m-1}$. Let $\mathbf{WOF}(\mathbf{p})$ be a set of all effective cost vectors $\widetilde{L}(\mathbf{x}) = (\tilde{\ell}_1(x_1), \ldots, \tilde{\ell}_m(x_m))$, whose Wardrop optimal flow is $\mathbf{p}$. Then it can be proved that the set $\mathbf{WOF}(\mathbf{p})$ is a convex cone.

## 3.2   Wardrop Optimal Flows on Dynamic Networks

Let $\langle \mathbf{x}, L_n(\frac{\mathbf{x}}{\mathbf{p}}) \rangle = \sum_{k=1}^m x_k \ell_n \left(\frac{x_k}{p_k}\right)$ be the average effective cost of the network at the flow vector $\mathbf{x} \in \mathbb{S}^{m-1}$. We assume that the network users may *dynamically* change the distribution of the total one unit flow over alternatively parallel links. Namely, if $\mathbf{x}^{(n)} = (x_1^{(n)}, \ldots, x_m^{(n)}) \in \mathbb{S}^{m-1}$ is the flow distribution of the users at the step $n$ then the relative growth rate $\frac{x_k^{(n+1)} - x_k^{(n)}}{x_k^{(n)}}$ of the flow on the link $k$ at the step $(n+1)$ is negatively proportional to the difference between the effective cost $\ell_n \left(\frac{x_k^{(n)}}{p_k}\right)$ of the link $k$ at the step $n$ and the average effective cost $\left\langle \mathbf{x}^{(n)}, L_n \left(\frac{\mathbf{x}^{(n)}}{\mathbf{p}}\right) \right\rangle = \sum_{k=1}^m x_k^{(n)} \ell_n \left(\frac{x_k^{(n)}}{p_k}\right)$ of the whole network at the step $n$.

We propose the dynamic approach to optimal flow distribution on dynamic networks as follows. Let $\mathbf{x}^{(n+1)} = \mathcal{R}_n(\mathbf{x}^{(n)})$, where $\mathcal{R}_n : \mathbb{S}^{m-1} \to \mathbb{S}^{m-1}$ is the discrete-time replicator equation on Wardrop optimal networks defined by

$$(\mathcal{R}_n(\mathbf{x}))_k = x_k \left[ 1 + \varepsilon \left( \ell_n \left( \frac{x_k}{p_k} \right) - \sum_{i=1}^m x_i \ell_n \left( \frac{x_i}{p_i} \right) \right) \right], \quad \forall\, k \in \mathbf{I}_m,\, n \in \mathbb{N}, \quad (1)$$

where $\{\ell_n\}_{n \in \mathbb{N}}$, $\ell_n : [0, \bar{p}] \to [0,1]$ is a sequence of continuously differentiable and uniformly strictly increasing functions, $\mathbf{p} = (p_1, \ldots, p_m) \in \mathrm{int}\mathbb{S}^{m-1}$ is any interior flow, $\bar{p} := \frac{1}{\min\limits_{i \in \mathbf{I}_m} p_i}$, $\varepsilon \in (-1, 0)$. Some particular cases of Eq. (1) were studied in [18,19].

We define the following constant

$$\mu := \sup_{n \in \mathbb{N}} \left[ \max_{x \in [0, \bar{p}]} \frac{d}{dx} \left( x f_n(x) \right) \right] < \infty.$$

Let $\mathbf{e}_i$ be the vertex of the simplex $\mathbb{S}^{m-1}$, $i \in \mathbf{I}_m$, and $\mathbf{p}_\alpha := \frac{1}{s_\alpha(\mathbf{p})} \sum_{i \in \alpha} p_i \mathbf{e}_i$ for all $\alpha \subset \mathbf{I}_m$, where $s_\alpha(\mathbf{p}) = \sum_{i \in \alpha} p_i$ and $\mathbf{p} = (p_1, \ldots, p_m) \in \mathrm{int}\mathbb{S}^{m-1}$.

Note that a flow $\mathbf{x} \in \mathbb{S}^{m-1}$ is called a **common Nash equilibrium** of the replicator equation given by (1) if

$$\left\langle \mathbf{x}, \varepsilon L_n \left( \frac{\mathbf{x}}{\mathbf{p}} \right) \right\rangle \geq \left\langle \mathbf{y}, \varepsilon L_n \left( \frac{\mathbf{x}}{\mathbf{p}} \right) \right\rangle$$

for all $\mathbf{y} \in \mathbb{S}^{m-1}$, $n \in \mathbb{N}$.

We denote by

$$\mathbf{Fix_{Com}} = \{ \mathbf{x} \in \mathbb{S}^{m-1} : \mathcal{R}_n(\mathbf{x}) = \mathbf{x} \}$$

a set of *common fixed* points (Appendix, Def. 6) of the replicator equation (1).

Let $\mathbb{S}^{|\alpha|-1} := \mathrm{conv}\{\mathbf{e}_i\}_{i \in \alpha}$ for $\alpha \subset \mathbf{I}_m$, where $\mathrm{conv}(\mathbf{A})$ is the convex hull of $\mathbf{A}$, and $\mathrm{int}\mathbb{S}^{|\alpha|-1} := \{ \mathbf{x} \in \mathbb{S}^{|\alpha|-1} : \mathrm{supp}(\mathbf{x}) = \alpha \}$ be an interior of the face $\mathbb{S}^{|\alpha|-1}$.

To study the stability of fixed points of the replicator equation (1) and the dynamics of (1) we employ a Lyapunov function.

**Proposition 4.** *Let $\varepsilon \in (-\frac{1}{\mu}, 0) \cap (-1, 0)$. Then the following statements hold true:*

**(i)** $\mathcal{M}_{\mathbf{p}:k}(\mathbf{x}) := \max\limits_{i \in \mathbf{I}_m} \{ \frac{x_i}{p_i} \} - \frac{x_k}{p_k}$ *for all $k \in \mathbf{I}_m$ ia a decreasing Lyapunov function over the interior $\mathrm{int}\mathbb{S}^{m-1}$ of the simplex $\mathbb{S}^{m-1}$;*

**(ii)** $\mathcal{M}_{\mathbf{p}_\alpha:k}(\mathbf{x}) := \max\limits_{i \in \alpha} \{ \frac{x_i}{p_i} \} - \frac{x_k}{p_k}$ *for all $k \in \alpha \subset \mathbf{I}_m$ is a decreasing Lyapunov function over the interior $\mathrm{int}\mathbb{S}^{|\alpha|-1}$ of the face $\mathbb{S}^{|\alpha|-1}$.*

The asymptotic stability and the dynamics of the replicator equation (1) can be described all over the simplex as in the following proposition.

**Proposition 5.** *Let $\varepsilon \in (-\frac{1}{\mu}, 0) \cap (-1, 0)$. Then an orbit of the replicator equation $\mathcal{R}_n : \mathbb{S}^{m-1} \to \mathbb{S}^{m-1}$ starting from any initial point $\mathbf{x} \in \mathbb{S}^{m-1}$ converges to the fixed point $\mathbf{p}_{\mathrm{supp}(\mathbf{x})}$ in the interior of the face $\mathbb{S}^{|\mathrm{supp}(\mathbf{x})|-1}$.*

The following proposition demonstrates the relationship between two distinct points of the simplex $\mathbb{S}^{m-1}$, and is needed for the proof of Theorem A..

**Proposition 6.** *Let* $\mathbf{x}, \mathbf{y} \in \mathbb{S}^{m-1}$ *be two **distinct** elements of the simplex* $\mathbb{S}^{m-1}$ *such that* $\mathbf{y} > 0$. *Let* $\frac{\mathbf{x}}{\mathbf{y}} := (\frac{x_1}{y_1}, \cdots, \frac{x_m}{y_m})$, $\bar{y} := \min_{k \in \mathbf{I}_m} y_k > 0$ *and* $\|\mathbf{x} - \mathbf{y}\|_1 := \sum_{k \in \mathbf{I}_m} |x_k - y_k|$. *Then the following statements hold true:*

(i) $\min_{k \in \mathbf{I}_m} \frac{x_k}{y_k} < 1 < \max_{k \in \mathbf{I}_m} \frac{x_k}{y_k}$;

(ii) $\bar{y} \left[ \max_{k \in \mathbf{I}_m} \frac{x_k}{y_k} - \min_{k \in \mathbf{I}_m} \frac{x_k}{y_k} \right] \leq \|\mathbf{x} - \mathbf{y}\|_1 \leq m \left[ \max_{k \in \mathbf{I}_m} \frac{x_k}{y_k} - \min_{k \in \mathbf{I}_m} \frac{x_k}{y_k} \right]$.

The main result of this paper presented in Theorem A., which describes the dynamics of the replicator equation (1) for sufficiently small $\varepsilon \in (-1, 0)$, is then proved by using the Propositions 4, 5 and 6.

**Theorem A.** *Let* $\varepsilon \in (-\frac{1}{\mu}, 0) \cap (-1, 0)$. *Then the following statements hold true:*

(i) *The common fixed points are* $\mathbf{Fix_{Com}}(\{\mathcal{R}_n\}) = \bigcup_{\alpha \subset \mathbf{I}_m} \{\mathbf{p}_\alpha\}$;

(ii) *The unique Wardrop optimal flow* $\mathbf{p}$ *is the only **common** Nash equilibrium;*

(iii) *The unique Wardrop optimal flow* $\mathbf{p}$ *is the only stable **common** fixed point;*

(iv) *Any interior orbit converges to the unique Wardrop optimal flow* $\mathbf{p}$.

## 4   Multi-agent Intelligent Transport System

Intelligent transport systems (ITS) are being developed to control and optimize network traffic flows. The technologies used are mainly intelligent technologies, that employ AI techniques, information technologies, and mathematical optimal transport methods. The main feature of modern ITS is their integration with methods of geoinformatics, spatial models, data mining, and geo/spatial knowledge acquisition methods. In this section, we propose a conceptual model of integrated multi-agent ITS and functional structures of some components of the system.   The multi-agent structure of ITS can be implemented through the usage of domain-oriented components: (1) *data collection component,* responsible for collecting, storing and retrieving statistical and real-time data. This component is considered as the core of the agent, which is accessed by other agents through certain interface protocols; (2) *analytical data processing component* that includes subcomponents: *model selection* intended for storing models, creating new models based on exisitng models and data and/or by using expert knowledge bases, as well as configuring models and evaluating the adequacy of models based on retrieved data and knowledge bases; *modeling and analysis* designed for express analysis of situations and quick decision making using the construction of model templates; the subcomponent of *probabilistic models,* *static models,* and *dynamic models* intended for direct computations and detailed analysis of transport tasks; *decision-making* allows one to find, prepare and conduct a rationale for control decisions that are necessary to achieve the goal.

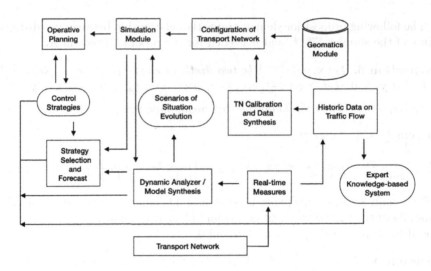

**Fig. 2.** Active Intelligent Control Subsystem of Transport Network

The main functions of the agent are storage of decisions, development of new ones based both on the model and on the basis of expert knowledge base, and evaluation of control decisions; (3) *information representation and visualization component*, whose main task is the preparation of documents for the decision maker. It is designed to present information in an efficient way, and it must perform data transformation, for example, from text to graphical form, plotting, creating animations or displaying using GIS technologies and 3D geomodeling.

The above components are implemented as agents and mapped onto a conceptual model of multi-agent ITS. The model has a multi-level structure and the number of agents at each level depends on the system configuration: (1) *user interaction level* within information representation and visualization component; (2) *data search and collection* within data collection component; (3) *data classification and transformation level* and (4) *data modeling and analysis level* both within analytical data processing component. The construction of multi-agent ITS is based on the distribution of functions between individual agents. Such a system is a combination of intelligent and traditional components, autonomous and interacting agents, where each solves its own "intelligent" task.

The subsystem of active intelligent control of transport network (Fig. 2) consists of the following: (1) *Measuring the traffic flow* and analyzing data that facilitates the transport network management; (2) *Operative Planning* including the study of transport network behavior under various scenarios (such as bad weather, accidents, road works, increased demand, etc.), as well as developing control strategies that, when needed, increase the productivity of the transport network and assess the suitability of the developed strategies in terms of their cost and potential efficiency; (3) *Strategy Selection* as implementation of the most promising strategies directly on the highways by installing the necessary equipment and software; (4) *Decision Support System* that filters incoming real-time measurements, predicts the behavior of the transport system for the next few hours and helps the dispatcher choose the control strategy that best suits the situation; (5) *Expert Knowledge* module that uses retrospective data and AI techniques in the process of developing of control strategies and their selection; (6) *Simulator* module based on mathematical transport models that uses operative planning to run a large number of simulations of various scenarios and potential traffic improvement actions, where scenarios may include redistribution of traffic flows due to possible road works, increased travel costs, maximum road capacity, etc.; (7) *Geomatics* module that incorporates telematics and geoinformation systems data is used for constructing dynamic transport model and its calibration based on data processing methods.

The adequate and efficient traffic flow allocation requires the system of traffic flow optimization and forecast whose structure is presented in Fig. 3. The complex traffic flow simulaton subsystem that supports the active control of transport network is shown in Fig. 4. It contains the components: (1) *Model/Map of TN* provides the map of transport network of a city (area) in the form of a directed graph; (2) *Crossroads* describes the configuration of crossroads and the rules of passage of it; (3) *Origin-Destination Traffic Flow* provides the traffic flow information and generates the flow distribution between fixed origin-destination pairs; (4) *Traffic Flow Simulator* provides the simulation of flows in transport network based on traffic light signals and current traffic flow in the network; (5) *Routing Module* transforms the flow distribution into actual traffic flow allocation/routes with the use of the current situation in the transport network provided by the Traffic Flow Simulator; (6) *Routes Scheduler* contains information on travels that are currently being performed, represented in the form of routes as a sequence of links over which either the users are traveling or going to travel; (7) *Historic Data* module provides information/data support and keeps

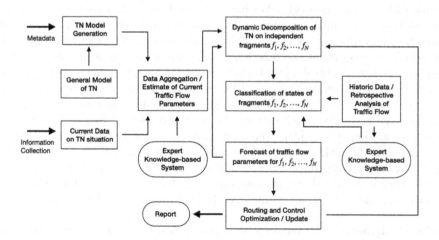

**Fig. 3.** Functional Structure of Traffic Flow Optimization and Forecast Subsystem

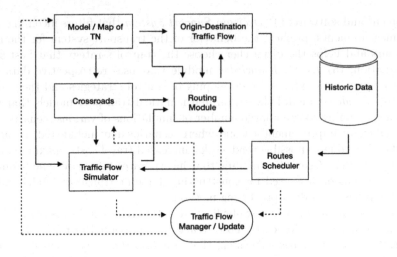

**Fig. 4.** The Structure of Traffic Flow Assignment Simulation Subsystem

track of all the journeys in the network; (8) *Traffic Flow Manager* implements the control of traffic flow assignment in the network.

The proposed generalized structures of ITS subsystems can serve as unified models for the development of perspective advanced AI-based ITS and intelligent control systems for dynamic traffic flow allocation in transportation networks.

## 5   Conclusion

We have introduced the notions of Wardrop optimal flows and Wardrop optimal networks and considered a dynamical model of optimal traffic flow distribution in parallel dynamic networks. We have provided an evolutionary game theory formulation of dynamic approach to Wardrop optimal flows using the model of discrete-time replicator dynamics on Wardrop optimal networks. We have also proposed the conceptual and functional structure of intelligent information system for intelligent control, optimization and forecast, and simulation of dynamic traffic flow assignment in transportation networks. Future research will address the study of Wardrop optimal flows on general dynamic networks and on general directed networks, which then can be employed for modeling and analysis of (mis)information spread [26], opinion dynamics and consensus models in complex networks [27,28], as well as for modeling of flow distribution and interaction in controlled dynamical systems and networks [29,30]. Another direction of future work is to extend and improve the traffic flow modeling and optimization algorithms, and perform algorithmic analysis of the developed models.

**Acknowledgments.** The authors wish to thank anonymous referees for useful commens and suggestions toward improvement of the presentation of this paper.

# A    Appendix

**Definition 4.** *A sequence* $\left\{\mathbf{x}^{(n)}\right\}_{n\in\mathbb{N}}$ *with* $\mathbf{x}^{(1)} := \mathbf{x}$ *is called an* **orbit** *of the point* $\mathbf{x} \in \mathbb{S}^{m-1}$.

Let $\mathcal{E}_{\varepsilon\mathbf{L}_m}(\mathbf{y},\mathbf{x}) := \varepsilon(\mathbf{y},\mathbf{L}_m(\mathbf{x})) = \varepsilon\sum_{i=1}^{m} y_i\ell_i(x_i)$ and $\mathcal{E}_{\varepsilon\mathbf{L}_m}(\mathbf{x},\mathbf{x}) := \varepsilon(\mathbf{x},\mathbf{L}_m(\mathbf{x})) = \varepsilon\sum_{i=1}^{m} x_i\ell_i(x_i)$ for any $\mathbf{x},\mathbf{y} \in \mathbb{S}^{m-1}$ and $\varepsilon \in (-1,0)$.

**Definition 5.** *A flow* $\mathbf{x}$ *is called a* **Nash equilibrium** *if one has* $\mathcal{E}_{\varepsilon\mathbf{L}_n}(\mathbf{x},\mathbf{x}) \geq \mathcal{E}_{\varepsilon\mathbf{L}_n}(\mathbf{y},\mathbf{x})$ *for any* $\mathbf{y} \in \mathbb{S}^{m-1}$. *A flow* $\mathbf{x}$ *is called a* **strictly Nash equilibrium** *if one has* $\mathcal{E}_{\varepsilon\mathbf{L}_n}(\mathbf{x},\mathbf{x}) > \mathcal{E}_{\varepsilon\mathbf{L}_n}(\mathbf{y},\mathbf{x})$ *for any* $\mathbf{y} \in \mathbb{S}^{m-1}$ *with* $\mathbf{y} \neq \mathbf{x}$.

**Definition 6.** *A point* $\mathbf{x} \in \mathbb{S}^{m-1}$ *is called a* **common fixed point** *of the sequence of the replicator equations* $\{\mathcal{R}_n\}_{n\in\mathbb{N}}$ *if one has* $\mathcal{R}_n(\mathbf{x}) = \mathbf{x}$ *for any* $n \in \mathbb{N}$.

**Definition 7.** *A continuous function* $\varphi : \mathbb{S}^{m-1} \to \mathbb{R}$ *is called a* **Lyapunov function** *if the number sequence* $\left\{\varphi\left(\mathbf{x}^{(n)}\right)\right\}_{n\in\mathbb{N}}$ *is a bounded monotone sequence for any initial point* $\mathbf{x}^{(1)} := \mathbf{x} \in \mathbb{S}^{m-1}$.

**Definition 8.** *A common fixed point* $\mathbf{x} \in \mathbb{S}^{m-1}$ *is called* **stable** *if for every neighborhood* $U(\mathbf{x}) \subset \mathbb{S}^{m-1}$ *of* $\mathbf{x}$ *there exists a neighborhood* $V(\mathbf{x}) \subset U(\mathbf{x}) \subset \mathbb{S}^{m-1}$ *of* $\mathbf{x}$ *such that an orbit* $\left\{\mathbf{y}^{(n)}\right\}_{n\in\mathbb{N}}$ *with* $\mathbf{y}^{(1)} := \mathbf{y}$ *of any initial point* $\mathbf{y} \in V(\mathbf{x})$ *remains inside of the neighborhood* $U(\mathbf{x})$.

**Definition 9.** *A common fixed point* $\mathbf{x} \in \mathbb{S}^{m-1}$ *is called* **attracting** *if there exists a neighborhood* $V(\mathbf{x}) \subset \mathbb{S}^{m-1}$ *of* $\mathbf{x}$ *such that an orbit an orbit* $\left\{\mathbf{y}^{(n)}\right\}_{n\in\mathbb{N}}$ *with* $\mathbf{y}^{(1)} := \mathbf{y}$ *of any initial point* $\mathbf{y} \in V(\mathbf{x})$ *converges to* $\mathbf{x}$. *A fixed point* $\mathbf{y} \in \mathbb{S}^{m-1}$ *is called asymptotically stable if it is both stable and attracting.*

**Definition 10.** *A common fixed point* $\mathbf{x} \in \mathbb{S}^{m-1}$ *is called* **asymptotically stable** *if it is both stable and attracting.*

# References

1. Acemoglu, D., Ozdaglar, A.: Competition and efficiency in congested markets. Math. Oper. Res. **32**(1), 1–31 (2007)
2. Köhler, E., Möhring, R.H., Skutella, M.: Traffic networks and flows over time. In: Lerner, J., Wagner, D., Zweig, K.A. (eds.) Algorithmics of Large and Complex Networks. LNCS, vol. 5515, pp. 166–196. Springer, Heidelberg (2009). https://doi.org/10.1007/978-3-642-02094-0_9
3. Köhler, Skutella, M.: Flows over time with load-dependent transit times. SIAM J. Optim. **15**(4), 1185–1202 (2005)
4. Hamacher, H., Heller, S., Rupp, B.: Flow location (flowloc) problems: dynamic network flows and location models for evacuation planning. Ann. Oper. Res. **207**(1), 161–180 (2013)
5. Chen, Y., Chin, H.: The quickest path problem. Comput. Oper. Res. **17**(2), 153–161 (1990)

6. Boland, N., Kalinowski, T., Waterer, H., Zheng, L.: Scheduling arc maintenance jobs in a network to maximize total flow over time. Discrete Appl. Math. **163**, 34–52 (2014)
7. Peis, B., Skutella, M., Wiese, A.: Packet routing: complexity and algorithms. In: Bampis, E., Jansen, K. (eds.) WAOA 2009. LNCS, vol. 5893, pp. 217–228. Springer, Heidelberg (2010). https://doi.org/10.1007/978-3-642-12450-1_20
8. Li, K., Yang, S.: Non-identical parallel-machine scheduling research with minimizing total weighted completion times: Models, relaxations and algorithms. Appl. Math. Model. **33**(4), 2145–2158 (2009)
9. Fleischer, L.K.: Faster algorithms for the quickest transshipment problem. SIAM J. Optim. **12**(1), 18–35 (2001)
10. Ford, L.R., Fulkerson, D.R.: Constructing maximal dynamic flows from static flows. Oper. Res. **6**(3), 419–433 (1958)
11. Hoppe, B., Tardos, E.: The quickest transshipment problem. Math. Oper. Res. **25**(1), 36–62 (2000)
12. Nash, J.F.: Equilibrium points in $n$-person games. Proc. Nat. Acad. Sci. USA **36**(1), 48–49 (1950)
13. Nash, J.F.: Non-cooperative games. Ann. Math. **54**, 287–295 (1951)
14. Hofbauer, J., Sigmund, K.: Evolutionary game dynamics. Bull. Amer. Math. Soc. **40**, 479–519 (2003)
15. Sigmund, K.: Evolutionary Game Dynamics. AMS, Providence (2010)
16. Hofbauer, J., Sigmund, K.: Evolutionary Games and Replicator Dynamics. Cambridge University Press, Cambridge (1998)
17. Cressman, R.: Evolutionary Dynamics and Extensive Form Games. MIT (2003)
18. Saburov, M.: On replicator equations with nonlinear payoff functions defined by the Ricker models. Adv. Pure Appl. Math. **12**, 139–156 (2021)
19. Saburov, M.: On discrete-time replicator equations with nonlinear payoff functions. Dyn. Games Appl. **12**, 643–661 (2022)
20. Patriksson, M.: The Traffic Assignment Problem: Models and Methods. VSP, The Netherlands (1994)
21. Acemoglu, D., Srikant, R.: Incentives and prices in communication networks. In: Algorithmic Game Theory. eds. N. Nisan, T. Roughgarden, E. Tardos, V. V. Vazirani. pp. 107–132, Cambridge University Press (2007)
22. Carlier, G., Jimenez, C., Santambrogio, F.: Optimal transportation with traffic congestion and Wardrop equilibria. SIAM J. Control. Optim. **47**, 1330–1350 (2008)
23. Beckmann, M., McGuir, C., Winsten, C.: Studies in Economics of Transportation. Yale University Press, New Haven (1956)
24. Larsson, T., Patriksson, M.: Equilibrium characterizations of solutions to side constrained traffic equilibrium models. Matematiche (Catania) **49**, 249–280 (1994)
25. Larsson, T., Patriksson, M.: Side constrained traffic equilibrium models: analysis, computation and applications. Transportation Res. **33**, 233–264 (1999)
26. Gavric, D., Bagdasaryan, A.: A fuzzy model for combating misinformation in social network twitter. Journal of Physics: Conf. Ser. **1391**, 012050 (2019) [8 pages]
27. Saburov, M., Saburov, K.: Reaching a nonlinear consensus: polynomial stochastic operators. Int. J. Control Autom. Syst. **12**, 1276–1282 (2014)
28. Saburov, M., Saburov, K.: Reaching a consensus: a discrete nonlinear time-varying case. Int. J. Syst. Sci. **47**, 2449–2457 (2016)
29. Bagdasaryan, A.: Optimal control synthesis for affine nonlinear dynamic systems. Journal of Physics: Conf. Ser. **1391**, 012113 (2019) [8 pages]
30. Bagdasaryan, A.: Optimal control and stability analysis of nonlinear control-affine systems, Journal of Physics: Conf. Ser. **1730**, 012076 (2021) [13 pages]

# Streamlined Training of GCN for Node Classification with Automatic Loss Function and Optimizer Selection

Sanaullah[1(✉)] , Shamini Koravuna[2] , Ulrich Rückert[2],
and Thorsten Jungeblut[1]

[1] Bielefeld University of Applied Sciences, Bielefeld, Germany
{sanaullah,thorsten.jungeblut}@fh-bielefeld.de
[2] Bielefeld University, Bielefeld, Germany
{skoravuna,rueckert}@techfak.uni-bielefeld.de

**Abstract.** Graph Neural Networks (GNNs) are specialized neural networks that operate on graph-structured data, utilizing the connections between nodes to learn and process information. To achieve optimal performance, GNNs require the automatic selection of the best loss and optimization functions, which allows the model to adapt to the unique features of the dataset being used. This eliminates the need for manual selection, saving time and minimizing the requirement for domain-specific knowledge. The automatic selection of loss and optimization functions is a crucial factor in achieving state-of-the-art results when training GNNs. In this study, we trained Graph Convolutional Networks (GCNs) and Graph Attention Networks (GAT) models for node classification on three benchmark datasets. To automatically select the best loss and optimization functions, we utilized performance metrics. We implemented a learning rate scheduler to adjust the learning rate based on the model's performance, which led to improved results. We evaluated the model's performance using multiple metrics and reported the best loss function and performance metric, enabling users to compare its performance to other models. Our approach achieved state-of-the-art results, highlighting the importance of selecting the appropriate loss and optimizer functions. Additionally, we developed a real-time visualization of the GCN model during training, providing users with a detailed understanding of the model's behavior. Overall, this study provides a comprehensive understanding of GNNs and their application to graph-structured data, with a specific focus on real-time visualization of GNN behavior during training.

**Keywords:** Graph convolutional networks · Graph-Structured Data · Los Functions · Node classification · Benchmark Datasets · Automatic Selection

This research was supported by the research training group "Dataninja" (Trustworthy AI for Seamless Problem Solving: Next Generation Intelligence Joins Robust Data Analysis) funded by the German federal state of North Rhine-Westphalia and the project SAIL. SAIL is funded by the Ministry of Culture and Science of the State of North Rhine-Westphalia under grant no. NW21-059B.

L. Iliadis et al. (Eds.): EANN 2023, CCIS 1826, pp. 191–202, 2023.
https://doi.org/10.1007/978-3-031-34204-2_17

# 1    Introduction

Graph Neural Network (GNN) is a type of neural network that is designed to operate on graph data structures [1]. In contrast to traditional neural networks that are designed to operate on vectors and matrices, GNNs operate on graphs, which can represent complex structured data, such as social networks, protein structures, and citation networks. GNNs use a message-passing approach to update node representations based on the features of its neighboring nodes and edges in the graph. This process is typically repeated multiple times to allow each node to gather information from its immediate neighbors and gradually incorporate information from more distant nodes. The selection of loss and optimization functions is crucial for achieving optimal performance in a given task. However, the process of selecting the best combination of these functions can be time-consuming and require significant domain expertise. Furthermore, manual selection can be prone to bias and can overlook potential combinations that may yield better results [2]. Therefore, an automatic approach for selecting loss and optimization functions can save time and effort, and potentially lead to better results by exploring a larger space of possibilities. This is especially important in the context of GNNs, where the task of selecting the best loss and optimization functions can be even more complex due to the inherent complexity of graph data [3].

In this study, we introduced an automatic approach for loss function and optimization in GNNs. One of the main types of GNNs we considered, GCN [4], which is a feedforward neural network designed to operate on graphs. GCNs apply a graph convolution operation to each node in the graph by aggregating the feature representations of its neighboring nodes, allowing for effective modeling of the local structure and neighborhood relationships of the graph data [5–7]. Another type of GNN we considered, GAT [8], uses attention mechanisms to weigh the importance of each neighbor node for a given node, allowing the network to selectively focus on the most relevant information for each node. To enhance the performance of GNNs, we proposed an automatic approach for optimizing the loss function. This approach can save significant amounts of time and resources that would otherwise be required for manual optimization. Our experiments on various datasets demonstrate the effectiveness of our approach and show that it outperforms existing methods in terms of accuracy and efficiency.

We also introduced real-time GCN training visualization as a tool to understand the model's behavior during the training process. The visualization provided insights into how the model learns and helped us identify any training process issues that might affect the model's performance. It is essential as it provides immediate feedback on the behavior and performance of a model during the learning process. This is particularly beneficial when working with complex models that require extended training time. Real-time visualization allows researchers and practitioners to diagnose and address any issues with the model promptly, leading to better performance. Various simulators in diverse fields, including computational biology [9], robotics [10], and game engines [11], have introduced real-time visualization to enhance their models' performance.

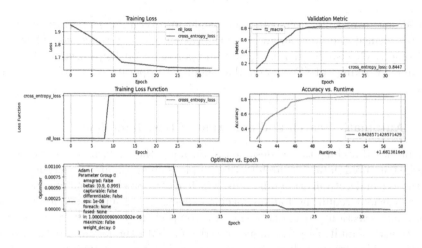

**Fig. 1.** Real-time visualization of GCN training process, which allows for immediate feedback on model performance and behavior during the learning process.

## 2   Proposed Architecture

In order to further optimize the performance of GNNs, we automated the selection process of the loss and optimization functions. In this study, we focused on automating this process by developing an approach that selects the best loss and optimization functions based on their respective performance metrics. This automatic selection eliminates the need for manual selection, saving time and minimizing the requirement for domain-specific knowledge. We trained and tested two types of GNNs, namely GCNs, and GATs, for node classification on three different benchmark datasets; Cora, CiteSeer, and PubMed [12]. During training, we implemented a ReduceLROnPlateau [13] learning rate scheduler that adjusts the learning rate based on the model's performance, leading to improved results. We evaluated the model's performance using multiple metrics and reported the best loss function, performance metric, and test accuracy. By doing so, we provided a comprehensive understanding of the model's behavior and how it compares to other models. This framework allows for the selection of the best loss and optimization functions based on their respective performance metrics, resulting in optimal model performance.

Additionally, we also investigated a real-time GCN visualization to provide a more comprehensive understanding of the model's behavior during training. The real-time GNN visualization of the GCN model allows users to track the model's training progress in real time, which is crucial for identifying and resolving any issues that may arise. It provides insights into how the model processes information through the graph structure and enables users to make informed decisions about the model's optimization and loss functions. Figure 1 shows an example of the GCN model training visualization during runtime, where the node embeddings are updated after each iteration. By observing the changes in the embeddings over time, users can gain insight into the model's performance and make informed decisions about its optimization and loss functions. Therefore, real-time GNN visualization is a powerful approach that helps users understand the inner workings of GNNs and their ability to operate on graph-structured data.

## 2.1   Automatic Search and Selection of Best Functions

The proposed architecture is designed to optimize the performance of GNNs on graph-structured data. The architecture employs an automated selection process for the loss and optimization functions, which allows for an optimal model performance without requiring domain-specific expertise or manual selection of functions. The selection process is based on a comprehensive evaluation framework that considers multiple performance metrics for both the loss and optimization functions. This framework enables the selection of the best functions based on their respective performance metrics, leading to improved model performance on graph-structured data. The automated selection process provides an effective and efficient method for selecting the most appropriate loss and optimization functions for GNNs. The use of multiple performance metrics ensures a comprehensive understanding of the model's behavior and performance, allowing for insights into its strengths and weaknesses. These insights can inform informed decisions about its optimization and lead to better model performance.

**Loss Search Phase.** Algorithm 1 provides a high-level description of our proposed architecture implementation. In order to train the GCN and GAT models effectively, we first conduct a loss search phase. During this phase, our algorithm automatically selects the best loss function based on the performance of the models on the training data. To achieve this, we used a loss functions dictionary that contains three types of loss functions: $nll\_loss$, $mse\_loss$, and $l1\_loss$ [14]. Each of these loss functions can be used to train the models. However, the choice of the loss function can have a significant impact on the performance of the models, and different loss functions may be more appropriate for different tasks.

In our implementation, we used a loss functions dictionary that contains three types of loss functions: $nll\_loss$, $mse\_loss$, and $l1\_loss$.

- $nll\_loss$ (negative log-likelihood loss) is often used in classification problems and measures the difference between the predicted probabilities and the true probabilities. It can be defined as:

$$nll\_loss(y_{\text{true}}, y_{\text{pred}}) = -\sum_{i=1}^{n} y_{\text{true},i} \log(y_{\text{pred},i}) \qquad (1)$$

where $y_{true}$ is the true label, $y_{pred}$ is the predicted label, and $n$ is the number of classes.

**Algorithm 1.** An Algorithm for Automatic Optimization and Loss Function Selection Using GNN Models

---

**Require:**
1: Start
   *Inputs* :
   *Dataset D*
   Number of epochs $N$
   List of loss functions $LF = [L_1, L_2, \ldots, L_m]$
   List of performance metrics $PM = [P_1, P_2, \ldots, P_n]$
   List of optimizers $OPT = [O_1, O_2, \ldots, O_k]$
   List of learning rates $LR = [lr_1, lr_2, \ldots, lr_k]$
**Require:**
   *Outputs* :
   GNN model accuracy
   Best loss function $L^*$
   Best optimizer $O^*$
   Learning rate history $LRH$
**Ensure:**
   Import the required packages and libraries
   Load the dataset using Planetoid
   Define the GNN model (GCN or GAT)
   Dictionary of loss functions and their corresponding performance metrics
      $LF\_PM = \{L_1 : [P_1, P_2, \ldots, P_n], L_2 : [P_1, P_2, \ldots, P_n], \ldots, L_m : [P_1, P_2, \ldots, P_n]\}$
   Define a list of optimizers and their corresponding learning rates
      $OPT\_LR = [(O_1, lr_1), (O_2, lr_2), \ldots, (O_k, lr_k)]$
   Initialize best loss function $L^*$ and best optimizer $O^*$ to None
   Initialize empty dictionary *loss_history*
   For each optimizer $O_i$ and learning rate $lr_i$ in $OPT\_LR$:
      a. For each loss function $L_j$ in $LF$
         i. Train the GNN model using $O_i$ and $L_j$ for $N$ epochs and record the training loss for each epoch
         ii. Compute the performance metrics in $PM$ for $L_j$ on the validation set
         iii. If $L^*$ and $O^*$ are None or the performance metric for $L_j$ and $O_i$ is better than the current best performance metric, update $L^*$ and $O^*$
         iv. Save the training loss history for $L_j$ and $O_i$ to *loss_history*
   Compute the loss using the best loss function $L^*$
   Backpropagate the loss and update the model weights using the selected optimizer $O^*$
   Adjust the learning rate using the ReduceLROnPlateau learning rate scheduler
   Repeat steps 8 to 11 for a fixed number of epochs $N$
   Record the learning rate history $LRH$
   Plot the training loss over epochs for each optimizer and loss function combination using *loss_history*
   Return the GNN models , best loss function L*, best optimizer O*, and learning rate history LRH
2: End

---

- *mse_loss* (mean squared error loss) is commonly used in regression problems and measures the average squared difference between the predicted values and the true values. It can be defined as:

$$mse\_loss(y_{\text{true}}, y_{\text{pred}}) = \frac{1}{n} \sum_{i=1}^{n} (y_{\text{true},i} - y_{\text{pred},i})^2 \qquad (2)$$

where $y_{true}$ is the true value, $y_{pred}$ is the predicted value, and $n$ is the number of samples.
- *l1_loss* (mean absolute error loss) is similar to *mse_loss*, but measures the average absolute difference between the predicted values and the true values. It can be defined as:

$$l1\_loss(y_{\text{true}}, y_{\text{pred}}) = \frac{1}{n} \sum_{i=1}^{n} |y_{\text{true},i} - y_{\text{pred},i}| \qquad (3)$$

where $y_{true}$ is the true value, $y_{pred}$ is the predicted value, and $n$ is the number of samples.

To automatically select the best loss function, our algorithm maps each loss function to a corresponding performance metric that evaluates the model. For example, *nll_loss* may be mapped to accuracy, *mse_loss* to mean squared error, and *l1_loss* to mean absolute error. Our algorithm then evaluates the models using these performance metrics and selects the loss function that yields the best performance on the training data. The selected loss function is then used to train the models for subsequent iterations. This automated approach to loss function selection can save significant time and effort, as it eliminates the need for manual experimentation with different loss functions. It also ensures that the best loss function is used for training the models, leading to improved performance.

**Optimizer Search Phase.** To automate the selection of the optimization function, we used a similar approach to the loss function selection process. We created a dictionary that contains various optimization functions such as Adam, RMSprop, and SGD. Each optimization function has different hyperparameters and can affect the model's performance in different ways. To select the best optimization function, we used a similar process to the loss function selection, where we mapped each optimization function to a corresponding performance metric. We then evaluated the models using these performance metrics and selected the optimization function that yields the best performance on the validation data. The selected optimization function was then used for subsequent iterations.

In the dictionary of optimization functions that we created, each optimizer has its own set of hyperparameters that can be tuned to improve the performance of the model. The Adam optimizer, for example, uses a combination of momentum and adaptive learning rates to update the model's parameters. It has been shown to perform well on a wide range of deep-learning tasks, including GNNs. The equations for the Adam optimizer are as follows:

$$m_t = \beta_1 m_{t-1} + (1 - \beta_1) g_t \tag{4}$$

$$v_t = \beta_2 v_{t-1} + (1 - \beta_2) g_t^2 \tag{5}$$

$$\theta_t = \theta_{t-1} - \frac{\eta}{\sqrt{v_t} + \epsilon} m_t \tag{6}$$

where $m_t$ and $v_t$ are the first and second moments of the gradient, $\beta_1$ and $\beta_2$ are exponential decay rates for the moments, $g_t$ is the gradient, $\theta_t$ is the parameter at time $t$, $\eta$ is the learning rate, and $\epsilon$ is a small constant added to the denominator for numerical stability.

The RMSprop optimizer, on the other hand, uses a moving average of the squared gradient to adjust the learning rate for each weight. It has been shown to be effective in handling non-stationary and sparse gradients. The equations for the RMSprop optimizer are as follows:

$$v_t = \beta v_{t-1} + (1 - \beta) g_t^2 \tag{7}$$

where $v_t$ is the moving average of the squared gradient, $\beta$ is the decay rate for the moving average, and the other symbols have the same meaning as in the Adam optimizer.

The SGD optimizer, or stochastic gradient descent, is a simple optimizer that updates the parameters by taking small steps in the direction of the negative gradient of the loss function. It has been shown to be effective in many deep learning tasks, although it may require more iterations to converge than more sophisticated optimizers. The equation for SGD optimizer is:

$$\theta_t = \theta_{t-1} - \eta g_t \tag{8}$$

where $\theta_t$ is the parameter at time $t$, $\eta$ is the learning rate, and $g_t$ is the gradient at time $t$.

Therefore, the automatic selection of the optimization function and the implementation of a learning rate scheduler can help improve the performance of GNNs and other deep-learning models. These techniques allow for more efficient training and can help prevent the model from getting stuck in local minima.

To further improve the training process, we implemented a ReduceLROnPlateau learning rate scheduler. This scheduler adjusts the learning rate during training based on the performance of the model on the validation data. Specifically, it reduces the learning rate by a factor of 0.1 if the validation loss does not improve for a certain number of epochs. This technique helps prevent the model from getting stuck in local minima and can lead to improved results.

## 2.2   Real-time Training Visualization

Real-time visualization is a powerful tool that allows users to observe the behavior of the GNN model during training in run-time. This approach provides a comprehensive understanding of how the model processes information through the graph structure and how it updates the node embeddings after each iteration. By monitoring the model's training progress in real-time, users can quickly identify and resolve any issues that may arise, ensuring that the model is optimized for its intended use.

In addition, our real-time visualization offers users the ability to observe the model's behavior with different combinations of optimizers, loss functions, and learning rates. This allows users to see the effect of each hyperparameter on the model's performance in real-time, and quickly identify the best combination for their specific use case. By monitoring the performance of the model with different hyperparameters, users can also gain valuable insights into the behavior of the model and how it responds to changes in the data or hyperparameters. As shown in Fig. 1, our real-time visualization provides a dynamic and interactive way of understanding the model's behavior during training. Users can explore the model's performance by adjusting the hyperparameters in real-time, and observing how the model responds to different changes. This allows users to experiment with different configurations and gain a deeper understanding of how the model works and what is necessary for optimal performance. Therefore, this real-time visualization is a powerful tool for understanding the GCN model's behavior, and it can be used to identify potential problems and fine-tune the model accordingly.

## 3   Dataset

The datasets used in our evaluation of the proposed architecture were carefully selected to represent different citation network scenarios. The Cora dataset comprises 2,708 scientific publications that are classified into one of seven classes. Each node in the graph is represented by a binary bag-of-words vector that captures the presence or absence of certain words in the corresponding publication, and the edges represent citation relationships between the publications. Similarly, the CiteSeer dataset contains 3,327 scientific publications that are classified into one of six classes. However, the features of each node are represented by a 3,703-dimensional sparse vector that indicates the presence or absence of certain words in the corresponding publication. Again, the edges in the graph represent citation relationships between the publications. Lastly, the PubMed dataset is a biomedical citation network consisting of 19,717 scientific publications classified into one of three classes. The features of each node are represented by a 500-dimensional sparse vector that captures the presence or absence of certain medical terms in the corresponding publication. The edges in the graph also represent citation relationships between the publications. The use of these datasets provides a diverse range of citation network scenarios, making our evaluation more comprehensive and meaningful.

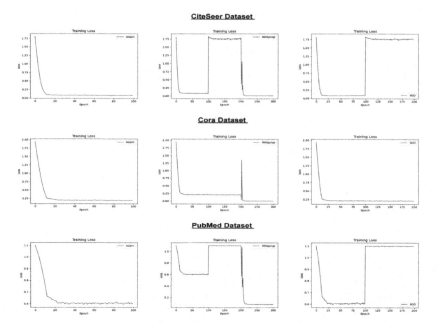

**Fig. 2.** GAT loss function search during training on three benchmark datasets. Each row shows the training process of the GAN model on a specific dataset

## 4    Findings and Analysis

The results of our evaluation of the proposed architecture are both interesting and promising. Through an automated selection process of loss and optimization functions, we were able to improve the performance of the GCN and GAT models compared to the traditional manual selection approach. This demonstrates the efficiency and effectiveness of automated approaches in selecting the best combinations of functions for a given task. Our comparison of the GCN and GAT models revealed that the former outperformed the latter in terms of accuracy on all three benchmark datasets. This result suggests that the GCN model is more suitable for node classification tasks in the context of citation networks. Figure 2 and 3, show the automated search for the best loss function during training on each dataset, highlighting the architecture's ability to choose the best loss function for each task. The plots demonstrate the effectiveness of our automated loss function selection approach in improving the performance of GAN models for node classification tasks in citation networks. Figure 4 displays the detailed results of each test case, providing insights into the performance of the proposed GNN architectural model on various datasets and under different experimental conditions.

Therefore, our evaluation of different optimization functions revealed that the Adam optimizer consistently performed better than other optimizers on all three datasets. This finding indicates that the Adam optimizer is a robust and reliable optimization function for GNNs in the context of node classification tasks. Therefore, our findings demonstrate the effectiveness of the proposed

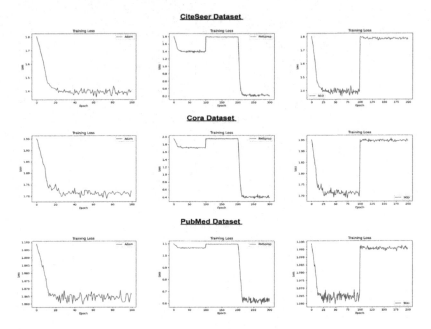

**Fig. 3.** GCN loss function search during training on three benchmark datasets. Each row shows the training process of the GCN model on a specific dataset

| Dataset | GNN Models | No. of Layers | Best metric | Epoch | Optimizer | Loss Function |
|---------|-----------|---------------|-------------|-------|-----------|---------------|
| Cora | GCN | 2 | 0.11 | 100 | Adam | nll_loss |
| | GAT | 2 | 0.129 | 100 | RMSprop | ll_loss |
| CiteSeer | GCN | 2 | 0.101 | 100 | SGD | nll_loss |
| | GAT | 2 | 0.163 | 100 | RMSprop | nll_loss |
| Pubmed | GCN | 2 | 0.297 | 100 | RMSprop | mse |
| | GAT | 2 | 0.345 | 100 | Adam | nll_loss |

**Fig. 4.** The detailed results of each test case, providing insights into the performance of the proposed GNN architectural model on various datasets

automated approach for selecting loss and optimization functions and provide valuable insights into the suitability of different functions for specific datasets. These insights can guide the development of more efficient and accurate GNN models for citation network analysis. Figure 5 visualizes a series of plots that provide insights into the performance of the GCN model with different combinations of optimizers and loss functions. The top left plot shows the total number of epochs run for each optimizer, while the top right plot displays the sum of the number of layers used by each loss function and the bottom left plot shows the same information for each optimizer. The bottom right plot displays the sum of the best metric achieved for each loss function. Finally, the central plot shows the total epochs for each loss function, indicating which combinations of optimizer and loss function produced the best results.

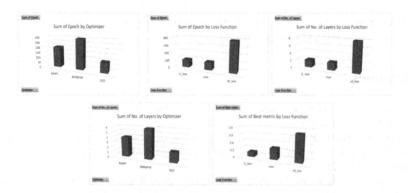

**Fig. 5.** Visualization of the sum of epochs by optimizer, sum of epochs by loss function, sum of number of layers by loss function, sum of number of layers by optimizer, and the sum of best metric by loss function plots.

# 5  Conclusion

To summarize, we have developed a simple yet effective Automatic Loss Function and Optimizer Selection architecture that is interactive, fast, and easy to use for understanding the mechanism of GNNs. The aim of this study was to optimize the performance of Graph Neural Networks (GNNs) by automating the selection of the best loss and optimization functions. By training Graph Convolutional Networks (GCNs) and Graph Attention Networks (GAT) models for node classification on three benchmark datasets, we have demonstrated the effectiveness of our approach in achieving state-of-the-art results. We have also implemented a ReduceLROnPlateau learning rate scheduler that adjusts the learning rate based on the model's performance, leading to improved results. The evaluation of the model's performance using multiple metrics has enabled users to compare its performance to other models, and the implementation of a real-time GNN visualization of the GCN model has allowed users to observe and understand the model's behavior in detail. Our results emphasize the importance of carefully selecting the loss and optimizer functions and providing a comprehensive understanding of GNNs and their application to graph-structured data.

This study serves as a foundational base for our future investigations, as we aim to develop a Spiking Neural Network architecture where the optimal hyperparameter values will be automatically selected by the model. We have gained valuable insights into the flow of Machine Learning architecture through this study, which will help guide our future research. By building on the findings of this study, we hope to improve the performance of Spiking Neural Networks and contribute to the advancement of the field.

**Availability.** In this study, we have made the code used in our experiments publicly available on GitHub [15]. This allows other researchers to replicate our experiments and build upon our work and to ensure the reproducibility of our results, we have used publicly available datasets for generating all the test cases.

# References

1. Zhou, J., et al.: Graph neural networks: a review of methods and applications. AI open **1**, 57–81 (2020)
2. Zheng, L., Zhou, J., Chen, C., Wu, B., Wang, L., Zhang, B.: Asfgnn: automated separated-federated graph neural network. Peer-to-Peer Network. Appl. **14**(3), 1692–1704 (2021)
3. Niknam, T., Narimani, M., Aghaei, J., Azizipanah-Abarghooee, R.: Improved particle swarm optimisation for multi-objective optimal power flow considering the cost, loss, emission and voltage stability index. IET Generation, Trans. Distrib. **6**(6), 515–527 (2012)
4. Zhang, S., Tong, H., Xu, J., Maciejewski, R.: Graph convolutional networks: a comprehensive review. Comput. Social Netw. **6**(1), 1–23 (2019). https://doi.org/10.1186/s40649-019-0069-y
5. Li, Q., Han, Z., Wu, X.M.: Deeper insights into graph convolutional networks for semi-supervised learning. In: Proceedings of the AAAI Conference on Artificial Intelligence, vol. 32 (2018)
6. Danel, T., et al.: Spatial graph convolutional networks. In: Yang, H., Pasupa, K., Leung, A.C.-S., Kwok, J.T., Chan, J.H., King, I. (eds.) ICONIP 2020. CCIS, vol. 1333, pp. 668–675. Springer, Cham (2020). https://doi.org/10.1007/978-3-030-63823-8_76
7. Wang, X., Zhu, M., Bo, D., Cui, P., Shi, C., Pei, J.: Am-gcn: Adaptive multi-channel graph convolutional networks. In: Proceedings of the 26th ACM SIGKDD International Conference on Knowledge Discovery & Data Mining, pp. 1243–1253 (2020)
8. Veličković, P., Cucurull, G., Casanova, A., Romero, A., Liò, P., Bengio, Y.: Graph Attention Networks. In: International Conference on Learning Representations (2018)
9. Sanaullah, Baig, H., Madsen, J., Lee, J.A.: A parallel approach to perform threshold value and propagation delay analyses of genetic logic circuit models. ACS Synth. Biol. **9**(12), 3422–3428 (2020)
10. Sanaullah, Koravuna, S., Rückert, U., Jungeblut, T.: Snns model analyzing and visualizing experimentation using ravsim. In: Engineering Applications of Neural Networks: 23rd International Conference, EAAAI/EANN 2022, Chersonissos, Crete, Greece, June 17–20, 2022, Proceedings. pp. 40–51. Springer (2022)
11. Yan, W., Culp, C., Graf, R.: Integrating bim and gaming for real-time interactive architectural visualization. Autom. Constr. **20**(4), 446–458 (2011)
12. Sen, P., Namata, G., Bilgic, M., Getoor, L., Galligher, B., Eliassi-Rad, T.: Collective classification in network data. AI Mag. **29**(3), 93–93 (2008)
13. Gabruseva, T., Poplavskiy, D., Kalinin, A.: Deep learning for automatic pneumonia detection. In: Proceedings of the IEEE/CVF Conference on Computer Vision and Pattern Recognition Workshops, pp. 350–351 (2020)
14. McCloskey, D.N.: The loss function has been mislaid: the rhetoric of significance tests. Am. Econ. Rev. **75**(2), 201–205 (1985)
15. Code availability. https://github.com/Rao-Sanaullah/GNN-Classification-with-Automatic-Loss-Function-and-Optimizer-Selection Accessed Apr 2023

# User Equilibrium and System Optimality Conditions for Flow Distributions on Congested Networks

Antonios Kalampakas[1]([⊠]), Armen Bagdasaryan[1], Mansoor Saburov[1], and Stefanos Spartalis[2,3]

[1] College of Engineering and Technology, American University of the Middle East, Egaila 54200, Kuwait
{antonios.kalampakas,armen.bagdasaryan,mansur.saburov}@aum.edu.kw
[2] Department of Production and Management Engineering, Laboratory of Computational Mathematics, School of Engineering, Democritus University of Thrace, V. Sofias 12, Prokat, Building A1, 67132 Xanthi, Greece
sspart@pme.duth.gr
[3] School of Science and Technology, Studies in Physics, Hellenic Open University, 18 Aristoteles Bystreet, 26335 Patra, Greece
spartalis.stefanos@ac.eap.gr

**Abstract.** Motivated by flow allocation in communication and transportation networks we examine user equilibrium and system optimal flows on networks of parallel links. User equilibrium is achieved when the journey times on all the used routes are equal and less than any other unused route. On the other hand the system optimal flow minimizes the average journey times for all used routes. In this paper we study the connection between user equilibrium and system optimums and investigate networks that have identical user equilibrium and system optimal flows. We identify a correspondence between the system optimum of a network and the user equilibrium of the associated Pigovian network and use it to show uniqueness of the system optimum. Using a characterization of Wardrop optimal flows for differentiable convex networks, we show that they are preserved via continuous, strictly increasing and convex functions, uniform increase or decrease of the latency functions and network addition and multiplication.

**Keywords:** Wardrop Equilibrium · System optimum · Resource allocation · Congestion externalities

## 1 Introduction

The optimal flow allocation in a network is a central problem with both theoretical and practical aspects in fields as economics [12,15], transportation [1,16] and communication [10,11]. In this respect, it was Wardrop in [16] who first identified the principles that capture two diverging notions of optimal flow inside networks: the *user equilibrium* and the *system optimum*.

L. Iliadis et al. (Eds.): EANN 2023, CCIS 1826, pp. 203–214, 2023.
https://doi.org/10.1007/978-3-031-34204-2_18

Wardrop's first principle, which describes the user equilibrium, states that the journey times on all routes actually used are equal, and less than those which would be experienced by a single vehicle on any unused route. A flow satisfying the above condition is also called a *Wardrop equilibrium* since users cannot reduce their journey time by selecting a different route [2]. The second principle states that the flow in the network minimizes the average journey times for all used routes. A flow satisfying Wardrop's second principle is clearly optimum from a network operator perspective.

Although for a given network in general, the flows that satisfy Wardrop's first and second principles don't coincide, there are networks that have identical user equilibrium and system optimal flows. A flow that satisfies both principles simultaneously is called *Wardrop optimal flow* and the corresponding networks *Wardrop optimal networks*.

In the present paper we investigate Wardrop optimal flows on networks of parallel links and the properties of the associated Wardrop optimal networks. The flow from the origin to the destination node is distributed among the alternative links of the network and creates congestion externalities which cause an increase in the time needed for the journey captured by a strictly increasing link-specific latency function. We show that the user equilibrium and system optimum of a given network are connected through the associated *Pigovian network* and using this important relation we prove existence and uniqueness for convex networks and obtain sufficient and necessary conditions characterizing the system optimum of the network.

The paper is organized as follows: in the next section, we describe the network framework and present the notions of user equilibrium, system optimum and Wardrop optimal flow of a network. In Sect. 3, we present some useful properties concerning the existence and uniqueness of user equilibrium optimum in our networks. The system optimum is investigated in Sect. 4. We introduce the corresponding Pigovian network, prove existence and uniqueness and obtain sufficient and necessary conditions for the system optimum. In Sect. 5 we examine networks that have Wardrop optimal flows. We provide a characterization of Wardrop optimal flows for differentiable convex networks and using this result we show that Wardrop optimal flows are preserved via continuous, strictly increasing, convex functions. Moreover, we prove that they are preserved by uniform increase or decrease of the latency functions. Furthermore, we illustrate a method to construct networks that admit any given point as Wardrop optimal flow and prove that Wardrop optimal flows are preserved by network addition and multiplication.

## 2    Preliminaries

We consider networks of $m$ parallel links $\mathbf{I}_m = \{1, 2, \ldots, m\}$ between the two nodes of origin and destination and denote by $x_i \geq 0$ the flow passing through the link $i$ of the network, for all $i \in \mathbf{I}_m$. In this setup, a unit total flow has to be distributed among all network links. All traffic of the network is routed in the sense that it holds

$$\sum_{i=1}^{m} x_i = 1.$$

We denote by $\mathbb{S}^{m-1} = \{x \in \mathbb{R}^m_+ : \sum_{i=1}^{m} x_i = 1\}$ the standard simplex and using this convention the points of the simplex represent flows of the network. For a given flow $x$, we define the support of $x$ by $supp(x) := \{i \in \mathbf{I}_m : x_i \neq 0\}$ and denote by $Int(\mathbb{S}^{m-1}) = \{x \in \mathbb{S}^{m-1} : supp(x) = \mathbf{I}_m\}$ the set of all internal points of the simplex. The flow in each link causes congestion which increases the delay while traversing the link. This is measured by flow dependent latency functions

$$\ell_i(x) : [0,1] \to [0,\infty), i \in \mathbf{I}_m,$$

which are assumed continuous and strictly increasing.

With this formalism, a network of $m$ parallel links between two nodes can be identified with the latency functions vector $\mathbf{L_m} = (\ell_1(x), \dots, \ell_m(x))$. A *differentiable network* (resp. *convex network*) is a network $\mathbf{L_m} = (\ell_1(x), \dots, \ell_m(x))$ with all the latency functions $\ell_i(x)$ differentiable (resp. convex).

A *user equilibrium* or *Wardrop equilibrium* of a network $\mathbf{L_m} = (\ell_1(x), \dots, \ell_m(x))$ is a flow $x = (x_1, \dots, x_m) \in \mathbb{S}^{m-1}$ such that

$$\ell_k(x_k) = \min_{i \in \mathbf{I}_m}\{\ell_i(x_i)\}, \text{ for all } k \in \mathbf{I}_m \text{ with } x_k > 0,$$

i.e., the delay is the same across all links with nonzero flow and smaller than the zero flow delay of the rest of the links [1]. The *average delay* of a network $\mathbf{L_m} = (\ell_1(x), \dots, \ell_m(x))$ at a flow $x = (x_1, \dots, x_m) \in \mathbb{S}^{m-1}$ is given by the sum

$$\sum_{i=1}^{m} x_i \ell_i(x_i).$$

A *system optimum* of a network $\mathbf{L_m} = (\ell_1(x), \dots, \ell_m(x))$ is a flow

$$x = (x_1, \dots, x_m) \in \mathbb{S}^{m-1}$$

that minimizes the average delay [1].

Given a network $\mathbf{L_m} = (\ell_1(x), \dots, \ell_m(x))$, a flow $x = (x_1, \dots, x_m) \in \mathbb{S}^{m-1}$ is called a *Wardrop optimal flow* if it is user equilibrium and system optimum of the network $\mathbf{L_m}$. A network that has a Wardrop optimal flow is called a *Wardrop optimal network*.

## 3 User Equilibrium and System Optimum

In this section we present the properties of the user equilibrium and the system optimum of a parallel network that we will need in the rest of the paper. The following lemma states that the user equilibrium is preserved by strictly increasing mappings.

**Lemma 1.** *Given a network* $\mathbf{L_m} = (\ell_1(x), \ldots, \ell_m(x))$ *and a continuous and strictly increasing function* $f(x) : [0, \infty] \rightarrow [0, \infty)$, *if a flow* $x = (x_1, \ldots, x_m) \in \mathbb{S}^{m-1}$ *is a user equilibrium of* $\mathbf{L_m}$ *then it is also a user equilibrium of the network* $f(\mathbf{L_m}) = (f(\ell_1(x)), \ldots, f(\ell_m(x)))$.

In general, the system optimum is not preserved even under continuous, strictly increasing and convex functions as opposed to user equilibrium. An important question that arises naturally at this point concerns whether Wardrop optimal flows are preserved by such transformations. This will be addressed in Theorem 7 of Sect. 4.

The following property regarding existence and uniqueness of a user equilibrium will be necessary for our construction later on.

**Proposition 1.** *Every network* $\mathbf{L_m}$ *has a unique user equilibrium.*

*Proof (Sketch of Proof).* For any network $\mathbf{L_m} = (\ell_1(x), \ldots, \ell_m(x))$, we prove that there is a unique flow $x = (x_1, \ldots, x_m) \in \mathbb{S}^{m-1}$ such that

$$\ell_k(x_k) = \min_{i \in \mathbf{I}_m}\{\ell_i(x_i)\}, \text{ for all } k \in \mathbf{I}_m \text{ with } x_k > 0$$

by showing that this can be obtained by taking the inverse of a stictly increasing function on an appropriate interval.

Now we proceed by examining internal points of the simplex $\mathbb{S}^1$ and we identify a necessary but not sufficient condition for such a flow to be system optimum. This can be proved by considering $\epsilon$-perturbations from one link to the other and show that a better total latency always exists unless if the following condition is satisfied.

**Proposition 2.** *Given two differentiable latency functions* $\ell_1(x), \ell_2(x)$, *if the flow* $(x_1, x_2) \in \text{Int}(\mathbb{S}^1)$ *is a system optimum of* $\mathbf{L}_2 = (\ell_1(x), \ell_2(x))$ *then it holds*

$$\ell_1(x_1) + x_1\ell_1'(x_1) = \ell_2(x_2) + x_2\ell_2'(x_2). \tag{1}$$

The above result can be generalized for $m$ parallel links as follows.

**Proposition 3.** *Given a differentiable network* $\mathbf{L_m} = (\ell_1(x), \ldots, \ell_m(x))$, *if the flow* $x = (x_1, \ldots, x_m) \in \text{Int}(\mathbb{S}^{m-1})$ *is a system optimum of* $\mathbf{L_m}$ *then for all* $i, j \in \mathbf{I}_m$ *it holds*

$$\ell_i(x_i) + x_i\ell_i'(x_i) = \ell_j(x_j) + x_j\ell_j'(x_j).$$

*Proof.* Using the result of Proposition 2, for any $i, j \in \mathbf{I}_m$, if

$$\ell_i(x_i) + x_i\ell_i'(x_i) > \ell_j(x_j) + x_j\ell_j'(x_j).$$

then we can obtain a lower total delay by $\epsilon$-reducing the flow of $x_i$ and simultaneously $\epsilon$-increasing it for $x_j$ and vice versa if the direction of the above inequality is the opposite. Since we assumed that $x$ is a system optimum this can not be the case so we get the result.

The general case of flow $x \in \mathbb{S}^{m-1}$ can be proved by taking into account zero flows.

**Theorem 1.** *Given a differentiable network* $\mathbf{L_m} = (\ell_1(x), \ldots, \ell_m(x))$, *if* $x = (x_1, \ldots, x_m) \in \mathbb{S}^{m-1}$ *is a system optimum of* $\mathbf{L_m}$ *then it holds*

$$\ell_i(x_i) + x_i \ell_i'(x_i) = \ell_j(x_j) + x_j \ell_j'(x_j), \quad \text{for all } i, j \in \mathbf{I}_m \text{ with } x_i, x_j > 0$$

*and*

$$\ell_i(0) \geq \ell_j(x_j) + x_j \ell_j'(x_j), \quad \text{for all } i, j \in \mathbf{I}_m \text{ with } x_i = 0, \text{ and } x_j > 0.$$

Given any differentiable latency function $\ell_i(x)$, we introduce the *Pigovian function*

$$g_i(x) = \ell_i(x) + x \ell_i'(x).$$

In this way, to every differentiable network $\mathbf{L_m} = (\ell_1(x), \ldots, \ell_m(x))$ we can associate the corresponding Pigovian network $\mathbf{PL}_m = (g_1(x), \ldots, g_m(x))$ and Theorem 1 can be reformulated illustrating the relation between a network and it's corresponding Pigovian network.

**Theorem 2.** *Given a differentiable network* $\mathbf{L_m} = (\ell_1(x), \ldots, \ell_m(x))$, *if a flow* $x = (x_1, \ldots, x_m) \in \mathbb{S}^{m-1}$ *is a system optimum of* $\mathbf{L_m}$ *then it is a user equilibrium of the corresponding Pigovian network* $\mathbf{PL}_m = (g_1(x), \ldots, g_m(x))$.

*Proof.* Direct result of Theorem 1 and the definition of the user equilibrium.

By employing Proposition 1 we obtain the following result regarding the uniqueness of a system optimum.

**Proposition 4.** *There exists a unique system optimum for a differentiable and convex network* $\mathbf{L_m} = (\ell_1(x), \ldots, \ell_m(x))$.

*Proof.* Since the functions $\ell_i(x)$ are differentiable in $[0, 1]$ we get that their total delay

$$\sum_{i=1}^{m} x_i \ell_i(x_i)$$

has at least one minimum, thus, by definition, there will be at least one system optimum of $\mathbf{L_m}$. Moreover since $\ell_i(x)$ are differentiable and convex we get that the functions $g_i(x)$ will be continuous and strictly increasing. Hence from Proposition 1 there will be a unique user equilibrium of the network $\mathbf{PL}_m = (g_1(x), \ldots, g_m(x))$. From Theorem 2, we get that every system optimum of $\mathbf{L_m}$ is a unique user equilibrium of $\mathbf{PL}_m$. Therefore there is a unique system optimum of $\mathbf{L_m}$ and it is the unique user equilibrium of $\mathbf{PL}_m$.

Combining Theorem 1 and Proposition 4 we obtain the following characterization of system optimums.

**Theorem 3.** *The flow* $x = (x_1, \ldots, x_m) \in \mathbb{S}^{m-1}$ *is the system optimum of a differentiable and convex network* $\mathbf{L_m} = (\ell_1(x), \ldots, \ell_m(x))$ *if and only if*

$$\ell_i(x_i) + x_i \ell_i'(x_i) = \ell_j(x_j) + x_j \ell_j'(x_j), \qquad \text{for all } i, j \in \mathbf{I}_m \text{ with } x_i, x_j > 0$$

*and*

$$\ell_i(0) \geq \ell_j(x_j) + x_j \ell_j'(x_j), \qquad \text{for all } i, j \in \mathbf{I}_m \text{ with } x_i = 0, \text{ and } x_j > 0.$$

The system optimum of a network can be characterized as the user equilibrium of the corresponding Pigovian network in the following way.

**Theorem 4.** *The flow* $x = (x_1, \ldots, x_m) \in \mathbb{S}^{m-1}$ *is the system optimum of a differential and convex network* $\mathbf{L_m} = (\ell_1(x), \ldots, \ell_m(x))$ *if and only if it is the user equilibrium of* $\mathbf{PL_m} = (g_1(x), \ldots, g_m(x))$, *i.e. if and only if it holds*

$$\ell_k(x_k) + x_k l'(x_k) = \min_{i \in \mathbf{I}_n} \{\ell_i(x_i) + x_i \ell_i'(x_i)\}, \qquad \text{for all } x_k > 0.$$

## 4    Wardrop Optimal Networks

In this section we examine Wardrop Optimal networks i.e., networks that have identical user equilibrium and system optimum. First we identify necessary conditions for a user equilibrium to be system optimum.

**Proposition 5.** *Given a differentiable network* $\mathbf{L_m} = (\ell_1(x), \ldots, \ell_m(x))$, *if a user equilibrium* $x = (x_1, \ldots, x_m) \in \mathbb{S}^{m-1}$ *of* $\mathbf{L_m}$ *is also a system optimum of* $\mathbf{L_m}$ *then it holds*

$$x_i \ell_i'(x_i) = x_j \ell_j'(x_j), \qquad \text{for all } i, j \in \mathbf{I}_m \text{ with } x_i, x_j > 0$$

*and*

$$\ell_i(0) \geq \ell_j(x_j) + x_j \ell_j'(x_j), \qquad \text{for all } i, j \in \mathbf{I}_m \text{ with } x_i = 0, \text{ and } x_j > 0$$

*Proof.* If $x = (x_1, \ldots, x_m) \in \mathbb{S}^{m-1}$ is a system optimum of $\mathbf{L_m}$ then, from Theorem 3 it holds

$$\ell_i(x_i) + x_i \ell_i'(x_i) = \ell_j(x_j) + x_j \ell_j'(x_j), \qquad \text{for all } i, j \in \mathbf{I}_m \text{ with } x_i, x_j > 0$$

and

$$\ell_i(0) \geq \ell_j(x_j) + x_j \ell_j'(x_j), \qquad \text{for all } i, j \in \mathbf{I}_m \text{ with } x_i = 0, \text{ and } x_j > 0$$

The result is obtained by taking into account that $x = (x_1, \ldots, x_m) \in \mathbb{S}^{m-1}$ is a user equilibrium i.e., that it holds

$$\ell_i(x_i) = \ell_j(x_j), \qquad \text{for all } i, j \in \mathbf{I}_m \text{ with } x_i, x_j > 0.$$

In the following Proposition we prove that if the network is in addition convex then the conditions of Proposition 5 are sufficient.

**Proposition 6.** *Given a differentiable and convex network* $\mathbf{L_m} = (\ell_1(x), \ldots, \ell_m(x))$, *if for a user equilibrium* $x = (x_1, \ldots, x_m) \in \mathbb{S}^{m-1}$ *of* $\mathbf{L_m}$ *it holds*

$$x_i \ell_i'(x_i) = x_j \ell_j'(x_j), \quad \text{for all } i, j \in \mathbf{I}_m \text{ with } x_i, x_j > 0$$

*and*

$$\ell_i(0) \geq \ell_j(x_j) + x_j \ell_j'(x_j), \quad \text{for all } i, j \in \mathbf{I}_m \text{ with } x_i = 0, \text{ and } x_j > 0,$$

*then it is a system optimum of* $\mathbf{L_m}$.

*Proof.* By considering Theorem 3 we only need to show that for $x = (x_1, \ldots, x_m) \in \mathbb{S}^{m-1}$ it holds

$$\ell_k(x_k) + x_k \ell'(x_k) = \min_{i \in \mathbf{I}_n} \{\ell_i(x_i) + x_i \ell_i'(x_i)\}, \quad \text{for all } x_k > 0.$$

or equivalently

$$\ell_i(x_i) + x_i \ell_i'(x_i) = \ell_j(x_j) + x_j \ell_j'(x_j), \quad \text{for all } i, j \in \mathbf{I}_m \text{ with } x_i, x_j > 0$$

and

$$\ell_i(0) \geq \ell_j(x_j) + x_j \ell_j'(x_j), \quad \text{for all } i, j \in \mathbf{I}_m \text{ with } x_i = 0, \text{ and } x_j > 0.$$

The result is obtained by taking into account that $x = (x_1, \ldots, x_m) \in \mathbb{S}^{m-1}$ is a user equilibrium i.e., it holds

$$\ell_i(x_i) = \ell_j(x_j), \quad \text{for all } i, j \in \mathbf{I}_m \text{ with } x_i, x_j > 0$$

and

$$\ell_i(0) \geq \ell_j(x_j), \quad \text{for all } i, j \in \mathbf{I}_m \text{ with } x_i = 0, \text{ and } x_j > 0.$$

Hence we obtain the following theorem describing the necessary and sufficient conditions for a user equilibrium to be system optimum.

**Theorem 5.** *Given a differentiable and convex network* $\mathbf{L_m} = (\ell_1(x), \ldots, \ell_m(x))$, *a user equilibrium* $x = (x_1, \ldots, x_m) \in \mathbb{S}^{m-1}$ *of* $\mathbf{L_m}$ *is a system optimum of* $\mathbf{L_m}$ *if and only if it holds*

$$x_i \ell_i'(x_i) = x_j \ell_j'(x_j), \quad \text{for all } i, j \in \mathbf{I}_m \text{ with } x_i, x_j > 0,$$

*and*

$$\ell_i(0) \geq \ell_j(x_j) + x_j \ell_j'(x_j), \quad \text{for all } i, j \in \mathbf{I}_m \text{ with } x_i = 0, \text{ and } x_j > 0.$$

On the other hand if $x$ is a system optimum, the requirements for $x$ to be a user equilibrium are more relaxed as it is illustrated in the following proposition.

**Proposition 7.** *Given a differentiable network* $\mathbf{L_m} = (\ell_1(x), \ldots, \ell_m(x))$, *if for a system optimum* $x = (x_1, \ldots, x_m) \in \mathbb{S}^{m-1}$ *of* $\mathbf{L_m}$ *it holds*

$$\ell_i(x_i) = \ell_j(x_j), \quad \text{for all } i, j \in \mathbf{I}_m \text{ with } x_i, x_j > 0$$

*then it is a user equilibrium of* $\mathbf{L_m}$.

*Proof.* By the definition of user equilibrium we only have to show that

$$\ell_i(0) \geq \ell_j(x_j), \quad \text{for all } i, j \in \mathbf{I}_m \text{ with } x_i = 0, \text{ and } x_j > 0.$$

Since $x$ is system optimum, by Theorem 1, we get that it holds

$$\ell_i(0) \geq \ell_j(x_j) + x_j \ell_j'(x_j), \quad \text{for all } i, j \in \mathbf{I}_m \text{ with } x_i = 0, \text{ and } x_j > 0,$$

which concludes the proof. ∎

The Wardrop optimal flows of a network can now be characterized as follows:

**Theorem 6.** *Given a differentiable and convex network* $\mathbf{L_m} = (\ell_1(x), \ldots, \ell_m(x))$ *a flow* $(x_1, \ldots, x_m) \in \mathbb{S}^{m-1}$, *is Wardrop optimal flow if and only if all the following conditions hold.*

*i)* $\ell_i(x_i) = \ell_j(x_j)$, *for all* $i, j \in \mathbf{I}_m$ *with* $x_i, x_j > 0$,
*ii)* $x_i \ell_i'(x_i) = x_j \ell_j'(x_j)$, *for all* $i, j \in \mathbf{I}_m$ *with* $x_i, x_j > 0$,
*iii)* $\ell_i(0) \geq \ell_j(x_j) + x_j \ell_j'(x_j)$, *for all* $i, j \in \mathbf{I}_m$ *with* $x_i = 0$, *and* $x_j > 0$.

For internal flows $(x_1, \ldots, x_m) \in \text{Int}(\mathbb{S}^{m-1})$ we obtain the following corollary of the previous Theorem.

**Corollary 1.** *Given a differentiable and convex network* $\mathbf{L_m} = (\ell_1(x), \ldots, \ell_m(x))$ *a flow* $(x_1, \ldots, x_m) \in \text{Int}(\mathbb{S}^{m-1})$, *is Wardrop optimal flow if and only if all the following conditions hold*

*i)* $\ell_i(x_i) = \ell_j(x_j)$, *for all* $i, j \in \mathbf{I}_m$ *with* $x_i, x_j > 0$,
*ii)* $x_i \ell_i'(x_i) = x_j \ell_j'(x_j)$, *for all* $i, j \in \mathbf{I}_m$ *with* $x_i, x_j > 0$.

We are now ready to settle the question we posed in Sect. 3 regarding the behavior of Wardrop optimal flows under strictly increasing and convex network transformations.

**Theorem 7.** *Given a differentiable and convex network* $\mathbf{L_m} = (\ell_1(x), \ldots, \ell_m(x))$ *and a continuous, strictly increasing and convex function* $f(x) : [0, \infty] \rightarrow [0, \infty]$, *if the flow* $x = (x_1, \ldots, x_m) \in \mathbb{S}^{m-1}$ *is a Wardrop optimal flow of* $\mathbf{L_m}$ *then it is also a Wardrop optimal flow of*

$$f(\mathbf{L_m}) = (f(\ell_1(x)), \ldots, f(\ell_m(x))).$$

*Proof (Sketch of Proof).* From Lemma 1 and given that $x$ is the user equilibrium of $\mathbf{L_m}$ we get that $x$ is the user equilibrium of the network $f(\mathbf{L_m})$. From $x$ being system optimum of $\mathbf{L_m}$ we prove the second condition of Theorem 6 for the set $f(\mathbf{L_m})$. Finally we need the convexity of $f(x)$ to prove the third condition of Theorem 6.

From Theorem 7 we obtain that a Wardrop optimal flow is preserved if the network is transformed by adding a constant toll price to the latency of each link or by increasing (resp. decreasing) the latency on every link by the same percentage. This is illustrated in the following corollaries.

**Corollary 2.** *If a flow* $x \in \mathbb{S}^{m-1}$ *is a Wardrop optimal flow of a differentiable and convex network* $\mathbf{L_m} = (\ell_1(x), \ldots, \ell_m(x))$ *then it is also a Wardrop optimal flow of the network*

$$\mathbf{L_m} + \mathbf{b} = (\ell_1(x) + b, \ldots, \ell_m(x) + b)$$

*for all* $b > 0$.

**Corollary 3.** *If a flow* $x \in \mathbb{S}^{m-1}$ *is a Wardrop optimal flow of a differentiable and convex network* $\mathbf{L_m} = (\ell_1(x), \ldots, \ell_m(x))$ *then it is also a Wardrop optimal flow of the network*

$$\mathbf{aL_m} = (a\ell_1(x), \ldots, a\ell_m(x)),$$

*for all* $a > 0$.

Moreover, since we only employ the convexity condition to prove the third part of Theorem 6, we obtain the following.

**Corollary 4.** *Given a differentiable and convex network* $\mathbf{L_m} = (\ell_1(x), \ldots, \ell_m(x))$ *and a continuous, strictly increasing function* $f(x) : [0, \infty] \to [0, \infty]$, *if the flow* $x = (x_1, \ldots, x_m) \in int\mathbb{S}^{m-1}$ *is a Wardrop optimal flow of* $\mathbf{L_m}$ *then it is also a Wardrop optimal flow of* $f(\mathbf{L_m}) = (f(\ell_1(x)), \ldots, f(\ell_m(x)))$.

Wardrop optimal flows are also preserved if a network is transformed by taking powers of the latency functions and this can be alternatively proved without using Theorem 7.

**Proposition 8.** *If the flow* $x = (x_1, \ldots, x_m) \in \mathbb{S}^{m-1}$ *is Wardrop optimal flow of the differentiable and convex network* $\mathbf{L_m} = (\ell_1(x), \ldots, \ell_m(x))$ *then it is also Wardrop optimal flow of* $\mathbf{L_m^k} = (\ell_1^k(x), \ldots, \ell_m^k(x))$, $k \in \mathbb{N}^*$.

*Proof.* Since $x$ is Wardrop optimal flow of $\mathbf{L_m}$, by the first condition of Theorem 6 we get

$$\ell_i^k(x_i) = \ell_j^k(x_j), \quad \text{for all } i, j \in \mathbf{I}_m \text{ with } x_i, x_j > 0 \tag{2}$$

Taking into account the first and the second condition of Theorem 6 we have

$$x_i(\ell_i^k(x_i))' = x_i \, k \, \ell_i^{k-1}(x_i) \, \ell_i'(x_i) = x_j \, k \, \ell_j^{k-1}(x_j) \, \ell_j'(x_j) = x_j(\ell_j^k(x_j))'. \tag{3}$$

At this point we note that all latency functions are defined on the domain $[0, 1]$, hence the functions $\ell_i^k(x)$ will be convex for all $k \in \mathbb{N}^*$ and we can used Theorem 6 to prove this proposition. From Eqs. 2 and 3 we get that the first two conditions of Theorem 6 are satisfied by $x$ for the network $\mathbf{L_m^k}$. It now remains to prove the third condition, i.e., that for all $i, j \in \mathbf{I}_m$ with $x_i = 0$ and $x_j > 0$ we have

$$\ell_i^k(0) \geq \ell_j^k(x_j) + x_j \left(\ell_j^k(x_j)\right)' = \ell_j^k(x_j) + x_j \, k \, \ell_j^{k-1}(x_j) \, \ell_i'(x)$$

Since $x$ is Wardrop optimal flow of $\mathbf{L_m}$, by taking the power of the third condition of Theorem 6, for all for all $i, j \in \mathbf{I}_m$ with $x_i = 0$ and $x_j > 0$ we have

$$\ell_i^k(0) \geq (\ell_j(x_j) + x_j\ell_j'(x_j))^k = \ell_j^k(x_j) + \binom{k}{1} \ell_j^{k-1}(x_j)x_j\ell_j'(x_j) + C,$$

where $C$ denotes the sum of the remaining terms of the binomial identity we used above. The result follows by observing that $C$ is positive.

Networks with identical flows admit the center of the simplex as the Wardrop optimal flow as it is shown in the below proposition.

**Proposition 9.** *A network* $\mathbf{L_m} = (l(x), \ldots, l(x))$ *with identical latency functions across all links has a uniformly distributed Wardrop optimal flow.*

*Proof.* It is easy to check that $x = (\frac{1}{n}, \ldots, \frac{1}{n})$. i.e., the center of the simplex $\mathbb{S}^{n-1}$, is the Wardrop optimal flow of $\mathbf{L_m}$.

In a similar way we get that for any a priori given internal flow $\mathbf{p} = (p_1, \cdots, p_n) \in \text{int}\mathbb{S}^{m-1}$, there exists always a network for which $\mathbf{p}$ is its Wardrop optimal flow.

**Proposition 10.** *Any internal flow* $\mathbf{p} = (p_1, \cdots, p_n) \in \text{int}\mathbb{S}^{m-1}$ *is the Wardrop optimal flow of the network* $\mathbf{L_m} = (\frac{x_1}{p_1}, \ldots, \frac{x_m}{p_m})$.

By combining the above result with Corollary 4, we can find more networks admitting any given user equilibrium.

**Proposition 11.** *An internal flow* $\mathbf{p} = (p_1, \cdots, p_n) \in \text{int}\mathbb{S}^{m-1}$ *is the Wardrop optimal flow of the network* $\mathbf{L_m} = (f(\frac{x_1}{p_1}), \ldots, f(\frac{x_m}{p_m}))$, *where* $f(x)$ *is any continuous, strictly increasing function.*

The product of two differentiable and convex latency functions is also a differentiable and convex function and thus we can use Theorem 6 to prove the following result.

**Proposition 12.** *If the flow* $x = (x_1, \ldots, x_m) \in \mathbb{S}^{m-1}$ *is Wardrop optimal flow of the differentiable and convex networks* $\mathbf{L_m} = (\ell_1(x), \ldots, \ell_m(x))$ *and* $\overline{\mathbf{L}}_\mathbf{m} = (\overline{\ell}_1(x), \ldots, \overline{\ell}_m(x))$ *then it is also Wardrop optimal flow of the network* $\mathbf{L_m}\overline{\mathbf{L}}_\mathbf{m} = (\ell_1(x)\overline{\ell}_1(x), \ldots, \ell_m(x)\overline{\ell}_m(x))$.

Similarly with the above, we can use again Theorem 6 to prove the following, since differentiable and convex functions are preserved by addition .

**Proposition 13.** *If the flow $x = (x_1, \ldots, x_m) \in \mathbb{S}^{m-1}$ is Wardrop optimal flow of the differentiable and convex networks $\mathbf{L_m} = (\ell_1(x), \ldots, \ell_m(x))$ and $\overline{\mathbf{L}}_{\mathbf{m}} = (\overline{\ell}_1(x), \ldots, \overline{\ell}_m(x))$ then it is also Wardrop optimal flow of the network $\mathbf{L_m} + \overline{\mathbf{L}}_{\mathbf{m}} = (\ell_1(x) + \overline{\ell}_1(x), \ldots, \ell_m(x) + \overline{\ell}_m(x))$.*

By using Corollary 4 we can construct networks for given internal flows as follows.

**Proposition 14.** *For any polynomial $P(x) = a_0 + a_1 x + \cdots + a_n x^n$, strictly increasing and continuous in [0,1] and any internal flow $\mathbf{p} = (p_1, \cdots, p_n) \in \text{int}\mathbb{S}^{m-1}$ we can construct a network $\mathbf{L_m} = (\ell_1(x), \ldots, \ell_m(x))$ with $\ell_1(x) = P(x)$ with Wardrop optimal flow $\mathbf{p}$.*

*Proof.* Assume $P(x) = a_0 + a_1 x + a_2 x^2 + \cdots + a_n x^n$ is a polynomial strictly increasing and continuous in [0,1] and $\mathbf{p} = (p_1, \cdots, p_n)$ any given flow. Then by taking the image of the network $\mathbf{L_m} = (\frac{x}{p_1}, \ldots, \frac{x}{p_m})$ via the function

$$f(x) = a_0 + a_1 p_1 x + a_2 p_1^2 x^2 + \cdots + a_n p_1^n x^n$$

we obtain a network that has $P(x)$ as latency function on the first link. The function $f(x)$ is also continuous and strictly increasing in $[0, 1]$ since from $f(x) = P(p_1 x)$ and $0 < p_1 < 1$ we get that $f(x)$ is the composition of two strictly increasing and continuous functions.

## 5    Conclusion and Future Work

We examined user equilibrium and system optimum in parallel networks with congestion externalities and obtained sufficient and necessary conditions for the system optimum. This leads to a characterization of Wardrop optimal flows for differentiable convex networks from which we obtained important closure properties preserving Wardrop optimal flows.

The importance of Wardrop optimal networks for transportation and communication networks stems from the integration of the interests of both users and system operators. Convergence to the Wardrop optimal flow inside such networks will allow us to simulate dynamic flow distribution in networks in the manner of [13, 14]. Wardrop optimal flows can be investigated in the framework of general directed graphs by identifying a fixed origin and destination node in the graph and considering all possible paths from origin to destination as this has been done using the path hyperoperation on directed graphs [7, 9]. This will allow us to model diffusion inside Wardrop networks as in [3] and moreover, as another future direction, the capacity of graph recognizability to identify graph properties (see [4–6, 8]) can be employed towards the recognition of Wardrop optimal networks.

# References

1. Beckmann, M.J., McGuire, C.B., Winsten, C.B.: Studies in the Economics of Transportation. RAND Corporation (1955)
2. Dafermos, S., Sparrow, F.: The traffic assignment problem for a general network. J. Res. National Bureau of Standards-B. Math. Sci. **73**(2), 91–118 (1969)
3. Kalampakas, A., Aifantis, E.: Random walk on graphs: an application to the double diffusivity model. Mech. Res. Commun. **43**, 101–104 (2012)
4. Kalampakas, A.: The syntactic complexity of eulerian graphs. Lecture Notes in Computer Science (including subseries Lecture Notes in Artificial Intelligence and Lecture Notes in Bioinformatics) 4728 LNCS, pp. 208–217 (2007)
5. Kalampakas, A.: Graph automata: The algebraic properties of abelian relational graphoids. Lecture Notes in Computer Science (including subseries Lecture Notes in Artificial Intelligence and Lecture Notes in Bioinformatics) 7020 LNCS, pp. 168–182 (2011)
6. Kalampakas, A.: Graph automata and graph colorability. Europ. J. Pure Appl. Mathe. **16**(1), 112–120 (2023)
7. Kalampakas, A., Spartalis, S.: Path hypergroupoids: Commutativity and graph connectivity. Europ. J. Combinat. **44**(PB), 257–264 (2015)
8. Kalampakas, A., Spartalis, S., Iliadis, L., Pimenidis, E.: Fuzzy graphs: algebraic structure and syntactic recognition. Artif. Intell. Rev. **42**(3), 479–490 (2014)
9. Kalampakas, A., Spartalis, S., Tsigkas, A.: The path hyperoperation. Analele Stiintifice ale Universitatii Ovidius Constanta, Seria Matematica **22**(1), 141–153 (2014)
10. Kelly, F.P., Maulloo, A.K., Tan, D.K.H.: Rate control for communication networks: shadow prices, proportional fairness and stability. J. Oper. Res. Soci. **49**(3), 237–252 (1998)
11. Low, S., Lapsley, D.: Optimization flow control. i. basic algorithm and convergence. IEEE/ACM Trans. Network.**7**(6), 861–874 (1999)
12. Pigou, A.C.: The Economics of Welfare. Macmillan, London (1920)
13. Saburov, M.: On replicator equations with nonlinear payoff functions defined by the ricker models. Adv. Pure Appl. Math. **12**, 39–156 (2021)
14. Saburov, M.: On discrete-time replicator equations with nonlinear payoff functions. Dyn. Games Appl. **12**, 643–661 (2022)
15. Sanghavi, S., Hajek, B.: Optimal allocation of a divisible good to strategic buyers. In: 2004 43rd IEEE Conference on Decision and Control (CDC) (IEEE Cat. No.04CH37601). vol. 3, pp. 2748–2753 Vol. 3 (2004)
16. Wardrop, J.G.: Some theoretical aspects of road traffic research. In: Proceedings of the Institute of Civil Engineers, Part II, 1, 325–378 3, pp. 325–362 (1952)

# Convolutional Neural Networks/Spiking Neural Networks

# Digital Transformation for Offshore Assets: A Deep Learning Framework for Weld Classification in Remote Visual Inspections

Luis Alberto Toral-Quijas[✉] , Eyad Elyan ,
Carlos Francisco Moreno-García , and Jan Stander

The Robert Gordon University, Aberdeen AB10 7AQ, UK
{soc-office,l.toral-quijas}@rgu.ac.uk

**Abstract.** Inspecting circumferential welds in caissons is a critical task in the offshore industry for ensuring the safety and reliability of structures. However, identifying and classifying different types of circumferential welds can be challenging in subsea environments due to low contrast, variable illumination, and suspended particles. To address this challenge, we present a framework for automating the classification of circumferential welds using deep learning-based methods. We used a dataset of 4,000 images for experimental purposes and utilised three state-of-the-art pretrained Convolutional Neural Network (CNN) architectures, including MobileNet V2, Xception, and EfficientNet. Our results showed superior performance of EfficientNet, with high levels of accuracy (86.75%), recall (91%), and F1-score (87.29%), as well as demonstrating efficient time. These findings suggest that leveraging deep learning-based methods can significantly reduce the time required for inspection tasks. This work opens a new research direction toward digitally transforming inspection tasks in the Oil and Gas industry.

**Keywords:** circumferential welds · offshore · remote visual inspections · EfficientNet

## 1 Introduction

Managing ageing offshore energy production infrastructure poses significant challenges for operating companies, particularly about caissons. Caissons are vertical tubes that hang beneath the platform topsides, often within the jacket's envelope. They are used for seawater intake, various discharge purposes, and as carriers for subsea infrastructure [7].

The Topside, Splash-zone, and Subsea are the three primary segments of a caisson (See Fig. 1). The Topside can be defined as the dry section zone located under the deck. The Splash-zone is the area of the structure intermittently in or out of seawater and is often submerged due to tides and winds. Finally, the underwater section is usually the longest section to inspect and where most anomalies are found.

Supported by Aisus Offshore LTD.

L. Iliadis et al. (Eds.): EANN 2023, CCIS 1826, pp. 217–226, 2023.
https://doi.org/10.1007/978-3-031-34204-2_19

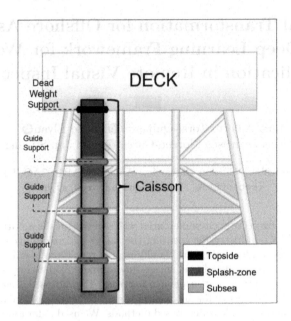

Fig. 1. Overview of the different caisson zones

Over the last few decades, caisson deterioration and failure have been significant problems in the United Kingdom Continental Shelf (UKCS) region, according to a recently published technical report [2]. Caissons are unlikely to lead
to overall structural collapse. Still, they may have negative consequences if a
failure occurs, which can escalate to a significant risk of dropped objects into
subsea structures. Examples include damage to jacket infrastructure, pipelines,
and risers. A failed caisson could hit the gas line resulting in gas release and
explosion from the ignition. The loss of a firewater caisson capability could also
disrupt operations, causing a shutdown of production platforms [2].

The vulnerability of caissons to internal corrosion is a major threat to their
structural integrity, and their internal inspection is essential to detect this type of
damage. General Visual Inspection (GVI) and Close Visual Inspection (CVI) are
the most commonly used inspection techniques. GVI is carried out by a remotely
operated vehicle (ROV) to detect major flaws and damages without prior asset
cleaning. On the other hand, a CVI is more accurate and used to detect local defects
or damages, which requires cleaning marine growth. The still images of anomalies
detected during a CVI are usually manually inspected and reported [1].

A full-caisson inspection commences with cleaning and surface preparation.
Subsequently, robotic ultrasonic inspection equipment is remotely deployed to
collect thickness measurements throughout the entire length of the caisson, giving real-time inspection data that can be analysed to provide an initial evaluation

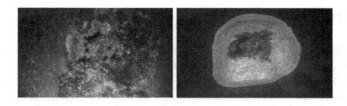

**Fig. 2.** Comparison between the same anomaly before cleaning (left) vs the post-cleaning (right)

of the caisson condition. Finally, inspection cameras are remotely deployed to offer visual confirmation of flaws and abnormalities discovered during the ultrasonic inspection and the condition of the caisson surface and welds.

Residual stresses are inherent in welded components, with the magnitude of the pressure reaching the yield strength of the material. The presence of tensile residual stress has a detrimental effect on the structural integrity of engineering constructions [13]. Therefore, during remote visual inspections of caissons, a crucial aspect is the evaluation of the welds. Caissons are typically joined through circumferential welds (CWs), which connect two round objects around their circumference. Since CWs are subjected to stress induced by surface tides and ocean currents, localised corrosion and fatigue are likely to occur [14] (Fig. 3).

The remote visual inspection of circumferential welds in caissons is challenging due to various factors that can affect the image quality, including lighting conditions, material reflectivity, water motion, and water turbidity when inspecting underwater. These challenges can lead to errors and significant time consumption during the inspection. In other words, existing inspection manual practices are prone to errors and are time-consuming.

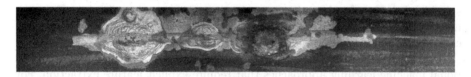

**Fig. 3.** Example of a 180° caisson panoramic view of a circumferential weld with defects.

This paper presents a deep learning-based framework to classify circumferential welds in caissons. An efficient classification system can help automate the inspection process and speed up the asset integrity assessment, which will be beneficial in the long run. The rest of the paper is organised as follows; Sect. 2 briefly presents related work, Sect. 3 explains the data collection process and procedures, Sect. 4 presents methods and the experimental validation, and Sect. 5 concludes the paper.

## 2    Related Work

Automating inspection tasks has been a crucial area of research, with several approaches developed to classify images and detect anomalies, mainly relying on computer vision and deep learning-based methods. In recent years, deep learning-based methods have shown promising results in image classification and anomaly detection tasks. Various techniques in the literature utilize deep-transfer learning and fine-tuning, where a pre-trained model is used as a starting point to train the model further for specific tasks.

Ren et al. [9] proposed a deep learning approach for automated surface inspection using a pre-trained deep learning model to extract patch features from images and generate a "efect heat map." Similarly, several other researchers have proposed deep-learning models for image classification. Luciane et al. [11] proposed a deep-learning approach to classify underwater images into four categories of corrosion severity. Bastian et al. [3] proposed a deep learning-based framework that utilizes Convolutional Neural Networks (CNN) for detecting and classifying corrosion in pipelines transporting water, oil, and gas. The study reported an overall classification accuracy of 98%, indicating the effectiveness of deep learning-based approaches for identifying pipeline defects.

Furthermore, Fu et al. [5] used a SqueezeNet pre-trained model to detect anomalies in steel surfaces, which outperformed state-of-the-art frameworks such as Enhanced Testing Machine (ETM) and Deep Convolutional Activation Features with Multiple Logistic Regression (DCAF-MLR). However, the proposed model was only evaluated on a single dataset(NEU), which may not represent all scenarios in real-world steel surface defect classification tasks.

In another study, [8], the authors presented an experimental framework for automating corrosion detection in subsea images using state-of-the-art computer vision and deep learning techniques. They compared three different architectures and image pre-processing methods and concluded that Mask R-CNN is the most suitable algorithm for detecting corrosion instances in subsea images. However, using a dataset not specifically tailored to subsea inspection may limit the generalizability of the results to other subsea inspection scenarios.

Despite recent advances in deep learning, some methods still rely on traditional machine learning approaches that require explicit feature extraction. For example, in a study by Hoang and Tran [6], Support Vector Machines (SVM) were employed to detect corrosion in pipelines, where the quality of the extracted features played a critical role in achieving accurate results. In such cases, the choice and design of the feature extraction method can be a crucial factor in the model's overall performance.

In summary, it can be said that most existing methods in the literature that handles inspection tasks of offshore or onshore energy assets rely heavily on deep-transfer learning methods, where models that have been trained on large public datasets (e.g. ImageNet) are then reused to perform specific inspection tasks.

# 3   Methods

Circumferential welds have varying sizes, thicknesses, and colours depending on various factors. However, all circumferential welds have a visible top and bottom horizontal line, resulting from the Heat-Affected Zone (HAZ) created during the welding process. The HAZ is a critical area of the weld that can have a different microstructure and properties than the parent material due to the heat generated during welding. Despite the horizontal line being a characteristic feature the human eye can quickly identify, CWs can be challenging to spot on the subsea section due to low contrast, suspended particles in the water, and highly variable illumination.

## 3.1   Data Collection

A database of hundreds of remote visual inspection jobs was filtered to ensure a representative sample of CWs covering different geographical regions and caissons' configurations. A Pareto chart was created to visualize the number of inspection jobs per global region. This approach aimed to develop a robust model with diverse CWs and background types. Afterwards, a team consisting of a mechanical engineer, senior inspection engineer, and offshore operation manager were consulted to establish clear guidelines for image classification under the labels "cw" and "non-cw" (See Fig. 4)

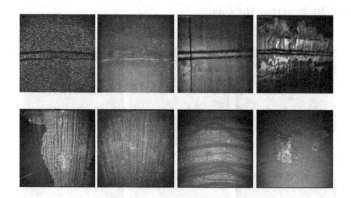

**Fig. 4.** Circumferential weld (top) and non-circumferential weld (bottom)

A total of 4,000 images were obtained from the filtered database. These images contained inspection stills in different format sizes and were manually selected and labelled. The dataset was split into two labels named *cw* and *non-cw*. Table 1 shows the data distribution between the training, validation and test sets.

Note that all annotated data (stills and labels) have been checked for annotation correctness three times; one from the inspection technician that collected

**Table 1.** Dataset distribution

| Label | Training | Validation | Test | Total |
|-------|----------|------------|------|-------|
| cw | 1400 | 400 | 200 | 2000 |
| non-cw | 1400 | 400 | 200 | 2000 |

and reported the data, subsequently on-shore by the senior inspection engineer for the approval of the report, and finally during the manual extraction of the dataset itself by the offshore operations manager.

## 3.2 Data Pre-processing

Internal inspections can be affected by challenging environmental conditions and lighting factors that negatively impact the quality of the captured images. To address this issue, previous research, such as the study conducted by Pirie et al. [8], has explored various filtering methods, including contrast-limited adaptive histogram equalization (CLAHE), Grayscale, and Inpainting, to improve image quality under such conditions. For our dataset, we found that a combination of these three techniques was the most effective. In Fig. 5, a comparison is presented between the different filters we tested and our final custom filter applied. The results show that the filter enhances the visibility of the top and bottom horizontal lines of the weld and attenuates light reflection, leading to a more uniform brightness across the image.

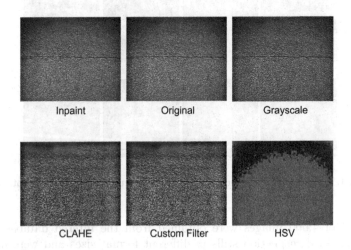

**Fig. 5.** Comparison of a circumferential weld using different filters.

### 3.3    Transfer Learning

Transfer learning is a popular machine learning technique used to transfer knowledge from pre-trained models to solve related problems. Instead of training a CNN from scratch, transfer learning allows the reuse of pre-trained model weights and adaptation for specific outputs by adding additional layers. This technique offers faster training and better prediction results. To assess the accuracy of state-of-the-art pre-trained CNN models in classifying CWs, experiments were conducted using MobileV2, Xception, and EfficientNet.

**MobileNet V2** is a highly efficient and simple CNN architecture commonly used for mobile applications. Its unique feature is the depth-wise convolution, which reduces model size and complexity with the low computational power required for transfer. The architecture has 32 filters followed by 19 residual bottleneck layers. Compared to its predecessor, MobileNetV1, this architecture uses 30% fewer parameters and half the operators, enhancing prediction speed performance while requiring minimal GPU requirements [10].

**Xception** is a CNN that contains 71 deep-layers and is considered a variation of Inception architecture. The Xception model is based entirely on depth-wise separable convolution layers. The main idea of this architecture is to fully decouple the cross-channel and spatial correlations in the feature map of the convolutional neural networks. Xception achieves a top-5 accuracy on the ImageNet database of 94.5%, outperforming state-of-the-art models such VGG16, ResNet-152 and Inception V3 [4].

**EfficientNet** is a CNN architecture designed to optimize the accuracy and efficiency trade-off by scaling the network's depth, width and resolution. It introduces a new compound scaling method that uniformly scales all three dimensions of depth, width, and resolution in a balanced way. EfficientNet-B0, the smallest variant, achieved a top-1 accuracy of 76.3% on the ImageNet dataset with only 5.3 million parameters, whereas EfficientNet-B7, the largest variant, achieved a top-1 accuracy of 86.5% with 66 million parameters, surpassing other models such as ResNet, DenseNet, and Inception-v3 on the same dataset. In this study, EfficientNet-B0 was chosen for the experiment [12].

## 4    Experiments and Results

### 4.1    Experiment Setup

Image augmentation techniques were applied to the training dataset to optimize the performance of the binary image classification models on detecting CWs. Random rotation and flip were used to account for the possibility of CWs appearing in different positions within the inspection image. As most CWs tend to appear horizontally in the middle of the image, the flip technique was used to create horizontal mirror images, and the rotation technique was used to make slight variations in the angle of the CWs. These techniques helped to generate additional training data, which allowed the model to learn to generalize better to new images and reduce over-fitting.

The batch size was set to 64 in this experiment. The models were compiled with the Adam optimizer, binary cross-entropy loss function, and accuracy metric. The learning rate for the optimizer was set to $10^{-4}$. The models were trained for 25 epochs.

## 4.2 Results

The binary image classification model was trained and evaluated using three CNN architectures: MobileNet V2, Xception, and EfficientNet. To present the performance of each model, this section features confusion matrices displayed in Fig. 6. Additionally, Table 2 provides a detailed comparison of each model's performance, measured by accuracy, recall, precision, and F1 score.

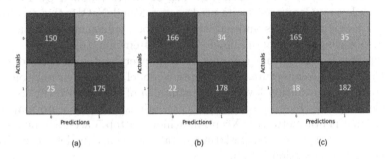

**Fig. 6.** Confusion Matrix (a) MobileNet V2, (b) Xception, and (c) EfficientNet

The presented results demonstrate that all three models achieve considerable accuracy, with EfficientNet performing the best, attaining the highest scores in accuracy, recall, and F1-score of 86.75%, 91.00%, and 87.26%, respectively. Regarding precision, Xception outperforms the other two architectures, while MobileNet V2 exhibits the lowest precision score among the three models.

**Table 2.** Comparison of CNN architectures for classification task

| Architecture | MobileNet V2 | Xception | EfficientNet |
|---|---|---|---|
| Accuracy | 0.8125 | 0.8600 | **0.8675** |
| Recall | 0.8750 | 0.8900 | **0.9100** |
| Precision | 0.7778 | **0.8396** | 0.8387 |
| F1 Score | 0.8235 | 0.8641 | **0.8729** |

Careful consideration of all relevant factors, including model performance and inference time, is necessary to select the most appropriate model for a given application. While Xception achieves slightly higher precision than EfficientNet, a thorough evaluation of model performance and inference time combination revealed that EfficientNet is the preferred model for the classification task.

# 5    Conclusion and Future Work

In this paper, we presented a framework for the automated classification of circumferential welds (CWs) in a caisson. A dataset of images representing inspection tasks was collected, labelled and enhanced using image processing methods. The prepared dataset was then used to train three state-of-the-art CNN architectures: MobileNet V2, Xception, and EfficientNet. Based on extensive experiments, EfficientNet emerged as the preferred model for the classification task due to its strong accuracy, sensitivity, and F1-score metrics performance while exhibiting a favourable trade-off with inference time. The methods developed in this paper were deployed in production and used for visual inspection jobs, achieving an average accuracy of 86.75%, a sensitivity of 91.00%, and an F1-score of 87.29%. Currently, the framework is being integrated into the company's data pipeline process under the supervision of senior inspection engineers. In future work, the authors plan to explore a multi-label classification model to automate the identification of other types of anomalies, including pitting, cracks, thru-wall defects, and localized wall loss commonly seen in caissons, especially in the underwater section.

**Acknowledgements.** We thank the North of Scotland KTP Centre, AISUS Offshore LTD, and Innovate UK for supporting this project. Their contributions were essential to this research.

# References

1. Structural integrity management framework for fixed jacket structures. HSE (2009 [Online]). https://www.hse.gov.uk/research/rrpdf/rr684.pdf
2. Caisson structural integrity. Offshore Safety Directive Regulator (2021 [Online]). https://www.hse.gov.uk/offshore/infosheets/is5-2019.pdf
3. Bastian, B.T.N.J., Ranjith, S.K., Jiji, C.: Visual inspection and characterization of external corrosion in pipelines using deep neural network. NDT & E Int. **107**, 102134 (2019). https://doi.org/10.1016/j.ndteint.2019.102134
4. Chollet, F.: Xception: Deep learning with depthwise separable convolutions. In: 2017 IEEE Conference on Computer Vision and Pattern Recognition (CVPR) (2017). https://doi.org/10.1109/cvpr.2017.195
5. Fu, G., et al.: A deep-learning-based approach for fast and robust steel surface defects classification. Opt. Lasers Eng. **121**, 397–405 (2019). https://doi.org/10.1016/j.optlaseng.2019.05.005
6. Hoang, N.D., Duc, T.: Image processing based detection of pipe corrosion using texture analysis and metaheuristic-optimized machine learning approach. Comput. Intell. Neurosci. In Press (2019). https://doi.org/10.1155/2019/8097213
7. Michael, J., Peter, J., P.S.L.I.A.N.P.M.: Hazards 25 (2015). https://www.icheme.org/media/8495/xxv-paper-28.pdf
8. Pirie, C., Moreno-Garcia, C.F.: Image pre-processing and segmentation for real-time subsea corrosion inspection. In: Iliadis, L., Macintyre, J., Jayne, C., Pimenidis, E. (eds.) EANN 2021. PINNS, vol. 3, pp. 220–231. Springer, Cham (2021). https://doi.org/10.1007/978-3-030-80568-5_19

9.  Ren, R., Hung, T., Tan, K.C.: A generic deep-learning-based approach for auto-mated surface inspection. IEEE Trans. Cybernet. **48**(3), 929–940 (2018). https://doi.org/10.1109/TCYB.2017.2668395

10. Sandler, M., Howard, A., Zhu, M., Zhmoginov, A., Chen, L.C.: Mobilenetv 2: Inverted residuals and linear bottlenecks. In: 2018 IEEE/CVF Conference on Computer Vision and Pattern Recognition (2018). https://doi.org/10.1109/cvpr.2018.00474

11. Soares, L., Botelho, S., Nagel, R., Drews, P.L.: A visual inspection proposal to identify corrosion levels in marine vessels using a deep neural network. In: 2021 Latin American Robotics Symposium (LARS), 2021 Brazilian Symposium on Robotics (SBR), and 2021 Workshop on Robotics in Education (WRE), pp. 222–227 (2021). https://doi.org/10.1109/LARS/SBR/WRE54079.2021.9605400

12. Tan, M., Le, Q.V.: Efficientnet: Rethinking model scaling for convolutional neural networks. In: Proceedings of the 36th International Conference on Machine Learning, pp. 6105–6114 (2019)

13. Zhang, Y., Smith, S., Wei, L., Johnston, C., Stacey, A.: Measurement and Modelling of Residual Stresses in Offshore Circumferential Welds, vol. 3 (2013). https://doi.org/10.1115/OMAE2013-10234

14. Zhang, Y., Smith, S., Wei, L., Johnston, C., Stacey, A.: Measurement and Modelling of Residual Stresses in Offshore Circumferential Welds, vol. 3 (2013). https://doi.org/10.1115/OMAE2013-10234

# Frameworks for SNNs: A Review of Data Science-Oriented Software and an Expansion of SpykeTorch

Davide L. Manna[1]([envelope]), Alex Vicente-Sola[1], Paul Kirkland[1],
Trevor J. Bihl[2], and Gaetano Di Caterina[1]

[1] Neuromorphic Sensor Signal Processing (NSSP) Lab, University of Strathclyde,
G1 1XW Glasgow, UK
davide.manna@strath.ac.uk
[2] Air Force Research Laboratory (AFRL), Wright-Patterson AFB, Ohio, USA
https://nssp.eee.strath.ac.uk

**Abstract.** The Neuromorphic (NM) field has seen significant growth in recent years, especially in the development of Machine Learning (ML) applications. Developing effective learning systems for such applications requires extensive experimentation and simulation, which can be facilitated by using software frameworks that provide researchers with a set of ready-to-use tools. The NM technological landscape has witnessed the emergence of several new frameworks in addition to the existing libraries in neuroscience fields. This work reviews nine frameworks for developing Spiking Neural Networks (SNNs) that are specifically oriented towards data science applications. We emphasize the availability of spiking neuron models and learning rules to more easily direct decisions on the most suitable frameworks to carry out different types of research. Furthermore, we present an extension to the SpykeTorch framework that enables users to incorporate a broader range of neuron models in SNNs trained with Spike-Timing-Dependent Plasticity (STDP). The extended code is made available to the public, providing a valuable resource for researchers in this field.

**Keywords:** frameworks · spiking neural networks · spiking neurons · neuromorphic · software · machine learning · unsupervised learning

## 1 Introduction

The development of Deep Learning (DL) algorithms was greatly eased by the introduction of purposely developed software packages. These packages, or frameworks, usually offer a wide range of software tools that aim to speed up the development of Machine Learning (ML) pipelines as well as make the algorithms available to a larger audience. When referring to conventional DL, i.e. non Neuromorphic (NM), several famous libraries exist, such as TensorFlow (TF) [2], PyTorch [43] or Caffe [32]. The field of Neuromorphic engineering has recently

L. Iliadis et al. (Eds.): EANN 2023, CCIS 1826, pp. 227–238, 2023.
https://doi.org/10.1007/978-3-031-34204-2_20

seen the emergence of several new software frameworks thanks to the renewed interest in its potential. However, these frameworks are often in an early development stage when compared to their conventional DL counterpart, being limited in the tools they offer, their documentation, and the support from the community. Some more established frameworks also exist, but they are often directed towards particular communities and use cases [48], or they are neuroscience-oriented frameworks rather than NM-ML development tools. Furthermore, effective data science algorithms that can close the gap with other conventional methodologies still need to be developed. Indeed, algorithms employing Spiking Neural Networks (SNNs) are already more energy efficient than conventional Convolutional Neural Networks (CNNs) [25], however, they are not as effective on ML tasks in terms of accuracy. Hence the importance of having good software frameworks that enable customization, simulation and deployment of SNNs. This requires combining a number of key elements into a pipeline such as learning rules, connectivity patterns, and spiking neurons. Regarding the spiking neurons, emerging NM chips such as Loihi 2 [41] allow the use of customized models. It has been shown in the literature that different types of neuron models can solve certain tasks more effectively than other models [22,36]. Therefore it can be beneficial for researchers to use a framework that enables seamless experimentation with different types of neurons.

This work contributes by providing a review of data science-oriented frameworks and highlighting the key features they offer. By restricting our review to this kind of frameworks, we hope to help boosting new research in NM for ML applications. Further to this, we develop an expansion[1] of the SpykeTorch [38] framework that enables the user to experiment on a wider variety of different spiking neuron models. By doing this, we aim to enlarge the scope of the research in SNNs to different spiking neuron models, and to thus build new algorithms that can leverage the latest advances in the NM hardware.

## 2   Related Works

When presenting a new software framework, authors often report other similar works and draw comparisons with them [27,38]. In these instances, differences in terms of offered features are highlighted, as well as the advantages of using the newly presented software over the existing ones. Other works specifically focus on reviewing the existing frameworks for the development of SNNs. One example is given by [45], where the authors make a subdivision of the software packages into three main groups depending on whether they are NM chips toolchains, SNN simulation frameworks or frameworks that integrate SNNs and DNNs. Another work [25] gives an introductory overview of SNNs and then reviews some prominent simulation frameworks. The authors also define a simple classification task and compare accuracy and execution time obtained by using the different frameworks. These previous two works consider frameworks regardless of their research orientation, i.e. they consider both neuroscience-oriented and

---

[1] Code available at https://www.github.com/daevem/SpykeTorch-Extended.

**Table 1.** Key elements of the reviewed frameworks. The "A-" stands for adaptive, whereas "H-" stand for heterogeneous.

| Framework | Nengo | Lava | SNN Toolbox | Norse | PySNN | snnTorch | SpikingJelly | BindsNet | SpykeTorch |
|---|---|---|---|---|---|---|---|---|---|
| Spiking Neurons | LIF<br>A-LIF<br>IZ | LIF<br>RF*<br>A-LIF*<br>A-RF*<br>A-IZ*<br>$\Sigma - \Delta$ | IF | LIF<br>AdEx<br>EIF<br>IZ<br>LSNN | IF<br>LIF<br>A-LIF | LIF<br>Recurrent LIF<br>2nd Order LIF<br>LSNN | IF<br>LIF<br>pLIF<br>QIF<br>EIF | IF<br>LIF<br>A-LIF<br>IZ<br>SRM | IF<br>LIF**<br>QIF**<br>EIF**<br>AdEx**<br>IZ**<br>H-Neurons** |
| Learning Rules | Oja<br>BCM<br>BP | SLAYER<br>STDP<br>3-Factor | Pre-trained | SuperSpike<br>STDP | STDP<br>MSTDP<br>MSTDPET | BPTT<br>RTRL | BP | STDP<br>Hebbian<br>MSTDPET | STDP<br>R-STDP |
| Conversion from | TF/Keras | PyTorch | TF/Keras<br>PyTorch<br>Caffe<br>Lasagne | – | – | – | PyTorch | PyTorch | – |
| Destination Backend/Platform | Loihi<br>FPGA<br>SpiNNaker<br>MPI<br>CPU/GPU | Loihi<br>CPU/GPU | SpiNNaker<br>Loihi<br>pyNN<br>Brian2<br>MegaSim | CPU/GPU | CPU/GPU | CPU/GPU | CPU/GPU | CPU/GPU | CPU/GPU |

\* Only available in Lava-DL.
\*\* Added in this work.

data science-oriented frameworks. In this work, we specifically highlight software packages that are data science-oriented and developed in Python or with a Python interface. Furthermore, we also include in our review other different frameworks and highlight some key features and neuron models that they offer for developing SNNs.

# 3  Software Frameworks

Many of the software libraries for the development of SNNs are oriented toward the needs of the neuroscience and neurobiology fields [25]. Because SNNs process inputs and communicate information in a way similar to the human brain, they are particularly suited for simulations of brain areas activations. Nevertheless, the recent emergence of NM engineering as a field for developing ML algorithms has highlighted the need for suitable frameworks. Consequently, following, we will present some of the most prominent software packages to develop data science-oriented SNNs along with their main features, which are also summarized in Table 1.

## 3.1  Nengo

Nengo [5] is a Python package for building and deploying neural networks. It is composed of several sub-packages to be used in case of different needs and destination platforms. NengoDL is to be used when aiming to convert a CNN built using TF/Keras into its Nengo spiking version. NengoLoihi allows to deploy NNs natively built in the Nengo Core package onto Loihi chips. Other packages are NengoFPGA, NengoSpiNNaker, NengoOCL and NengoMPI. Nengo builds on top of a theoretical framework called the Neural Engineering Framework (NEF)

[50]. Computations are based on the three principles of the NEF: neural representation, transformation, and neural dynamics. Neurons in Nengo are organized in Ensembles, and different types of neuron models are available, among which the Leaky Integrate-and-Fire (LIF) [33], and Izhikevich's (IZ) [30] models. Connections between ensembles are designed to allow a transformation of the information from one ensemble to another. Training in Nengo is possible with the Oja [40], BCM [7] and backpropagation (BP) learning rules. Using Nengo as a tool for the development of SNNs has the main advantage of having the possibility to target a wide variety of backends and to convert conventional DNNs into a spiking equivalent [25]. Nengo also allows for a certain degree of customization of the components; however, it remains very oriented towards the NEF structure.

## 3.2   SNN Toolbox

SNN Toolbox [46] provides a set of tools to perform automated conversion from conventional Artificial Neural Network (ANN) models into SNNs. Conversion is possible from three different DL frameworks, namely TF/Keras, PyTorch, Caffe and Lasagne [16]. The framework supports conversion to models for PyNN [15], Brian2 [51], MegaSim [35], SpiNNaker [24], and Loihi [14] where the SNN can be simulated or deployed. However, depending on the components used in the original ANN, some of the target platforms might not be available. During the conversion phase, Integrate-and-Fire (IF) neurons are used for a one-to-one substitution. These are then tuned so that their mean firing rate approximates the activation of the corresponding neuron in the original ANN. Neural networks must be pre-trained in their original framework. Tuning conversion parameters and performing inference is possible either through the command line or through a simple GUI.

## 3.3   Lava

Lava [1] is a relatively recent framework built by Intel's Neuromorphic Computing Lab (NCL). The framework results from an evolution from the Nx SDK software for Loihi chips, but aims to target other hardware platforms as well. Lava is composed of 4 main packages, namely Lava (core), Lava-DL, Lava Dynamic Neural Fields (DNF) and Lava Optimization. The current state of the platform includes the development of deep SNNs trained with SLAYER [49], and of SNNs converted from PyTorch. On-chip training through SLAYER is currently not available. Instead, models need to be trained off-chip, and weights must be exported to be used within the Lava core package. Within Lava-DL, a number of neuron models are defined, such as the LIF, Resonate-and-Fire (RF) [31], RF Izhikevich, Adaptive LIF [26], Adaptive RF, and Sigma-Delta [12] modulation models. The core package currently supports LIF and Sigma-Delta modulation neurons. Recent developments in the framework have seen the implementation of on-chip learning functionalities through STDP and customized 3-factor learning rules.

## 3.4   PyTorch-Based Frameworks

### Norse

Norse [44] is a relatively recent PyTorch-based framework. It was developed with the aim of easing the construction of SNNs for ML solutions. This framework offers a wide range of neuron models, such as the LIF, LIF variants and extensions, and Izhikevich's model. It also provides a LSNN [6], a spiking version of the LSTM (Long Short-Term Memory) [28]. Norse has a functional programming style. Neurons are mainly implemented as functions and do not hold an internal state. Instead, the previous state of the neuron needs to be provided as an argument at each iteration. The framework mainly allows for two types of learning: STDP [37], and SuperSpike [53]. Therefore, both local unsupervised learning and surrogate gradient learning are possible. Overall, Norse provides a good degree of flexibility and allows leveraging all of the features of PyTorch, such as GPU acceleration.

### PySNN

PySNN [8] is another framework based on PyTorch aimed at developing ML algorithms. Similarly to Nengo, connections between two neurons are modelled as separate objects that have properties and can affect the transmission of a signal. For instance, they can explicitly account for connection delays. Neuron models in PySNN embed the concept of spike trace, which can be used for learning purposes. Some available neuron models are the IF, LIF and ALIF. Concerning the learning rules, it is possible to use either STDP or MSTDPET (Modulated STDP with Eligibility Traces) [20]. The framework also provides some useful utilities to load some NM datasets. A downside of using PySNN is that the documentation is not complete.

### SnnTorch

SnnTorch [18] also bases its architecture on PyTorch. Connectivity between layers is enabled by leveraging PyTorch standard layers. Spiking neurons are thought to be used as intermediate layers between these. Spiking neurons are modelled as classes that hold their own internal state. Available models include LIF-based models, second-order LIF models, recurrent LIF models, and LSTM memory cells. Learning in snnTorch takes place with BP Through Time (BPTT) using surrogate gradient functions to calculate the gradient of the spiking neurons. The framework also offers the possibility to use a Real-Time Recurrent Learning (RTRL) rule, which applies weight updates at each time step, rather than at the end of a sequence of inputs. The network output can be interpreted using both a rate-based approach and a time-to-first-spike (TTFS) approach. Finally, snnTorch provides access to the N-MNIST [42], DVS Gestures [3], and the Spiking Heidelberg Digits [13] datasets, and includes useful network activity visualization tools.

## SpikingJelly

SpikingJelly [19] is a framework using PyTorch as a backend and adopting its coding style throughout. It provides implementations of IF, LIF, parametric LIF (pLIF), Quadratic IF (QIF), and Exponential IF neuron [21] models. The firing of neurons in SpikingJelly is approximated by a surrogate function (such as the sigmoid) that allows differentiation. The framework provides several utilities to read NM and non-NM datasets. Concerning the NM datasets, it is possible to both read them with a fixed integration time-window and with a fixed number of frames. Among the available datasets, there are the CIFAR10-DVS [34] dataset, the DVS Gestures dataset, the N-Caltech101 [42] dataset, and the N-MNIST dataset. Finally, SpikingJelly also provides functionality for ANN to SNN conversion from PyTorch.

## BindsNet

BindsNet [27] is a library for the development of biologically inspired SNNs. Despite having PyTorch as a backend, the coding style differs slightly. Execution is implemented by running the network for a certain amount of time on some input rather than explicitly looping through the dataset. BindsNet supports several types of neuron models: IF, LIF, LIF with adaptive thresholds, Izhikevich's, and Spike Response Model (SRM)-based [26] models. Connections are modelled explicitly and link one node of the network with another. Recurrent connections are also possible. The provided learning rules are biologically inspired and can be either two-factor (STDP or Hebbian) or three-factor (MST-DPET); hence no BP-based learning rule is proposed. Through sub-classing, it is possible to customize neurons, input encoding and learning rules. The framework also provides utility tools to load datasets, such as the spoken MNIST, and DAVIS [9] camera-based datasets. Finally, BindsNet includes a conversion system to convert neural networks developed in PyTorch into SNNs.

## SpykeTorch

SpykeTorch is PyTorch-based library for building SNNs with at most one spike per neuron. This means that for each sequence of inputs, each neuron is allowed to fire only once. Because of this, tensor operations can be easily used to compute neuron activations. Because NM data includes the concept of time, what is normally treated as the batch dimension in PyTorch, it is interpreted as the time dimension in SpykeTorch. The framework is built to support STDP and Reward-modulated STDP (R-STDP) with a Winner Takes All (WTA) paradigm, and using convolutions as a connection scheme. The only available neuron model is the IF, which is provided as a function. Finally, the framework provides functionalities to encode non-NM input through difference of Gaussians and intensity to latency transforms, as well as some inhibition functions.

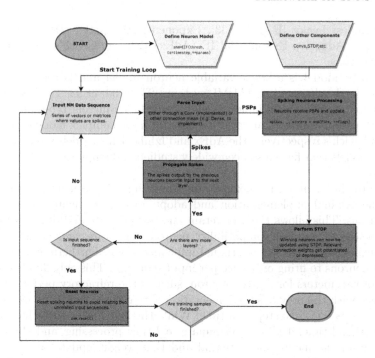

**Fig. 1.** Example flowchart for SpykeTorch-Extended. After the definition of the components of the SNN, each data sample is required to be decomposed into its forming time steps before being processed by the SNN. This ensures that learnt parameters will influence the result of the next iteration.

## 4    SpykeTorch Spiking Neurons

For the purpose of developing NM-ML algorithms based on STDP, SpykeTorch allows a high degree of customization and flexibility to the user. However, as mentioned in Sect. 3.4, the framework originally provides a single spiking neuron model, the IF. This does not have a voltage leakage factor, which means that its internal state can only increase until it is reset. In order to augment the usage potential of SpykeTorch, we expand the library by implementing a new set of spiking neuron models, for a total of 8 new models, as show in Table 2. By introducing more complex neuron models, the original workflow and implementation patterns adopted in the original framework cannot be easily utilized. Therefore, the following are some details about the differences introduced to accommodate such neuron models in the library. We refer to the framework resulting from our changes as SpykeTorch-Extended.

### 4.1    Spiking Neurons Implementation Details

In our implementation of spiking neurons, we consider a subset from the phenomenological family of neuron models due to their computational efficiency [36].

This includes: Leaky IF (LIF) [33], Exponential IF (EIF) [21], Quadratic IF (QIF) [17], Adaptive Exponential IF (AdEx) [10], Izhikevich's [30], Heterogeneous Neurons.

The LIF model is a single-variable neuron model and is the most widely used for the development of NM-ML systems [23, 29, 36, 39, 52]; the EIF and QIF models are other single-variable models that include different types of complexities in their equation, and are also the base for more complex models, the AdEx and Izhikevich's respectively; the AdEx and Izhikevich's models are two-variable neuron models that have also been widely studied and employed in the literature [4, 11, 47].

Due to the greater complexity of the newly introduced neurons, we deviate from the original implementation and adopt an object-oriented approach for the neurons. This allows them to retain an internal state and other properties. Nevertheless, to maintain compatibility, neuron objects are callable and share the same output format as in the original implementation. Furthermore, we do not restrict neurons to firing only once per input sequence. This only depends on the choice of parameters for a given neuron, such as the refractory period. Another difference with the previous implementation is that the neurons are expected to receive events one time-step at a time. While this introduces a overhead on the computational time, it allows to simulate real-time processing, and also ensures the decay of the membrane potential and that weight updates due to STDP affect every subsequent moment in time, thus making the system more realistic. A neuron layer in SpykeTorch-Extended is characterized by at least the set of parameters of a LIF neuron; however, more complex neuron models will require more parameters. A layer of neurons in this system can be better depicted as a set of neuronal populations. The number and size of the population reflect that of the input that is processed by the layer. Thus, a single population is intended as the group of neurons corresponding to one of the feature maps produced by a convolutional layer.

As a result of the changes above, the standard workflow in SpykeTorch-Extended requires some adjustments with respect to the original version. In Fig. 1, we report an example flowchart of how a pipeline using the new neuron models could look like. As the flowchart highlights, each input is expected to be unravelled into all the time steps it is composed of and, for each time step, all the events that took place in such a time span are to be fed forward to the SNN.

## 4.2   Heterogeneous Neuron Classes

The implemented neuron classes create a layer of spiking neurons that share the same hyper-parameters. We refer to this as being a homogeneous layer of neurons because they all react in the same way to the same sequence of inputs. However, it might be useful to have neurons reacting differently to one input, since this could mean being able to learn different kinds of temporal patterns within the same layer. Because of this, we further implement heterogeneous neuron classes for the LIF, EIF, and QIF classes. Specifically, they provide a set of $\tau_{rc}$ values that are uniformly distributed within a range specified by the user through the parameter `tau_range`. We limited the current implementation to a uniform distribution for simplicity, and limit the heterogeneity to the $\tau_{rc}$ parameter since this directly influences the time scale to which the neuron is sensitive. Nevertheless, future developments will consider other types of distributions and parameters.

**Table 2.** Summary of newly added spiking neurons to SpykeTorch. All the neurons share a base set of parameters with the LIF, but they may require more depending on the neuron type, which are briefly reported in the short description.

| Neurons | Short Description |
|---|---|
| LIF [33] | Uses the integral solution to the differential equation in [26]. |
| EIF [21] | Single-variable model with an exponential dependency. Has parameters `delta_t` for the sharpness of the curve, and `theta_rh` as a cut-off threshold for the upswing of the curve [26]. |
| QIF [17] | Single-variable model with a quadratic dependency. Has parameters **a** for the steepness of the quadratic curve, and `u_c` as the negative-to-positive updates crossing point of the membrane potential [26]. |
| AdEx [10] | Two-variables model similar to the EIF, but with an adaptation variable. It adds parameters **a** and **b**, respectively for adaptation-potential coupling and adaptation increase upon spike emission. |
| IZ [30] | Two-variables model similar to the QIF, but with an adaptation variable. It adds parameters **a** for the time scale of the adaptation variable, **b** for the sub-threshold sensitivity of the adaptation, and **d** for the adaptation increase upon spike emission. |
| H-Neurons | Heterogeneous versions of LIF, EIF, and QIF neurons with uniformly distributed `tau_rc` parameter |

## 5   Conclusions

In this work we have presented a review of 9 Python frameworks for the development of spiking neural networks oriented towards data science applications. We have seen that several of them use PyTorch as a base to leverage the GPU acceleration, to exploit the existing functionalities it offers, and to ease the transition for users that come from a conventional DL background. Nevertheless, they all differ slightly in their implementations and in the SNN development tools they offer. Other frameworks like Nengo and Lava do not have such a base, but provide conversion methods to increase usability. This review also highlights how, despite restricting our field of view to data science-oriented libraries, there is a wide variety of frameworks. This is possibly due to growing interest that SNNs have lately received, however this also reflects the lack of an established and widespread framework like in the case of PyTorch or TF/Keras for conventional DL. Finally, we report our extension to a specific framework, SpykeTorch, that includes several new spiking neurons to use for simulations. Our additions require a modification of the original workflow, but enable real-time processing simulation with STDP. By doing this, we hope to promote and speed up future research in this direction, as well as to contribute to the development of richer software frameworks.

# References

1. Lava: A software framework for neuromorphic computing (2021). https://github.com/lava-nc/lava
2. Abadi, M., et al.: Tensorflow: a system for large-scale machine learning. In: 12th USENIX Symposium on Operating Systems Design and Implementation (OSDI 2016), pp. 265–283 (2016)
3. Amir, A., et al.: A low power, fully event-based gesture recognition system. In: 2017 IEEE Conference on Computer Vision and Pattern Recognition (CVPR), pp. 7388–7397 (2017)
4. Barton, A., Volna, E., Kotyrba, M.: The application perspective of izhikevich spiking neural model – the initial experimental study. In: Matoušek, R. (ed.) MENDEL 2017. AISC, vol. 837, pp. 223–232. Springer, Cham (2019). https://doi.org/10.1007/978-3-319-97888-8_19
5. Bekolay, T., et al.: Nengo: a python tool for building large-scale functional brain models. Front. Neuroinf. **7** (2014)
6. Bellec, G., Salaj, D., Subramoney, A., Legenstein, R., Maass, W.: Long short-term memory and learning-to-learn in networks of spiking neurons. In: Bengio, S., Wallach, H., Larochelle, H., Grauman, K., Cesa-Bianchi, N., Garnett, R. (eds.) Advances in Neural Information Processing Systems, vol. 31. Curran Associates, Inc. (2018)
7. Bienenstock, E.L., Cooper, L.N., Munro, P.W.: Theory for the development of neuron selectivity: orientation specificity and binocular interaction in visual cortex. J. Neurosci. **2**(1), 32–48 (1982)
8. Büller, B.: Pysnn (2019). https://github.com/BasBuller/PySNN
9. Brandli, C., Berner, R., Yang, M., Liu, S.C., Delbruck, T.: A 240 × 180 130 db 3 $\mu$s latency global shutter spatiotemporal vision sensor. IEEE J. Solid-State Circ. **49**, 2333–2341 (2014)
10. Brette, R., Gerstner, W.: Adaptive exponential integrate-and-fire model as an effective description of neuronal activity. J. Neurophysiol. **94**(5), 3637–3642 (2005)
11. Chaturvedi, S., Titre, R.N., Sondhiya, N.: Review of handwritten pattern recognition of digits and special characters using feed forward neural network and izhikevich neural model. In: 2014 International Conference on Electronic Systems, Signal Processing and Computing Technologies. IEEE (2014)
12. Cheung, K., Tang, P.: Sigma-delta modulation neural networks. In: IEEE International Conference on Neural Networks, vol. 1, pp. 489–493 (1993)
13. Cramer, B., Stradmann, Y., Schemmel, J., Zenke, F.: The heidelberg spiking data sets for the systematic evaluation of spiking neural networks. IEEE Trans. Neural Netw. Learn. Syst. **33**, 1–14 (2020)
14. Davies, M., et al.: Loihi: a neuromorphic manycore processor with on-chip learning. IEEE Micro **38**(1), 82–99 (2018)
15. Davison, A.P.: PyNN: a common interface for neuronal network simulators. Front. Neuroinf. **2** (2008)
16. Dieleman, S., et al.: Lasagne: First release (2015)
17. Ermentrout, G.B., Kopell, N.: Parabolic bursting in an excitable system coupled with a slow oscillation. SIAM J. Appl. Math. **46**(2), 233–253 (1986)
18. Eshraghian, J.K., et al.: Training spiking neural networks using lessons from deep learning. arXiv preprint arXiv:2109.12894 (2021)
19. Fang, W., et al: Spikingjelly (2020). https://github.com/fangwei123456/spikingjelly

20. Florian, R.V.: Reinforcement learning through modulation of spike-timing-dependent synaptic plasticity. Neural Comput. **19**(6), 1468–1502 (2007)
21. Fourcaud-Trocmé, N., Hansel, D., van Vreeswijk, C., Brunel, N.: How spike generation mechanisms determine the neuronal response to fluctuating inputs. J. Neurosci. **23**(37), 11628–11640 (2003)
22. Frady, E.P., et al.: Efficient neuromorphic signal processing with resonator neurons. J. Signal Process. Syst. **94**(10), 917–927 (2022)
23. Friedl, K.E., Voelker, A.R., Peer, A., Eliasmith, C.: Human-inspired neurorobotic system for classifying surface textures by touch. IEEE Rob. Autom. Lett. **1**(1), 516–523 (2016)
24. Furber, S., Bogdan, P.: SpiNNaker: A Spiking Neural Network Architecture. Now publishers, Inc., Delft (2020)
25. García-Vico, Á.M., Herrera, F.: A preliminary analysis on software frameworks for the development of spiking neural networks. In: Sanjurjo González, H., Pastor López, I., García Bringas, P., Quintián, H., Corchado, E. (eds.) HAIS 2021. LNCS (LNAI), vol. 12886, pp. 564–575. Springer, Cham (2021). https://doi.org/10.1007/978-3-030-86271-8_47
26. Gerstner, W., Kistler, W.M., Naud, R., Paninski, L.: Neuronal Dynamics. Cambridge University Press, Cambridge (2009)
27. Hazan, H., et al: BindsNET: a machine learning-oriented spiking neural networks library in python. Front. Neuroinf. **12** (2018)
28. Hochreiter, S., Schmidhuber, J.: Long short-term memory. Neural Comput. **9**(8), 1735–1780 (1997)
29. Hunsberger, E., Eliasmith, C.: Spiking deep networks with lif neurons. arXiv preprint arXiv:1510.0882 (2015)
30. Izhikevich, E.: Simple model of spiking neurons. IEEE Trans. Neural Netw. **14**(6), 1569–1572 (2003)
31. Izhikevich, E.M.: Resonate-and-fire neurons. Neural Netw. **14**(6–7), 883–894 (2001)
32. Jia, Y., et al.: Caffe. In: Proceedings of the 22nd ACM International Conference on Multimedia. ACM (2014)
33. Lapicque, L.: Recherches quantitatives sur l'excitation electrique des nerfs traitée comme une polarization. J. de Physiologie et Pathologie General **9**, 620–635 (1907)
34. Li, H., Liu, H., Ji, X., Li, G., Shi, L.: Cifar10-dvs: an event-stream dataset for object classification. Front. Neurosci. **11** (2017)
35. Linares-Barranco, B.: Modular event-driven growing asynchronous simulator (megasim) (2018). https://bitbucket.org/bernabelinares/megasim
36. Manna, D.L., Vicente-Sola, A., Kirkland, P., Bihl, T., Di Caterina, G.: Simple and complex spiking neurons: perspectives and analysis in a simple stdp scenario. In: Neuromorphic Computing and Engineering (2022)
37. Masquelier, T., Thorpe, S.J.: Unsupervised learning of visual features through spike timing dependent plasticity. PLoS Comput. Biol. **3**(2), e31 (2007)
38. Mozafari, M., Ganjtabesh, M., Nowzari-Dalini, A., Masquelier, T.: SpykeTorch: efficient simulation of convolutional spiking neural networks with at most one spike per neuron. Front. Neurosci. **13** (2019)
39. Mozafari, M., Kheradpisheh, S.R., Masquelier, T., Nowzari-Dalini, A., Ganjtabesh, M.: First-spike-based visual categorization using reward-modulated STDP. IEEE Trans. Neural Netw. Learn. Syst. **29**(12), 6178–6190 (2018)
40. Oja, E.: Simplified neuron model as a principal component analyzer. J. Math. Biol. **15**(3), 267–273 (1982)
41. Orchard, G., et al.: Efficient neuromorphic signal processing with loihi 2. In: 2021 IEEE Workshop on Signal Processing Systems (SiPS), pp. 254–259. IEEE (2021)

42. Orchard, G., Jayawant, A., Cohen, G.K., Thakor, N.: Converting static image datasets to spiking neuromorphic datasets using saccades. Front. Neurosci. **9** (2015)

43. Paszke, A., et al.: Pytorch: an imperative style, high-performance deep learning library. In: NeurIPS (2019)

44. Pehle, C., Pedersen, J.E.: Norse - a deep learning library for spiking neural networks (2021). https://norse.ai/docs/

45. Qu, P., Yang, L., Zheng, W., Zhang, Y.: A review of basic software for brain-inspired computing. CCF Trans. High Perf. Comput. (2022)

46. Rueckauer, B., Lungu, I.A., Hu, Y., Pfeiffer, M., Liu, S.C.: Conversion of continuous-valued deep networks to efficient event-driven networks for image classification. Front. Neurosci. **11** (2017)

47. Schemmel, J., Billaudelle, S., Dauer, P., Weis, J.: Accelerated analog neuromorphic computing. ArXiv abs/2003.11996 (2020)

48. Schuman, C.D., Kulkarni, S.R., Parsa, M., Mitchell, J.P., Date, P., Kay, B.: Opportunities for neuromorphic computing algorithms and applications. Nat. Comput. Sci. **2**(1), 10–19 (2022)

49. Shrestha, S.B., Orchard, G.: SLAYER: spike layer error reassignment in time. In: Bengio, S., Wallach, H., Larochelle, H., Grauman, K., Cesa-Bianchi, N., Garnett, R. (eds.) Advances in Neural Information Processing Systems, vol. 31, pp. 1419–1428. Curran Associates, Inc. (2018)

50. Stewart, T.C.: A technical overview of the neural engineering framework. Technical report, Centre for Theoretical Neuroscience (2012)

51. Stimberg, M., Brette, R., Goodman, D.F.: Brian 2, an intuitive and efficient neural simulator. eLife **8** (2019)

52. Vicente-Sola, A., Manna, D.L., Kirkland, P., Caterina, G.D., Bihl, T.: Keys to accurate feature extraction using residual spiking neural networks. Neuromorp. Comput. Eng. **2**(4), 044001 (2022)

53. Zenke, F., Ganguli, S.: Superspike: supervised learning in multilayer spiking neural networks. Neural Comput. **30**(6), 1514–1541 (2018)

# Hierarchical Prediction in Incomplete Submetering Systems Using a CNN

Serafín Alonso[✉][iD], Antonio Morán[iD], Daniel Pérez[iD], Miguel A. Prada[iD],
Juan J. Fuertes[iD], and Manuel Domínguez[iD]

Grupo de Investigación En Supervisión, Control Y Automatización de Procesos
Industriales (SUPPRESS), Escuela de Ing. Industrial, Informática Y Aeroespacial,
Universidad De León, Campus de Vegazana S/n, 24007 León, Spain
{saloc,a.moran,dperl,dperl,jjfuem,manuel.dominguez}@unileon.es
https://suppress.unileon.es

**Abstract.** Energy market liberalization brings new opportunities, since
large consumers have direct access to energy trading to buy energy for
the next day. However, that requires a good estimation of the expected
amount of energy and its hourly distribution in advance. On the other
hand, smart energy meters are being installed in many facilities with
the aim of achieving holistic submetering systems. These systems consist
of a set of meters structured in several levels, so that there are hierarchical relations among upstream and downstream meters. This information could be exploited for achieving accurate one-day-ahead energy
predictions. However, submetering systems might be incomplete due to
unavailable meters or lost energy. In this paper, we propose a hierarchical prediction method for incomplete submetering systems that is based
on 2D convolutional neural network (2D CNN) and is able to perform
day ahead prediction of power consumption. This method exploits the
hierarchical relations among meters and considers periodicity in order
to forecast the power consumption for the next day. The proposed hierarchical method has proved to be more accurate and fast to forecast
power consumption in incomplete submetering systems than using an
individual predictions.

**Keywords:** Hierarchical prediction · Power consumption ·
Submetering systems · Convolutional Neural Networks

## 1 Introduction

Since energy markets are liberalized, large consumers can resort to energy auc-
tions to buy the necessary energy for the next day. For that purpose, they need
to estimate in advance the amount of energy and its hourly distribution, since
energy prices vary each hour. Typically, energy trading takes place in the middle of each day (at noon). Thus, having an accurate one-day-ahead prediction
becomes vital for an adequate purchase. As a baseline prediction, buyers could

Grant PID2020-117890RB-I00 funded by MCIN/AEI/10.13039/501100011033.

L. Iliadis et al. (Eds.): EANN 2023, CCIS 1826, pp. 239–250, 2023.
https://doi.org/10.1007/978-3-031-34204-2_21

use the energy consumption from the previous day or from the same day of the past week, considering the periodicity of energy consumption. However, they could make use of specific prediction methods to obtain the power consumption with more accuracy.

It is interesting to note that smart energy meters are being installed in many facilities, achieving holistic submetering systems [12]. These meters measure, storage and communicate data [24] and are placed at strategic points in the energy supply systems, establishing hierarchical relations among upstream and downstream meters. Note that the sum of measurements from individual lower meters should be equal to a measurement from the aggregated higher meter and this information could be useful for achieving more accurate energy predictions. In a submetering system, it could be also required to predict the energy consumption in several downstream meters (bottom level), not only in the main one (top level), i.e., energy consumption could be analyzed at a more granular level. However, not all meters might be available in the submetering system or the sum of individual consumption might not match with the aggregated consumption due to lost energy. Therefore, classic bottom-up and top-down approaches for hierarchical prediction would fail since they rely on complete submetering systems.

For that reason, in this paper we propose a method to perform a hierarchical prediction of the power consumption in incomplete submetering systems. This method aims to yield forecasts which are coherent across the particular meters at different levels of a submetering system. It is based on a convolutional neural network that exploits the periodicity of the power consumption and the hierarchy of the meters in the submetering system.

The structure of this paper is as follows: the state of the art is reviewed in Sect. 2. The proposed method is presented in Sect. 3. Section 4 describes the experiments, presents the results and discusses them. Finally, in Sect. 5, conclusions are exposed.

## 2   Related Work

Energy prediction or load forecasting has become a key aspect for electricity management. Although an accurate forecast in lower levels is more difficult than in higher levels, the use of smart meters contributes to improve the performance of prediction models. In general, several techniques for smart meter data analytics can be found in literature [2, 26]. Other reviews have studied methods in load forecasting [5], time-series [10], machine learning techniques for building load prediction [28], or also focused on using artificial neural networks [17]. Assuming the prediction problem as a time-series analysis, the autoregressive integrated moving average (ARIMA) is a widely-used method [6]. The addition of external variables to the model through exogenous inputs (ARIMAX) have improved accuracy, e.g., the use of occupancy data allowed a slight improvement of the accuracy when applied to the forecast of power demand in an office building [19]. A methodology was also developed for forecasting daily electric power load in Kuwait [3] based on decomposition and segmentation of time-series analyzed with methods such as moving average, exponential smoothing or ARIMA.

Other machine learning techniques have been studied for prediction of next day electricity load in public buildings [11]. In that work, several models were developed for energy forecasting of different equipment (air, lighting, power, etc.), showing the support vector regression (SVR) model the best results. SVR was also applied to develop a generic strategy for short-term load forecasting [8], using feature selection and particle swarm global optimization for hyperparameter tuning, and for an energy forecasting model of multi-family residential buildings in order to study the impact temporal and spatial granularity has on model accuracy [13].

Artificial neural networks, including the advances of deep learning, have been widely implemented to build energy prediction models [17], being feed forward neural networks (FFNN) the most popular architecture because of its easy implementation. Since energy data are temporal-oriented, another preferred network class is that of recurrent neural networks (RNN). They can be seen in examples such as nonlinear autoregressive neural network with exogenous inputs (NARX) applied to an institutional building [16], a hybrid model based on long short term memory networks (LSTM) and an improved sine cosine algorithm to optimize hyperparameters [23], and a Gate-Recurrent Unit (GRU) model [27]. Moreover, convolutional neural networks (CNN) have been shown as an efficient time-series model for day-ahead building-level load forecasting [7], which has also been used in combination with fuzzy time-series analysis [21]. Being hybrid models an alternative to enhance performance of other baseline methods, a common combination includes RNN and CNN. For instance, a CNN-LSTM neural network was proposed to extract spatial and temporal features [15], CNN with GRU was used as an effective alternative in terms of preciseness and efficiency [22], and RNN for past preservation and 1D convolutional inception module helped to calibrate the prediction time and the hidden state vector values [14].

Finally, another approach for load forecasting is to consider the hierarchical structure of the power grid. In [25], the load of a root node of a subtree was forecasted using a wavelet neural network. The child nodes were categorized based on similarities, so that the forecast of a *regular* child node was proportional to the parent node load forecast, while the *irregular* child nodes were calculated individually using neural networks. Another novel approach using hierarchical information for load forecasting was proposed in [4], where three methods based on combined aggregation (bottom-up aggregation, top-down aggregation and regression aggregation) were devised to obtain overall consumption. Two case studies were conducted and results showed that aggregative model combination is an effective forecasting technique in smart grids.

## 3    The Proposed Method

Classic bottom-up and top-down approaches for hierarchical prediction require complete data in all levels of the submetering system. Unlike them, the proposed

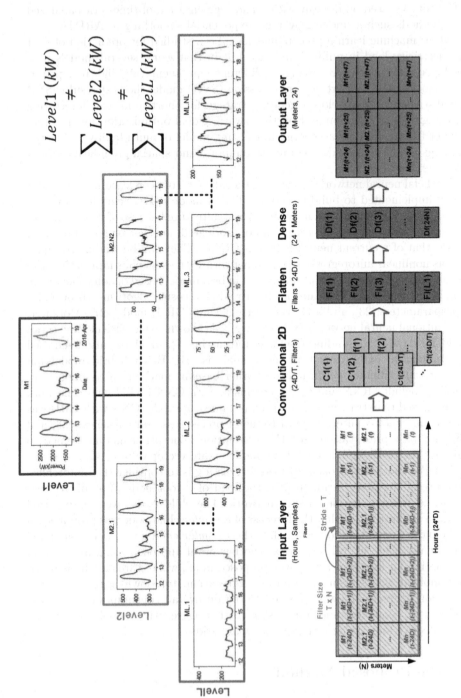

**Fig. 1.** Hierarchical prediction based on CNN.

method is able to predict the energy consumption for the next day in incomplete submetering systems. For that purpose, on the one hand, the method should exploit the hierarchical structure of the data, i.e., the hierarchical relations among upstream and downstream meters. On the other hand, it should also consider the periodicity (daily, weekly, monthly, etc.) of energy consumption in order to perform the day ahead prediction. Therefore, the method should learn both from hierarchical and temporal patterns. Figure 1 shows the proposed method, which is based on 2D convolutional neural network (2D CNN) that processes time (hours of the day) and levels of the hierarchy (submetering structure).

Let us define a submetering structure with $L$ levels from the top to the bottom, being $N$ the total number of meters. The top level contains one main meter ($M1$) and the bottom level includes $NL$ meters ($ML.1, ML.2, \ldots ML.NL$). Intermediate levels consist of different number of meters, i.e., $N2, N3, N4, \ldots$. Each meter provides hourly measurements of power consumption (24 samples per day). Let us assume that there could be some zones without meters (where data are unavailable), especially in the intermediate and bottom levels, so the proposed method could exploit existing data to predict the next power consumption.

Data from several previous days ($D$) is used due to the periodicity of the power consumption. Therefore, input data contains hourly power consumption of certain past days ($D$) for several meters ($N$) belonging to the submetering structure. Width and height dimensions of the input data correspond to past hours ($24 \cdot D$) and meters ($N$), respectively, so the size of the input will be ($24 \cdot D \times N$). In order to consider relationships among different levels of the hierarchy $L$, the kernel height of the 2D convolutions should include all meters along this dimension, so it should be fixed to $N$. On the contrary, different kernel widths could be used in order to capture the periodicity of the power consumption, so it will be an adjustable parameter ($T$). Thus, the size of the kernel will be $T \times N$. Finally, the width of the strides in the convolutions should be equal to kernel width ($T$), avoiding overlap in time dimension (maximizing extracted temporal patterns). Note that there are no strides in the meters dimension. The output of the proposed method will be one day ahead prediction of hourly power consumption for several meters, so its size is ($24 \times N$).

The proposed method comprises an input layer whose dimensions (width and height) are past hours and meters ($24 \cdot D \times N$). A unique channel is used. The main layer is based on a 2D CNN layer in which the input is convolved with the kernel ($T \times N$) producing the output filters with dimension $24 \cdot D/T$. The kernel must include all meters, so the height dimension of the convolution must be equal to number of meters ($N$). Furthermore, with the aim of extracting independent temporal patterns along the day, the strides must have the same width dimension (hours) than the kernel ($T$). Relu activation function will be added to process nonlinearities. Then, the output of the 2D CNN is flattened ($Filters \times 24 \cdot D/T$). Next, a dense layer is required to combine all features, so every features should influence each value of the output vector. The number of neurons should be multiple of number of ahead predicted hours and meters ($24 \cdot N$). A linear activation function is used here in order to provide the predictions. Finally, an output layer reshapes the output data to ($24 \times N$) dimensions.

**Table 1.** Electrical meters at the Hospital of León used in the experiments.

| Meter No. | Meter location | Submetering level |
|-----------|----------------|-------------------|
| #0 | Main supply | Level 0 |
| #1 | Module 10 | Level 2 |
| #2 | North Zone Elevators | Level 3 |
| #3 | Module 2 | Level 2 |
| #4 | North Zone HVAC | Level 3 |
| #5 | Module 3 | Level 2 |
| #6 | South Zone Elevators | Level 3 |
| #7 | Air Handling Units | Level 3 |

# 4    Experiments and Results

## 4.1    Submetering System and Dataset

The submetering system deployed in the Hospital of León [18] is used to assess the proposed approach. This system consists of more than 30 electrical meters installed in several strategic points of the electricity supply system (in the main supply point, in transformation centers, in the distribution panels, etc.) To perform the experiment, 7 representative submeters corresponding to zones with high consumption (more than 10% of the total consumption each) were selected among those submeters. This experiment design shows the ability of the proposed approach to be used even for incomplete submetering systems. Table 1 lists the representative meters. Although these meters measure and store several variables, only power consumption [KW] is used in the experiments. Power data were collected from 2018 March to 2019 July using a sampling period of 1 min. Daily electricity profiles were obtained by resampling data each 1 h. Therefore, the size of the dataset is 507 electricity profiles with 24 samples from 8 m (including the main meter).

## 4.2    Experiments

The dataset was standardized between [-1, 1] and split into training, validation and test datasets. Data corresponding to 1 year (365 d, 72%) were used to train and validate the proposed approach and the remaining data (142 d, 28%) were used to test it. Weekly periodicity was considered, by setting D to 7 past days. A 3-fold cross-validation was performed to tune the hyperparameters of the hierarchical 2D CNN. The hyperparameters were the number of filters, the kernels and the strides of the convolutions. After several preliminary runs, a range of hyperparameters was established and then, a grid search was performed. The number of filters were chosen between 8 and 128 and the kernels and strides were chosen between 24 and 3 h, i.e., from (24,8) to (3,8) for the kernel and (24,1) to (3,1) for the strides. Filters, kernel and strides were established to 64, (24,8) and (24,1), respectively, through

**Table 2.** Prediction errors using the validation dataset (average values).

| Filter | Kernel | Strides | Average Forecasting | | | |
|---|---|---|---|---|---|---|
| | | | RMSE | | MAE | |
| | | | Hierarchical | Individual | Hierarchical | Individual |
| 8 | 24 | 24 | 35.32 ± 1.02 | 39.43 ± 0.37 | 23.64 ± 0.16 | 26.17 ± 0.42 |
| | 12 | 12 | 33.42 ± 0.69 | 36.90 ± 0.84 | 21.62 ± 0.41 | 23.38 ± 0.54 |
| | 8 | 8 | 33.82 ± 0.85 | 36.47 ± 0.95 | 22.15 ± 0.51 | 23.12 ± 0.67 |
| | 6 | 6 | 33.54 ± 1.16 | 35.77 ± 0.58 | 21.90 ± 0.98 | 22.49 ± 0.49 |
| | 3 | 3 | 33.45 ± 0.66 | 35.22 ± 0.84 | 21.93 ± 0.27 | 21.92 ± 0.57 |
| 16 | 24 | 24 | 34.05 ± 0.61 | 36.38 ± 0.82 | 22.81 ± 0.50 | 22.90 ± 0.69 |
| | 12 | 12 | 33.17 ± 1.25 | 35.44 ± 0.60 | 21.60 ± 0.66 | 22.02 ± 0.60 |
| | 8 | 8 | 33.03 ± 1.42 | 34.89 ± 0.93 | 21.33 ± 0.71 | 21.63 ± 0.60 |
| | 6 | 6 | 33.39 ± 0.85 | 35.48 ± 0.65 | 21.60 ± 1.05 | 21.87 ± 0.39 |
| | 3 | 3 | 34.04 ± 0.45 | 34.84 ± 0.84 | 22.05 ± 0.54 | 21.34 ± 0.49 |
| 32 | 24 | 24 | 33.28 ± 0.99 | 35.14 ± 0.66 | 21.58 ± 0.74 | 21.40 ± 0.39 |
| | 12 | 12 | 32.68 ± 1.35 | 34.76 ± 0.60 | 21.03 ± 0.48 | 21.35 ± 0.30 |
| | 8 | 8 | 33.61 ± 0.96 | 34.68 ± 0.59 | 21.66 ± 0.56 | 21.39 ± 0.55 |
| | 6 | 6 | 33.50 ± 1.18 | 34.84 ± 0.74 | 21.74 ± 0.85 | 21.49 ± 0.44 |
| | 3 | 3 | 34.08 ± 1.75 | 35.07 ± 0.74 | 22.05 ± 0.77 | 21.65 ± 0.25 |
| 64 | 24 | 24 | **32.56 ± 1.16** | 35.14 ± 0.75 | **20.95 ± 0.69** | 21.58 ± 0.27 |
| | 12 | 12 | 34.22 ± 0.98 | 34.75 ± 0.48 | 22.32 ± 0.84 | 21.39 ± 0.25 |
| | 8 | 8 | 34.51 ± 1.61 | 34.86 ± 0.30 | 22.56 ± 0.70 | 21.57 ± 0.20 |
| | 6 | 6 | 34.81 ± 1.30 | 34.79 ± 0.73 | 22.30 ± 0.89 | 21.27 ± 0.50 |
| | 3 | 3 | 34.34 ± 1.46 | 35.58 ± 0.28 | 22.32 ± 0.38 | 22.08 ± 0.39 |
| 128 | 24 | 24 | 33.30 ± 1.39 | **34.60 ± 0.66** | 21.78 ± 0.22 | **21.09 ± 0.52** |
| | 12 | 12 | 34.91 ± 1.24 | 35.07 ± 0.42 | 22.27 ± 0.13 | 21.57 ± 0.21 |
| | 8 | 8 | 35.94 ± 0.60 | 35.06 ± 0.82 | 23.85 ± 0.68 | 21.54 ± 0.62 |
| | 6 | 6 | 35.78 ± 1.95 | 35.53 ± 0.47 | 23.17 ± 0.67 | 21.81 ± 0.28 |
| | 3 | 3 | 34.54 ± 0.45 | 35.46 ± 0.97 | 22.43 ± 0.22 | 22.05 ± 0.63 |

cross-validation. An individual 2D CNN per meter was also trained in order to compare both methods. Using the same procedure, filters, kernel and strides were set to 128, (24,1) and (24,1), respectively. Training epochs were set to 50 for all models (hierarchical and individual ones).

The experiments were executed on a PC equipped with an Intel Core i7-6700 3.40GHz CPU and 16GB RAM. Python 3.10.6, Keras 2.10.0 [9], Tensorflow 2.10.0 [1], pandas 1.5.1 and scikit-learn 1.1.3 [20] are used to implement them.

### 4.3 Results and Discussion

RMSE (Root Mean Square Error) and MAE (Mean Absolute Error) have been chosen as evaluation metrics. Table 2 shows the result of the validation pro-

**Table 3.** Prediction errors with the optimal hyperparameters using the validation dataset.

| | | RMSE | | MAE | |
|---|---|---|---|---|---|
| | | Hierarchical | Individual | Hierarchical | Individual |
| | Filters | 64 | 128 | 64 | 128 |
| | Kernel | 24 | 24 | 24 | 24 |
| | Strides | 24 | 24 | 24 | 24 |
| Meters | #0 | 105.76 ± 5.36 | 113.88 ± 6.53 | 71.62 ± 2.23 | 73.75 ± 3.49 |
| | #1 | 25.03 ± 1.86 | 26.12 ± 1.26 | 16.08 ± 1.20 | 16.61 ± 1.00 |
| | #2 | 6.42 ± 0.44 | 6.20 ± 0.24 | 3.79 ± 0.12 | 3.69 ± 0.16 |
| | #3 | 71.29 ± 4.20 | 76.47 ± 4.88 | 48.13 ± 4.44 | 46.89 ± 4.82 |
| | #4 | 3.88 ± 0.38 | 3.13 ± 0.32 | 2.70 ± 0.18 | 2.04 ± 0.14 |
| | #5 | 34.84 ± 3.21 | 37.46 ± 1.57 | 17.08 ± 0.73 | 17.93 ± 0.35 |
| | #6 | 6.83 ± 0.82 | 7.35 ± 0.32 | 3.29 ± 0.20 | 3.44 ± 0.17 |
| | #7 | 6.47 ± 0.11 | 6.20 ± 0.41 | 4.86 ± 0.11 | 4.36 ± 0.23 |
| | #Avg | 32.56 ± 1.16 | 34.60 ± 0.66 | 20.95 ± 0.69 | 21.09 ± 0.52 |

cess. The prediction average errors for the 8 m were computed. The hierarchical method yields the lowest errors (RMSE and MAE) using 64 filters, (24,8) kernel and (24,1) strides. The average prediction errors are 32.56±1.16 and 20.95±0.69, respectively. On the contrary, the individual method provides the lowest errors (RMSE and MAE) using 128 filters, (24,1) kernel and (24,1) strides. The average prediction errors are 34.60 ± 0.66 and 21.09 ± 0.52, respectively. Note that the hierarchical method yields slightly higher errors than the individual method. These optimal hyperparameters are used for hierarchical and individual methods in order to compare validation and test results for each meter.

Table 3 shows the prediction errors for each meter using the validation dataset. As it can be seen, the hierarchical method provides lower RMSE errors for five meters (#0, #1, #3, #5, #6) whereas the individual method only has lower RMSE errors for three meters (#2, #4, #7). According to MAE, the hierarchical method is lower for four meters (#0, #1, #5, #6) and the individual method also yields lower errors for other four meters (#2, #3, #4, #7).

Table 4 shows the prediction errors for each meter using the test dataset. Average values were also computed. The hierarchical method gives an average RMSE error of 39.02 whereas the individual method yields a higher value (40.16). However, the hierarchical method provides slightly higher average MAE error (26.08) than the individual method (25.57). As expected, test average errors are higher than validation average errors (both RMSE and MAE errors), so there exist coherence in the results. Analyzing each meter, it can be stated the hierarchical method provides lower RMSE errors for five meters (#1, #2, #3, #5, #6) whereas the individual method only has lower RMSE errors for three meters (#0, #4, #7). Regarding to MAE error, the hierarchical method provides

**Table 4.** Prediction errors using the test dataset.

|        |        | RMSE | | MAE | |
|--------|--------|------|------|------|------|
|        |        | **Hierarchical** | **Individual** | **Hierarchical** | **Individual** |
|        | **Filters** | 64 | 128 | 64 | 128 |
|        | **Kernel** | 24 | 24 | 24 | 24 |
|        | **Strides** | 24 | 24 | 24 | 24 |
| Meters | **#0** | 148.50 | 148.04 | 96.91 | 97.36 |
|        | **#1** | 25.48 | 27.42 | 18.65 | 18.18 |
|        | **#2** | 6.47 | 6.61 | 4.29 | 4.32 |
|        | **#3** | 80.18 | 85.43 | 57.17 | 57.34 |
|        | **#4** | 4.94 | 3.47 | 3.74 | 2.51 |
|        | **#5** | 31.61 | 36.83 | 17.76 | 17.16 |
|        | **#6** | 6.39 | 7.72 | 3.30 | 3.44 |
|        | **#7** | 8.58 | 5.76 | 6.82 | 4.25 |
|        | **#Avg** | 39.02 | 40.16 | 26.08 | 25.57 |

lower errors for four meters (#0, #2, #3, #6) and the individual method also yields lower errors for other four meters (#1, #4, #5, #7).

As expected, meter #0 in the top level of the hierarchy has the highest RMSE and MAE errors (using validation and test datasets). In contrast, meters #2, #4, #6, #7 in the bottom level possess the lowest RMSE and MAE errors. Thus it can be remarked, meters located in a a higher level of the submetering structure measure more power consumption and, consequently, their prediction errors are greater.

In addition to the errors, training and inference times were evaluated. Training a hierarchical method takes only 2.68 s whereas training an individual method per meter takes 10.58 s in total, i.e., an average time of 1.32 s per model. On the other hand, the hierarchical method is able to predict the test dataset in 0.14 s whereas forecasting the test dataset for each meter using the individual method lasts 0.84 s in total. Therefore, it can be remarked the hierarchical method can predict faster with acceptable errors. In short, the hierarchical method provides predictions either comparable or slightly superior to those provided by the individual method, but more efficiently.

Although the proposed hierarchical method is able to perform accurate and fast predictions of the power consumption in incomplete submetering systems, it presents some drawbacks. Figure 2 shows the prediction of the power consumption for different zones (#0-main supply, #6-south elevators and #7-air handling units) using both hierarchical and individual methods during one week. Note that, selected meters #0, #6 and #7 are located at different levels of the submetering structure (level 0 or top and 3 or bottom). For meter #0, it can be seen that there are small differences between hierarchical prediction (in red) and individual prediction (in green), nevertheless, the hierarchical prediction is

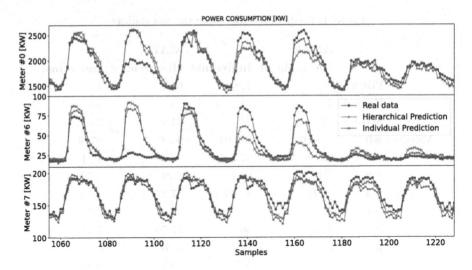

**Fig. 2.** Prediction of the power consumption in different meters.

closer to the real data (in blue), since it is more accurate than individual prediction. However, both predictions clearly fail when forecasting power consumption for a holiday (samples between 1080 and 1110). That is due to the fact that both methods use a similar kernel (24-width) that learns periodic patterns of the past power consumption, but not singular behaviours. Meter #6 shows the same problem, since the use of elevators depends on the activity in the building (there are few people on holidays). On the contrary, air handling units work continuously during a year (heating and cooling), so both methods are able to predict power consumption more accurate corresponding to meter #7. Thus, it leads to the conclusion that exogenous variables (holidays, activity, occupation, etc.) should be introduced to the model in order to take into account this scenario.

Another drawback of the proposed hierarchical method is dealing with noise introduced by some meters, which is especially true for those located at the bottom level, which measure lower power consumption. In this paper, seven representative submeters measuring high power consumption have been used, discarding the remaining ones. The proposed method should be able to tackle this problem by filtering the noise and extracting the meaningful patterns.

## 5    Conclusions

In this paper, we propose a hierarchical prediction method for incomplete submetering systems. It is based on 2D convolutional neural network (2D CNN) and is able to perform day ahead prediction of the power consumption. This method exploits the hierarchical relations among meters (submetering structure) and considers the periodicity (temporal patterns) of the power consumption in order to forecast the power consumption for the next day.

The proposed hierarchical method has proved to be more accurate and efficient for forecasting power consumption in incomplete submetering systems than using an individual method for each meter. RMSE errors are lower for the most of the meters and MAE errors are at least similar. Furthermore, both training and predicting times are much shorter.

As future work, a dilated CNN could be trained to create dependencies among power consumption corresponding to the same previous hours, considering different periodicities (daily, weekly, monthly, etc.) in one step. Furthermore, exogenous variables could be processed by the method in order to improve the predictions, especially those corresponding to singular consumption patterns, such as holidays. The method should also be adapted to filter the noise corresponding to lower power consumptions and to exploit all available meters in the submetering system. Additionally, the results and subsequent discussion could be extended by considering longer or shorter previous samples, by predicting more values ahead (e.g., two days ahead) or by analyzing errors in different levels of the submetering structure.

# References

1. Abadi, M., Agarwal, A., et al., P.B.: TensorFlow: Large-scale machine learning on heterogeneous systems (2015). https://www.tensorflow.org/ software available from tensorflow.org
2. Alahakoon, D., Yu, X.: Smart electricity meter data intelligence for future energy systems: a survey. IEEE Trans. Industr. Inf. **12**(1), 425–436 (2016). https://doi.org/10.1109/TII.2015.2414355
3. Almeshaiei, E., Soltan, H.: A methodology for electric power load forecasting. Alex. Eng. J. **50**(2), 137–144 (2011)
4. Borges, C.E., Penya, Y.K., Fernandez, I.: Evaluating combined load forecasting in large power systems and smart grids. IEEE Trans. Industr. Inf. **9**(3), 1570–1577 (2012)
5. Bourdeau, M., qiang Zhai, X., Nefzaoui, E., Guo, X., Chatellier, P.: Modeling and forecasting building energy consumption: a review of data-driven techniques. Sustainable Cities Society **48**, 101533 (2019)
6. Box, G.: Box and Jenkins: time series analysis, forecasting and control. In: A Very British Affair: Six Britons and the Development of Time Series Analysis during the 20th Century, pp. 161–215. Springer (2013). https://doi.org/10.1057/9781137291264_6
7. Cai, M., Pipattanasomporn, M., Rahman, S.: Day-ahead building-level load forecasts using deep learning vs. traditional time-series techniques. Appl. Energy **236**, 1078–1088 (2019). https://doi.org/10.1016/j.apenergy.2018.12.042
8. Ceperic, E., Ceperic, V., Baric, A.: A strategy for short-term load forecasting by support vector regression machines. IEEE Trans. Power Syst. **28**(4), 4356–4364 (2013)
9. Chollet, F., et al.: Keras. https://keras.io (2015)
10. Deb, C., Zhang, F., Yang, J., Lee, S.E., Shah, K.W.: A review on time series forecasting techniques for building energy consumption. Renew. Sustain. Energy Rev. **74**, 902–924 (2017)

11. Fu, Y., Li, Z., Zhang, H., Xu, P.: Using support vector machine to predict next day electricity load of public buildings with sub-metering devices. Procedia Eng. **121**, 1016–1022 (2015). https://doi.org/10.1016/j.proeng.2015.09.097

12. Halstenberg, F., Lindow, K., Stark, R.: Implementation of an energy metering system for smart production. In: Technologies and Eco-innovation towards Sustainability II. Springer, Singapore (2019). https://doi.org/10.1007/978-981-13-1196-3_11

13. Jain, R.K., Smith, K.M., Culligan, P.J., Taylor, J.E.: Forecasting energy consumption of multi-family residential buildings using support vector regression: Investigating the impact of temporal and spatial monitoring granularity on performance accuracy. Appl. Energy **123**, 168–178 (2014)

14. Kim, J., Moon, J., Hwang, E., Kang, P.: Recurrent inception convolution neural network for multi short-term load forecasting. Energy Build. **194**, 328–341 (2019)

15. Kim, T.Y., Cho, S.B.: Predicting residential energy consumption using cnn-lstm neural networks. Energy **182**, 72–81 (2019)

16. Kim, Y., Son, H.g.: KimShort term electricity load forecasting for institutional buildings. Energy Rep. **5**, 1270–1280 (2019)

17. Lu, C., Li, S., Lu, Z.: Building energy prediction using artificial neural networks: a literature survey. Energy Build. **262**, 111718 (2022). https://doi.org/10.1016/j.enbuild.2021.111718

18. Morán, A., Alonso, S., Pérez, D., Prada, M.A., Fuertes, J.J., Domínguez, M.: Feature extraction from building submetering networks using deep learning. Sensors **20**(13) (2020). https://doi.org/10.3390/s20133665

19. Newsham, G.R., Birt, B.J.: Building-level occupancy data to improve arima-based electricity use forecasts. In: Proceedings of the 2nd ACM Workshop on Embedded Sensing Systems for Energy-Efficiency in Building, pp. 13–18 (2010)

20. Pedregosa, F., et al.: Scikit-learn: machine learning in Python. J. Mach. Learn. Res. **12**, 2825–2830 (2011)

21. Sadaei, H.J., de Lima e Silva, P.C., Guimarães, F.G., Lee, M.H.: Short-term load forecasting by using a combined method of convolutional neural networks and fuzzy time series. Energy **175**, 365–377 (2019). https://doi.org/10.1016/j.energy.2019.03.081

22. Sajjad, M., et al.: A novel cnn-gru-based hybrid approach for short-term residential load forecasting. Ieee Access **8**, 143759–143768 (2020)

23. Somu, N., MR, G.R., Ramamritham, K.: A hybrid model for building energy consumption forecasting using long short term memory networks. Appl. Energy **261**, 114131 (2020)

24. Sun, Q., Li, H., Ma, Z., Wang, C., Campillo, J., Zhang, Q., Wallin, F., Guo, J.: A comprehensive review of smart energy meters in intelligent energy networks. IEEE Internet Things J. **3**(4), 464–479 (2016). https://doi.org/10.1109/JIOT.2015.2512325

25. Sun, X., et al.: An efficient approach to short-term load forecasting at the distribution level. IEEE Trans. Power Syst. **31**(4), 2526–2537 (2016). https://doi.org/10.1109/TPWRS.2015.2489679

26. Wang, Y., Chen, Q., Hong, T., Kang, C.: Review of smart meter data analytics: applications, methodologies, and challenges. IEEE Trans. Smart Grid **10**(3), 3125–3148 (2018)

27. Wen, L., Zhou, K., Yang, S.: Load demand forecasting of residential buildings using a deep learning model. Electric Power Syst.Res. **179**, 106073 (2020)

28. Zhang, L., Wen, J., Li, Y., Chen, J., Ye, Y., Fu, Y., Livingood, W.: A review of machine learning in building load prediction. Appl. Energy **285**, 116452 (2021)

# Pruning for Power: Optimizing Energy Efficiency in IoT with Neural Network Pruning

Thomas Widmann[ID], Florian Merkle[(✉)][ID], Martin Nocker[ID], and Pascal Schöttle[ID]

MCI Management Center Innsbruck, Innsbruck, Austria
{th.widmann,florian.merkle,martin.nocker,
pascal.schoettle}@mci.edu

**Abstract.** The Internet of Things (IoT) has rapidly emerged as a crucial driver of the digital economy, generating massive amounts of data. Machine learning (ML) is an important technology to extract insights from the data generated by IoT devices. Deploying ML on low-power devices such as microcontroller units (MCUs) improves data protection, reduces bandwidth, and enables on-device data processing. However, the requirements of ML algorithms exceed the processing power, memory, and energy consumption capabilities of these devices. One solution to adapt ML networks to the limited capacities of MCUs is network pruning, the process of removing unnecessary connections or neurons from a neural network. In this work, we investigate the effect of unstructured and structured pruning methods on energy consumption. A series of experiments is conducted using a Raspberry Pi Pico to classify the FashionMNIST dataset with a LeNet-5-like convolutional neural network while applying unstructured magnitude and structured APoZ pruning approaches with various model compression rates from two to 64. We find that unstructured pruning out of the box has no effect on energy consumption, while structured pruning reduces energy consumption with increasing model compression. When structured pruning is applied to remove 75 % of the model parameters, inference consumes 59.06 % less energy, while the accuracy declines by 3.01 %. We further develop an adaption of the TensorFlow Lite framework that realizes the theoretical improvements for unstructured pruning, reducing the energy consumption by 37.59 % with a decrease of only 1.58 % in accuracy when 75 % of the parameters are removed. Our results show that both approaches are feasible to significantly reduce the energy consumption of MCUs, leading to various possible sweet spots within the trade-off between accuracy and energy consumption.

The second and fourth author are supported by the Austrian Science Fund (FWF) under grant no. I 4057-N31 ("Game Over Eva(sion)"). The third author is supported under the project "Secure Machine Learning Applications with Homomorphically Encrypted Data" (project no. 886524) by the Federal Ministry for Climate Action, Environment, Energy, Mobility, Innovation and Technology (BMK) of Austria.

L. Iliadis et al. (Eds.): EANN 2023, CCIS 1826, pp. 251–263, 2023.
https://doi.org/10.1007/978-3-031-34204-2_22

## 1   Introduction

Driven by the shift towards Industry 4.0 and the Internet of Things (IoT), machine learning (ML) on edge devices has gained increasing attention. It has huge potential to increase energy efficiency, privacy, responsiveness, and autonomy of edge devices. Until today, research in edge ML has focused mainly on mobile devices, but there is also a lot of interest in microcontroller-based devices [2]. Tiny machine learning (TinyML) brings machine learning to low-power devices such as microcontroller units (MCUs), enabling many new applications. However, this area also brings challenges [2]. The most critical challenge is that microcontrollers have few computational resources compared to traditional ML devices. Exemplary, the RP2040[1] microcontroller, developed by *Raspberry Pi Foundation* has 264 KB of SRAM, a dual-core ARM Cortex-M0+ CPU with 133 MHz clock frequency, and 2 MB of flash memory. Most of today's deep learning models exceed the storage capacity of such MCUs. Additionally, TinyML systems often use batteries to enable applications like augmented reality glasses [2]. To achieve a long battery life of these systems, very low energy consumption is crucial.

Neural network pruning is a promising approach to simultaneously tackle restrictions regarding storage capacity and energy consumption. It refers to the deletion of selected connections, nodes, or layers of neural networks to improve memory usage and computational efficiency while having moderate to no effects on the accuracy [6], robustness [17], and explainability [21]. It is conceivable that the energy consumption of MCUs decreases when the deployed neural network is pruned. We run a series of experiments to examine the impact of neural network pruning on the energy consumption of a convolutional neural network (CNN) for two types of neural network pruning and nine compression rates.

Our contribution is twofold. First, we show that structured neural network pruning out of the box decreases the energy consumption of the CNN, while unstructured pruning does not substantially decrease the energy consumption of the CNN. Further, we propose an adaption to the matrix multiplication method of the TensorFlow Lite framework that allows realizing of theoretical improvements regarding the inference time and the energy consumption. The remainder of this work is structured as follows. The next section introduces the theoretical concepts relevant to this work. Section 3 describes our initial experiments, whose results are presented in Sect. 4. In Sect. 5, we propose our approach to realize the theoretical improvements of unstructured pruning with TensorFlow Lite before we conclude our work in Sect. 6.

## 2   Theoretical Background

In this section, we provide a brief background on TinyML and neural network pruning, two important areas of machine learning research due to their potential in deploying ML models on resource-constraint devices.

---

[1] https://datasheets.raspberrypi.com/rp2040/rp2040-datasheet.pdf.

## 2.1  TinyML

TinyML is a paradigm that deals with ML models running on ultra-low-power devices like embedded systems [2,18]. Today's ML models are frequently hosted on cloud systems that offer powerful hardware systems, but they frequently experience challenges with excessive energy consumption, privacy concerns, latency, and reliability issues. TinyML enables microcontroller units to process data on-chip instead of outsourcing the computation to external cloud systems. This results in better energy efficiency, improved privacy, low latency, and minimal connectivity dependencies [18].

The main challenges TinyML systems are facing are energy constraints and computational resources (CPU power and memory capacity). TinyML systems often rely on limited energy sources to keep the energy consumption as low as possible, such as batteries in the range of 10 – 100 mAh or on energy-harvesting approaches. Additionally, dedicated hardware accelerators and compact software are used to tackle these restrictions [18]. Due to limited hardware capacities, TinyML systems can have as little as four orders of magnitude less processing power available compared to typical ML systems [2]. Most CPUs used in TinyML systems have a clock speed of 10 – 1000 MHz [18].

## 2.2  Neural Network Pruning

Network pruning involves removing unnecessary parameters from a deep neural network (DNN) to reduce storage, memory usage, and computational resources. Overparameterization is common in modern NNs, resulting in redundancy in the models and excessive resource requirements. However, carefully selecting the parameters to be pruned, i.e. removed, can not only minimize resource requirements but also improve accuracy. This highlights the significance of network pruning in optimizing the performance and efficiency of DNNs [4,7]. Neural network pruning was initially proposed in 1989 by LeCun et al. [16] and later refined by Hassibi et al. [8].

Multiple methods exist to create a pruned model from an untrained model [3]. Most of them follow or derive from the algorithm described by the researchers in [5]. For generalization, Blalock et al. defined four dimensions to categorize different pruning methods: *structure, scoring, scheduling,* and *fine-tuning* [3].

The pruning structure defines whether individual or grouped parameters are removed [3,7]. In unstructured pruning, parameters with lower importance are set to zero, resulting in a sparse network. The size of the network with respect to the number of parameters stays the same [3]. Without modern libraries or hardware, the computational effort is not reduced [7]. Structured pruning removes entire neurons, filters, or channels, resulting in a new network structure with fewer parameters [3]. To select parameters with lower importance, different scoring methods are used. This selection is performed either globally or locally with different strategies. Furthermore, the selection is distinguished whether the selection is weight-based or activation-based [10]. Scheduling refers to when pruning is applied. Pruning can be conducted in small pruning steps or in one big step [3].

It is common to continue training after pruning, a process referred to as fine-tuning. One approach is to reinitialize the network. Another approach is to continue with the previously trained parameters [3].

Even though previous work considered the energy efficiency of pruned neural networks [7, e.g.], to the best of our knowledge, no work has examined this issue in the context of MCUs, that come with their own specific implications.

## 3    Experiments

The aim of this section is to evaluate the impact of model pruning on energy consumption. Specifically, the effect of various levels of network pruning on energy consumption will be measured while running a model with an architecture similar to the LeNet-5 model [15] on the RP2040 microcontroller. This will provide insights into the energy-efficiency trade-offs of model pruning. As recommended in [3], the model compression rate is defined as follows:

$$\text{CR} := \frac{\text{original number of parameters}}{\text{new number of parameters}} \tag{1}$$

The consumed energy of the MCU is given as a scaled value in joules and depends on the CR in the experiment.

### 3.1    Experimental Setup

A Raspberry Pi Pico (RPP) was selected as the MCU under analysis as its ARM Cortex-M0+ architecture is the most energy-efficient in the ARM Cortex-M series. To measure the current $I_{\mu C}$ consumed by the MCU we apply the widely used approach of a shunt resistor with a dimension of $R_{\text{shunt}} = 1\Omega$ [12]. The consumed energy is calculated by $E = \int_{t_1}^{t_2} v(t) \cdot i(t)\, dt$. The voltage drop on the shunt resistor $R_{\text{shunt}}$ is measured by an oscilloscope. The image data is transmitted to the RPP via the Universal Asynchronous Receiver Transmitter (UART) interface. The schematics of the measurement setup is shown in Fig. 2 in Appendix A.

Due to the limited resources of the Raspberry Pi Pico the Fashion-MNIST dataset[2], a standard dataset commonly used in research, is selected for comparability. The dataset consists of 60 000 training images and 10 000 test images of garments distributed over ten distinct classes (T-shirt/top, Trouser, Pullover, Dress, Coat, Sandal, Shirt, Sneaker, Bag, Ankle boot). Each image has a size of $28 \times 28$ pixels with one channel.

The model architecture is based on the architecture of a LeNet-5 network [15]. To reach a compression rate of up to 64, the architecture was modified. The first convolutional layer was increased to twelve channels (from six) and the second layer to 32 channels (from 16) to prevent the accidental removal of all channels in a single layer. The remaining layer dimensions remain unchanged, resulting

---

[2] https://github.com/zalandoresearch/fashion-mnist .

in a model architecture with 110 742 parameters. For the model training, we follow the authors of [13,20]. Therefore, we use the categorical cross entropy loss function, the RMSprop optimizer and an early stopping callback (based on the model's validation accuracy).

We implement one unstructured and one structured pruning approach to the model. Both approaches are applied iteratively, globally, and the models are fine-tuned after each pruning step with the remaining weights. For unstructured pruning the weights are selected based on their magnitude [7] and for structured pruning we apply the average percentage of zero (APoZ) approach [11]. The set of compression rates to be examined is {2, 3, 4, 8, 16, 24, 32, 48, 64}.

## 3.2 Implementation

The models are implemented in TensorFlow [1]. Unstructured pruning is conducted with the TensorFlow pruning utility and structures are eliminated from the network with the *keras-surgeon*[3] library before the model is converted into a TensorFlow Lite model. To run the pruned models on the RPP, we use the MicroInterpreter from the TensorFlow Lite framework. Image samples are transmitted to the RPP via the UART interface. After the image is received, the model classifies it, and the RPP returns the predicted class. To increase the accuracy of the energy and time measurements, we classify 30 different images and average over all results. During the classification, we utilize an oscilloscope to observe the current consumed by the RPP. Eventually, we calculate the consumed energy as described in Sect. 3.1. The accuracy values are computed for the whole testset.

# 4   Experimental Results

This section summarizes the results of our experiment described in the previous section. We analyze both pruning approaches with regard to the models' accuracy, inference speed, and energy consumption. The results are illustrated in Fig. 1. Further, we provide a table of all results in Appendix B.

Figure 1a shows that both, unstructured and structured pruning decrease the accuracy moderately for compression rates up to four. The base models have accuracy values from 89.37 % to 89.29 %. We report a decrease in accuracy of approximately 1.6 % (unstructured pruning) and 3.0 % (structured pruning), respectively. For lower compression rates, unstructured pruning leads to slightly better accuracy values, while beyond this point the accuracy of the unstructured pruned model decreases faster. At a maximum compression rate of 64, the compressed model using unstructured pruning achieves an accuracy of 42.9 % while the model pruned with structured pruning reaches 77.4 %. These findings are in line with existing research that has shown that moderate pruning does not reduce a model's accuracy significantly, while extensive pruning leads to a sharp decrease in the model's performance. However, no increase in accuracy was observable for moderate pruning which contrasts prior work (e.g. [9,11,17]), but this might be due to the small network capacity considering the problem difficulty.

---

[3] https://github.com/BenWhetton/keras-surgeon/tree/b0b892988e725b9203afc48e639c49d06155 b59b.

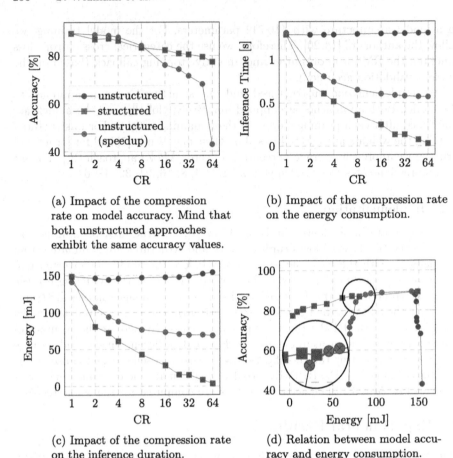

(a) Impact of the compression rate on model accuracy. Mind that both unstructured approaches exhibit the same accuracy values.

(b) Impact of the compression rate on the energy consumption.

(c) Impact of the compression rate on the inference duration.

(d) Relation between model accuracy and energy consumption.

**Fig. 1.** Overview of the results comparing unstructured pruning, structured pruning, and unstructured pruning with our framework adaption.

The base model has an inference time of 1.29 s. In Fig. 1b it is visible that the inference time for the model pruned with unstructured pruning (blue) remains steady over all compression rates. In contrast, the inference time of the model pruned with structured pruning (red) decreases linearly with an increasing compression rate, reaching a low of 27 milliseconds at a compression rate of 64.

Figure 1c shows that the energy consumption of one inference run evolves similarly to the inference time with increasing model compression. The base model consumes 149 mJ. Unstructured pruning slightly increases the expenditure up to 154 mJ for a compression rate of 64, while structured pruning leads to a linear decrease down to 4 mJ, effectively reducing the consumption by 97 %.

Finally, Fig. 1d shows the trade-off between energy consumption and accuracy. Data points to the upper left are strictly more desirable as they relate to higher accuracy and lower energy usage. It is visible that structured pruning (red) outperforms the unstructured approach (blue) in every instance, due to the non-reduced energy consumption of unstructured pruning.

# 5  Unstructured Pruning Speedup

In order to exploit the potential of unstructured pruning for low compression rates where it outperforms the structured approach accuracy-wise we analyze why unstructured pruning does not improve energy consumption. We propose an optimization of the TensorFlow Lite framework to partially realize its theoretical improvements.

## 5.1  Performance Bottleneck and Improvements

The implementation of the dense layer involves a multiply-accumulate (MAC) operation nested within three loops and includes an activation function. The runtime complexity of the three nested loops is $O(d_{in} \cdot d_{out} \cdot b)$, where $d_{in}$ is the input depth, $d_{out}$ is the output depth, and $b$ is the number of batches. In numerical terms, the base model necessitates 10 692 MAC operations for the dense layers.

Concerning the convolutional layer, we first describe the calculation of a single feature map at a specific location in the image. The calculation consists of a MAC operation nested within three loops. Therefore, the runtime complexity of calculating a single feature map at one location is $O(d_{in} \cdot f_x \cdot f_y)$, where $f_x$ is the filter width, and $f_y$ is the filter height. This feature map calculation is required on every location in the image and for every channel, leading to a total runtime complexity of $O(d_{in} \cdot f_x \cdot f_y \cdot d_{out} \cdot x_{out} \cdot y_{out} \cdot b)$, where $x_{out}$ is the output width, and $y_{out}$ is the output height. In numerical terms, the unpruned model needs 491 184 MAC operations for a convolutional layer to calculate the output.

Weights that are removed by unstructured pruning are set to zero, nevertheless, each activation calculation is performed regardless of whether the weight was removed by unstructured pruning and therefore its value was set to zero, or not. Therefore, no reduction in energy consumption is achieved when unstructured pruning is utilized. The idea of our framework improvement is to skip costly MAC operations for zero-weights and thereby reducing the number of MAC operations. A TensorFlow Lite floating-point model is represented using IEEE-754 floating-point numbers. Simply checking weights for zero would require complex floating-point comparisons. To avoid this, we only check the exponent of the IEEE-754 representation for zero, resulting in a more efficient check without floating-point comparisons. As a consequence, numbers with a zero exponent but with a non-zero fraction part are also classified as zero in our check. This simplification classifies numbers in the range [-1.17549421069e-38, 1.17549421069e-38] as zero. However, as low-magnitude weights are commonly removed by pruning, especially with low-magnitude pruning as used in our case, this effect is negligible. Eventually, for zero-valued weights we skip computing the product between the weight and the corresponding activation of the previous layer, resulting in

**Listing 1.1.** TensorFlow Dense layer implementation[4]. The dark-gray code lines (5–6) were replaced by our improvement (light-gray, 7–10).

```
 1  for (int b = 0; b < batches; ++b) {
 2    for (int out_c = 0; out_c < output_depth; ++out_c) {
 3      float total = 0.f;
 4      for (int d = 0; d < accum_depth; ++d) {
 5        total += input_data[b * accum_depth + d] *          // TensorFlow code
 6                 weights_data[out_c * accum_depth + d];
 7        const float fWeight = weights_data[out_c * accum_depth + d];  // improved dense layer
 8        if (float_check_exponent_not_zero(fWeight)) {               // with zero weights
 9          total += input_data[b * accum_depth + d] * fWeight;
10        }
11      }
12      float bias_value = 0.0f;
13      if (bias_data) {
14        bias_value = bias_data[out_c];
15      }
16      output_data[out_c + output_depth * b] = ActivationFunctionWithMinMax(
17          total + bias_value, output_activation_min, output_activation_max);
18    }
19  }
```

**Listing 1.2.** Simplified IEEE-754 zero check added to common.h[5].

```
 1  inline bool float_check_exponent_not_zero(float f) {
 2    short* p = (short*)&f;
 3    p++;
 4    short c = *p;
 5    c = c << 1;
 6    char* pe = (char*)&c;
 7    pe++;
 8    char e = *pe;
 9    return e != 0;
10  }
```

a significant runtime improvement. The improved performance is evident in the code block of Listing 1.1, which highlights the optimizations we implemented for the dense layer to reduce the number of MAC operations. Our simplified exponent zero-check is illustrated in Listing 1.2. The improvement for the convolutional layer is implemented analogous.

## 5.2 Results

Applying the framework optimization described in the previous subsection leads to the following result: As expected, the imprecision of minor values around zero

---

[4] https://github.com/tensorflow/tensorflow/blob/b6fee828d995ae13d6083e37b597df766904cacd/tensorflow/lite/kernels/internal/reference/fully_connected.h

[5] https://github.com/tensorflow/tensorflow/blob/b6fee828d995ae13d6083e37b597df766904cacd/tensorflow/lite/kernels/internal/common.h

does not impact the model's accuracy. Therefore the curves for unstructured pruning with and without the framework adaption are identical in Fig. 1a. However, the adaption causes a significant improvement in terms of inference time (Fig. 1b) and energy consumption (Fig. 1c). Specifically, for a compression rate of four, the energy consumption is 88 mJ which amounts to a decrease of 40 % compared to standard unstructured pruning and is only 27 mJ higher than the structured approach. When applying compression at the rate of 64 the model consumes 68 mJ, which is a decrease of 56 % relative to the standard approach but still one order of magnitude higher than structured pruning.

The results with regard to the inference time are similar: at the compression rate of four, inference takes 0.745 s, which is a 37 % decrease compared to standard unstructured pruning and only 0.227 s slower than the structured approach. For a compression rate of 64, inference takes still 0.569 s, which is an 57 % improvement over the standard approach, but again one order of magnitude higher than the structured approach.

Obviously, these improvements do influence the trade-off between accuracy and energy consumption. Figure 1d shows that unstructured pruning with our proposed framework improvement is strictly better than standard unstructured pruning, and is superior to structured pruning in some cases.

## 6  Conclusion

This work analyzes the impact of pruning convolutional neural networks in the TinyML domain on energy consumption. In detail, unstructured and structured pruning approaches are applied to a LeNet-5-like network. We perform inference on a Raspberry Pi Pico, which uses an RP2040 chip and measure energy consumption, inference speed, and accuracy on the FashionMNIST dataset. Our results show that structured pruning out of the box decreases energy consumption and inference time up to over 97% for a compression rate of 64, while standard unstructured pruning has no (positive) impact on energy usage and inference speed.

We further analyze why unstructured pruning did not improve energy consumption in our experiment setting and found that the computationally expensive MAC operations are also performed for zero-valued weights. As the examined ARM Cortex-M0+ architecture does not have a floating-point unit, all floating-point operations are emulated by software. Therefore we develop an adaption of the TensorFlow implementation, where all MAC operations with zero-valued weights are suppressed. This results in a substantial speedup and reduction of energy usage. Checking weights, represented in the IEEE-754 format, for zero would also induce a costly floating point operation. To make the check as efficient as possible, only the exponent of the weight is checked for zero. With this optimization, we achieve a reduction of up to 54 % in energy consumption and inference speed for a compression rate of 64 compared to standard unstructured pruning.

## 6.1 Recommendations

Our experiments show that out of the box, structured pruning provides a significant improvement in energy consumption, while unstructured pruning does not. However, with our framework adaption, we also realize improvements in inference speed and energy consumption for unstructured pruning. This results in situations where the trade-off between accuracy and energy consumption is more favorable when unstructured magnitude pruning is applied. That is, while for higher compression rates > 8, structured pruning is favorable in terms of both accuracy and energy consumption, for lower compression rates, unstructured pruning with our framework adaption provides a feasible option to decrease energy consumption without offering up significant classification performance.

While only one unstructured pruning approach – magnitude-based pruning – was examined in this work, it is noted that our framework adaption will increase the efficiency of other methods (on the same hardware). This is especially notable as research [17,19] shows that in other settings, unstructured pruning approaches outperform structured pruning for a wide range of compression rates with stable accuracy values for high compression rates. Nevertheless, it must be considered that strong compression reduces the model's accuracy when deciding on the trade-off between energy consumption, inference speed and accuracy.

## 6.2 Delimitation and Further Research

As this work analyzes only the impact of pruning on the energy consumption of a CNN on the Raspberry Pi Pico , further research is necessary to answer whether the observed results are generalizable to other network architectures, pruning methods, data sets, and microcontroller architectures, with and without hardware FPUs. Furthermore, the influence of a hardware FPU should be investigated, as well as the application of network quantization, which has the potential to improve energy consumption [14], especially for MCUs without hardware FPU. Finally, it should be investigated whether the performed adaptation of the TensorFlow Lite framework is also applicable to quantized networks.

# A    Measurement Setup

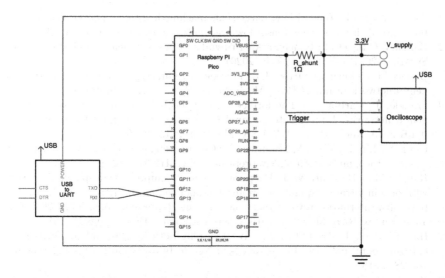

**Fig. 2.** Measurement setup to measure the energy consumption of the Raspberry Pi Pico during execution. Both the oscilloscope and the USB-to-UART converter are connected to a PC, which evaluates the results.

# B    Experimental Results

**Table 1.** Results of the conducted experiments. Classification accuracy, energy consumption and inference time are measured for various compression rates (CR) for three different pruning techniques each: unstructured magnitude pruning (UMP), average percentage of zero structured pruning (APoZ SP), and unstructured magnitude pruning with our adaption (UMP-A).

| CR | Accuracy [%] | | | Energy Consumption [J] | | | Inference Time [s] | | |
|---|---|---|---|---|---|---|---|---|---|
| | UMP | APoZ SP | UMP-A | UMP | APoZ SP | UMP-A | UMP | APoZ SP | UMP-A |
| 1 | 89.37 | 89.29 | 89.37 | 0.149 | 0.149 | 0.141 | 1.292 | 1.292 | 1.313 |
| 2 | 88.79 | 86.89 | 88.79 | 0.146 | 0.081 | 0.107 | 1.289 | 0.713 | 0.935 |
| 3 | 88.48 | 87.22 | 88.48 | 0.144 | 0.072 | 0.094 | 1.289 | 0.609 | 0.808 |
| 4 | 87.79 | 86.28 | 87.79 | 0.146 | 0.061 | 0.088 | 1.290 | 0.518 | 0.745 |
| 8 | 84.21 | 83.31 | 84.21 | 0.147 | 0.043 | 0.076 | 1.297 | 0.361 | 0.652 |
| 16 | 76.10 | 82.29 | 76.10 | 0.147 | 0.028 | 0.073 | 1.301 | 0.247 | 0.604 |
| 24 | 74.31 | 80.87 | 74.31 | 0.147 | 0.016 | 0.070 | 1.303 | 0.132 | 0.589 |
| 32 | 71.56 | 80.45 | 71.56 | 0.149 | 0.015 | 0.069 | 1.304 | 0.131 | 0.580 |
| 48 | 68.11 | 79.45 | 68.11 | 0.152 | 0.009 | 0.069 | 1.308 | 0.073 | 0.572 |
| 64 | 42.90 | 77.41 | 42.90 | 0.154 | 0.004 | 0.068 | 1.309 | 0.028 | 0.569 |

# References

1. Abadi, M., et al.: TensorFlow: Large-scale machine learning on heterogeneous systems (2015). https://www.tensorflow.org/ software available from tensorflow.org
2. Banbury, C.R., et al.: Benchmarking tinyml systems: Challenges and direction. In: SysML 2020, Proceedings. York (2020)
3. Blalock, D., Gonzalez Ortiz, J.J., Frankle, J., Guttag, J.: What is the state of neural network pruning? Proc. Mach. Learn. Syst. **2**, 129–146 (2020)
4. Frankle, J., Carbin, M.: The lottery ticket hypothesis: Finding sparse, trainable neural networks. In: 7th International Conference on Learning Representations, ICLR 2019, New Orleans, LA, USA, May 6–9, 2019 (2019)
5. Gong, Y., Liu, L., Yang, M., Bourdev, L.: Compressing deep convolutional networks using vector quantization. arXiv preprint arXiv:1412.6115 (2014)
6. Han, S., Mao, H., Dally, W.J.: Deep compression: Compressing deep neural network with pruning, trained quantization and huffman coding. In: Bengio, Y., LeCun, Y. (eds.) 4th International Conference on Learning Representations, ICLR 2016, San Juan, Puerto Rico, May 2–4, 2016, Conference Track Proceedings (2016)
7. Han, S., Pool, J., Tran, J., Dally, W.: Learning both weights and connections for efficient neural network. In: Advances in Neural Information Processing Systems, vol. 28 (2015)
8. Hassibi, B., Stork, D.: Second order derivatives for network pruning: Optimal brain surgeon. In: Advances in Neural Information Processing Systems, vol. 5 (1992)
9. He, K., Zhang, X., Ren, S., Sun, J.: Deep residual learning for image recognition. In: Proceedings of the IEEE Conference on Computer Vision and Pattern Recognition (CVPR) (2016)
10. He, Y., Ding, Y., Liu, P., Zhu, L., Zhang, H., Yang, Y.: Learning filter pruning criteria for deep convolutional neural networks acceleration. In: Proceedings of the IEEE/CVF Conference on Computer Vision and Pattern Recognition, pp. 2009–2018 (2020)
11. Hu, H., Peng, R., Tai, Y.W., Tang, C.K.: Network trimming: A data-driven neuron pruning approach towards efficient deep architectures. arXiv preprint arXiv:1607.03250 (2016)
12. Janković, S.P., Drndarević, V.R.: Microcontroller power consumption measurement based on psoc. In: 2015 23rd Telecommunications Forum Telfor (TELFOR), pp. 673–676. IEEE (2015)
13. Kadam, S.S., Adamuthe, A.C., Patil, A.B.: Cnn model for image classification on mnist and fashion-mnist dataset. J. Sci. Res. **64**(2), 374–384 (2020)
14. Kim, M., Saad, W., Mozaffari, M., Debbah, M.: On the tradeoff between energy, precision, and accuracy in federated quantized neural networks. In: ICC 2022-IEEE International Conference on Communications, pp. 2194–2199. IEEE (2022)
15. LeCun, Y., Bottou, L., Bengio, Y., Haffner, P.: Gradient-based learning applied to document recognition. Proc. IEEE **86**(11), 2278–2324 (1998)
16. LeCun, Y., Denker, J., Solla, S.: Optimal brain damage. In: Advances in Neural Information Processing Systems, vol. 2 (1989)
17. Merkle, F., Samsinger, M., Schöttle, P.: Pruning in the face of adversaries. In: International Conference on Image Analysis and Processing, pp. 658–669. Springer (2022). https://doi.org/10.1007/978-3-031-06427-2_55
18. Ray, P.P.: A review on TinyML: State-of-the-art and prospects. J. King Saud Univ.-Comput. Inform. Sci. **34**(4), 1595–1623 (2021)

19. Renda, A., Frankle, J., Carbin, M.: Comparing rewinding and fine-tuning in neural network pruning. arXiv preprint arXiv:2003.02389 (2020)
20. Tabik, S., Peralta, D., Herrera, A.H.P.F.: A snapshot of image pre-processing for convolutional neural networks: case study of mnist. Int. J. Comput. Intell. Syst. **10**, 555–568 (2017)
21. Weber, D., Merkle, F., Schöttle, P., Schlögl, S.: Less is more: The influence of pruning on the explainability of cnns. arXiv preprint arXiv:2302.08878 (2023)

# Deep Learning Modeling

# Advanced Skin Cancer Detection Using Deep Learning

Mai Alzamel[1]([⊠])(iD), Seba Alhejaili[1], Fatimah Alhumaidhi[1], Joud Alismail[1],
Lama Almubarak[1], Halah Altammami[1], Costas Iliopoulos[2](iD), and Zara Lim[2](iD)

[1] Computer Science Department, King Saud University, Riyadh, Saudi Arabia
malzamel@ksu.edu.sa,
{441200901,441200921,441201002,441200964,441201366}@student.ksu.edu.sa
[2] Department of Informatics, King's College London, London, UK
{csi,zara.lim}@kcl.ac.uk

**Abstract.** Skin cancer is one of the most dangerous forms of cancer and can be lethal. In general an early diagnosis in the preliminary stages can significantly determine the probability of fully recovering. Nonetheless, early detection of skin cancer is an arduous and expensive process. Although this type of cancer is visible, this does not simplify the diagnosis, as cancerous tumours look extremely similarity to normal lesions. Examining all pigmented skin lesions via surgical treatments causes significant soreness and scarring. Consequently, there is a need for an automatic and painless skin cancer detection system with high accuracy. Recently, Machine Learning (ML) and Deep Learning (DL) have demonstrated promising results in prediction and classification, skin cancer detection has been performed exceptionally well by them. This paper compares the effectiveness of several DL models which tackle the problem of automatic skin cancer detection using pre-trained models of Convolutional Neural Networks (CNNs), namely ResNetv2, VGG16, EfficientNet-B5, and EfficientNet-B7. These are compared with a ML model, namely the Support Vector Machine (SVM), in order to determine whether or not the examined skin sample is cancerous. The results show that the four CNN models outperform the SVM in accuracy, precision, recall and F1-score, especially EfficientNet-B7 provides the highest F1-score to reach 84.22%.

**Keywords:** Skin Cancer · SVM · CNN · Deep learning · Machine Learning

## 1 Introduction

Skin cancer is a common type of cancer where abnormal growth of skin cells occurs and spreads, invading other parts of the body [1]. A number of recent studies have revealed that skin cancer is among the most dangerous types of cancer [2]. Although the skin is an easily accessible site for examination, it is often difficult to diagnose skin cancers as many benign lesions visually resemble malignant ones. Consequently, an accurate clinical diagnosis can only be concluded

© The Author(s), under exclusive license to Springer Nature Switzerland AG 2023
L. Iliadis et al. (Eds.): EANN 2023, CCIS 1826, pp. 267–278, 2023.
https://doi.org/10.1007/978-3-031-34204-2_23

from a biopsy and subsequent histopathological examination. Two challenges that arise are: i) determining how many biopses to perform and ii) which skin lesions should be tested; these are both typically based on visual inspection and haptic response. Despite many efforts, there remains a need for an automated, noninvasive diagnostic method capable of directing biopsies to characterize skin lesions [3]. As with all types of cancer, it has been demonstrated that screening and preliminary detection of skin cancer is the most reliable indicator of complete recovery. Early detection of skin cancer results in a 94% ten-year survival rate [4]. Recent technology can now detect skin cancer at an early stage. Such methods utilise computer vision as part of the medical image diagnosis [2]. Using ML and DL, clinicians and patients can streamline diagnostic and therapeutic procedures in a single visit [3]. As one of the most threatening forms of cancer, skin cancer detection will be the focus of our research. We will display the performance of the ML model using SVM, and DL models using CNN.

SVM is a supervised learning algorithm that was invented by Vapnik and Chervonenkis [5]. Statistical learning theory states that SVMs are considered one of the most effective ML algorithms for classification and regression. It has been successfully applied to the recognition of images, categorizing texts, diagnosing medical conditions, remote sensing, and classifying motions [6]. Further details of SVM are represented in [7]. CNN is a DL network with an architecture designed for image analysis trained through supervised learning [8]. CNNs use labelled data such as dermoscopic images with their corresponding diagnoses or ground truths to determine a relationship between the input data and the labels. As a result, CNNs can apply learned operations to unknown images and classify them using the extracted features [8]. Clinical dermatology and dermatopathology diagnose largely through the recognition of visual patterns. Therefore, using CNNs can help develop additional and/or improved clinically meaningful databases [9].

**Proposed Solution.** This research seeks to identify skin lesions using Computer-Aided Diagnosis (CAD) systems created by a CNN classifier, as they have proven effective for image classification tasks. We will build our system to take the input image, resize it and remove any noise. The model then segments the input image to separate the lesion from the surrounding skin. Finally, the model will classify the lesion into one of two categories: either benign or malignant. Our model was trained using a dataset of images taken from the International Image Collaboration Archive (ISIC) [10]. Eventually, the purpose of this research is to develop and train these DL models, as well as present results that indicate the performance of the various approaches on specific medical classification tasks.

The rest of the paper is organized as follows. Section 2 reviews different approaches used in previous works on skin cancer detection. Section 3 presents our methodology to tackle the problem. Section 4 includes the experimental design. Section 5 presents the implementation of our methodology and the limitations and issues that accrued during this phase. Section 6 shows the details of the experiments and a discussion of the results. Lastly, Sect. 7 concludes this research paper.

## 2   Literature Review

A growing number of studies have used ML and DL to detect skin cancer in recent years. This section aims to provide a summary of previous related works, describing the models, datasets, techniques, and performance of each case.

Sarkar et al. [11] proposed a Deep Depthwise Separable Residual Convolutional Network model. The model was trained and validated using a subset of the ISIC dataset, and was also tested on 3 other datasets (PH2, DermIS, and MED-NODE). The authors used multiple pre-processing methods such as image denoising using the Non-local Means denoising technique, image enhancement using the CLAHE-DWT algorithm, and selecting multiple color channels [12]. The channels selected were RGB color space channels, saturation channels of the HSV color space, the b* channel of the CIELAB color space, and finally the inverted grey scale color space channel. The model's performance was observed with various kernel sizes, with the best performance being 99.49% accuracy and a 0.9948 F1 Score on the ISIC dataset using a $4 \times 4$ kernel and 4 residual blocks. Garg et al. proposed in [13] a system using CNNs to identify skin cancer and categorize it. A MNIST HAM-10000 dataset was used for skin cancer images. For the classification task, the authors trained a CNN network to classify the given images in the dataset in their respective classes. Moreover, transfer learning was used as well by applying models such as ResNet and VGG16 to increase the classification accuracy of the images, and to compare the accuracy of the model with that of the proposed DL model [14]. Furthermore, to accomplish the optimization purpose, the authors used Adaptive Moment Estimation (Adam) optimizer [15]. They found that the ResNet model which is pre-trained in ImageNet dataset could be beneficent, and found that it is the successful classification of cancer lesions in the HAM1000 dataset. Also, they mentioned that learning algorithms such as Random Forest, XGBoost, and SVMs were not very effective for classification tasks, and do not give promising results, where the accuracy of Random Forest was 65.9%, XGBoost was 65.15%, and SVM was 65.86%. On the other hand, their CNN model gave a weighted average precision of 0.88, a weighted recall average of 0.74, and a weighted F1 Score of 0.77. The transfer learning approach applied using VGG model gave an accuracy of 78%, whereas the ResNet model gave an accuracy of 90.5%.

Daghrir et al. [16] used a CNN and two ML classifiers, KNN and SVM to train a set of features describing the borders, texture, and color of a skin lesion. The authors employed a color enhancement technique known as Gaussian (DOG) for pre-processing and noise reduction in order to remove hair from lesion images, as well as Morphological Active Contours without Edges (MorphACWE) for lesion segmentation. The authors chose 640 lesion images from the ISIC Archive for models' training. The models' accuracy results were 57.3% for the KNN model, 71.8% for the SVM model, 85.5% for the CNN model, and 88.4% on majority voting.

Al-masni et al. [17] proposed a model for lesion segmentation using a Full-resolution Convolutional Network (FrCN). The segmented images were classified using a Deep Residual Network, namely ResNet-50 [18]. The authors used the

International Skin Image Collaboration (ISIC) 2017 dataset for training and testing and used rotation transformation on training data to augment more images. In addition, they used transfer learning and fine-tuning to address the shortcomings of their models. The classifier achieved 81.57% accuracy and 75% F1 Score. The classifier was compared to two other classifiers that did not use segmentation to demonstrate the superior performance of the model.

Nataha et al. [19], developed a skin cancer detection CNN model that can classify skin cancer types and detect them early. The model was trained and tested on the state-of-art CNNs, namely Inception V3, ResNet50, VGG16, MobileNet, and InceptionResnet [20–23] and performed a seven-class classification of the skin lesion images. The models were tested on the following two datasets: ISIC 2018, and ISIC 2019. They measured the accuracy, precision, recall, F1 score, and support for every class of skin lesion disease. The results of the average metrics achieved by all final CNNs were as follows. In ResNet, researchers got an accuracy of 85%, a precision of 0.86, a recall of 0.85, and an F1 Score of 0.85. In MobileNet, researchers got an accuracy of 85%, a precision of 0.86, a recall of 0.85, an F1 Score of 0.85, and support of 6944. In VGG16, researchers got an accuracy of 87%, a precision of 0.87, a recall of 0.87, and an F1 Score of 0.87. In Inception V3, researchers got an accuracy of 90%, a precision of 0.90, a recall of 0.90, and an F1 Score of 0.90. Lastly, in InceptionResnet, researchers got an accuracy of 91%, a precision of 0.91, a recall of 0.91, and an F1 Score of 0.91. Fu'adah et al. [24] built a system that used a CNN with three hidden layers, $3 \times 3$ filter sizes, and output channels of 16, 32, and 64, respectively, to automatically diagnose skin cancer and benign tumor lesions. The used dataset in this study is an augmentation of the ISIC dataset composed of four classes: Dermatofibroma, Nevus Pigments, Squamous-Cell Carcinoma (SCC), and Melanoma. In total 4,000 images were used, of these 3000 were training images and 1000 were validation images. These images were trained using the CNN model with several optimization techniques, such as Stochastic Gradient Descent (SGD), Root Mean Square Propagation (RMSprop), Adam and Nesterovaccelerated Adaptive Moment Estimation (Nadam) optimizer with a learning rate of 0.001 and using loss categorical cross-entropy [25–27]. Their results showed that the Adam optimizer provides the highest performance, with an accuracy value of 99%, a loss of 0.0346, and precision, recall, and F1 Score values of 0.91. Moreover, they noted that the proposed model has promising usage as an existing tool for medical personnel.

## 3   Methodology

After evaluating the related works, the analysis has established that CNN and SVM are the most appropriate models for this challenge. To evaluate their performance, we first preprocess the lesion images, and then we segment them. After that, we evaluate the performance of the CNN and the SVM models. An overview of our proposed models is presented below in Fig. 1.

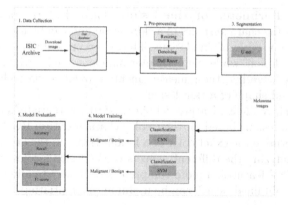

**Fig. 1.** Graphical Representation of the Proposed Methodology.

## 3.1 Preprocessing and Segmentation

We denoised the skin lesion dataset, using the DullRazor algorithm, a method used to tackle the issue of hair detection and removal based on the result in [28]. DullRazor algorithm stages are specified as follows: converting the original image to grayscale. Closing to the grayscale image, using a linear or cross-shaped kernel. Calculating the difference between the resulting image and the original. Apply binary thresholding to obtain a mask with the hairs in the image. Finally, Replace the pixels in common between the mask and the original image, with pixels from the latter. Later, we apply U-Net which is a neural network architecture designed for image segmentation to separate the image from the studied regions and unwanted regions [29].

## 3.2 CNN Classifiers

For the classification task, we use the following four CNN pre-trained models, which are ResNet50V2, VGG16, EfficientNet-B5 and EfficientNet-B7. These four chosen models provide diverse architectures, computational requirements and performance characteristics, making them suitable for our task. Mathematical details about ResNet50V2, VGG16, EfficientNet-B5 and EfficientNet-B7 can be found in, [18,22,30].

## 3.3 SVM Classifier with Feature Extraction

The technique of feature extraction will be employed for the SVM. This method proves to be efficient in decreasing the dimensionality of large datasets, particularly when utilized in conjunction with SVM algorithms, which require a significant amount of computational resources [31]. Reducing the number of features in the dataset can make the training process more efficient and manageable. The following features will be extracted from lesion images for skin cancer classification:

- **Area and Perimeter of the lesion**: These features provide valuable insights into the characteristics of a skin lesion and can be used to distinguish between various types of skin lesions. The area represents the two-dimensional extent of the lesion, while the perimeter indicates the length of the boundary of the lesion. Together, these measurements provide a comprehensive picture of the size and shape of a skin lesion.
- **RGB and HSV**: These features will be used to differentiate between different types of skin lesions based on their color characteristics. RGB values can be used to determine the exact color of a lesion. HSV, on the other hand, can be useful in analyzing the different aspects of the lesion's color. By using both RGB and HSV features, a more comprehensive understanding of the lesion's color can be obtained, which can be useful in differentiating between different types of skin lesions.
- **Mean and Standard Deviation of RGB and HSV**: These features provide information about the distribution of color intensity values in the image and can be used to distinguish between subtle differences in color. By measuring the mean and standard deviation of the RGB and HSV channels, we can quantify the distribution of color information in the image and use that information to differentiate between different types of skin lesions. This information can be especially useful in cases where the differences in color between lesions are subtle, but still important to consider in making a diagnosis.

## 4    Experimental Design

### 4.1    Dataset

In this research, we use the International Skin Imaging Collaboration (ISIC) dataset [10]. ISIC is a public provided dataset for academia and industry partnerships which designed to facilitate the application of digital skin imaging to help reduce melanoma mortality. We split the dataset as follows: 80% for the training set, 10% for the validation set, and 10% for the test set. Dataset's Images Ground-Truth was based on each lesion's medical diagnosis. A total of 20,092 images were used. 11063 images of benign types, and 8732 images of malignant types. Following the pre-processing of the dataset described in the Subsect. 3.1, the segmentation task will be deployed on 10,015 of the 20,092 images as that was provided with a mask and was used to train a U-Net model to segment the rest of the images as described in the Subsect. 3.1.

### 4.2    Experiments

We have conducted two different experiments using the two models mentioned in the methodology. First, we use the CNN classifiers, we conduct the first experiment by taking a subset of images and preprocessing them by resizing, and then denoise them using the DullRazor technique. A U-Net network will be used to output a mask for each image, and the mask will be applied to the images to remove the background, and finally, the output dataset will be used to train the CNN classifiers. Secondly, we use the SVM classifier, in this experiment, we implement an SVM model using our pre-processed and segmented images to compare the results with our CNN models.

# 5   Implementation Details

In order to implement our experiments, we have chosen Python as it is the most suitable programming language for ML and DL experiments. It provides a variety of libraries to support the implementation process. As implementing these experiments consumes a lot of hardware resources, Google Colaboratory was our choice to run them [32]. The reason for this is that it provides cloud-based resources like GPUs. We used several libraries, including TensorFlow's Keras, OpenCV, Scikit-Learn, and SciPy. **Keras** is a Python-based DL API that runs on top of TensorFlow and provides a high-level interface for developing DL neural networks [33]. **OpenCV** is an open-source Python library used for image processing and computer vision. Many algorithms are available that can be used to identify objects, detect and recognize faces, and more [34]. **Scikit-Learn** is an open-source Python library for ML and statistical modelling. Among its features are algorithms for classification, regression, clustering, and dimension reduction, as well as unsupervised and supervised learning techniques [35]. **SciPy** is a library that takes on standard problems, and mathematical computations, using arrays and manipulations [36]. We provide below a pseudocode of algorithms used throughout these experiments. Our experiments with the DullRazor algorithm have produced intriguing results, which demonstrate its effectiveness in detecting and removing hair from images. Below algorithm 1 explains the details steps of DullRazor. Algorithm 2 shows a pseudocode for U-Net which is used in the segmentation task. In the image classification task using SVM, the model is available in Scikit-learn. For an image classification task using CNN, the four chosen models are available in tensorflow.keras.applications module.

---

**Algorithm 1:** DullRazor

---

   **Input**   : Image Array
   **Output:** Image Array After Applying DullRazor Algorithm
   $grayimage = $ **RGB2GRAY**$(image)$
   $blackhat = $
   **MorphologyEx**$(grayimage, MORPH\_BLACKHAT, filter_{9 \times 9})$
   $blurredimage = $ **GaussianBlur**$(blackhat, filter_{3 \times 3})$
   $mask = $ **BinaryThreshold**$(blurredimage, threshold = 15, maxval = $
   $255)$
   $output = $ **Inpaint**$(image, mask, inpaintRadius = $
   $6, INPAINT\_TELEA)$

---

---

**Algorithm 2:** U-Net Model Training Function

---

**Input** : DIR "Dataset directory"
**Output:** masks for images with no available mask
(trainingData, trainingMasks), (validationData, validationMasks) ←
loadDataset(DIR=DIR)
*model* ← getUNet()
callbacks ← CSVLogger and ModelCheckpoint callbacks
model.fit(trainingData, trainingMasks, batchSize=32, epochs=30,
  validationData=(validationData, validationMasks), callbacks=callbacks)
images ← loadDatasetWithNoMask()
masks ← empty set
**for** *image* ∈ *images* **do**
  | prediction ← *model*.predict(image)
  | mask ← applyOtsuThreshold(prediction)
  | append mask to masks
**end**

---

## 6    Results and Discussion

In this section, we explain the SVM and CNN hyperparameter tuning results and later we demonstrate compassion between SVM and CNN of the testing results.

### 6.1    Parameters Tuning

Hyperparameter tuning is one of the fundamental ways to enhance the performance of ML and DL models. During the learning process of a model, hyperparameters are passed in order to make corrections or adjustments. Diverse data patterns may necessitate distinct constraints, weights, or learning rates for the same ML model. These kinds of measurements are referred to as hyperparameters [37]. We tuned the hyperparameters of our SVM model by using Grid Search. Grid Search, also known as the Estimator, is a tuning technique aiming to calculate hyperparameters' optimal values. It is an exhaustive search that is performed on specific parameter values of a specific model [38]. The ranges of values to tune the hyperparameter in SVM are as follows: C: [0.001, 0.01, 0.1, 1, 10, 100, 1000], kernel: [linear, poly, rbf, sigmoid] and gamma: [0.0001, 0.001, 0.01, 0.1, 1, 10, scale, auto]. After performing the grid search, the optimal hyperparameters for our SVM model were found to be C = 1000, gamma = auto, and kernel = rbf. This indicates that a high value of C, the radial basis function (RBF) kernel, and an automatic setting for gamma were the best choices for our problem.

To tune the hyperparameters of the four CNN models, we use KerasTuner, which is a scalable, easy-to-use hyperparameter optimization framework that alleviates the difficulties associated with hyperparameter search. KerasTuner comes with Bayesian Optimization, Hyperband, and Random Search algorithms, and is designed to be extensible so that researchers can experiment with new search algorithms [39]. The hyperparameters we tuned are Dropout, Dense layers sizes, Learning Rate and Pooling type. Each hyperparameter has a range of values to make the tuner decide which value is more suitable, the ranges of values are as follows: Dropout 1: Range [0, 0.8], Dsense layer 1: [4096, 512, 256], Dropout 2: Range [0, 0.6], Dsense layer 2: [128, 64, 32], Learning Rate: Range [1e-4, 1e-7] and Pooling type: [Average, Max]. Using the above mentioned processing techniques and model parameter tuning libraries. We present the results of the CNN models in Table 1 on the test set using the preprocessed dataset.

**Table 1.** CNN Parameters Tuning Results.

| Model | Dropouts | Dense layers | Learning Rate | Pooling type |
|---|---|---|---|---|
| EfficientNetB5 | [.4, .2] | [256, 32] | 1e-05 | Average pooling |
| EfficientNetB7 | [.8, .6] | [512, 256] | 7e-5 | Max pooling |
| ResNet50V2 | [.3, .1] | [4096, 32] | 9e-06 | Average pooling |
| VGG16 | [.3, .0] | [4096, 64] | 5e-06 | Max pooling |

## 6.2  Results

As the primary objective of our research is to investigate the effectiveness of SVM and CNN models of skin lesions classification. We provide a detailed analysis of the performance metrics of the proposed trained models and compare them with existing methods. Table 2 demonstrates the Accuracy, Recall, Precision and F1-Score for each model. The results show that EfficientNet-B7 provide the highest Accuracy which reaches 85% and Recall which is 88% among the other 4 models. On the other hand, the EfficientNet-B5 gives the highest Precision which is 88% with respect to the other compared models. For the four chosen CNN models there is a slight difference in the performance measurement results including Accuracy, Recall and Precision leading to the F1-Score for EfficientNet-B7 being the superior result with a minor difference among the others, whereas the F1-score for EfficientNet-B7, EfficientNet-B5, ResNet50V2, VGG16 and SVM are 84%, 80%, 80%, 80%, 67%, respectively. Ultimately, the CNN models give greater Accuracy, Precision, Recall and F1-score compared with the SVM model.

Table 3 shows the time complexity for SVM model and for each of the CNN models using datasets and without augmented data. Additionally, we used Google's colab that have over 500 GPUs to speed up the run.

**Table 2.** SVM and CNN Models Testing Results.

| Model | Dataset | Accuracy | Recall | Precision | F1 Score |
|---|---|---|---|---|---|
| EfficientNet-B7 | Segmented | 0.856219 | 0.882151 | 0.805643 | 0.842163 |
| EfficientNet-B5 | Segmented | 0.843781 | 0.737986 | 0.883562 | 0.804239 |
| ResNet50V2 | Segmented | 0.831343 | 0.779176 | 0.823458 | 0.800705 |
| VGG16 | Segmented | 0.840796 | 0.779176 | 0.842822 | 0.809750 |
| SVM | Segmented | 0.748693 | 0.657175 | 0.738796 | 0.695600 |

**Table 3.** Models' Training Time

| Model | Dataset | Training Time |
|---|---|---|
| EfficientNetB7 | Segmented | 1253 s |
| EfficientNetB5 | Segmented | 6003 s |
| ResNet50V2 | Segmented | 787 s |
| VGG16 | Segmented | 915 s |
| SVM | Segmented | 3983 s |

## 7    Conclusion and Future Work

In this research, we tackled the problem of detecting skin cancer automatically using four CNN models. The proposed solution starts with some image pre-processing: image resizing and image denoising using DullRazor. Later, tumour segmentation from skin lesions is applied to the images using U-Net. Finally, a classification stage is deployed using four pre-trained CNN models: ResNetV2, VGG16, EfficientNet B5, and EfficientNet B7, and compared their performance with SVM. After presenting and analyzing the models' performance, we found that EfficientNet-B7 has the highest accuracy which is 86.91%. Our experiments show that the CNN model outperforms the SVM model in Accuracy, Recall, Presecion and F1-Score. The results show that EfficientNet-B7 provides the highest accuracy and Recall with respect to the other compared models, having 85.62% Accuracy and 88.21% Recall. However, the results provide that the EfficientNet-B5 gives the highest Precision compared with observed models which reachs up to 88.35%. Notably, there is a need for larger and more diverse datasets to further improve the performance of DL algorithms in this domain. Consequently, as future work will study image augmentation using GAN models and how can help complex DL models' performance measurements in detecting malignant skin lesions.

## References

1. Narayanamurth, et al.: Skin cancer detection using non-invasive techniques. RSC Adv. **8**(49), 28095–28130 (2018)

2. Jain, S., Pise, N., et al.: Computer aided melanoma skin cancer detection using image processing. Proc. Comput. Sci. **48**, 735–740 (2015)
3. Lieber, C.A., Majumder, S.K., Billheimer, D.D., Ellis, D.L., Mahadevan-Jansen, A.: Raman microspectroscopy for skin cancer detection in vitro. J. Biomed. Opt. **13**(2), 024013 (2009)
4. Dubal, P., Bhatt, S., Joglekar, C., Patil, S.: Skin cancer detection and classification. In: 2017 6th International Conference on Electrical Engineering and Informatics (ICEEI), pp. 1–6, IEEE (2017)
5. Ghosh, S., Dasgupta, A., Swetapadma, A.: A study on support vector machine based linear and non-linear pattern classification. In: 2019 International Conference on Intelligent Sustainable Systems (ICISS), IEEE (2019)
6. Yuan, R., Li, Z., Guan, X., Xu, L.: An SVM-based machine learning method for accurate internet traffic classification. Inf. Syst. Front. **12**, 149–156 (2010)
7. Alzubi, J., Nayyar, A., Kumar, A.: Machine learning from theory to algorithms: an overview. J. Phys: Conf. Ser. **1142**, 012012 (2018)
8. Haggenmüller, et al.: Skin cancer classification via convolutional neural networks: systematic review of studies involving human experts. Eur. J. Cancer **156**, 202–216 (2021)
9. Tschandl, et al.: Expert-level diagnosis of nonpigmented skin cancer by combined convolutional neural networks. JAMA Dermatol. **155**, 58–65 (2019)
10. The International Skin Imaging Collaboration (ISIC), "Melanoma Project." https://www.isic-archive.com/ Accessed 10 Jan 2021
11. Sarkar, R., Chatterjee, C.C., Hazra, A.: Diagnosis of melanoma from dermoscopic images using a deep depthwise separable residual convolutional network. IET Image Process. **13**, 2130–2142 (2019)
12. Lidong, H., Wei, Z., Jun, W., Zebin, S.: Combination of contrast limited adaptive histogram equalisation and discrete wavelet transform for image enhancement. IET Image Proc. **9**(10), 908–915 (2015)
13. Garg, R., Maheshwari, S., Shukla, A.: Decision support system for detection and classification of skin cancer using CNN. arXiv e-prints (2019)
14. Torrey, L., Shavlik, J.: Transfer learning. In: Handbook of Research on Machine Learning Applications and Trends: Algorithms, Methods, and Techniques, pp. 242–264, IGI global (2010)
15. Kingma, D.P., Ba, J.: Adam: A method for stochastic optimization. arXiv preprint arXiv:1412.6980 (2014)
16. Daghrir, J., Tlig, L., Bouchouicha, M., Sayadi, M.: Melanoma skin cancer detection using deep learning and classical machine learning techniques: A hybrid approach. In: 2020 5th International Conference on Advanced Technologies for Signal and Image Processing (ATSIP), IEEE (2020)
17. Al-Masni, M.A., Al-Antari, M.A., Park, H.M., Park, N.H., Kim, T.S.: A deep learning model integrating FrCN and residual convolutional networks for skin lesion segmentation and classification. In: 2019 IEEE Eurasia Conference on Biomedical Engineering, Healthcare and Sustainability (ECBIOS), IEEE, May (2019)
18. He, K., Zhang, X., Ren, S., Sun, J.: Deep residual learning for image recognition In: 2016 IEEE Conference on Computer Vision and Pattern Recognition (CVPR), pp. 770–778 (2016)
19. Nahata, H., Singh, S.P.: Deep learning solutions for skin cancer detection and diagnosis. In: Learning and Analytics in Intelligent Systems, pp. 159–182, Cham: Springer International Publishing, 2020

20. Szegedy, C., Vanhoucke, V., Ioffe, S., Shlens, J., Wojna, Z.: Rethinking the inception architecture for computer vision. In: Proceedings of the IEEE Conference on Computer Vision and Pattern Recognition, pp. 2818–2826 (2016)
21. He, K., Zhang, X., Ren, S., Sun, J.: Deep Residual Learning for Image Recognition. In: Proceedings of the IEEE Conference on Computer Vision and Pattern Recognition, pp. 770–778 (2016)
22. Simonyan, K., Zisserman. Vgg-16, arXiv Prepr (2014)
23. Howard, et al.: Mobilenets: Efficient convolutional neural networks for mobile vision applications, arXiv preprint arXiv:1704.04861 (2017)
24. Fu'adah, Y.N., Pratiwi, N.K.C., Pramudito, M.A., Ibrahim, N.: Convolutional neural network (CNN) for automatic skin cancer classification system. IOP Conf. Ser. Mater. Sci. Eng. **982**, 012005 (2020)
25. Robbins, H., Monro, S.: A stochastic approximation method. The annals of mathematical statistics, pp. 400–407 ( 1951)
26. Duchi, J., Hazan, E., Singer, Y.: Adaptive subgradient methods for online learning and stochastic optimization. J. Mach. Learn. Res. **12**(7) (2011)
27. Dozat, T.: Incorporating nesterov momentum into adam (2016)
28. Lee, T., Ng, V., Gallagher, R., Coldman, A., McLean, D.: Dullrazor®: a software approach to hair removal from images. Comput. Biol. Med. **27**(6), 533–543 (1997)
29. Siddique, N., Paheding, S., Elkin, C.P., Devabhaktuni, V.: U-net and its variants for medical image segmentation: a review of theory and applications. Ieee Access **9**, 82031–82057 (2021)
30. Agarwal, V.: Complete architectural details of all efficientnet models. Medium Toward Data Science, 2020
31. Hira, Z.M., Gillies, D.F.: A review of feature selection and feature extraction methods applied on microarray data. In: Advances in Bioinformatics, vol. 2015 (2015)
32. Colaboratory. https://research.google.com/colaboratory/faq.html. Verified: 2022-03-24
33. Manaswi, N.K., Manaswi, N.K.: Understanding and working with keras, Deep learning with applications using Python: Chatbots and face, object, and speech recognition with TensorFlow and Keras, pp. 31–43, (2018)
34. Bradski, G., Kaehler, A.: Learning OpenCV: Computer vision with the OpenCV library. O'Reilly Media, Inc., (2008)
35. Pedregosa, F., et al.: Scikit-learn: Machine learning in python. J. Mach. Learn. Res. **12**, 2825–2830 (2011)
36. Bressert, E.: Scipy and numpy: an overview for developers (2012)
37. Pon, M.Z.A., KK, K.P.: Hyperparameter tuning of deep learning models in keras. In: Sparklinglight Trans. Artif. Intell. Quant. Comput. (STAIQC), **1**(1), 36–40 (2021)
38. Malik, F.: What is grid search. Medium, FinTechExplained (2020)
39. Chollet, F., et al.: Keras (2015)

# Cross-Learning-Based Sales Forecasting Using Deep Learning via Partial Pooling from Multi-level Data

José Manuel Oliveira[1,2] and Patrícia Ramos[2,3(✉)]

[1] Faculty of Economics, University of Porto,
rua Dr. Roberto Frias, 4200-464 Porto, Portugal
`jmo@fep.up.pt`
[2] INESC TEC – Institute for Systems and Computer Engineering,
Technology and Science, rua Dr. Roberto Frias, 4200-465 Porto, Portugal
`patricia@iscap.ipp.pt`
[3] ISCAP, Polytechnic University of Porto,
rua Jaime Lopes Amorim, 4465-004 S. Mamede de Infesta, Portugal

**Abstract.** Sales forecasts are an important tool for inventory management, allowing retailers to balance inventory levels with customer demand and market conditions. By using sales forecasts to inform inventory management decisions, companies can optimize their inventory levels and avoid costly stockouts or excess inventory costs. The scale of the forecasting problem in the retail domain is significant and requires ongoing attention and resources to ensure accurate and effective forecasting. Recent advances in machine learning algorithms such as deep learning have made possible to build more sophisticated forecasting models that can learn from large amounts of data. These global models can capture complex patterns and relationships in the data and predict demand across multiple regions and product categories. In this paper, we investigate the cross-learning scenarios, inspired by the product hierarchy frequently utilized in retail planning, which enable global models to better capture interdependencies between different products and regions. Our empirical results obtained using M5 competition dataset indicate that the cross-learning approaches exhibit significantly superior performance compared to local forecasting benchmarks. Our findings also suggest that using partial pooling at the lowest aggregation level of the retail hierarchical allows for a more effective capture of the distinct characteristics of each group.

**Keywords:** Deep learning · Time series forecasting · Cross-learning · Retailing · Hierarchical aggregation · Intermittent data

## 1 Introduction

Sales forecasts play a critical role in inventory management, as they provide insights into the expected demand for a product or service [6]. They help businesses to determine the quantity of products they need to order and the amount of stock they need to hold. If the forecast predicts strong demand, a company may

L. Iliadis et al. (Eds.): EANN 2023, CCIS 1826, pp. 279–290, 2023.
https://doi.org/10.1007/978-3-031-34204-2_24

choose to increase inventory levels to avoid stockouts and lost sales. Conversely, if the forecast predicts weaker demand, a company may choose to decrease inventory levels to avoid excess inventory costs. By forecasting future demand, businesses can plan their production schedules and produce the right amount of inventory to meet customer demand without overproducing, which could lead to overstocking or wastage. Sales forecasts can also help businesses prepare for seasonal fluctuations in demand.

The forecasting problem in the retail domain is large-scale because it involves predicting sales for a vast number of products, across multiple channels, with numerous variables affecting demand [15,18]. Retailers often have an extensive product catalog with thousands of unique items, ranging from perishable goods like fresh produce to non-perishable goods like electronics and clothing. Each of these products has unique demand patterns, which can vary by region, season, day of the week, time of day, and promotional events. Forecasting sales for each of these items is a complex and challenging task. Moreover, typically they sell products through multiple channels, including physical stores, online stores, mobile apps, marketplaces, and more. Each of these channels has its own set of challenges and opportunities that must be taken into account when forecasting sales. Furthermore, in the retail domain, demand forecasting must be done frequently, often weekly or even daily, to ensure that inventory levels are optimized. This means that the forecasting problem requires advanced models and techniques that must be: (1) automatic, minimizing the need for manual intervention or expert knowledge, (2) robust i.e. capable to handle different types of data and scenarios, such as missing values, outliers, and non-linear relationships between variables, and (3) efficiently scaleable to handle large volumes of data and be easily adapted to changing business needs [16,17].

The traditional approach to time series forecasting has been to treat each series as a separate entity, resulting in local forecasting models that forecast each series in isolation. Examples of such models include the Exponential Smoothing State Space model (ETS) [9] and AutoRegressive Integrated Moving Average Model (ARIMA) [4]. However, in recent times, many companies collect large volumes of time series data from similar sources, such as sales data for thousands of products in retail. While local forecasting techniques can still be applied to these situations, they fail to exploit the potential for pattern learning across multiple time series. Global forecasting models (GFM), on the other hand, are a more recent development that attempt to capture more complex patterns in the data, such as nonlinear relationships and interactions between variables [10]. These models are often based on machine learning algorithms, such as neural networks, support vector machines, or gradient boosting. GFM can capture those dependencies by analyzing multiple time series simultaneously, taking into account the interdependencies between the time series [7]. Specifically in the retail domain they can potentially capture cross-product and cross-region dependencies, leading to more accurate predictions across the entire product catalog. Cross-product dependencies refer to the relationship between different products, where changes in one product can impact the demand or performance of another product (the sales of one product may influence the sales of another product, particularly if they are complementary or substitutable). Cross-region dependencies refer to the relationship between different regions or locations, where changes in one region (impacted by regional factors such as weather patterns or economic conditions) may influence the demand or performance of another region.

In contrast to local models that have unique parameters for each individual series, GFM utilize a common set of parameters (such as weights, in the case of neural networks) that are applied to all time series being analyzed. GFM are currently being developed and implemented with success, as evidenced by the works of [2], and have emerged victorious in prominent forecasting competitions like the M4 [12] and M5 competitions [13], as well as all recent Kaggle competitions focused on forecasting [3]. The fundamental concept on which these studies are based, and which explains the efficacy of global models, is that there must be some form of relationship between the series, allowing the global model to identify patterns across them. However, none of these studies attempts to explain or establish the properties of this relationship. While certain research has linked high levels of relatedness between series with greater similarity in their shapes/patterns and stronger cross-correlation [19], other studies have proposed that higher relatedness is associated with greater similarity in the extracted features of the series under consideration [1]. The first research to provide some insights into the problem is the recent study by [14], which theoretically proves that, despite the heterogeneity of the data, there is always a GFM that can perform equally well, or even better, than a set of local models for any dataset. Furthermore, in an extensive empirical research, the authors show that a slightly increase in the complexity of global models makes them extremely competitive, surpassing the performance of local state-of-the-art ones on the majority of datasets. Therefore, according to this work, in theory GFM's performance is not dependent on the relationship between series. However, it is worth to reinforce that this work concentrates on the complexity of the model rather than examining relatedness, and on this matter the authors conclude that the complexity of global models can be achieved by incorporating more lags, using non-linear/non-parametric models and implementing data partitioning.

Hence, when it comes to global models, the key is to determine the optimal level of complexity that surpasses local methods. More recently, [7] made a simulation study to compare the accuracy of global models with traditional time series forecasting methods on datasets with different characteristics. Their results indicate that GFM's better performance is related to the availability of data, the complexity of patterns in the series and the complexity of the model used, and underpin that having complex non-linear modelling capabilities and the ability to exploit more data, GFM are more competitive under difficult forecasting conditions such as short series, heterogeneous series and minimal prior knowledge of the data patterns. Despite these efforts, there has been a lack of research on how the relatedness between series impacts the effectiveness of GFM in real-world demand forecasting problems, especially when dealing with challenging conditions such as highly lumpy or intermittent data very common in retail.

The research conducted in this study was driven precisely by this motivation: to investigate the cross-learning scenarios driven by the product hierarchy commonly employed in retail planning, which enable global models to better capture interdependencies across products and regions. The layout of the remainder of this paper is as follows. Section 2 describes our forecasting framework developed for the evaluation of the cross-learning approaches and Sect. 3 provides the details about its implementation. Section 4 presents and discusses the results obtained, and Sect. 5 provides some concluding remarks and promising areas for further research.

# 2    Deep Learning Model

Deep learning has had remarkable success in computer vision and has since been applied to various fields, such as natural language processing and robot control, making it a popular choice for machine learning tasks. However, the adoption of deep learning in time series forecasting has been relatively slower compared to other areas, and the lack of a clear experimental protocol makes it challenging to compare with other forecasting methods. Despite this, deep learning has shown excellent performance in multiple domains when trained on large datasets, which gave us confidence in its potential for time series forecasting. Nevertheless, there has been limited research on deep learning approaches for intermittent demand [11], which involves forecasting sequences with sporadic values and a significant number of zeros [5]. To address this, we chose to use DeepAR, an autoregressive recurrent neural network model introduced by Amazon in 2018 [19], which has demonstrated success in various time series applications and is considered a leading deep-learning forecasting model.

## 2.1    DeepAR

Formally, denoting the value of item $i$ at time $t$ by $z_{i,t}$, the goal of DeepAR model is to predict the conditional probability $P$ of future sales $z_{i,t_0:T}$ based on past sales $z_{i,1:t_0-1}$ and covariates $\mathbf{x}_{i,1:T}$, where $t_0$ and $T$ are respectively the first and last time points of the future

$$P(z_{i,t_0:T}|z_{i,1:t_0-1}, \mathbf{x}_{i,1:T}). \tag{1}$$

Note that the time index $t$ is relative, i.e. $t = 1$ may not correspond to the first time point of the time series. During training, $z_{i,t}$ is available in both time ranges $[1, t_0-1]$ and $[t_0, T]$, known respectively as conditioning range and prediction range (corresponding to the encoder and decoder in a sequence-to-sequence model), but during inference $z_{i,t}$ is not available in the prediction range. The network output at time $t$ can be expressed as

$$\mathbf{h}_{i,t} = h(\mathbf{h}_{i,t-1}, z_{i,t-1}, \mathbf{x}_{i,t}; \Theta) \tag{2}$$

where $h$ is a function that is implemented by a multi-layer RNN with long short-term memory (LSTM) cells [8] parameterized by $\Theta$. The model is autoregressive in the sense that it uses the sales value at the previous time step $z_{i,t-1}$ as an input, and recurrent in the sense that the previous network output $\mathbf{h}_{i,t-1}$ is fed back as an input at the next time step. During training, given a batch of $N$ items $\{z_{i,1:T}\}_{i=1,...,N}$ and corresponding covariates $\{\mathbf{x}_{i,1:T}\}_{i=1,...,N}$, the model parameters are learned by maximizing the log-likelihood of a fixed probability distribution as follows

$$L = \sum_{i=1}^{N} \sum_{t=t_0}^{T} \log l(z_{i,t}|\theta(\mathbf{h}_{i,t})) \tag{3}$$

where $\theta$ denotes a linear mapping from the function $\mathbf{h}_{i,t}$ to the distribution's parameters, while $l$ represents the likelihood of the distribution. Since the encoder model is the same as the decoder, DeepAR uses the all the time range $[0, T]$ to calculate this loss (i.e., $t_0 = 0$ in Eq. 3). The primary aim of DeepAR is to forecast a single future value in each step. In order to forecast multiple future steps during the inference phase, the model produces forecasts for the following period repeatedly until the end of the forecast horizon. The model is first given past sequences ($t < t_0$), and it generates the forecast for the initial period by drawing samples from the trained probability distribution. The forecast for the first period is then used as an input to the model to generate the forecast for the second period, and so on for each succeeding period. Since the forecast is based on prior samples from the predicted distribution, the output of the model is probabilistic and represents a distribution of sampled sequences rather than a deterministic value. This sampling approach has the benefit of creating a probability distribution of forecasts, which can be utilized to assess the accuracy of the predictions.

## 2.2 Tweedie Loss

To tackle the problem of zero-inflated distribution in sales, we used the negative log-likelihood of the Tweedie distribution for the loss function. The Tweedie distribution's probability density function is defined as follows:

$$f(y; \mu, \phi, p) = \frac{y^{p-1} \exp\left(\frac{y\mu^{1-p}}{\phi(1-p)}\right)}{\phi(1-p)y^p \Gamma\left(\frac{1}{1-p}\right)}, \quad y > 0 \tag{4}$$

where $\Gamma$ is the gamma function and $\mu$, $\phi$ and $p$ are the mean, dispersion and power parameters, respectively. When $1 < p < 2$, it takes the form of a compound Poisson-gamma distribution frequently applied to data sets exhibiting positive skewness and numerous zeros. The extent of diversity or heterogeneity in the data is regulated by the dispersion parameter $\phi$. If $\phi$ is small, the data is described as having high dispersion, while a large value of $\phi$ suggests homogeneity in the data.

# 3   Empirical Study

This section provides information on the empirical evaluation of this study, including the selection of data, performance metrics, benchmarks, and the framework used as the basis for implementing cross-learning forecasting models.

## 3.1   Dataset

For a study's findings to have significance, they need to be reproducible and comparable to other relevant studies. With this in mind, we used the M5 competition's data, a widely recognized, established, and openly accessible dataset. The aim of the M5 Accuracy competition was to generate point forecasts for time series that depict the hierarchical unit sales of Walmart, the largest retail company in the world in terms of revenue [13]. The M5 dataset comprises unit sales data for 3,049 products that are categorized into three categories - Hobbies, Foods, and Household - and seven product departments that disaggregate the aforementioned categories. The products are sold across 10 stores located in three states - California (CA), Texas (TX), and Wisconsin (WI). The most granular level of data, i.e., product-store unit sales, can be grouped based on either location (state and store) or product-related information (category and department). The M5 dataset covers a period of approximately 5.4 years, starting from January 29, 2011 to June 19, 2016, on a daily basis, totaling 1969 days. Figure 1 and Fig. 2 show the time series plots of the unit sales for the 30,490 items (3,049 products × 10 stores), grouped by six aggregation levels: Total, State, Category, Store, Department and State-Department.

## 3.2   Partial Pooling of Multi-level Data

The framework that is being presented implements a partial pooling approach, which is inspired by the different levels of aggregation found in the hierarchical structure of Walmart. From the provided multi-level data, six different levels of data such as total, state, store, category, department and state-department are first prepared. Second, we obtain five levels of partial pools: 3 state pools, 10 store pools, 3 category pools, 7 department pools and 21 state-department pools. Although complete pooling, which involves using a single forecasting model for the entire dataset, can capture interdependencies among products and regions, partial pooling, which uses a separate forecasting model for each pool, is often better suited for capturing the unique characteristics of each group.

## 3.3   Model Selection

We maintained the M5 competition's framework preserving the final 28 days of each series for out-of-sample testing (May 23, 2016 to June 19, 2016) and utilizing the remaining data for in-sample training (January 29, 2011 to May 22, 2016, 1941 days). Finding the appropriate model that performs well during testing is

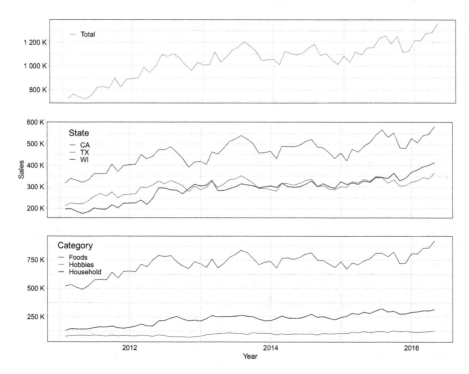

**Fig. 1.** Monthly aggregate unit sales time series over all items (top), states (center) and categories (bottom).

crucial in order to attain the highest level of accuracy. In general, the validation set is used to select a model. The effectiveness of a deep learning model, specifically, relies on several settings, including hyperparameters and initial weights. The last 28 days of the in-sample training were used for validation (April 25, 2016 to May 22, 2016). We implemented our DeepAR models in GluonTS using Pytorch. Table 1 presents the hyperparameters and their range of values used in the model selection. The hyperparameters optimization process was carried out using Optuna optimization framework. In Table 2, the data pools are listed along with the optimal hyperparameter values selected for each corresponding DeepAR model. The Root Mean Squared Error (RMSE) [17] was used to measure model selection.

## 3.4 Results

The cross-learning approaches for each level of aggregation were evaluated by calculating the Mean of the Root Mean Squared Scaled Error (MRMSSE) [13], where RMSSE is defines as follows:

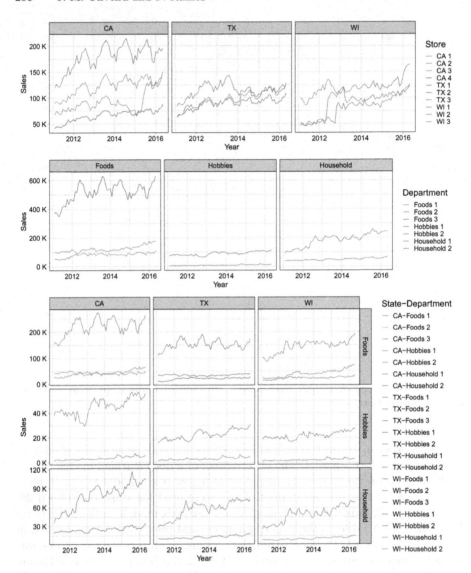

**Fig. 2.** Monthly aggregate unit sales time series over stores, presented by state (top), departments, presented by category (center) and departments, presented simultaneously by state and category (bottom).

**Table 1.** Range of values for DeepAR hyperparameters used in the optimization process.

| Hyperparameter | Values considered |
|---|---|
| Context length | 28 |
| Prediction length | 28 |
| Number of hidden layers (HL) | $\{1, 2, 3, 4\}$ |
| Hidden size (HS) | $\{20, 40, 60, 80, 100, 120, 140\}$ |
| Learning rate (LR) | $[1e^{-5}, 1e^{-1}]$ |
| Dropout rate (DR) | $[0, 0.2]$ |
| Batch size (BS) | $\{16, 32, 64, 128\}$ |
| Scaling | True |
| Number of epochs | 100 |
| Number of parallel samples | 100 |
| Number of trials | 50 |

$$\text{RMSSE}_i = \sqrt{\frac{\frac{1}{h}\sum_{t=n+1}^{n+h}\left(z_{i,t} - \hat{z}_{i,t}\right)^2}{\frac{1}{n-1}\sum_{t=2}^{n}\left(z_{i,t} - z_{i,t-1}\right)^2}}, \tag{5}$$

where $z_{i,t}$ is the value of item $i$ at time $t$, $\hat{z}_{i,t}$ is the corresponding forecast, $n$ is the length of the in-sample training and $h$ is the forecast horizon, 28 days in this case study. The RMSSE is scale-independent and hence suitable for comparing the forecasts across multiple products of different scales and units. This is achieved by scaling the forecasts errors by the Mean Squared Error (MSE) of the 1-step ahead in-sample naïve forecast errors, to match the quadratic loss of the numerator. Squared errors favour forecasts that track the mean of the target series. In the field of forecasting, it is common to use forecast averaging as a complementary approach to using multiple models. Numerous studies have demonstrated the effectiveness of averaging the forecasts generated by individual models in enhancing the accuracy of forecasts. Based on this idea, we computed the arithmetic mean of forecasts generated by the various cross-learning approaches that were developed from the available data pools, and denoted this as DeepAR-Ensemble. The results show that the cross-learning approaches outperform significantly the benchmarks. Our results indicate that the cross-learning approaches exhibit significantly superior performance compared to the benchmarks. As expected, the DeepAR-Ensemble exhibited the most superior performance among the various cross-learning approaches. It is surprising to note that the performance differences among the various cross-learning approaches that were evaluated are not significant, implying that DeepAR-Total could serve as a suitable and straightforward solution in this case. It is noteworthy that the DeepAR-State-Department approach performs better than other cross-learning methods, indicating that utilizing partial pooling at the lowest aggregation level

**Table 2.** Data pools built from multi-level data and optimal hyperparameters values found for the corresponding DeepAR model.

| Aggregation level | Data pool | Size | RMSE | HL | HS | LR | DR | BS |
|---|---|---|---|---|---|---|---|---|
| Total (1) | | 30490 | 2.147 | 3 | 100 | 0.00562 | 0.1077 | 16 |
| State (3) | CA | 12196 | 2.130 | 3 | 120 | 0.00339 | 0.0515 | 32 |
| | TX | 9147 | 1.921 | 1 | 140 | 0.00449 | 0.0955 | 128 |
| | WI | 9147 | 2.348 | 3 | 100 | 0.00076 | 0.1039 | 16 |
| Store (10) | CA 1 | 3049 | 2.212 | 4 | 120 | 0.00180 | 0.1549 | 16 |
| | CA 2 | 3049 | 2.044 | 3 | 100 | 0.01287 | 0.1281 | 32 |
| | CA 3 | 3049 | 2.652 | 3 | 140 | 0.00806 | 0.1993 | 128 |
| | CA 4 | 3049 | 1.450 | 3 | 120 | 0.00733 | 0.1309 | 32 |
| | TX 1 | 3049 | 1.781 | 1 | 80 | 0.00213 | 0.1009 | 16 |
| | TX 2 | 3049 | 1.913 | 2 | 60 | 0.01639 | 0.0021 | 128 |
| | TX 3 | 3049 | 2.052 | 3 | 40 | 0.00655 | 0.1279 | 64 |
| | WI 1 | 3049 | 1.706 | 3 | 80 | 0.00869 | 0.1720 | 128 |
| | WI 2 | 3049 | 3.092 | 2 | 120 | 0.00178 | 0.0115 | 64 |
| | WI 3 | 3049 | 2.079 | 3 | 140 | 0.00537 | 0.0258 | 64 |
| Category (3) | Foods | 14370 | 2.686 | 4 | 140 | 0.00513 | 0.0168 | 16 |
| | Hobbies | 5650 | 1.650 | 4 | 40 | 0.00271 | 0.0481 | 16 |
| | Household | 10470 | 1.409 | 3 | 60 | 0.00322 | 0.0011 | 32 |
| Department (7) | Foods 1 | 2160 | 2.644 | 3 | 20 | 0.01331 | 0.0389 | 128 |
| | Foods 2 | 3980 | 1.882 | 2 | 120 | 0.00094 | 0.0735 | 16 |
| | Foods 3 | 8230 | 2.996 | 4 | 100 | 0.00040 | 0.0524 | 16 |
| | Hobbies 1 | 4160 | 1.855 | 2 | 120 | 0.00157 | 0.0169 | 16 |
| | Hobbies 2 | 1490 | 0.829 | 3 | 60 | 0.00038 | 0.1250 | 32 |
| | Household 1 | 5320 | 1.793 | 4 | 100 | 0.00243 | 0.0646 | 32 |
| | Household 2 | 5150 | 0.837 | 4 | 100 | 0.00003 | 0.1635 | 64 |
| State-Department (21) | CA-Foods 1 | 864 | 2.687 | 3 | 40 | 0.00002 | 0.1187 | 128 |
| | CA-Foods 2 | 1592 | 1.671 | 2 | 100 | 0.02818 | 0.1600 | 32 |
| | CA-Foods 3 | 3292 | 2.826 | 3 | 80 | 0.00471 | 0.0718 | 32 |
| | CA-Hobbies 1 | 1664 | 2.231 | 3 | 60 | 0.00172 | 0.0229 | 16 |
| | CA-Hobbies 2 | 596 | 0.847 | 4 | 20 | 0.03534 | 0.0028 | 128 |
| | CA-Household 1 | 2128 | 1.925 | 3 | 20 | 0.00465 | 0.1048 | 32 |
| | CA-Household 2 | 2060 | 0.955 | 2 | 20 | 0.00622 | 0.1640 | 64 |
| | TX-Foods 1 | 648 | 2.270 | 1 | 120 | 0.00003 | 0.0440 | 64 |
| | TX-Foods 2 | 1194 | 1.473 | 1 | 140 | 0.09178 | 0.1924 | 64 |
| | TX-Foods 3 | 2469 | 2.718 | 3 | 120 | 0.00537 | 0.0475 | 32 |
| | TX-Hobbies 1 | 1248 | 1.612 | 2 | 140 | 0.01623 | 0.0602 | 32 |
| | TX-Hobbies 2 | 447 | 0.907 | 4 | 80 | 0.00023 | 0.0870 | 128 |
| | TX-Household 1 | 1596 | 1.722 | 1 | 120 | 0.00859 | 0.0426 | 16 |
| | TX-Household 2 | 1545 | 0.770 | 1 | 100 | 0.00148 | 0.1987 | 128 |
| | WI-Foods 1 | 648 | 2.810 | 4 | 40 | 0.00002 | 0.1893 | 128 |
| | WI-Foods 2 | 1194 | 2.431 | 3 | 80 | 0.00100 | 0.0059 | 16 |
| | WI-Foods 3 | 2469 | 3.464 | 2 | 140 | 0.00091 | 0.0762 | 16 |
| | WI-Hobbies 1 | 1248 | 1.498 | 1 | 40 | 0.00032 | 0.1963 | 32 |
| | WI-Hobbies 2 | 447 | 0.707 | 1 | 80 | 0.05757 | 0.0489 | 64 |
| | WI-Household 1 | 1596 | 1.695 | 3 | 120 | 0.00597 | 0.0703 | 16 |
| | WI-Household 2 | 1545 | 0.705 | 2 | 100 | 0.00629 | 0.0120 | 16 |

**Table 3.** Performance of the cross-learning approaches according to MRMSSE and its improvement against two benchmarks: ARIMA and Seasonal Naïve.

|  | MRMSSE | Improvement over ARIMA | Improvement over SNaive |
|---|---|---|---|
| Cross-learning approaches |  |  |  |
| DeepAR-Total | 0.783405 | 16.16% | 36.70% |
| DeepAR-State | 0.781190 | 16.39% | 36.88% |
| DeepAR-Store | 0.782332 | 16.27% | 36.79% |
| DeepAR-Category | 0.780938 | 16.42% | 36.90% |
| DeepAR-Department | 0.781195 | 16.39% | 36.88% |
| DeepAR-State-Department | 0.780556 | 16.46% | 36.93% |
| DeepAR-Ensemble | 0.776851 | 16.86% | 37.23% |
| Benchmarks |  |  |  |
| ARIMA | 0.934364 | - | 24.50% |
| Seasonal Naïve | 1.237630 | −32.46% | - |

allows for a more effective capture of the distinct characteristics of each group (Table 3).

## 4 Conclusions

Sales forecasts are essential for inventory management in the retail industry, enabling retailers to balance inventory levels with customer demand and market conditions. Recent advancements in machine learning algorithms, such as deep learning, have allowed for the development of more sophisticated forecasting models that can capture complex patterns and relationships in data and predict demand across various regions and product categories. This paper investigates cross-learning scenarios, inspired by the product hierarchy used in retail planning, which enable global models to better capture interdependencies between different products and regions. The empirical results obtained using the M5 competition dataset indicate that cross-learning approaches outperform local forecasting benchmarks, and utilizing partial pooling at the lowest aggregation level of the retail hierarchy can better capture the unique characteristics of each group.

## References

1. Bandara, K., Bergmeir, C., Smyl, S.: Forecasting across time series databases using recurrent neural networks on groups of similar series: a clustering approach. Exp. Syst. Appl. **140**, 112896 (2020). https://doi.org/10.1016/j.eswa.2019.112896
2. Bandara, K., Hewamalage, H., Liu, Y.H., Kang, Y., Bergmeir, C.: Improving the accuracy of global forecasting models using time series data augmentation. Pattern Recogn. **120**, 108148 (2021). https://doi.org/10.1016/j.patcog.2021.108148

3. Bojer, C.S., Meldgaard, J.P.: Kaggle forecasting competitions: an overlooked learning opportunity. Int. J. Forecast. **37**(2), 587–603 (2021). https://doi.org/10.1016/j.ijforecast.2020.07.007

4. Box, G.E.P., Jenkins, G.M., Reinsel, G.C., Ljung, G.M.: Time Series Analysis: Forecasting and Control, 5th edn. Wiley (2015)

5. Croston, J.D.: Forecasting and stock control for intermittent demands. J. Oper. Res. Soc. **23**(3), 289–303 (1972). https://doi.org/10.1057/jors.1972.50

6. Fildes, R., Ma, S., Kolassa, S.: Retail forecasting: research and practice. Int. J. Forecast. **38**, 1283–1318 (2019). https://doi.org/10.1016/j.ijforecast.2019.06.004

7. Hewamalage, H., Bergmeir, C., Bandara, K.: Global models for time series forecasting: a simulation study. Pattern Recogn. **124**, 108441 (2022). https://doi.org/10.1016/j.patcog.2021.108441

8. Hochreiter, S., Schmidhuber, J.: Long short-term memory. Neural Comput. **9**(8), 1735–1780 (1997). https://doi.org/10.1162/neco.1997.9.8.1735

9. Hyndman, R.J., Koehler, A.B., Ord, J.K., Snyder, R.D.: Forecasting with exponential smoothing: the state space approach. Springer Series in Statistics. Springer, Heidelberg (2008). https://doi.org/10.1007/978-3-540-71918-2

10. Januschowski, T., et al.: Criteria for classifying forecasting methods. Int. J. Forecast. **36**(1), 167–177 (2020). https://doi.org/10.1016/j.ijforecast.2019.05.008, m4 Competition

11. Kourentzes, N.: Intermittent demand forecasts with neural networks. Int. J. Prod. Econ. **143**(1), 198–206 (2013). https://doi.org/10.1016/j.ijpe.2013.01.009

12. Makridakis, S., Spiliotis, E., Assimakopoulos, V.: The M4 competition: 100,000 time series and 61 forecasting methods. Int. J. Forecast. **36**(1), 54–74 (2020). https://doi.org/10.1016/j.ijforecast.2019.04.014

13. Makridakis, S., Spiliotis, E., Assimakopoulos, V.: The M5 competition: background, organization, and implementation. Int. J. Forecast. (2021). https://doi.org/10.1016/j.ijforecast.2021.07.007

14. Montero-Manso, P., Hyndman, R.J.: Principles and algorithms for forecasting groups of time series: locality and globality. Int. J. Forecast. **37**(4), 1632–1653 (2021). https://doi.org/10.1016/j.ijforecast.2021.03.004

15. Oliveira, J.M., Ramos, P.: Assessing the performance of hierarchical forecasting methods on the retail sector. Entropy **21**(4), 436 (2019). https://doi.org/10.3390/e21040436

16. Ramos, P., Oliveira, J.M.: A procedure for identification of appropriate state space and ARIMA models based on time-series cross-validation. Algorithms **9**(4), 76 (2016). https://doi.org/10.3390/a9040076

17. Ramos, P., Oliveira, J.M., Kourentzes, N., Fildes, R.: Forecasting seasonal sales with many drivers: Shrinkage or dimensionality reduction? Appl. Syst. Innov. **6**(1), 3 (2023). https://doi.org/10.3390/asi6010003

18. Ramos, P., Santos, N., Rebelo, R.: Performance of state space and ARIMA models for consumer retail sales forecasting. Robot. Comput. Integr. Manuf. **34**, 151–163 (2015). https://doi.org/10.1016/j.rcim.2014.12.015

19. Salinas, D., Flunkert, V., Gasthaus, J., Januschowski, T.: DeepAR: probabilistic forecasting with autoregressive recurrent networks. Int. J. Forecast. **36**(3), 1181–1191 (2020). https://doi.org/10.1016/j.ijforecast.2019.07.001

# Discrimination of Attention Deficit Hyperactivity Disorder Using Capsule Networks and LSTM Networks on fMRI Data

Arunav Dey[✉], Jigya Singh, Manaswini Rathore, Roshni Govind, and Vandana M. Ladwani

PES University, Bangalore 560100, Karnataka, India
{pes2ug19cs066,pes2ug19cs167,pes2ug19cs217,pes2ug19cs339}@pesu.pes.edu,
vandanamd@pes.edu

**Abstract.** Attention deficit/hyperactivity disorder (ADHD) is a neurodevelopmental disorder that is typically diagnosed in young children. ADHD is heterogeneous by nature with subjects exhibiting various combinations of inattention, impulsiveness, and hyperactivity. ADHD typically persists into adulthood and increases the likelihood of diverse mental health issues and comorbid disorders such as depression, anxiety and learning disabilities. The ramifications of ADHD may worsen with age. In this paper, we propose a novel approach for the diagnosis of ADHD from resting-state fMRI (rs-fMRI) images using Capsule Network paired with LSTM Network. Combining the predictions of the Capsule Network along with the LSTM Network with the help of a voting classifier ensures that both aspects of the data - the sequential features for every subject's scan from the LSTM Network along with the attributes of the entire scan itself from the Capsule Network can be combined to fill in some gaps between each of their predictions and give a better prediction as a whole. Our proposed model achieves an accuracy of 80% on the KKI dataset and 73.33% on Peking-I dataset which is an improvement over the existing approaches.

**Keywords:** Attention Deficit/Hyperactivity Disorder · Deep Learning · Machine Learning · Capsule Network · LSTM Network

## 1 Introduction

Attention Deficit/Hyperactivity Disorder (ADHD) is one of the most widespread neurodevelopmental diseases in children and is typically first detected in infancy. Children with ADHD have acute and/or severe behavior difficulties that interfere with their capacity to lead regular lives.

Standard methods of detecting ADHD include taking a characteristic interview of the individual, gathering information about possible symptoms from friends and family, DSM-5 checklists, behavioral rating scales and other psychometric tests if deemed necessary. Recently, advances in the imaging and neural

L. Iliadis et al. (Eds.): EANN 2023, CCIS 1826, pp. 291–302, 2023.
https://doi.org/10.1007/978-3-031-34204-2_25

networks fields have enabled the automatic diagnosis of ADHD with Blood Oxygen Level Dependent (BOLD) functional Magnetic Resonance Imaging (fMRI) [2,6]. Functional MRI is a noninvasive technique used to measure and map the brain activity. Examining not only brain structure but also brain activity during a task could reveal particulars about the causes of ADHD.

In the proposed approach, we present a deep learning model that combines the results from two different networks - a capsule network and an LSTM network. The ADHD-200 dataset was used to train the models [1]. This dataset consists of fMRI scans, using which we prepare a CSV with the preprocessed features for each subject. We train the capsule network using fMRI scans and the LSTM network is trained on the preprocessed features using the prepared CSV. The results from both the networks are then combined using an average probability classifier to derive the final inference.

We discuss the existing approaches for ADHD detection in Sect. 2. We describe the dataset in Sect. 3. We present our proposed approach and methodology in Sect. 4. Section 5 presents the obtained results, and Sect. 6 concludes the paper.

## 2   Literature Survey

Kuang et al. proposed a deep belief Network (DBN) comprising three hidden layers with greedy RBMs to determine the presence of ADHD and its subtypes, using the ADHD-200 dataset. Multiple restrained Boltzmann machines (RBMs) stacked on top of each other, represented each layer in the DBN hierarchy. The DBN architecture consisted of multiple layers represented by Restricted Boltzmann Machines (RBMs). Methods such as the Brodmann mask, Fast Fourier Transform algorithm (FFT) and max-pooling frequencies were used to lower the dimensionality of fMRI data. DBN was applied to different DMN areas in fMRI such as the Prefrontal cortex, Visual cortex and Cingulate cortex [7].

Hao et al. used the Deep Bayesian Network, which is a combination of Deep Belief Network proposed by [7] along with the Bayesian Network. In their work, features of relationships were drawn out using the Bayesian network and the Deep Belief Network was used for normalization and dimension reduction of fMRI data in every Brodmann area. Finally, an SVM classifier was used to discriminate between ADHD subtypes and classify them into control, combined, inattentive or hyperactive. The combination of the two networks performed better than a deep belief network single. The deep belief network is a stack of RBMs whereas the foundation of the Bayesian network is a directed acyclic graph (DAG). Max-Min Hill Climbing (MMHC) algorithm was applied to efficiently learn the structure of the Bayesian network [4].

Zou et al. noticed that functional and structural data in the brain are complementary to each other, they proposed "multi-modality CNN architecture" to assimilate both, functional along with structural MRI data. Their work mentions six types of 3D features, comprising three types of morphological features and three types of functional features. The high-level characteristics from each modality were extracted using a 3D CNN-based method. Low-level features were preserved in tensors of the third-order and 3D CNN was trained on them, unlike earlier techniques that largely regarded these features as vectors and thus ignored potential 3D local patterns [15].

Mao et al. developed a deep learning system based on granular computing termed 4-D CNN, which was trained using changes that are derivative in entropy and allow the granularity to be computed at a sequential level by stacking the layers. For rs-fMRI images, which typically constitute a temporal series of 3-D frames, methods such as feature pooling, long short-term memory (LSTM) and spatio-temporal convolution were presented for temporal and granular processing and integration. To begin with, 3-D CNNs were used to scale 3-D spatial features. Subsequently, feature pooling and long short-term memory (LSTM) were used to fuse features together in the time dimension. A 4-D CNN architecture was suggested to concurrently learn the spatio-temporal features [9].

Riaz et al. applied an end-to-end network to classify ADHD. They proposed DeepFMRI model that comprises three components: a feature extractor, a similarity network, and a classification network. Backpropogation algorithm was used to train the model to differentiate between healthy controls and subjects with ADHD. This trained end-to-end model predicts the classification characterization directly from the raw fMRI time-series signals [10].

In [8], a multi-network of long short-term memory (multi-LSTM) was proposed by Liu et al. to identify ADHD. They used GMM-based ROIs clustering method to identify the clusters and a multi-LSTM model to collaboratively extract the crucial signal between various clusters. They included phenotypic information in the model to improve the results of the classification.

In [13], Wang et al. proposed two deep learning approaches for ADHD classification using fMRI scans. The first method employed ICA-CNN architecture. This method utilized independent component analysis to separate distinct components from each subject. Separate components were then given as input features into a convolutional neural network to differentiate ADHD patients from the usual controls. The second method, learns the latent features from the correlations between the regions of interest of the brain and these latent features are then used by new neural network to solve the classification task. They showed that with empirical results both methods are able to outperform the classical methods such as logistic regression, support vector machines etc.

Kim et al. presented a system consisting of a separate channel attention convolutional network (SC-CNN), which directly encodes the time series of the region of interest (ROI) to detect ADHD on the rs-fMRI data. This framework consisted of two stages in the network, where the first stage of the SC-CNN network encoded the time-series signal of the fMRI data for each area of the brain (channel signal) and a second attention network which captured the temporal interaction features between the extract fusion and the regions [5].

Zhang et al. used a Separate Channel CNN - RNN Architecture, 'SCCNN-RNN' can extract spatial and temporal information from fMRI data. Specifically, 'SCCNN-RNN' can be divided into two parts with different purposes. The SCCNN part can extract the features of the BOLD signal in each ROI with

1-D CNN and the RNN part can learn the spatial relation of the ROIs. Three modified models were also explored: (1) Separate Channel CNN - RNN with Attention (ASCRNN), (2) Separate Channel dilate CNN - RNN with Attention (ASDRNN), (3) Separate Channel CNN - slicing RNN with Attention (ASS-RNN). All the three modified models had the attention mechanism in common [14].

## 3   Dataset

Data from the ADHD-200 Consortium was used for the proposed approach[1]. A total of 776 MRIs and phenotypic data were collected from various centers (including NYU Child Study Center, Peking, OHSU, KKI, NI, BHBU, Pitt, and WUSTL) to build this dataset. This dataset comprises an "unrestricted public release of resting-state fMRI (rs-fMRI) and anatomical datasets aggregated across 8 independent imaging sites, 491 of which were obtained from typically developing individuals and 285 in children and adolescents with ADHD (ages: 7–21 years old)". This dataset also includes each subject's phenotypic information, such as their age, sex, diagnostic status, dimensional ADHD symptom measures, different IQ measures and their lifetime medication status. Based on visual time-series inspections, the resting-state functional MRI scans are also subject to preliminary quality control assessments. The ADHD-200 Consortium hosted a competition in 2011 to identify ADHD biomarkers [3]. By preprocessing the data and sharing the results openly, the Preprocessed Connectomes Project (PCP) makes the competition more accessible to a wider range of researchers. Using their preferred tools, the three teams preprocessed the ADHD-200 data. Athena pipelines use tools from the FSL and AFNI software packages, NIAK pipelines employ CBRAIN's Neuroimaging Analysis Kit, and Burner pipelines use SPM8 for voxel-based morphometry. Each dataset contains no protected health information and is anonymous in accordance with the HIPAA guidelines and the 1000 Functional Connectomes Project/INDI protocols.

## 4   Proposed System

### 4.1   Preprocessing and Feature Extraction

The fMRI images in the ADHD-200 dataset are 4-dimensional images. Thus, the dimensions need to be reduced and converted into feature vectors. The scans went through multiple preprocessing steps such as realignment, normalization, smoothing and slice time correction. We have primarily used the data which were preprocessed using the Athena pipeline under the PCP to perform the preprocessing and feature extraction stages for the fMRI scans [1]. The AFNI and FSL neuroimaging toolkits were combined in a shell script used to process the

---

[1] http://preprocessed-connectomes-project.org/adhd200/

images in this pipeline. The Athena preprocessing scripts and the preprocessed ADHD-200 data set are available on the official Neuro Bureau website[2].

The following steps are included in the Athena pipeline:

- Slice time correction
- Motion correction to reduce the noise introduced while scanning
- Creating a standard mean image by averaging the volumes
- Preprocessing anatomical information to obtain down-sampled WM and CSF masks
- Using EPI volumes to extract WSM and CSF time-courses
- Using Band-pass filter (0.009 < f > 0.08 Hz) voxel time courses to exclude certain frequencies
- Using a Gaussian filter with an FWHM of 6 mm to blur the filtered and unfiltered data

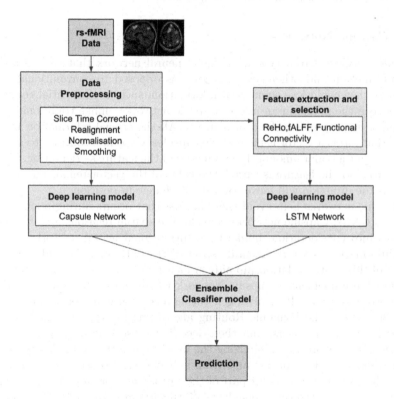

**Fig. 1.** High Level Design

Analyzing abnormal brain activity was done using aberrant ReHo signals that are connected to modifications in local brain region neuronal activity. The fractional amplitude of low-frequency fluctuations (fALFF) was used to assess the

---

[2] https://www.nitrc.org/projects/neurobureau.

relative contribution of low-frequency fluctuations in a specific frequency band. AFNI was used to extract ReHo and fALFF. Seed-Based Correlation (SBC) was performed on the scans, where connectivity was estimated using correlations between time series for all remaining brain voxels. The Nilearn library in Python was used to calculate this connectivity. The atlas of the brain was also used since it captures the regions of the brain in a common coordinate space, and this is useful for mapping the features to their respective regions. A CSV file with the preprocessed features is prepared, which is then used as an input in the further stages to train the model. The columns of the CSV file include the coordinates of the points in each fMRI scan, 10 functional connectivity features, ReHo features, fALFF features along with the age, gender, handedness, verbal IQ and performance IQ values of each subject. The rows of the CSV contain every point of each scan for every subject, one after the other. Figure 1 depicts the high level design of our proposed approach.

## 4.2 Capsule Networks

Capsule Networks are a type of artificial neural network that can retain spatial information and other key properties as opposed to convolutional neural networks that could lose some vital information, such as the spatial connectivity between the points in an image. Capsule networks, unlike traditional neural networks, use capsules instead of neurons. All the crucial information from an image that forms a vector is included in capsules. Capsules, contrary to neurons, which output a scalar amount, keep a record of the feature's orientation. Thus, if the location of the feature is varied, the value of the vector remains unchanged, whereas the direction will move toward the change in position.

Capsule networks help avoid the data loss that occurs during pooling operations in CNNs. Capsule networks consider the spatial relationship between the features into consideration, unlike the convolutional neural networks (CNNs). This information is a fundamental aspect of the data analysis, and the examination of this spatial relationship aids in identifying images in a more improved manner. We implement a Capsule Network where the fMRI scans are fed into the network as inputs. It involves generating inverse graphics of the input image with the help of the Dynamic Routing algorithm [11] amongst the lower and higher level capsule layers, and then decoding these inverse graphics back to the original input image, minimizing the loss between the original scan and the regenerated scan. The routing algorithm is being run 4 times (Figs. 2 and 3).

As shown in Fig. 2, the first part of the capsule network architecture consists of 3 layers: (1) a 3-D convolutional layer (2) the primary capsule layer (3) the final capsule layer. The second part of the architecture includes a Decoder network, which is shown in Fig. 3. The Decoder network has 4 connected layers, the first 3 layers being dense layers, which use ReLU with an alpha value of 0.1 for their activation functions and the final layer, also a dense layer, utilizes a Sigmoid activation function. We have eliminated the pooling layer and instead have used larger kernel sizes of 15 in the convolution layers. For capsule networks, we have

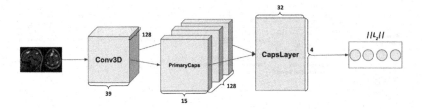

**Fig. 2.** 3 Layered Capsnet

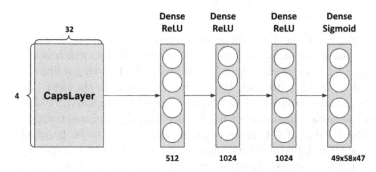

**Fig. 3.** Decoder Architecture

augmented 16 time slices from each subject's fMRI scan and used a learning rate scheduler and run it for a greater number of epochs where:

$$LearningRate_{new} = LearningRate_{old} \times LearningRateCoefficient^{EpochNo.}$$

### 4.3   LSTM Networks

Long short-term memory (LSTM) is a special type of recurrent neural network that enables the learning of long-term data and establishes relationships over time [12]. A sequential feed of data into the network is the best way for them to perform effectively. As opposed to RNNs that suffer from vanishing gradients or long-term dependence problems, LSTMs do not come with these drawbacks. An example of gradient vanishing may be found in a neural network where information is lost as connections recur from time to time over a long period. In short, LSTMs ignore useless data/information in the network to avoid a vanishing gradient in its network.

The LSTM Network consists of 3 parts as depicted in Fig. 4.

A decision is made in the first part, which determines whether the prior timestamp's information should be remembered, or whether it is irrelevant and should be forgotten. A cell will then learn new information from the input it receives in the second part of the algorithm. In the third and final part, the cell communicates its updated information from the current time stamp to the data in the next time stamp.

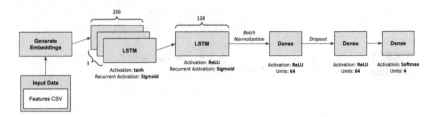

**Fig. 4.** LSTM Network

The input from the CSV file consisting of the extracted features and the phenotypic information is used to generate embeddings, which are fed as the input to an LSTM network. Three LSTM layers, each having a dimension of 64, are stacked together, with each layer being the input to the next one, and the third layer is then provided as the input to another singular LSTM layer. This layer has the same dimension of 64, having a Leaky ReLu activation function with an alpha value of 0.1, since negative values need to be handled. We end the network with 3 Dense layers having 64, 64, and 4 units respectively, using a Leaky ReLU activation function with an alpha value of 0.1 for the first 2 layers, and a Softmax activation function for the third layer. Finally, we compile the model with a Sparse Categorical Cross Entropy loss function and an Adam optimizer. And at last, we trained the model for 100 epochs with a batch size of 32.

For the final step, an average prediction classifier is used as an ensemble model which combines the prediction from each model equally. The output from the capsule network and the LSTM network is combined to give a better prediction on average than the individual models.

## 5    Results and Discussion

This section highlights the performance of the proposed Capsule-LSTM model on discriminating ADHD in the rs-fMRI data obtained from the ADHD-200 dataset. We chose to use dataset from two sites for training, validating and testing our model, the KKI and Peking-I site, since they yielded the highest accuracy as per the existing literature. For training, 80% of the dataset was used from each site, that is 64 subjects from both the KKI and Peking-I datasets, and the remaining 20% of the dataset was used for validation and hyperparameter tuning, that is 16 subjects for both the KKI and Peking-I datasets. For testing, 15 subjects from the test dataset of both the sites KKI and Peking-I was used. Table 1 compares the performance accuracy of our model on the test set for the sites KKI and Peking-I with similar approaches already existing in literature.

A confusion matrix is a way to visualize and summarize the performance of a classification algorithm on test data. A confusion matrix for binary classification is depicted by Fig. 5. For a classifier model, it creates a table with predicted values on one axis and true values on the other. The cells of the table correspond to True

Positive (TP), False Negative (FN), False Positive (FP) and True Negative (TN) values. The term true positive (TP) indicates the number of positive samples classified correctly, the term true negative (TN) indicates the number of negative samples classified correctly, the term false positive (FP) indicates the number of true negative samples which were classified as positive, and the term false negative (FN) indicates the number of true positive samples which were classified as negative. Accuracy, precision, sensitivity, specificity, and F-score are the most popular metrics for measuring the performance of a classification model.

$$Accuracy = \frac{TP + TN}{TP + TN + FP + FN}$$

$$Precision = \frac{TP}{TP + FP}$$

$$Sensitivity/Recall = \frac{TP}{TP + FN}$$

$$Specificity = \frac{TN}{TN + FP}$$

$$F1 - Score = \frac{2 * Precision * Recall}{Precision + Recall}$$

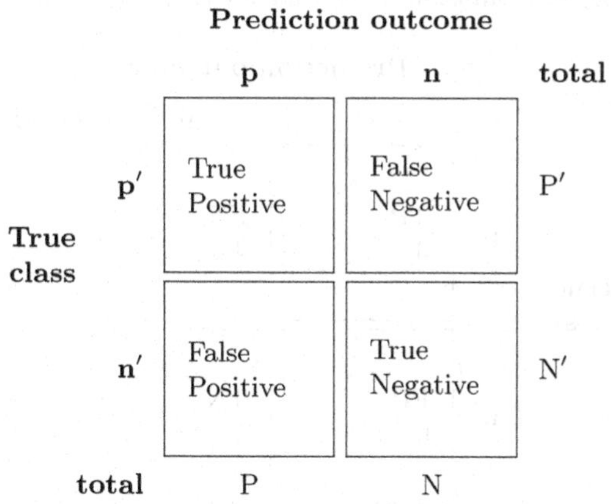

**Fig. 5.** Confusion Matrix for Binary Classification

The confusion matrices depicted in Figs. 6 and 7 take into account 15 test subjects each from the KKI and Peking-I sites respectively.

For the KKI data, the average prediction classifier reported an accuracy of 80.00%, sensitivity of 66.67%, specificity of 88.89%, precision of 80.00% and an F1-Score of 72.73% for the discrimination of ADHD.

Using Peking-I data, the average prediction classifier could identify ADHD with an accuracy of 73.33%, sensitivity of 42.86%, specificity of 100%, precision of 100% and a 60.00% F1-Score.

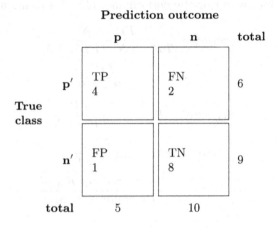

**Fig. 6.** Confusion Matrix for KKI testing dataset

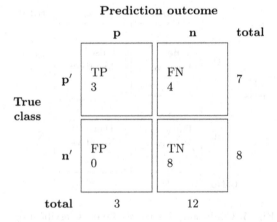

**Fig. 7.** Confusion Matrix for Peking-I testing dataset

**Table 1.** Performance comparison of ADHD prediction models on the 'ADHD-200' dataset

| Paper | Model | Accuracy | Year |
|---|---|---|---|
| [15] | 3D CNN | 69.25% | 2017 |
| [9] | 4D CNN | 71.3% | 2019 |
| [10] | DeepfMRI | 73.1% | 2018 |
| [8] | Multi LSTM | 73.7% | 2020 |
| [13] | ICA-CNN | 67% | 2022 |
| [13] | Corr-AE | 69% | 2022 |
| [7] | Deep Belief Network | 72.72% | 2014 |
| [4] | Deep Bayesian Network | 72.73% | 2015 |
| [5] | SC-CNN-Attention | 68.6% | 2021 |
| [14] | SCCNN-RNN | 70.6% | 2020 |
| Proposed System | Capsule-LSTM | 80% (KKI) 73.3% (Peking-I) | 2022 |

## 6    Conclusion and Future Scope

We present a pioneering deep learning and classification framework using Capsule Network and LSTM, based on the ADHD-200 dataset to detect the presence of ADHD using rs-fMRI scans. Data from the KKI and Peking-I sites in the ADHD-200 dataset are used. With a classic CNN being the most prevalent model used, choosing a Capsule Network instead allowed us to retain the spatial connections between the features. We also used an LSTM network to remember and preserve the important features extracted from the scans. The rs-fMRI scans are four-dimensional and undergo multiple preprocessing steps such as slice time correction, realignment, smoothing and normalization using the Athena pipeline. These images then undergo feature extraction through the same pipeline where features like ReHo, fALFF and the functional connectivity features are extracted, using which a CSV file with these features and additional phenotypic information is prepared. This data is given as an input to the LSTM Network to perform sequential model training on. A Capsule Network is trained on the fMRI images directly. These models are then fed testing data from the testing datasets, both giving an accuracy metric each. The accuracy metrics obtained from both of these networks are then fed into an average probability classifier to give the final and overall accuracy of the Capsule-LSTM network. The training and validation split of the dataset is 80% and 20% respectively, and the final accuracies obtained for the KKI and Peking-I datasets are 80% and 73.33% respectively, obtained by feeding the testing data for each of the sites into the trained model.

In the future, Capsule Networks can be combined with a range of other models to further improve classification performance, as well as make use of sMRI scans for added information. The decoder network can be optimized to better suit the dimensions of the MRI scans. It can also be used to predict ADHD index rather than ADHD type using a form of Capsule Network regression.

# References

1. Bellec, P., Chu, C., Chouinard-Decorte, F., Benhajali, Y., Margulies, D.S., Craddock, R.C.: The neuro bureau ADHD-200 preprocessed repository. Neuroimage **144**, 275–286 (2017)
2. Castellanos, F.X., et al.: Cingulate-precuneus interactions: A new locus of dysfunction in adult attention-deficit/hyperactivity disorder. Biol. Psychiat. **63**(3), 332–337 (2008)
3. Consortium, A.: The ADHD-200 consortium: A model to advance the translational potential of neuroimaging in clinical neuroscience. Front. Syst. Neurosci. **6**, 62 (2012)
4. Hao, A.J., He, B.L., Yin, C.H.: Discrimination of ADHD children based on deep bayesian network. In: 2015 IET International Conference on Biomedical Image and Signal Processing (ICBISP 2015), pp. 1–6. IET (2015)
5. Kim, B., Park, J., Kim, T., Kwon, Y.: Finding essential parts of the brain in RS-FMRI can improve diagnosing ADHD by deep learning. arXiv preprint arXiv:2108.10137 (2021)
6. Konrad, K., Eickhoff, S.B.: Is the ADHD brain wired differently? A review on structural and functional connectivity in attention deficit hyperactivity disorder. Human Brain Map. **31**(6), 904–916 (2010)
7. Kuang, D., Guo, X., An, X., Zhao, Y., He, L.: Discrimination of ADHD based on fMRI data with deep belief network. In: Huang, D.-S., Han, K., Gromiha, M. (eds.) ICIC 2014. LNCS, vol. 8590, pp. 225–232. Springer, Cham (2014). https://doi.org/10.1007/978-3-319-09330-7_27
8. Liu, R., Huang, Z.A., Jiang, M., Tan, K.C.: Multi-LSTM networks for accurate classification of attention deficit hyperactivity disorder from resting-state fMRI data. In: 2020 2nd International Conference on Industrial Artificial Intelligence (IAI), pp. 1–6. IEEE (2020)
9. Mao, Z., et al.: Spatio-temporal deep learning method for ADHD FMRI classification. Inf. Sci. **499**, 1–11 (2019)
10. Riaz, A., et al.: Deep fMRI: An end-to-end deep network for classification of fMRI data. In: 2018 IEEE 15th International Symposium on Biomedical Imaging (ISBI 2018), pp. 1419–1422. IEEE (2018)
11. Sabour, S., Frosst, N., Hinton, G.E.: Dynamic routing between capsules. Adv. Neural Inf. Process. Syst. **30** (2017)
12. Sherstinsky, A.: Fundamentals of recurrent neural network (RNN) and long short-term memory (LSTM) network. Physica D: Nonlin. Phenomena **404**, 132306 (2020)
13. Wang, D., Hong, D., Wu, Q.: Attention deficit hyperactivity disorder classification based on deep learning. IEEE/ACM Trans. Comput. Biol. Bioinform. (2022)
14. Zhang, T., et al.: Separated channel attention convolutional neural network (SC-CNN-attention) to identify ADHD in multi-site RS-FMRI dataset. Entropy **22**(8), 893 (2020)
15. Zou, L., Zheng, J., Miao, C., Mckeown, M.J., Wang, Z.J.: 3D CNN based automatic diagnosis of attention deficit hyperactivity disorder using functional and structural MRI. IEEE Access **5**, 23626–23636 (2017)

# Gaussian-Based Approach for Out-of-Distribution Detection in Deep Learning

Thiago Carvalho[1]([✉]) [iD], Marley Vellasco[1] [iD], and José Franco Amaral[2] [iD]

[1] Pontifical Catholic University of Rio de Janeiro, Rio de Janeiro, Brazil
`tmedeiros@aluno.puc-rio.br`, `marley@ele.puc-rio.br`
[2] Rio de Janeiro State University, Rio de Janeiro, Brazil
`franco@eng.uerj.br`

**Abstract.** When dealing with Deep Learning applications for open-set problems, detecting unknown samples is crucial for ensuring the model's robustness. Numerous methods aim to distinguish between known and unknown samples by analyzing different patterns generated by the model. Among these methods, those that utilize the model's output are considered the most widely applicable and practical for pre-trained models. Despite their effectiveness, there are also other techniques that can enhance Out-of-distribution detection methods by calibrating or transforming logit scores. In this study, we propose two approaches for out-of-distribution detection using logit transformation. One approach is based on the likelihood from a Gaussian distribution of logits. Additionally, we extend our method to a multivariate perspective using a mixture of Gaussian distributions to obtain better score disentanglement for traditional out-of-distribution detection methods. Our approaches were evaluated in various multi-class classification scenarios. The results showed that our logit transformation method using Gaussian distribution led to an improvement of up to 11% in terms of AUROC, and up to 32.6% in FPR95 if compared to other methods.

**Keywords:** Deep Learning · Out-of-Distribution detection · Gaussian distribution

## 1 Introduction

Deep Learning (DL) models have found widespread use in various applications, ranging from autonomous driving [18] and pest detection, to speech recognition [21]. However, in an open-set scenario, accuracy is not the only aspect that matters, but also safety and reliability [7]. Depending on the problem at hand, other aspects may also become relevant. Some aspects can be optional but highly desirable, such as explainability, or essential, such as the ability to handle unseen data robustly [25].

Most Deep Learning models are trained to recognize only a specific set of classes, referred to as In-distribution (ID) classes. Typically, these are the same classes that the model is used in the test phase [3]. However, this approach

L. Iliadis et al. (Eds.): EANN 2023, CCIS 1826, pp. 303–314, 2023.
https://doi.org/10.1007/978-3-031-34204-2_26

assumes that the model will only encounter input data from those classes, which is not always true in an open-set scenario. In reality, it is difficult (or even impossible) to guarantee that all input data will belong to known classes [20]. As a result, the model needs to be robust and able to handle Out-of-distribution (OOD) samples, which can come in various forms depending on the problem.

To identify OOD samples, auxiliary methods are often employed. These methods use patterns from the model to distinguish between ID and OOD samples. Because the goal is to identify whether a sample belongs to any known class, traditional methods often rely on the model's output, such as Maximum Softmax Probability (MSP) [8] and MaxLogit [6].

Although these techniques are widely used, they may contain limitations. For instance, some models can generate overconfident scores for unseen classes, which can lower the effectiveness of these methods for OOD detection [11]. To mitigate this issue, additional techniques are often applied with these methods to generate more reliable scores for OOD detection. These techniques may involve different strategies, such as modifying the training strategy to reduce confidence in unseen data [10] or calibrating the output scores [4].

In this article, we introduce two approaches for OOD detection that utilize the output space. These methods are inspired by the standardization of logits in semantic segmentation [13] and involve adapting the logit using Gaussian distribution-based techniques. The contributions of this work are threefold:

1. We introduce two straightforward approaches for OOD detection in multi-class classification. The first approach transforms the logits into a likelihood for a class-specific multivariate Gaussian distribution. We also propose adapting this approach, based on a mixture of Gaussian distributions, to generate an average likelihood.
2. We evaluate the effectiveness of our approach as an extension to two existing OOD detection methods, namely MSP and MaxLogit. Because these methods rely on the logit vector, our approach can be easily adapted to work in a similar manner.
3. We assess our approaches in different tasks, datasets, and model architectures. The proposed methods showed effectively better capability for OOD detection, compared to similar approaches.

## 2   Related Works

Out-of-Distribution (OOD) detection is a critical aspect of building robust Deep Learning models that can perform well in an open-set scenario. The specific applications and methods of OOD detection vary according to the task at hand, but they typically involve identifying and labeling unknown samples appropriately for complex problems such as autonomous driving [6] and farmland crop segmentation.

One of the most common methods for Out-of-Distribution (OOD) detection involves using the softmax output as an OOD score, known as Maximum Softmax

Probability (MSP) [8]. This method is based on the idea that unknown class samples would generate lower confidence scores for each known class, which are then used to distinguish ID and OOD data. However, using softmax output can sometimes lead to overconfident scores on unknown data or exploit in adversarial attacks [24], which has led to the development of adaptations to address these problems. For example, in [15], the authors proposed an adaptation that uses input perturbation to transform the output score for OOD detection.

To avoid the issues associated with the softmax, some authors have suggested using the logit and other scoring functions directly for OOD detection. For instance, [16] proposes using an entropy-based function to transform the logit into a score for OOD detection. Additionally, [6] suggests using the maximum logit value directly for OOD detection, similar to MSP. The key difference is that the logit space is unnormalized, which can emphasize differences between known and unknown samples.

Although many OOD detection techniques rely on the output space, some researchers have explored ways to adapt traditional methods to address the challenges of OOD detection. One approach involves adjusting the training process to improve OOD detection, such as by exposing models to unknown samples [19] or simply modifying the loss function [22]. However, these methods may have limited applicability to pre-trained models. Another common approach is to use various logit transformations in traditional OOD detection methods. For example, temperature scaling can be used to recalibrate output scores, as proposed in [4]. Additionally, [13] suggests standardizing logits before using the Max Logit method, which normalizes class-wise scores and ensures the same OOD threshold for each known class.

The ease and applicability of using the logit to compute the OOD score have led to various efforts to adjust the output of Deep Learning models for better OOD detection. While strategies exist to improve the results of the aforementioned methods by adjusting the logits, there are still gaps that require further investigation, such as exploring multivariate logit transformations or experimenting with other functions to recalibrate them.

# 3   Our Proposed Approaches

In this section, we propose two methods to enhance Out-of-Distribution (OOD) detection using a Gaussian density estimator to recalibrate the logit scores. Additionally, we introduce a modification that uses a univariate Gaussian distribution, based on the Standardized Max Logit technique.

Our approaches focus on class-wise normalization to rescale the different scales and distributions of the logits. To achieve this, we fit a distribution for each class and transform the logits into likelihoods, putting all values on the same scale. Inspired by [13], we propose using a Gaussian distribution to fit the logits. For better understandability, the authors in [13] proposed an adaptation to the logit scores by using a standardization method, described in Eq. 1.

$$s_c = \frac{l_c - \mu_c}{\sigma_c} \tag{1}$$

where $s_c$, $l_c$, $\mu_c$ and $\sigma_c$ are the new score, logit value, mean, and standard deviation corresponding to class $c$. In that case, $\mu_c$ and $\sigma_c$ are obtained using the logit scores from the training set.

The remaining of this section presents new approaches that utilize the idea of logit transformation with a Gaussian distribution. These techniques are variants of the Standardized Max Logit method, aimed at producing OOD scores that can more effectively distinguish between known and unknown samples.

### 3.1 Gaussian Max Likelihood

Instead of using standardization to recalibrate the logit scores, we propose the Gaussian Max Likelihood (GML), which transforms the logit value into likelihood. Let $L$ be the set of logit vectors related to the training set and $L_c$ a subset of logit value $l_c$ at position $c$, corresponding to the known class $c$ with $C$ known classes. To fit a Gaussian distribution for each known class, we calculate the mean $\mu_c$ and the standard deviation $\sigma_c$ using $L_c$, which is repeated for every known class $c$.

In test time, we consider a logit vector $l$ and recalibrate each value according to the Eq. 2. In that case, we need to change each value of the logit, which may recalibrate the scores for OOD detection.

$$s_c = \frac{1}{\sqrt{2\pi\sigma_c^2}} \exp\left(-\frac{(l_c - \mu_c)^2}{2\sigma_c^2}\right) \tag{2}$$

where $l_c$ is the logit value at position $c$, $\mu_c$ and $\sigma_c$ are the mean and standard deviation corresponding to class $c$, and $s_c$ is the score after the gaussian transformation. If the logit belongs to a known class, the likelihood would be high in this position and approximately zero in all other positions. The transformed logit's norm approaches zero for an unknown class, as the likelihood of each class would be nearly zero.

On further examination of the mathematical formulation, it can be observed that this method bears similarities to the Standardized Max Logits approach. However, this method places a significant penalty on samples that lie outside the distribution, which can aid in differentiating the scores of known and unknown samples.

### 3.2 Gaussian Mixture Max Likelihood

Based on the Gaussian distribution, we tested another approach by transforming the logits into likelihood by using a mixture of multivariate Gaussian distributions, denoted as Gaussian Mixture Max Likelihood (GMML). In that case, we follow the standard procedure to fit the Gaussian Mixture Model [17], and then use the probability density function of a Gaussian distribution to transform the logit score, as stated in Eq. 3:

$$s_c = \ln \sum_{k=1}^{K} \pi_k \mathcal{N}(\mathbf{l} \mid \boldsymbol{\mu}_k, \boldsymbol{\Sigma}_k) \tag{3}$$

where $\pi_k$ is the mixing coefficient for the $k$-th component, $\boldsymbol{\mu}_k$ and $\boldsymbol{\Sigma}_k$ are the mean vector for the $k$-th component and the covariance matrix for the $k$-th component and class $c$, respectively, and $\mathcal{N}(\mathbf{l} \mid \boldsymbol{\mu}, \boldsymbol{\Sigma})$ is the multivariate Gaussian probability density function with mean $\boldsymbol{\mu}$ and covariance matrix $\boldsymbol{\Sigma}$ evaluated at logit l. Depending on the problem, a mixture of Gaussian distributions can be a better approach to estimating the class-wise likelihood of the logits, instead of only a multivariate Gaussian distribution.

Using a multivariate Gaussian distribution can capture the relationship between the logit value and the known class and all other logits. To illustrate this advantage, Fig. 1 shows an example of binary classification, using a two-dimensional logit vector $l$, with $l_1$ and $l_2$ axis. For the GMML method, logit vectors that don't lie in any multivariate distribution for each class are more likely to be considered an OOD, even if the logit values individually can be closer to ID logits.

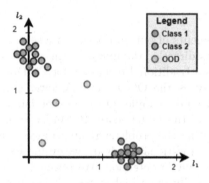

**Fig. 1.** Examples of OOD samples in label space.

## 4   Experiments

This section presents the experimental protocol to evaluate our proposed approaches, such as the chosen OOD methods, auxiliary techniques, datasets, and metrics. In this work, we focused on multi-class classification problems for image and text classification.

### 4.1  Datasets

For image classification, we followed the same procedure for dataset selection as related works in OOD detection [8, 20], choosing both the ID dataset $D^{in}$ and OOD datasets $D^{out}$. We selected the CIFAR-10 dataset for $D^{in}$, which consists of 10 known classes in relatively low resolution. For $D^{out}$, we chose four benchmark datasets with classes that differ from those in CIFAR-10. Two of these datasets are semantically different, namely the Textures and House Numbers (SVHN) datasets, while the other two are closer in proximity: the iNaturalist and Places 365 datasets. Each pair of $D^{in}$ and $D^{out}$ denote an experiment, using OOD detection methods to distinguish them. Hence, it's essential to guarantee that there is no overlap between these two datasets.

For text classification, we evaluated the proposed approaches in experiments considering two $D^{in}$ datasets individually: i) the Emotion dataset, which consists of phrases extracted from the internet and labeled into six basic emotions; and ii) the AG News, which is a collection of news headlines divided into four classes (World, Business, Sports, and Science/Technology). For $D^{out}$, we select two traditional datasets for text classification: Stanford Sentiment Tree (SST) and IMDB datasets, which are datasets related to sentiment analysis of film reviews. Therefore, an experiment consists of a pair of $D^{in}$ and $D^{out}$, in which we evaluate the capability to distinguish between known and unknown samples.

### 4.2  OOD Methods

To demonstrate the benefits of our approaches, we selected two strong baseline methods that use logits directly, Maximum Softmax Probability (MSP) [8] and Max Logit [6]. MSP is a traditional technique for OOD detection that exploits the softmax probability as the OOD score. A lower score indicates a higher likelihood of being an OOD sample. On the other hand, Max Logit uses the maximum logit value as the OOD score. It can be seen as an unnormalized version of MSP, alleviating the problems related to overconfidence in MSP.

In addition to these traditional methods, we evaluated techniques that apply logit transformation for OOD detection. We selected Standardized Max Logit (SML) [13], mathematically described in Sect. 3. Furthermore, we chose Temperature scaling [4], a traditional output-calibration technique, as an auxiliary technique to the MSP. The Temperature scaling strategy adjusts the output probabilities by a constant $T$ as shown in Eq. 4.

$$s_c = \frac{e^{l_c/T}}{\sum_{j=1}^{C} e^{l_j/T}} \tag{4}$$

where $l_c$ is the value of logit $l$ at position $c$, $C$ is the total number of classes, $T$ is the temperature scaling and $s_c$ is the calibrated softmax output at position $c$.

### 4.3  Metrics

We have selected two standard metrics to evaluate the OOD detection task in multi-classification problems.

**AUROC** (Area Under Recall Operating Curve) is probably the most common metric to evaluate the OOD detection methods. For the OOD detection problem, we consider our task as a binary problem, considering only $ID$ and $OOD$ classes. This metric summarizes the Recall Operating Curve by using the area under the curve. Therefore, the higher the AUROC, the better the model to distinguish those classes.

**FPR95** is another metric used to evaluate how well the method behaves on a threshold-defined value. This metric indicates the False Positive Rate (FPR) when the True Positive Rate (TPR) is 95%. In other terms, the FPR95 highlights the capability to distinguish OOD samples and most of the $ID$ samples.

### 4.4 Experimental Details

To evaluate our proposed approach, we used the same experimental procedure in all experiments. During the testing phase, we randomly selected 1000 samples from each set of $D^{in}$ and $D^{out}$ (when applicable) and computed the average metrics over 10 runs. We chose three different model architectures for image classification and four different $D^{out}$ datasets for CIFAR10 as $D^{in}$. Also, we selected two datasets as $D^{in}$ in the text classification task and used the same model architecture for both.

Our proposed approach using univariate Gaussian distribution is a parameter-free method, making it an advantage as it eliminates the need for hyperparameter tuning. However, for the GMML approach, we tested a narrow range of numbers of components, varying from 2 to 4. To tune the hyperparameter of the MSP with temperature scaling, we used a grid search with values ranging from 0.5 to 2, with increments of 0.1.

We also assess the impact of these OOD detectors across different model architectures. In image classification, we used a pre-trained Vision Transformer (ViT) model [2] on the CIFAR-10 dataset, and two traditional models, ResNet [5] and DenseNet [12], which were fine-tuned on the CIFAR-10 dataset using a similar approach as presented in [23]. Since we were already evaluating the OOD detection in two $D^{in}$ datasets for text classification, we chose to use only one model architecture in our experiments. We opted for the BERT model architecture [1], pre-trained on different datasets according to the $D^{in}$.

## 5   Results and Discussion

This section presents the results of our multi-class classification experiments, where we evaluate our approaches against methods that rely solely on the output space and calculate the OOD score in a single forward run during inference. Although Temperature Scaling is not typically considered an OOD method, as explained in Sect. 4, we have included MSP with temperature scaling as a variant method in the experiments.

## 5.1 Image Classification

For image classification, Tables 1 and 2 show the results for OOD detection using AUROC and FPR95 metrics, respectively.

**Table 1.** OOD detection for image classification - AUROC ↑

| Model | $D^{out}$ | MSP | Temp | MaxLogit | SML | GMML | GML |
|---|---|---|---|---|---|---|---|
| ViT | SVHN | 0.9922 | 0.9950 | **0.9978** | 0.9968 | 0.9965 | 0.9975 |
| | iNaturalist | 0.9782 | 0.9782 | 0.9825 | 0.9840 | 0.9737 | **0.9899** |
| | Places365 | 0.9673 | 0.9795 | 0.9673 | 0.9795 | 0.9853 | **0.9945** |
| | Textures | 0.9993 | 0.9995 | **0.9997** | 0.9994 | **0.9997** | 0.9994 |
| DenseNet | SVHN | 0.6767 | 0.6767 | 0.6843 | 0.7365 | **0.7445** | 0.7202 |
| | iNaturalist | 0.6581 | 0.6221 | 0.6190 | 0.6220 | **0.7103** | 0.6220 |
| | Places365 | 0.7138 | 0.6865 | 0.6839 | 0.6865 | 0.7177 | **0.6815** |
| | Textures | 0.6824 | 0.7289 | 0.6679 | 0.6670 | **0.7418** | 0.7073 |
| ResNet | SVHN | 0.6979 | 0.6979 | 0.6826 | 0.6816 | **0.7507** | 0.5955 |
| | iNaturalist | 0.6952 | 0.6941 | 0.6952 | 0.6941 | **0.7584** | 0.6012 |
| | Places365 | 0.6786 | 0.6168 | 0.6626 | 0.6617 | **0.7221** | 0.5816 |
| | Textures | 0.7058 | 0.6334 | 0.6880 | 0.6866 | **0.7536** | 0.5974 |

**Table 2.** OOD detection for image classification - FPR95 ↓

| Model | $D^{out}$ | MSP | Temp | MaxLogit | SML | GMML | GML |
|---|---|---|---|---|---|---|---|
| ViT | SVHN | 0.0095 | 0.0060 | 0.0053 | 0.0070 | 0.0051 | **0.0050** |
| | iNaturalist | 0.1283 | 0.1283 | 0.0975 | 0.0907 | 0.1233 | **0.0807** |
| | Places365 | 0.0632 | 0.00570 | 0.0552 | 0.0470 | 0.0504 | **0.0370** |
| | Textures | 0.0016 | 0.0001 | 0.0011 | 0.0005 | 0.0001 | **0.0001** |
| DenseNet | SVHN | 0.6285 | 0.6310 | 0.6581 | 0.6221 | **0.6003** | 0.7220 |
| | iNaturalist | 0.6843 | 0.7365 | 0.6710 | 0.6702 | **0.7571** | 0.6702 |
| | Places365 | 0.6427 | 0.7022 | 0.6274 | 0.6264 | **0.7198** | 0.6264 |
| | Textures | 0.6574 | 0.7289 | **0.6319** | 0.6335 | 0.8920 | 0.8372 |
| ResNet | SVHN | 0.7670 | 0.7661 | 0.7928 | 0.7669 | **0.7018** | 0.7309 |
| | iNaturalist | 0.7881 | 0.7569 | 0.7573 | 0.7549 | **0.7041** | 0.9337 |
| | Places365 | 0.8135 | 0.7879 | 0.7901 | 0.7879 | **0.6253** | 0.9482 |
| | Textures | 0.7798 | 0.7569 | 0.7612 | 0.7537 | **0.7064** | 0.9346 |

At first glance, we observed that transformer-based models performed better than other methods, even for baseline models, for detecting out-of-distribution (OOD) data. While the reported accuracy metrics for multi-class classification tasks didn't show a significant difference, some authors suggest that transformer-based models can have superior OOD detection capabilities, regardless of the

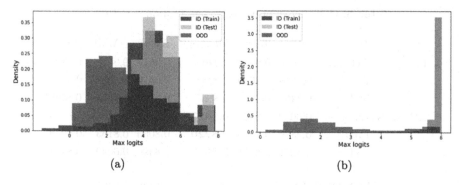

**Fig. 2.** Max logit density distribution for (a) ResNet model; (b) ViT model architectures

specific task [9,14]. This advantage resulted in better OOD-based metrics and slight improvements by using the auxiliary techniques, especially in terms of the AUROC. Notably, we found that our approaches consistently outperformed other methods for OOD detection using the Vision Transformer model.

Regarding the other two architectures, we had a better understanding of why auxiliary techniques could be beneficial. We found that one of the primary differences was the significant dissimilarity in the scale of logits from both ID and OOD data, which was not as pronounced in the ResNet architecture, illustrated in Fig. 2. This discrepancy was reflected in more entangled max logit values, which made it challenging to develop an effective OOD detector relying solely on uncalibrated scores using the MaxLogit method. However, methods that use class-wise calibration of logit scores could mitigate this issue, especially if the entire logit vector was taken into consideration instead of just the maximum value, as GMML does. For ResNet, the GMML increased up to 10.7% in terms of AUROC if compared to the MSP method, reported in the iNaturalist as $D^{out}$. Similar results are found for the DenseNet architecture, which showed that our approaches outperformed similar methods for OOD detection.

## 5.2   Text Classification

For text classification, we changed the $D^{in}$ while maintaining the same model architecture. We also evaluated the same methods for OOD detection, whose results are presented in Tables 3 and 4.

For the first set of experiments, using the Emotion dataset as $D^{in}$, we observed that all of the logit recalibration strategies enhanced the OOD detection, for both AUROC and FPR95 metrics. However, our approach outperformed those strategies, increasing the AUROC up to 11.0% and decreasing the FPR95 up to 32.6% using AG News as $D^{out}$, if compared to the SML method. The proposed approaches provided a better disentanglement to generate an OOD score in the fuzzy region between OOD samples and ID ones with lower confidence.

For the experiments using AG News as $D^{in}$, however, we noticed a more controversial problem. For all of these experiments, the usage of logit transformation techniques lowered the capability of such methods for OOD detection.

**Table 3.** OOD detection for text classification - AUROC ↑

| $D^{in}$ | $D^{out}$ | MSP | Temp | MaxLogit | SML | GMML | GML |
|---|---|---|---|---|---|---|---|
| Emotion | AG News | 0.9018 | 0.9410 | 0.9464 | 0.9610 | 0.9690 | **0.9680** |
| | IMDB | 0.9018 | 0.9690 | 0.9464 | 0.9610 | **0.9692** | 0.9667 |
| | SST | 0.8460 | 0.8672 | 0.8851 | 0.9144 | 0.9313 | **0.9393** |
| AG News | Emotion | 0.8669 | 0.8669 | **0.9017** | 0.8836 | 0.6496 | 0.8876 |
| | IMDB | 0.7839 | 0.7839 | **0.8220** | 0.8093 | 0.8163 | 0.8038 |
| | SST | 0.8271 | 0.8271 | **0.8653** | 0.8496 | 0.6049 | 0.8408 |

**Table 4.** OOD detection for image classification - FPR95 ↓

| $D^{in}$ | $D^{out}$ | MSP | Temp | MaxLogit | SML | GMML | GML |
|---|---|---|---|---|---|---|---|
| Emotion | AG News | 0.7617 | 0.3384 | 0.3476 | 0.2479 | 0.1678 | **0.1425** |
| | IMDB | 0.7617 | 0.3384 | 0.3476 | 0.2479 | 0.1673 | **0.1671** |
| | SST | 0.8380 | 0.5407 | 0.5511 | 0.4570 | **0.3281** | 0.3299 |
| AG News | Emotion | 0.6055 | 0.6055 | **0.4695** | 0.8720 | 0.9765 | 0.4905 |
| | IMDB | 0.8596 | 0.8596 | 0.8220 | 0.8093 | 0.8163 | **0.8038** |
| | SST | 0.6882 | 0.6882 | 0.8653 | 0.8496 | 0.6208 | **0.6049** |

One of the issues that we found is that logit distribution for some of the known classes behaved in an odd manner, as illustrated in Fig. 3. Controversy from the literature, where, generally, training samples produce higher logits than test set or unknown samples, in this example, we can see that the opposite happened. This could generate a problem in the logit recalibration strategies, which can make an OOD sample more likely to be an ID class, especially for the multivariate Gaussian approach, in which logits from its class may impact the likelihood for other classes as well.

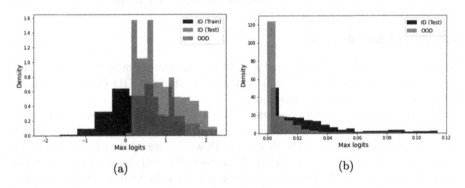

**Fig. 3.** The distribution problem for AG News dataset experiment; (a) Max logit distribution for the training set, test set and OOD samples; (b) Max logit after GMM transformation

# 6  Conclusion

This paper introduced two strategies that utilize output space-based methods to improve OOD detection, based on the use of the Gaussian distribution, either through a univariate Gaussian or a mixture of Gaussian. Our experiments showed that our strategies effectively distinguished between known and unknown classes, thereby improving the baseline methods. However, we also observed that logit transformation alone could not be used without additional analysis of the logit distribution, as seen in the last experiment of the text classification section. We plan to further evaluate our approaches in various scenarios to better understand these methods for OOD detection.

**Acknowledgements.** This work was supported in part by the Coordenação de Aperfeiçoamento de Pessoal de Nível Superior - Brasil (CAPES) - Finance Code 001, Conselho Nacional de Desenvolvimento e Pesquisa (CNPq) under Grant 140254/2021-8, and Fundação de Amparo à Pesquisa do Rio de Janeiro (FAPERJ).

# References

1. Devlin, J., Chang, M.W., Lee, K., Toutanova, K.: Bert: Pre-training of deep bidirectional transformers for language understanding. arXiv preprint arXiv:1810.04805 (2018)
2. Dosovitskiy, A., et al.: An image is worth 16x16 words: Transformers for image recognition at scale. arXiv preprint arXiv:2010.11929 (2020)
3. Geng, C., Huang, S.J., Chen, S.: Recent advances in open set recognition: A survey. IEEE Trans. Pattern Anal. Mach. Intell. **43**(10), 3614–3631 (2020)
4. Guo, C., Pleiss, G., Sun, Y., Weinberger, K.Q.: On calibration of modern neural networks. In: International Conference on Machine Learning, pp. 1321–1330. PMLR (2017)
5. He, K., Zhang, X., Ren, S., Sun, J.: Deep residual learning for image recognition. In: Proceedings of the IEEE Conference on Computer Vision and Pattern Recognition, pp. 770–778 (2016)
6. Hendrycks, D., et al.: Scaling out-of-distribution detection for real-world settings. In: International Conference on Machine Learning, pp. 8759–8773. PMLR (2022)
7. Hendrycks, D., Carlini, N., Schulman, J., Steinhardt, J.: Unsolved problems in ml safety. arXiv preprint arXiv:2109.13916 (2021)
8. Hendrycks, D., Gimpel, K.: A baseline for detecting misclassified and out-of-distribution examples in neural networks. arXiv preprint arXiv:1610.02136 (2016)
9. Hendrycks, D., Liu, X., Wallace, E., Dziedzic, A., Krishnan, R., Song, D.: Pretrained transformers improve out-of-distribution robustness. arXiv preprint arXiv:2004.06100 (2020)
10. Hendrycks, D., Mazeika, M., Dietterich, T.: Deep anomaly detection with outlier exposure. arXiv preprint arXiv:1812.04606 (2018)
11. Holm, A.N., Wright, D., Augenstein, I.: Revisiting softmax for uncertainty approximation in text classification. arXiv preprint arXiv:2210.14037 (2022)
12. Huang, G., Liu, Z., Van Der Maaten, L., Weinberger, K.Q.: Densely connected convolutional networks. In: Proceedings of the IEEE Conference on Computer Vision and Pattern Recognition, pp. 4700–4708 (2017)

13. Jung, S., Lee, J., Gwak, D., Choi, S., Choo, J.: Standardized max logits: A simple yet effective approach for identifying unexpected road obstacles in urban-scene segmentation. In: Proceedings of the IEEE/CVF International Conference on Computer Vision, pp. 15425–15434 (2021)

14. Koner, R., Sinhamahapatra, P., Roscher, K., Günnemann, S., Tresp, V.: Oodformer: Out-of-distribution detection transformer. arXiv preprint arXiv:2107.08976 (2021)

15. Liang, S., Li, Y., Srikant, R.: Enhancing the reliability of out-of-distribution image detection in neural networks. arXiv preprint arXiv:1706.02690 (2017)

16. Liu, W., Wang, X., Owens, J., Li, Y.: Energy-based out-of-distribution detection. Adv. Neural Inf. Process. Syst. **33**, 21464–21475 (2020)

17. McLachlan, G.J., Rathnayake, S.: On the number of components in a gaussian mixture model. Wiley Interdiscip. Rev.: Data Mining Knowl. Discov. **4**(5), 341–355 (2014)

18. Muhammad, K., et al.: Vision-based semantic segmentation in scene understanding for autonomous driving: Recent achievements, challenges, and outlooks. IEEE Trans. Intell. Transp. Syst. (2022)

19. Papadopoulos, A.A., Rajati, M.R., Shaikh, N., Wang, J.: Outlier exposure with confidence control for out-of-distribution detection. Neurocomputing **441**, 138–150 (2021)

20. Salehi, M., Mirzaei, H., Hendrycks, D., Li, Y., Rohban, M.H., Sabokrou, M.: A unified survey on anomaly, novelty, open-set, and out-of-distribution detection: Solutions and future challenges. arXiv preprint arXiv:2110.14051 (2021)

21. Swetha, P., Srilatha, J.: Applications of speech recognition in the agriculture sector: A review. ECS Trans. **107**(1), 19377 (2022)

22. Wei, H., Xie, R., Cheng, H., Feng, L., An, B., Li, Y.: Mitigating neural network overconfidence with logit normalization. In: International Conference on Machine Learning, pp. 23631–23644. PMLR (2022)

23. Wightman, R., Touvron, H., Jégou, H.: Resnet strikes back: An improved training procedure in timm. arXiv preprint arXiv:2110.00476 (2021)

24. Wu, Y., et al.: Disentangling confidence score distribution for out-of-domain intent detection with energy-based learning. arXiv preprint arXiv:2210.08830 (2022)

25. Yang, J., Zhou, K., Li, Y., Liu, Z.: Generalized out-of-distribution detection: A survey. arXiv preprint arXiv:2110.11334 (2021)

# LoockMe: An Ever Evolving Artificial Intelligence Platform for Location Scouting in Greece

Eleftherios Trivizakis[1]([envelope]) [ID], Vassilios Aidonis[2,3], Vassilios C. Pezoulas[2,3] [ID],
Yorgos Goletsis[3,4] [ID], Nikolaos Oikonomou[5], Ioannis Stefanis[1,5] [ID],
Leoni Chondromatidou[1], Dimitrios I. Fotiadis[2,3], Manolis Tsiknakis[1,5] [ID],
and Kostas Marias[1,5] [ID]

[1] Computational BioMedicine Laboratory (CBML), Foundation for Research and Technology, Hellas (FORTH), 70013 Heraklion, Greece
trivizakis@ics.forth.gr
[2] Biomedical Research Institute (BRI), Foundation for Research and Technology, Hellas (FORTH), 45110 Ioannina, Greece
[3] Unit of Medical Technology and Intelligent Information Systems, Department of Materials Science and Engineering, University of Ioannina, 45110 Ioannina, Greece
[4] Laboratory of Business Economics and Decisions, Department of Economics, University of Ioannina, 45110 Ioannina, Greece
[5] Department of Electrical and Computer Engineering, Hellenic Mediterranean University, 71410 Heraklion, Greece

**Abstract.** LoockMe is an artificial intelligence-powered location scouting platform that combines deep learning image analysis, cutting-edge machine learning natural language processing (NLP) for automated content annotation, and intelligent search. The platform's objective is to label input images of local landscapes, and/or any other assets that regional film offices want to expose to those interested in identifying potential locations for the film production industry. The deep learning-based image analysis achieved high classification performance with an AUC score of 99.4%. Moreover, the state-of-the-art machine learning NLP module enhances the platform's capabilities by analyzing text descriptions of the locations and thus allowing for automated annotation, while the intelligent search engine combines image analysis with NLP to extract relevant context from available data. The proposed artificial intelligence platform has the potential to substantially assist asset publishers and revolutionize the location scouting process for the film production industry in Greece.

**Keywords:** artificial intelligence · deep learning · transfer learning · natural language processing · location scouting · film production · search engine

## 1 Introduction

Artificial intelligence (AI) has the potential to revolutionize various industries by streamlining and automating complex tasks. In recent years, deep learning (DL) has made significant strides in the fields of image analysis and natural language processing, making it possible to extract meaningful insights from vast amounts of raw data. One potential application of AI is in location scouting for film production, where identifying suitable locations can be a crucial aspect of the filmmaking process.

DL has also been utilized in location recognition based on image classification tasks, where the objective is to identify photos of a certain area or site. A variety of studies have investigated the performance of DL analysis for location classification. Kim et al. [1] propose a method of automatically classifying tourist photos by attractions using DL models and feature vector clustering, which allows for the flexible extraction of categories for each tourist destination and improves classification performance with a small dataset. D'Haro et al. [2] present a system that uses a CNN-based model to automatically recognize landmarks in Singapore through images, which is combined with metadata information to provide information about specific places. The proposed model achieved an F1 score of 81% over a set of six different landmarks. Hettiarachchi et al. [3] presented a hierarchical place recognition system that fuses visual and location information using DL models, achieving a recall of 95.7% on the Tokyo Outdoor Places dataset. These results demonstrate the potential of DL models for location image classification tasks, which can have practical applications in fields such as tourism, urban planning, and location scouting.

Text annotation is the process of assigning labels to documents and their contents. Such annotation supported by machine learning (ML) tools has been applied in domains such as the biomedical domain [4], social network post analysis [5], and emotion detection [6].

In this paper, an AI platform that integrates DL image analysis and ML NLP to label images of locations in Greece is presented. LoockMe is designed to perform DL- and ML-based data analysis, including images and text descriptions, respectively, and extract relevant information about locations that might be of interest to film production companies.

The contributions of this study can be summarized as follows:

- The proposed transfer learning framework for image analysis is a high-performing, easy-to-deploy, and effective methodology for domain adaptation tasks.
- Extend the publicly available imaging and NLP pre-trained models by adapting them to new domains.
- The interplay between the NLP and the AI image annotation component can significantly accelerate the location registration process on the LoockMe platform.
- The proposed platform architecture will allow the ML models to improve over the life cycle of the service, despite the data shift as the language and imaging databases get larger.

## 2    Material and Methods

### 2.1    Data Collection

Data collection is crucial to building robust and highly accurate image recognition models. Public and open imaging datasets can provide a diverse and representative sampling of sites for highly precise analysis and classification. For legal and ethical reasons, collecting license-free images is important because using copyrighted images without permission for model development could be prohibited in many areas. An open-source image scraper [7] was used to automatically download data from Google Search (www. google.com) based on specific criteria such as the size of the pixel array of the image, keywords relevant to Greek landmarks, and the availability of a creative commons license. The search was performed on the Google search website with the abovementioned constraints, and the link was passed to the image scraper software. Terms in both Greek and English were used to search for imaging categories such as "ancient amphitheater" (164), "ancient temple" (171), "Byzantine architecture" (43), "Greek urban landscape" (29), "village (island)" (129), "old port" (39), "olive grove" (57), "ancient ruins" (33), "traditional Greek architecture" (23), "traditional stone bridge" (89), "vineyard" (136), "windmill" (107), "saltpan" (18), as presented in Fig. 1. Assessing image quality and discarding images based on the relevancy of the search term was key to enhancing the robustness of the dataset. In particular, from the twenty terms, three returned irrelevant or low-quality images, and four returned fewer than seven images per term. Finally, thirteen classes were used to develop the DL model. The model is available online[1].

**Fig. 1.** Samples of the collected LoockMe imaging dataset

## 2.2  Deep Learning-Based Image Analysis

**Image Pre-processing and Data Stratification.** All images were resized to a pixel array of 256 by 256 pixels as required by the DL analysis. The statistics of the pixel distribution of the collected dataset used for the standardization of the images were extracted exclusively from the training set and applied to the other sets. In particular, after standardization, the final pixel distribution is characterized by unit variance and a zero mean. Five-fold cross-validation was used to split the convergence and testing sets. The convergence set was further split into training (80%) and validation (20%) sets by

---

[1] http://www.github.com/trivizakis/loockme-model/.

applying holdout cross-validation. In particular, the training set was used for fitting the model, and the validation set was used for early stopping of the training phase. Finally, the testing set remained unseen across experiments to avoid data leaks and fairly evaluate the models. The class balances were preserved across sets.

**Transfer Learning.** Transfer learning (TL) is a popular technique in DL that involves using pre-trained models as a starting point for training with less data. Adapting ImageNet [8] weights is a commonly used solution in DL image analysis [9–11]. This is because the source models were trained on a large dataset with a wide variety of images, and consequently the learned filters, which are low-level texture detectors, are transferable across domains. Therefore, TL with such pre-trained models allows for better and faster convergence on a much smaller dataset. The convolutional part of the source model was transferred to a target model with new input and neural network layers, as depicted in Fig. 2, enabling the adaptation of the source model to a new classification domain. In the context of location identification, TL was used to train DL models to classify images of local landscapes as potential filming locations. This approach can save significant amounts of time and resources since the pre-trained model already has learned low-level features that are useful for the new problem. Part of the transferred convolutional neural network remained frozen, while the new layers were adapted on the relatively size-limited LoockMe dataset, improving the target model's accuracy and reducing the risk of overfitting. In this study, eight models with different architectures and layer types were used, including the most prominent: a) VGG [12], b) Inception [13], c) Xception [14], d) ResNet [15], e) NasNet [16], f) MobileNet [17], and g) DenseNet [18], available in the Keras [19] online repository.

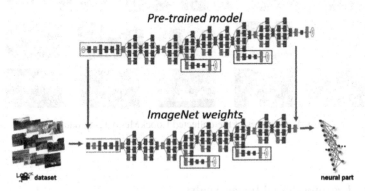

**Fig. 2.** The TL implementation for image analysis. Three settings for neurons were tested including 256, 512 and 1024 neurons in the hidden layer.

**Hyper-parameters Optimization.** TL does not require optimizing the parameters of the architecture except for the neural network part of the deep model. The convolutional part of the model was transferred to the target model, while new input and neural layers were added. Several neural network settings were tested. In particular, a single hidden layer with either 256, 512, or 1024 neurons was examined. The criteria for assessing the convergence status of the deep models was the minimum loss that maximizes the prediction accuracy in the validation set. Additionally, for the same task, learning curves for loss and accuracy were also considered for evaluating each model's convergence status.

### 2.3 Natural Language Processing Service

**Service Functionalities.** The natural language processing service was designed to provide a solution both to the content provider and to the end-user. The former provides a description of an image and receives intelligent suggestions for annotation, while the latter provides a query of a desired location and receives a collection of relevant images. By utilizing a pre-defined set of ontology terms, a pre-trained unsupervised algorithm, and distance algorithms, the service is capable of capturing the semantic relationships within a given text. As a result, it provides intelligent methods for the user.

**Data Collection – Film Offices.** Since the service relies on a pre-trained ML algorithm, data collection was focused on ontology development. To this end, relevant search vocabularies were identified by examining existing solutions on the internet. Data were collected by employing Python programming language tools and web scraping techniques to extract information from various film offices. The sites were categorized into logical categories and subcategories, which included flat and multi-level categorization with each category further divided into individual subcategories.

**The Creation of the Ontology.** The ontology constitutes a main, static component of the NLP service. The creation of such a file required the implementation of certain steps that are described below:

1. Aggregation of all the terms of the existing Film Offices.
2. Addition of terms that correspond to the unique geographical, architectural features of Greece and its history.
3. Refinement and cleaning of the ontology after multiple quality checks to ensure it was efficient and accurate.
4. Ontology optimization.
5. Creation of a final version of the ontology after continuous conversions and evaluations.

The final version was comprised of 13 categories, 31 subcategories (Table 1), and 649 terms. The ontology terms were originally stored in XLS file format and transformed into XML file format with Python programming language scripts.

**General Approach and Description of the Techniques Used.** The NLP service manages and understands term representations at a programming level using vector word embeddings. Word embeddings are fixed-length vectors constructed using word co-occurrence statistics based on the distributional hypothesis [5]. This hypothesis states that words appearing in the same contexts tend to have similar meanings, and mathematical operations such as (e.g., addition, subtraction) can be used [6].

Another component of the service is GloVe (Global Vectors for Word Representation), a log-bilinear model with a weighted least-squares objective. GloVe is trained on aggregated global statistics of word co-occurrence, allowing it to represent words as

**Table 1.** The LoockMe ontology: Main categories and subcategories.

| Categories | Subcategories | Categories | Subcategories |
|---|---|---|---|
| Facilities | Agriculture, Educational, Healthcare, House Type, Industrial, Institutional/Government, Sport Facilities, Tourist accommodation, Worship-Religious Buildings | Culture-Leisure | Museum-Exhibits-Art, Recreation, Theatre-Auditorium |
| | | CHRONOLOGICAL-Period | Modern Greece |
| Trade Facilities | Individual shops, Shopping Areas | REGIONAL-Administrative Region | Attica, Central Greece, Central Macedonia, Crete, East Macedonia and Thrace, Epirus, Ionian Islands, North Aegean, Peloponnese, South Aegean, Thessaly, West Greece, West Macedonia |
| Environment-Landscapes-City Areas | | | |
| Transportation | | | |
| Ancient-Historic Monuments | | REGIONAL-Proximity | |
| Architectural | Appearance and Condition, Architectural Style, Special Interest | REGIONAL-Coordinates | |
| | | Film Genre-Mood | |
| | | Background View | |

linear sub-structures in the vector space. Thus, using mathematical functions such as Euclidean distance, it is possible to calculate the percentage of linguistic or semantic similarity between two words based on GloVe's word representations [7].

The service combines all necessary components to construct a comprehensive NLP tool capable of processing text and extracting meaning, capturing the semantic relationships of a given text and specific terms within the ontology. An overview of the service's functionality:

The content provider or end-user writes a description/sentence.

1. The service receives an API request.
2. The NLP pipeline processes the request.
3. The service returns an API response.

The response includes a set of terms for annotation or a collection of images, depending on the use case. A more detailed representation is shown in Fig. 3.

The set of functions that were applied for the operation of the service is analyzed individually and descriptively in the next steps. If necessary, the input is split into separate sentences depending on the use case.

1. The function takes a string of words as input and converts them to lowercase, while also handling capital letters and dashes (-, _).
2. It uses the word_tokenize() function from the NLTK library to remove all punctuation from the input.
3. It splits the resulting string into a list of unique words.
4. It lemmatizes the words in the list using the WordNetLemmatizer class from the nltk.stem package.
5. It removes all stopwords from the list using the stopword corpus from the nltk.copus package.

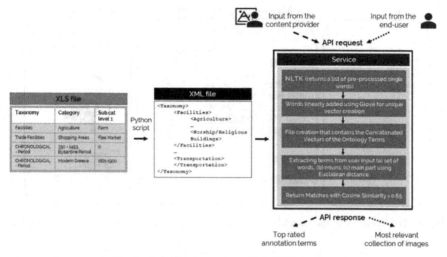

**Fig. 3.** A detailed overview of the NLP service.

6. It returns the modified list of words.

After the pre-processing steps, the input will undergo three separate NLP pipelines, each referred to as processes (a), (b), and (c).

- The first process (a) uses the set of words proposed by the user to find embeddings.
- The second process (b) uses the set of all nouns found in the user's input.
- The third process (c) uses the main part of the sentence that comes before determiners, adverbs, or subordinating conjunctions, if they exist.

The parts of the sentence are identified using the pos_tag function of the NLTK library, which tags each word in the input text with a part of speech. This allows the service to extract the main part of the sentence for use in the third process. To measure text similarity to the ontology terms, cosine similarity was employed in all three processes with a threshold of 65%. This choice of metric and threshold was determined after experimentation and analysis of the results.

## 2.4 LoockMe Platform

The LoockMe platform was designed on the same principles that big film offices [20–22] were built upon. In particular, key features of these successful services were integrated into LoockMe with the ambition of extending their baseline functionality and usability by incorporating AI analysis tools, such as NLP and DL image analysis, as depicted in Fig. 4. The LoockMe database offers information to film/content professionals and producers about the accommodations, auxiliary support services, other technical infrastructure required, and other metadata of the depicted location.

Two main use case scenarios are available on the platform: a) content upload, and b) location recommendation. During the content upload, the input images are analyzed by the DL-based module, and a list of relevant terms are recommended for approval to the

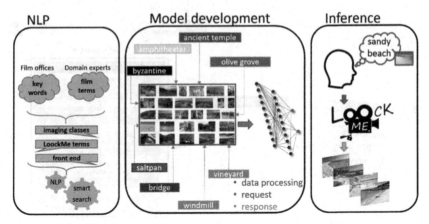

**Fig. 4.** The workflow of the LoockMe smart search engine. NLP, natural language processing.

user. Multiple models are leveraged for this task including the custom LoockMe model, an ImageNet model with reduced outputs only to relevant classes, and the Place356 model [23, 24]. For the location recommendation, the NLP module of the platform can detect the most relevant keywords from the search query of the user. Then, these are matched to the database of LoockMe, and the best locations are returned to the front-end.

## 3   Results

**Image Analysis.** The DL analysis was conducted on a computational node integrating an Intel Xeon central processing unit with twenty threads, thirty-two gigabytes of random access memory, and an NVidia Quadro M4000 graphics processing unit with eight gigabytes of video memory. The dataset splits and experimental protocol were kept constant across all experiments, with the key differentiating factors being the number of neurons, and the transferred layers of the pre-trained models. In total, 120 unique models were evaluated, including 24 architectures (eight architectures by three neural network settings) in five different splits of the LoockMe dataset (k-fold cross-validation). The dataset consists of 1038 samples across 13 classes. Four types of data augmentation transformations were performed: 1) flipping from right to left, 2) flipping from top to bottom, 3) rotation at 90°, and 4) rotation at 270°. The training sets consisted of approximately 650 samples, which were augmented to more than 3250 images. 90% of the transferred convolutional layers remained frozen, while the rest were adapted to the new domain. A batch size of 16 samples and a learning rate of $10^{-4}$ were used. All the metrics are presented in the mean $\pm$ standard deviation% format.

The top-performing architectures in terms of F1 score include Inception v3 (88.0 $\pm$ 2.2), Xception (89.0 $\pm$ 1.6), and DenseNet (89.8 $\pm$ 1.0). The latter achieved the highest accuracy with the lowest prediction variability in its 512-neuron layer architecture, as presented in Table 2. It is worth noting that despite the fact that the examined dataset is highly imbalanced, the convolutional layers of the DenseNet architecture learned an invariance feature representation that was highly transferable to the examined study's

**Table 2.** The performance of each deep model on the unseen testing sets based on the five-fold cross-validation methodology.

| Architecture | Accuracy | | | AUC (OvR) | | |
|---|---|---|---|---|---|---|
| Number of Neurons | 256 | 512 | 1024 | 256 | 512 | 1024 |
| DenseNet121 | 90.0 ± 2.7 | **90.3 ± 0.7** | 88.9 ± 2.2 | 99.3 ± 0.2 | **99.4 ± 0.5** | 98.9 ± 0.4 |
| Inception v3 | 89.6 ± 2.4 | 88.4 ± 1.7 | 85.5 ± 3.4 | 99.1 ± 0.3 | 99.3 ± 0.4 | 98.8 ± 0.5 |
| Inception Residual v2 | 88.7 ± 1.8 | 88.3 ± 1.5 | 87.4 ± 2.5 | 99.4 ± 0.2 | 99.4 ± 0.2 | 99.1 ± 0.4 |
| MobileNet v2 | 84.6 ± 1.8 | 85.3 ± 1.5 | 86.3 ± 0.7 | 99.0 ± 0.3 | 98.8 ± 0.3 | 98.7 ± 0.2 |
| NasNetm | 85.0 ± 3.5 | 86.3 ± 3.0 | 86.2 ± 3.3 | 98.6 ± 0.6 | 98.8 ± 0.7 | 98.7 ± 0.3 |
| ResNet50 | 68.8 ± 1.5 | 69.0 ± 1.8 | 71.0 ± 3.9 | 95.0 ± 0.9 | 94.7 ± 1.0 | 95.2 ± 0.9 |
| VGG16 | 87.5 ± 1.8 | 88.4 ± 3.0 | 86.1 ± 4.3 | 99.2 ± 0.2 | 99.2 ± 0.2 | 99.0 ± 0.4 |
| Xception | 89.5 ± 2.0 | 89.2 ± 1.4 | 88.7 ± 2.7 | 99.2 ± 0.1 | 98.9 ± 0.6 | 99.1 ± 0.4 |

domain. In contrast, the rest of the architectures' most common misclassification classes were those with the least representation in the dataset, as presented in the confusion matrix of the ResNet in Fig. 5b.

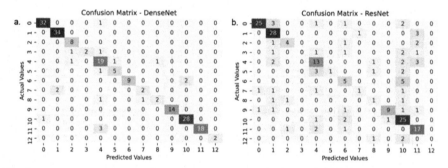

**Fig. 5.** Confusion matrices of the best- (a) versus the worst-case convergence (b) model. The class numbers represent: 0. Ancient amphitheater, 1. Ancient temple, 2. Byzantine architecture, 3. Greek urban landscape, 4. Village (island), 5. Old port, 6. Olive grove, 7. Ancient ruins, 8. Traditional greek architecture, 9. Traditional stone bridge, 10. Vineyard, 11. Windmill, 12. Saltpan.

The transferability of the DensetNet layers was superb, especially when compared to the poorly converged ResNet. For the latter architecture, the validation loss remained very high (Fig. 6e), greater than 1 during the training phase, which explains the very low prediction accuracy on the unseen testing set. Figure 6 also highlights the impact of the pre-trained weights in the proposed DL model, since the convergence of these models is performed in just a few epochs despite the size-limited LoockMe dataset. The low performance of some classes (Fig. 5. Classes: 3, 7, 8) can be attributed to the very low sample size per class and the visual similarities with other classes. In particular, the class "Greek urban landscape" is miscategorized as "Byzantine architecture" and "village (island)". This is because the background in some samples of "Byzantine architecture" is often a Greek city, for instance when a church is depicted. Similarly, "ancient ruins" are classified as "ancient amphitheater", and "Ttraditional Greek architecture", which mostly consists of old stone buildings, as "ancient ruins" or "village (island)". Nevertheless, despite the superior performance of the DenseNet-based models, it is clear that there is room for an even better convergence with a lower loss than the one that was achieved (loss of 0.27), as seen in the learning curves in Fig. 6d. This will be addressed by integrating retraining routines in LoockMe that will alleviate any data drifting issues during the platform's life cycle.

**Natural Language Processing Service.** The NLP service and pipelines were developed and refined through continuous evaluation and validation, including rigorous testing on two separate validation sets pro-vided by field experts coming the Greek National Centre of Audiovisual Media and Communication (EKOME) and a private production company. In addition, the processes were designed to generalize well beyond the specific da-ta used in the validation sets, with the goal of creating an NLP service that can effectively process natural language input in real-world scenarios. The overall effective-ness of the NLP service on the validation sets have a total of 88% accuracy.

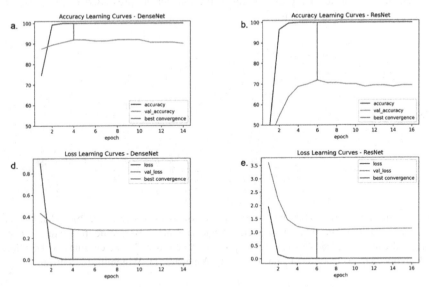

**Fig. 6.** Two types of learning curves are presented based on: a) accuracy (top), and b) loss (bottom). The convergence of the high performing DenseNet (a, d) is compared to the poorly fitted ResNet (d, e).

# 4 Discussion

The present study introduced an artificial intelligence (AI) platform that integrates DL image analysis and NLP processing to label raw input data for location scouting in Greece. The LoockMe platform is aiming to automate and streamline the process of identifying potential locations for film production companies by analyzing large volumes of raw data, including images and text descriptions, and extracting relevant information about the location. LoockMe offers several benefits, such as accurate image classification, time-, and cost-effective location scouting.

One of the main advantages of the platform is its ability to accurately identify locations that may meet the specific requirements of film production companies. This was achieved through the use of DL models, which can analyze unseen images and extract relevant information with high accuracy. LoockMe can lead to time and cost effectiveness as it automates the process of identifying potential locations, which will save resources for film production companies. This will allow them to focus on other more creative and demanding aspects of the production process. Additionally, LoockMe can alleviate the drawbacks of filming in a foreign country, where language and cultural barriers may require additional resources. By adapting text descriptions and collecting a custom imaging dataset of locations in Greece, the proposed DL model was able to identify key features and characteristics of the locations, such as sites of historical and cultural significance.

The proposed infrastructure automates the process of identifying potential locations by using production terminology. In particular, the use of AI reduces the need for manual labor, which can be costly. Therefore, the LoockMe platform offers a cost-effective solution for location scouting in Greece, allowing filmmakers to identify suitable locations without having to hire large teams of expert scouts.

One of the few limiting factors of LoockMe is that the prediction accuracy of the platform depends on the quality of the data being used. If the data is of low quality, the platform may not be able to accurately identify suitable locations. Therefore, mechanisms for retraining and fine-tuning current versions of the models will be integrated and will be triggered based on the presence of new data on the platform. Additionally, limitations in understanding local languages and dialects could lead to errors in the analysis of text descriptions and, therefore, the annotation of imaging data. The models, such as Places365, that were developed with open datasets may not be able to fully capture the cultural differences of Greek architecture and cityscapes that could affect the suitability of a location for film production.

In future iterations of LoockMe, the DL analysis module should be expanded to give a comprehensive and accurate understanding of the locations and multiple landmarks in an image that are being considered. This would help filmmakers make better decisions about possible locations.

# 5 Conclusion

The use of an artificial intelligence platform that integrates DL image analysis and natural language processing for location scouting in Greece offers significant benefits such as accuracy, time-savings, cost effectiveness, and a comprehensive understanding of the locations being considered. Overall, the platform fulfills an important unmet need in Greece, and offers a user-friendly solution for location scouting in Greece.

**Authors' Contributions.** E.T. conceived and designed the DL image analyses of the study. V.A, V.C.P., and Y.G. conceived and designed the NLP part of the study. E.T. and N.O contributed to the image collection. I.S. deployed the imaging module on the LoockMe platform. E.T., V.A, V.C.P., and Y.G contributed to the performed analysis, and drafted the manuscript. E.T., V.A, V.C.P., Y.G., D.I.F., M.T. and K.M. contributed to the literature research, interpretation of data and revised the manuscript. Y.G., D.I.F., and M.T. contributed to the critical revision of the paper. K.M. contributed to the critical revision of the paper and was the guarantor of the integrity of the entire study. All authors have read and agreed to the published version of the manuscript.

**Funding.** This research has been co-financed by the European Regional Development Fund of the European Union and Greek national funds through the Operational Program Competitiveness, Entrepreneurship and Innovation, under the call "RESEARCH – CREATE – INNOVATE (project code:T2EDK-1346)".

# References

1. Kim, J., Kang, Y.: Automatic classification of photos by tourist attractions using deep learning model and image feature vector clustering. ISPRS Int. J. Geo-Inf. **11**, 245 (2022)
2. D'Haro, L.F., Banchs, R.E., Leong, C.K., Daven, L.G.M., Yuan, N.T.: Automatic labelling of touristic pictures using CNNs and metadata information. In: 2017 IEEE 2nd International Conference on Signal Image Process, pp. 292–296. IEEE (2017)
3. Hettiarachchi, D., Kamijo, S.: Visual and location information fusion for hierarchical place recognition. In: 2022 IEEE International Conference on Consumer Electronics, pp. 1–6. IEEE (2022)
4. Neves, M., Ševa, J.: An extensive review of tools for manual annotation of documents. Brief Bioinform. **22**, 146–163 (2021)
5. Meddeb, A., Ben, R.L.: Using topic modeling and word embedding for topic extraction in Twitter. Procedia Comput. Sci. **207**, 790–799 (2022)
6. Saffar, A.H., Mann, T.K., Ofoghi, B.: Textual emotion detection in health: advances and applications. J. Biomed. Inform. **137**, 104258 (2023)
7. Techwithtim: Image Scraper and Downloader (2021). https://github.com/techwithtim/Image-Scraper-And-Downloader/blob/main/tutorial.py. Accessed 15 Feb 2023
8. Deng, J., Dong, W., Socher, R., Li, L.-J., Li, K., Fei-Fei, L.: ImageNet: a large-scale hierarchical image database. In: CVPR 2009 (2009)
9. Trivizakis, E., et al.: Advancing Covid-19 differentiation with a robust preprocessing and integration of multi-institutional open-repository computer tomography datasets for deep learning analysis. Exp. Ther. Med. **20**, 1 (2020)
10. Ioannidis, G.S., Trivizakis, E., Metzakis, I., Papagiannakis, S., Lagoudaki, E., Marias, K.: Pathomics and deep learning classification of a heterogeneous fluorescence histology image dataset. Appl. Sci. **11**, 3796 (2021)
11. Trivizakis, E., Souglakos, I., Karantanas, A.H., Marias, K.: Deep radiotranscriptomics of non-small cell lung carcinoma for assessing molecular and histology subtypes with a data-driven analysis. Diagnostics **11**, 1–15 (2021)
12. Simonyan, K., Zisserman, A.: Very deep convolutional networks for large-scale image recognition. arXiv Prepr. arXiv:1409.1556 (2014)

13. Szegedy, C., Vanhoucke, V., Ioffe, S., Shlens, J., Wojna, Z.: Rethinking the inception architecture for computer vision. In: Proceedings of the IEEE Computer Society Conference on Computer Vision and Pattern Recognition, pp. 2818–2826. IEEE Computer Society (2016)

14. Chollet, F.: Xception: deep learning with depthwise separable convolutions. In: Proceedings of the 30th IEEE Conference on Computer Vision and Pattern Recognition, CVPR 2017, pp 1800–1807. Institute of Electrical and Electronics Engineers Inc. (2017)

15. He, K., Zhang, X., Ren, S., Sun, J.: Deep residual learning for image recognition. In: Proceedings of the IEEE Conference on Computer Vision and Pattern Recognition, pp 770–778. IEEE Computer Society (2016)

16. Zoph, B., Vasudevan, V., Shlens, J., Le, Q.V.: Learning transferable architectures for scalable image recognition. arXiv Prepr. arXiv:1707.07012 (2017)

17. Howard, A.G., et al.: MobileNets: efficient convolutional neural networks for mobile vision applications. arXiv Prepr. arXiv:1704.04861 (2017)

18. Huang, G., Liu, Z., van der Maaten, L., Weinberger, K.Q.: Densely connected convolutional networks. arXiv Prepr. arXiv:1608.06993 (2016)

19. Chollet, F., et al.: Keras (2015). https://keras.io

20. Tokyo Location Box. In: Tokyo Film Commission. https://www.locationbox.metro.tokyo.lg.jp/english/. Accessed 1 Feb 2020

21. Barcelona Film Commission. In: Dep. Cult. https://www.bcncatfilmcommission.com/en. Accessed 1 Feb 2020

22. Film LA. https://filmla.com/. Accessed 1 Feb 2020

23. Places365. In: MIT CSAIL Computer Vision. https://github.com/CSAILVision/places365. Accessed 14 Sept 2022

24. Zhou, B., Lapedriza, A., Khosla, A., Oliva, A., Torralba, A.: Places: a 10 million image database for scene recognition. IEEE Trans. Pattern Anal. Mach. Intell. **40**, 1452–1464 (2018)

# Object Detection for Functional Assessment Applications

Alessandro Melino-Carrero(✉) , Álvaro Nieva Suárez ,
Cristina Losada-Gutierrez , Marta Marron-Romera ,
Irene Guardiola Luna , and Javier Baeza-Mas

Universidad de Alcalá, Department of Electronics, Edificio Politécnico, Ctra.
Madrid-Barcelona Km 33,600, 28805 Alcalá de Henares, Spain
alessandro.melino@uah.es

**Abstract.** This paper presents a proposal for object detection as a first stage for the analysis of Human-Object Interaction (HOI) in the context of automated functional assessment. The proposed system is based in a two-step strategy, thus, in the first stage there are detected the people in the scene, as well as large objects (table, chairs, etc.) using a pre-trained YOLOv8. Then, there is defined a ROI around each person that is processed using a custom YOLO to detect small elements (forks, plates, spoons, etc.). Since there are no large image datasets that include all the objects of interest, there has also been compiled a new dataset including images from different sets, and improving the available labels. The proposal has been evaluated in the novel dataset, and in different images acquired in the area in which the functional assessment is performed, obtaining promising results.

**Keywords:** Image processing · Object detection · Occupational therapy · Functional assessment · Human-Object Interaction

## 1 Introduction

In the field of occupational therapy, there is a branch of study in which patients are evaluated according to criteria related to the quality with which certain types of actions are carried out. These actions are household chores or daily routines with which the patients are familiarized, hence, they are used to perform them, easing the execution of the tasks. The specialists are responsible of evaluate these tasks using prompts or truth tables, with which the quality of the actions is quantitatively set, to get a functional assessment. They do this just by observing the patients, without any supporting tool to automate the procedure.

One of the methods used for this objective is called AMPS (Assessment of Motor and Process Skills) [9]. The AMPS is a tool that allows a thorough and unbiased evaluation of an individual's ability to perform Activities of Daily

L. Iliadis et al. (Eds.): EANN 2023, CCIS 1826, pp. 328–339, 2023.
https://doi.org/10.1007/978-3-031-34204-2_28

Living (ADLs) in real-life situations. It includes over 125 tasks that can be done in different settings and with varying levels of difficulty, ranging from simple self-care tasks to more complex ones in various environments such as at home, supermarkets or parks.

In physiotherapy, professionals use the clinical assessment of the degree of functional limitation of individuals through automated analysis of the performance of ADLs. However, the evaluation of the performance of these ADLs can be subjective and strongly depends on the person who is doing the evaluation.

During the execution of the ADLs, one of the evaluated aspects are the interactions of the patients with different objects, determining if the chosen objects are correct or not, if the patient pick it up adequately, etc. It this context, this paper is focused on the detection and classification of Human-Object Interaction (HOI) as a part of a system for automatic functional assessment from image sequences, in which HOI analysis consist on finding people and things and recognizing the intricate relationships between them [16].

Due to the characteristic of the analyzed ADLs, the proposed system must be able to detect the different involved objects such as: tables, chairs, cupboards, forks, clothes, etc. that can be very small in the images. Furthermore, the system must be non-intrusive, preventing the execution of the actions from being affected, thus the cameras are located in fixed positions in the environment.

There are numerous works related to HOI in different contexts, what can be divided into sequential and parallel approaches [17,25]. The sequential methods first detect the object in the scene and then analyze the interactions, whereas the parallel ones detect interactions directly from image sequences. In the sequential approaches, interactions can be detected by appearance [11] or using graphs [23,24] and connecting them by context, relationships or structural information.

In [5] the authors use RGBD-HOI descriptors to evaluate ADLs, however, the camera is located in front of the patients, what can be intrusive and modify they behaviour. There also exist some datasets with different ADLs such us Toyota Smarthome [7], but it does not include the ADLs of interest.

Due to the characteristics of the objects and interactions, the proposed system is sequential, and it is divided into different steps as it can be seen in the general block diagram in Fig. 1.

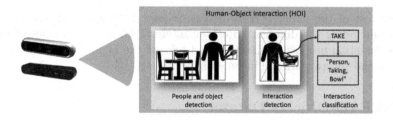

**Fig. 1.** General block diagram of the Human-Object Interaction proposal.

The first module consists of detecting people and the objects with which they may interact. Then, the second one searches for possible connections between the person and the detected objects and generates an association that links them. Finally, the last module analyzes the context of the scene and the connections to classify the interactions and obtain the final output.

This work is develop under the EYEFUL project [1], that aims to develop a methodology to design, implement and evaluate automated clinical tests of functional limitations, which give objective assessments with clinical validity, and eliminate the interference in test performance caused by the physical presence of the assessor. Furthermore, the subjectivity of the human assessor will be replaced by an automatic system that extracts multisensory information from the environment during the functional assessment of the user.

The set up for the EYEFUL project is installed in a simulated apartment located in the Rey Juan Carlos University (URJC), distributed as shown in Fig. 2). It includes a living room, a kitchen, a bathroom and a bedroom, but the chosen ADLs take place in the kitchen and the bedroom. Besides, there are different cameras Stereolabs Zed 2i [4] and Intel Realsense D455 [3] located in the environment as shown in Fig. 2.

**Fig. 2.** URJC apartment map.

The rest of the paper is organized as follows: Sect. 2 present the collected dataset including the different objects of interest. Then, Sect. 3.1 describes the object detection proposal. Finally, Sect. 4 present the main results and the conclusions and future work are included in Sect. 5.

## 2    GEFAD-Objects Dataset

For this paper, we have compiled images and annotations from some existing datasets to get enough quantity of instances for fine-tuning a model to the objects needed for the applications of interest. We have named this compilation as Geintra Functional Assessment Dataset - Objects (GEFAD-Objects). Below, there are described the analyzed Datasets.

- **Microsoft COCO** [18]. Common Objects in Context is a dataset created with the goal of advance in the object recognition task in the context of the scene. It gathers images of everyday scenes in their natural context. It accumulates a total of 91 object classes, with 2.5 million instances labelled in 328k images. This dataset includes image classification, object detection and semantic segmentation. The dataset is interesting for this work because it includes almost every kitchen object under study (bowl, chair, wine glass, knife, spoon, fork and table). COCO provides the labels in JSON format (based on dictionaries), the same chosen for the GEFAD-Objects dataset.
- **ImageNet** [8]. It is the very first large-scale image ontology published in 2009 and based on the WordNet framework. It provides approximately from 500 to 1000 images for the synsets in WordNet. At the beginning, it included 5247 synsets and 3.2 million images, but now it provides 14,197,122 images and 21841 synsets indexed [2]. Despite the number of images and synsets, from ImageNet it has not been possible to get more than 1000 instances for every object (except for the class "chair"). The format in which the labels are present is XML so it require a conversion.
- **Open Images** [15]. It includes 1.9 million and over these images, it provides more than 15 million bounding boxes that are each assigned to 600 different item categories, with unified annotations for image classification, object detection and visual relationship detection. It is noteworthy that this dataset annotates visual relationships between them, which support visual relationship detection. This dataset is very complete and provides a lot of instances for our purpose, mainly for the classes of chair and table, but it is not so useful for other less common categories. Labels are provided in CSV format.
- **LVIS** [12]. It is a Large Vocabulary Instance Segmentation dataset published in 2019, able to recognize more than 1000 object categories. LVIS has emphasized learning from few examples, but it presents over 2 million instances in 164k images. The objects are segmented with high-quality masks, but it also includes the labels of the bounding boxes. Besides, this dataset also uses the JSON format.
- **Epic-kitchens** [6]. This is a first-person point of view dataset, consisting of videos recorded by 32 participants doing kitchen chores. It includes 55 h of video, divided into 11.5M frames, where 454.3K object bounding boxes are labelled. Although the characteristics of this dataset can be interesting for this work, the labels were incorrect, so it has been discarded.

Table 1, summarizes the classes that appear in each dataset. It is work highlighting that, all datasets are open source within Creative Commons Attribution license.

**Table 1.** Classes present in each of the used datasets.

| Object | COCO | ImageNet | OpenImages | LVIS |
|--------|------|----------|------------|------|
| Plates |      | X        | X          | X    |
| Fork   | X    | X        | X          | X    |
| Glass  | X    | X        |            | X    |
| Knife  | X    | X        | X          | X    |
| Shoe   |      | X        |            | X    |
| Spoon  | X    | X        | X          | X    |

Since there were detected some problems in the annotations of the collected datasets, such as not including the label "person", a label propagation algorithms has been used to avoid problems.

To do that, all the chosen images were classified using a pre-trained neural network. The obtained results were compared to the available labels by computing the intersection over union (IoU). This procedure allows adding between the annotations obtained. After doing this, there were added more than 40k new instances to the dataset (taking into account "person").

Once all datasets are collected, the labels are transformed into JSON format to standardize them and ease the process of managing the data. In summary, GEFAD-Objects dataset includes the categories shown in Table 2, where there is also shown the number of instances and the percentage of labels belonging to each class.

**Table 2.** List of categories in GEFAD-Objects dataset.

| Category | Id | Number of instances | Percentage |
|----------|-----|--------------------|-----------|
| Plates   | 0   | 34083              | 32.1%     |
| Fork     | 1   | 10513              | 9.9%      |
| Glass    | 2   | 25675              | 24.2%     |
| Knife    | 3   | 13947              | 13.1%     |
| Shoe     | 4   | 11354              | 10.7%     |
| Spoon    | 5   | 10708              | 10.1%     |
| Total    | –   | 106280             | 100%      |

# 3    Object Detection for Functional Assessment Evaluation

The object detection module requires detecting several specific objects involved in the analyzed ADLs, such as the kitchen objects (plates, glasses, cutlery, etc.) or the bedroom ones (underwear, shoes, socks, etc.), as well as other more common elements as people, chairs or tables.

Most of the available pre-trained models are able to detect the common elements, however there have problems detecting specific objects, specially if there are small in the image (such as the kitchen objects), so it is needed to adapt the model for detecting the objects involved in the analyzed ADLs, using the collected dataset described in Sect. 2 as described below. Furthermore, some elements such as the tablecloth and napkins, can not be detected using these networks, thus, there has been proposed an approach for detecting these elements based on their color.

## 3.1    Object Detection by Pattern

There are numerous approaches for object detection based on neural networks, that can include one or two stages. One-stage models, such as You Only Look Once (YOLO) [20,21] and Single Shot Detector (SSD) [19], search in a single step for both candidate regions containing objects and the classes and coordinates of the objects. Two-stages models first identify candidate regions to contain objects, and then refine the location and identification of object classes in the second step, i.e. Fast RCNN [10], Faster RCNN [22] or Mask RCNN [13].

In this work, there is used YOLO, due to its high accuracy with a low computation time. Specifically, it is used YOLO v8 [14]. However, this YOLO architecture present a lack of detections of small objects, due to the input image sizes used for training the network. To avoid these problem, after detecting people and common elements with a pretrained YOLO, a region of interest (ROI) around each person is cropped and processed again, using a customized YOLOv8 to improve detection of small objects, as shown in Fig. 3. Furthermore, the second stage has been fine-tunned including the objects of interest.

To get better training results, it is recommended to use at least 1500 images and 10000 instances per class, as well as to include background images, which are images with no objects of the dataset. Image variety and label consistency, accuracy and verification are also recommended.

The base neural network is a light version YOLOv8s to avoid overfitting due to the reduced size of the dataset.

We found that the higher is the number of epochs for training, the networks obtains better metrics, but qualitatively, the results obtained in our images are not improving. In Table 3 there are presented the training metrics after 100 and 500 epochs.

## 3.2    Object Detection by Colour

As commented before, some objects can not be detected with AI methods, because they are difficult to differentiate using characteristics related to shape

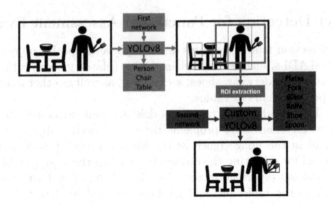

**Fig. 3.** Representation of the levels object detection for the functional assessment context.

**Table 3.** Metrics of YOLOv8 after fine-tuning with GEFAD-Objects.

| Epochs | Precision | Recall | mAP50 | mAP50-95 |
|---|---|---|---|---|
| 100 | 0.76435 | 0.52489 | 0.60366 | 0.44413 |
| 500 | 0.85721 | 0.59349 | 0.6801 | 0.52387 |

or size, specially with fabrics, such as napkins, tablecloth and socks. In these cases, the classification is based on color, since the evaluation is carried out in a controlled environments, and the colors of the different elements are known.

The classification is carried out in the HSV colour space, since it is possible to delimit the colours by its hue. For example, in Fig. 4, there must be detected the tablecloth (green) and the napkins (pink), that can be segmented in the HSV colour spectre shown in Fig. 5.

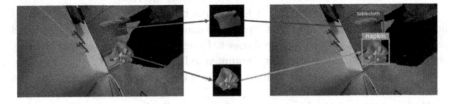

**Fig. 4.** Object detection differentiating by colours (Color figure online).

This allows detecting objects that the Deep Neural Networks (DNN) can not obtain.

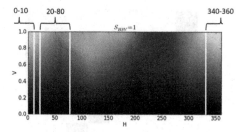

**Fig. 5.** Segmentation of the HSV colour space.

## 4    Experimental Results

This section presents the results obtained with the proposal for object detection with two stages shown in Fig. 3, and with the colour classification.

As it has been explained in Sect. 3, first there are detected the common objects (table, chairs) and people using YOLOv8. These objects can be detected with high accuracy. An example of the obtained detections in an image acquired in the URJC apartment is shown in Fig. 6.

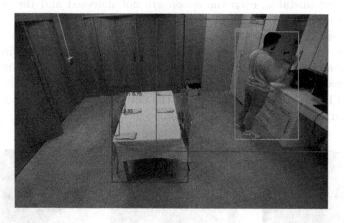

**Fig. 6.** First stage detections. People in green, chairs in red and tables in blue (Color figure online).

In the second stage, there is only analyzed a ROI centered in the detection of the person (purple point), with a $640 \times 480$ pixels shape (purple rectangle), and it has been trained for detecting only the objects of interest.

The confusion matrix of this model is shown in Fig. 7. Here it is possible to check that the plates is the category which the model best performance, but the correlation between "the predicted background" and the true positives is high. This fact means that the objects are not being detected, so they are false negatives.

In spite of the confusion matrix obtained, the metrics related to train and validation loss and precision are good and they improve every epoch.

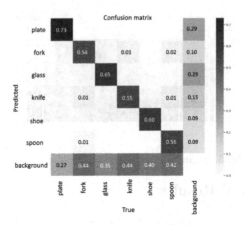

**Fig. 7.** YOLOv8 confusion matrix fine-tuned with GEFAD-Objects (500 epochs).

However, we test the network in real environments and the results are shown in Fig. 8. In the confusion matrix, the diagonal is very highlighted and the metrics are acceptable, so theoretically we have to receive relative good results.

We get some detections for every object, but they have low confidence, being imprecise and unstable, even the spoon are not detected and the network is confusing the spoons with the plates.

These results are due to the quality and the perspective of the images of the dataset. We noticed that most of the images are taken with a first person point of view, that hence, differ from the one of interest. Trying the model in a complex image with such characteristics gives the result shown in Fig. 9.

Finally, in Fig. 10 there is presented the detection of the napkin, which has green colour, applying the method explained in the Sect. 3.2.

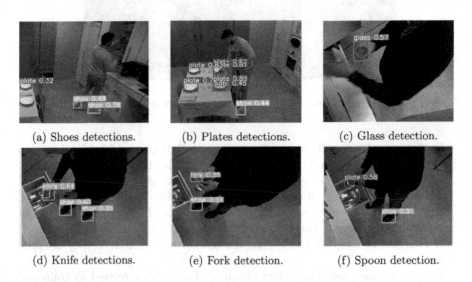

| (a) Shoes detections. | (b) Plates detections. | (c) Glass detection. |
| (d) Knife detections. | (e) Fork detection. | (f) Spoon detection. |

**Fig. 8.** Results of the second stage of the object detector.

**Fig. 9.** Detections of YOLOv8-GEFAD-Objects with a better point of view.

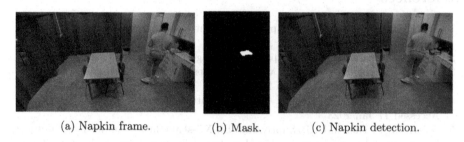

(a) Napkin frame.          (b) Mask.          (c) Napkin detection.

**Fig. 10.** Results of the detection by colour extraction.

## 5    Conclusions and Future Works

This paper presents the work developed with the projection of detecting and classifying Human Object Interactions (HOIs) in controlled scenes, where physiotherapists evaluate Activities of Daily Living (ADLs), and it is focused on the objects detection stage.

Since there are not large image datasets including all the objects involved in the analyzed ADLs, there has been compiled a dataset named GEFAD-Objects, including images for different available dataset, and adapting their labels to JSON format.

There has also been proposed a two-step approach for detecting the objects that the person in the scene may interact with. In the first stage, there are detected chairs, tables and people with a YOLOv8 trained with COCO. Then, there is cropped a ROI of size $640 \times 480$ pixels that is used as input in the second stage. This stage is based on a YOLOv8 model trained with GEFAD-Objects dataset that allows detecting other objects of interest (shoe, plate, glass, knife, spoon and fork).

Furthermore, a color based detector has also been proposed for those elements that can not be detected by the neural network, such as the tablecloth or napkins.

The detected objects, will be used for HOI analysis in a future work, focused on the functional assessment environment.

With this work, we set the structure of a HOI detector, but some aspect must be improved, in order to allow it obtaining enough accuracy with the point of view of the cameras in the URJC apartment. Furthermore, also the color classification algorithm can help to improve the object detection results, since different elements have different colors.

**Acknowledgements.** This work has been partially supported by the Spanish Ministry of Science and Innovation MICINN/AEI/10.13039/501100011033 under projects EYEFUL-UAH (PID2020-113118RB-C31) and ATHENA (PID2020-115995RB-I00), by CAM under project CONCORDIA (CM/JIN/2021-015), and by UAH under projects ARGOS+ (PIUAH21/IA-016) and METIS (PIUAH22/IA-037).

# References

1. Eyeful project webpage. https://www.geintra-uah.org/eyeful/es/informaci'on. Accessed 9 Jan 2023

2. ImageNet dataset webpage. https://www.image-net.org/. Accessed 2 Feb 2023

3. Intel RealSense D455 camera webpage. https://www.intelrealsense.com/depth-camera-d455/. Accessed 17 Jan 2023

4. Stereolabs: ZED 2i camera webpage. https://www.stereolabs.com/zed-2i/. Accessed 17 Jan 2023

5. As'ari, M.A., Sheikh, U.U., Supriyanto, E.: XZ-shape histogram for human-object interaction activity recognition based on kinect-like depth image. WSEAS Trans. Sig. Process. Arch. **10**, 382–391 (2014)

6. Damen, D., et al.: Scaling egocentric vision: the dataset. In: Ferrari, V., Hebert, M., Sminchisescu, C., Weiss, Y. (eds.) ECCV 2018. LNCS, vol. 11208, pp. 753–771. Springer, Cham (2018). https://doi.org/10.1007/978-3-030-01225-0_44

7. Das, S., et al.: Toyota smarthome: real-world activities of daily living. In: Proceedings of the IEEE/CVF International Conference on Computer Vision, pp. 833–842 (2019)

8. Deng, J., Dong, W., Socher, R., Li, L.J., Li, K., Fei-Fei, L.: ImageNet: a large-scale hierarchical image database. In: 2009 IEEE Conference on Computer Vision and Pattern Recognition, pp. 248–255. IEEE (2009)

9. Fisher, A.G., Jones, K.B.: Assessment of Motor and Process Skills: Development, Standardization, and Administration Manual. Three Star Press, Incorporated (2001)

10. Girshick, R.: Fast R-CNN. In: Proceedings of the IEEE International Conference on Computer Vision, pp. 1440–1448 (2015)

11. Gkioxari, G., Girshick, R., Dollár, P., He, K.: Detecting and recognizing human-object interactions. In: Proceedings of the IEEE Conference on Computer Vision and Pattern Recognition, pp. 8359–8367 (2018)

12. Gupta, A., Dollar, P., Girshick, R.: LVIS: a dataset for large vocabulary instance segmentation. In: Proceedings of the IEEE Conference on Computer Vision and Pattern Recognition (2019)

13. He, K., Gkioxari, G., Dollár, P., Girshick, R.: Mask R-CNN. In: Proceedings of the IEEE International Conference on Computer Vision, pp. 2961–2969 (2017)

14. Jocher, G., Chaurasia, A., Qiu, J.: YOLO by Ultralytics, January 2023. https://github.com/ultralytics/ultralytics

15. Kuznetsova, A., et al.: The Open Images Dataset V4: unified image classification, object detection, and visual relationship detection at scale. Int. J. Comput. Vis. **128**(7), 1956–1981 (2020)

16. Li, F., Wang, S., Wang, S., Zhang, L.: Human-object interaction detection: a survey of deep learning-based methods. In: Fang, L., Povey, D., Zhai, G., Mei, T., Wang, R. (eds.) Artificial Intelligence. CICAI 2022. Lecture Notes in Computer Science, vol. 13604. Springer, Cham (2022). https://doi.org/10.1007/978-3-031-20497-5_36

17. Liao, Y., Liu, S., Wang, F., Chen, Y., Qian, C., Feng, J.: PPDM: parallel point detection and matching for real-time human-object interaction detection. In: Proceedings of the IEEE/CVF Conference on Computer Vision and Pattern Recognition, pp. 482–490 (2020)

18. Lin, T.-Y., et al.: Microsoft COCO: common objects in context. In: Fleet, D., Pajdla, T., Schiele, B., Tuytelaars, T. (eds.) ECCV 2014. LNCS, vol. 8693, pp. 740–755. Springer, Cham (2014). https://doi.org/10.1007/978-3-319-10602-1_48

19. Liu, W., et al.: SSD: single shot multibox detector. In: Leibe, B., Matas, J., Sebe, N., Welling, M. (eds.) ECCV 2016. LNCS, vol. 9905, pp. 21–37. Springer, Cham (2016). https://doi.org/10.1007/978-3-319-46448-0_2

20. Redmon, J., Divvala, S., Girshick, R., Farhadi, A.: You only look once: unified, real-time object detection. In: Proceedings of the IEEE Conference on Computer Vision and Pattern Recognition, pp. 779–788 (2016)

21. Redmon, J., Farhadi, A.: YOLO9000: better, faster, stronger. In: 2017 IEEE Conference on Computer Vision and Pattern Recognition (CVPR), pp. 6517–6525 (2017)

22. Ren, S., He, K., Girshick, R., Sun, J.: Faster R-CNN: towards real-time object detection with region proposal networks. In: Advances in Neural Information Processing Systems, vol. 28 (2015)

23. Ulutan, O., Iftekhar, A., Manjunath, B.S.: VSGNet: spatial attention network for detecting human object interactions using graph convolutions. In: Proceedings of the IEEE/CVF Conference on Computer Vision and Pattern Recognition, pp. 13617–13626 (2020)

24. Wang, H., Zheng, W., Yingbiao, L.: Contextual heterogeneous graph network for human-object interaction detection. In: Vedaldi, A., Bischof, H., Brox, T., Frahm, J.-M. (eds.) ECCV 2020. LNCS, vol. 12362, pp. 248–264. Springer, Cham (2020). https://doi.org/10.1007/978-3-030-58520-4_15

25. Wang, T., Yang, T., Danelljan, M., Khan, F.S., Zhang, X., Sun, J.: Learning human-object interaction detection using interaction points. In: Proceedings of the IEEE/CVF Conference on Computer Vision and Pattern Recognition, pp. 4116–4125 (2020)

# Performance Analysis of Digit Recognizer Using Various Machine Learning Algorithms

Lakshmi Alekya Chittem, Doina Logofatu[✉], and Sheikh Sharfuddin Mim

Frankfurt University of Applied Sciences, Frankfurt am Main, Germany
{lakshmi.chittem,smim}@stud.fra-uas.de, logofatu@fb2.fra-uas.de

**Abstract.** In the field of pattern recognition, researchers are trying to figure out how to make a machine that can accurately recognize and predict handwritten digits. The problem falls into the category of object detection and multi-class classification. Several machine learning (ML) algorithms have been used and optimized to achieve effective prediction results for digit recognition. A generic research question that comes up in this context is the usage of specific ML algorithms for performing this task. The purpose of this work is to build efficient deep learning (DL) algorithms to recognize digits and compare their performance with that of conventional ML algorithms. Two of the most common DL algorithms, convolutional neural network (CNN) and multilayer perceptron (MLP) or artificial neural network (ANN), are used here. A widely used conventional ML algorithm, Support Vector Machine (SVM), which usually provides robust performance in general classification tasks, is also used. The performance of these algorithms is compared and analyzed based on accuracy and test results. The MNIST dataset from Kaggle's Digit Recognizer competition is used here for training and testing the model. A graphical user interface (GUI) is constructed, in which the implemented ML model can be used to predict real-time user input of handwritten digits.

**Keywords:** Pattern Recognition · Object Detection · Classification · Supervised Machine Learning · Digit Recognition · Deep Learning (DL) · Convolutional Neural Network (CNN) · Multilayer Perceptron (MLP) · Support Vector Machine (SVM) · MNIST Dataset · Graphical User Interface (GUI) · Performance Analysis

## 1 Introduction

Handwriting-digit recognition is when a computer can read the numbers that a person writes by hand. As we know, these handwritten digits are not always so legible and can be written in many different styles, so it will be a hard task to make the machine recognize them [1]. Handwriting recognition and optical character recognition (OCR) can be done with a number of programs and technologies that are available right now. Digit recognition is a subset of the handwritten text identification problem. It encompasses a variety of image processing, computer vision, and ML approaches. One of the key difficulties associated with digit recognition is that different users write the digits with a varying degree of difference in shape, size, and orientation of the digits. Hence, it is essential to extrapolate appropriate image processing and computer vision techniques in effect so that the handwritten digit images can be converted to an appropriate pixel format and subsequently to a time series dataset [2]. In this project, the main emphasis would be given to the already-recorded MNIST dataset of handwritten data. One of the primary objectives of this project would be to apply appropriate classification problems to a few of the conventional and wisely used ML algorithms and assess relevant performance metrics for each one of them. The following ML algorithms would be used for the classification tasks: convolutional neural network (CNN), multilayer perceptrons (MLP), and support vector machine (SVM). Implementing highly optimized classifier models based on each of the ML algorithms and comparing their accuracy scores are the fundamental objectives of this project. An imperative task associated with this objective is to create an appropriate user interface where the handwritten data of the user can be provided as input. To accommodate this feature, a GUI is created through which users can provide digitally recorded handwritten data in the respective interface slab.

## 2    Related Work

Character recognition is a very good example of pattern recognition. An important research problem in this aspect is the problem of handwritten digit recognition. The ML algorithms can be applied to perform classification on the MNIST data available for digit recognition. The work by M. Jain et al. gives a detailed approach to handwritten digit recognition using a CNN [3]. In their work, 70000 handwritten images containing digits in the range of 0-9 from the MNIST database are used for building the classification model. The implementation is carried out using the Tensorflow library in a Python environment. An adaptive moment estimation (ADAM) was used for the optimization of the model. The CNN system validation accuracy of 99.16% was achieved for a particular MNIST dataset.

In this other paper by Saeed Al Mansoori [4], ANN was used to classify 5000 samples from the MNIST database in a way that was similar to the task above. A MLP neural network is made, which has 25 hidden neurons and can go through a maximum of 250 iterations. First, the geometric mean method was used, and then the cross-validation technique was used to find the best number of hidden neurons. Back propagation, which is based on gradient descent, is used to train 4000 samples from the MNIST database. The remaining 1000 samples were used for testing through the feed-forward algorithm.

Several conventional ML approaches have been used by various researchers. In the work by Hafiz Ahamed et al. [5], a very powerful classification technique called SVM is used. This method achieved a test accuracy of 97.8%.

# 3    Algorithms Overview

A brief overview of the theoretical ideas behind the ML models used in this project is discussed in this section.

## 3.1    Convolutional Neural Network (CNN)

A CNN is a deep learning algorithm that takes an image as input and assigns parameters like weight, bias, etc. to different parts of the image so that it can be distinguished from other images. The fundamental motivation to use CNN for handwritten digit image recognition comes from the fact that CNN is one of the most powerful ML techniques for image classification. The efficacy of CNN lies in the fact that it can successfully capture the spatial dependencies in an image through the application of particular filters. CNN learns the features automatically without mentioning them explicitly, and this way it can accurately extract the right and relevant features from the input vectors. The architecture of a convolutional network (Fig. 1) contains three types of layers: convolutional layer, pooling layer, and output layers [6, 7].

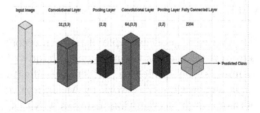

**Fig. 1.** Basic CNN architecture.

## 3.2    Multilayer Perceptron (MLP)

MLP is a type of ANN where neurons are grouped in layers and only forward connections exist. A typical MLP consists of an input layer followed by one or several hidden layers and output layers, including neurons, weights, and transfer functions [8]. Signals are usually transmitted in one direction throughout the network: from input to output without any loop. This architecture is called feedforward [9]. Each neuron (noted i) transforms the weighted sum (weight $w_{ij}$, bias $b_i$ of inputs $x_j$ into an output $y_i$ using a transfer or activation function (f). We can combine the output $y_i$ from all the neurons together and get the resultant output y as:

$$y = f(Wx + b) \tag{1}$$

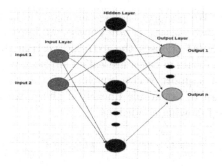

**Fig. 2.** MLP with one hidden layer.

If there is only one input layer and one output layer in the model above (Fig. 2), this is called a perceptron. MLP is composed of an input layer, at least one hidden layer, and an output layer. The calculations are the same as for a perceptron, but there are now more hidden layers to integrate before the output y is reached [9].

$$h^1 = f(W^1x + b^1) \tag{2}$$

$$y = f(W^2h^1 + b^2) \tag{3}$$

### 3.3 Support Vector Machine (SVM)

SVM comes under the category of supervise machine learning algorithms. It can be used for classification as well as regression problems, but it's widely used for classification. The primary goal of SVM is to identify the optimal hyperplane, which is the plane that is most distant from both classes (green and blue) (Fig. 3). This is achieved by identifying multiple hyperplanes that best classify the labels, then selecting the one that is most remote from the data points or has the maximum margin [10]. In this, we generally plot data items in n-dimensional space, where n is the number of features and a particular coordinate represents

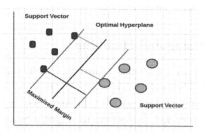

**Fig. 3.** Optimal Hyperplane using the SVM algorithm. (Color figure online)

the value of a feature. We perform the classification by finding the hyperplane that distinguishes the two classes. It will choose the hyperplane that separates the classes correctly. SVM chooses the extreme vectors that help in creating the hyperplane. These extreme cases are called support vectors, and hence the algorithm is termed a support vector machine [5]. A set of labeled training patterns like $(x_i, y_i)$ can be separable linearly if there exists a vector w and a scalar b such that the following conditions

$$wx_i + b \geq 1 \quad if \; y_i = 1 \tag{4}$$

$$wx_i + b \leq 1 \quad if \; y_i = -1 \tag{5}$$

are valid for all the elements contained in the training set. The optimal hyperplane that separates the training set with maximal margin can be expressed as:

$$w_0 x + b_0 = 0 \tag{6}$$

Since the goal is to increase the margin as much as possible, Hyperplane should be as far away from instances of both classes as possible. The SVM algorithm tries to construct a decision boundary in such a way that the separation between the classes becomes as wide as possible [5].

## 4    Implementation

This section contains the articulation of various steps to preprocess the data and implement as well as test the classifier model. The implementation is discussed in detail below.

### 4.1    Package Import

All algorithms are implemented in the Python programming language using the PyCharm IDE. CNN and MLP models are implemented using software libraries such as Tensorflow and Keras. SVM is implemented using the Scikit-Learn package in the Python language. Numpy, Pandas, and Matplotlib packages are used for data pre-processing and visualization.

### 4.2    Data Preprocessing and Handling

The dataset comes in two CSV files (source Kaggle [12]), which are training and testing data. The Python OS Library is used to load the dataset from the base folders. The first column of the dataset, which contains the labels, is removed. The training dataset is loaded in a pandas dataframe as a variable named 'train', and the testing dataset is the same in 'test'. To visualize the distribution of corresponding labels in our dataset, `matplotlib` function is used to plot a graphical representation as in Fig. 4.

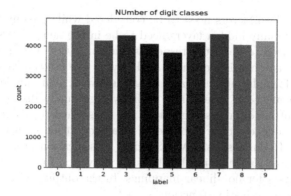

**Fig. 4.** Distribution of Digit Labels in Dataset.

**CNN.** The pixel values in the dataset are in the range of (0, 255). We normalize this data to the range of (0, 1) since this range is a good format for working with neural network models. This normalization is achieved by dividing the value of each pixel by 255 and converting it to a numpy array. The length of the array is 784 (28 × 28) pixels. To feed the data into the Keras model, this array is reshaped to have dimensions 28 × 28 × 1 (height × weight × channel). The additional dimension is used as 1 in the case of the greyscale channel. The training dataset is divided into a training set and a validation set with an 80% to 20% ratio.

**MLP.** Since ANN can process input in vector format, the training dataset is normalized to the range (0, 1) with a dimension of (42000, 7784) and stored in a variable X_train. Also, corresponding labels are created and stored in a variable, Y_train. The training and validation set is divided into 80% to 20% ratio.

**SVM** The training dataframe is normalized and stored in a variable called source, and the corresponding labels dataframe is stored in a variable 'target'. The scikit-learn train_test_split function is used to split the dataset into a training and validation set ratio of 75% to 25% ratio.

### 4.3 Model Creation

The ML model or architecture and the parameters that go with it can be set up based on what is needed.

**CNN Model.** Sequential and functional models can be constructed using Keras. When a simple stack of layers with precisely one input tensor and one output tensor is required, the sequential API model works best. Since the aforementioned factor satisfies our requirement, we used it in the construction of our CNN model. The activation function in the convolution is the Rectified Linear Unit (ReLU).

**MLP Model.** Two factors need to be considered while passing values in this parameter: how many hidden layers need to be in the neural network and how many neurons need to be in the respective hidden layers. The proposed neural network model here consists of three MLP layers. We use the Keras Sequential class here for formulating the basic neural network. This model in Keras is considered a sequence of layers, and each layer gradually distills the input to generate the output data. As suggested, the dense layer is a linear operation, and hence the sequence of the same would be a good fit for a linear functionality approximation. In our task, the MNIST digit classification problem is a highly non-linear process. Hence, using ReLU as an activation function performs best in the dense layers for non-linear mappings. In the output layer, a unit of size 10 with a softmax activation function is used.

**SVM Model.** The SVM algorithm is carried out by a kernel that changes a data space into the form that is needed. In our architecture, we apply the kernel trick to transform low-dimensional input space into a higher-dimensional space. In this way, it converts non-separable problems into separable problems, implying more dimensions. Radial Basis Function Kernel (RBF) is used in our architecture. Theoretically, RBF can map an input space in infinite dimensional space, as can be inferred from the equation below:

$$K(x, x_i) = e^{(-\gamma \sum (x - x_i^2))} \tag{7}$$

Here, $\gamma$ is the parameter that has the range of (0,1) [11]. In scikit-learn, the SVM model is built using the SVC function. The gamma parameter indicates how far the training reaches. C is a hyperparameter in SVM that controls error. Both C and gamma need to be set before training the model. In our architecture, C value has been set to 400, and gamma value is set to 'scale' mode.

### 4.4   Model Compilation, Evaluation and Optimization

Until a reasonable level of efficiency and accuracy is achieved, the model should be calibrated with hyperparameter tuning and model optimization as discussed below:

**CNN Model.** The following enhancements and model validation techniques have been used in our CNN model:

- **Data Augmentation:** To improve accuracy and prevent overfitting, we used the data augmentation technique, which generates data from existing samples by applying different transformation techniques to the original dataset. In the Keras package, this task is performed via the keras preprocessing ImageDataGenerator class. This increases the number of distinct samples as input images and allows the model to show better validation accuracy.

- **Optimization:** The RMSprop algorithm is used in Optimizer. The basic functionality of the algorithm is to maintain a moving (discounted) average of the square of gradients and divide the gradient by the root of this average. We used callback functionality to invoke a checkpoint so that when the learning process stops improving with the given parameters, it stops. This way, by setting a large number of epochs, we can make sure optimal results are obtained.
- **Model Fitting and Validation:** At first, the number of steps is defined by normalizing training length by batch size. The model is compiled with the defined optimizer and categorical cross-entropy as the loss function. The model is fitted with the determined parameters, like augmented functions, steps, callbacks, etc. For model evaluation, a prediction on the validation set is performed, and the same is checked with the highest probability scale. The predicted class is compared with actual values of the output, and validation accuracy is obtained. A confusion matrix with the predicted model and the actual model is constructed and plotted with relevant labels.

**MLP Model.** The following are used in our MLP model:

- **Loss Function:** Categorical cross entropy is used as the loss function since the nature of the classification is multi-class.
- **Optimizer:** Adam, an adaptive learning rate optimization, is used for weight optimization. It can automatically calibrate the amount to update and fine-tune parameters based on adaptive estimates of lower-order moments. As per the Sklearn guidelines, Adam works quite well with large datasets for training and validation.
- **Metrics:** In our model, during training, validation, and testing, the accuracy metric is used. Accuracy is the percent of correct predictions compared to the actual true values of the data.

**SVM Model.** The SVM parameter selection has been done by calibrating the hyperparameters several times over different settings and determining the optimal value obtained by manual tuning. For model evaluation, an accuracy score and confusion matrix are created.

### 4.5  Testing and Saving Model

Once the model is validated with reasonable accuracy, it is tested with Kaggle's competition test dataset, which is part of the MNIST main dataset of the same. The models don't know anything about the test dataset, so the result would show how well the model works. The data frame containing the test result is stored in a CSV file. The trained models are stored in TF or Pickle format.

### 4.6 Graphical User Interface (GUI)

The idea is to create a GUI through which a user can enter one or more English digits in the widget, which will then generate one or more images. The pixels will be converted to numerical arrays and predicted by the previously trained ML model. The accuracy of the prediction score would also be displayed in the widget.

**Packages Used.** The following packages and libraries are used for this:

- Pyscreenshot package to copy the contents of the screen to a pillow image memory.
- Tkinter package for the Python interface to the GUI toolkit.
- OpenCV to perform necessary image processing operations.
- Numpy for handling the image in array format for the ML model to process.
- Keras to load the ML models.

**GUI Design.** The Tkinter package provides a variety of GUI elements like buttons, widgets, entry fields,display areas, etc. Tk() is the main method that is used to create the main window of the function. At first, the saved ML model is loaded with the Keras package. In our design, two widget classes-Canvas and Button-are used. Canvas is used in our application to draw the digit. Buttons map directly to the user interface. Two buttons, **Recognize Digit** and **Clear Widget**, are used in our design. The following functions are used to trigger the mainloop():

- clear_window(): Used to clear the canvas window.
- start_event(): Binds event called <B1-Motion> which signals that a mouse cursor is moved in the widget.
- draw_lines(): Used for drawing lines on the canvas.

**Computer Vision Tasks.** We implement the function Recognize_Digit() which inherently performs the task of recognizing the digit drawn on the canvas. First, we use ImageGrab module from Pyscreenshot library to take a screenshot of the screen, crop the rectangular region containing the drawing, and store it as an image in PNG format. Subsequently, OpenCV is used to determine the contour of the saved image, which would be useful for object detection and recognition. The last part of this section contains the creation of bounding boxes for contours and extracting regions of interest. The image is pre-processed to $28 \times 28$ pixels to support ML model input. Finally, model.predict() method is used to recognize the digit drawn in the canvas by drawing a bounding box surrounding the drawing and predicting the image classification outcome.

## 5   Results

All the models were trained and tested in an Intel Core i7 CPU and NVIDIA 1050 Ti GPU hardware environment.

## 5.1   CNN

After performing the training with the specified and tuned parameters, the CNN model achieved a training accuracy of 97.5% and a validation accuracy of 99.21%.

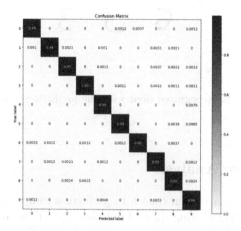

**Fig. 5.** CNN Model Confusion Matrix.

The confusion matrix (Fig. 5) generated from the post-validation assessment indicates all the labels (here the digits 0, 1,..., 9) received true positive values of more than 99%. The CNN model scores **0.99110** out of 1.0.

## 5.2   MLP

The trained MLP model achieved a training accuracy of 99.6% and a validation accuracy of 97.6%. The MLP model scores **0.97417** out of 1.0.

## 5.3   SVM

The trained SVM model achieved an overall validation accuracy of 97.83%. This model scores **0.97907** out of 1.0, which indicates a highly accurate outcome.

## 5.4   Real Time Detection from GUI

The GUI is tested with real-time digit inputs that are drawn over the canvas. The recognized digit with the prediction score in percentage is displayed in the next window (Fig. 6). It can be observed that all the digits drawn, even if slanted to some extent, have been predicted accurately by the model.

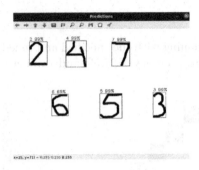

**Fig. 6.** Recognized digit with the prediction score.

## 6   Performance Analysis

Accuracy and scores have been chosen to perform a comparative analysis of the respective models in detecting digits from the MNIST database and displayed in Table 1. Accuracy is the best way to measure how well a model has learned to classify. The score here is an important parameter that tests how well the model can predict from a completely new dataset. As per the comparison analysis, it can be inferred that the convolutional network has the best score in accuracy as well as the highest Kaggle test score by margin compared to MLP and SVM, and gives us the best performance for detecting handwritten digits based on the MNIST datasets. Whereas the performances of the MLP and SVM models are quite similar based on their scores. Both MLP and SVM do significantly well.

**Table 1.** Performance Analysis of Models.

| ML Model | Accuracy (%) | Score out of 1.0 |
|----------|--------------|------------------|
| CNN      | 99.21        | 0.99110          |
| MLP      | 97.61        | 0.97417          |
| SVM      | 97.83        | 0.97907          |

## 7   Conclusion

In this study, three machine learning (ML) algorithms were used to recognize handwritten numbers from the MNIST database from the Kaggle competition. Two of the algorithms were based on deep learning, and the other was a more traditional ML method. The performance of all the models was compared based on their overall accuracy and ability to correctly predict results for new datasets. Different hyper-parameter tuning and optimization techniques were tried and tested, and the best-fit models were implemented. Additionally, a GUI-based real-time digit recognition platform was designed, and the ML model produced accurate predictions for all the user inputs where the user drew digits in the Tkinter user interface window. It is observed that CNN provided the most accurate prediction, whereas MLP and SVM performed on a similar scale. Hence, it can be concluded that CNN would serve as the best-fit model for image-based classification problems, including handwritten digit recognition.

# References

1. Chychkarova, Y., Serhiienkob, A., Syrmamiikha, I., Karginc, A.: Handwritten Digits Recognition Using SVM, KNN, RF and Deep learning Algorithms. https://ceur-ws.org/Vol-2864/paper44.pdf. Accessed 23 Feb 2023
2. Niu, X.X., Suen, C.Y.: A novel hybrid CNN-SVM classifier for recognizing handwritten digits. Pattern Recogn. **45**(4), 1318–1325 (2012)
3. Jain, M., Kaur, G., Quamar, M.P., Gupta, H.: Handwritten digit recognition using CNN. In: 2021 International Conference on Innovative Practices in Technology and Management (ICIPTM), Noida, India, pp. 211–215 (2021)
4. Al Mansoori, S.: Intelligent handwritten digit recognition using artificial neural network. Int. J. Eng. Res. Appl. **5**(5(Part -3)), 46–51 (2015). https://www.ijera.comISSN. ISSN : 2248–9622
5. Ahamed, H., Alam, S.M.I., Islam, M.M.: SVM based real time hand-written digit recognition system. In: Conference: International Conference on Engineering Research and Education School of Applied sciences & Technology, Sylhet (2019). ] https://www.researchgate.net/publication/330684489_SVM_Based_Real_Time_Hand-Written_Digit_Recognition_System
6. Zargar, S.A.: Introduction to Convolutional Neural Networks (2021). https://www.researchgate.net/publication/350955402_Introduction_to_Convolutional_Neural_Networks
7. IBM: Convolutional Neural Networks. https://www.ibm.com/topics/convolutional-neural-networks. Accessed 14 Feb 2023
8. Voyant, C., et al.: Time series modeling with pruned multi-layer perceptron and 2-stage damped least-squares method. In: International Conference on Mathematical Modeling in Physical Sciences, IC-MSQUARE, Czech Republic (2013)
9. Popescu, M., Balas, V.E., Perescu-Popescu, L., Mastorakis, N.E.: Multilayer perceptron and neural networks. WSEAS Trans. Circ. Syst. Arch. **8**, 579–588 (2009)
10. Saini, A.: Support Vector Machine(SVM): a complete guide for beginners (2021). https://www.analyticsvidhya.com/blog/2021/10/support-vector-machinessvm-a-complete-guide-for-beginners/. Last Accessed 24 Feb 2023
11. Aiman Ngadilan, M.A., Ismail, N., Rahiman, M.H.F., Taib, M.N., Mohd Ali, N.A., Tajuddin, S.N.: Radial Basis Function (RBF) tuned Kernel Parameter of Agarwood Oil Compound for Quality Classification using Support Vector Machine (SVM). In: 9th IEEE Control and System Graduate Research Colloquium (ICSGRC), Shah Alam, Malaysia 2018, pp. 64–68 (2018)
12. Kaggle: MNIST Dataset Description, Digit Recognizer-Learn computer vision fundamentals with the famous MNIST data. https://www.kaggle.com/competitions/digit-recognizer/data

# Towards Automatic Assessment of Quiet Standing Balance During the Execution of ADLs

Irene Guardiola-Luna[✉], Leticia Monasterio-Exposito,
Javier Macias-Guarasa, Alvaro Nieva-Suarez, Marina Murillo-Teruel,
Jose Luis Martin-Sanchez, and Sira Elena Palazuelos-Cagigas

Universidad de Alcalá, Department of Electronics, Edificio Politécnico, Ctra.
Madrid-Barcelona km 33,600, 28805 Alcalá de Henares, Spain
`irene.guardiola@edu.uah.es`

**Abstract.** The current method used to estimate the balance a person has during the performance of Activities of Daily Life (ADLs) is through the application of standardized scales used by occupational therapists to evaluate a person's motor skills and performance quality during those activities, such as the Assessment of Motor and Process Skills scale (AMPS). In this paper, we propose a method to automate the evaluation of a person's balance during the stage of quiet standing still while a person is completing an ADL. Our proposal is aimed to first estimate the projection of the person's center of mass (CoM) from the 3D position of the body joints by applying theoretical and deep learning approaches. Then, we aim to predict a clinically validated objective balance score from previous estimations of the CoM and the Center of Pressure (CoP), using different neural network models. While there are other proposals in the literature, the lack of publicly available datasets makes it difficult to do an extensive comparison, so we compare our proposal with state-of-the-art results in two publicly available datasets, improving their results.

**Keywords:** Quiet standing still balance · Automatic Estimation · Deep learning

## 1 Introduction

The Assessment of Motor and Process Skills (AMPS) is an observational evaluation tool that allows occupational therapists to simultaneously assess a person's motor skills and the quality of their performance while carrying out activities of daily living (ADLs) [12].

One of the motor skills that is evaluated in AMPS is whether the patient stabilizes their body position. The occupational therapist would give a subjective score from 1 to 4, based on the task being performed by the person [13].

L. Iliadis et al. (Eds.): EANN 2023, CCIS 1826, pp. 352–363, 2023.
https://doi.org/10.1007/978-3-031-34204-2_30

In order to remove the subjectivity of the occupational therapist and the disturbance that the presence of the therapist exerts on the patients who are performing the ADLs, we propose to use an automatic system that provides clinically validated objective assessments. This would allow us to detect limitations in people's stabilization skills at an early stage, which may be due to a specific pathology or to physical and/or cognitive changes caused by aging. In the latter case, the poor standing posture is due to the deterioration in the function of the sensory organs over the years, with the visual system being the one that most affect posture control. To compensate for the loss of vision, the vestibular and somatosensory systems intervene so that the person can maintain a stable posture, but not without increasing the sway [2].

The assessment of the balance of the patient during the execution of ADLs has to be done in different stages since while executing a task there will be sequences in which the balance is static and others where the balance is dynamic. The final system we are pursuing will use information from video and depth sequences of the user performing ADLs, to automatically estimate an objective balance score. However, as a first stage, in the present paper we are proposing a system to evaluate the balance during the quiet standing still stage, aimed at being consistent with the score given by an occupational therapist with the help of different clinical balance assessment tools, such as the Balance Error Scoring System (BESS) [4] or the Balance Evaluation Systems Tests (BESTest) [17].

## 2   Related Work

The assessment of the balance has been studied previously, but not so much how to obtain a quantitative assessment of the balance (a score), as opposed to the direct consequence of the loss of balance, referred to as fall risk assessment, where people are classified as fallers or non-fallers [24,30].

To assess the balance quantitatively, different technologies have been used to obtain different types of data: balance boards [27], inertial sensors [1,3], accelerometers [25] and depth sensors [5,14,23].

An indicator of loss of balance is the position and displacement of the projection of the center of mass (CoM). This must be within the base of support, which is the polygon formed between the outer sides of the feet. From the base of support, it is possible to define the limits of stability, the area within the base of support in which the person can remain stable, limits that decrease with age. The most frequently used parameter to assess the quiet standing still posture is the body sway, directly related to the measure of the center of pressure (CoP) displacement, which is the most common posturographic value used in the literature. More specifically, it is the CoM displacement that indicates the body's sway and the CoP is the neuromuscular response to the displacement of the CoM [10].

To the best of our knowledge, there are very few research works that propose an automatic system capable of scoring the balance of a person. The ones with the highest accuracy on the prediction use private datasets [5,23,33]. In [3] they use the trunk sway data to determine a score between 1 and 5, stating that they obtain an 83% of accuracy. In [27] they get a mean absolute error between 0.642 and 2.658 *points* from features obtained from CoP data while using as a ground truth simplified BESTest scores.

The position of the CoP has been previously automatically estimated from the body joints as in [6], or by employing graph convolutional networks [9] and 3D body landmark sequences as the input.

Many studies use CoP-derived parameters (displacement, velocity, path length and/or area) to estimate the postural sway and, hence, the balance. These parameters could give us information about neural or sensorimotor dysfunctions, yet the CoM can eventually be stabilized through the movement of the CoP. It would be more accurate to use the CoM, but it is difficult to determine and it is usually an estimated parameter. Some studies claim that combining the CoM and CoP displacement values provides more information on balance than either of them alone. Therefore, they propose the variable $\|CoP-CoM\|$ as the distance between the CoP and CoM, as it provides a better estimate of the effectiveness of postural control, being more decisive than other metrics [20].

The CoM of a person during a static stance can be estimated:

1. From anthropometric parameters: Direct (or whole body approach), using experimental techniques on living subjects to obtain anthropometric values; and indirect (or segmental) through, for example, corpse studies [15]. In this paper we will apply the two most commonly used estimations, either considering the body as a set of segments or a simplified version that only monitors one marker, assuming that it represents CoM position (typically located at the $5^{th}$ lumbar vertebra (L5)).
2. By low-pass filtering the CoP signal, with a cut-off frequency estimated according to the anthropometric characteristics of the body, usually $0.5\,\mathrm{Hz}$ [10].

To estimate the CoM position of the body, two classical reference anthropometric tables can be used. One from De Leva [7], who adapted the inertial parameters from the Zatsiorsky studies [34], and another from Dempster [8], modified by Winter [32]. The most used model was that of De Leva as it had a larger sample size of living subjects. However, since Winter improved Dempster's model by incorporating in vivo measurements into the small sample size of corpses, it has become the most widely used model. They contain information about the weight of each segment as a percentage of the total body weight, and the position of the CoM relative to the length of each segment. The body CoM is calculated as the weighted sum of each body segment's CoM [32], Eq. 1.

$$\mathbf{com} = \frac{1}{M}\sum_{i=1}^{N_S} f_i \mathbf{p}_i, \quad \mathbf{p}_i = (x_p, y_p, z_p) + l_d[(x_d, y_d, z_d) - (x_p, y_p, z_p)], \quad (1)$$

where **com** is the body's CoM 3D position; $M$ is the total body's weight; $\mathbf{p}_i$ is the 3D position of the CoM for each body segment; $(x_p, y_p, z_p)$ and $(x_d, y_d, z_d)$ are the 3D coordinates of the proximal and distal joints of each segment, respectively; $l_d$ is the factor of CoM per segment length; $f_i$ are the fractions of the total body mass determined by the corresponding studies; and $N_S$ is the number of considered segments.

This strategy is referred to as the *segmental method*, and its downside is that the estimations may be wrong when the subjects do not have the same characteristics as the studies population, such as in the case of children or people with pathologies, and to a lesser extent women and non-Caucasians.

In [31], the authors propose to obtain the location of a human's CoM from the information captured by a depth camera, achieving a Root Mean Squared Error (RMSE) of 0.89 cm on the x-axis (anterior-posterior) and 1.72 cm on the y-axis (medio-lateral).

In this paper, we aim at evaluating the feasibility of obtaining a clinically validated assessment of quiet standing balance based on the 3D position of the joints of the human body obtained by a depth camera. In order to achieve this, and taking into account that there are no public databases available that include both, the 3D joints positions of subjects performing ADLs not static balance tests, and the associated balance score, we describe an approach with two different models that are tested separately. We first evaluate a system to obtain the position of the projection of a human's CoM from the 3D positions of the body's joints (Sect. 3). Then, we evaluate a proposal to obtain an estimation of a clinically validated standing still balance score from values derived from the CoM and CoP estimations (Sect. 4). The diagram of the system is shown in Fig. 1.

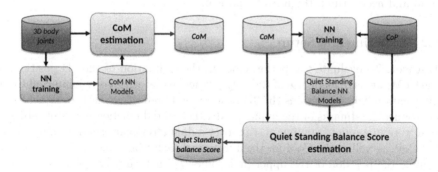

**Fig. 1.** Diagram of the full system proposal.

# 3   CoM Estimation

## 3.1   System Proposal

Our proposal is the use of a neural network that behaves as a CoM estimator (regressor) from the 3D positions of simplified 15 body joints. The multilayer network architecture proposed consists of a fully connected layer at the input, one or two fully connected hidden layers, and a final fully connected layer. Each of the intermediate layers is followed by batch normalization, with dropout and ReLU activation functions. The optimizer selected was Adam [19] and the loss metric used was the mean squared error (MSE), Eq. 2. It calculates the average of the $l_2$ norm between the CoM ground truth and the predicted values.

$$MSE = \frac{1}{N} \sum_{i=1}^{N} ||\mathbf{com}_{GT} - \mathbf{com}_{EST}||^2, \tag{2}$$

where $\mathbf{com}_{GT}$ and $\mathbf{com}_{EST}$ are the CoM ground truth and predicted values, respectively.

To further assess the accuracy of our proposal, we compare it with the segmental methods described above using Eq. 1, based on the fractions provided by the two classical anthropometric tables references, De Leva's and Dempster's (referred to below as DeLeva and Dempster). We will also provide a comparison with the simplification of using the marker located at the $5^{th}$ lumbar vertebra (referred to as L5 below).

For consistency reasons in the comparison, the body has been segmented into the same amount of parts to compare the use of the two anthropometric tables: head and neck, trunk, thigh, calf, and feet.

## 3.2   Experimental Setup

**Dataset.** To evaluate the performance in the estimation of the 3D position of the CoM, we have made use of the only public dataset with body joints and CoM information [29]. It contains the 3D position of 42 reflective markers attached to anatomical landmarks of the human body, the ground reaction forces of subjects that were in a quiet standing posture over a dual force platform during 60 s, and the CoP, as well as the CoM for the duration of each trial. The database does not include the position of the upper limb joints, as each subject had to keep their arms close to their trunk during the recording. The ground truth CoM position they provide was calculated by applying Dempster's model to an altered trunk segment, in which they include the arms, head, and trunk.

The database contains 12 trials of 49 persons, 27 young people between 21.8 and 37.9 years old, and 22 older people between 61.14 and 84.7 years old. Four tasks were defined. In all of them, the person was requested to stand still, and there were 4 variations, combining the use of a firm surface or a surface covered with foam, and the state of the eyes, either opened or closed. For each of the tasks, each person had up to three attempts to execute it.

The database partition considers 81% of the full dataset for training, 9% for validation, and 10% for testing, with no common users between the test and train+validation subsets. We also roughly forced half of the components of each subset to belong to the young people cohort and the other half to the older people cohort.

As previously indicated, in the real implementation of the system, the 3D position of the body joints will be obtained by a depth camera. Therefore, a mapping was made between the position of the markers provided in this database, obtained using reflective markers [21,22], and the position of the joints provided by a depth camera (such as the Microsoft Kinect[TM] v2). Thus, excluding the upper limbs, we went from 42 to a simplified version of 15 joints.

**Performance Metrics.** We will be using the following evaluation metrics:

- The Mean Absolute Error ($MAE$, Eq. 3), which is the mean of the absolute value difference between the predicted value and the ground truth.

$$MAE = \frac{1}{2N} \sum_{i=1}^{N} \sum_{j \in \{x,z\}} |c_{j,\text{com}_{GT}} - c_{j,\text{com}_{EST}}|, \tag{3}$$

where $N$ is the number of predictions, $c_j$ with $j \in \{x, z\}$ is the $(x, z)$ coordinates of the corresponding CoM ground truth or its estimation (the $1/2$ in the equation normalizes as we only consider two coordinates in the CoM projection to the ground).

- Additionally, we have added the Percentage of Correct Keypoints ($PCK$, Eq. 4), calculated as the percentage of the predicted CoM that fall within a certain threshold distance to the ground truth position.

$$PCK_{thr} = \frac{1}{N} \sum_{i=1}^{N} c_i, \text{ where } c_i = \begin{cases} 1 \text{ if } \|\text{com}_{GT} - \text{com}_{EST}\| < thr \\ 0 \text{ otherwise} \end{cases}, \tag{4}$$

where $thr$ is the given threshold.

## 3.3   Results

The results for $MAE$ and $PCK_{1\,\text{cm}}$ obtained with the proposed network are shown on the left side of Fig. 2, as a function of the network architecture. Training parameters were optimized in preliminary experiments on the training + validation subsets: Dropout was set to 0.5, and rectified linear unit activation functions (ReLU) were used. The optimizer selected was Adam [19] and the best results were obtained with a batch size of 100, and a learning rate of $10^{-2}$.

Figure 2 shows the results with the best ones enclosed in red rectangles. As we can see in the left graphic, the best average $MAE$ obtained was 0.35 cm with an $PCK_{1\,\text{cm}}$ of 76.40% when the network topology is 1024-1025-512-3. This suggests that an architecture with two hidden layers is effectively capturing the

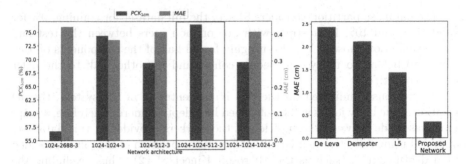

**Fig. 2.** (Left) $PCK_{1cm}$ (the higher the better) and $MAE$ (the lower the better) depending on the network layer sizes (input-hidden-output). (Right) $MAE$ results comparison for different systems. Best results are enclosed in red rectangles (Color figure online).

relation between the input data and the CoM position. If we change the accuracy threshold to 2.5 cm, $PCK_{2.5\,cm}$ increases to 100%.

The right graphic of Fig. 2 shows a comparison between our proposed network and the segmental and simplified methods described above. The neural network shows the highest performance (red rectangle), with a $MAE$ of 0.35 cm, followed by the L5 simplification with a $MAE$ four times bigger, of 1.43 cm. This implies that the deep learning approach is more suitable for accurately estimating the CoM position, hence, the possible use of this model to obtain the CoM position in a different environment. Between the two theoretical models, `Dempster` gives a slightly better result because the CoM ground truth of this database was calculated using Dempster's anthropometric model (with the full set of joints).

Additionally, we have calculated the RMSE, obtaining a value of 0.51 cm to get an idea of where our results stand in comparison to [31], where they achieved 0.89 cm, clearly improving their performance.

## 4    Score Estimation of the Quiet Standing Postural Stability

### 4.1    System Proposal

Before describing the system, we first checked the performance of a simpler CoM estimation procedure. Since the database used does not provide 3D joint positions, we have obtained the CoM by low-pass filtering of the provided CoP signal from the database used in Sect. 3.2. When applied to the network described in Sect. 3.1, a $MAE$ of 0.62 cm and an $PCK_{2.5\,cm}$ of 98.17% were obtained. The error is acceptable and similar to that of [6], that obtained 0.5 cm, and better than the 1.1 cm to 2.5 cm of other studies, as reported by [6]. Our RMSE value of 0.84 cm is also better than the 0.89 cm of [31].

Our proposal is again using a neural network approach. Given that the assigned scores vary between 0 and 6 (in increasing values of good balance behavior), the problem can be posed as a classification or a regression task. The different network architectures that have been evaluated are:

- Regressor model: Composed by a fully connected layer as the input, one hidden and one at the output.
- Classifier model: Using the same architecture as the regressor model, but implementing a softmax function at the output layer.
- CNN model: Consisting of an input and hidden 1D convolutional layer, followed by two hidden and output fully connected layers. At the output, we apply a softmax function.

The optimizer used in all the models was Adam [19]. Each intermediate layer is followed by batch normalization and a ReLU function as the activation layer. In terms of the loss metric, the one used in the training was $MAE$ (Eq. 3).

In addition to these architectures, experiments were also carried out using the *auto-sklearn* toolkit [11], in which we tested 15 different machine learning classification algorithms, to provide additional comparison elements.

## 4.2   Experimental Setup

**Dataset.** In our state-of-the-art revision, we only found two public datasets that included clinically validated scores using clinical balance assessment tools. One of them [26], provides the scores of multiple motor scales of individuals with Parkinson's disease. The other one [28], which was the one we finally selected, also provides multiple motor scale scores, including the Mini-BESTest scale scores, but considering healthy subjects, and interesting data such as raw data of the force, moments of forces, and centers of pressure of subjects that were in a quiet standing posture over a force platform during 60 s in four different conditions. The clinical balance score was also provided with information about the subjects and balance conditions and the results of all the evaluation tests. This database contains 12 trials of 163 persons (116 females and 47 males), between 18 and 85 years old. The task conditions were the same as those described in Sect. 3.2 for the dataset provided by [29].

We will compare our results with those achieved in [27]. To ensure consistency in the comparison, we have followed the same data handling procedure, for both the data processing and the database splitting tasks. As we did in the dataset splitting described in Sect. 3.2, we selected approximately the same number of older and young people in each subset. We have also used the same input features proposed by [27] (statistics on the provided signals) but calculated on the $||CoP-CoM||$ distance, instead of just using the CoP signals.

Our comparison will be focused on the estimation of the Sensory Orientation subscale within the BESTest (that gets values from 0 to 6), as the CoP data is only recorded for this Sensory Orientation task.

**Performance Metrics.** For this system, we will provide details on the $MAE$ metric of Eq. 3, as it is the same one provided in [27], to ease the comparison task.

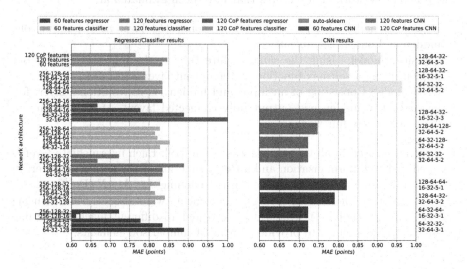

**Fig. 3.** $MAE$ of the test set for different models, architectures, and batch sizes. On the left are the results for the classifier and regressor models and on the right are the results of the CNN model. The best result is enclosed in a red rectangle (Color figure online).

### 4.3    Results

For every model, we evaluated the performance of three different feature sets: the statistics for the $\|CoP-CoM\|$ distance (60 features), the statistics from the $\|CoP-CoM\|$ distance in the z-axis (anterior-posterior) and x-axis (medio-lateral) dimensions (120 features), and the statistics from the CoP signal (120 features).

The results for $MAE$ obtained with each network are shown in Fig. 3, as a function of the network architecture. Training parameters of the network were optimized in preliminary experiments on the training + validation subsets. Next to every bar, you can find the architecture and batch size information of the classification and regression model in this order: input layer-hidden layer-batch size. The order for the CNN model is: 1D convolutional input layer - hidden 1D convolutional layer - hidden fully connected layers - size of the kernel - stride.

Analyzing Fig. 3, we can see how the regressor approach is better than the classifier one, and how the CNN does not improve the results obtained by the regressor, as well as informing us that the choice of hyperparameters greatly affects the performance. The best result is obtained with a batch size of 64, a learning rate of $10^{-1}$, an input layer size of 128, an intermediate layer size of 64, and using 60 input features, i.e. the $\|CoP-CoM\|$ distance statistics, which is in line with the conclusions of [20]. The lowest $MAE$ value obtained with this model for the Sensory Orientation subscale within BESTest is 0.611 *points*, which is slightly better than the one obtained in [27], which was 0.642 *points*, becoming the best-published estimate with this database so far. If we normalize per score range, our model obtains a normalized mean absolute error of 10.18% which means an accuracy of 89.82%. This is an acceptable error, so the model could be applied under a different environment.

## 5    Conclusions and Future Work

In this paper, we have proposed two systems. The first one, aimed at estimating the CoM from the 3D positions of human body joints, and the second one to estimate a clinically validated balance score from features derived from the CoM and CoP estimations. In both cases, we are addressing the standing still balance assessment task, as a previous stage to evaluate the balance behavior of users performing ADLs in functional evaluation tasks such as AMPS.

Regarding the first system proposal, we have obtained promising results of the estimation of a human's CoM ground projection based on the position of the human body joints, achieving an MAE of 0.35 cm on the public database provided in [29]. Our proposal clearly outperforms traditional segmental estimators and those using the simplified L5 assumption.

Regarding the standing still balance score estimation task, we have improved the state-of-the-art results in the Sensory Orientation estimation task using this subscale within the BESTest scale, achieving a prediction very close to the clinically validated score provided by occupational therapists.

These initial results, when completed with the estimation of dynamic balance score values, will be very useful for the objective assessment of the stability of subjects during the performance of ADLs in functional evaluation tasks, oriented toward the early identification of balance deficiencies in patients. Overall, these results are promising and suggest that the technology can play an important role in the objective assessment of human body stability.

As for future work, we plan to explore the use of temporal models such as LSTMs [16] or ESNs [18] to improve the results obtained for the assessment of the human body stability during the quiet standing phase. We will also address the exploitation of the $||CoP-CoM||$ 2D and 3D trajectory images by using image-based processing by CNNs. Our main final target will be the derivation of static+dynamic balance assessment in ADL-related evaluations, including the systems proposed in this paper.

**Acknowledgments.** This work has been partially supported by the Spanish Ministry of Science and Innovation MICINN/AEI/10.13039/501100011033 under projects EYE-FUL (PID2020-113118RB-C31) and ATHENA (PID2020-115995RB-I00), by CAM under project CONDORDIA (CM/JIN/2021-015), and by UAH under projects ARGOS+ (PIUAH21/IA-016) and METIS (PIUAH22/IA-037).

# References

1. Noamani, A., Vette, A.H., Rouhani, H.: Instrumented functional test for objective outcome evaluation of balance rehabilitation in elderly fallers: a clinical study. Gerontology **68**, 1233–1245 (2022)
2. Aoki, H., Demura, S., Hirai, H.: Age-related changes in body sway when standing with eyes closed or open and on stable and unstable surfaces. Am. J. Sports Sci. Med. **6**, 33–38 (2018)
3. Bao, T., Klatt, B.N., Whitney, S.L., Sienko, K.H., Wiens, J.: Automatically evaluating balance: a machine learning approach. IEEE Trans. Neural Syst. Rehabil. Eng. **27**(2), 179–186 (2019)
4. Bell, D.R., Guskiewicz, K.M., Clark, M.A., Padua, D.A.: Systematic review of the balance error scoring system. Sports Health **3**(3), 287–95 (2011)
5. Chakravarty, K., Suman, S., Bhowmick, B., Sinha, A., Das, A.: Quantification of balance in single limb stance using kinect. In: 2016 IEEE International Conference on Acoustics, Speech and Signal Processing (ICASSP), pp. 854–858, March 2016
6. Chen, S.C., Hsieh, H.J., Lu, T.W., Tseng, C.H.: A method for estimating subject-specific body segment inertial parameters in human movement analysis. Gait Posture **33**(4), 695–700 (2011)
7. de Leva, P.: Adjustments to Zatsiorsky-Seluyanov's segment inertia parameters. J. Biomech. **29**(9), 1223–1230 (1996)
8. Dempster, L.: Patterns of Human Motion. Prentice Hall Inc., Englewood Cliffs, New Jersey (1971)
9. Du, C., Graham, S., Depp, C., Nguyen, T.: Multi-task center-of-pressure metrics estimation with graph convolutional network. IEEE Trans. Multimedia **24**, 2018–2033 (2022)
10. Duarte, M., Freitas, S.M.S.: Revision of posturography based on forceplate for balance evaluation. Braz. J. Phys. Ther. **14**(3), 183–192 (2010)
11. Feurer, M., Klein, A., Eggensperger, K., Springenberg, J., Blum, M., Hutter, F.: Efficient and robust automated machine learning. In: Advances in Neural Information Processing Systems, vol. 28, pp. 2962–2970 (2015)
12. Fisher, A.G., Jones, K.B.: Assessment of Motor and Process Skills: Development, Standardization, and Administration Manual, vol. 1, 7th edn. Three Star Press (2012)
13. Fisher, A.G., Jones, K.B.: Assessment of Motor and Process Skills: User Manual, vol. 2, 7th edn. Three Star Press (2012)
14. Glass, S.M., Napoli, A., Thompson, E.D., Obeid, I., Tucker, C.A.: Validity of an automated balance error scoring system. J. Appl. Biomech. **35**(1), 32–36 (2019)
15. Hay, J.G.: The center of gravity of the human body. Kinesiology **3**, 20–44 (1973)
16. Hochreiter, S., Schmidhuber, J.: Long short-term memory. Neural Comput. **9**, 1735–80 (1997)
17. Horak, F.B., Wrisley, D.M., Frank, J.: The balance evaluation systems test (BESTest) to differentiate balance deficits. Phys. Ther. **89**(5), 484–498 (2009)
18. Jaeger, H., Haas, H.: Harnessing nonlinearity: predicting chaotic systems and saving energy in wireless communication. Science **304**(5667), 78–80 (2004)
19. Kingma, D.P., Ba, J.: Adam: a method for stochastic optimization (2014)
20. Lafond, D., Duarte, M., Prince, F.: Comparison of three methods to estimate the center of mass during balance assessment. J. Biomech. **37**(9), 1421–1426 (2004)
21. Leardini, A., Biagi, F., Merlo, A., Belvedere, C., Benedetti, M.G.: Multi-segment trunk kinematics during locomotion and elementary exercises. Clin. Biomech. **26**(6), 562–571 (2011)

22. Leardini, A., Sawacha, Z., Paolini, G., Ingrosso, S., Nativo, R., Benedetti, M.G.: A new anatomically based protocol for gait analysis in children. Gait Posture **26**(4), 560–571 (2007)
23. Mazumder, O., Chakravarty, K., Chatterjee, D., Sinha, A., Das, A.: Posturography stability score generation for stroke patient using kinect: fuzzy based approach. In: 2017 39th Annual International Conference of the IEEE Engineering in Medicine and Biology Society (EMBC), pp. 3052–3056, July 2017
24. Montesinos, L., Castaldo, R., Pecchia, L.: Wearable inertial sensors for fall risk assessment and prediction in older adults: a systematic review and meta-analysis. IEEE Trans. Neural Syst. Rehabil. Eng. **26**(3), 573–582 (2018)
25. Noamani, A., Nazarahari, M., Lewicke, J., Vette, A.H., Rouhani, H.: Validity of using wearable inertial sensors for assessing the dynamics of standing balance. Med. Eng. Phys. **77**, 53–59 (2020)
26. de Oliveira, C.E.N., et al.: A public data set with ground reaction forces of human balance in individuals with Parkinson's disease. Front. Neurosci. **16**, 865882 (2022)
27. Ren, P., et al.: Assessment of balance control subsystems by artificial intelligence. IEEE Trans. Neural Syst. Rehabil. Eng. **28**(3), 658–668 (2020)
28. dos Santos, D.A., Duarte, M.: A public data set of human balance evaluations (2016). https://doi.org/10.6084/m9.figshare.3394432.v2
29. dos Santos, D.A., Fukuchi, C.A., Fukuchi, R.K., Duarte, M.: A data set with kinematic and ground reaction forces of human balance. PeerJ **5**, e3626 (2017)
30. Sun, R., Sosnoff, J.J.: Novel sensing technology in fall risk assessment in older adults: a systematic review. BMC Geriatr. **18**(14), 1471–2318 (2018)
31. Wei, W., Dey, S.: Center of mass estimation for balance evaluation using convolutional neural networks, pp. 1–7 (2019)
32. Winter, D.A.: Biomechanics and Motor Control of Human Movement, 4th edn. Wiley, September 2009
33. Wu, J., et al.: Automated assessment of balance: a neural network approach based on large-scale balance function data. Front. Pub. Health **10**, 882811 (2022)
34. Zatsiorsky, V.: Methods of determining mass-inertial characteristics of human body segments. In: Contemporary Problems of Biomechanics (1990)

# Deep/Machine Learning in Engineering

# Adaptive Model for Industrial Systems Using Echo State Networks

José Ramón Rodríguez-Ossorio[1]([✉]) [iD], Antonio Morán[1] [iD], Juan J. Fuertes[1] [iD], Miguel A. Prada[1] [iD], Ignacio Díaz[2] [iD], and Manuel Domínguez[1] [iD]

[1] SUPPRESS research group, Escuela de Ingenierías, Universidad de León, Campus de Vegazana, León 24007, Spain
{jrodro,a.moran,jj.fuertes,ma.prada,mdomg}@unileon.es
[2] Electrical Engineering Department University of Oviedo, Edif. Departamental Oeste 2, Campus de Viesques s/n, Gijón 33204, Spain
idiaz@uniovi.es
https://suppress.unileon.es

**Abstract.** When a model of an industrial system is developed, it is expected that this model performs consistently when applied to other identically designed systems. However, different operating hours, degradation or maintenance, among other circumstances, cause a change in the dynamics of the system and result in the model not performing as expected. For this reason, it is necessary to build a model that continuously adapts to changes in the dynamics of the system, in order to handle such deviations and thus reduce the estimation error.

This paper proposes the development of an adaptive model based on Echo State Networks to estimate the level of a water tank. For this purpose, two identically designed industrial pilot plants are used, taking one of them as a reference for the parameterization, training and validation of the model, and applying the developed model to the other one in order to evaluate the adaptation to changes in the dynamics of the system.

**Keywords:** Echo State Networks · Dynamics · Data-based Modelling · Online Learning

## 1 Introduction

Physical systems modelling in the industrial sector is a relevant task, since it allows the behaviour of these systems and their evolution over time to be analysed and understood in depth, and it is essential to detect anomalous behaviours and to improve the efficiency and optimization of processes in the context of an increasingly competitive industry, that aims to maximise production at lowest possible costs. However, modelling real industrial systems is extremely complex, since a large amount of process data is available in a relatively simple way, but extracting knowledge about system dynamics from this data is not so straightforward.

L. Iliadis et al. (Eds.): EANN 2023, CCIS 1826, pp. 367–378, 2023.
https://doi.org/10.1007/978-3-031-34204-2_31

In this context, what is known as Industry 4.0 [4,9] comes into focus, a new paradigm considered as the fourth industrial revolution, which involves the introduction of digital twins among other technologies. These digital twins are virtual models of real systems that allow the aforementioned objectives of efficiency improvement or detection of anomalous situations to be achieved [14]. For a proper implementation of a digital twin, it will be necessary to develop a model as faithful as possible to the real system: the closer the model is to reality, the better the digital twin will work and the better these objectives can be achieved.

Moreover, the generated model should be as flexible and adaptable as possible, allowing generalisation and adjustment to identical systems with similar characteristics. This adaptation is an additional challenge, as models are developed for particular systems with specific peculiarities, and, although they are expected to generalise system main characteristics, they are very sensitive to small differences or variations and will start to fail if applied to a different system.

There are few modelling algorithms that allow this adaptive learning, but most of these require complex, resource-intensive and time-consuming trainings. As an example, *Long Short Term Memory* (LSTM) algorithm, an special *Recurrent Neural Network* (RNN) approach, made possible effective training for large datasets, but implies a harder training, slow convergence and other kind of stability problems [8]. As an alternative, *Echo State Networks* (ESN) are another variation of RNN proposal, which have the same power and advantages as RNNs but require much simpler and lightweight training [16] and include the posibility of online training for easier adaptation to changes in the modelled physical system.

This paper proposes the application of *Echo State Networks* for the modelling of industrial pilot plants, using one plant as a reference for the parameterisation, training and validation of the model, with both offline and online training, and then testing the online adaptation of the developed model to another plant identical to the first one.

The paper is structured as follows: Sect. 2 describes the basics of ESN, their operating principles and the main training methods used; Sect. 3 presents the pilot plant used and the methodology for working with ESN; Sect. 4 shows the results obtained with the developed model and its adaptation to another identically designed system; and finally concludes in Sect. 5.

## 2    Echo State Networks

Recurrent neural networks of the type called Echo State Networks (ESN) enable the modeling of non-linear systems through supervised learning [5]. ESNs respond to an input signal with a fixed, randomly created recurrent neural network that consists of a *reservoir* of neurons with non-linear response signals, generating the desired output signal by a trainable linear combination of all these responses [6]. ESNs are a very interesting approach to recurrent neural networks as they are a particular form of a state-space model. A set of first-order differential equations is used in the generic state-space model of a non-linear dynamical system to generate a vector of outputs $\mathbf{y}(k) \in \mathbb{R}^q$ from a vector of inputs $\mathbf{u}(k) \in \mathbb{R}^p$ and from a vector of states $\mathbf{x}(k) \in \mathbb{R}^n$, as it can be observed in the expression:

$$\mathbf{x}(k + 1) = f(\mathbf{x}(k), \mathbf{u}(k)) \tag{1}$$
$$\mathbf{y}(k) = g(\mathbf{x}(k), \mathbf{u}(k))$$

where $f$ and $g$ are, typically, non-linear functions. Echo State Networks, based on the idea of *nonlinear expansion* [11], are a specific type of state-space model in which a high-dimensional vector of states $\mathbf{x}(k) \in \mathbb{R}^n$, a nonlinear model in the state equation, and a linear model of the output from the state are taken into consideration, as it can be seen below:

$$\mathbf{x}(k) = \sigma(\mathbf{W}_{res}\mathbf{x}(k - 1) + \mathbf{W}_{in}\mathbf{u}(k)) \tag{2}$$
$$\mathbf{y}(k) = \mathbf{W}_{out}\mathbf{x}(k)$$

where $\mathbf{W}_{res} \in \mathbb{R}^{n \times n}$ is the *reservoir* matrix, $\mathbf{W}_{in} \in \mathbb{R}^{n \times p}$ is an input matrix and $\mathbf{W}_{out} \in \mathbb{R}^{q \times n}$ is the output matrix. This model given in (2) is a particular case of the state-space representation shown in (1), where the state equation uses the common sigmoid nonlinear function $\sigma$. In this state-space model, matrices $\mathbf{W}_{res}$ and $\mathbf{W}_{in}$ are constructed using random values, with minor adjustments to drive the system's stability edge. This is the basic and most straightforward form of the ESNs. However, there are other more intricate variations, such as the usage of a feedback term, including $\mathbf{y}(k)$ in the system state equation, or also the use of direct connections from the input to the readout, which are represented in the output equation [10]

The model shown in (2) can be applied recursively to produce a sequence of state vectors $\{\mathbf{x}(k)\}$ of size $n$ from an input or excitation sequence $\{\mathbf{u}(k)\}$ that, when combined with $N$ samples, can be arranged into a matrix: $\mathbf{X} = (\mathbf{x}(1), \mathbf{x}(2), \ldots, \mathbf{x}(N)) \in \mathbb{R}^{n \times N}$.

The matrix X thus constitutes a *reservoir* of dynamic transient modes $x_i(k)$, since it represents the evolution over time of each of the $n$ states within the states vector $\mathbf{x}(k)$. If the $\mathbf{W}_{res}$ and $\mathbf{W}_{in}$ matrices have been generated with the appropriate parameters, this matrix of states $\mathbf{X}$ thus provides a great richness and variety of dynamic behaviors. When ESNs are used to model non-linear dynamic systems, one of their main applications, the $n$ dynamical modes obtained must be combined to estimate the system output. Thus, the output matrix can be defined as: $\mathbf{Y} = (\mathbf{y}(1), \mathbf{y}(2), \ldots, \mathbf{y}(N)) \in \mathbb{R}^{q \times N}$.

With this matrix $\mathbf{Y}$, the output equation of the ESN model in (2) implies a linear regression problem $\mathbf{Y} = \mathbf{W}_{out}\mathbf{X}$, that can be tackled with usual least squares techniques. Among the regression methods available for obtaining the readout of the model, two groups can be distinguished:

- **Offline methods**: the entire input sequence is processed in order to calculate the $W_{out}$ weights and thus obtain the output [10]. Offline regression methods

comprise *ridge regression* or *Moore-Penrose pseudo-inverse*, among others, where *ridge regression* is the most recommended option, as it requires less computational load, and is therefore the offline method used in this paper.
- **Online methods**: the weights of the output matrix are constantly adjusted, allowing adaptation to changes in system dynamics over time [16]. Online training methods include the *Least Mean Squares* (LMS) algorithm, and also the *Recursive Least Squares* (RLS) algorithm, among others. Of these methods, LMS converges very slowly, but RLS works quite well and it is, therefore, the online option used in this paper.

In RLS method, the output weights are recursively adapted in order to converge to the desired output signal [8], as shown in the following equations:

$$\mathbf{P}(0) = \frac{1}{\alpha}\mathbf{I} \tag{3}$$

$$\mathbf{e}(k) = \mathbf{W}_{out}(k-1)\mathbf{x}(k) - \mathbf{y}_{teach}(k) \tag{4}$$

$$\mathbf{P}(k) = \frac{\mathbf{P}(k-1)}{\lambda} - \frac{\mathbf{P}(k-1)\mathbf{x}(k)\mathbf{x}^T(k)\mathbf{P}(k-1)}{\lambda(\lambda + \mathbf{x}^T(k)\mathbf{P}(k-1)\mathbf{x}(k))} \tag{5}$$

$$\mathbf{W}_{out}(k) = \mathbf{W}_{out}(k-1) - \mathbf{e}(k)\mathbf{P}(k)\mathbf{x}(k) \tag{6}$$

where $\mathbf{P}(k)$ is usually referred to as covariance matrix, $\mathbf{I}$ is the identity matrix, $\mathbf{e}(k)$ is the error between current ESN output ($\mathbf{W}_{out}(k-1)\mathbf{x}(k)$) and desired output $\mathbf{y}_{teach}(k)$, $\alpha$ represents how much is initially known about the system, and $\lambda$ is the forgetting factor that models the weight of most recent data samples compared with previous ones.

When constructing an ESN model, there are several hyperparameters that can be adjusted, among which the most relevant are: the reservoir internal units (the number of states within the reservoir), the spectral radius, $\rho$, of matrix $\mathbf{W}_{res}$ (maximum absolute eigenvalue of the reservoir matrix), the leaking rate (lower or higher recall of previous states), the $\mathbf{W}_{res}$ connectivity (density of reservoir internal matrix, defined as the proportion of non-zero values within the matrix) and the $\mathbf{W}_{in}$ connectivity (density of the input matrix). A more detailed explanation of the different ESN hyperparameters and their selection can be found at [10].

There are many use cases for *Echo State Networks* in the field of industrial engineering. As examples, in [2] are used for the identification of harmonics in power supply systems, in [13] the health of rechargeable vehicle batteries is monitored, in [12] ESN are used for motor control and monitoring, and in [1] are dedicated to the detection of pressure downholes in oil wells. ESNs are also implemented with online adaptation in instances such as in [16], where monitoring of wide areas of power systems is developed, or in [8], where the control of an oil production platform is addressed.

# 3  Methodology

## 3.1  Quadruple-Tank Process

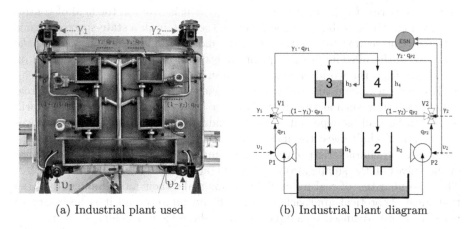

(a) Industrial plant used                    (b) Industrial plant diagram

**Fig. 1.** Industrial plant and its diagram

For the experiments presented in this paper, two pilot plants with real indus-trial instrumentation were used, which were designed at the Remote Laboratory of Automatic Control of the University of León [3], based on the well-known four-tank process proposed by Karl Henrik Johansson [7]. The design is composed of four water tanks that are positioned vertically in pairs so that the drains from the upper tanks eventually reach the lower ones. In addition, the plant has two twin pumps that deliver water to the tanks from a supply tank at the bottom. These pumps have the possibility to regulate their power by means of a variable speed drive.

The water flow supplied by the pumps is distributed between the tanks with two three-way valves, crossing the flows so that the left pump supplies its flow to lower left and upper right tanks, while the right pump supplies its flow to lower right and upper left tanks. This peculiar flow distribution makes the system more interesting in terms of control, since the level of each of the lower tanks will be influenced by the set points of both the adjacent pump and valve and the opposite pump and valve, each one with different dynamics.

To measure the level of the tanks, each tank is equipped with a pressure sensor at the base, which allows the height of the water to be calculated. These sensors are used to perform experiments controlling the level of the tanks with the pumps and valves as actuators. Finally, each of the tanks also has a solenoid valve at the base, which makes it possible to introduce disturbances in the flow of water that each of the tanks discharges. Figure 1 shows an image of the industrial plant implemented at University of León, and also its schematic representation, where $v_j$ is the ratio of pump j, $\gamma_j$ is the ratio of the valve j, $q_{P,j}$ is the total flow of pump j, and $h_i$ is water level in tank i.

The four-tank process is mathematically defined in a simple way with the combination of Bernoulli's and mass balance laws, obtaining the corresponding differential equations for the level of each tank. In addition, the system can also be easily described with a state space model, as it is usual in the field of control engineering. The possibility of representing the system in a state-space design is extremely interesting for relating it to the model developed by means of *Echo State Networks*, allowing a subsequent analysis of the model obtained based on knowledge from the world of control engineering.

However, it should also be borne in mind that, when working with a real industrial system such as this pilot plant, the theoretic mathematical model will not be as faithful as expected, since the industrial instrumentation introduces new technical challenges: the noise generated by sensors in the measurements, the non-linear characteristic curves of the pumps, the non-symmetrical response of the valves or the small ratio between the area of the tanks and their drains. These peculiarities of real industrial systems make their modelling complex, so that ideal theoretical approaches do not fit adequately and it is necessary to resort to more advanced techniques, such as those using machine learning.

With the design proposed by the University of León, two plants were built: the one created for the University of León itself, and the one built for its usage at the Polytechnic School of Engineering in Gijón (University of Oviedo), adopting the original instrumentation, dimensions and configuration. Of the two plants, the one at the University of León has been used extensively, its current state is known in detail and several previous experiments have been carried out on it. However, the plant in Gijón is known in less detail, less data is available from previous experiments and its current status is not well determined. Although the two plants were designed in the same layout, they have had different operating hours, different degradation, different maintenance, and a series of other circumstances that mean that their operation is not identical in both instances. Therefore, the system in León can be considered as the reference system, the one that works under normal conditions, and the system in Gijón as the one with differences with respect to the original, in which the adaptation of the model is evaluated.

### 3.2  Adaptive Model

In order to develop an adaptive model of the industrial plant, it is proposed to work with the upper tank 3, using tank level as model output and setpoint of pump 2 and valve 2 as model inputs. The input signals as well as the output signal are percentage scaled with values ranging from 0 to 100. The representation of the ESN model and its connection with industrial plant variables is shown in Fig. 1b. The modelling would be analogous for the prediction of tank 4 level, using the setpoints of pump 1 and valve 1 as inputs in this situation.

Data from the system needed to develop the model were obtained by conducting an experiment in a closed loop, with a proportional controller to regulate the

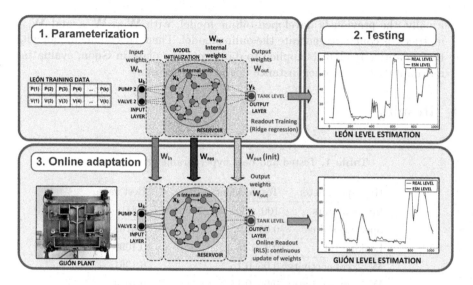

**Fig. 2.** Proposed methodology

tank level, as this is a more realistic situation with respect to the typical operation of an industrial plant. This experiment consists of different phases lasting 60 s, in which at least the regulator setpoint, the valve opening, or both variables simultaneously, are changed. It is decided that the aforementioned phases of the experiment will be 60 s, as it is enough time to reach a steady state in the level of the tank. Data used have been obtained with an application developed in Python, with a sampling rate of 100 milliseconds, and then resampled to 1 s and filtered. Out of the captured data, 70% was used for training and validation, and the remaining 30% was left for testing.

The programming, setup and training of the ESN model has been developed with the Python programming language, using the *ReservoirPy* library [15], a modular library that allows working with different elements of the ESN model as independently parameterizable nodes that are subsequently joined together. The search and optimization of the hyperparameters for the developed ESN model was carried out with the *hyperopt* library, integrated in *ReservoirPy*, which allows a random search for the best hyperparameters within a defined range of values, selecting the ones that produce the lowest error in the model output.

The experiment described above was conducted at both León and Gijón plants, with the same equipment and data acquisition configurations. The methodology followed to develop an adaptive model of the tank level is shown in Fig. 2, and consists of steps described below:

1. First, a search for hyperparameters, initialization, training and validation of the offline model with data from León is performed.
2. Next, the offline model is tested with the plant in León, to evaluate its performance in estimating the tank level.

3. Finally, the previously developed offline model, with $\mathbf{W}_{in}$, $\mathbf{W}_{res}$ and $\mathbf{W}_{out}$ matrices, is copied to generate the online model. Then, this online model with RLS adaptive readout is applied to data from the plant in Gijón, evaluating its adaptation to another instance of the same system.

# 4    Results

**Table 1.** Tested and best hyperparameter values

| Hyperparameter | Tested values | Best value |
|---|---|---|
| Internal units | 100, 250, 500, 750, 1000 | 1000 |
| Spectral radius | 0.01–1.5 | 0.6708 |
| Leaking rate | 0.1–0.25 | 0.1090 |
| $\mathbf{W}_{res}$ connectivity | 0.05–0.15 | 0.1361 |
| $\mathbf{W}_{in}$ connectivity | 0.05–0.15 | 0.1064 |

For the ESN model parameterisation, 200 random sets of hyperparameters have been generated, performing 3 trials with each of these sets. Table 1 shows the hyperparameter ranges tested, as well as the best ones obtained after the search. Once the best hyperparameters have been found after training and validation, the model is run with test data from both León and Gijón plants. To analyse and visualise the performance of the developed model with the industrial plant, the residuals are calculated, defined as the absolute value of the difference between the system's real output (real tank level) and the model estimated output (estimated level). These residuals are shown in a colour map, assigning a colour to the residual in each sample according to its magnitude. In addition, for a more quantitative assessment of model performance, the Root Mean Square Error (RMSE) has been calculated, defined as:

$$RMSE = \sqrt{\sum_{i=1}^{n} \frac{(\hat{y}_i - y_i)^2}{n}} \tag{7}$$

where $n$ is the number of samples used, $\hat{y}_i$ is the estimated output at sample $i$ and $y_i$ is the real output at sample $i$. Both outputs are scaled to the range of values used for the tank level, from 0% to 100%. RMSE values obtained for each of the presented scenarios are shown in Table 2.

In first scenario, the model with the offline readout (*ridge regression*) is applied to the test data from León plant, obtaining the results shown in Fig. 3a. Analysing these results, it can be seen that there is not much difference between the real level of the tank and the estimated one, as is also reflected in the residuals map. In this instance, an RMSE of 3.3489 is obtained, as shown in Table 2.

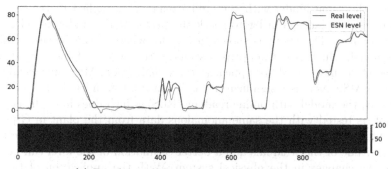

(a) Results with León plant and Ridge method

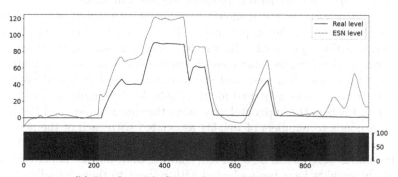

(b) Results with Gijón plant and Ridge method

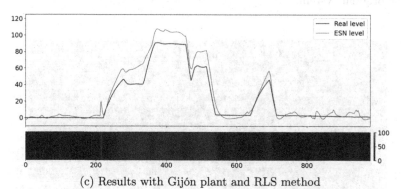

(c) Results with Gijón plant and RLS method

**Fig. 3.** Results obtained with ESN model

**Table 2.** RMSE values obtained

| Scenario | RMSE |
|---|---|
| Ridge with León plant | 3.3489 |
| Ridge with Gijón plant | 18.1924 |
| RLS with Gijón plant | 7.8649 |

Next, the same model with the offline readout is applied to the test data from the Gijón plant, in order to check the performance of the model against system changes. The result is shown in Fig. 3b, where it can be seen that the offline model, which is not adaptive, estimates the output of the system worse and, therefore, more residuals appear in the visualisation. More specifically, this time the RMSE increases significantly, as it can be seen in Table 2.

Finally, the model with online readout (RLS), which does have the capacity to adapt, is tested with the same anomalous data from the plant in Gijón. By observing the results obtained on this instance, shown in Fig. 3c, a reduction in the magnitude of the residuals and a better estimation of the level can be seen, despite the changes in the physical system. With the application of the RLS model, the RMSE is considerably reduced, as shown in Table 2.

In the latter case, as the readout of the model is adapted, it is decided to visualise the change in the output matrix $\mathbf{W}_{out}$, since the fitting in the online model involves the adjustment of the weights within this matrix. In order to track these changes, the differences between the current states of the $\mathbf{W}_{out}$ matrix and its initial states are calculated, and the results are displayed in a colour map similar to the one previously used for the residuals. The result obtained can be seen in Fig. 4, where the horizontal axis shows the time samples, and the vertical axis corresponds to numbers of weights associated with each of the neurons in the reservoir. In this colour map, an increase in the magnitude of the differences with the initial weights can be observed, showing that, due to changes modelled system, the weights have been adapted with respect to those initially obtained for the original system.

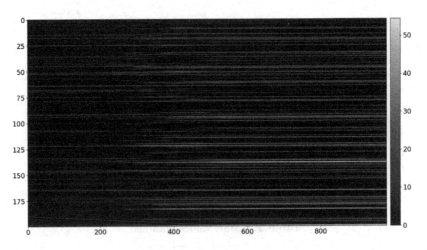

**Fig. 4.** Adaptation of the $\mathbf{W}_{out}$ matrix with RLS method applied to Gijón plant

# 5   Conclusions

This paper has presented the use of *Echo State Networks* (ESN) for modelling real industrial systems, such as tank plants with circulating fluids, adapting the model to other identically designed systems. This modelling is particularly challenging, as real systems have certain characteristics that make their modelling highly complex: non-linearities, lack of symmetry, sensor noise, among other singularities. In addition, when a model is applied to a system identical to that for which the model was designed, although it is expected to work correctly, errors are observed to occur and the model needs to be adapted in real time.

The use of ESNs for the modelling of this kind of systems is of great interest, due to their easy training, only for readout, as well as including online training possibilities for real-time adaptation to changes in system dynamics. ESNs are also of interest because of their similarity to state-space models, which are commonly used in the field of control engineering, making it easier to establish a relationship with this field.

More specifically, in this paper it has been tested the performance of ESNs for modelling tank water level in an industrial pilot plant, and also the online adaptation of the model to another identically designed plant. To analyse the performance of the models in the different case studies, RMSE errors have been calculated and the absolute value of the errors has been visualised through colour maps.

Based on the results, it can be concluded that the offline model works correctly with the system used for training and validation but the error increases considerably when applied to another identical system. On the other hand, the online model is able to adapt to the identical system and reduce the error in the output estimation.

As future work, it is still pending to improve the adjustments of the online model with the RLS method, regulating the weight of short-term and long-term memory with forgetting factor, in order to achieve adequate adaptation times. On the other hand, the use and evaluation of online adaptive models for the detection of anomalies in the modelled systems is also an ongoing task.

**Acknowledgements.** This work was supported by the Spanish State Research Agency, MCIN/ AEI/ 10.13039/ 501100011033 under Grant PID2020-117890RB-I00 and Grant PID2020-115401GB-I00. The work of José Ramón Rodríguez-Ossorio was supported by a grant from the *2020 Edition of Research Programme of the University of León*.

# References

1. Antonelo, E.A., Camponogara, E., Foss, B.: Echo state networks for data-driven downhole pressure estimation in gas-lift oil wells. Neural Netw. **85**, 106–117 (2017)
2. Dai, J., Venayagamoorthy, G.K., Harley, R.G.: Harmonic identification using an echo state network for adaptive control of an active filter in an electric ship. In: 2009 International Joint Conference on Neural Networks, pp. 634–640. IEEE (2009)

3. Fuertes, J., Prada, M.A., Domínguez, M., Reguera, P., Díaz, I., Díez, A.: Visualization of dynamic parameters of a multivariable system using self-organizing maps. IFAC Proc. Volumes **41**(2), 11001–11006 (2008)
4. Fuertes, J.J., Prada, M.A., Rodríguez-Ossorio, J.R., González-Herbón, R., Pérez, D., Domínguez, M.: Environment for education on industry 4.0. IEEE Access **9**, 144395–144405 (2021). https://doi.org/10.1109/ACCESS.2021.3120517
5. Jaeger, H.: The "echo state" approach to analysing and training recurrent neural networks-with an erratum note. Bonn, Germany: German National Research Center for Information Technology GMD Technical Report **148**(34), 13 (2001)
6. Jaeger, H.: Echo state network. Scholarpedia **2**, 2330 (2007). https://doi.org/10.4249/SCHOLARPEDIA.2330
7. Johansson, K.H.: The quadruple-tank process: a multivariable laboratory process with an adjustable zero. IEEE Trans. Control Syst. Technol. **8**(3), 456–465 (2000). https://doi.org/10.1109/87.845876
8. Jordanou, J.P., Antonelo, E.A., Camponogara, E.: Online learning control with echo state networks of an oil production platform. Eng. Appl. Artif. Intell. **85**, 214–228 (2019)
9. Lasi, H., Fettke, P., Kemper, H.-G., Feld, T., Hoffmann, M.: Industry 4.0. Bus. Inf. Syst. Eng. **6**(4), 239–242 (2014)
10. Lukoševičius, M.: A practical guide to applying echo state networks. In: Montavon, G., Orr, G.B., Müller, K.-R. (eds.) Neural Networks: Tricks of the Trade. LNCS, vol. 7700, pp. 659–686. Springer, Heidelberg (2012). https://doi.org/10.1007/978-3-642-35289-8_36
11. Lukoševičius, M., Jaeger, H.: Reservoir computing approaches to recurrent neural network training. Comput. Sci. Rev. **3**(3), 127–149 (2009)
12. Salmen, M., Ploger, P.G.: Echo state networks used for motor control. In: Proceedings of the 2005 IEEE International Conference on Robotics and Automation, pp. 1953–1958. IEEE (2005)
13. Sánchez, L., Anseán, D., Otero, J., Couso, I.: Assessing the health of LiFePO4 traction batteries through monotonic echo state networks. Sensors **18**(1), 9 (2018). https://doi.org/10.3390/s18010009
14. Tao, F., Cheng, J., Qi, Q., Zhang, M., Zhang, H., Sui, F.: Digital twin-driven product design, manufacturing and service with big data. Int. J. Adv. Manuf. Technol. **94**(9-12), 3563–3576 (2018). https://doi.org/10.1007/s00170-017-0233-1
15. Trouvain, N., Pedrelli, L., Dinh, T.T., Hinaut, X.: ReservoirPy: an efficient and user-friendly library to design echo state networks. In: ICANN 2020 - 29th International Conference on Artificial Neural Networks. Bratislava, Slovakia (Sep 2020)
16. Venayagamoorthy, G.K.: Online design of an echo state network based wide area monitor for a multimachine power system. Neural Netw. **20**(3), 404–413 (2007)

# DNN-Driven Gradient-Based Shape Optimization in Fluid Mechanics

Konstantina G. Kovani$^{(\boxtimes)}$, Marina G. Kontou⑩, Varvara G. Asouti⑩,
and Kyriakos C. Giannakoglou⑩

Parallel CFD & Optimization Unit (PCOpt), School of Mechanical Engineering,
National Technical University of Athens,
9, Iroon Polytechniou Street, 15772 Zografou, Greece
k.kovani99@gmail.com, {mkontou,vasouti,kgianna}@mail.ntua.gr

**Abstract.** The implementation of differentiated Deep Neural Networks
(DNNs), within a gradient-based optimization method in fluid mechanics, for predicting the objective function values and its gradient, is
demonstrated and assessed. In the proposed method, DNNs, after being
trained on a set of patterns for which the objective function values are
available, are used to replace both the code simulating the fluid flow
and its adjoint solver computing gradients in problems governed by partial differential equations. The derivatives of the responses of the trained
DNNs with respect to its inputs (which are the design variables of the
optimization problem) are computed using automatic differentiation in
reverse accumulation mode. Prior to successfully and efficiently supporting the optimization loop, gradients are verified against finite differences
as well as the adjoint method. The proposed, DNN-driven shape optimization method is used to design an isolated airfoil (inviscid flow) and
an S-bend duct (laminar flow); its efficiency is compared with an adjoint-based optimization.

**Keywords:** Deep Neural Networks · Computational Fluid Dynamics ·
Gradient-based Shape Optimization · Aerodynamics

## 1 Introduction

Nowadays, Computational Fluid Dynamics (CFD) tools and optimization methods are very attractive in various engineering fields involving fluid dynamics. CFD-based optimization tools for large scale applications usually rely on
gradient-based techniques supported by the adjoint method, [5,6]. The latter
computes the gradient of the objective function with respect to (w.r.t.) the design
variables at a cost which is independent of their number $N$.

At the same time, DNNs and their integration within simulations (CFD-based, in our case) are gaining ground due to their ability to handle large volumes
of complex data at low computational cost and resources. Trained DNNs may
accelerate the simulation process by replacing part of or the entire CFD tool.
For instance, [14] uses conditional variational autoencoders and an integrated
generative network for the inverse design of supercritical airfoils. [4] presents a

ⓒ The Author(s), under exclusive license to Springer Nature Switzerland AG 2023
L. Iliadis et al. (Eds.): EANN 2023, CCIS 1826, pp. 379–390, 2023.
https://doi.org/10.1007/978-3-031-34204-2_32

solver based on Machine Learning (ML) models that predict the required numerical fluxes, in compressible fluid flows, based on high-resolution runs; the solver was fully differentiated using automatic differentiation (AD). A toolkit based on complex-step finite differences for the numerical differentiation of neural networks was proposed in [12], making it computationally lightweight by overcoming the high-order chain rule. In [7], the authors of this paper proposed a DNN-based surrogate for the turbulence closure of the Reynolds-Averaged Navier Stokes (RANS) equations; the role of the DNN is to replace the numerical solution of the turbulence and transition models. The DNN-assisted RANS solver was combined with an evolutionary algorithm to optimize the shape of a transonic turbine blade and a car model. ML surrogates were used in aerodynamic shape optimization of transonic airfoils, in [11].

The cost of the aerodynamic shape optimization is highly affected by the dimensionality of the design space and the cost of the aerodynamic analysis. In [8], the performance of ML models used in aerodynamic shape optimization is reviewed, and the efficiency of more advanced models using appropriate geometry parameterization so as to reduce the dimensionality of the design space, is presented. In [9], a numerical methodology based on modal decomposition coupled with the regression analysis for creating reduced-order models of fluid flows is demonstrated. In [15], the efficiency of the adjoint-based optimization is accelerated using DNNs to predict the mapping between the adjoint vector and the local flow variables.

In this work, DNNs are used to assist gradient-based shape optimization problems in fluid mechanics, by undertaking the computation of both the objective function and its gradients. The DNNs use the values of the design variables determining the shape to be designed (according to the selected parameterization) as inputs and are trained to compute the objective and constraint (if any) functions of the optimization. Once trained, these are also differentiated to additionally provide the gradient of their response(s) w.r.t. the design variables to drive the optimization. The proposed method is compared with a (continuous) adjoint-based optimization in terms of effectiveness and cost, since the latter is widely used in industrial applications. A parametric study on the DNN activation functions, regarding the accuracy of the computed gradients is included.

## 2    Methods and Tools

This section describes the constituents of the proposed gradient-based optimization method that makes use of differentiated DNNs. Initially, the CFD code used to simulate the flow problems is briefly described; this software runs on Graphics Processing Units (GPUs). Then, topics related to the DNNs and their implementation in the gradient-based shape optimization loop are discussed.

### 2.1    CFD and Shape Parameterization Tools

All flow simulations are performed using the in-house GPU-accelerated CFD solver PUMA, [2,13] which numerically solves the Navier-Stokes equations for compressible and incompressible fluids; herein the compressible flow variant is used. The flow and their (continuous) adjoint equations are discretized on unstructured/hybrid grids, using the vertex-centered finite volume technique. The viscous flow equations for compressible fluids are written in the form

$$R_n = \frac{\partial f_{nk}^{\text{inv}}}{\partial x_k} - \frac{\partial f_{nk}^{\text{vis}}}{\partial x_k} = 0 \tag{1}$$

where $f_k^{inv} = [\rho v_k \quad \rho v_k v_1 + p\delta_{1k} \quad \rho v_k v_2 + p\delta_{2k} \quad \rho v_k v_3 + p\delta_{3k} \quad \rho v_k h_t]^T$ are the inviscid and $f_k^{vis} = [0 \quad \tau_{1k} \quad \tau_{2k} \quad \tau_{3k} \quad v_\ell \tau_{\ell k} + q_k]^T$ the viscous fluxes. $\rho$, $p$, $v_k$ and $h_t$ stand for the fluid's density, pressure, velocity components, total enthalpy and $\delta_{km}$ is the Kronecker symbol, respectively. The viscous stress tensor is given by $\tau_{km} = \mu \left( \frac{\partial v_k}{\partial x_m} + \frac{\partial v_m}{\partial x_k} - \frac{2}{3}\delta_{km}\frac{\partial v_\ell}{\partial x_\ell} \right)$ where $\mu$ is the bulk viscosity and $q_k$ the heat flux. All computations are made with second-order accuracy.

The adjoint method (which is used to compare with) is based on the definition of a Lagrangian function; this is formed by adding the objective function to be minimized to the integral (over the flow domain) of the residuals of the flow equations multiplied by the adjoint variables (or Lagrange multipliers). It is evident that objective and Lagrangian functions take on the same value as the flow equations are always satisfied and, thus, their residuals are zero. Therefore, the gradient of the Lagrangian, rather than the objective function, can be computed. This is differentiated w.r.t. to the design variables and terms multiplying the derivatives of flow variables w.r.t. to the design variables are set to zero, leading to the adjoint equations. PUMA implements the continuous adjoint approach in which the adjoint equations are derived in the form of partial differential equations which are, then, discretized and numerically solved [13].

In both the flow and adjoint solvers of PUMA, high parallel efficiency is achieved by the use of Mixed Precision Arithmetics (MPA), [2]. MPA reduces the memory footprint of the code and the memory transactions of the GPU threads with the device memory, without affecting code's accuracy. In particular, the memory demanding computations of the coefficient matrices of the linearized systems is performed with double, though these are stored in single, precision accuracy. The residuals of the equations, determining the accuracy of the simulation, are always computed and stored in double precision.

In addition to the flow and adjoint solvers, PUMA contains a set of shape and mesh morphing and parameterization techniques based on volumetric Non-Uniform Rational B-Splines (NURBS), [10]. The geometry to be optimized and (part of) the grid are encapsulated within a NURBS lattice. A knot vector and a degree must be defined for each parametric direction. Each time the NURBS lattice points (a.k.a. control points) are displaced, the geometry changes and the CFD grid is adapted to it.

## 2.2  DNNs - Training and Differentiation

Working with DNNs, the first step is to collect the necessary training data and create the database (to be referred to DB$_{DNN}$) which the DNN will be trained on. Herein, the $DB_{DNN}$ is formed by sampling the design space using the Latin Hypercube Sampling (LHS) technique, generating the corresponding geometries and evaluating them on the CFD solver. The LHS is effective in case the number of samples must be kept small, and it is widely used in DNNs. In this paper, reducing the size of the $DB_{DNN}$ is important as all of its entries should be evaluated on the costly CFD code.

To increase the prediction accuracy of the DNN, its hyperparameters must carefully be determined. The number of layers and neurons per layer as well as the most appropriate activation function(s) must be selected, see Sect. 3. In all problems, fully connected networks are used. Given that the DNN output practically results from operations involving the networks's weights and the activation functions, the derivatives of the DNN can be obtained through automatic differentiation in reverse mode [3]. Setup, training and differentiation of the DNNs is carried out in the TensorFlow framework (v2.6.0), [1], using Python.

### 2.3   The Proposed DNN-Driven Gradient-Based Algorithm

In CFD-based optimization based on the adjoint method, each cycle comprises the numerical solution of the Navier-Stokes equations, that of the adjoint equations and the computation of the gradient of sensitivity derivatives (SDs) used to update the design variables vector. Without loss of generality, in this work, all updates are computed by steepest descent.

Alternatively, this work proposes to replace the flow and the adjoint equations solvers with the trained DNN which predicts both the objective function value (used to monitor the progress of the optimization) and the SDs. Once the initial $DB_{DNN}$ resulting from the LHS is available (see Sect. 2.2), each round (this term is used to distinguish this loop and the gradient-based descent loop of step 2, in which optimization cycles are performed by updating the design vector and the gradient) of the proposed algorithm comprises the following steps:

1. Train the DNN using the data available in $DB_{DNN}$.
2. Iteratively optimize (till convergence) by applying gradient-based descent using, exclusively, the DNN-based sensitivities. A number of entries selected from the $DB_{DNN}$ can be used as starting points (starting designs) and perform as many runs as the number of starting points.
3. Re-evaluate (all or part of) the "optimized" solution(s) on the CFD tool; the use of quotes ("optimized") makes clear that this is the best solution according to the DNN.
4. Update the $DB_{DNN}$ with all the recently evaluated solutions, if necessary, and repeat all four steps starting from step 1. The termination criterion is related to the DNN prediction accuracy.

In step 1, the DNN is configured differently in each problem. Experience has shown that, the use of a single DNN in all problems is not a viable solution, in CFD-based analysis. Regarding the paper, one may notice that the two problems involve different physics (the one is an inviscid whereas the other is a viscous flow problem) and it is reasonable to have different DNN configurations. An optimization algorithm could have been used to find the optimal set of hyperparameters, as in [7]. However, since in this work emphasis is laid on the computation and use of the DNN gradient, it was decided to perform parametric studies and discuss their outcome rather than optimizing the network hyperparameters and, then, just using the optimal configuration to get results.

## 3    Applications in Aerodynamic Shape Optimization

Two aerodynamic shape optimization problems are selected to demonstrate the capabilities of the proposed algorithm. These are related to the shape optimization of an isolated airfoil and that of an S-bend duct. The first problem assumes an inviscid fluid flow (so, the flow solver is faster than the second one since the part of the flow solver dealing with the viscous terms is omitted and, also, the CFD grid is coarser). In all problems, the gradient (computed by the trained DNN) is verified against the outcome of Finite Differences (FDs) and the continuous adjoint of PUMA.

Since the potential of the proposed method should mainly be assessed in terms of computational cost, one time unit (TU) is set equal to the cost of numerically solving the flow equations. Also, the absolutely realistic assumption that the solution of the adjoint equations has practically the cost of solving the flow equations is made. Thus, one adjoint-based optimization cycle costs 2 TUs. Apart from the cost of forming the $DB_{DNN}$ (as many TUs as the number of its entries), the cost of a DNN-driven optimization should also include the re-evaluation of some of the "optimized" solutions on the CFD tool.

### 3.1    Problem I: Inviscid Flow Around an Airfoil

The first problem performs an optimization starting from the NACA0012 isolated airfoil. The flow is inviscid with free-stream Mach number and flow angle equal to $M_\infty = 0.50$ and $\alpha_\infty = 2°$, respectively. An unstructured grid with $\sim 7.8K$ nodes is used; the farfield boundaries of the computational domain are located about 10 chords away from the airfoil. The optimization aims at designing a new airfoil with a user-defined lift coefficient value ($C_{L,target}$). The objective function (to be minimized) is

$$F = \frac{1}{2} \left( C_L - C_{L,target} \right)^2 \tag{2}$$

where $C_L$ is the lift force ($L$) exerted by the flow on the airfoil normalized by the dynamic pressure coefficient multiplied by the airfoil's chord (c), as $C_L = L/(\frac{1}{2}\rho U_\infty^2 c)$, where $U_\infty$ is the farfield velocity. In this problem, $C_{L,target}$ is set twice as high as the $C_L$ of the baseline profile. The $10 \times 7$ NURBS lattice of Fig. 1 controls both the airfoil shape and part of the surrounding grid. 16 out of the 70 control points are allowed to be displaced in the normal-to-the chord (vertical) direction, resulting in $N = 16$ design variables (and, thus, 16 are the inputs to

the DNN), in total. The design variables ($b \in R^N$) are allowed to change within
the $\pm 0.05c$ around their initial values, so as to avoid the overlapping of the
lattice lines. The LHS technique was used to generate 20 different combinations
of the design variables, corresponding to 20 different airfoil shapes. Each sampled
geometry was evaluated on the CFD solver and $C_L$ was computed. Thus, the
DNN model's input was a [20 × 16] tensor with the sampled coordinates of the
lattice control points, with the [20 × 1] tensor of the corresponding $C_L$ values as
output.

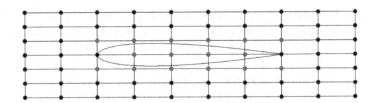

**Fig. 1.** *Problem I*: NURBS control lattice parameterizing the airfoil contour. Control
points in blue are fixed; red ones can be displaced in the normal-to-the-chord direction.
(Color figure online)

The DNN's configuration was derived after a parametric study/trial-and-
error procedure for the model's hyperparameters, focusing mainly on the number
of the hidden layers, the number of neurons per layer and the activation functions. For this first problem, the selected configuration has four hidden layers,
with 32, 32, 64 and 32 neurons, respectively. This DNN architecture was assessed
in terms of accuracy (of both $C_L$ and its gradient) by combining different activation functions. Four DNNs using the ReLU, the GELU, the sigmoid and the tanh
activation functions in all hidden layers are trained and compared. The results
are summarized in Fig. 2. The DNN-based SDs for the baseline geometry using
GELU are in good agreement with FDs. Small discrepancies are observed in the
derivatives w.r.t. some design variables, preserving though the sign of the SDs,
in contrast to other activation functions that yield even wrongly signed SDs.

The shape optimization follows. Two runs were carried out; the first run relied
exclusively on the DNN using the GELU activation function (as concluded after
the previously presented parametric study), while the second one on PUMA
and its adjoint solver. Once the DNN-based optimization run converged, the
"optimized" solution was re-evaluated on PUMA. This was then added to the
$DB_{DNN}$, the DNN was re-trained, and the optimization was repeated. Three
rounds (each of them including re-evaluations of one "optimized" solution per
cycle and DNN re-training) were sufficient to reach the optimal solution with
a deviation in the $C_L$ values (w.r.t. to the $C_{L,target}$) less than 1%. Given that
the cost of a DNN-based optimization as well as that of the DNN training is
practically negligible (w.r.t. the cost of a CFD run, even if the less costly inviscid
flow model is used), the optimization turnaround time was 23 TUs. This includes
the cost to form the $DB_{DNN}$ (20 TUs) and the three CFD based re-evaluations.

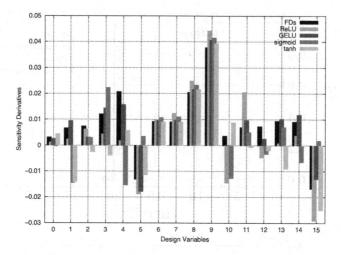

**Fig. 2.** _Problem I_: SDs of $C_L$ (w.r.t. the design variables) for the baseline geometry computed with FDs (black) and derived from the DNN's differentiation for the different activation functions: ReLU (red), GELU (blue), sigmoid (green), tanh (orange). The SDs computed by the adjoint method of PUMA are omitted as these are practically identical to those computed by FDs. (Color figure online)

On the other hand, the adjoint-based run (with cost of 2 TUs per cycle) needs 32 TUs for reaching the target $C_{L,target}$ value. The convergence histories of the optimization runs are presented in Fig. 3. Overall, the DNN-based optimization is by $\sim 31\%$ less expensive than the adjoint-based run.

The optimized airfoil shapes resulted from both optimization runs and the Mach number fields around them are compared with the baseline airfoil in Fig. 4; overall, the flow speed increased (pressure decreased) over the suction side of the optimized airfoils in order to match $C_{L,target}$.

### 3.2 Problem II: Laminar Flow Within an S-Bend Duct

The second problem is dealing with the re-design of an S-bend duct for min. mass-averaged total pressure losses between the inlet $(I)$ and the outlet $(O)$. The objective to minimize is

$$F = \frac{\int\limits_{S_I} p_t \rho v_n dS + \int\limits_{S_O} p_t \rho v_n dS}{\int\limits_{S_I} \rho v_n dS} \tag{3}$$

where $p_t$, $v_n$ are the total pressure and the normal velocity pointing outwards to the CFD domain (this is why in the numerator of Eq. 3, the sum, rather than the difference of two integrals appears). $F$ stands for the losses occurring in the flow due to the viscous effects. The flow is laminar with $Re = 1.84 \cdot 10^4$ (Reynolds number based on the duct width) and inlet velocity $U = 20$ m/s; a

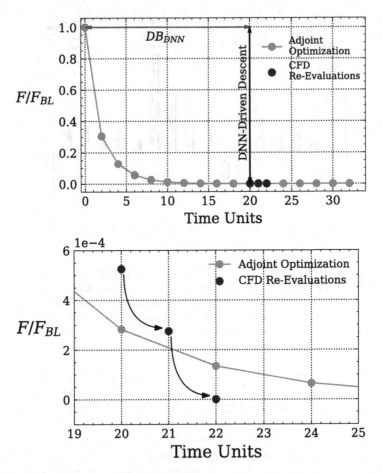

**Fig. 3.** _Problem I_: Top: Convergence history of the optimization runs based on the adjoint method (red) and the differentiated DNN (black). Solutions of the DNN-based optimization which are re-evaluated on the CFD tool are shown in filled blue circles. Bottom: Close-up view of the previous curve between TU 19 and 25, in order to make a clear comparison between the adjoint curve and the three solutions "optimized" by the DNN-driven run and re-evaluated on the CFD. (Color figure online)

structured grid of $\sim 90K$ nodes was generated. The duct shape is parameterized using a $8 \times 9$ NURBS lattice, Fig. 5. 20, (out of the 72) control points are allowed to move in the $y$ direction, yielding $N = 20$ design variables (20 inputs to the DNN).

A $DB_{DNN}$ consisting of 50 duct geometries was used to train the DNN. The DNN gets the $[50 \times 20]$ tensor of the $y$ coordinates of the control points of all samples as input and computes the $[50 \times 1]$ tensor of the $F$ values (Eq. 3). As in Problem I, the model's configuration was decided after comparing various hyper-parameter combinations, and is made of 7 layers with $32, 64, 128, 256, 128, 64, 32$

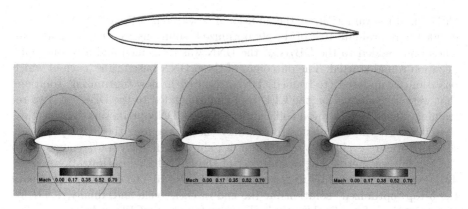

**Fig. 4.** _Problem I_: Top: Shape of the baseline (black) and optimized airfoils based on the adjoint method (blue) and the differentiated DNN (red). Bottom: Mach number field for the baseline (left) and optimized airfoil resulted from the adjoint method (center) and the differentiated DNN (right). (Color figure online)

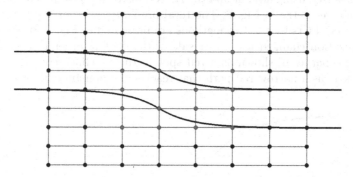

**Fig. 5.** _Problem II_: Control points of the volumetric NURBS control lattice, parameterizing the S-bend duct. Blue points are kept fixed, whereas red ones can be displaced in the $y$ direction. (Color figure online)

neurons; the GELU activation function was used for all hidden layers and the sigmoid for the output one.

Since the descent phase of the DNN-driven optimization algorithm is of negligible cost, it was decided to perform optimization runs starting from all sampled geometries forming the $DB_{DNN}$, i.e. 50 runs in total. Though this is not what this paper generally proposes, such a decision was made since it allows an exhaustive exploitation of the design space and showcases the appearance of many local minima in this kind of problems. Upon completion of the 50 optimization runs, the designer may decide which of the "optimized" solutions should undergo a

CFD-based re-evaluation, at the additional cost of one TU each. Herein, it was decided to re-evaluate 10% of the 50 "optimized" solutions, i.e. the top 5 of them. These were added to the $DB_{DNN}$, the DNN was re-trained and a second optimization round started. The outcomes of the 5 DNN-based runs, each of which based on an updated (re-trained) DNN, resulted in new "optimized" solutions that were re-evaluated on the CFD tool and appended to the $DB_{DNN}$. Two re-trainings of the DNN proved sufficient to obtain a DNN prediction accuracy less than 0.5%. At the end of this round, only the best among the five "optimized" solutions was re-evaluated, resulting in a reduction in $F$ by 4.6% compared to the baseline geometry. The overall cost of the DNN-based optimization was 61 TUs, consisting of: 50 TUs to generate the $DB_{DNN}$, 10 TUs ($= 2 \times 5$) to evaluate the 5 top "optimized" solutions at the end of each cycle and, finally, 1 TU for the evaluation of the final "optimized" geometry on the CFD code.

For comparison, an adjoint-based optimization was also performed. The optimization loop resulted in a reduction in $F$ by 4.6%, compared to the baseline geometry and required 30 cycles till convergence, at the cost of 60 TUs. The duct shapes optimized using adjoint and the DNN-assisted method are compared with the baseline geometry in Fig. 6. The total pressure losses for the baseline, and the optimized ducts by the two methods are presented in Fig. 7. It is clear that the optimization changed the upper side of the duct in order to avoid a small (incipient) separation, shown as a red spot in the baseline geometry. This red spot develops as a narrow red path that reaches the domain exit.

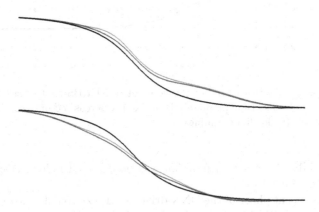

**Fig. 6.** *Problem II*: Shape of the baseline (black), the adjoint-based (red) and the DNN-based (blue) optimized ducts. Axes not in scale ($x : y = 1 : 2$). (Color figure online)

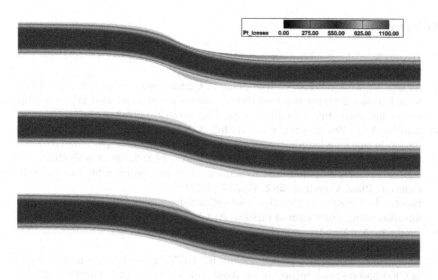

**Fig. 7.** _Problem II_: Total pressure losses for the baseline (top) , the optimized by the adjoint method (center) and the optimized by the proposed DNN-driven method (bottom) geometries.

## 4  Conclusions

A gradient-based optimization framework for CFD problems relying exclusively on differentiated DNNs was presented and tested. The DNN was trained to predict the objective function value and, then, differentiated based on reverse mode AD; the optimization loop was exclusively driven by derivatives provided by the differentiated DNN. This was demonstrated in the shape optimization of an isolated airfoil (inviscid flow) and an S-bend duct (laminar flow). Since the objective function values and their derivatives resulting from CFD simulations can vary significantly w.r.t the flow properties and the geometric parameterization of the design space, different DNN configurations were tested, depending on the case. A parametric study on the models hyperparameters designated that, for the examined problems, the GELU activation function is the most appropriate for achieving high accuracy of both the objective function and its gradient. The performance of the DNN-assisted optimizations were compared with those based on the (continuous) adjoint method in terms of computational cost and solution quality. In the first flow problem, the DNN-driven optimization achieved a solution of the same quality as the adjoint-based one, at $\sim 70\%$ of the computational cost of the latter. Similar conclusions were drawn in the second problem too. Here, in addition, the developed software was asked to perform more than one (concurrent) DNN-driven optimizations, given their negligible costs. Overall, the obtained results sound very encouraging; on-going work focuses on the extension of this method to many-objective and/or constrained optimization, even for turbulent flow problems.

# References

1. TensorFlow: large-scale machine learning on heterogeneous systems (2015). https://www.tensorflow.org/
2. Asouti, V., Trompoukis, X., Kampolis, I., Giannakoglou, K.: Unsteady CFD computations using vertex-centered finite volumes for unstructured grids on graphics processing units. Int. J. Numer. Meth. Fluids **67**(2), 232–246 (2011)
3. Baydin, A.G., Pearlmutter, B.A., Radul, A.A., Siskind, J.M.: Automatic differentiation in machine learning: a survey. J. Mach. Learn. Res. **18**, 1–43 (2018)
4. Bezgin, D.A., Buhendwa, A.B., Adams, N.A.: JAX-fluids: a fully-differentiable high-order computational fluid dynamics solver for compressible two-phase flows. Comput. Phys. Commun. **282**, 108527 (2023)
5. Elliott, J., Peraire, J.: Practical three-dimensional aerodynamic design and optimization using unstructured meshes. AIAA J. **35**(9), 1479–1485 (1997)
6. Jameson, A.: Aerodynamic design via control theory. J. Sci. Comput. **3**, 233–260 (1988)
7. Kontou, M., Asouti, V., Giannakoglou, K.: DNN surrogates for turbulence closure in CFD-based shape optimization. Appl. Soft Comput. **134**, 110013 (2023)
8. Li, J., Du, X., Martins, J.R.: Machine learning in aerodynamic shape optimization. Prog. Aerosp. Sci. **134**, 100849 (2022)
9. Lui, H.F.S., Wolf, W.R.: Construction of reduced-order models for fluid flows using deep feedforward neural networks. J. Fluid Mech. **872**, 963–994 (2019)
10. Piegl, L., Tiller, W.: The NURBS Book, 2nd edn. Springer, Heidelberg (1997). https://doi.org/10.1007/978-3-642-97385-7
11. Renganathan, S.A., Maulik, R., Ahuja, J.: Enhanced data efficiency using deep neural networks and gaussian processes for aerodynamic design optimization. Aerosp. Sci. Technol. **111**, 106522 (2021)
12. Shen, S., Shao, T., Zhou, K., Jiang, C., Luo, F., Yang, Y.: HoD-Net: high-order differentiable deep neural networks and applications. In: Proceedings of the AAAI Conference on Artificial Intelligence, vol. 36, no. 8, pp. 8249–8258 (2022)
13. Trompoukis, X.S., Tsiakas, K.T., Asouti, V.G., Giannakoglou, K.C.: Continuous adjoint-based shape optimization of a turbomachinery stage using a 3D volumetric parameterization. Int. J. Numer. Meth. Fluids (2023). https://doi.org/10.1002/fld.5187
14. Wang, J., et al.: An inverse design method for supercritical airfoil based on conditional generative models. Chin. J. Aeronaut. **35**(3), 62–74 (2022)
15. Xu, M., Song, S., Sun, X., Chen, W., Zhang, W.: Machine learning for adjoint vector in aerodynamic shape optimization. Acta. Mech. Sin. **37**(9), 1416–1432 (2021)

# Residual Error Learning for Electricity Demand Forecasting

Achilleas Andronikos, Maria Tzelepi[✉], and Anastasios Tefas

Aristotle University of Thessaloniki, Thessaloniki, Greece
{aandroni,mtzelepi,tefas}@csd.auth.gr

**Abstract.** Electricity demand forecasting describes the challenging task of predicting the electricity demand by employing historical load data. In this paper, we propose a novel method, named *RESidual Error Learning for Forecasting* (RESELF) for improving the performance of a deep learning model towards the electricity demand forecasting task. The proposed method proposes to train a model with the actual load values and compute the residual errors. Subsequently, RESELF proposes to train a second model using as targets the computed residual errors. Finally, the prediction of the proposed methodology is defined as the sum of the first model's and second model's predictions. We argue that if the errors are systematic, the proposed method will provide improved results. The experimental evaluation on four datasets validates the effectiveness of the proposed method in improving the forecasting performance.

**Keywords:** Residual Error Learning · Electricity Demand Forecasting · Greek Energy Market · Deep Learning

## 1 Introduction

Electricity demand forecasting (also known as electric load demand forecasting) describes the task of predicting the electricity demand by utilizing historical load data, as well as exogenous variables like temperature. Based on the time-scale, it can be discriminated into three categories: short-term load forecast with a time frame of a few hours up to one-day ahead or a week ahead, mid-term load forecast with a time frame of a week to one year ahead, and the long-term forecast with a time frame of up to several years ahead. In this work, we mainly deal with a short-term forecasting task, and particularly the one-day-ahead forecasting (i.e., 24 h of the next day). Additionally, we perform experiments considering also a similar problem, that is we also apply the proposed method for improving the personalized energy consumption prediction considering the one-year-ahead task.

Generally, electricity demand forecasting has been a vivid research area in recent years [11], since it is linked with many critical applications ranging from power system operation and planning to energy trading [8], allowing power companies to accomplish an efficient balance between demand and supply, avoiding excess reserve of power generation or power interruptions due to load shedding.

© The Author(s), under exclusive license to Springer Nature Switzerland AG 2023
L. Iliadis et al. (Eds.): EANN 2023, CCIS 1826, pp. 391–402, 2023.
https://doi.org/10.1007/978-3-031-34204-2_33

In this paper, we mainly deal with short-term electricity demand forecasting focusing attention to the *Greek Energy Market*. We propose a novel residual error learning methodology for improving the forecasting performance of deep learning models, named *RESidual Error Learning for Forecasting* (RESELF). Generally, the *residuals* are a useful tool in traditional time-series analysis for analyzing the properties of a forecasting model. In this paper, we introduce residual error learning in deep learning models in a novel way. More specifically, we propose to train a model with the actual load values, considering the electricity demand task and then compute the residual errors from the actual load values. Subsequently, we propose to train a second model using as targets the computed residual errors. Then, the final predictions of the proposed methodology are defined as the sum of the first model's prediction and the second model's prediction. We argue that, if the errors are systematic, then the proposed methodology will provide improved performance. This is experimentally validated through extensive experiments.

The remainder of the manuscript is structured as follows. Section 2 presents previous relevant works. Section 3 presents in detail the proposed residual error learning methodology for electricity demand forecasting. Subsequently, in Sect. 4 the experimental evaluation of the proposed method is provided. Finally, the conclusions are drawn in Sect. 5.

## 2    Relevant Work

The problem of electricity demand forecasting has been extensively studied since the past decades. Earlier works for tackling the problem include statistical models [10,16] and machine learning models [4,13]. Subsequently, motivated by the outstanding results of DL models in a wide variety of problems, ranging from image classification and retrieval [18] to financial time-series forecasting [14], they have been proposed so as to address the electricity demand problem [1,2,6,7] accomplishing notable performance.

Surveying the existing literature, we come across several works addressing the electricity demand forecasting problem on the Greek Energy Market [5]. For instance, a fuzzy-based ensemble that uses hybrid DL networks is proposed for load demand prediction of the next week in [15]. More specifically, initially, a fuzzy clustering technique creates an ensemble prediction and after that a pipeline of radial basis function neural network transforms the data in order to be fitted in a convolutional neural network. Furthermore, the effect of dimensionality reduction methods in the day-ahead forecasting performance of neural networks is investigated in [12]. Additionally, a method that assists the exploitation of the statistical properties of each time series with main focus the optimization of CNN's hyper-parameters is proposed in [3].

Subsequently, in a recent work, a realistic approach for the electricity demand forecasting considering the Greek Energy Market is developed in [9]. More specifically, the vast majority of the existing methods make two assumptions. Firstly, it is assumed that any past load data before the day whose load demand we want to predict are available and can be used. Secondly, real weather information (i.e., temperature) of the aforementioned day is also considered available.

On the contrary, in [9], a more realistic setup is followed, considering an information gap between the prediction day and the past load data, retaining however the assumption regarding the weather information, and a strategy for filling the information gap is proposed, along with a novel loss function.

Next, in [19], an evaluation study regarding the optimal input features and an effective model architecture considering the electricity demand forecasting task is performed, and then using the optimal features and model, a novel regularization method is proposed, improving the baseline forecasting. Finally, a novel online self-distillation method considering electricity demand forecasting tasks is proposed in [17].

In this paper, we propose a novel method for improving the forecasting performance of DL models towards the electricity demand task, using the residual errors of the model. It should be emphasized that the proposed methodology can also be combined with several methods for electricity demand forecasting, further improving their performance.

## 3   Proposed Method

In this paper, we deal with electricity demand forecasting. Our goal is to improve the forecasting performance of a DL model towards this task. To achieve this goal we utilize the concept of *residuals*, and propose a methodology named *RESidual Error Learning for Forecasting* (RESELF). More specifically, as illustrated in Fig. 1, we first train a model to predict the actual load values (ground truth). Then we compute the residual errors from the actual load values. In the second stage, we use the computed residual errors as targets to train a second model. That is, the second model is trained to predict the residual errors. Finally, the prediction of the proposed method is formulated as the sum of the first model's prediction and the second model's prediction. We argue that if the errors have any underlying structure, and hence are systematic, then the proposed methodology will provide enhanced performance.

More specifically, we consider the input data $\{\mathbf{x}_i, \mathbf{y}_i\}_{i=1}^{N}$, where $\mathbf{x}_i \in \Re^D$ is an input vector and $D$ its dimensionality (as it is presented in the subsequent Section, D=171 for the main problem of electricity demand forecasting), while $\mathbf{y}_i \in \Re^d$ corresponds to its $d$-dimensional ground truth vector (d=24 for one-day-ahead problem in an hourly basis). Thus, we fist train the first model, using a common loss function considering forecasting tasks, that is, Mean Absolute Percentage Error (MAPE) loss:

$$MAPE = \frac{1}{N} \sum_{i=1}^{N} \left| \frac{\mathbf{y}_i - \hat{\mathbf{y}}_i}{\mathbf{y}_i} \right|, \tag{1}$$

where $\mathbf{y}_i$ is the ground truth and $\hat{\mathbf{y}}_i$ is the model's prediction.

Then, the we compute the residual errors for each sample $i$ between its predicted values $\hat{\mathbf{y}}_i$ and its actual values $\mathbf{y}_i$ as follows:

$$\mathbf{e}_i = \mathbf{y}_i - \hat{\mathbf{y}}_i. \tag{2}$$

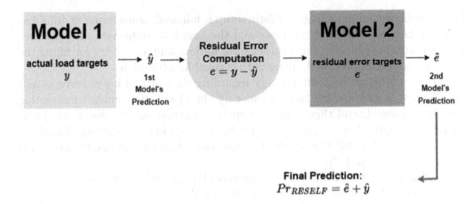

**Fig. 1.** Proposed Method

Subsequently, we use the computed residual errors of Eq. (2) in order to train the second model, using the same input features. Note, that any loss function considering regression tasks can be used for training both the models. In a preliminary investigation we noticed that marginally better results can be obtained using Mean Absolute Error (MAE) loss for training the second model.

After the convergence of the second model, we can acquire the final prediction, $Pr_{RESELF}$ by summing the prediction of the initial model $\hat{y}$ and the prediction of the second model $\hat{e}$, and evaluate the performance of the proposed method. That is, for a sample $i$ the final prediction is computed as follows:

$$Pr^i_{RESELF} = \hat{e}_i + \hat{y}_i. \tag{3}$$

Finally, it should be emphasized that the two models of the proposed pipeline can be of different architecture. As it will be presented in the Experimental Evaluation, we can use a more lightweight model to train with the residual errors, achieving further improvements, while limiting at the same time the additional computational cost of the proposed pipeline.

## 4   Experimental Evaluation

In this Section, we present the experiments conducted in order to evaluate the proposed RESELF method for time-series forecasting. First the descriptions of the utilized datasets are provided followed by the description of the utilized models. Subsequently, the experimental setup and the implementation details are presented and finally the experimental results are provided and discussed.

### 4.1   Datasets

In this paper, we use four different datasets to evaluate the proposed RESELF method. More specifically, we use three datasets considering the main task of this paper, that is the one-day-ahead electricity demand prediction problem. We use data from the Greek energy market, and also electricity data from Spain[1] and New England[2]. Furthermore, we perform indicative experiments considering a similar task, that is the personalized electricity consumption forecasting, considering MV and HV costumers. The descriptions of the datasets follow bellow.

**Greek Energy Market.** The dataset of Greek energy market consists of historical load data, provided by the Greek Public Power Corporation (these data are not publicly available), as well as weather information (i.e., temperature), derived from OpenWeather[3]. Seven years of data are used in total. Specifically, load and temperature data from years 2012–2016 are used for training, the corresponding data from year 2017 are used for validation, while data from year 2018 are used for testing.

**Spain.** The dataset of Spain energy data contains historical load data, provided by ENTSO-E Transparency Platform, and weather information (i.e., temperature), obtained from OpenWeather. Data from four years are used. Data from years 2015–2017 are used for training, data from year 2017 are used for validation, and finally data from year 2018 are used for testing.

**ISO-NE.** ISO-NE consists of historical load and weather data from totally eight years. Data from years 2007–2012 are used for training, data from year 2013 are used for validation, and finally data from year 2018 are used for testing.

**MV/HV Personalized Consumption.** The MV/HV Personalized Consumption dataset consists of historical load data, provided by the Greek Public Power Corporation, and is based on MV and HV individual customer load data, as well as weather information (i.e., temperature), derived from OpenWeather. Five years of data in period 2016–2021 are used in total. For the MV customers problem data from the years 2016–2019 are used for training, while 2020 and 2021 are used for validation and training respectively. For the HV customers problem the 2015–2018 years are used for training while the 2019 year year is used for testing. We note that in this case, we deal with the problem of the one-year-ahead prediction (12 values, each for the 12 months of the year ahead), and thus the data are in a monthly basis.

## 4.2   Models

In our experiments, we use two different model architectures. That is, in the first case we use a certain model architecture for both the models of our pipeline,

---

[1] https://www.kaggle.com/datasets/nicholasjhana/energy-consumption-generation-prices-and-weather.

[2] https://github.com/yalickj/load-forecasting-resnet.

[3] https://openweathermap.org/.

and in the second case we use a more lightweight model for training with the residual errors. The first, relatively more heavyweight model consists of three hidden layers each with 64 neurons. This model contains 20,824 parameters. The second, more lightweight model consists of two hidden layers, each with 32 neurons. This model contains 7,320 parameters. In the main focus of this paper, which concerns the one-day-ahead forecasting task, the outputs of the models are 24 neurons, for each hour of the next day. The input features are described in the Table 1. Finally, considering the one-year-ahead forecasting of personalized consumption, the outputs of the models are 12 neurons for each of the 12 months of the year ahead. The input features for this case are described in Table 2.

**Table 1.** Description of Input Features - One-day-ahead Forecasting Task.

| Abbreviation | Dim | Description |
|---|---|---|
| $L_d$ | 24 | Load of the day that is 1 day before Target Day (TD) |
| $L_w$ | 24 | Load of the day that is 7 days before TD |
| $L_m$ | 24 | Load of the day that is 28 days before TD |
| $T_d$ | 24 | Corresponding temperature for $L^d$ |
| $T_w$ | 24 | Corresponding temperature for $L^w$ |
| $T_m$ | 24 | Corresponding temperature for $L^m$ |
| T | 24 | Corresponding temperature for TD |
| D | 1 | Indicator of which day of the week is the TD |
| W | 1 | Indicator of TD being weekend |
| H | 1 | Indicator of TD being holiday |

**Table 2.** Description of Input Features - One-year-ahead Forecasting Task.

| Abbreviation | Dim | Description |
|---|---|---|
| $L_m$ | 12 | Consumption of 12 months before TD |
| $T_m$ | 12 | Corresponding temperature for $L^m$ |
| $Hu_m$ | 12 | Corresponding humidity for $L^m$ |
| $S_m$ | 12 | Corresponding season indicator for $L^m$ |
| $H_m$ | 12 | Corresponding holiday indicator for $L^m$ |
| $M_m$ | 12 | Corresponding month indicator for $L^m$ |
| $Y_m$ | 12 | Corresponding year indicator for $L^m$ |
| $DY_m$ | 12 | Corresponding day of year indicator for $L^m$ |
| Avg | 1 | Average Consumption of 12 months before TD |
| Std | 1 | Standard Deviation of Consumption of 12 months before TD |
| Min | 1 | Minimum consumption of 12 months before TD |
| Max | 1 | Maximum consumption of 12 months before TD |
| Skew | 1 | Skewness of consumption of 12 months before TD |

## 4.3   Evaluation Metrics

MAPE, as defined in Eq. (1) is utilized as evaluation metric, since it is the most common evaluation metric considering time-series forecasting tasks. Experiments are repeated ten times, and we report the mean value and standard deviation.

## 4.4   Experimental Setup

In order to validate the effectiveness of the proposed RESELF method we perform three sets of experiments. In the first set of experiments, we deal with one-day-ahead electricity demand task and we use the same architecture for the two models of the proposed pipeline. In this case, we evaluate the performance of the method against baseline, which concerns the evaluation of the same model architecture trained with the actual load values (this is the case of training only the first model of the pipeline).

In the second set of experiments, we explore different model architectures for the two models of the proposed pipeline, considering the one-day-ahead electricity demand task. More specifically, we use a more lightweight model for training with the residual errors. In this case, we perform comparisons with both architectures trained using the actual load targets, denoted as baseline 1 and baseline 2 in the experimental results.

Finally, in the third set of experiments, we perform indicative experiments considering the second problem of personalized one-year-ahead forecasting task, using a more lightweight second model.

## 4.5   Implementation Details

Both models are trained with Adam optimizer with initial learning rate of 0.001 for the first model and 0.005 for the second model respectively, with a learning decay factor of 0.5 every 500 epochs. Mini-batch size is set to 32 samples. Input features are normalized using max scaler. Each model was trained for 2,000 epochs. We have implemented the proposed method using the Pytorch framework.

## 4.6   Experimental Results

In this Section we provide the experimental results for the proposed method. In Table 3 we provide the experimental results considering the first set of experiments. As it is demonstrated the proposed RESELF method remarkably improves the baseline performance on the three utilized datasets. Subsequently, the corresponding results for each of the three datasets are provided in Figs. 2, 3 and 4 where the steadily better performance of the proposed method is illustrated.

Next, in Table 4, the corresponding results considering the second set of experiments, where the second model for training with the residual errors is more lightweight, are provided. As it can be observed this practice provides further improvements. That is, apart from the fact that it achieves lower errors as compared to the baselines, it also achieves reduced errors as compared to the first approach, where the second model is identical to the first one, that is more heavyweight. The same remarks can be drawn with the corresponding Figs. 5, 6 and 7.

**Table 3.** Test MAPE (%) for the proposed method against baseline, where the two models are of identical architectures.

| Method | Greek Energy Market | Spain | ISO-NE |
|---|---|---|---|
| Baseline | 3.36 ± 0.08 | 5.62 ± 0.07 | 2.56 ± 0.15 |
| RESELF | **2.63 ± 0.15** | **4.66 ± 0.14** | **2.15 ± 0.06** |

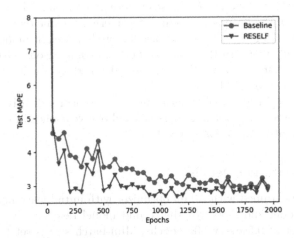

**Fig. 2.** Greek Energy Market: Test MAPE throughout training epochs for the proposed method against baseline, where the two models are of identical architectures.

Finally, in Table 5 the experimental results considering the one-year-ahead forecasting task for one MV and one HV costumer are provided. We can observe that the proposed RESELF method improves the forecasting performance on this task too.

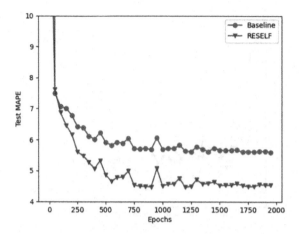

**Fig. 3.** Spain: Test MAPE throughout training epochs for the proposed method against baseline, where the two models are of identical architectures.

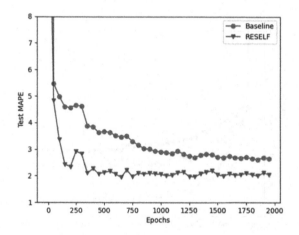

**Fig. 4.** ISO-NET: Test MAPE throughout training epochs for the proposed method against baseline, where the two models are of identical architectures.

**Table 4.** Test MAPE (%) for the proposed method against baseline, where the second model is lightweight.

| Method | Greek Energy Market | Spain | ISO-NE |
|---|---|---|---|
| Baseline 1 (Heavyweight) | $3.36 \pm 0.08$ | $5.62 \pm 0.07$ | $2.56 \pm 0.15$ |
| Baseline 2 (Lightweight) | $3.39 \pm 0.100$ | $6.05 \pm 0.06$ | $3.43 \pm 0.300$ |
| RESELF | $\mathbf{2.52 \pm 0.08}$ | $\mathbf{4.50 \pm 0.05}$ | $\mathbf{1.91 \pm 0.01}$ |

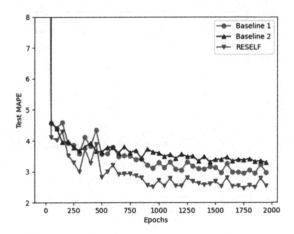

**Fig. 5.** Greek Energy Market: Test MAPE throughout training epochs using various architectures.

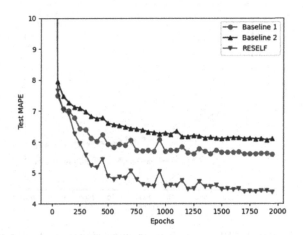

**Fig. 6.** Spain: Test MAPE throughout training epochs using various architectures.

**Table 5.** Test MAPE (%) for the proposed method against baseline for two MV and HV consumers, considering the one-year-ahead prediction task.

| Method | MV | HV |
|---|---|---|
| Baseline | 8.27 | 1.66 |
| RESELF | **6.19** | **1.60** |

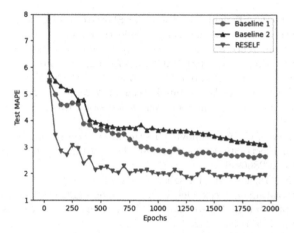

**Fig. 7.** ISO-NET: Test MAPE throughout training epochs using various architectures.

## 5   Conclusions

In this work, we proposed a novel methodology for improving the forecasting performance, focusing on the one-day-ahead electricity demand forecasting task. More specifically, the proposed RESELF method proposes to train a model with the actual load targets, compute then the residual errors, and train a second model for predicting these errors. Finally, the prediction of the proposed pipeline is computed by summing the two models' predictions. As it is also experimentally validated through extensive experiments on four datasets, if the errors are systematic, then this approach provides improved forecasting performance.

**Acknowledgements.** This work is co-financed by the European Regional Development Fund of the European Union and Greek national funds through the Operational Program Competitiveness, Entrepreneurship and Innovation, under the call RESEARCH - CREATE - INNOVATE (project code: T2EDK-03048).

## References

1. Abeysingha, A., Sritharan, A.S., Valluvan, R., Ahilan, K., Jayasinghe, D.: Electricity load/demand forecasting in sri lanka using deep learning techniques. In: 2021 10th International Conference on Information and Automation for Sustainability (ICIAfS), pp. 293–298 (2021). https://doi.org/10.1109/ICIAfS52090.2021.9606057
2. Amarasinghe, K., Marino, D.L., Manic, M.: Deep neural networks for energy load forecasting. In: Proceedings of the IEEE 26th International Symposium on Industrial Electronics (ISIE), pp. 1483–1488 (2017)
3. Andriopoulos, N., et al.: Short term electric load forecasting based on data transformation and statistical machine learning. Appl. Sci. **11**(1), 158 (2021)
4. Cheng, Y.Y., Chan, P.P., Qiu, Z.W.: Random forest based ensemble system for short term load forecasting. In: Proceedings of the 2012 International Conference on Machine Learning and Cybernetics, vol. 1, pp. 52–56 (2012)

5. Emmanouilidis, G., Tzelepi, M., Tefas, A.: Short-term electric load demand forecasting on greek energy market using deep learning: a comparative study. In: 2022 Panhellenic Conference on Electronics & Telecommunications (PACET), pp. 1–4 (2022). https://doi.org/10.1109/PACET56979.2022.9976351

6. Gasparin, A., Lukovic, S., Alippi, C.: Deep learning for time series forecasting: the electric load case. CAAI Trans. Intell. Technol. **7**(1), 1–25 (2022)

7. He, W.: Load forecasting via deep neural networks. Procedia Comput. Sci. **122**, 308–314 (2017)

8. Jacob, M., Neves, C., Vukadinović Greetham, D.: Forecasting and Assessing Risk of Individual Electricity Peaks. Springer, Heidelberg (2020). https://doi.org/10.1007/978-3-030-28669-9

9. Maragkos, N., Tzelepi, M., Passalis, N., Adamakos, A., Tefas, A.: Electric load demand forecasting on greek energy market using lightweight neural networks. In: 2022 IEEE 14th Image, Video, and Multidimensional Signal Processing Workshop (IVMSP), pp. 1–5. IEEE (2022)

10. Nie, H., Liu, G., Liu, X., Wang, Y.: Hybrid of arima and svms for short-term load forecasting. Energy Procedia **16**, 1455–1460 (2012)

11. Nti, I.K., Teimeh, M., Nyarko-Boateng, O., Adekoya, A.F.: Electricity load forecasting: a systematic review. J. Electr. Syst. Inf. Technol. **7**(1), 1–19 (2020)

12. Panapakidis, I.P., Perifanis, T., Dagoumas, A.S.: The effect of dimensionality reduction methods in short-term load forecasting performance. In: Proceedings of the 2018 15th International Conference on the European Energy Market (EEM), pp. 1–5 (2018)

13. Setiawan, A., Koprinska, I., Agelidis, V.G.: Very short-term electricity load demand forecasting using support vector regression. In: Proceedings of the 2009 International Joint Conference on Neural Networks, pp. 2888–2894 (2009)

14. Sezer, O.B., Gudelek, M.U., Ozbayoglu, A.M.: Financial time series forecasting with deep learning: a systematic literature review: 2005–2019. Appl. Soft Comput. **90**, 106181 (2020)

15. Sideratos, G., Ikonomopoulos, A., Hatziargyriou, N.D.: A novel fuzzy-based ensemble model for load forecasting using hybrid deep neural networks. Electr. Power Syst. Res. **178**, 106025 (2020)

16. Taylor, J.W.: Short-term electricity demand forecasting using double seasonal exponential smoothing. J. Oper. Res. Soc. **54**(8), 799–805 (2003)

17. Tzelepi, M., Sapountzaki, A., Maragkos, N., Tefas, A.: Online self-distillation for electric load demand forecasting on Greek energy market. In: 2022 Panhellenic Conference on Electronics & Telecommunications (PACET), pp. 1–5 (2022). https://doi.org/10.1109/PACET56979.2022.9976318

18. Tzelepi, M., Tefas, A.: Deep convolutional learning for content based image retrieval. Neurocomputing **275**, 2467–2478 (2018)

19. Tzelepi, M., Tefas, A.: Forecasting day-ahead electric load demand on greek energy market. In: Thirteen IEEE International Conference on Information, Intelligence, Systems and Applications (IISA). IEEE (2022)

# Strain Prediction of a Bridge Deploying Autoregressive Models with ARIMA and Machine Learning Algorithms

Anastasios Panagiotis Psathas$^{(\boxtimes)}$ ⓘ, Lazaros Iliadis ⓘ, and Antonios Papaleonidas ⓘ

Department of Civil Engineering-Lab of Mathematics and Informatics (ISCE),
Democritus University of Thrace, 67100 Xanthi, Greece
{anpsatha,liliadis,papaleon}@civil.duth.gr

**Abstract.** Lately, there is an increasing demand for resilient infrastructure assets. To support the documentation of resilience, Structural Health Monitoring (SHM) data is a necessity, as well as traffic loads. Those diagnosis and function data can be the basis for the prognosis of future prediction for the performance of the assets. In this research, the authors present an approach based on nineteen (19) Machine Learning (ML) techniques for the prediction of the future strain values in a Dutch Highway Bridge depending on previous measurements of the strain. For the evaluation of the algorithms the indices Root Mean Square Error (RMSE), Mean Absolute Error (MAE) and R square ($R^2$) were chosen and Fast Fourier Transform (FFT) and Averaged Standardized Values were chosen for the time series pre-processing. The results are extremely promising, with almost every algorithm to predict the fluctuations of strain values and the indexes are quite satisfactory. The results ensure that those who are responsible for the maintenance of the bridge or for its repairs, could use these models to determine which time that should take action.

**Keywords:** Machine Learning · ARIMA · Univariate · Autoregression · Strain · Bridge · Infrastructure

## 1 Introduction

Structures, including bridges, buildings, dams, pipelines, aircraft, ships, among others, are complex engineered systems that ensure society's economic and industrial prosperity. To design structures that are safe for public use, standardized building codes and design methodologies have been created [18, 19]. Critical Transport Infrastructures (CTIs) such as highway Reinforced Concrete bridges (RC) have a crucial socio-economic impact [47, 48]. The ageing RC bridges are deteriorated by diverse stressors, e.g. increased traffic load, corrosion and multiple hazards, e.g. extreme temperatures, seismic events, floods [47, 48]. Therefore, maintenance and retrofitting measures are necessary to ensure the asset's safety [49]. Though, according to the European Union (EU) Road Federation, the maintenance of damaged CTIs due to natural hazards is significantly expensive and reaches approximately €20 billion per year [50], accompanied with bridges' disruption and further economic losses [48, 50].

© The Author(s), under exclusive license to Springer Nature Switzerland AG 2023
L. Iliadis et al. (Eds.): EANN 2023, CCIS 1826, pp. 403–419, 2023.
https://doi.org/10.1007/978-3-031-34204-2_34

The adaptation of the decaying highway RC bridges to the ever-changing environment and increased traffic demands are incorporated into the concept of the forthcoming EU Adaptation Strategies [51]. In particular, the main goal of the new strategies is to guarantee the resilience of CTIs, especially to climate change [51, 52].

With the development of detection and data processing techniques, monitoring of physical systems with a network of sensor network is possible for many fields [1]. The modern Structural Health Monitoring and Functionality systems (SHM and SHFM) provide useful data, e.g. early warnings of damages, damage location, deformations, deflections and information about the structural integrity, functionality or traffic level of the CTIs over time [48, 49]. This is a challenging and critical problem that can positively affect the manner how a public infrastructure is being managed and maintained [16]. A typical SHM implementation requires the infrastructure to be equipped with a network of sensors, continuously measuring and collecting various structural and climate features such as vibration, strain and weather conditions [3, 4]. This continuous measuring process generates a massive amount of streaming data which can be further analyzed in order to deduce knowledge about the asset's lifetime and maintenance demand. In a real-time SHM systems, catching long-term informative data helps to diagnose health problems under different conditions. In most studies, laboratory tests of simple structural systems are considered, rather than real structures in their operating environment [10]. Although some studies work on real structures, they just consider a short period of data, and assume that various environmental conditions remain the same during this period [11].

Today, with the 4th technological evolution the sensors' cost is decreased and a new era of emerging digital technologies has been introduced, e.g. Artificial Intelligence (AI), Machine Learning (ML), Finite Element (FE), Internet of Things (IoT) [53, 54]. As a result, there are numerous sophisticated methods to collect and combine diverse data [54, 55].

In this paper, the authors use a public dataset which derived from InfraWatch project, a large monitoring project in the Netherlands [9]. The data was obtained from a sensor network installed on a highway bridge. The sensor network was installed on this bridge during a renovation launched in 2007, to monitor the condition of the bridge. There are three kinds of sensors (145 in total) involved in the sensor network: temperature, vertical movement (vibration) and horizontal stress (strain) [5]. Furthermore, there is a weather station and a video-camera to measure the weather and the actual traffic on the bridge. The aim of this research effort is the prediction of the future strain values of a specific sensor on the aforementioned Bridge. Thus, the deployment of autoregressive models using the well-known forecasting method Autoregressive Integrated Moving Average (ARIMA) and Machine Learning (ML) techniques. The dataset consists of a times series acquired from the strain sensor. To the best of our knowledge this is the first time that the development of autoregressive models is attempted in this dataset and to such an extent using ARIMA and ML algorithms.

The rest of the paper is organized as follows. Section 2 describes the area of research and pinpoints some notable research efforts. Section 3 describes the dataset, its features and the pre-processing process. Section 4 provides the architecture of the proposed models. Section 5 presents the experimental results and the evaluation of the model. Finally, Sect. 6 concludes the research.

## 2 Area of Research

The proposed research approach was implemented for a case study bridge in the Netherlands, named the Hollandse Brug. This bridge is located between the provinces Flevoland
and Noord-Holland in the Netherlands, which is where the Gooimeer joins the IJmeer
(see Fig. 1a) [57]. The bridge was opened in June 1969, and since then is used by national
Road A6. There is also a connection for rail parallel to the highway bridge, as well as
a lane for cyclists on the west side of the car bridge [56]. In 1980, the development
of Almere's city led to an increase in the traffic load and the bridge was considered
overloaded [57]. Thus, in 1993 and 1999 it was widened to the south and the north
respectively. Though, eight years later (2007), the Hollandse Brug was inspected by the
Dutch Organisation for Applied Scientific Research and was considered unsafe to carry
traffic loads over 12 tons [57, 58]. Therefore, heavy loads were prohibited to pass the
bridge causing significant economic losses [58]. In April 2007 it was announced that
measurements would have shown that the bridge did not meet the quality and security
requirements. Therefore, the bridge was closed in both directions to freight traffic on
April 27, 2007. The repairs were launched in August 2007 and a consortium of companies, Strukton, RWS and Reef has installed a monitoring configuration underneath
the first south span of the Hollandse Brug with the intent of obtaining a SHM system
(Fig. 1b) [9]. However, the continuous increase of the traffic load resulted from 2011 to
2014 in further actions and finally in the reconstruction of the bridge and the building
of a second one as it is represented in Fig. 1a.

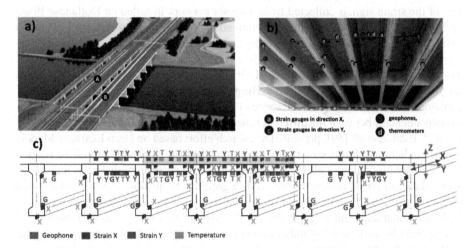

**Fig. 1.** Hollandse Brug bridge **a)** in 2015 where **A** is the old bridge and **B** is the new, **b)** photograph
of part of the sensor's network and **c)** representation of the 1st bridge span with sensors [57]

The monitoring system that was established during Hollandse Brug bridge's renovation comprises 145 sensors that measure different aspects of the condition of the bridge, at several locations on the bridge (Fig. 1c). The following types of sensors are employed:

- 34 geo-phones (vibration sensors) that measure the vertical movement of the bottom of the road-deck as well as the supporting columns.
- 16 strain-gauges embedded in the concrete, measuring horizontal longitudinal strain, and an additional 34 gauges attached to the outside.
- 28 strain-gauges embedded in the concrete, measuring horizontal strain perpendicular to the first 16 strain-gauges, and an additional 13 gauges attached to the outside.
- 10 thermometers embedded in the concrete, and 10 attached on the outside.

Furthermore, there is a weather station and a video-camera, which provides a continuous video stream of the actual traffic on the bridge [20].

The 145 sensor network collects data at a frequency of 100 Hz from the bridge, which not only contains vehicles with various weights, lengths, speeds, and directions, but also includes environmental factors such as wind, temperature, rain and so on. They produce around 56 kB of data per second. This amounts to about 5 GB per day, and over 1.7 TB on a yearly basis. The video camera produces a data stream in a similar range, with 46 kB/s of compressed video, for a typical daytime situation. The current data available for analysis consists of short snapshots of strain and video data, which is being manually transported from the site to the monitoring location (typically an office environment or Leiden University) [15].

In 2014, Miao et al. [5], present a baseline correction method to deal with the baseline of the strain signals collected from a sensor network installed on Hollandse Brug. In 2012, Vespier et al. [8], propose a combination of the Minimum Description Length (MDL) principle, feature selection strategies, and convolution techniques for decomposition of a time series on artificial data and the aforementioned Bridge. In 2010, Koopman et al. [17], describe a method for pattern selection in collections of patterns discovered in time series of Hollandse Brug. The method presented selects a subset of equations, while optimizing the relevance of variables within the equations, and captures the dependencies between the different time-series well, while minimizing redundancy. In 2022, Psathas et al. [59], presented a research effort based on Deep Learning Models for the prediction of future strain values in Hollandse Brug, achieving promising results. In 2022, Achillopoulou et al. [57], develops a new methodology that uses real monitoring data and Artificial Intelligence (AI) algorithms to quantify the resilience based on future traffic load predictions of functionality. Resilience is derived as a function of both functional and structural parameters throughout the lifecycle. The quantification is supported by sustainability indices and key performance indicators representing the traffic flow, the structural integrity and the sustainability level of the asset. Furthermore attempts for analyzing the Hollandse Brug time series were performed in [6, 7, 13, 14].

## 3  Dataset

As it was mentioned before the dataset used in this research on the measurements of a strain sensor attached on the Hollandse Brug, a Dutch Highway Bridge. This specific sensor collects data at 10 Hz. The dataset deals with finite sequences of numerical measurements (samples), collected by observing some property of a system with a sensor and represented as time series [6]. A time series of length n is an ordered sequence of values x = x[1],..., x[n] of finite precision. A subsequence x[a: b] of x is defined as follows

$$x[a : b] = (x[a], x[a + 1], \ldots, x[b]), \quad 1 \le a < b \le n \tag{1}$$

More specifically, the dataset comprises of 10,280,939 strain measurements over a period of 12 days, from Saturday 2008/11/15 to Wednesday 2008/11/26. The time series is presented in Fig. 2.

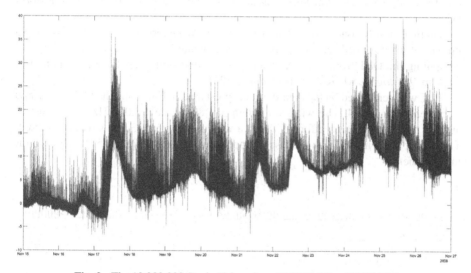

**Fig. 2.** The 10,280,939 Strain Values from 2008/11/15 to 2008/11/26

The dataset is publicly available and can be found at the following website: https://infrawatch.liacs.nl/

### 3.1 Dataset Preprocessing

As it is already mentioned, the sensor collects data at frequency of 10 Hz. This means that there are 10 values for 1 s. The measurements are very dense and in Infrastructures it does not make much sense to predict the value for the next second. The forecast usually refers to specific times of the day when conditions are harsher, such as traffic jams, or very high and very low temperature conditions. The variable data segmentation was performed by using Fast Fourier Transform (FFT).

Fourier analysis converts a signal from its original domain (often time or space) to a representation in the frequency domain and vice versa. FFT is a specific implementation that computes the Discrete Fourier Transform (DFT) of a sequence. It is an extremely powerful mathematical tool that allows to observe the obtained signals in a different domain, inside which several difficult problems become very simple to analyse [21].

The DFT is obtained by decomposing a sequence of values into components of different frequencies. Any periodic function g(x) integrable in the domain $D = [-\pi, \pi]$ can be written as an infinite sum of sine and cosine as follows:

$$g(x) = \sum_{k=-\infty}^{\infty} \tau_k e^{jkx} \tag{2}$$

$$\tau_k = \frac{1}{2\pi} \int_D g(x)e^{-jkx}dx \tag{3}$$

where $e^{j\theta} = \cos(\theta) + j\sin(\theta)$. The idea that a function can be broken down into its constituent frequencies is a powerful one and forms the backbone of the Fourier transform [22].

An FFT rapidly computes such transformations by factorizing the DFT matrix into a product of sparse (mostly zero) factors. As a result, it manages to reduce the complexity of computing the DFT from $O(N^2)$, which arises if one simply applies the definition of DFT, to $O(N.logN)$, where $N$ is the data size [23].

FFT was performed on the dataset as it is presented in Fig. 3 and the FFT time series id presented in Fig. 4. The windows length is 1,800 s, i.e. 18,000 Hz, in contrast of authors previous research effort in which a window length of 3,600 s was performed. Thus, after applying FFT, the dataset comprises of a time series of 571 half an hour measurements.

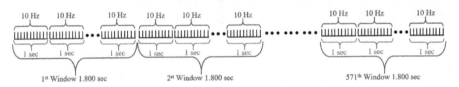

**Fig. 3.** Applying FFT for Window Length of 1,800 s (18,000 Hz)

As can be seen from Fig. 4, the processed dataset still captures the flow of strain values without much deviation. Usually in such time series there is almost always seasonality or trending that makes the time series non-stationary, i.e. it does not follow Normal (Gaussian) Distribution $N(\mu, \sigma^2)$ [24]. In such cases one can use stationarity tests or unit roots tests to check if a time series is stationary. There are two different approaches:

- Stationarity tests such as the Kwiatkowski-Phillips-Schmidt-Shin (KPSS) Test [25] that consider as null hypothesis H0 that the series is stationary
- Unit root tests, such as the Dickey-Fuller (ADF) test [26] and its augmented version, the augmented Dickey-Fuller test (ADF) [27], or the Phillips-Perron test (PP) [28], for which the null hypothesis H0 is that the series possesses a unit root and hence is not stationary.

In this research effort, the authors use the 3 more used tests: ADF, KPSS and PP. Their description is presented in Table 1.

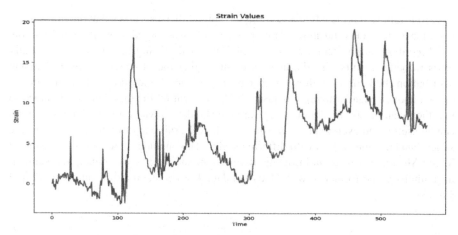

**Fig. 4.** Strain values after FFT is applied

**Table 1.** H0 is the null hypothesis, H1 is the alternative hypothesis, Description is how the test works, and alpha is the significance value

| Stationarity/Unit Root Test | Ho | H1 | Description | alpha |
|---|---|---|---|---|
| ADF | There is a unit root for the series | There is not unit root for the series. The series is stationary | If p-value is lower than the significance level alpha = 0.05, H0 is rejected and the alternative is accepted | 0.05 |
| PP | | | | |
| KPSS | The series is stationary | The series is not stationary | | |

For the autoregression problem the authors test the time series for the range of lags 0–23. Table 2 presents the p-values of the times series for all lags.

**Table 2.** Stationarity tests p-values of the time series for 24 different lags

| Lag | 0 | 1 | 2 | 3 | 4 | 5 | 6 | 7 | 8 | 9 | 10 | 11 |
|---|---|---|---|---|---|---|---|---|---|---|---|---|
| p-value ADF | 0.001 | 0.009 | 0.029 | 0.041 | 0.035 | 0.003 | 0.001 | 0.001 | 0.001 | 0.001 | 0.002 | 0.003 |
| p-value PP | 0.001 | 0.001 | 0.001 | 0.001 | 0.001 | 0.001 | 0.001 | 0.001 | 0.001 | 0.001 | 0.001 | 0.001 |
| p-value KPSS | **0.01** | **0.01** | **0.01** | **0.01** | **0.018** | **0.033** | 0.052 | 0.081 | 0.1 | 0.1 | 0.1 | 0.1 |
| Lag | **12** | **13** | **14** | **15** | **16** | **17** | **18** | **19** | **20** | **21** | **22** | **23** |
| p-value ADF | 0.003 | 0.001 | 0.003 | 0.002 | 0.004 | 0.002 | 0.003 | 0.004 | 0.006 | 0.007 | 0.010 | 0.018 |
| p-value PP | 0.001 | 0.001 | 0.001 | 0.001 | 0.001 | 0.001 | 0.001 | 0.001 | 0.001 | 0.001 | 0.001 | 0.001 |
| p-value KPSS | 0.1 | 0.1 | 0.1 | 0.1 | 0.1 | 0.1 | 0.1 | 0.1 | 0.1 | 0.1 | 0.1 | 0.1 |

From Table 2 it is clear that according to Table 1, all 3 tests agree that the times series is stationary for 6 lags and above. Thus, our data follows Normal (Gaussian) distribution.

According to the literature review [29, 30], standardizing time series data usually leads to better results. Standardization assumes that the observations fit a Gaussian distribution (bell curve) with a well behaved mean and standard deviation (as already proved above). Standardizing a dataset involves rescaling the distribution of values so that the mean of observed values is 0 and the standard deviation is 1. Standardization can be useful, and even required in some machine learning algorithms when your time series data has input values with differing scales. This includes algorithms like Support Vector Machines, Linear and Logistic Regression, and other algorithms that assume or have improved performance with Gaussian data. For the standardization process Eq. 3 was used.

$$y = \frac{x - \hat{x}}{\sigma} \tag{4}$$

where, $x$ is the value of the FFT time series, $\hat{x}$ is the mean value of all $x$, $\sigma$ is the Standard Deviation of the FFT time series and $y$ is the value of the Standardized Dataset. Thus, Fig. 5 presents the strain values after FFT and standardization was performed.

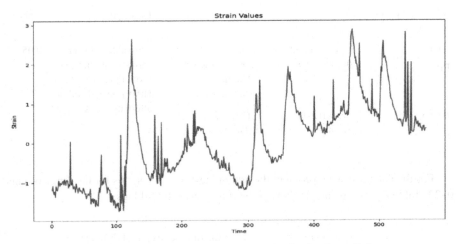

**Fig. 5.** Strain values after FFT and standardization is applied

Data handling was performed in Matlab with code written from scratch.

## 4    Algorithms and Evaluation Indices

Both standardized and non-standardized datasets will be used in this research. The data sets consists of a time series of 571 values. The goal of this research effort is to predict the future values of based on the previous ones. Predicting the trend of the strain values, it would help to monitor when the bridge will receive more stress to be maintained by the by the responsible staff. Or even schedule any other action to ensure the longevity and the safe operating conditions of the bridge. Forecasting the high strain values can even help in better managing actions at that time.

Thus, for the purpose of this research the datasets were fed in 19 ML algorithms named *Linear Regression, Interactions Linear, Robust Linear, Stepwise Linear, Fine Tree, Medium Tree, Coarse Tree, Linear Support Vector Regression (SVM), Quadratic SVM, Cubic SVM, Fine Gaussian SVM Medium Gaussian SVM, Coarse Gaussian SVM, Boosted trees, Bagged Trees, Squared Exponential Gaussian Process Regression (GPR), Matern 5/2 GPR, Exponential GPR, Rational Quadratic GPR* and the well know methodology for univariate forecasting Autoregressive Integrated Moving Average (ARIMA) [31]. Due to the limited extent of the manuscript, a brief description of the algorithms will be provided. The detailed description and the mathematical foundations of the algorithms can be done by a simple internet search or by visiting the respective references.

### 4.1 Machine Learning Algorithms and ARIMA Description

Linear regression is an approach for modelling the relationship between a scalar response (dependent variable) and one or more explanatory variables (independent variables). This relationship is modeled using linear predictor functions whose unknown model parameters are estimated from the data. In Interactions Linear apart from a constant and linear terms, interaction parameters are used. In Robust Linear, a robust objective function is used to make the model less sensitive to outliers. Stepwise linear regression starts with an initial model and systematically adds and removes terms to the model based on the explanatory power of these incrementally larger and smaller models [32].

Tree algorithms are widely used abstract data type that simulates a hierarchical tree structure, with a root value and subtrees of children with a parent node, represented as a set of linked nodes. A tree data structure can be defined recursively as a collection of nodes, where each node is a data structure consisting of a value and a list of references to nodes. To predict a response of a regression tree, follow the tree from the root (beginning) node down to a leaf node. The leaf node contains the value of the response. Fine, Medium and Coarse Trees are subcategories of Tree algorithms, where there are Many small leaves, medium-sized leaves and few large leaves respectively [33, 34]. Boosted Trees and Bagged Trees are Ensemble models that combine results from many weak learners into one high-quality ensemble model [41].

SVM Models for Regression (commonly known as Support Vector Regression-SVR) use the same principle as the SVMs for Classification [35]. The basic idea behind SVR is to find the best fit line. In SVR, the best fit line is the hyperplane that has the maximum number of points. Unlike other Regression models that try to minimize the error between the real and predicted value, the SVR tries to fit the best line within a threshold value. The threshold value is the distance between the hyperplane and boundary line. Linear, Quadratic, Cubic and Gaussian SVMs are using the Linear, Quadratic, Cubic and Gaussian of Radial Basis Function (RBF) respectively. The difference between Fine, Medium and Coarse Gaussian SVM are the Kernel Scale is set to $\frac{\sqrt{p}}{4}$, $\sqrt{p}$ and $4\sqrt{p}$, where p is the number of the predictors [36, 37].

GPR models are nonparametric kernel-based probabilistic models based on Gaussian Process (GP) [38] governed by prior covariance. Spatial inference, or estimation, of a quantity at an unobserved location is calculated from a linear combination of the observed values and weights. The kernel function determines the correlation in the response as a function of the distance between the predictor values. The Kernels chosen for this attempt are Rational Quadratic, Squared Exponential, Matern 5/2 and Exponential [39, 40].

ARIMA model belongs to the one of the most used methodology approaches for analyzing time series. This is mostly because of it offers great flexibility in analyzing various time series and because of achieving accurate forecasts, too. Its other advantage is that for analyzing single time series it uses its own historical data. This approach analyzes univariate stochastic time series, i.e. error term of this time series. For this to be possible, the analyzed time series must be stationary [31].

### 4.2 Evaluation of Deep Learning Algorithms.

For the evaluation of the aforementioned DL algorithms 3 evaluation indices were use. The following Table 3 presents the validation indexes, their abbreviation and the corresponding calculation manner.

**Table 3.** Calculated indices for the evaluation of the binary classification approach

| Index | Abbreviation | Calculation |
|-------|--------------|-------------|
| Root Mean Square Error | RMSE | $\sqrt{\frac{\sum_{i=1}^{N}(y_i-\hat{y}_i)^2}{N}}$ |
| Mean Absolute Error | MAE | $\frac{1}{N}\sum_{i=1}^{N}\left|y_i-\hat{y}_i\right|$ |
| R Square | $R^2$ | $1-\frac{\sum_i(y_i-\hat{y}_i)^2}{\sum_i(y_i-\overline{y})^2}$ |

where $y_i$ is the actual value, $\hat{y}_i$ is the predicted value, $\overline{y}$ is the mean value, and N is the total number of the instances. $R^2$ measures how much variability in dependent variable can be explained by the model. $R^2$ is valued in closed interval [0, 1] and a bigger value indicates a better fit between prediction and actual value R Square is a good measure to determine how well the model fits the dependent variables [42]. RMSE is an absolute measure of the goodness for the fit. It gives an absolute number on how much your predicted results deviate from the actual number. You cannot interpret many insights from one single result but it gives you a real number to compare against other model results and help you select the best regression model [43]. MAE is similar to RMSE. Instead of the sum of square of error in RMSE, MAE is taking the sum of the absolute value of error. MAE is a more direct representation of sum of error terms. RMSE gives larger penalization to big prediction error by square it while MAE treats all errors the same [43].

## 5    Evaluation and Experimental Results

All algorithms, their evaluation and the training-testing process was made in Python and Matlab. The Keras [44] and Tensorflow [45] libraries have been employed to build the model's architecture in Python. Both datasets were split in **Train Data** (80% of the data) and **Test Data** (20% of the data). Training of all models was performed for 30 epochs. The algorithms were trained for 16 lags, videlicet for the prediction of the next price, the 16 previous measurements are taken into account. The values of all hyperparameters for each algorithm were chosen using the 10-fold cross validation method in **Train Data** [46]. Figure 6 and 7 present the true values vs the predicted values for ARIMA and the best ML algorithm (Medium Gaussian SVM in both cases) for non-standardized and standardized **Test Data** respectively. Table 4 and 5 present the evaluation indices RMSE, MAE and $R^2$ for each algorithm on both **Test Data**.

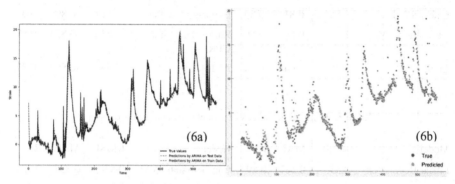

**Fig. 6.** True Strain vs Predicted Strain values for ARIMA (6a) and Medium Gaussian SVM (6b) for the non-standardized dataset

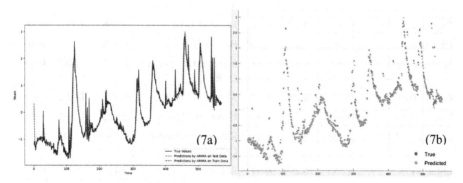

**Fig. 7.** True Strain vs Predicted Strain values for ARIMA (7a) and Medium Gaussian SVM (7b) for the standardized dataset

**Table 4.** Evaluation Indices of models on non-standardize dataset

| Model | RMSE | MAE | $R^2$ | Model | RMSE | MAE | $R^2$ |
|---|---|---|---|---|---|---|---|
| Linear Regression | 1.548 | 0.886 | 0.89 | Fine Gaussian SVM | 2.391 | 1.54 | 0.74 |
| Interactions Linear | 2.917 | 1.457 | 0.61 | Medium Gaussian SVM | 1.508 | 0.878 | **0.9** |
| Robust Linear | 1.617 | 0.808 | 0.88 | Coarse Gaussian SVM | 1.607 | 0.883 | 0.88 |
| Stepwise Linear | 1.573 | 0.891 | 0.89 | Boosted Trees | 1.588 | 0.909 | 0.89 |
| Fine Tree | 1.747 | 1.037 | 0.86 | Bagged Tress | 1.676 | 1.009 | 0.87 |
| Medium Tree | 1.764 | 1.067 | 0.86 | Squared Exponential GPR | 1.539 | 0.891 | 0.89 |
| Coarse Tree | 1.808 | 1.076 | 0.85 | Matern 5/2 GPR | 1.533 | 0.89 | 0.89 |
| Linear SVM | 1.545 | **0.817** | 0.89 | Exponential GPR | 1.511 | 0.898 | 0.9 |
| Quadratic SVM | 1.553 | 0.863 | 0.89 | Rational Quadratic GPR | 1.538 | 0.894 | 0.89 |
| Cubic SVM | 3.257 | 1.644 | 0.52 | ARIMA | **1.39** | 0.869 | 0.87 |

**Table 5.** Evaluation Indices of models on standardize dataset

| Model | RMSE | MAE | $R^2$ | Model | RMSE | MAE | $R^2$ |
|---|---|---|---|---|---|---|---|
| Linear Regression | 0.33 | 0.187 | 0.89 | Fine Gaussian SVM | 0.524 | 0.337 | 0.72 |
| Interactions Linear | 0.537 | 0.284 | 0.71 | Medium Gaussian SVM* | **0.316** | 0.182 | **0.9** |
| Robust Linear | 0.342 | **0.171** | 0.88 | Coarse Gaussian SVM | 0.34 | 0.187 | 0.88 |
| Stepwise Linear | 0.339 | 0.192 | 0.88 | Boosted Trees | 0.338 | 0.2 | 0.88 |
| Fine Tree | 0.381 | 0.227 | 0.85 | Bagged Tress | 0.375 | 0.222 | 0.86 |
| Medium Tree | 0.367 | 0.225 | 0.86 | Squared Exponential GPR | 0.325 | 1.883 | 0.89 |
| Coarse Tree | 0.38 | 0.23 | 0.85 | Matern 5/2 GPR | 0.325 | 0.189 | 0.89 |
| Linear SVM | 0.327 | 0.173 | 0.89 | Exponential GPR | 0.322 | 0.191 | **0.9** |
| Quadratic SVM | 0.328 | 0.181 | 0.89 | Rational Quadratic GPR | 0.326 | 0.19 | 0.89 |
| Cubic SVM | 0.533 | 0.294 | 0.71 | ARIMA | 0.427 | 0.228 | 0.716 |

[*] Best overall Model (c = 1.083, ε = 0.108, Kernel Scale = 4, Predictors = 16)

As Fig. 5 and 6 indicates, ARIMA and Medium Gaussian SVM, can predict the fluctuations of the strain in both datasets, which is the main object of the research. Essentially, the diagrams show that whatever model is used by those who are responsible for the maintenance of the bridge or for its repairs, it is clear which time there will be a higher value of the strain and which one will be lower. Furthermore, this research effort verifies the findings of the literature review. Indeed, all ML algorithms and ARIMA performs better in the second standardized dataset. Both RMSE and MAE indices range at noticeably better levels.

ARIMA seem to outperform the ML algorithms in the non-standardized dataset, but lags behind in standardized dataset. This leads to the conclusion that APIMA obviously recognizes the value pattern better in the standardize dataset, but can recognize the fluctuation of the values in their normal form. Medium Gaussian SVM has in both datasets the better performance of all ML Algorithms, and generally speaking the SVM algorithms outperforms the other approaches. The Ensembles methods, Boosted Trees and Bagged Trees, have excellent performance, but cannot take advantage of the many learners and the majority vote to get better results. Finally, almost all algorithms could be used for this task with few exceptions such as Interactions Linear, Cubic SVM, and Fine Gaussian SVM for both datasets.

**Table 6.** Evaluation Indices for Deep Learning Algorithms in [59]

| Model | RMSE | MAE | $R^2$ | Model | RMSE | MAE | $R^2$ |
|---|---|---|---|---|---|---|---|
| **Vanilla LSTM** | **1.369** | 0.917 | **0.880** | **MLP** | 1.807 | 1.304 | 0.805 |
| **Bi-LSTM** | 1.413 | **0.864** | 0.871 | **CNN-LSTM** | 1568 | 1.003 | 0.842 |
| **Stacked LSTM** | 4.350 | 3.770 | -0.749 | **DC-CNN** | 1.496 | 0.983 | 0.856 |
| **Stacked Bi-LSTM** | 3.380 | 2.701 | 0.570 | **SeriesNet** | 1.769 | 1.098 | 0.793 |
| **RNN** | 2.611 | 1.874 | 0.373 | **WaveNet** | 3.138 | 2.441 | 0.093 |
| **GRU** | 1.835 | 1.101 | 0.774 | | | | |

Table 6 presents the evaluation indices of the previous innovative research effort of the authors for the bridge strain prediction. It is clear that ARIMA stands at the same level as the Deep Learning Algorithms for the non-standardized data. However, after the standardization of the dataset, ML Algorithms dominate the ARIMA method and the Deep Learning Algorithms paving the way for more experiments and new approaches.

## 6  Conclusions and Future Work

In this paper, the authors deal with a univariate problem (auto regression problem). They try to predict the future strain values of a Dutch Highway Bridge, the Hollandse Brug, using the 16 previous strain values. Authors used FFT for the signal processing, to create half-hour measurements. For the autoregression problem, authors recruited 19 ML algorithms and the well-known for autoregression problems method ARIMA. The research effort shows promising results as all algorithms seem to be able to predict the fluctuation of strain values. RMSE, MAE and $R^2$ were chosen for evaluation indices. The values of the aforementioned indices are adequate for the majority of the models, especially for Medium Gaussian SVM which respond better for the both datasets and problem, according to the indexes and diagrams. Additionally, this paper verifies that the standardized records on a dataset which follows Gaussian Distribution could lead to better results. The predicted values of all models have a deviation from the actual values. This may be because the strain values are not only depend to their previous values, but also depend on other factors such as traffic jam and weather conditions according to literature.

Although the results were very good, there is always room for improvement. There are already plans for future expansion of this research. The first scenario is to find out if there is a better number of time lags that increase the quality of the models. Additionally, authors could use a different window length for applying FFT. Another scenario could be to obtain more values from the same dataset in order to use more values for training and testing of the models. Last but not least, authors could obtain more variates for the specific time series (temperature conditions or traffic jam data), which will likely increase the performance of the models. After all, no model is perfect, a model is good when it is practically useful.

# References

1. Fallahian, M., Khoshnoudian, F., Meruane, V.: Ensemble classification method for structural damage assessment under varying temperature. Struct. Health Monit. **17**(4), 747–762 (2018)
2. Cunha, A., Caetano, E., Magalhes, F., Moutinho, C.: Recent perspectives in dynamic testing and monitoring of bridges. Struct. Control Health Monit. **20**, 853877 (2013)
3. Li, H., Li, S., Ou, J., Li, H.: Modal identification of bridges under varying environmental conditions: Temperature and wind effects. Struct. Control Health Monit. **17**, 495512 (2010)
4. Xia, Y., Chen, B., Zhou, X.Q., Xu, Y.L.: Field monitoring and numerical analysis of Tsing Ma suspension bridge temperature behavior. Struct. Control. Health Monit. **20**(4), 560–575 (2013). https://doi.org/10.1002/stc.515
5. Miao, S., Koenders, E.A.B., Knobbe, A., Automatic baseline correction of strain gauge signals. Struct. Control Health Monit. **22**(1), 36–49 (2014). ISSN 1545-2263
6. Vespier, U., Nijssen, S., Knobbe, A.: Mining characteristic multi-scale motifs in sensor-based time series. In: Proceedings of the International Conference on Information and Knowledge Management, pp. 2393–2398 (2013). https://doi.org/10.1145/2505515.2505620
7. Miao, S., Vespier, U., Vanschoren, J., Knobbe, A., Cachucho, R.: Modeling Sensor Dependencies between Multiple Sensor Types (2013)
8. Vespier, U., Knobbe, A.J., Nijssen, S., Vanschoren, J.: MDL-based identification of relevant temporal scales in time series (2012)
9. Knobbe, A., et al.: InfraWatch: Data Management of Large Systems for Monitoring Infrastructural Performance. In: Cohen, P.R., Adams, N.M., Berthold, M.R. (eds.) IDA 2010. LNCS, vol. 6065, pp. 91–102. Springer, Heidelberg (2010). https://doi.org/10.1007/978-3-642-13062-5_10
10. Farrar, C., Hemez, F., Shunk, D., Stinemates, D., Nadler, B.: A review of structural health monitoring literature, pp. 1996–2001 (2004)
11. Kim, C.-Y., Jung, D.-S., Kim, N.-S., Kwon, S.-D., Feng, M.: Effect of vehicle weight on natural frequencies of bridges measured from traffic-induced vibration. Earthq. Eng. Eng. Vib. **2**, 109–115 (2003). https://doi.org/10.1007/BF02857543
12. Witkin, A.P.: Scale-Space Filtering. In: IJCAI (1983)

13. Miao, S., Knobbe, A., Vanschoren, J., Vespier, U., Chen, X.: A range of data mining techniques to correlate multiple sensor types (2011)
14. Vespier, U., et al.: Traffic events modeling for structural health monitoring. In: Gama, J., Bradley, E., Hollmén, J. (eds.) IDA 2011. LNCS, vol. 7014, pp. 376–387. Springer, Heidelberg (2011). https://doi.org/10.1007/978-3-642-24800-9_35
15. Knobbe, A.J., Koopman, A., Kok, J.N., Obladen, B., Bosma, C., Koenders, E.: Large data stream processing for bridge management systems (2010)
16. Li, X., Yu, W., Villegas, S.: Structural health monitoring of building structures with online data mining methods. IEEE Syst. J. **10**, 1–10 (2015). https://doi.org/10.1109/JSYST.2015.2481380
17. Koopman, A., Knobbe, A., Meeng, M.: Pattern selection problems in multivariate time-series using equation discovery. In: Proceedings of the ACM SIGKDD International Conference on Knowledge Discovery and Data Mining (2010). https://doi.org/10.1145/1816112.1816122
18. Lynch, J.P., Loh, K.J.: A summary review of wireless sensors and sensor networks for structural health monitoring. Shock Vibr. Dig. **38**(2), 91–130 (2006)
19. Liu, S.-C., Tomizuka, M., Ulsoy, A.: Strategic issues in sensors and smart structures. Struct. Control. Health Monit. **13**, 946–957 (2006). https://doi.org/10.1002/stc.88
20. Knobbe, A., Koopman, A., Kok, J.N., Obladen, B., Bosma, C., Galenkamp, H.: The role of fielded applications in machine learning education. In: Proceedings 20th Belgian Dutch Conference on Machine Learning (BENELEARN) (2010)
21. Brigham, E.O.: The Fast Fourier Transform and Its Applications. Prentice-Hall, Inc. (1988)
22. Zhang, Z.: Photoplethysmography-based heart rate monitoring in physical activities via joint sparse spectrum reconstruction. IEEE Trans. Biomed. Eng. **62**(8), 1902–1910 (2015)
23. Nussbaumer, H.J.: The fast Fourier transform. In: Fast Fourier Transform and Convolution Algorithms, pp. 80–111. Springer, Heidelberg (1981). https://doi.org/10.1007/978-3-642-818 97-4_4
24. Rhif, M., Ben Abbes, A., Farah, I.R., Martínez, B., Sang, Y.: Wavelet transform application for/in non-stationary time-series analysis: a review. Appl. Sci. **9**(7), 1345 (2019)
25. Baum, C.: KPSS: Stata module to compute Kwiatkowski-Phillips-Schmidt-Shin test for stationarity (2018)
26. Lopez, J.H.: The power of the ADF test. Econ. Lett. **57**(1), 5–10 (1997)
27. Paparoditis, E., Politis, D.N.: The asymptotic size and power of the augmented Dickey-Fuller test for a unit root. Economet. Rev. **37**(9), 955–973 (2018)
28. Cheung, Y.W., Lai, K.S.: Bandwidth selection, prewhitening, and the power of the Phillips-Perron test. Economet. Theor. **13**(5), 679–691 (1997)
29. Boeva, V., Tsiporkova, E.: A multi-purpose time series data standardization method. In: Sgurev, V., Hadjiski, M., Kacprzyk, J. (eds.) Intelligent Systems: From Theory to Practice. Studies in Computational Intelligence, vol. 299, pp. 445–460. Springer, Heidelberg (2010). https://doi.org/10.1007/978-3-642-13428-9_22
30. Batyrshin, I.: Constructing time series shape association measures: Minkowski distance and data standardization. In: 2013 BRICS Congress on Computational Intelligence and 11th Brazilian Congress on Computational Intelligence, pp. 204–212. IEEE, September 2013
31. Peter, Ď., Silvia, P.: ARIMA vs. ARIMAX–which approach is better to analyze and forecast macroeconomic time series. In: Proceedings of 30th International Conference Mathematical Methods in Economics, vol. 2, pp. 136–140, September 2012
32. King, M.L.: Testing for autocorrelation in linear regression models: a survey. In: Specification Analysis in the Linear Model, pp. 19–73. Routledge (2018)
33. Chethana, C.: Tree based predictive modelling for prediction of the accuracy of diabetics. In: 2021 International Conference on Intelligent Technologies (CONIT), pp. 1–6. IEEE, June2021

34. Patel, H.H., Prajapati, P.: Study and analysis of decision tree based classification algorithms. Int. J. Comput. Sci. Eng. **6**(10), 74–78 (2018)
35. Psathas, A. P., Papaleonidas, A., Iliadis, L.: Machine learning modeling of human activity using PPG signals. In: International Conference on Computational Collective Intelligence, pp. 543–557. Springer, Cham, November 2020
36. Kalita, D.J., Singh, V.P., Kumar, V.: A survey on svm hyper-parameters optimization techniques. In: Shukla, R.K., Agrawal, J., Sharma, S., Chaudhari, N.S., Shukla, K.K. (eds.) Social Networking and Computational Intelligence. LNNS, vol. 100, pp. 243–256. Springer, Singapore (2020). https://doi.org/10.1007/978-981-15-2071-6_20
37. Xiao, J., Yu, L., Bai, Y.: Survey of the selection of kernels and hyper-parameters in support vector regression. J. Southwest Jiaotong Univ. **43**(3), 297–303 (2008)
38. Dudley, R.M.: Sample functions of the Gaussian process. Selected Works of RM Dudley, pp. 187–224 (2010)
39. Quinonero-Candela, J., Rasmussen, C.E.: A unifying view of sparse approximate Gaussian process regression. J. Mach. Learn. Res. **6**, 1939–1959 (2005)
40. Swiler, L.P., Gulian, M., Frankel, A.L., Safta, C., Jakeman, J.D.: A survey of constrained Gaussian process regression: approaches and implementation challenges. J. Mach. Learn. Model. Comput. **1**(2), 119–156 (2020)
41. Ganjisaffar, Y., Caruana, R., Lopes, C.V.: Bagging gradient-boosted trees for high precision, low variance ranking models. In: Proceedings of the 34th International ACM SIGIR Conference on Research and Development in Information Retrieval, pp. 85–94, July 2011
42. Israeli, O.: A shapley-based decomposition of the R-square of a linear regression. J. Econ. Inequality **5**(2), 199–212 (2007)
43. Chai, T., Draxler, R.R.: Root mean square error (RMSE) or mean absolute error (MAE)?–Arguments against avoiding RMSE in the literature. Geosci. Model Dev. **7**(3), 1247–1250 (2014)
44. Ketkar, N.: Introduction to Keras. In: Deep learning with Python, pp. 97–111. Apress, Berkeley, CA (2017)
45. Dillon, J.V., et al.: Tensorflow distributions (2017). arXiv preprint arXiv:1711.10604
46. Papaleonidas, A., Psathas, A.P., Iliadis, L.: High accuracy human activity recognition using machine learning and wearable devices' raw signals. J. Inf. Telecommun., 1–17 (2021)
47. Gaitanidou, E., Bellini, E., Ferreira, P.: European Resilience Management Guidlines (2018)
48. Gkoumas, K., Marques Dos Santos, F.L., Van Balen, M., Tsakalidis, A., Ortega Hortelano, A., Pekár, F.: Research & innovation in bridge maintenance, inspection & monitoring. Publication Office of the EU (2019)
49. Haq, G., et al.: Research & innovation in bridge maintenance, inspection & monitoring: a European perspective based on the Transport Research & Innovation Monitoring & Information System (TRIMIS): study (2019)
50. Nicodème, C., Diamandouros, K., Diez, J., Durso, C., Arampidou, K., Nuri, A.K.: Road statistics yearbook (2017)
51. Eurocodes: Building the future-The European Commission website on the Eurocodes 631 (2019). https://eurocodes.jrc.ec.europa.eu/showpage.php?id=631. Accessed 8 Mar 2023
52. Tsionis, G.: Seismic resilience: concept, metrics & integration with other hazards. Joint Research Centre, Public. Office of the EU, Luxembourg (2014). https://doi.org/10.2788/713724
53. Achillopoulou, D.V., Mitoulis, S.A., Argyroudis, S.A., Wang, Y.: Monitoring of transport infrastructures exposed to multiple hazards: a roadmap for building resilience. Sci. Total Environ. **746**, 141001 (2020)
54. Argyroudis, S.A., et al.: Digital technologies can enhance climate resilience of critical infrastructure. Clim. Risk Manage. **35**, 100387 (2022)

55. Li, X., Yu, W., Villegas, S.: Structural health monitoring of building structures with online data mining methods. IEEE Syst. J. **10**, 1–10 (2015)
56. Wegenwiki.nl: Hollandse Brug-Wegenwiki (2022). https://cutt.ly/uFnOV4r. Accessed 8 Mar 2023
57. Achillopoulou, D.V., Stamataki, N.K., Psathas, A.P., Iliadis, L., Karabinis, A.I.: Quantification of resilience of bridges using artificial intelligence (AI) algorithms & structural health monitoring (SHM). In: IABSE Congress Nanjing 2022 Bridges and Structures: Connection, Integration and Harmonization, Data, 21–23 September 2022 (2022)
58. Veerman, R.: Deflections & natural frequencies as parameters for structural health monitoring: the effect of fatigue and corrosion on the deflections and the natural frequencies of reinforced concrete beams. Repository.tudelft.nl (2017)
59. Psathas, A.P., et al. Autoregressive deep learning models for bridge strain prediction. In: Iliadis, L., Jayne, C., Tefas, A., Pimenidis, E. (eds.) Proceedings of the 23rd International Conference on Engineering Applications of Neural Networks. EAAAI/EANN 2022, Chersonissos, Crete, Greece, 17–20 June 2022, pp. 150–164. Springer, Cham, June 2022. https://doi.org/10.1007/978-3-031-08223-8_13

# Verification of Neural Networks Meets PLC Code: An LHC Cooling Tower Control System at CERN

Ignacio D. Lopez-Miguel[1]([✉]) [ID], Borja Fernández Adiego[2], Faiq Ghawash[3], and Enrique Blanco Viñuela[2]

[1] TU Wien, Vienna, Austria
ignacio.lopez@tuwien.ac.at
[2] European Organization for Nuclear Research (CERN), Geneva, Switzerland
borja.fernandez.adiego@cern.ch
[3] Norwegian University of Science and Technology, Trondheim, Norway
faiq.ghawash@ntnu.no

**Abstract.** In the last few years, control engineers have started to use artificial neural networks (NNs) embedded in advanced feedback control algorithms. Its natural integration into existing controllers, such as programmable logic controllers (PLCs) or close to them, represents a challenge. Besides, the application of these algorithms in critical applications still raises concerns among control engineers due to the lack of safety guarantees. Building trustworthy NNs is still a challenge and their verification is attracting more attention nowadays. This paper discusses the peculiarities of formal verification of NNs controllers running on PLCs. It outlines a set of properties that should be satisfied by a NN that is intended to be deployed in a critical high-availability installation at CERN. It compares different methods to verify this NN and sketches our future research directions to find a safe NN.

**Keywords:** Verification of neural networks · PLCs · Control system

## 1 Introduction

Programmable logic controllers (PLCs) are widely used in the process industry. In critical industrial installations, where a failure in the control system could have dramatic consequences, PLCs are used to control and protect industrial plants. This is mainly due to their hardware robustness, communication capabilities, their modularity, but also the simplicity of PLC programming compared with other programmable devices, giving them a high-reliability characteristic.

Using neural networks (NNs) as controllers is not novel [34], but it has seen exponential growth over the last years due to the increase in computation power (e.g., [28]). NNs are fast, they can operate in non-linear domains, and there is no need to know the dynamics of the systems as long as data are available. However, control engineers are still reluctant to use them in critical industrial installations due to the lack of safety, stability and robustness guarantees.

© The Author(s), under exclusive license to Springer Nature Switzerland AG 2023
L. Iliadis et al. (Eds.): EANN 2023, CCIS 1826, pp. 420–432, 2023.
https://doi.org/10.1007/978-3-031-34204-2_35

Whereas it is possible to prove certain properties in classic controllers (like efficiency, monotonicity, stability, robustness, etc.) and their behavior can be explained, it is not yet the complete case for NN-based controllers.

The goal of this paper is to analyze and compare different approaches to formally verify a NN for critical applications encoded in a PLC program. We will specifically focus on PLC code running on Siemens SIMATIC S7 PLCs. This paper makes special emphasis on the type of safety guarantees (verification properties) for this specific domain and the limitations of each verification method. The approaches are tested in an ongoing work for a NN-based controller for a cooling tower of the Large Hadron Collider (LHC) at CERN. The used NN is not the final version to be deployed in production, but this verification work will help us to find the appropriate one.

The main contributions of this paper can be summarized as follows:

- Provision of different properties that can be verified for a NN-based controller that is implemented on a PLC.
- Verification of a NN-based controller directly on PLC code using PLCverif.
- Verification of the same NN-based controller using a state-of-the-art NN verifier, nnenum, and using a state-of-the-art SMT solver, Z3.
- Comparison of the different techniques.
- Application of the previous methods in a real case study of a safety-critical system at CERN.

## 2  Background

### 2.1  Verification of NNs

Over the last years, the verification of NNs has raised its popularity due to the increasing number of applications of NNs in critical systems[1]. Robustness, especially against adversarial attacks, as well as reachability have been some of the main topics that have been targeted. Overapproximation of the activation functions and encoding the neural network as a mixed integer linear program [6], symbolic interval propagation [32,33], and SMT encoding [9] are some of the approaches to verify this type of properties.

Since neural networks can be used as feedback controllers, different reachability properties shall be checked. A wide variety of approaches exists, such as using a MILP encoding [2], modeling the systems with a neural network [8], and including perturbations [1].

The Verification of Neural Networks COMpetition (VNN-COMP) [23], shows the existance of many efficient tools like nnenum [3], VeriNet [16] or $\alpha,\beta$-CROWN [35]. Normally, these tools are not very flexible, i.e., they only accept one type of activation function, one predefined architecture type, and a specific data type.

If during the NN verification, one finds a problem, it is necessary to repair it. For example, in [5] they re-train the neural network guided by the counterexamples until reaching a safe network. Other approaches do not reuse the training

---

[1] For a complete overview of this topic, please see [18].

data [17]. However, this is an open research topic and there is no clear way to repair neural networks. Besides, when an engineer finds a counterexample, it helps them to better understand the behavior of the system [12].

## 2.2  PLCverif

PLCverif[2] is a plugin-oriented tool that allows the formal verification of PLC programs [7,22,31]. It has been used to verify various safety-critical programs [10–12]. In PLCverif, different requirement specification methods can be used. Moreover, different formal verification tools can be integrated. The PLCverif verification workflow consists of five main steps, as shown in Fig. 1:

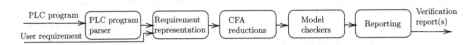

**Fig. 1.** Formal verification workflow of PLCverif

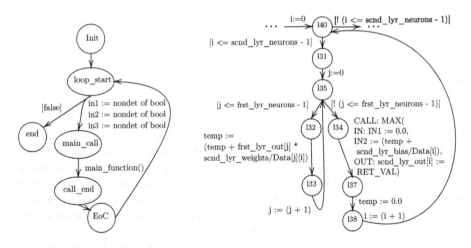

**Fig. 2.** CFA–Main PLC cycle.          **Fig. 3.** CFA–Part of a NN.

1. **PLC program parser.** The PLC program is parsed and translated into a control flow-based representation, producing a so-called Control Flow Automata (CFA) [4]. Figure 2 shows a PLC cycle represented as a CFA, which calls its main function in every cycle (Fig. 3). This main function expresses as a CFA a part of a feedforward NN with ReLU functions (listing 1.1).

---

[2] PLCverif is publicly available under https://gitlab.com/plcverif-oss.

2. **Requirement representation.** The PLCverif user describes precisely the requirement to be checked in a natural manner. Thanks to the CFA representation, different types of properties can be included.
3. **CFA reductions.** The CFA is reduced to speed up the verification process.
4. **Model checkers.** A state-of-the-art model checker is executed.
5. **Reporting.** The results are given to the user in a human-readable manner.

```
1 scnd_lyr_neurons := 8;
2 FOR i := 0 TO scnd_lyr_neurons - 1 DO
3  FOR j := 0 TO frst_lyr_neurons - 1 DO
4   temp := temp + frst_lyr_out[j] * scnd_lyr_weights.Data[j, i];
5  END_FOR;
6  scnd_lyr_out[i]:=MAX(IN1:=0,IN2:=(temp+scnd_lyr_bias.Data[i])); temp:=0;
7 END_FOR;
```

**Listing 1.1.** First hidden layer processing of the NN for the LHC cooling tower.

## 3 Case Study: The LHC Cooling Towers Controls

At CERN, large-scale chilled water cooling facilities are installed at various locations along the LHC site to meet the cooling requirements of different clients (e.g chillers, cryogenics, air handling units, etc.). Among various components of a large-scale cooling facility, induced draft cooling towers (IDCTs) are employed to cool the incoming hot water by rejecting the excess heat into the atmosphere. The typical arrangement of an IDCT involves the water entering the IDCT from the top and the ambient air enters from the bottom. The main components of an IDCT includes a fan, distribution system, spray nozzles, fill (packing), and collection basin. The cooled water is collected in the shared water collection basin before being supplied to different clients. Figure 4 shows multiple IDCTs with a shared water collection basin [15].

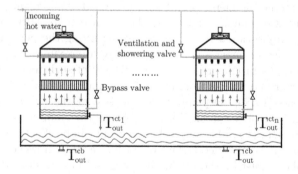

**Fig. 4.** Multiple induced draft cooling towers with a shared water collection basin.

The working principle of an IDCT is mainly based on simultaneous heat and mass transfer taking place between the hot water and the (cool) ambient air.

Depending on the cooling requirement and ambient air temperature, an IDCT can be operated in different operational modes namely: *ventilation, showering,* and *bypass*. In the ventilation and showering mode, the bypass valve remains off and the hot water is sprayed downwards through spray nozzles. In the showering mode, the fan remains off and the cooling of the hot water takes place through a natural draft. The mathematical model of the outlet water temperature under different operational modes is proposed in [19] [29]. Moreover, a switched system representation is presented in [14] to compactly represent the dynamics in different operational modes of the IDCT.

## 3.1   Control Design for the Cooling Towers

The primary objective of the cooling tower control design is to keep the outlet water temperature within strict limits ensuring the requirements of the downstream clients while utilizing the minimum amount of energy. The energy-optimal operation of the cooling towers requires the simultaneous determination of the best operational mode and optimal fan speed which poses a challenging control design problem.

The MPC (model predictive control) framework provides a structured way of designing the energy optimal control for the cooling towers. *The main idea behind MPC is to utilize the model of the system to predict future process behavior and minimize a given cost index subject to different physical and operational constraints.* It is based on solving a finite horizon-constrained optimal control problem at each sampling instant, resulting in the so-called *receding horizon control* [30]. Despite the advantages provided in terms of performance and energy optimization, the memory and computational resources required restrict their applicability to resource-constrained embedded hardware.

## 3.2   Approximate MPC Using Neural Networks

In order to overcome the memory and computational requirements, approximate MPC is becoming a popular choice [27]. The approximate MPC requires lower memory and computational resources while preserving the performance of the controller. The idea of using a neural network to approximate the solution of a MPC has its origins in [25]. However, the efficacy of such techniques has been recently demonstrated for controlling nonlinear multiple-input multiple-output (MIMO) systems [13,26]. Depending on the size of the neural networks, the neural network controller can significantly reduce the computational times and memory requirement to traditional techniques and can be effectively deployed on resource-constrained embedded hardware, such as a PLC. However, the behavior of such controllers must be thoroughly investigated in terms of safety, stability, and robustness to be deployed in the production environment.

The preliminary version of the NN consists of 4 hidden layers with 8 neurons per layer. It combines a classification problem for the mode selection and a regression problem for the fan speed calculation. This is an initial version of the NN and will be improved in subsequent work.

# 4    Verification of a NN-Based Controller on a PLC

Different properties with respect to the previously mentioned NN that approximates a MPC will be verified using different methods.

## 4.1    Properties to Verify

1. **Operational modes reachability.** Is there a combination of inputs (measurements from sensors) that reach mode $M_i$? This property is analyzed for the three previously introduced modes. Each of the counterexamples gives a combination of inputs that leads to each mode. If there would not be a counterexample for a certain mode, it would mean that mode is never going to be selected by the system, which is possibly an error in the design.
2. **Fan speed reachability.** Is there a combination of inputs that reach a certain range of the fan speed $[v_{min}, v_{max}]$? Different ranges are analyzed: $[0, 20)$, $[20, 60)$, $[60, 80)$, and $[80, 100]$. A counterexample gives a combination of inputs that leads to a fan speed in those ranges.
3. **Fan speed constraint satisfaction.** In *ventilation* mode, the fan should always operate within the desired range [60% - 100%], which can be verified. That is, is there a combination of inputs that leads to a fan speed lower than 60% or bigger than 100% when the mode is *ventilation*? If there is a counterexample, this could mean there is a problem in the network since the behavior is different than expected.
4. **Monotonicity.** If the mode is *ventilation* and all the temperatures increase, is the mode changing? It is expected that if all the temperatures increase, the mode remains at *ventilation*. A counterexample would show a case in which the temperatures increase and the mode is not *ventilation*.
5. **Softmax overflow.** Is there a combination of inputs that leads to a negative value of any of the outputs of the softmax layer of the modes? By definition of the softmax, since the exponential functions are always positive, the output of all the softmax layers should be always positive. If it is negative, it means there was an overflow in one of the components of the softmax formula.
6. **Robustness.** If the inputs are slightly changed, does the selected mode change? The counterexamples given by this property show the borders between the selection of the different modes. This could help the control engineer better understand if the controller is behaving as expected.

## 4.2    Verification of a NN with PLCverif

In order to tell PLCverif which variables should be non-deterministic so that the model checker explores all their possible values, we need to include those as input variables (VAR_INPUT) as shown in Listing 1.2. Instead of following the approach from [21], input variables are defined as integers but divided by 10 so that the input to the neural network has one decimal place.

```
1  VAR_INPUT
2   in_lyr_0, in_lyr_1, in_lyr_2 : Int; // non—deterministic
3  END_VAR
4  BEGIN // one decimal place
5   in_lyr[0]:=in_lyr_0/10; in_lyr[1]:=in_lyr_1/10; in_lyr[2]:=in_lyr_2/10;
```

**Listing 1.2.** PLC code for the input variables.

Since the input variables have a limited possible range (temperatures), we can tell CBMC not to explore all the possible values and assume they are in a given range as shown in Listing 1.3. This is done for all the inputs.

```
1  instance.input_layer_0 = nondet_int16_t();
2  __CPROVER_assume(instance.input_layer_0 >=200 &&
3                              instance.input_layer_0 <=250);
```

**Listing 1.3.** C code for CBMC to limit the range of the input variables.

Listing 1.4 shows how the previous properties can be encoded in PLC code so that they can be verified with PLCverif. Notice that property 6. has included the variable max_mode_prev_cycle from the previous cycle, which is defined as a temporary variable. This value is retained at the end of the cycle by adding an extra assignment after the assertions.

```
1  //#ASSERT NOT max_mode=0 : modesReachability0; // same for the other modes
2  //#ASSERT NOT (speed_layer_output[0]>=0 AND speed_layer_output[0]<20):
        fan_speed_reachability_0_20; // same for the other ranges
3  //#ASSERT max_mode=0 AND (speed_layer_output[0]>1 OR speed_layer_output
        [0]<0.6): fan_speed_constraint_satisfaction;
4  //#ASSERT NOT (in0>23.6 AND in1>23.0 AND in2>14.1 AND max_mode!=2) :
        monotonicity;
5  //#ASSERT NOT (modes_nn[0]<0 OR modes_nn[1]<0 OR modes_nn[2]<0):overflow;
6  //#ASSERT NOT (max_mode_prev_cycle!=max_mode) : robustness;
```

**Listing 1.4.** Translation of the properties into assertions.

Listing 1.5 shows the command to unwind the loops of the neural network 9 times (the maximum number of layers and of neurons in a layer is 8), and the global loop of the PLC cycle 2 times. The unwinding of 2 times of this loop is necessary to verify properties across 2 consecutive cycles.

```
1    cbmc neuralNetwork_prop7.c --unwind 9 --unwindset VerificationLoop.0:2
```

**Listing 1.5.** Command to execute CBMC unwinding the loops of the neural network 9 times, and the loop of the PLC cycle 2 times.

### 4.3 Verification of a NN Using Other Methods

*NN Verifier.* It was decided to use **nnenum** [3] since it is the best fully open-source neural network verifier according to the VNN-COMP (Report) [23] and due to its simplicity. It was needed to manually translate the NN weights given in the PLC code to the .nnet format in order to finally transform it to ONNX. Since the original NN had softmax functions in the output layers, they had to be ignored as **nnenum** cannot handle them. Furthermore, the original NN had to be split into two according to the different outputs (mode and fan speed) since **nnenum** only accepts NNs with one output. This led to the impossibility of verifying the properties in which both outputs are involved. In addition to **nnenum**, VeriNet [16] and $\alpha, \beta$-CROWN [35] were tested without success due to compatibility and reproducibility issues.

*SMT Solver.* Due to the numeric nature of the NN, an SMT solver (Z3 [24]) was used. According to the SMTcompetition, Z3 is one of the best and is open-source. All the loops were unwinded and the Python API for Z3 was used.

*Exhaustive Testing.* Another possibility is to test every single combination of the inputs. Since we are limiting the number of possible input values by using integers and the number of inputs is small, this option was feasible.

## 5   Empirical Results

All the previously presented properties were verified using the described different methods. Table 1 shows the results from these experiments. Since the first two properties are composed of more than one property, the mean and the standard deviation from those cases are shown. Clearly, **nnenum** is the fastest one since it is designed to work with NNs. PLCverif is the one with the lowest performance but it is the only one in which we can express all properties. Z3 is in the middle way between PLCverif and **nnenum**. A more detailed comparison of the different methods is presented in the next Subsect. 5.1.

**Table 1.** Results with the three approaches. Mean and standard deviation when different properties were checked. "-" means that it is not possible to verify that property with that method.

| property | time (s) | | | cex. found |
|---|---|---|---|---|
| | PLCverif | Z3 | nnenum | |
| modes reachability | $4932 \pm 5908$ | $454 \pm 88$ | $< 1$ | yes |
| fan speed reachability | $6162 \pm 5909$ | $1741 \pm 1588$ | $< 1$ | yes |
| fan speed constraint satisfaction | 2469 | 1049 | – | yes |
| monotonicity | 144 | 727 | $< 1$ | yes |
| softmax overflow | 11 | – | – | no |
| robustness | 3517 | 2820 | – | yes |

The code to run these experiments can be found in [20], as well as the results of their executions with the counterexamples. The experiments were done using CBMC 5.10, the Docker image of **nnenum** as of commit `cf7c0e7`, and the Python

API of Z3 version 4.12.1.0. They were run on an AMD Ryzen 7 2700X at 4 GHz with 48 GB RAM memory, running Ubuntu 20.4.

The results from exhaustive testing are not presented in the table since all the properties were checked simultaneously. We built our own testing infrastructure in Python, and the execution time for $51 \cdot 41 \cdot 131 = 273921$ tests (all combinations of the inputs) was 288 s.

The counterexamples given by PLCverif have been tested in the original PLC code to make sure the counterexamples were not spurious. This has been done using the integrated simulator *S7-PLCSIM Advanced* in the TIA portal PLC programming environment. As an example, the counterexample given by nnenum for property 3 is shown in Fig. 5. The three inputs corresponding to the three temperatures are forced to the values given by the counterexample and the expected output values for the fan speed and the operation modes (*ventilation, showering,* and *bypass*) are checked. The simulation shows that the counterexample is real and the problem exists in the NN.

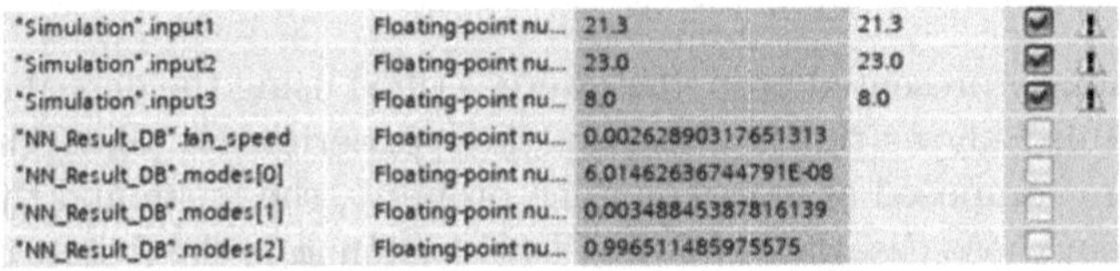

| "Simulation".input1 | Floating-point nu... | 21.3 | 21.3 | ☑ ! |
| "Simulation".input2 | Floating-point nu... | 23.0 | 23.0 | ☑ ! |
| "Simulation".input3 | Floating-point nu... | 8.0 | 8.0 | ☑ ! |
| "NN_Result_DB".fan_speed | Floating-point nu... | 0.00262890317651313 | | ☐ |
| "NN_Result_DB".modes[0] | Floating-point nu... | 6.01462636744791E-08 | | ☐ |
| "NN_Result_DB".modes[1] | Floating-point nu... | 0.00348845387816139 | | ☐ |
| "NN_Result_DB".modes[2] | Floating-point nu... | 0.996511485975575 | | ☐ |

**Fig. 5.** Fan speed constraint satisfaction: Counterexample tested in S7-PLCSIM Advanced.

### 5.1   Comparison of the Different Approaches

Table 2 compares the different methods that were used. By using PLCverif, one can express more complex properties, such as the ones over time cycles. There is also no restriction on the architecture of the NN and the verification is done on the final model that will be deployed. Besides, there is no need to translate the NN to run a verification case. However, performance is low since it was not designed for this purpose. Nevertheless, since it is plug-in based, integrating an SMT solver such as Z3 without using a model checker could improve this issue.

**Table 2.** Comparison of different methods to verify a NN.

| | performance | scalability | expressiveness | same types? | plug-and-play? |
|---|---|---|---|---|---|
| PLCverif | low | low | **high** | yes | yes |
| nnenum | **very high** | **high** | low | no | no |
| Z3 | medium | medium | low | no | no |
| Testing | high[a] | very low | medium | no | no |

[a] For this particular example due to the limited number of inputs and their values.

On the other hand, nnenum is the opposite of PLCverif. That is, its performance was the best but it is not flexible, the type of properties that can be expressed is limited, the data types differ from the ones of a PLC, and a manual translation from the PLC code to ONNX is needed.

The verification with Z3 is in the middle way, where the performance is better than PLCverif, but worse than nnenum. As well, its expressiveness is worse than with PLCverif but better than with nnenum. Finally, the performance of testing was excellent in this particular example. It also gives all the counterexamples and it is relatively flexible. However, it will become unfeasible after a small increase in the number of variables or their possible values due to the exponential growth of the search space. This is independent of the NN architecture. PLCverif and Z3, on the contrary, suffer due to the NN architecture complexity.

## 6    Conclusions and Future Work

Different approaches to verify the ongoing work of a NN running on a PLC that will approximate a MPC for a real installation at CERN have been analyzed. Given the empirical results and the process to obtain them, the ideal approach would be to verify as much as possible with PLCverif. Once it becomes unfeasible due to performance issues, a NN verifier should be used. Finally, especially for the NN verifier due to the discrepancy in data types, the results should be checked using, for example, a simulator to avoid spurious counterexamples.

It is extremely important to verify a NN that will be deployed in a critical system to be sure that it will behave as expected. Verification can help with this endeavor and should be done together as part of the training of the NN until a safe NN is reached. This process will also help the control engineers to better understand the NN behavior as a feedback controller.

To the best of our knowledge, this is the first attempt to verify a neural network controller encoded on a PLC program. This initial study will help us to find a NN that satisfies the properties shown in this paper and new ones. Other future research directions include the analysis of how counterexamples can help improve the NN and the verification of closed-loop system properties.

## References

1. Akintunde, M.E., Botoeva, E., Kouvaros, P., Lomuscio, A.: Formal verification of neural agents in non-deterministic environments. Auton. Agents Multi-Agent Syst. **36**(1), 1–36 (2021). https://doi.org/10.1007/s10458-021-09529-3
2. Akintunde, M., Lomuscio, A., Maganti, L., Pirovano, E.: Reachability analysis for neural agent-environment systems. In: International Conference on Principles of Knowledge Representation and Reasoning (2018)

3. Bak, S.: nnenum: verification of ReLU neural networks with optimized abstraction refinement. In: Dutle, A., Moscato, M.M., Titolo, L., Muñoz, C.A., Perez, I. (eds.) NFM 2021. LNCS, vol. 12673, pp. 19–36. Springer, Cham (2021). https://doi.org/10.1007/978-3-030-76384-8_2

4. Beyer, D., Henzinger, T.A., Jhala, R., Majumdar, R.: The software model checker Blast. Int. J. Softw. Tools Technol. Transf. **9**(5–6), 505–525 (2007). https://doi.org/10.1007/s10009-007-0044-z

5. Boetius, D., Leue, S., Sutter, T.: A robust optimisation perspective on counterexample-guided repair of neural networks. CoRR (2023)

6. Botoeva, E., Kouvaros, P., Kronqvist, J., Lomuscio, A., Misener, R.: Efficient verification of relu-based neural networks via dependency analysis. In: AAAI Conference on Artificial Intelligence (2020)

7. Darvas, D., Fernández Adiego, B., Blanco Viñuela, E.: PLCverif: a tool to verify PLC programs based on model checking techniques. In: Proceedings of ICALEPCS'15 (2015). https://doi.org/10.18429/JACoW-ICALEPCS2015-WEPGF092

8. Dutta, S., Jha, S., Sankaranarayanan, S., Tiwari, A.: Learning and verification of feedback control systems using feedforward neural networks. IFAC-PapersOnLine **51**(16), 151–156 (2018). https://doi.org/10.1016/j.ifacol.2018.08.026

9. Ehlers, R.: Formal verification of piece-wise linear feed-forward neural networks. In: Automated Technology for Verification and Analysis (2017)

10. Fernández Adiego, B., Blanco Viñuela, E.: Applying model checking to critical PLC applications: an ITER case study. In: Proceedings of ICALEPCS 2017 (2017). https://doi.org/10.18429/JACoW-ICALEPCS2017-THPHA161

11. Fernández Adiego, B., et al.: Applying model checking to industrial-sized PLC programs. IEEE Trans. Ind. Inf. **11**, 1400–1410 (2015). https://doi.org/10.1109/TII.2015.2489184

12. Fernández Adiego, B., Lopez-Miguel, I.D., Tournier, J.C., Blanco Viñuela, E., Ladzinski, T., Havart, F.: Applying model checking to highly-configurable safety critical software: the SPS-PPS PLC program. In: Proceedings of ICALEPCS 2021 (2022). https://doi.org/10.18429/JACoW-ICALEPCS2021-WEPV042

13. Georges, D.: A simple machine learning technique for model predictive control. In: 2019 27th Mediterranean Conference on Control and Automation (MED), pp. 69–74. IEEE (2019)

14. Ghawash, F., Hovd, M., Schofield, B.: Optimal control of induced draft cooling tower using mixed integer programming. In: 2021 IEEE Conference on Control Technology and Applications (CCTA), pp. 214–219. IEEE (2021)

15. Ghawash, F., Hovd, M., Schofield, B.: Model predictive control of induced draft cooling towers in a large scale cooling plant. IFAC-PapersOnLine **55**(7), 161–167 (2022)

16. Henriksen, P., Lomuscio, A.: Efficient neural network verification via adaptive refinement and adversarial search. In: European Conference on Artificial Intelligence (2020)

17. Henriksen, P., Leofante, F., Lomuscio, A.: Repairing misclassifications in neural networks using limited data. In: Proceedings of the 37th ACM/SIGAPP Symposium on Applied Computing, SAC 2022, pp. 1031–1038. Association for Computing Machinery, New York (2022). https://doi.org/10.1145/3477314.3507059

18. Huang, X., et al.: A survey of safety and trustworthiness of deep neural networks: verification, testing, adversarial attack and defence, and interpretability. Comput. Sci. Rev. **37**, 100270 (2020). https://doi.org/10.1016/j.cosrev.2020.100270

19. Jin, G.Y., Cai, W.J., Lu, L., Lee, E.L., Chiang, A.: A simplified modeling of mechanical cooling tower for control and optimization of hvac systems. Energy Conv. Manag. **48**(2), 355–365 (2007)
20. Lopez-Miguel, I.D.: Verification of a neural network controller encoded on a PLC program. TU Wien Research Data (2023). https://doi.org/10.48436/fww3h-2y402
21. Lopez-Miguel, I.D., Adiego, B.F., Tournier, J.C., Viñuela, E.B., Rodriguez-Aguilar, J.A.: Simplification of numeric variables for plc model checking. In: Proceedings of the 19th ACM-IEEE International Conference on Formal Methods and Models for System Design, MEMOCODE 2021, pp. 10–20. Association for Computing Machinery, New York (2021). https://doi.org/10.1145/3487212.3487334
22. Lopez-Miguel, I.D., Tournier, J.C., Fernández Adiego, B.: PLCverif: status of a formal verification tool for programmable logic controller. In: Proceedings of ICALEPCS 2021 (2022). https://doi.org/10.18429/JACoW-ICALEPCS2021-MOPV042
23. Müller, M.N., Brix, C., Bak, S., Liu, C., Johnson, T.T.: The third international verification of neural networks competition (vnn-comp 2022): summary and results (2022). https://doi.org/10.48550/ARXIV.2212.10376
24. de Moura, L., Bjørner, N.: Z3: an efficient SMT solver. In: Ramakrishnan, C.R., Rehof, J. (eds.) TACAS 2008. LNCS, vol. 4963, pp. 337–340. Springer, Heidelberg (2008). https://doi.org/10.1007/978-3-540-78800-3_24
25. Parisini, T., Zoppoli, R.: A receding-horizon regulator for nonlinear systems and a neural approximation. Automatica **31**(10), 1443–1451 (1995)
26. Pasta, E., Carapellese, F., Mattiazzo, G.: Deep neural network trained to mimic nonlinear economic model predictive control: an application to a pendulum wave energy converter. In: 2021 IEEE Conference on Control Technology and Applications (CCTA), pp. 295–300. IEEE (2021)
27. Pin, G., Filippo, M., Pellegrino, F.A., Fenu, G., Parisini, T.: Approximate model predictive control laws for constrained nonlinear discrete-time systems: analysis and offline design. Int. J. Control **86**(5), 804–820 (2013)
28. Poznyak, A., Chairez, I., Poznyak, T.: A survey on artificial neural networks application for identification and control in environmental engineering: biological and chemical systems with uncertain models. Ann. Rev. Control **48**, 250–272 (2019). https://doi.org/10.1016/j.arcontrol.2019.07.003
29. Schofield, B., Peljo, M., Blanco, E., Booth, W.: Waste heat recovery for lhc cooling towers control system validation using digital twins. In: 17th International Conference on Accelerator and Large Experimental Physics Control Systems on and Information, New York, USA (2019)
30. Schwenzer, M., Ay, M., Bergs, T., Abel, D.: Review on model predictive control: an engineering perspective. Int. J. Adv. Manuf. Technol. **117**(5–6), 1327–1349 (2021)
31. Viñuela, E.B., Darvas, D., Molnár, V.: PLCverif Re-engineered: an open platform for the formal analysis of PLC programs. In: Proceedings of ICALEPCS 2019, International Conference on Accelerator and Large Experimental Physics Control Systems, no. 17, pp. 21–27. JACoW Publishing, Geneva (2020). https://doi.org/10.18429/JACoW-ICALEPCS2019-MOBPP01
32. Wang, S., Pei, K., Whitehouse, J., Yang, J., Jana, S.: Efficient formal safety analysis of neural networks. In: Proceedings of the 32nd International Conference on Neural Information Processing Systems, NIPS 2018, pp. 6369–6379. Curran Associates Inc., Red Hook (2018)

33. Wang, S., Pei, K., Whitehouse, J., Yang, J., Jana, S.: Formal security analysis of neural networks using symbolic intervals. In: Proceedings of the 27th USENIX Conference on Security Symposium, SEC 2018, pp. 1599–1614. USENIX Association, USA (2018)
34. Werbos, P.: An overview of neural networks for control. IEEE Control Syst. Maga. **11**(1), 40–41 (1991). https://doi.org/10.1109/37.103352
35. Xu, K., et al.: Fast and Complete: Enabling complete neural network verification with rapid and massively parallel incomplete verifiers. In: International Conference on Learning Representations (2021). https://openreview.net/forum?id=nVZtXBI6LNn

# Virtual Flow Meter for an Industrial Process

Raúl González-Herbón[(✉)] [ID], Guzmán González-Mateos[ID], Serafín Alonso[ID],
Miguel A. Prada[ID], Juan J. Fuertes[ID], Antonio Morán[ID],
and Manuel Domínguez[ID]

Suppress Research Group, Escuela de Ingenierías, Universidad de León,
Campus de Vegazana s/n, 24007 León, Spain
{rgonzh,ggonzm,saloc,ma.prada,jj.fuertes,a.moran,mdomg}@unileon.es
https://suppress.unileon.es

**Abstract.** The digitalization process has emerged strongly in the industry, causing an increase of connected sensors and IIoT devices, which produce a great amount of varied data. However, some industrial variables are hard to measure because of its high cost, complex installation mechanisms or non-stop production requirements. These variables could be indirectly estimated based on other related variables available in the process. Data-driven methods would be appropriate for this purpose, modelling real and potentially complex industrial processes. In this paper, a methodology to develop a virtual flow meter for industrial processes is presented. It assumes the impossibility of installing a flow meter in the process, so a non-invasive flow meter is used punctually to measure and capture data for training data-driven methods. Three different methods have been trained to obtain the model function: multiple linear regression (MLR), multilayer perceptron (MLP) and long-short term memory (LSTM). The developed virtual flow meter has been tested on a pilot plant built with real industrial equipment. LSTM method yields the best performance in the flow estimation, providing the lowest MAE and RMSE errors. It is able to consider temporal dependencies, besides modelling the nonlinear nature of industrial processes.

**Keywords:** Data-driven models · Digitalization · Industry 4.0 ·
Virtual sensor · Deep learning

## 1 Introduction

In the last years, a digitalization process has emerged strongly in the industry. This process introduces cutting-edge advances in industrial automation, combined with a deeper application of information technologies (IT) [19]. In this context, the increasing number of connected sensors and IIoT devices plays an important role, generally producing a large volume of non-centralised data [20], which is significant for process control and monitoring or virtual representation of the process using digital twins [16].

© The Author(s), under exclusive license to Springer Nature Switzerland AG 2023
L. Iliadis et al. (Eds.): EANN 2023, CCIS 1826, pp. 433–444, 2023.
https://doi.org/10.1007/978-3-031-34204-2_36

Therefore, this digitalization process entails the measurement and storage of huge amounts of varied data. However, some industrial variables are hard-to-measure because of its high cost, complex installation mechanisms or non-stop production requirements [10]. Portable sensors could be used in order to address this issue. Nevertheless, it might be unaffordable for small companies. On the contrary, these hard-to-measure variables could also be estimated based on other related variables available in the process [2]. This indirect approach to measurement can be carried out by using physical principles and equations. However, adverse conditions in the industrial environments could influence the process. Data-driven models would be more appropriate for this purpose when applied to real and potentially complex industrial processes, due to the difficulty to model from first principles all the nonlinearities that are introduced by industrial elements such as pumps, variable frequency drives or valves [17].

Measuring flow is challenging since its regime can be turbulent due to rough conditions in the processes, and nonlinearities can be introduced by propelling elements such as pumps. The theological properties of the fluids also influence the flow measurements [3]. On the other hand, flow meters are scarcely installed in the industry due to budget constraints or space limitations [13]. Moreover, their installation usually requires stopping the process.

For these reasons, a methodology is proposed in this paper to develop a virtual flow meter for industrial environments, which should be able to provide flow observations based on other process variables. For that purpose, it relies on a data-driven model built using stored data from the industrial process. The paper is structured as follows: a literature review of virtual sensors in industry and alternatives to implement them is presented in Sect. 2. In Sect. 3, the problem and the methodology adopted to develop a virtual flow meter are described. In Sect. 4, the experiment and the results are explained and discussed. Finally, conclusions are drawn and future work is discussed in Sect. 5.

## 2    Literature Review

Virtual or soft sensors are software applications based on inferential models that use available process variables to indirectly estimate other unavailable variables [9]. Thus, virtual sensors can be used when the corresponding real sensor is expensive, inaccurate or out of service. They are not invasive and do not require a physical modification of the system where are deployed [13]. Furthermore, virtual sensors can be easily changed and reconfigured anytime whereas real sensors usually require stopping the process when they are installed [11].

Soft sensors can be classified into model-driven and data-driven categories [21]. The first group comprises soft sensors built from first-principle and mathematical models [12], whereas the second group contains those models built with data-based methods, ranging from linear regression methods to more sophisticated deep learning methods [8]. A multivariable statistical analysis where there is some statistical characteristics are constant can be used [1]. Finally, machine learning methods, especially deep learning ones with different architectures such

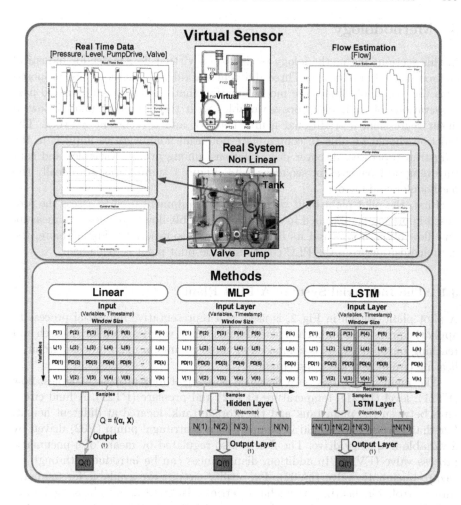

**Fig. 1.** Methodology

as dense neural networks, recurrent networks or convolutional networks, are an interesting approach to learn models from real data [14].

Virtual sensors have been applied to several fields in the industry. For instance, different solutions have been proposed to measure flow of non Newtonian fluids [3], pH [18], or volatile fatty acids concentrations [15]. In building automation systems, they have also been used to improve monitoring, diagnosis and efficiency [9]. In this paper, we propose to develop a virtual flow meter using three data-driven methods: a multi-linear regression, and multilayer perceptron and a long-short term memory.

# 3   Methodology

In this section, the methodology to develop a virtual flow meter for industrial environments is presented. Three different data-driven methods are proposed with the aim of obtaining the model function that relates the current and past observations of available process variables with the desired estimated flow: a linear regression, a traditional neural network and a recurrent network. The function should be able to contemplate potential nonlinearities implicit in the industrial processes, discover deep relations among process variables and capture temporal patterns in sequence data. Figure 1 summarizes graphically the methodology adopted.

First, the pilot plant built with industrial equipment used to assess the proposed approach is described in detail. The portable flow meter used to measure true flow observations and its installation are also described. Furthermore, the data acquisition from the PLC controlling the pilot plant is explained.

## 3.1   The Industrial System: A Pilot Plant

A pilot plant, shown in Fig. 2, is used as a representative industrial process to apply the proposed approach. This industrial plant was designed for research and teaching purposes [4]. It is composed of three circuits: a main process circuit, a heating circuit and a cooling circuit.

The main circuit has been designed to control four process variables: flow (FT21), level (LT21), temperature (TT22) and pressure (PT21). A fluid circulates between the main tank and the storage tank, located at different height. For that purpose, the liquid is pumped by a centrifugal pump (P02) driven by a variable frequency drive. The flow is also regulated by means of a pneumatic process valve (FV21). In addition, disturbances can be introduced through an electro-pneumatic valve (FV02). Two utility circuits are available for temperature control. The heating circuit has electric resistors (JZ21), to heat the liquid, and a high-performance heat exchanger, to transfer this heat to the process liquid. The hot water flow that transfers the heat to the process is controlled by a three-way valve (TV21). The cooling circuit makes use of an external cooling unit to cool the process liquid. The cool transfer is carried out by means of an exchanger similar to the one in the heating circuit. Recirculation of chilled water is again controlled by a three-way valve (TV22).

The pilot plant has a flexible architecture, so that several controllers from different manufacturers can be used. In this case, the control strategy was programmed on a Schneider Electric Modicon M340 PLC (Programmable Logic Controller), with I/O interfaces connected to the transmitters and actuators of the pilot plant. This PLC communicates through the Modbus TCP standard.

The variables corresponding to sensors and actuators of the pilot plant are wired to the I/O cards. Additionally, an ultrasonic sensor (UltS) has been connected in order to measure the flow of the main process circuit. All variables wired to the PLC I/O interfaces are listed in Table 1.

**Fig. 2.** Pilot plant, built with industrial equipment

## 3.2 Measurement of Flow and Data Acquisition

A flow meter is not usually available in industrial processes, being difficult to install them quickly. To replicate this scenario, a portable ultrasonic meter has been used, a FLUXUS F601 by Flexim (see Fig. 3). This meter makes use of external transducers that are capable of measuring the flow through ultrasonic signals, so it is non-invasive. It has been installed on the pipe surface in the main process circuit. This flow meter allows us to measure flow rates between 0.01 and 25 m/s in pipes whose size can range from 6mm to 6500 mm mm. The measurement configuration is not trivial due to the need of specifying multiple parameters such as: pipe roughness and pipe wall thickness (highly susceptible to perturbations caused by dirt and usage); sound velocity and kinematic viscosity of the medium (processes working with poorly known fluids or with mixes of fluids and/or solids make it hard to define these parameters); as well as parameters related to the used transducers, such as sound paths (the number of bounces that the ultrasonic beam does). This meter gives a typical 4-20 mA analog signal, which can be directly connected to the PLC I/O interfaces.

Among the sensors and actuators of the pilot plant, five variables are selected to build the dataset needed by the proposed data-driven methods: ultrasonic sensor (UltS), main process pressure (PT21), level of the main tank (LT21), main process valve (FV21) and pump setpoint (P02). These data are requested to the Modicon M340 PLC of the pilot plant by means of a multithreaded acquisition application that has been programmed in Python. This application offers

**Table 1.** Pilot plant variables

| Type | TAGs | Variables | Unit |
|---|---|---|---|
| Digital Input | LSH21 | High Level Tank D02 | |
| | LSL21 | Low Level Tank D02 | |
| | LSH22 | High Level Tank D04 | |
| | LSL22 | Low Level Tank D04 | |
| | TSH21 | High Temperature Tank D01 | |
| | ES24 | ACK Pump 1 | |
| | ES25 | ACK Pump 2 | |
| | ES26 | ACK Heat Resistors | |
| Digital Output | FY21 | On/Off Pump 1 | |
| | FY22 | Electrovalve | |
| | FY23 | On/Off Pump 2 | |
| | FY24 | On/Off Heat Resistors | |
| Analog Input | TT21 | Heating Circuit Temperature | °C |
| | TT22 | Main Process Temperature | °C |
| | TT23 | Cooling Circuit Temperature | °C |
| | LT21 | Tank Level D03 | % |
| | FT21 | Main Process Flow | l/min |
| | PT21 | Main Process Pressure | bar |
| | **UltS** | **Ultrasonic Sensor** | l/min |
| Analog Output | JZ21 | Heat Resistors Setpoint | % |
| | TV21 | Heating Circuit Valve | % |
| | TV22 | Cooling Circuit Valve | % |
| | FV21 | Main Process Valve | % |
| | P02 | Pump 2 Setpoint | % |

multiprotocol support (Modbus TCP is used in this case), allowing unified reading and preprocessing of data, regardless of the manufacturer and nature of the equipment involved in the experiments. A thread requests the specified data from the equipment at the sampling time previously set through a web user interface of the application. The requested datasets will be temporally stored in memory, until their later storage in a specific database.

### 3.3 Developing a Virtual Flow Meter

The industrial process should be analyzed in detail in order to proceed with the development of a virtual flow meter. This virtual meter should be able to provide current flow observations based on values from those process variables that influence on flow. Both current and past observations from these process variables are considered in order to model temporal patterns [2]. Therefore, developing a virtual flow meter could be understood as a regression problem (see Eq. 1), where the estimated flow observations $\hat{y}_t$ are a function of current and past observations from related process variables $\mathbf{X}_t, \mathbf{X}_{t-1}, \ldots, \mathbf{X}_{t-w}$, being $\mathbf{X} = [x_1, x_2, \ldots, x_n]$ the process variables and $w$ the temporal window.

$$\hat{y}_t = f(\mathbf{X}_t, \mathbf{X}_{t-1}, \ldots, \mathbf{X}_{t-w}) \tag{1}$$

The challenge is to achieve the model function $f$ indicated in Eq. 1, which relates the output $\hat{y}_t$ to process variables $\mathbf{X} = [x_1, x_2, \ldots, x_n]$. Note that the true flow observations needed to train the models are captured by the portable flow meter.

Three different methods have been selected in order to obtain function $f$. The aim is to assess different methods, observing advantages and drawbacks of each of them. First, a **multiple linear regression** (MLR) [5] is chosen as the baseline method. MLR assumes a linear relationship between each of the inputs (explanatory variables) and the output (flow in this case). For that reason, it might be unsuitable to model the nonlinearities usually present in industrial processes. However, it is still interesting as a baseline model.

Second, a **multilayer perceptron** (MLP) [6], a shallow neural network with a single hidden layer is chosen due to its higher suitability to accurately model those nonlinearities. MLPs achieve this goal through nonlinear activation functions. In order to obtain a faster computational performance, a shallow structure is tested. The MLP is composed of input and output layers, a flatten layer, together with a single hidden layer. Finally, a **long-short term memory** (LSTM) [7] is selected because of its ability to processing sequences of data. This is possible thanks to the recurrent or feedback connections that let the network use their internal state as a memory. Unlike regular recurrent neural networks, LSTMs have a larger memory capacity, making them a more robust alternative for modelling dynamic behaviour. However, they become difficult to train as the number of parameters is large and so they could present convergence problems, in spite of handling the vanishing/exploding gradient problems.

The desired virtual meter is in charge of estimating the flow of the main process circuit in the pilot plant. In this case, flow depends on pressure (PT21), level in the main tank (LT21), the setpoint of the main process pump (P02) and the process valve opening (FV21). Since a window with $w$ previous observations is used to take into account the dynamic of the system, the dimension of the input data is $n \times w$, where $n = 4$: pressure, level, pump and valve. The settling times of the system are considered to appropriately establish the window size $w$.

## 4   Experimental Results and Discussion

Three experiments, with a length of one hour, have been performed to collect the data. In them, step changes of 5% in the process valve opening (FV21) combined with pseudorandom pump setpoints (P02) have been introduced to the pilot plant. This way, a dataset with a variety of situations that consider the inertia associated with filling the main tank is built.

The input to the virtual flow meter is given by:

$$\mathbf{X} = \begin{bmatrix} PT21, LT21, P02, FV21 \end{bmatrix}.$$

And the output of the proposed approach will be the predicted flow:

$$\hat{y} = \widehat{UltS}.$$

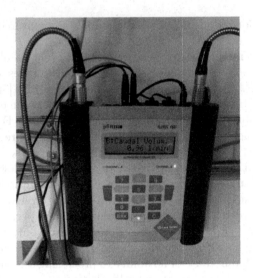

**Fig. 3.** Portable ultrasonic flow meter

**Table 2.** Hyperparameter tuning

| Hyperparameters | Range | Value |
|---|---|---|
| MLP Neurons | 5,10,20,40,80,160 | 20 |
| LSTM Neurons | 5,10,20,40,80,160 | 80 |

The size of the sliding window used to capture the system dynamics is a model parameter. To select it appropriately, the time constants of the system have been empirically computed. Since the maximum settling time obtained was 5 s and the sampling time is 100 ms, the dimension of the input vector was set 50.

The dataset was divided in 2 subsets: training (66%) and testing dataset (34%). For MLP and LSTM training, 10 epochs were used, introducing data in batches of 32 samples. A grid search over a range of hyperparameters (the number of units in the neural networks) was performed using a 10-fold cross-validation on the training dataset. Table 2 shows the range and the optimal value of these hyperparameters. Among values of 5, 10, 20, 40, 80, and 160, the optimal number of neurons in the MLP hidden layer was set to 20 neurons, whereas it was set to 80 in the LSTM network.

The MAE (Mean Absolute Error), RMSE (Root Mean Square Error) and $R^2$ (coefficient of determination) have been chosen as evaluation metrics. These errors have been computed using test dataset. In Table 3, it can be seen that LSTM method had the lowest MAE and RMSE errors since it is able to consider temporal dependencies, besides capturing the nonlinear nature of the industrial process. MAE and RMSE errors using MLP regression are only slightly higher than those obtained by LSTM, showing the strength of nonlinear functions to

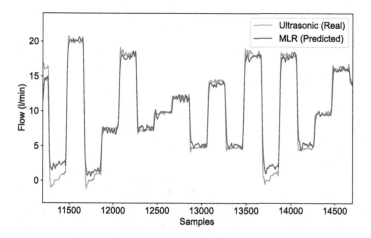

**Fig. 4.** Comparison between the real ultrasonic and the MLR virtual flow meter.

model complex relations. As expected, the virtual flow meter based on linear method (MLR) provided the worst results, roughly doubling the MLP errors. These results revealing its poorer suitability for modelling behaviours in industrial processes. Also, R-squared is in agreement with the results obtained, observing that the closest to 1 is the LSTM, slightly below is the MLP and with a poor result is the MLR.

Additionally, the performance of the virtual flow meter developed with each method (MLR, MLP and LSTM) is assessed through the comparison of its estimations with real data from the ultrasonic flow meter, as shown in Figs. 4, 5 and 6, respectively. In Fig. 4, it can be seen how the sensor response with the linear method did not follow well with the actual flow, producing significant differences between the steady state of predicted and real flows. The comparison with the MLP method shown in Fig. 5, shows more similar responses where the greatest differences are found for flow values that are close to zero. Last, Fig. 6 shows that the flow estimated by the LSTM provides a better fit than the others, and shows a behaviour that is more insensitive to the disturbances associated with the real ultrasonic meter. This results in the ability of the virtual flow meter to extract the trend of the real flow without being influenced by measurement noise.

These results are consistent with the hypothesis that linear modelling leads to unacceptable errors in industrial processes due to existing non-linear characteristics in their elements. And so, nonlinear methods are needed to match the dynamic behaviour of the systems. Both nonlinear methods allowed modelling accurately the dynamic behaviour of the flow variable, although the shallow neural network was more sensitive to noise and disturbances. The use of recurrent networks is proven to be a more robust and capable solution for predicting complex dynamic behaviours, since it learns deep relations and temporal patterns.

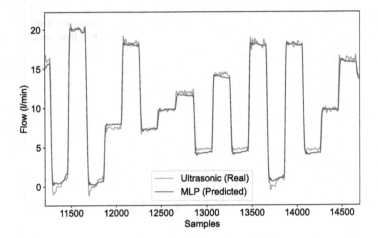

**Fig. 5.** Comparison between the real ultrasonic and the MLP virtual flow meter.

**Table 3.** Results on the test dataset

| Método | MAE | RMSE | $R^2$ |
|--------|------|------|--------|
| MLR    | 1.16 | 1.67 | 0.9284 |
| MLP    | 0.61 | 0.56 | 0.9830 |
| LSTM   | 0.45 | 0.33 | 0.9970 |

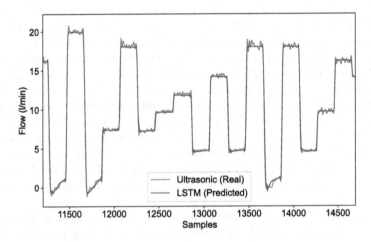

**Fig. 6.** Comparison between the real ultrasonic and the LSTM virtual flow meter.

## 5   Conclusions

In this paper, a methodology to develop a virtual flow meter for industrial processes is presented. It relies on indirect measurements of related process variables.

Furthermore, it assumes the impossibility of installing a flow meter in the process, so a non-invasive flow meter should be used punctually to measure and capture data for training data-driven methods. Three different methods have been used to obtain a model function: multiple linear regression (MLR), multilayer perceptron (MLP) and long-short term memory (LSTM) network.

The developed virtual flow meter has been tested on a pilot plant built with real industrial equipment. The LSTM network yielded the best performance in the flow estimation, i.e., it gave the lowest MAE and RMSE errors and the highest R-squared. Furthermore, it proved to be the most robust implementation against noise and disturbances. MLP method had problems dealing with noise and disturbances in comparison with LSTM and linear regressions (MLR) should be dismissed because its assumptions of linearity make it unsuitable for real industrial environments.

Future research will focus on the deployment of the developed virtual flow meter on a low-cost hardware and its integration in the pilot plant, so that it could actually replace the real flow sensor when its measurement is nonexistent. This way, it could be used as redundant sensor in a flow control loop, avoiding the control degradation. The methodology could also be extended to the development of a data-driven model of the whole pilot plant in the context of a digital twin of the complete system.

**Acknowledgements.** This work was supported by the Spanish State Research Agency, MCIN/ AEI/ 10.13039/ 501100011033 under Grant PID2020-117890RB-I00. The work of Guzmán González-Mateos was supported by a grant of the *Research Programme of the University of León 2021*.

# References

1. Abeykoon, C.: Design and applications of soft sensors in polymer processing: a review. IEEE Sens. J. **19**(8), 2801–2813 (2018)
2. Alonso, S., Morán, A., Pérez, D., Prada, M.A., Díaz, I., Domínguez, M.: Estimating cooling production and monitoring efficiency in chillers using a soft sensor. Neural Comput. Appl. **32**(23), 17291–17308 (2020). https://doi.org/10.1007/s00521-020-05165-2
3. Chhantyal, K., Jondahl, M.H., Viumdal, H., Mylvaganam, S.: Upstream ultrasonic level based soft sensing of volumetric flow of non-Newtonian fluids in open Venturi channels. IEEE Sens. J. **18**(12), 5002–5013 (2018). https://doi.org/10.1109/JSEN.2018.2831445
4. Domínguez, M., Fuertes, J.J., Reguera, P., González, J.J., Ramón, J.M.: Maqueta industrial para docencia e investigación. Rev. Iberoamericana Automática Informática Ind. **1**(2), 58–63 (2010)
5. Hastie, T., Tibshirani, R., Friedman, J.: The Elements of Statistical Learning, 2nd edn. Springer, New York (2009). https://doi.org/10.1007/978-0-387-84858-7
6. Haykin, S.: Neural Networks: A Comprehensive Foundation. Prentice Hall PTR, Hoboken (1994)
7. Hochreiter, S., Schmidhuber, J.: Long short-term memory. Neural Comput. **9**(8), 1735–1780 (1997). https://doi.org/10.1162/neco.1997.9.8.1735

8. Kadlec, P., Gabrys, B., Strandt, S.: Data-driven soft sensors in the process industry. Comput. Chem. Eng. **33**(4), 795–814 (2009). https://doi.org/10.1016/j.compchemeng.2008.12.012

9. Li, H., Yu, D., Braun, J.E.: A review of virtual sensing technology and application in building systems. HVAC&R Res. **17**(5), 619–645 (2011). https://doi.org/10.1080/10789669.2011.573051

10. Liu, Y., Xie, M.: Rebooting data-driven soft-sensors in process industries: a review of kernel methods. J. Process Control **89**, 58–73 (2020). https://doi.org/10.1016/j.jprocont.2020.03.012

11. Martin, D., Kühl, N., Satzger, G.: Virtual sensors. Bus. Inf. Syst. Eng. **63**(3), 315–323 (2021)

12. Mattera, C.G., Quevedo, J., Escobet, T., Shaker, H.R., Jradi, M.: A method for fault detection and diagnostics in ventilation units using virtual sensors. Sensors **18**(11), 3931 (2018)

13. McDonald, E., Zmeureanu, R.: Development and testing of a virtual flow meter tool to monitor the performance of cooling plants. Energy Procedia **78**, 1129–1134 (2015). https://doi.org/10.1016/j.egypro.2015.11.071

14. Márquez-Vera, M.A., López-Ortega, O., Ramos-Velasco, L.E., Ortega-Mendoza, R.M., Fernández-Neri, B.J., Zúñiga-Peña, N.S.: Diagnóstico de fallas mediante una LSTM y una red elástica. Rev. Iberoamericana Automática Informática Ind. **18**(2), 160–171 (2021). https://doi.org/10.4995/riai.2020.13611

15. Nair, A.M., Fanta, A., Haugen, F.A., Ratnaweera, H.: Implementing an extended Kalman filter for estimating nutrient composition in a sequential batch MBBR pilot plant. Water Sci. Technol. **80**(2), 317–328 (2019). https://doi.org/10.2166/wst.2019.272

16. de Prada, C., Galán-Casado, S., Pitarch, J.L., Sarabia, D., Galán, A., Gutiérrez, G.: Gemelos digitales en la industria de procesos. Rev. Iberoamericana Automática Informática Ind. **19**(3), 285–296 (2022). https://doi.org/10.4995/riai.2022.16901

17. Sun, Q., Ge, Z.: A survey on deep learning for data-driven soft sensors. IEEE Trans. Ind. Inf. **17**(9), 5853–5866 (2021)

18. Thürlimann, C.M., Dürrenmatt, D.J., Villez, K.: Soft-sensing with qualitative trend analysis for wastewater treatment plant control. Control Eng. Pract. **70**, 121–133 (2018). https://doi.org/10.1016/j.conengprac.2017.09.015

19. Xu, L.D., Xu, E.L., Li, L.: Industry 4.0: state of the art and future trends. Int. J. Prod. Res. **56**(8), 2941–2962 (2018). https://doi.org/10.1080/00207543.2018.1444806

20. Yan, J., Meng, Y., Lu, L., Li, L.: Industrial big data in an industry 4.0 environment: challenges, schemes, and applications for predictive maintenance. IEEE Access **5**, 23484–23491 (2017). https://doi.org/10.1109/ACCESS.2017.2765544

21. Yuan, X., Wang, Y., Yang, C., Ge, Z., Song, Z., Gui, W.: Weighted linear dynamic system for feature representation and soft sensor application in nonlinear dynamic industrial processes. IEEE Trans. Ind. Electron. **65**(2), 1508–1517 (2018). https://doi.org/10.1109/TIE.2017.2733443

# Wind Energy Prediction Guided by Multiple-Location Weather Forecasts

Charalampos Symeonidis[✉] and Nikos Nikolaidis

Artificial Intelligence and Information Analysis Lab, Department of Informatics,
Aristotle University of Thessaloniki, Thessaloniki, Greece
{charsyme,nnik}@csd.auth.gr

**Abstract.** In recent years, electricity generated from renewable energy sources has become a significant contributor to power supply systems over the world. Wind is one of the most important renewable energy sources, thus accurate wind energy prediction is a vital component of the management and operation of electric grids. This paper proposes a novel method for wind energy forecasting, which relies on a novel variant of the scaled-dot product attention mechanism, for exploring relations between the generated energy and a set of multiple-location weather forecasts/measurements. The conducted experimental evaluation on a dataset consisting of the hourly generated wind energy in Greece along with hourly weather forecasts for 18 different locations, demonstrated that the proposed approach outperforms competitive methods.

**Keywords:** Wind energy prediction · Renewable energy · Scaled-dot product attention

## 1 Introduction

Electricity generated from renewable energy sources, has been proven an effective solution against the energy shortage and the environmental pollution caused by conventional (e.g. fossil fuels) energy production methods. Wind energy is one of the most important renewable energy sources. However, wind energy is a highly fluctuating resource, mainly due to the respective unpredictable nature of weather conditions, mainly wind speed and direction. Accurate wind energy prediction is vital for lowering the impact of uncertainty, thus achieving a smoother integration of the respective energy sources (wind farms/parks) into the grid.

Most approaches for wind energy generation prediction can be classified based on either the applied methodology or the time horizon of the prediction [4]. Based on the predictive horizon, the methods are usually classified into the following four categories:

- Very short-term (up to 30 min) forecasting
- Short-term (30 min to 6 h) forecasting
- Medium-term (6 h to 1 day) forecasting
- Long-term (1 day to a month) forecasting

L. Iliadis et al. (Eds.): EANN 2023, CCIS 1826, pp. 445–457, 2023.
https://doi.org/10.1007/978-3-031-34204-2_37

Regarding the applied methodology, wind energy prediction methods are categorized as physical or statistical. The first, explore the physical relations between the wind speed, climate conditions, topological information and the energy generated from the corresponding wind power plant. Usually, physical models [2,19] rely on numerical weather prediction models (NWP) that simulate atmospheric physics by utilizing boundary conditions and physical laws, in order to determine wind speed. The predicted wind speed is then used along with the related wind turbine power curve, usually provided by the turbine manufacturer, in order to predict the generated wind energy. Physical models are generally suitable for long-term wind energy forecasting, but their short-term precision remains low.

Statistical models/approaches [6,18] are more appropriate for short-term wind energy prediction compared to physical models. Their aim is not to describe the physical steps involved in the wind power conversion process, but to directly obtain wind energy predictions, by exploring statistical relations between historical wind energy data and other relevant input data. A sub-class of statistical models are Deep Learning (DL) based methods. In recent years, several DL-based methods, including approaches utilizing convolutional neural networks (CNNs) [17,20], autoencoders [16], recurrent neural networks (RNNs) [10] and spatio-temporal attention-based networks [11], have been proposed as suitable solutions for wind energy forecasting.

In [17], the authors mapped data collected from wind turbines into a grid space, which they called scene. The scene time series is a multi-channel image, which represents the spatio-temporal characteristics of wind in a certain area and time. Therefore, they developed a DL model based on CNN to extract features from these images, in order to predict the generated energy. The results showed that the proposed model achieves better accuracy than other existing methods. The authors in [11] proposed a sequence-to-sequence model for multi-step-ahead wind power forecasting, namely prediction of multiple future wind power values. The model architecture consists of two groups of Gated Recurrent Units (GRU) blocks, which work as encoder and decoder. The authors proposed the Attention-based GRU (AGRU) for embedding the task of correlating different forecasting steps by hidden activations of GRU blocks. The AGRU model achieved top performance against other competitive wind energy forecasting methods. In [13], the authors modified the N-BEATS [12] model towards making it suitable for the f wind energy forecasting task and proposed a loss function capable to confront the issue of forecast bias. The method, mostly evaluated on very-short term wind energy prediction datasets, was able to compete against other state-of-the-art approaches and even outperform them in terms of accuracy in most cases. In [20], the authors proposed a DL-based architecture, based on Temporal Convolutional Networks (TCNs) for short-term wind energy prediction. An experimental evaluation of the method on a dataset consisting of 5000 hourly wind power and meteorological data samples collected from a single wind energy power plant, showed promising results against the competitive methods. In [16] the authors proposed an architecture named SIRAE (Staked Independently Recurrent Auto-Encoder), suitable for ultra-short wind energy forecasting. According to the authors, this approach can accommodate a large volume of data in an efficient manner while also overcoming the effects of random changes in the natural environment. To verify the effectiveness and stability of SIRAE, two comparative experiments, in which it outperformed several popular models, were conducted. In [10], the authors proposed DWT_LSTM, a short-term wind energy forecasting method based on Discrete Wavelet Transform (DWT) and Long Short-Term Memory (LSTM) networks. The method adopts a divide and conquer strategy, in which DWT is used to decompose original wind power data into sub-signals, while several independent LSTMs are employed to approximate the temporal dynamic behaviors of these sub-signals. The proposed method achieved top prediction accuracy rates against other state-of-the-art methods.

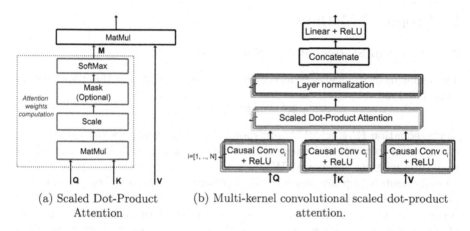

(a) Scaled Dot-Product Attention

(b) Multi-kernel convolutional scaled dot-product attention.

**Fig. 1.** (a): Scaled Dot-Product Attention, (b): the novel Multi-kernel convolutional scaled dot-product attention. $c_i$ denotes the $i$-th convolutional kernel size, employed in the temporal domain whereas $N$ denotes the number of convolutional kernels.

The method proposed in this paper relies on the scaled dot-product attention mechanism, initially proposed in [15]. Several methods [9] in the relevant literature have applied this mechanism in time-series forecasting for exploring temporal dependencies. More recently, spatio-temporal attention networks [3] have been introduced to wind energy forecasting, aiming to predict the generated energy of multiple, spatially neighboring, wind farms. Compared to methods in the relevant literature, our approach provides the following contributions:

– Utilizes past and future wind-related weather measurements/forecasts from multiple locations, aiming to explore temporal patterns between the time instances in the past and prediction windows. In addition, the method is able to explore pseudo-spatial relations between the energy generation location/region and the multiple locations of the weather measurements/forecasts, aiming to find how the weather in each of the locations for which weather data are available

affects the energy generation prediction in the region under study. To achieve this, the method doesn't rely on any spatial information (e.g., geographic coordinates, or geographic distances) as input.
- Proposes a variant of scaled dot-product attention, which employs *causal convolutions* of multiple kernel sizes, for exploring context-based similarities, instead of point-based similarities, as proposed in [15]. To the best of our knowledge, this approach is novel. Indeed, although a similar approach has been proposed in [8], the corresponding authors employed *Causal Convolutions* with single sized kernels.
- Achieves top results, compared to SoA time-series forecasting methods, on a dataset suitable for wind energy generation prediction in Greece at hour-level resolution.

## 2    Proposed Method

### 2.1    Problem Statement and Notations

The problem of wind energy forecasting that is addressed in this paper can be formulated as:

$$\hat{\mathbf{E}}^f = g(\mathbf{E}^h, \mathbf{W}^h, \mathbf{W}^f) \tag{1}$$

In this equation $\mathbf{E}^h \in \mathbb{R}^{1 \times H \times 1}$ corresponds to the past/history ($h$: history) wind energy measurements of a single region or power plant, $H$ being the size of the past time window. Moreover, $\mathbf{W}^h \in \mathbb{R}^{B \times H \times D_{w^h}}$ corresponds to past weather measurements which are provided for $B$ distinct locations or regions and $D_{w^h}$ is the number of input weather variables, for the past. Also, $\mathbf{W}^f \in \mathbb{R}^{B \times F \times D_{w^f}}$ corresponds to weather forecasts (predictions in the future), where $F$ is the size of the future time window and $D_{w^f}$ is the number of input weather variables, for the future. Finally, $\hat{\mathbf{E}}^f \in \mathbb{R}^{1 \times F \times 1}$ corresponds to the wind energy predictions that are generated by the method for the region of interest.

In short, given past energy measurements for a region or location and wind-related weather data from $B$ distinct locations, our aim is to find how the energy generation is related to the weather on each of the $B$ locations. Once those pseudo-spatial relations are estimated, wind energy predictions can be obtained by exploring temporal patterns between the past weather measurements and weather forecasts.

Adopting the typical attention mechanism [14], the single-time step prediction $\hat{e}^f$, namely one of the elements of $\hat{\mathbf{E}}^f = [\hat{e}_1^f, ..., \hat{e}_F^f]$ can be defined as:

$$\hat{e}^f = \mathbf{C}^T \sum_{j=1}^{H} \alpha_j \mathbf{e}_j^{h,r}$$

$$\text{where } \sum_{j=0}^{H} \alpha_j = 1 \tag{2}$$

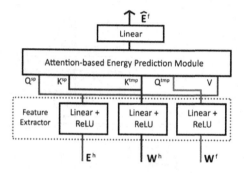

**Fig. 2.** The architecture of the proposed wind energy prediction method.

In the above formulas, $\boldsymbol{\alpha} \in \mathbb{R}^{1 \times H}$ corresponds to the attention weights, $\mathbf{e}_j^{h,r} \in \mathbb{R}^{1 \times D_{e^{h,r}}}$ corresponds to the hidden representations ($r$: representations) of past energy measurements at the $j^{th}$ time instance in the past. $D_{e^{h,r}}$ corresponds to size each hidden representation. Moreover, $\mathbf{C} \in \mathbb{R}^{D_{e^{h,r}} \times 1}$ are learnable parameters of a linear operator. In this formulation, wind energy is predicted based on the temporal patterns imposed by attention weights $\boldsymbol{\alpha}$, between the time step being predicted and past energy measurements (more specifically their internal representations) within the respective temporal window. It shall be noted that a multi-time step prediction formulation would involve a matrix $\mathbf{A} \in \mathbb{R}^{1 \times F \times H}$ rather than $\boldsymbol{\alpha}$. Our objective is to explore, the previously described, pseudo-spatial and temporal relations between $\mathbf{E}^h$, $\mathbf{W}^h$ and $\mathbf{W}^f$ in order to efficiently approximate $\mathbf{A}$.

### 2.2 Multi-Kernel Convolutional Scaled Dot-Product Attention

The Scaled Dot-Product Attention, was presented in [15] and formulated as follows:

$$Attention(\mathbf{Q}, \mathbf{K}, \mathbf{V}) = \mathbf{MV}, \qquad (3)$$

where

$$where \ \ \mathbf{M} = softmax(\frac{\mathbf{QK}^T}{\sqrt{D_K}}) \qquad (4)$$

$\mathbf{Q} \in \mathbb{R}^{N_Q \times D_Q}$, $\mathbf{K} \in \mathbb{R}^{N_K \times D_Q}$ and $\mathbf{V} \in \mathbb{R}^{N_K \times D_V}$ are the queries, keys and values respectively. Queries and keys have a dimension of $D_K$, while values have a dimension of $D_V$. $N_Q$ is the number of queries while $N_K$ is the number of keys and values. An illustration of the mechanism is depicted in Fig. 1a. Multi-head attention was also proposed in [15], allowing various attention mechanisms, including scaled dot-product attention, to run in parallel. To this end, instead of performing a single attention computation on queries, keys, and values of size $D_L$, the authors proposed their transformation with $N$ independently learned linear projections. The attention computation is then performed, in parallel, on

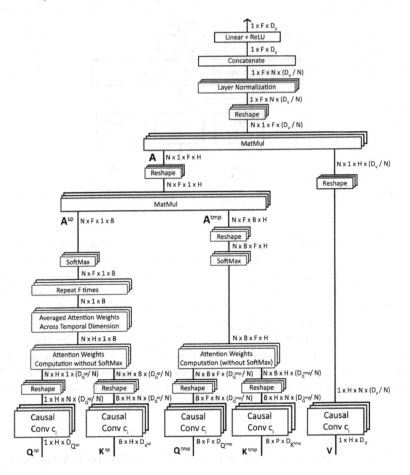

**Fig. 3.** The architecture of the core attention-based energy prediction module.

those $N$ projected queries, keys, and values. More specifically, the multi-head attention module can be formulated as:

$$Multihead(\mathbf{Q}, \mathbf{K}, \mathbf{V}) = [\mathbf{p_1}, ..., \mathbf{p_N}]\mathbf{S}^O, \tag{5}$$

$$\mathbf{p}_i = Attention(\mathbf{Q}\mathbf{S}_i^Q, \mathbf{K}\mathbf{S}_i^K, \mathbf{V}\mathbf{S}_i^V). \tag{6}$$

In this formulation, $\mathbf{S}_i^Q \in \mathbb{R}^{D_L \times D_K}$, $\mathbf{S}_i^K \in \mathbb{R}^{D_L \times D_K}$, $\mathbf{S}_i^V \in \mathbb{R}^{D_L \times D_V}$, $\mathbf{S}_i^O \in \mathbb{R}^{ND_V \times D_L}$ are projection parameter matrices, $N$ is the number of heads, $D_K = D_V = \frac{D_L}{N}$, and the operator [...] implies concatenation.

On the original formulation, the scaled dot-product attention was designed to explore point-wise similarities between queries and keys. However, in most time-series analysis tasks, information regarding the surrounding context of observed points is vital for exploring patterns among the series. The authors in [8], were

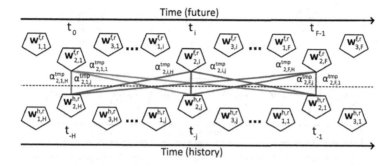

**Fig. 4.** The temporal attention mechanism captures correlations in weather forecasts between the time instances in the prediction window and the history (past) window. In this example, the number of weather forecasts/measurements $B$ is set to 3.

able to employ *causal convolutions* of kernel size $c$ to transform inputs into queries and keys. Thus, local context was exploited in the query-key matching, improving the way temporal patterns among the corresponding time series are explored. The authors experimented with various values of $c$ in order to find the optimal one. To avoid selecting a specific kernel size, as well as for allowing the method to detect patterns in various kernel sizes, we propose the multi-kernel convolutional scaled dot-product attention. In our formulation, *causal convolutions* with $N$ different kernel sizes are applied on $\mathbf{Q}$, $\mathbf{K}$ and $\mathbf{V}$, resulting in $N$ heads. The scaled dot-product attention is computed separately for each head. Layer normalization is then applied to the output of each head. Finally, the outputs are concatenated and projected, resulting in the final values, as depicted in Fig. 1b.

### 2.3 Model Architecture

The overall architecture of our proposed method is depicted on Fig. 2. The method receives as input $\mathbf{E}^h$, $\mathbf{E}^F$ and $\mathbf{W}^f$, and process those modalities through linear layers with the Rectified Linear Unit (ReLU) as activation function. Then, the hidden representations of all modality are fed into the Attention-based Energy Prediction module. Its architecture is depicted on Fig. 3. The module is motivated by the typical attention mechanism, defined in Eq. 2, utilizing the multi-kernel convolutional scaled dot-product attention, previously described in Sect. 2.2. Its aim is to generate future energy representations, based on (i) temporal relations within past and future weather predictions, (ii) pseudo-spatial relations between the region of wind energy prediction and the locations of the weather forecasts. The temporal relations are imposed by $\mathbf{A}^{tmp} \in \mathbb{R}^{N \times B \times F \times H}$. The formulation of $\mathbf{A}^{tmp}$ involves a query-key matching of $\mathbf{W}^{f,r}$ and $\mathbf{W}^{h,r}$. An illustration of the described temporal attention mechanism is depicted on Fig. 4. The pseudo-spatial relations are imposed by $\mathbf{A}^{sp} \in \mathbb{R}^{N \times F \times 1 \times B}$ and in the query-key matching $\mathbf{E}^{h,r}$ and $\mathbf{W}^{h,r}$ are involved. Illustrations of the described

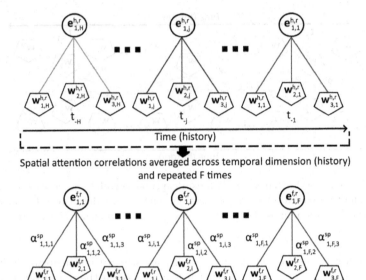

**Fig. 5.** The pseudo-spatial attention mechanism captures correlations between the generated energy and the multiple-location weather forecasts in the history window. In this example, the number $B$ of locations for which weather forecasts/measurements are available is set to 3.

pseudo-spatial relations are depicted on Fig. 5. The final attention weights $\mathbf{A}$ can be defined as:

$$\mathbf{A} = u(\mathbf{A}^{sp} \otimes u(\mathbf{A}^{tmp})) \tag{7}$$

where $\mathbf{A} \in \mathbb{R}^{N \times 1 \times F \times H}$ and $u(.)$ denotes a tensor reshaping function. In particular, element $a_{n,1,j,l}$ of $\mathbf{A}$ is computed as:

$$a_{n,1,l,j} = \sum_{i=1}^{B} \alpha^{sp}_{n,l,1,i} \cdot \alpha^{tmp}_{n,i,l,j} \tag{8}$$

$$\text{where } \sum_{i=1}^{B} \alpha^{sp}_{n,l,1,i} = 1, \ \sum_{j=1}^{H} \alpha^{tmp}_{n,i,l,j} = 1, \ 1 \leq l \leq F, \ 1 \leq j \leq H, \ 1 \leq n \leq N$$

The output of the attention-based module are the hidden representations of the wind energy values $\hat{\mathbf{E}}^{f,r}$. Finally, a lineal layer is applied for generating the wind energy predictions.

## 3   Experimental Evaluation

### 3.1   Dataset Description

The dataset employed in the experimental evaluation was initially proposed in [7]. It consists of (i) hourly wind energy generation data for Greece (the entire country), collected by the European Network of Transmission System Operators for Electricity[1], and (ii) hourly wind-related weather data, which correspond to 18 separate locations in Greece, retrieved by the Storm Glass weather API[2]. The weather data consist of forecasts regarding the wind speed, wind direction and gust. The dataset spans the period 2017–2020. The training set contains data for the period 2017–2019, while the data from the final year form the test set.

The provided wind energy generation values are not normalized/standardized and no information is provided for wind energy generation bounds within regular time intervals (e.g. per annum). Table 1 depicts the large differences between various statistics of the generated energy at annual level. This is indeed a common real-world issue, since the number of wind stations/turbines of a region changes over time (usually increases due to the installation of new ones, as is obviously the case for Greece) and no information regarding this number is provided at country level in regular intervals. A method employed to predict power generation under these circumstances must have a high generalization ability, and be able to overcome such significant data distribution shifts. Being fair to the corresponding dataset split, wind energy data used as input were scaled explicitly based on the minimum and maximum energy values of the training set. However, the metrics used in the evaluation were computed on output data (predictions) that were re-scaled on the min/max values of the overall dataset.

**Table 1.** Statistics derived from wind energy generation data (in MW) for Greece in the period 2017–2020.

| Year | Mean | Std. | Median | Max. |
|------|---------|---------|--------|--------|
| 2017 | 482.312 | 336.052 | 369.0  | 1702.0 |
| 2018 | 554.554 | 384.459 | 466.0  | 1695.0 |
| 2019 | 662.747 | 457.254 | 545.0  | 2107.0 |
| 2020 | 849.010 | 595.726 | 696.0  | 2630.0 |

Based on this dataset, two evaluation/benchmarking scenarios were formed. The first scenario assumes a forecast horizon of one hour and historic (past) data availability of up to 120 h. Weather data are available for both input (past measurements, 120 measurements) and target (future forecasts) windows. Past energy production measurements for 72 h are provided as input, starting 48 h prior to the target period. This 48-h gap in past energy data is due to the fact that measurements are not released immediately by the transmission system operators, i.e. it reflects the real situation. The second scenario assumes a 24-h forecast horizon, in 1-h intervals and data availability of up to 384 h. In a similar fashion to the first scenario, weather data are available for both input (past measurements, 384 measurements) and target (future forecasts, 24 values)

---

[1] https://transparency.entsoe.eu.
[2] https://stormglass.io/.

windows. Past energy production measurements for 336 h are provided as input, starting 48 h prior to the target period (48-h gap).

## 3.2   Baseline Methods

Three SoA time series forecasting methods were trained and evaluated on each of the described wind energy prediction scenarios. The first employed method is N-BEATS [12], implemented by [5]. Compared to the original method, the implemented model can receive as input both historic wind energy measurements, as well as historic wind-related weather data for the corresponding time instances. This is accomplished by flattening the model inputs to a 1-D series.

The performance of a deterministic implementation of DeepTCN [1] was also evaluated in our scenaria. In addition to the historic wind energy measurements, we provide as input the historical wind-related weather data, since the method allows the use of past covariates. Finally, an implementations of TFT [9] was also employed in our experimental evaluation. Information regarding the type of input covariates of each method is provided in Table 2. In particular, TFT and our method are the only ones incorporating future weather forecasts as input. Aiming to achieve a fair comparison, the weather data from all 18 locations, as well as weather data corresponding formed as an aggregated weather forecast from those 18 locations, were fed as input covariates to the three baseline methods. Furthermore, all four methods, including ours, were trained incorporating the 48-h gap within the scenario specific prediction window (i.e., in the first scenario the methods were trained using a 49 prediction window). However, the predictions corresponding to the 48-h gap were excluded during the evaluation process.

All methods, including our proposed method, were trained of 8 epochs. The learning rate was initially set to $5 \times 10^{-4}$ and it was decreased twice by multiplying it with 0.1 at epochs 4 and 6, respectively. Regarding our proposed method, the number of kernels $N$ in the multi-kernel convolutional scaled dot-product attention was set to 6, using 1, 3, 5, 9, 13 and 17 sized kernels. In addition, $D_{e^{h,r}}$, $D_{w^{h,r}}$, $D_{w^{f,r}}$ and $D_{e^{f,r}}$ were set to 66.

**Table 2.** Covariates used as input for each of the compared methods.

| Method | Covariates | |
| --- | --- | --- |
| | Past Weather Measurements | Future Weather Forecasts |
| N-BEATS [12] | ✓ | |
| DeepTCN [1] | ✓ | |
| TFT [9] | ✓ | ✓ |
| Ours | ✓ | ✓ |

### 3.3  Experimental Results

This subsection presents the results of the forecasting experiments for each method along with a commentary on the findings. To be consistent with the literature [10,20], Root Mean Square Error (RMSE) and Mean Absolute Error (MAE) were used to measure the performance of the models. Each experiment was executed four times, and the mean value and standard deviation are reported.

**Table 3.** MAE and RMSE values for the two evaluation scenarios.

| Method | Scenario 1 | | Scenario 2 | |
|---|---|---|---|---|
| | MAE | RMSE | MAE | RMSE |
| N-BEATS | $0.201 \pm 0.003$ | $0.262 \pm 0.006$ | $0.202 \pm 0.002$ | $0.262 \pm 0.003$ |
| DeepTCN | $0.189 \pm 0.008$ | $0.243 \pm 0.017$ | $0.226 \pm 0.027$ | $0.301 \pm 0.030$ |
| TFT | $0.113 \pm 0.008$ | $0.154 \pm 0.012$ | $0.118 \pm 0.008$ | $0.159 \pm 0.012$ |
| Ours | $\mathbf{0.103 \pm 0.002}$ | $\mathbf{0.139 \pm 0.003}$ | $\mathbf{0.085 \pm 0.001}$ | $\mathbf{0.112 \pm 0.003}$ |

Table 3 shows the MAE and RMSE of all compared methods for the two wind energy prediction scenarios. In both scenarios, methods which employ future weather forecasts as input covariates, i.e. TFT and the proposed method, demonstrate significant performance gains. In both scenarios our proposed method achieved top results, compared to the three baseline methods. In particular, more significant results were attained in the second scenario achieving mean MAE and RMSE, among 4 experiments, of 0.085 and 0.112, respectively.

It is worth noting that the performance of our proposed method was better in the second scenario, compared to the first, in all metrics. This behaviour is exactly the opposite compared to the rest of the methods, where their performances downgraded in the second scenario. The improved performance of the proposed method, on a scenario in which data from a larger temporal window were used as input, highlights that the implemented temporal attention-based mechanism is able to effectively capture relations between distant samples within the sequences. Future work will focus on conducting more experiments, in respect to the size of input and prediction windows, as well as to extend the method, aiming to process and predict wind energy time-series from multiple stations or regions.

## 4   Conclusions

Energy generation from wind exhibits inherent uncertainties due to its intermittent nature. The accurate wind energy prediction can assist its integration, operation and management within the electric grids. This paper proposes a novel wind energy forecasting method, which relies on a novel variant of the scaled-dot product attention mechanism, for exploring relations between the generated energy and a set of multiple-location weather forecasts/measurements. The results of the conducted preliminary experimental evaluation against SoA time-series forecasting methods on a dataset consisting of the hourly generated wind energy in Greece, highlighted the potential of the proposed method.

**Acknowledgements.** This work is co-financed by the European Regional Development Fund of the European Union and Greek national funds through the Operational Program Competitiveness, Entrepreneurship and Innovation, under the call RESEARCH - CREATE - INNOVATE (project code: T2EDK-03048).

# References

1. Chen, Y., Kang, Y., Chen, Y., Wang, Z.: Probabilistic forecasting with temporal convolutional neural network. Neurocomputing **399**, 491–501 (2020)
2. Focken, U., Lange, M., Waldl, H.P.: Previento-a wind power prediction system with an innovative upscaling algorithm. In: Proceedings of the European Wind Energy Conference, vol. 276 (2001)
3. Fu, X., Gao, F., Wu, J., Wei, X., Duan, F.: Spatiotemporal attention networks for wind power forecasting. In: 2019 International Conference on Data Mining Workshops (ICDMW), pp. 149–154. IEEE (2019)
4. Hanifi, S., Liu, X., Linand, Z., Lotfian, S.: A critical review of wind power forecasting methods-past, present and future. Energies **13**, 3764 (2020)
5. Herzen, J., et al.: Darts: user-friendly modern machine learning for time series. J. Mach. Learn. Res. **23**(124), 1–6 (2022)
6. Hodge, B.M., Zeiler, A., Brooks, D., Blau, G., Pekny, J., Reklatis, G.: Improved wind power forecasting with ARIMA models. Comput. Aided Chem. Eng. **29**, 1789–1793 (2011)
7. Vartholomaios, A., Karlos, S., Kouloumpris, E., Tsoumakas, G.: Short-term renewable energy forecasting in Greece using prophet decomposition and tree-based ensembles. In: Kotsis, G., et al. (eds.) DEXA 2021. CCIS, vol. 1479, pp. 227–238. Springer, Cham (2021). https://doi.org/10.1007/978-3-030-87101-7_22
8. Li, S., et al.: Enhancing the locality and breaking the memory bottleneck of transformer on time series forecasting. In: Advances in Neural Information Processing Systems, vol. 32 (2019)
9. Lim, B., Arık, S.O., Loeff, N., Pfister, T.: Temporal fusion transformers for interpretable multi-horizon time series forecasting. Int. J. Forecast. **37**, 1748–1764 (2021)
10. Liu, Y., et al.: Wind power short-term prediction based on LSTM and discrete wavelet transform. Appl. Sci. **9**(6), 1108 (2019)
11. Niu, Z., Yu, Z., Tang, W., Wu, Q., Reformat, M.: Wind power forecasting using attention-based gated recurrent unit network. Energy **196**, 117081 (2020)
12. Oreshkin, B.N., Carpov, D., Chapados, N., Bengio, Y.: N-BEATS: neural basis expansion analysis for interpretable time series forecasting. In: Proceedings of the International Conference on Learning Representations (2020)
13. Putz, D., Gumhalter, M., Auer, H.: A novel approach to multi-horizon wind power forecasting based on deep neural architecture. Renew. Energy **178**, 494–505 (2021)

14. Shih, S.Y., Sun, F.K., Lee, H.Y.: Temporal pattern attention for multivariate time series forecasting. Mach. Learn. **108**, 1421–1441 (2019)
15. Vaswani, A., et al.: Attention is all you need. In: Proceedings of the International Conference on Neural Information Processing Systems (NIPS) (2017)
16. Wang, L., Tao, R., Hu, H., Zeng, Y.R.: Effective wind power prediction using novel deep learning network: stacked independently recurrent autoencoder. Renew. Energy **164**, 642–655 (2021)
17. Yu, R.: Scene learning: deep convolutional networks for wind power prediction by embedding turbines into grid space. Appl. Energy **238**, 249–257 (2019)
18. Zhang, J., Yan, J., Infield, D., Liu, Y., Lien, F.S.: Short-term forecasting and uncertainty analysis of wind turbine power based on long short-term memory network and gaussian mixture model. Appl. Energy **241**, 229–244 (2019)
19. Zhao, J., Guo, Z.H., Su, Z.Y., Zhao, Z.Y., Xiao, X., Liu, F.: An improved multi-step forecasting model based on WRF ensembles and creative fuzzy systems for wind speed. Appl. Energy **162**, 808–826 (2016)
20. Zhu, R., Liao, W., Wang, Y.: Short-term prediction for wind power based on temporal convolutional network. Energy Rep. **6**, 424–429 (2020)

# Learning (Reinforcemet - Federated - Adversarial - Transfer)

# An Autonomous Self-learning and Self-adversarial Training Neural Architecture for Intelligent and Resilient Cyber Security Systems

Konstantinos Demertzis[1]([⊠]) and Lazaros Iliadis[2]

[1] School of Science and Technology, Informatics Studies, Hellenic Open University, Patras, Greece
demertzis.konstantinos@ac.eap.gr
[2] Department of Civil Engineering, Faculty of Mathematics Programming and General Courses, School of Engineering, Democritus University of Thrace, Kimmeria, Xanthi, Greece
liliadis@civil.duth.gr

**Abstract.** Cybersecurity systems have become increasingly important as businesses and individuals rely more on technology. However, the increasing complexity of these systems and the evolving nature of cyber threats require innovative solutions to protect against cyber attacks. One promising approach is the idea of autonomous self-learning and auto-training neural architectures. Autonomous self-learning refers to the ability of the system to adapt to new threats and learn from past experiences without human intervention. Auto-training, on the other hand, refers to the ability of the system to improve its performance over time by automatically adjusting its parameters and algorithms. This research proposes an autonomous Self-Learning and Self-Adversarial Training (SLSAT) neural architecture for intelligent and resilient cyber security systems. It is an extension of the next-generation Continuous-Time Reservoir Computing (CTRC) that was proposed by the authors recently. The CTRC is a time-series anomaly detection system controlled by time-varying differential equations. It uses Reinforcement Learning (RL) to dynamically fine-tune the reservoir computing parameters in order to identify the aberrant changes in the data. The proposed method in this research improves the CTRC's architecture by including a Conditional Tabular Generative Adversarial Network (CTGAN). Specifically, including CTGAN allows the SLSAT architecture to generate synthetic data based on the identified abnormalities to improve the model's performance and adapt to new and evolving threats without manual intervention. This, as proved experimentally, helps the model identify aberrant changes in the data and fend off poison and zero-day attacks.

**Keywords:** Reservoir Computing · Continuous-Time Reservoir Computing · Cyber Defense · Time Series Analysis

# 1 Introduction

Cyber security is a constantly evolving field, and the threat landscape is constantly changing. Attackers are becoming more sophisticated and are constantly developing new techniques and strategies to bypass traditional security measures [1]. This means the cybersecurity industry must continually innovate and develop more advanced and proactive security solutions to stay ahead of attackers. One approach that is gaining popularity in the cybersecurity industry is using artificial intelligence and machine learning [2]. Machine learning algorithms can be trained to detect anomalies in network traffic and identify behavior patterns indicative of an attack. These algorithms can be trained using large network traffic and attack data datasets and continuously updated to adapt to new attack techniques. The cybersecurity industry needs to take a proactive security approach rather than relying on reactive measures. By using advanced technologies such as artificial intelligence and machine learning [3], sharing threat intelligence, and collaborating with other organizations, the industry can stay ahead of the evolving threat landscape and better protect against cyber-attacks [4, 5].

The proposed approach is an extension of the next-generation Continuous-Time Reservoir Computing (CTRC) that was proposed by the authors recently [6, 7]. Reservoir computing is a machine learning algorithm that uses the dynamics of a high-dimensional, randomly connected network to process and learn from input signals. It is an efficient and powerful technique for solving complex machine-learning tasks, particularly those involving time-series data. At the heart of the system is a reservoir, which is a randomly connected network of nodes. The input signal is fed into the reservoir, and the state vector is fed into a readout layer, which is trained using linear regression or another simple learning algorithm. Next-generation automated RC is an emerging technology that has the potential to enhance cyber defense greatly, using the basic principles of RC to analyze network traffic and identify anomalies indicative of cyberattacks or other security threats [8, 9].

The CTRC is an extension of the RC paradigm that operates in continuous rather than discrete time. In a traditional discrete-time reservoir computing system, input signals are fed into the reservoir at discrete intervals. In a CTRC system, the input signal drives the reservoir dynamics, producing an output signal. The continuous-time nature of the system enables the reservoir to process input signals in real-time without discretization, which is particularly useful in applications where the input signal is a continuous data stream. However, it can be more difficult to train and optimize than discrete-time RC due to the complexity of the reservoir dynamics [8, 10]. The proposed CTRC's system parameters are optimized using the RL method to overcome these challenges.

This paper extends the above architecture and proposes an autonomous self-healing neural architecture for cyber security that leverages advanced machine learning techniques to detect, respond to, and mitigate cyber threats automatically. Specifically, the proposed method enhances the architecture by adding a CTGAN [11] to the CTRC. It creates a model that can withstand poison and zero-day attacks by enhancing the network's capacity for self-learning and self-training based on the identified abnormalities. The STSAT refers to the system's ability to detect and respond to security incidents without human intervention. This is important in cyber security, where threats can emerge and spread quickly, making it difficult for human operators to respond quickly.

## 2  Methodology

The proposed CTRC system is modelled using continuous-time differential equations, and the system parameters are optimized using the RL method and, specifically, the Q-Learning approach. The CTRC system's architecture comprises input, reservoir, and output layers. In RC, the connection and input weights are assigned at random. The Echo State Property (ESP) [12, 13], the condition in which the reservoir is an "echo" of the complete input history, is ensured by scaling the reservoir weights in a fashion that does just that. The input u(n) and output y(n) discrete layers of the CTRC follow the problem's definitions. The number of hidden layers is grouped in an RC zone [14, 15]. The amount to which the RC's neurons, x(n), are coupled defines how sparse the RC will be.

The CTRC system can record temporal and spatial patterns of the network's data thanks to differential equations $dx1$ and $dx2$, which control how state vectors $x1(t)$ and $x2(t)$ behave as follows [16, 17]:

$$dx1/dt = -x1(t) + f1(W1x1(t) + \text{Win}\,1u(t))$$
$$dx2/dt = -x2(t) + f2(W2x2(t) + \text{Win}\,2u(t) + Vx1(t))$$

While $x2(t)$ represents the state vector that captures the spatial patterns of the data, $x1(t)$ represents the state vector that captures the temporal patterns of the network traffic data in equations $dx1$ and $dx2$, respectively. The state vectors $x1(t)$ and $x2(t)$ change over time in response to the input signal u(t) and the reservoir's current state, as shown by the differential equations above. A depiction of the CTRC architecture is presented in Fig. 1.

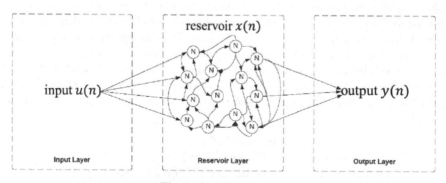

**Fig. 1.** CTRC architecture

In order to model the drift phenomenon, identify the abnormal changes in the data, and adaptively stabilize the learning system, the weight matrices W1, W2, Win1, Win2, and V are optimized using the Q-Learning algorithm [18, 19] to minimize the difference between the predicted output of the system and the true labels in a training dataset. The state space is defined in the first step of the Q-learning algorithm. The state space records pertinent data about the cyber defense scenario's current network traffic analysis. The Q-learning algorithm's action space is then based on the potential steps the agent could take to counteract cyberattacks. The agent's performance in the cyber defense task is then used as the basis for the reward function for the Q-learning algorithm. The reward function motivates the agent to counter cyberattacks effectively and dissuades ineffective or harmful behavior. The Q-table is a lookup table associating expected rewards with states and actions. The Q-table is updated using the Q-learning algorithm to choose actions iteratively based on the current state and the values in the Q-table. The Bellman equation calculates the expected future reward from the present state and action and is used to update the Q-table [20]. The Q-table modifies the weight matrices and bias terms of the CTRC system. The Q-table estimates train the CTRC system to optimize the expected future reward. A test dataset implements the trained CTRC system's performance evaluation process. Based on the evaluation outcomes, the parameters of the CTRC algorithm are adjusted. This entails automatically modifying the group of parameters that the Q-learning process optimized.

In order to increase the CTRC's capacity for self-learning and self-training and create a model that can thwart poison and zero-day attacks, the proposed method in this research incorporates a CTGAN into the CTRC's architecture. CTGAN is a Generative Adversarial Network (GAN) for generating synthetic tabular data. GAN is a type of deep learning algorithm used to generate new data by learning the patterns and features in a given dataset. GANs are composed of two main components: a generator and a discriminator. The generator inputs random noise and produces a fake sample that resembles the original data. The discriminator, on the other hand, is trained to distinguish between real and fake samples. The generator is trained to fool the discriminator by producing samples that are indistinguishable from the real ones. The discriminator, in turn, is trained to identify whether a sample is real or fake correctly.

The training process involves alternating between training the generator to produce better fake samples and training the discriminator to better distinguish between real and fake samples. This process continues until the generator can produce samples that are difficult to distinguish from the real ones. Its objective is to learn the underlying probability distribution of the input data and then generate new samples that closely resemble the original data. The CTGAN consists of a generator and discriminator networks, similar to GANs. However, CTGAN is conditioned on the values of a subset of the input features. The generator network takes both a random noise vector and the conditioned input features as input. The objective function of CTGAN can be expressed as follows [11, 21]:

$$
min_G max_D V(D, G)
$$
$$
= Ex{\sim}pdata(x)[log\, D(x|condition)
$$
$$
+ Ez{\sim}pnoise(z), c{\sim}pcondition(c)\, [log(1 - D(G(z, c)|c))]
$$

where, $G$ is the generator network, $D$ is the discriminator network, $x$ is a real sample from the input data distribution $pdata$, $z$ is a noise vector sampled from a prior distribution $pnoise$, c is a conditioned subset of the input features sampled from the conditioning distribution $pcondition$, $condition$ is a function that maps the input data $x$ to the conditioned subset of input features $c$, $D(x|condition)$ is the discriminator's probability of assigning a real sample $x$ a score of 1 (indicating that it is real) given the conditioning features condition, $G(z, c)$ is the generator's output, which is a synthetic sample generated by the generator network, conditioned on the input features $c$ and $1 - D(G(z, c)|c)$ is the discriminator's probability of assigning a synthetic sample $G(z, c)$ a score of 1 (indicating that it is real), given the conditioning features $c$. The objective function is optimized iteratively between the generator and discriminator networks until the generator produces synthetic samples that are indistinguishable from real samples according to the discriminator [11, 22]. A depiction of the CTGAN architecture is presented in Fig. 2.

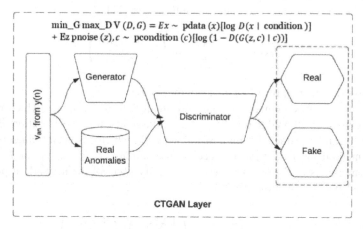

**Fig. 2.** CTGAN architecture

Because there is no sufficient defence mechanism capable of fully protecting against novel attacks, as these lie in the ingenuity of the attackers, this process extends the so far techniques in a prototype way, protecting not only against zero-day but also against poison attacks. Including CTGAN allows the SLSAT architecture to generate synthetic data based on the identified abnormalities. Specifically, as the adversary wants to find the least possible $x^{adv}$ that is closest to $x$ to generate a contradictory sample, the proposed mechanism pushes this $x^{adv}$ as far away from the legitimate sample as possible. In particular, during the training of this particular neural architecture, it learns to successfully recognize samples that belong to the distribution of the training data. Still, it recognizes large changes in its outputs for samples at a short distance but outside the specific distribution. By introducing to the training set patterns that are a linear combination of the original patterns, the neural network learns to recognize contradictory disturbances [23]. Specifically for $\lambda \in [0, 1]$ and $x_i, x_j$ two instances of the training set, introducing the case $x_{new}$ to the training set for which applies [22, 24, 25]:

$$x_{new} = \lambda x_i + (1 - \lambda)x_j \text{ και } f(x_{new}) = \lambda f(x_i) + (1 - \lambda)f(x_j)$$

Thus the training set acquires a more generalized distribution, with the result that the network generalizes better and does not have large changes in points of the input space outside the distribution of the original training set. The method improves the network's performance even on datasets where you expect the classification function to exhibit significant non-linearities.

The defense method is based on the observation that the aggressive cases do not belong to the distribution field to which the input data belongs. At the same time, they are closer to the subfield to which the cases of their true class belong. Considering that the outputs of the last layers of the neural network are feature vectors that are entered as inputs to the network, the distribution to which the feature vectors that result as outputs of the neural network belong, when real data is present as input, is calculated. Specifically, suppose $Y_c$ is the set of training vectors belonging to class $c$. In that case, $y$ is the vector of input features, calculating $\hat{f}_c(y)$, which is the estimate of the density of the distribution of the real features of class $c$ at point $y$ as follows [26, 27]:

$$\hat{f}_c(y) = \frac{1}{|Y_c|} \sum_{y_i \in Y_c} exp\left(\frac{-\|y - y_i\|_2^2}{\sigma^2}\right)$$

where with $|Y_c|$ the number of elements of the set $Y_c$.

According to this method, an aggressive input with real class $c_1$, which is recognized as class $c_2$, will hold that $\hat{f}_{c_1}(x) > \hat{f}_{c_2}(x)$. Extending this consideration, Bayesian uncertainty can be extracted from a neural network, which has been trained using the dropout method, so that an input $x$ receives the outputs $y_1, y_2, \ldots, y_T$ for $T$ different sets of parameters of the network. The uncertainty $U(x)$ of the network at point $x$ is calculated from the equation [28, 29]:

$$U(x) = \frac{1}{T} \sum_{i=1}^{T} y_i^T y_i - \left(\frac{1}{T} \sum_{i=1}^{T} y_i\right)^T \left(\frac{1}{T} \sum_{i=1}^{T} y_i\right)$$

Given the assumption that aggressive inputs appear in regions of the network with high uncertainty, $U(x)$ is a useful metric for determining whether an input $x$ is aggressive. A depiction of the proposed architecture is presented in Fig. 3 (Appendix 1).

## 3   Dataset and Results

Factry.io and InfluxDB were used to provide a perfect simulation environment [30, 31]. Factry.io is a data collection and visualization platform that enables users to easily collect, monitor, and analyze data from various sources, such as machines, sensors, and devices. InfluxDB is a time-series database designed to handle high volumes of time-stamped data. It supports various data types and formats, including numerical, string, and Boolean data, and provides a SQL-like query language to access and manipulate data. The goal was to gather data about the industrial environment using the open-source OPC-UA collector protocol [32].

Data for one year was gathered from three sensors' hourly quantifiable values within a machine condition that runs continuously. There is a tank specifically for raw water storage, and a valve opens when the sensor detects a level of less than or equal to 0.5 m. This research suggests a trustworthy heuristic approach of selection, based only on assessment criteria, to identify an ideal threshold for binary class separation (normal or abnormal). The proposed algorithm calculates the density around each data point to identify the dynamic threshold. This is achieved by counting the number of points in a user-defined neighborhood (Eps-Neighbourhood) with the definition of thresholds. The extra data points are added to the center of the regions if they are densely accessible. The neighborhood area of a point $p$ is defined as the set of points for which the Euclidean distance between the points $p, q$ is smaller than the parameter Eps [33, 34]:

$$N_{Eps}(p) = \{q \in D | dist(p, q) \leq Eps\}$$

provided that $p = (p1, p2)$ and $q = (q1, q2)$, the Euclidean distance is defined as:

$$\sqrt{(q_1 - p_1)^2 + (q_2 - p_2)^2}$$

So, a point $p$ is considered to be reachable from a point $q$ based on a density determined by the parameters *Eps, MinPts* if:

$$p \in N_{Eps}(q) \text{ and } N_{Eps}(q) \geq MinPts$$

Two plots to visualize the dynamic threshold calculation depicted in the following Fig. 4.

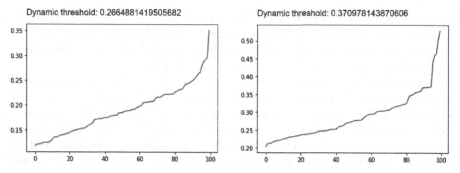

**Fig. 4.** Dynamic threshold calculation

Samples (outliers) are considered abnormal when the anomaly score departs from the expected behaviour by applying the dynamic threshold.

In order to easily make a comparison between the real and synthetic data, a visual evaluation method is used to generate a plot that allows comparing the distributions of the datasets visually. The plot consists of two panels, one for the real dataset and one for the synthetic dataset. Each panel shows the dataset's values distribution using a kernel density estimate (KDE) plot [11]. The Fig. 5 shows a dataset's absolute log mean and standard deviation of each numeric column.

The KDE plot shows the probability density function of the data, which represents the relative frequency of values in each interval of the range of the variable. The x-axis of the plot represents the values of the variable, and the y-axis represents the probability density of those values. The more similar the distributions of the real and synthetic datasets are, the more the two KDE plots will overlap. If the two datasets are very similar, the two KDE plots will overlap significantly. If the two datasets have very different distributions, the two KDE plots will not overlap much. By comparing the KDE plots for the real and synthetic datasets, one can understand how similar the two datasets are in their statistical

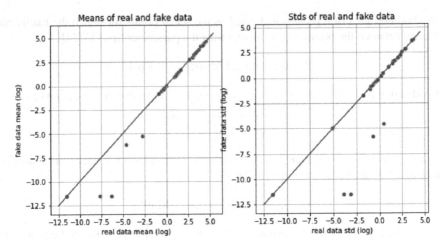

**Fig. 5.** Absolute Log Mean and STDs of real and fake data

properties. If the KDE plots are very similar, it suggests that the synthetic dataset has been generated successfully and has similar statistical properties to the real dataset. If the KDE plots are very different, it suggests that the synthetic dataset does not represent the real dataset well may not be suitable for the intended use.

Specifically, the blue line in the left plot represents the absolute log of the mean for each column. The mean is a measure of central tendency representing the average value of the data in that column. Taking the absolute value of the log of the mean ensures that we are looking at differences in magnitude rather than direction, making it easier to compare the means of columns with different scales. The blue line in the right plot represents the absolute log of the standard deviation for each column. The standard deviation is a measure of variability that represents the spread out of the data in each column. Taking the absolute value of the log of the standard deviation ensures that we are looking at differences in magnitude rather than direction and makes it easier to compare the standard deviations of columns with different scales. By looking at the plot, we can quickly identify columns with significantly different means or standard deviations. These columns may indicate outliers or other issues in the data that should be investigated further. In addition, columns with very low or zero values may be problematic for some types of analysis, as their logarithms can be undefined or very large negative numbers. Overall, the plot provides a quick overview of the numeric columns in the dataset and can help identify potential issues or areas for further investigation [35]. Figure 6 shows the cumulative sum of a column over time from 8 features. The plot's x-axis shows the time of each value in the column, and the y-axis shows the cumulative sum of those values up to that point.

The blue line (real data) represents the current cumulative sum values of the column, and the orange line (fake data) represents the column's expected feature cumulative sum values. The expected features cumulative sum values are obtained by shifting the blue line forward by a certain number of time periods. By comparing the blue and orange lines, it is easy to see how the cumulative sum of the column is expected to change

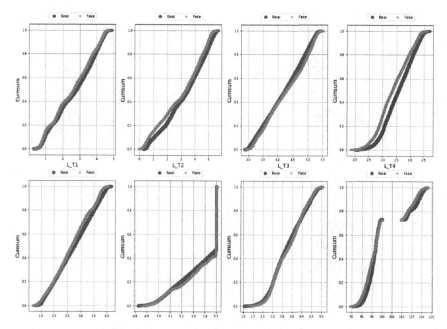

**Fig. 6.** Cumulative sums per feature (8 features)

over time. If the orange line is significantly higher than the blue line, it suggests that the cumulative sum of the column is expected to increase rapidly in the future. If the orange line is significantly lower than the blue line, it suggests that the cumulative sum of the column is expected to decrease rapidly in the future. The plot provides a way to visualize the trend of the data over time and how it is expected to change cumulatively in the future. It can be useful for predicting future trends or identifying patterns in the data that may be useful for making decisions [36]. Figure 7 shows the distribution per future time period.

The x-axis of each histogram shows the value of the column, and the y-axis shows the frequency of each value. The plot consists of multiple histograms, one for each feature time period. Each histogram shows the distribution of values in the column for that time period and provides a way to visualize how the distribution of values is expected to change over time. By comparing the histograms for different time periods, it is easy to see how the distribution of values in the column is expected to change over time. For example, if the histograms shift to the right over time, it suggests that the values in the column are expected to increase in the future. If the histograms shift to the left over time, it suggests that the values in the column are expected to decrease in the future. If the histograms remain relatively stable over time, it suggests that the values in the column are expected to remain relatively constant. The plot provides a way to visualize how the distribution of values in the column is expected to change over time, and can be useful for predicting future trends or identifying patterns in the data that may be useful for making decisions. It can also be used to identify potential outliers or other issues in the data that may affect its analysis [37].

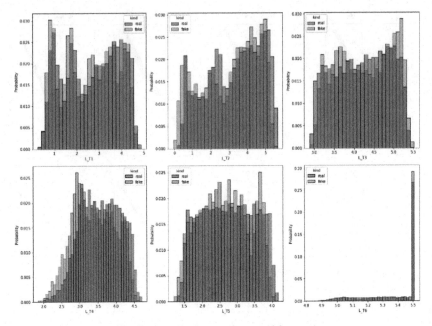

**Fig. 7.** Distribution per feature (6 features)

Figure 8 shows the correlation matrices of real and fake data and the differences between them.

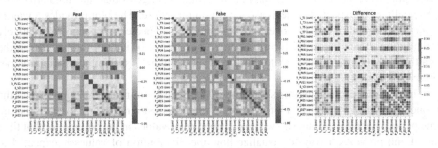

**Fig. 8.** Correlation matrices of real data, fake data and the differences

This plot concatenates the real and synthetic datasets and computes their difference. The x-axis and y-axis of each heatmap show the column names of the dataset, and each cell in the heatmap represents the correlation between a pair of columns. The color of each cell represents the strength and direction of the correlation, with blue indicating a negative correlation and red indicating a positive correlation. White cells indicate no correlation. The first heatmap shows the correlation matrix for the real data, allowing to see the correlation between pairs of columns in the real data. The second heatmap shows the correlation matrix for the synthetic data, allowing to see the correlation between pairs of columns in the synthetic data. Finally, the third heatmap shows the difference in correlation matrices between the synthetic and real data, allowing to see where the synthetic data's correlation structure deviates from the real data's correlation structure. This can be useful for identifying areas where the synthetic data may not accurately represent the real data [11].

Finally, Fig. 9 shows a scatter plot of the first two principal components of a dataset using Principal Component Analysis (PCA).

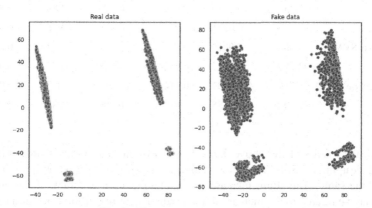

**Fig. 9.** First two components of PCA

The left plot represents the first principal component (PC1), and the right plot represents the second principal component (PC2). Each data point in the plot represents a row in the dataset, and its position on the plot represents its values in the first two principal component directions. The position of each data point on the plot is determined by the values of the data in the first two principal component directions, which are calculated by the PCA algorithm [38, 39]. The plot can be useful for identifying patterns and trends in the data, as well as for visualizing the similarity and differences between different data points. Data points that are close together on the plot are similar to each other in terms of their values in the first two principal component directions, while data points that are far apart are dissimilar.

The plot can also be used to identify potential outliers or other issues in the data that may affect its analysis. Outliers may appear as data points that are far away from the main cluster of data points on the plot and may be worth investigating further to determine if they represent genuine data points or errors in the data. In summary, the plot provides a useful visualization of the main directions of variation in the data and can be a useful tool for exploratory data analysis.

In order to perform analytical tests that will prove the value and capability of the proposed scheme, three datasets were created. The initial one includes only the real data where in this case, the last layer of the proposed architecture works, but it is not possible to evaluate its capabilities in detecting poisoning-induced anomalies. The evaluation performance metrics in all cases used to compare the anomaly detection algorithms are Accuracy, RMSE, Precision, Recall (Sensitivity), F-Score, and AUC [35, 36]. Tables 1, 2 and 3 shows the classification accuracy and performance metrics in real, fake and mix datasets of six different classifiers: SLST, CTRC, One Class SVM, Long Short-Term Memory (LSTM), Isolation Forest and k-NN.

**Table 1.** Classification Accuracy and Performance Metrics in real data

| Classifier | Accuracy | RMSE | Precision | Recall | F-Score | AUC |
|---|---|---|---|---|---|---|
| SLSAT | 97.95% | 0.0819 | 0.980 | 0.985 | 0.984 | 0.9902 |
| CTRC | 97.89% | 0.0821 | 0.980 | 0.980 | 0.978 | 0.9887 |
| One Class SVM | 93.66% | 0.0912 | 0.937 | 0.936 | 0.937 | 0.9752 |
| LSTM | 93.17% | 0.0932 | 0.932 | 0.933 | 0.933 | 0.9703 |
| Isolation Forest | 91.38% | 0.1007 | 0.914 | 0.914 | 0.913 | 0.9588 |
| k-NN | 87.99% | 0.1185 | 0.880 | 0.880 | 0.880 | 0.9502 |

From the results of the above Table 1, it is evident that, there is little difference between the upgraded SLSAT scheme and the previous CTRC method, as the architecture remains the same. The slight increase in the classification accuracy of the proposed model may be related to the increase in the predictive ability of the algorithm based on the additional samples added to the dataset after finding some anomalies. In addition, the training processes' randomness which is used to calculate the density around each data point to identify the dynamic threshold. This is achieved by counting the number of points in a user-defined neighbourhood (Eps-Neighbourhood) with the definition of thresholds. This means that if the algorithm is run multiple times on the same dataset, it may produce slightly different accuracy scores due to this randomness.

**Table 2.** Classification Accuracy and Performance Metrics in fake data

| Classifier | Accuracy | RMSE | Precision | Recall | F-Score | AUC |
|---|---|---|---|---|---|---|
| SLSAT | 94.12% | 0.0903 | 0.941 | 0.940 | 0.941 | 0.9689 |
| CTRC | 83.71% | 0.1566 | 0.837 | 0.838 | 0.837 | 0.9124 |
| One Class SVM | 86.38% | 0.1207 | 0.865 | 0.865 | 0.870 | 0.9341 |
| LSTM | 82.97% | 0.1632 | 0.830 | 0.830 | 0.830 | 0.9108 |
| Isolation Forest | 80.26% | 0.1981 | 0.801 | 0.805 | 0.805 | 0.8894 |
| k-NN | 81.58% | 0.1873 | 0.816 | 0.816 | 0.816 | 0.8943 |

From the results of Table 2 above, it is evident that in this particular case, there is a significant difference between the proposed algorithm and the other methods, which mostly showed very low performance. This fact is obviously due to the inability of the other models to cope with the inability to find unknown patterns which, although very similar to the real ones, differ significantly. The fake data generated by CTGAN contain noise or uncertainty does not present in the real data. This can be due to several factors, including the inherent stochasticity of the generative model, the use of random seeds, or other sources of variability in the training process. This makes it more difficult for the machine learning model to accurately distinguish between real and fake examples, especially if the noise is correlated with the target variable. This can lead to lower performance on the fake data than the real data. The proposed model uses self-learning and self-adversarial training to address this issue. The SLSAT model is self-training in order to distinguish between real and fake examples more accurately. This enhances the model's performance to recognize and handle the noise or uncertainty in the fake data and improves its overall performance on real and fake examples, as proved by results.

**Table 3.** Classification Accuracy and Performance Metrics in mix data

| Classifier | Accuracy | RMSE | Precision | Recall | F-Score | AUC |
|---|---|---|---|---|---|---|
| SLSAT | 99.05% | 0.0697 | 0.991 | 0.991 | 0.991 | 0.9938 |
| CTRC | 90.15% | 0.1123 | 0.900 | 0.905 | 0.905 | 0.9416 |
| One Class SVM | 89.81% | 0.1131 | 0.898 | 0.898 | 0.898 | 0.9409 |
| LSTM | 89.76% | 0.1136 | 0.898 | 0.897 | 0.897 | 0.9397 |
| Isolation Forest | 90.04% | 0.1127 | 0.905 | 0.905 | 0.905 | 0.9403 |
| k-NN | 84.12% | 0.1513 | 0.841 | 0.841 | 0.841 | 0.9073 |

The enormous superiority of the proposed system is confirmed in the mixed dataset. The table shows that the SLSAT classifier has the highest accuracy at 99.05% and the highest AUC at 0.9938. It also has high precision, recall, and F-score. The CTRC, One Class SVM, LSTM, and Isolation Forest classifiers have similar accuracies ranging from 89.76% to 90.15% and AUCs ranging from 0.9403 to 0.9416. The k-NN classifier has the lowest accuracy at 84.12% but still has a decent AUC of 0.9073. The reasons for this superiority could be attributed to the following:

1. Self-Learning Capability: SLSAT incorporates a CTGAN to enhance the model's self-learning capability. By generating synthetic data that mimics real data, SLSAT can improve its accuracy and generalization capabilities, which makes it better equipped to identify abnormal behavior in the data.
2. Self-Adversarial Training: The self-adversarial training approach in SLSAT allows the model to learn from attacks and adapt its defense strategy in real-time. This capability enables the model to detect and fend off zero-day attacks, a significant advantage in the current threat landscape.
3. Robustness to Poisoning Attacks: Poisoning attacks are a type of cyber-attack in which an attacker manipulates the training data to introduce biases or cause the model to make incorrect predictions. SLSAT's self-learning and self-adversarial training capabilities make it more robust to such attacks. By continuously learning from the data and adapting its defense strategy, SLSAT can detect and mitigate the effects of poisoning attacks.
4. Reinforcement Learning (RL): SLSAT employs RL to dynamically fine-tune the parameters of the Continuous-Time Reservoir Computing (CTRC) algorithm. This

allows SLSAT to optimize its performance continuously and adapt to changing conditions in the data.
5. Robustness: SLSAT is designed to be robust to noise and other perturbations in the data. By using CTRC, SLSAT can handle time-series data more effectively and efficiently, making it more robust than other algorithms.
6. Capacity for Self-Learning: Including CTGAN in the SLSAT architecture allows it to self-learn, meaning it can learn from data without supervision. This is particularly useful in cyber security applications, where anomalies can be hard to define or may change over time. SLSAT's ability to learn without supervision gives it an advantage over other algorithms that rely on labeled data.
7. Ability to Detect and Handle Complex Patterns: SLSAT's architecture, which includes CTRC and CTGAN, enables it to detect and handle complex patterns in the data. This is important in cyber security applications where anomalies may not be easily discernible or hidden within the noise of the data. SLSAT's ability to handle complex patterns gives it an advantage over other algorithms that may struggle to identify such anomalies.

These features enable the model to learn continuously, adapt to new threats, and perform well in various conditions, making it an effective tool for detecting and mitigating cyber threats.

## 4 Conclusion

The paper proposes an autonomous SLSAT neural architecture for intelligent and resilient cyber security systems. The proposed architecture extends the CTRC algorithm, incorporating a CTGAN to increase the network's capacity for self-learning and self-adversarial training. The proposed method allows for real-time adaptation to new and evolving cyber threats. The SLSAT model, as proved experimentally, outperforms other competitor algorithms in all performance metrics, including accuracy, RMSE, precision, recall, F-score, and AUC. The model's self-learning and self-adversarial approach enables it to detect and fend off zero-day and poison attacks, making it a valuable tool for next-generation cyber security applications [40].

Furthermore, the SLSAT architecture's capacity for self-learning and robustness to poisoning attacks make it a powerful tool for handling complex patterns in the data, which is crucial for detecting and mitigating advanced persistent cyber threats.

While the proposed SLSAT model has demonstrated superior performance in the current research, further development could be made in several areas:

1. Scalability: The current research evaluates the SLSAT model on a specific dataset. Future research could investigate the model's scalability and performance on larger datasets with a broader range of cyber threats.
2. Real-time Performance: The SLSAT model's ability to adapt to new and evolving threats in real time is a significant advantage. However, future research could further explore optimizing the model in streaming data performance.
3. Robustness: While the SLSAT model is designed to be robust to noise and other perturbations in the data, future research could further investigate ways to improve

its robustness. For instance, they are exploring new adversarial training techniques or enhancing the CTGAN's capacity to generate synthetic data that mimics rare events or evolving complex patterns in the data.

4. Explainability: While the SLSAT model's superior performance is clear, it is essential to understand how it arrives at its conclusions. Future research could investigate ways to make the model's decision-making process more transparent and interpretable, especially for regulatory compliance.

5. Deployment: The SLSAT model's real-world deployment raises several challenges, such as integrating it with existing cyber security infrastructure, managing the model's computational resources, and ensuring data privacy and security. Future research could address these deployment challenges to make the model more practical and useful in real-world applications.

6. The proposed SLSAT model has demonstrated excellent performance in cybersecurity applications. It is a significant contribution to the field of cyber defense, as it provides an intelligent and resilient solution for detecting and mitigating cyber threats in real time.

## Appendix 1

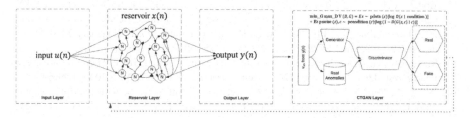

**Fig. 3.** The autonomous self-learning and self-adversarial training neural architecture

## References

1. Alhasan, S., Abdul-Salaam, G., Bayor, L., Oliver, K.: Intrusion detection system based on artificial immune system: a review. In: 2021 International Conference on Cyber Security and Internet of Things (ICSIoT), pp. 7–14, September 2021. https://doi.org/10.1109/ICSIoT 55070.2021.00011

2. Elmrabit, N., Zhou, F., Li, F., Zhou, H.: Evaluation of machine learning algorithms for anomaly detection. In: 2020 International Conference on Cyber Security and Protection of Digital Services (Cyber Security), pp. 1–8, June 2020. https://doi.org/10.1109/CyberSecurity49315. 2020.9138871

3. Demertzis, K., Iliadis, L.S., Anezakis, V.-D.: An innovative soft computing system for smart energy grids cybersecurity. Adv. Build. Energy Res. 12(1), 3–24 (2018). https://doi.org/10. 1080/17512549.2017.1325401

4. Alromaihi, S., Elmedany, W., Balakrishna, C.: Cyber security challenges of deploying IoT in smart cities for healthcare applications. In: 2018 6th International Conference on Future Internet of Things and Cloud Workshops (FiCloudW), pp. 140–145, December 2018. https://doi.org/10.1109/W-FiCloud.2018.00028.

5. Coulter, R., Han, Q.-L., Pan, L., Zhang, J., Xiang, Y.: Data-driven cyber security in perspective—intelligent traffic analysis. IEEE Trans. Cybern. **50**(7), 3081–3093 (2020). https://doi.org/10.1109/TCYB.2019.2940940

6. Hart, A.: Generalised synchronisation for continuous time reservoir computers. Rochester, NY, 17 December 2021. https://doi.org/10.2139/ssrn.3987856

7. Bala, A., Ismail, I., Ibrahim, R., Sait, S.M.: Applications of metaheuristics in reservoir computing techniques: a review. IEEE Access **6**, 58012–58029 (2018). https://doi.org/10.1109/ACCESS.2018.2873770

8. Cuchiero, C., Gonon, L., Grigoryeva, L., Ortega, J.-P., Teichmann, J.: Discrete-time signatures and randomness in reservoir computing. IEEE Trans. Neural Netw. Learn. Syst. **33**(11), 6321–6330 (2022). https://doi.org/10.1109/TNNLS.2021.3076777

9. Demertzis, K., Iliadis, L., Pimenidis, E.: Geo-AI to aid disaster response by memory-augmented deep reservoir computing. Integr. Comput.-Aided Eng. **28**(4), 383–398 (2021). https://doi.org/10.3233/ICA-210657

10. Al Jallad, K., Aljnidi, M., Desouki, M.S.: Anomaly detection optimization using big data and deep learning to reduce false-positive. J. Big Data **7**(1), 68 (2020). https://doi.org/10.1186/s40537-020-00346-1

11. Xu, L., Skoularidou, M., Cuesta-Infante, A., Veeramachaneni, K.: Modeling tabular data using conditional GAN. arXiv, 27 October 2019. https://doi.org/10.48550/arXiv.1907.00503

12. Abu, U.A., Folly, K.A., Jayawardene, I., Venayagamoorthy, G.K.: Echo State Network (ESN) based generator speed prediction of wide area signals in a multimachine power system. In: 2020 International SAUPEC/RobMech/PRASA Conference, pp. 1–5, January 2020. https://doi.org/10.1109/SAUPEC/RobMech/PRASA48453.2020.9041236

13. Manjunath, G.: An echo state network imparts a curve fitting. IEEE Trans. Neural Netw. Learn. Syst. **33**(6), 2596–2604 (2022). https://doi.org/10.1109/TNNLS.2021.3099091

14. Wang, Z., Yao, X., Huang, Z., Liu, L.: Deep echo state network with multiple adaptive reservoirs for time series prediction. IEEE Trans. Cogn. Dev. Syst. **13**(3), 693–704 (2021). https://doi.org/10.1109/TCDS.2021.3062177

15. Whiteaker, B., Gerstoft, P.: Memory in echo state networks and the controllability matrix rank. In: ICASSP 2022 - 2022 IEEE International Conference on Acoustics, Speech and Signal Processing (ICASSP), pp. 3948–3952, February 2022. https://doi.org/10.1109/ICASSP43922.2022.9746766.

16. Kidger, P.: On neural differential equations. arXiv, 4 February 2022. https://doi.org/10.48550/arXiv.2202.02435

17. Raissi, M., Perdikaris, P., Karniadakis, G.E.: Physics-informed neural networks: a deep learning framework for solving forward and inverse problems involving nonlinear partial differential equations. J. Comput. Phys. **378**, 686–707 (2019). https://doi.org/10.1016/j.jcp.2018.10.045

18. Shi, Y., Rong, Z.: Analysis of Q-Learning like algorithms through evolutionary game dynamics. IEEE Trans. Circuits Syst. II Express Briefs **69**(5), 2463–2467 (2022). https://doi.org/10.1109/TCSII.2022.3161655

19. Yin, Z., Cao, W., Song, T., Yang, X., Zhang, T.: Reinforcement learning path planning based on step batch Q-learning algorithm. In: 2022 IEEE International Conference on Artificial Intelligence and Computer Applications (ICAICA), June 2022, pp. 630–633. https://doi.org/10.1109/ICAICA54878.2022.9844553

20. Huang, D., Zhu, H., Lin, X., Wang, L.: Application of massive parallel computation based Q-learning in system control. In: 2022 5th International Conference on Pattern Recognition and Artificial Intelligence (PRAI), pp. 1–5, December 2022. https://doi.org/10.1109/PRAI55 851.2022.9904213

21. Habibi, O., Chemmakha, M., Lazaar, M.: Imbalanced tabular data modelization using CTGAN and machine learning to improve IoT Botnet attacks detection. Eng. Appl. Artif. Intell. **118**, 105669 (2023). https://doi.org/10.1016/j.engappai.2022.105669

22. Chauhan, R., Heydari, S.S.: Polymorphic adversarial DDoS attack on IDS using GAN. In: 2020 International Symposium on Networks, Computers and Communications (ISNCC), pp. 1–6, July 2020. https://doi.org/10.1109/ISNCC49221.2020.9297264

23. Demertzis, K., Tziritas, N., Kikiras, P., Sanchez, S.L., Iliadis, L.: The next generation cognitive security operations center: adaptive analytic lambda architecture for efficient defense against adversarial attacks. Big Data Cogn. Comput. **3**(1), Article no. 1, March 2019. https://doi.org/10.3390/bdcc3010006

24. Akhtar, N., Mian, A.: Threat of adversarial attacks on deep learning in computer vision: a survey. IEEE Access **6**, 14410–14430 (2018). https://doi.org/10.1109/ACCESS.2018.280 7385

25. Demertzis, K., Iliadis, L., Kikiras, P.: A Lipschitz - shapley explainable defense methodology against adversarial attacks. In: Maglogiannis, I., Macintyre, J., Iliadis, L. (eds.) AIAI 2021. IAICT, vol. 628, pp. 211–227. Springer, Cham (2021). https://doi.org/10.1007/978-3-030-79157-5_18

26. Dong, Y., et al.: Benchmarking adversarial robustness on image classification. In: 2020 IEEE/CVF Conference on Computer Vision and Pattern Recognition (CVPR), pp. 318–328, June 2020. https://doi.org/10.1109/CVPR42600.2020.00040

27. Bousmalis, K., Silberman, N., Dohan, D., Erhan, D., Krishnan, D.: Unsupervised pixel-level domain adaptation with generative adversarial networks. arXiv, 23 August 2017. https://doi.org/10.48550/arXiv.1612.05424

28. Han, K., Li, Y., Xia, B.: A cascade model-aware generative adversarial example detection method. Tsinghua Sci. Technol. **26**(6), 800–812 (2021). https://doi.org/10.26599/TST.2020.9010038

29. Mahmood, K., Nguyen, P.H., Nguyen, L.M., Nguyen, T., Van Dijk, M.: Besting the Black-Box: barrier zones for adversarial example defense. IEEE Access **10**, 1451–1474 (2022). https://doi.org/10.1109/ACCESS.2021.3138966

30. InfluxDB Times Series Data Platform, InfluxData, 15 January 2022. https://www.influxdata.com/home/. Accessed 28 Feb 2023

31. Industrial IoT (IIoT) solutions for smart industries – Factry, Factry - Open Manufacturing Intelligence. https://www.factry.io/. Accessed 28 Feb 2023

32. Nguyen, Q.-D., Dhouib, S., Chanet, J.-P., Bellot, P.: Towards a web-of-things approach for OPC UA field device discovery in the industrial IoT. In: 2022 IEEE 18th International Conference on Factory Communication Systems (WFCS), pp. 1–4, April 2022. https://doi.org/10.1109/WFCS53837.2022.9779181

33. Wang, H., Wang, Y., Wan, S.: A density-based clustering algorithm for uncertain data. In: 2012 International Conference on Computer Science and Electronics Engineering, vol. 3, pp. 102–105, March 2012. https://doi.org/10.1109/ICCSEE.2012.91

34. Khan, M.M.R., Siddique, Md.A.B., Arif, R.B., Oishe, M.R.: ADBSCAN: adaptive density-based spatial clustering of applications with noise for identifying clusters with varying densities. In: 2018 4th International Conference on Electrical Engineering and Information & Communication Technology (iCEEiCT), pp. 107–111, September 2018. https://doi.org/10.1109/CEEICT.2018.8628138

35. Botchkarev, A.: Performance metrics (Error Measures) in machine learning regression, forecasting and prognostics: properties and typology. Interdiscip. J. Inf. Knowl. Manag. **14**, 045–076 (2019). https://doi.org/10.28945/4184

36. Koyejo, O.O., Natarajan, N., Ravikumar, P.K., Dhillon, I.S.: Consistent binary classification with generalized performance metrics. In: Advances in Neural Information Processing Systems, vol. 27 (2014). https://papers.nips.cc/paper/2014/hash/30c8e1ca872524fbf7ea5c519ca 397ee-Abstract.html. Accessed 24 Oct 2021

37. Liu, Y., Zhou, Y., Wen, S., Tang, C.: A strategy on selecting performance metrics for classifier evaluation. Int. J. Mob. Comput. Multimed. Commun. IJMCMC **6**(4), 20–35 (2014). https://doi.org/10.4018/IJMCMC.2014100102

38. Li, X.: Fault data detection of traffic detector based on wavelet packet in the residual subspace associated with PCA. Appl. Sci. **9**(17), 3491 (2019). https://doi.org/10.3390/app9173491

39. Shamili, A.S., Bauckhage, C., Alpcan, T.: Malware detection on mobile devices using distributed machine learning. In: 2010 20th International Conference on Pattern Recognition, pp. 4348–4351, December 2010. https://doi.org/10.1109/ICPR.2010.1057

40. Demertzis, K., Kikiras, P., Tziritas, N., Sanchez, S.L., Iliadis, L.: The next generation cognitive security operations center: network flow forensics using cybersecurity intelligence. Big Data Cogn. Comput. **2**(4), Article no. 4, December 2018. https://doi.org/10.3390/bdcc2040035

# Deep Transfer Learning Application for Intelligent Marine Debris Detection

Kai Yuan Chia[1], Cheng Siong Chin[1(✉)], and Simon See[2]

[1] Faculty of Science, Agriculture, and Engineering, Newcastle University in Singapore, 599493 Singapore, Singapore
cheng.chin@newcastle.ac.uk

[2] Department of Computer Science and Engineering, DongchuanRD. Minhang District, Shanghai Jiao Tong University, Shanghai 200240, China

**Abstract.** This paper aims to evaluate the state-of-the-art object detection network; YOLOv5s (You Only Look Once version 5 small) for the detection of underwater marine debris using AUVs. The development of machine learning and AUVs for detecting marine debris is reviewed. In the paper, the YOLOv5s model is trained on a marine debris dataset using transfer learning. Several other object detection models are also trained on the same dataset for comparison. The results of the trained models are evaluated and the YOLOv5s model is deployed on an Android device to determine its suitability for real-time marine debris detection onboard AUVs. Overall, the YOLOv5s was able to achieve high accuracy scores of up to 91.2% and fast detection speeds of up to 20FPS on a Poco X3 Pro.

**Keywords:** Autonomous Underwater Vehicles · YOLOv5s · Marine Debris Detection · Intelligent

## 1 Introduction

In recent years, the pollution of oceans through the form of marine debris has been increasing at a rapid rate. Multiple efforts have been implemented to curb the global marine debris situation. Trawlers are the primary mode of monitoring/removing marine debris, but this method can be labor-intensive and expensive. Additionally, there are regions in the sea where trawling cannot be done e.g., regions where explosives or ammunition have been disposed [1]. Thus, there is an increasing trend to develop AUVs (Autonomous Underwater Vehicles) for monitoring marine debris. Currently, the main limitations of AUV marine debris detection are the need for quantitative datasets and the usage of an object detection model that is well-suited for real-time deployment onboard AUVs. This paper will evaluate using the YOLOv5s object detection model for detecting marine debris. At the same time, four other established object detection networks, namely Tiny-YOLOv3 (You Only Look Once version 3), Tiny-YOLOv4 (You Only Look Once version 4), RetinaNet, and Faster R-CNN (Faster Regional-Convolutional Neural Network), will also be trained under the same image dataset for comparison. The YOLOv5s will subsequently be deployed on an Android application and tested on a mobile device to determine its suitability to be deployed on an AUV for real-time marine debris detection. AUVs are deployed for various marine applications, such as surveying seabed environments and monitoring marine life. Several works have been done in recent years to develop ROVs/AUVs for underwater object detection. The FeelHippo AUV developed [2] can perform underwater object detection for both optical camera and FLS (Forward Looking Sonar) images using the Faster R-CNN and SSD (Single Shot Multibox Detector) object detection networks. The Intel Neural Compute Stick 2 and the NVIDIA Jetson Nano GPU were used to process the networks.

A Proof-of-Concept was implemented by [3] for an object detection network deployed on an ROV tethered to a surface vessel. The R-CNN (Regions with Convolutional Neural Networks) object detection model was trained using MATLAB to locate and detect lionfish in live underwater footage. The ROV camera captures the video sent to the surface vessel for processing and detection. Researchers [4] also developed an ROV to perform object detection underwater. The experiment was conducted in an inhouse aquarium, with a Raspberry Pi camera system placed in the ROV and tethered to a computer for object detection. The experiment utilized both transfer learning and learning from scratch. Transfer learning achieved 4% higher accuracy overall than training the model from scratch.

The 'SAILFISH' AUV developed in 2021 [5] uses a Side-scan Sonar (SSS) for object detection. The SC-CNN (Self Cascaded Convolutional Neural Network) is proposed to perform image segmentation of SSS images. The sonar sends the images to an Nvidia Jetson TX2 GPU onboard the AUV for object detection and image segmentation. The PENGUIN AUV [6], a modified version of a drone that is available on the market, was developed in 2020. The prototype PENGUIN AUV utilizes an augmented camera device to perform real-time marine debris detection using deep learning training methods and an optical sensor to detect the type of debris material.

The research and development of marine debris detection have been increasing lately. To detect marine debris autonomously, machine learning is applied to train object detection networks for marine debris detection and mapping. Researchers [7] developed four object detection models (YOLOv2, TinyYOLO, Faster R-CNN, SSD) for marine debris detection using transfer learning on an Nvidia Jetson TX2 GPU. The models were trained based on images from the JAMSTEC J-EDI (E-Library of Deep-sea Images) database, comprising videos and images of deep-sea environments captured by submersibles and ROVs.

A CNN (Convolutional Neural Network) model was developed by [8] that could detect marine debris in FLS (Forward-Looking Sonar) images based on the traditional sliding window approach. The images were captured using an imaging sonar inside a water tank. Another team of researchers [9] trained the EfficientDet, DETR (Detection Transformer), and Mask R-CNN networks to perform object detection on multiple surfaces and underwater debris datasets such as the TACO (Trash Annotations in Context) and Trashcan Dataset.

A custom ResNet50-YOLOv3 network was developed [10] for detecting submerged marine debris based on an image dataset curated from the JAMSTEC E-Library of Deep-sea Images (J-EDI). Similarly, a YOLOv3 object detection network was trained by [11] for detecting marine debris and animals using an image dataset collected by air and underwater drones. The YOLOv3 network in this case utilizes the default Darknet-53 CNN backbone.

Several works have been done to develop marine debris datasets for machine learning usage, such as the dataset gathered by [12], which consists of seabed litter images captured using a TUC (Towed Underwater Camera). A Forward-Looking Sonar marine debris dataset was done by [13], which was captured in a water tank using an imaging sonar. The MARIDA (Marine Debris Archive), created by [14], consists of marine debris images captured through satellite data. Also, a surface marine debris dataset was developed by [15] from aerial surveys using a UAV (Unmanned Aerial Vehicle). It is noted that artificial environments such as tanks may have differences compared to the actual marine environments in terms of lighting and water opacity. Also, marine debris datasets captured using satellites or UAVs are unsuitable for underwater (ROV or AUV) deployment.

Numerous studies have been done to deploy object detection networks on mobile devices/Raspberry Pi/Nvidia Jetson GPUs onboard ROVs/AUVs for other underwater detection purposes, demonstrating the feasibility of using AUVs to detect marine debris. There are limitations regarding the deployment of AUVs for marine debris detection. This paper aims to address the current limits of marine debris detection using AUVs by providing the following main contributions:

- To train the networks (YOLOv5s, Tiny-YOLOv4, Tiny-YOLOv3, RetinaNet, and Faster R-CNN) for marine debris detection using a standard dataset through transfer learning.
- To compare the trained networks using mA P0.5and mAP0.5:0.95 scores, inference speed, and model size.
- To deploy the YOLOv5s on a POCO X3 Pro Android device that can be augmented on an AUV. Subsequently, the performance of the deployed YOLOv5s will be evaluated based on inference speed and application size.

## 2  Methodology

The training and testing of the object detection networks are done using Google Colab (Google Collaboratory), which allows the running of programs using Google's resources. It is best suited for machine learning applications, where Google provides GPUs (Graphics Processing Units). A total of five object detection networks will be trained on the marine debris dataset: YOLOv5s, Tiny-YOLOv4, Tiny-YOLOv3, RetinaNet, and Faster R-CNN. The training parameters are kept constant as much as possible for a fair comparison of the networks.

### 2.1  Image Dataset

The marine debris image dataset used for this paper was obtained from the open-source Trashcan dataset . It contains images of marine debris ROVs and marine animals/plants taken from videos in the JAMSTEC (Japan Agency of Marine-Earth Science and Technology) E-Library of Deep-sea Images (J-EDI) which were captured by ROVs. Each image is annotated to label the ground truth of any objects within the image as shown in the image (see Fig.1). The annotations for the ground truth bounding boxes in this dataset are annotated in the form: 'Class', 'centre x-coordinate', 'centre y-coordinate', 'width', and 'height'. The Roboflow platform was used to pre-process the images into input sizes of 416 × 416 pixels and export them to respective formats for training the five networks.

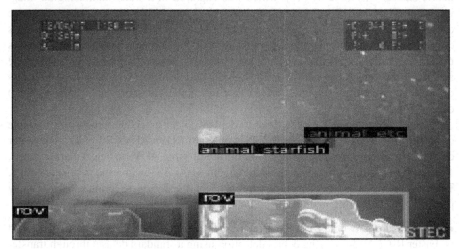

**Fig. 1.** Ground truth bounding boxes

There are 16 classes of objects. The classes include marine animals, plants, trash, and ROVs. The 'Animal etc.' and 'Trash etc.' classes refer to instances that are not substantial enough to be labeled as a single class in the dataset e.g., partially buried marine debris, unknown/deformed trash objects, and other animals such as crab, eel, fish and etc. A total of 7212 images were split into a training set, validation set, and test set in proportions of 70%, 20%, and 10%, respectively. The images in the test set should not be from the images used in the training and validation sets. Also, the dataset should contain a fair distribution of classes to ensure proper training and evaluation. Transfer learning was applied to train the models using the same marine debris dataset. The training and evaluation were also carried out with the same input size of 416 × 416 pixels. Transfer learning is a branch of machine/deep learning where a pre-trained object detection network is further trained to detect objects of a specific application. To perform transfer learning, an established pre-trained object detection network is selected. The network is usually trained on a large object detection dataset beforehand. The Microsoft COCO (Common Objects in Context) object detection dataset is an example. The COCO dataset serves as a popular benchmark to evaluate the performance metrics of different object detection networks. The YOLOv5 object detection model is a pre-trained model that has been trained on the COCO dataset.

All five models (YOLOv5s, Tiny-YOLOv4, Tiny-YOLOv3, RetinaNet, Faster R-CNN) were trained using the same dataset on Google Colab Pro with a single Nvidia Tesla P100 GPU. Using the same GPU allows for a fair comparison of inference speeds and performance. The main performance metric used to measure the accuracy of the models is the mAP (Mean Average Precision). mAP is the mean of all AP (Average Precision) scores across all classes. AP represents the area under the Precision-Recall curve and is calculated based on two metrics: Precision and Recall.

The precision and recall metrics are calculated using an IoU (Intersection Over Union) threshold. IoU is a metric that calculates the area of overlap between the model's prediction and the ground truth. For example, if the IoU for a certain prediction is 0.9, and the specified IoU threshold is 0.5, the prediction would be classified as a True Positive. On the other hand, if the IoU for a prediction is 0.4 with a specified IoU threshold of 0.5, then the prediction would be classified as a False Positive. The mA P0.5 metric is primarily used to compare the accuracy of the networks in this paper, and it represents the mAP score of a network, based on an IoU threshold of 0.5. Another metric used to evaluate the training process is the loss function, which represents the difference between the ground truth and the prediction made by the model. The lower the loss value, the more accurate the model is.

## 3   Transfer Learning of Models

A typical object detection network consists of three main parts: a backbone, a neck, and a head. The backbone is a CNN that serves as the primary feature extractor. The neck is an additional model that can be used for feature fusion to improve communication within the network. The feature maps generated by the backbone and neck are fed to the head. As stated earlier, transfer learning takes a pre-trained network and trains it on a new set of data, which is the method applied in this paper.

CNNs operate based on the same concept as neurons in a human brain, with the main function being the convolutional layers. Convolutional layers are equipped with kernels/filters, and a kernel is essentially a grid of discrete numbers/weights. At the start of the CNN training process, the kernel consists of random numbers. These numbers/weights are then tuned as the input is processed during training, to extract features from the input more effectively. The convolutional operation is performed by sliding the kernel over the input. For example, a $2 \times 2$ random weight-initialized kernel is processed over a $4 \times 4$ input image, the dot products between the kernel and input matrices are calculated, and the resulting vector is then summed to generate a single scalar value. The entire process is repeated until the kernel slides over the entire input.

There are several variants of ResNet (Residual Network), with a varying number of layers. The more layers, the deeper and more accurate the network will be. However, this also results in increased computational requirements. ResNet50 is one of the more popular ResNet variants, consisting of 49 convolutional layers with a Fully-Connected layer. The central concept behind ResNet is the usage of shortcut connections, also known as residual links, to enhance connectivity between layers, which is obtained by plotting the Resnet50 layers through MATLAB's Deep Learning Toolbox and Deep Learning Network Analyzer.

YOLOv5 is a family of state-of-the-art object detection networks, comprising five different sizes; YOLOv5n, YOLOv5s, YOLOv5m, YOLOv5l, and YOLOv5x. YOLOv5s was selected due to its fast detection speeds and sufficiently high accuracy. The model is compound scaled in a similar method as EfficientNet. The backbone of

YOLOv5 features the utilization of the Cross Stage Partial (CSP) network. The key to using CSP is the ability to reduce computation costs by reducing the parameters involved. This is done by partitioning the feature map outputs in the CNN into two parts using a cross-stage hierarchy. An SPP (Spatial Pyramid Pooling) layer is placed at the end of the CNN to allow input images of different sizes into the CNN. Furthermore, a PANet (Path Aggregation Network) is implemented as the neck of YOLOv5. Data is fed in a bottom-up path, followed by an additional top-down path from the backbone to combine the features from each level. Finally, the head of the YOLOv5 network creates three different-sized feature maps to predict objects of different sizes.

Firstly, the content required for YOLOv5s and Pytorch is installed in the coding environment as the YOLOv5s model is developed on the Pytorch framework. Next, the marine debris dataset is uploaded to Roboflow, and imported in Pytorch YOLOv5 format to the Google Colab notebook. After the content has been installed and imported, the training can be carried out. A batch size of 16, along with 150 epochs, was selected for training. The batch size indicates the number of images in the training set fed into the object detection network before updating the network weights. Completion of an epoch suggests that the network has processed the entire training set for one pass. In this case, a batch size of 16 would mean that the training dataset is split into batches of 16 images each, while 150 epochs would imply that the network has to process all the images in the training dataset for a total of 150 times. The COCO pre-trained YOLOv5s weights are then specified to be used for training. The training took place on a Tesla P100 GPU, as mentioned, achieving a mAP0.5 (Mean Average Precision) of 0.896 for the validation set on the 150th epoch, which shows a steep rise in mAP at the start while gradually stabilizing at the end as the learning rate decay starts to prevent overfitting.

After training, the Tensorboard toolkit was imported to plot training metrics such as precision, recall, mAP, and loss graphs. The validation loss and mAP graphs are used to evaluate the training process, and to determine if the model is overfitted or insufficiently trained. The mAP and loss values started to plateau at a certain number of epochs, and overfitting did not occur, which indicates an appropriate training duration. Upon completion of training, the final weights at the 150th epoch were exported in Pytorch format. Then, the trained YOLOv5s weights were evaluated based on the test dataset with an example prediction as shown in the images (see Fig. 2). After evaluation, the YOLOv5s achieved a test mA P0.5 score of 0.912 and inference speed of approximately 4.1 ms per image for the test set.

Also, the $AP_{0.5}$ (Average Precision at an IoU threshold of 0.5) scores for each class were evaluated. It was observed that the YOLOv5s model attained high AP0.5 scores for all classes, with the lowest AP0.5 of 0.726 and the highest AP0.5 of 0.992 as shown in Table 1.

Overall, the trained YOLOv5s model was able to generate a high number of true positive predictions across all classes. Among all the classes, the 'rubber' and 'paper' classes achieved nearly 100% true positive predictions as shown in the confusion matrix in Fig. 3. On the other hand, the 'shells' and 'animal" class achieved the lowest percentage of true positive predictions of 75% and 77% respectively. It can also be observed that the 'thrash etc.' class has the widest range of false positive and false negative predictions. This would mean the 'trash etc.' class is easily confused by the YOLOv5s model with

**Fig. 2.** YOLOv5s ground truth (left) and prediction (right)

**Table 1.** Top and Bottom Three $AP_{0.5}$ Scores for Yolov5s

| Class | $AP_{0.5}$ |
| --- | --- |
| Shells | 0.726 |
| Starfish | 0.826 |
| Trash etc. and Animal etc | 0.841 |
| Fabric | 0.938 |
| Rubber | 0.988 |
| Paper | 0.992 |

other classes during inference. This is expected as many possible objects can belong to the 'trash' class and it is difficult to accurately train the model to predict all the possibilities.

The YOLOv3 object detection network is a one-stage object detector developed in 2018. The CNN backbone for the YOLOv3 is the Darknet-53 network, which has 53 convolutional layers. An FPN (Feature Pyramid Network) functions as the neck, where information is fed in a top-down path from the backbone. The FPN combines the output from the CNN with a top-down path, along with side-by-side connections. This effectively forms a dense, multi-scale feature pyramid, and the pyramid can be used to output feature maps of varying scales to the YOLOv3 detector head for classification and prediction.

The YOLOv4 object detection network is a successor to the previous YOLO networks. It utilizes the CSP (Cross Stage Partial) network like YOLOv5, along with the Darknet-53 CNN as the backbone. RetinaNet is a one-stage object detection model developed based on a ResNet (Residual Neural Network) and FPN (Feature Pyramid Network) backbone. The key feature introduced in RetinaNet is the usage of focal loss, which targets to remove the imbalance between classes by reducing the weights for easy detections and increasing weights for harder detections. As a result, this reduces the total loss contribution from easy detections, and more emphasis is placed to correct the harder detections. In contrast to the previous models, Faster R-CNN is a two-stage object

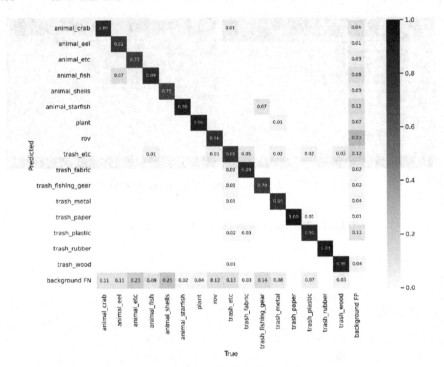

**Fig. 3.** YOLOv5s confusion matrix

detection network that utilizes the technique of RPNs (Region Proposal Networks) to perform detection. A region proposal network in the CNN processes an input image and produces region proposals based on the likelihood that an object is in that region, also known as an objectness score.

## 4 Comparison of Models

The accuracy metric used to compare the five models is the mA P0.5 Mean Average Precision based on an IoU threshold of 0.5), as shown in Table 2. The mA P0.5 values are the mA P0.5scores achieved by the trained models when performing on the test dataset. Table 2 shows that the YOLOv5s achieved the highest test mA P0.5 of 0.912, with the Tiny-YOLOv4 coming second with a mA P0.5 of 0.874. The Faster R-CNN model has a slightly lower mA P0.5 of 0.808 despite being a two-staged detection network. On the other hand, the Tiny-YOLOv3 scored the lowest mAP0.5 of 0.700 out of the five models. As the mA P0.5 metric is used to evaluate the accuracy of a model, with higher mA P0.5 representing higher accuracy, it can be deduced that the YOLOv5s is the most accurate out of all five models, when evaluated using an IoU threshold of 0.5.

As seen in Table 2, the Tiny-YOLOv4 and Tiny-YOLOv3 networks have the fastest inference speeds of 3.1ms and 3.3ms, respectively. The YOLOv5s model has a slightly longer inference time of 4.1 ms. On the other hand, the RetinaNet and Faster R-CNN have significantly slower inference speeds of 53 ms and 54 ms, respectively. This indicates that the YOLO object detection networks (YOLOv5s, Tiny-YOLOv4, Tiny-YOLOv3) are more suited for deployment on smaller devices due to their fast inference speeds. To be suitable for real-time deployment onboard an AUV, the object detection network must be fast, lightweight, and utilize minimal processing power simultaneously. Smaller AUVs may only have space for smaller processing units with less storage space. After training, the weights of the five trained networks are exported and downloaded. Table 2 shows the size of the model weights after export in MB (megabytes).

Based on the comparisons made in the previous sections, it is evident that the YOLOv5s and Tiny-YOLOv5 networks excel in accuracy, speed, and size. The YOLOv5s weights have the smallest size of 14.1 MB, followed by the Tiny-YOLOv4, with a size of 22.5 MB. On the other hand, the Faster R-CNN and RetinaNet models have a significantly large size of 315 MB and 278 MB, respectively. Again, this indicates that the YOLO networks are better suited for deployment on smaller processing units. As such, a further comparison is made for the two networks using another accuracy evaluation metric known as the mA P0.5$_{0.95}$, the average of Mean Average Precision scores calculated over an IoU threshold range of 0.5 to 0.95, with a step size of 0.05.

**Table 2.** Comparison of all Metrics with Top Scores

| Object Detection Model | mAP 0.5 | Inference Speed (ms) | Size (MB) |
|---|---|---|---|
| YOLOv5s | **0.912** | 4.1 | **14.1** |
| Tiny-YOLOv4 | 0.874 | **3.1** | 22.5 |
| Tiny-YOLOv3 | 0.700 | 3.3 | 34.7 |
| RetinaNet | 0.851 | 53 | 278 |
| Faster R-CNN | 0.808 | 54 | 315 |

YOLOv5s network generally performs better at higher IoU thresholds, indicating that the YOLOv5s is more accurate at predicting the locations of the bounding boxes closer to the ground truth. After evaluating the results, it was observed that all the models were able to achieve high AP scores for most of the classes in the 'trash' category, with the only exception being the 'trash' class, which appeared in the bottom three AP scores for YOLOv5s, Tiny-YOLOv4, and RetinaNet. The 'trash etc.' class can be easily confused with other classes, as proven by the YOLOv5s confusion matrix. Also, it was observed that all the models scored lower AP scores for classes in the 'animals' category, with the 'shells' class appearing in the bottom three AP scores for all five models. However, this is not a huge concern as the primary aim of the models is to detect marine debris accurately. Overall, it was observed that most of the one-stage detectors performed better. Besides the Tiny-YOLOv3, all the one-stage detectors outperformed the Faster R-CNN two-stage detector in terms of accuracy. YOLOv5s is the best performer in accuracy with mA P0.5:0.95 of 0.663 compared to Tiny-YOLOv4 of 0.589. In terms of processing speed, the YOLOv5s is slightly slower than the Tiny-YOLOv4, but it is better at predicting the exact locations of the bounding boxes, as proven by its higher mA P0.5$_{:0.95}$ score, as well as a smaller model size.

488     K. Y. Chia et al.

## 5  Deployment

Development of the application was done on Android Studio, along with Android SDK (Software Development Kit), as shown in Fig. 4. Firstly, the YOLOv5s model was converted to TFLite (Tensorflow Lite) FP16 (Half Precision Floating Point) format, which allows for Android deployment using the Tensorflow Lite framework. The converted YOLOv5s TFLite FP16 format has a size of 13.87 MB. The code for the Android application was written on Android Studio and is based on the official Tensorflow Android object detection example. The Android project file is based on Tensorflow, with amendments made to the codes to support the trained YOLOv5s model. Firstly, the YOLOv5s TFLite model was imported into the Android project. The final build is built through Android wireless debugging. The Android application was tested on video footage from the JAMSTEC JEDI dataset. Overall, the average inference time was about 50 to 80ms on a POCO X3 Pro Android device with a Qualcomm Adreno 640 GPU. This speed is approximately 12.5 to 20 FPS (Frames Per Second). The application's performance varies greatly across different devices, depending on the GPU of the device. There is also an option to configure the application to run on CPU or GPU. However, running on CPU results in much slower inference speeds of 360 to 400ms on the POCO X3 Pro, which translates to approximately 2.5 to 2.7 FPS. The HYPER-DOLPHIN ROV used to capture images and video footage for the JEDI dataset has a maximum forward speed of 3knots (approximately 1.54m/s). Similarly, if an AUV moves across the seabed at an average speed of 1.5 to 2 m/s in a straight-line path for surveying, this means that the Android application would be able to process a range of between 8.33 to 10 frames per meter of seabed based-on a detection speed range of 12.5 to 20FPS.

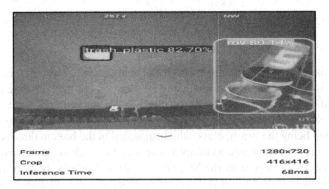

**Fig. 4.** Android Application real-time inference

## 6  Conclusion

This paper developed and evaluated the performance of five object detection networks for marine debris detection onboard AUVs. Among the five models, it was concluded that the YOLOv5s model was best suited for underwater marine debris detection due to its high accuracy, speed, and size. The YOLOv5s model was successfully deployed on a

POCO X3 Pro, demonstrating decent speeds of 12.5 to 20FPS, with high accuracy scores of up to 91.2%. Object detection networks can also be trained to perform other functions, such as hull inspection and ship navigation. The object detection software onboard the AUV can be programmed to process images at a specific interval. Each processed image is subsequently tagged with geolocation data. This information can then be evaluated to identify locations with a higher concentration of marine debris so that removal can be performed efficiently. Further work will allow the Android application to utilize geotagging algorithms to assign latitude and longitude data to a predicted image.

# References

1. Canals, M., Pham, C.K., Bergmann, M., et al.: The quest for seafloor macrolitter: A critical review of background knowledge, current methods, and future prospects. Environm. Res. Lett. (2020)
2. Zacchini, L., Ridolfi, A., Topini, A., et al.: Deep learning for on-board auv automatic target recognition for optical and acoustic imagery. IFAC-PapersOnLine **53**, 14589–14594 (2020)
3. Naddaf-Sh, M., Myler, H., Zargarzadeh, H.: Design and implementation of an assistive real-time red lionfish detection system for AUV/ROVs. Complexity **2018**, 1–10 (2018)
4. Wang, C.C., Samani, H.: Object Detection using Transfer Learning for Underwater Robot. In: International Conference on Advanced Robotics and Intelligent Systems (ARIS), pp. 1–4 (2020)
5. Song, Y., He, N., Liu, P.: Real-time object detection for AUVs using self-cascaded convolutional neural networks. IEE J. Oceanic Eng. **46**(1) (2021)
6. Flores, H., Zuniga, A., Motlagh, N.H., et al.: PENGUIN: aquatic plastic pollution sensing using AUVs. In: Proceedings of the 6th ACM Workshop on Micro Aerial Vehicle Networks, Systems, and Applications (DroNet 2020), Article 5, pp. 1–6. Association for Computing Machinery, New York (2020)
7. Fulton, M., Hong, J.S., Islam, M.J., et al.: Robotic detection of marine litter using deep visual detection models.In: 2019 International Conference on Robotics and Automation (2019)
8. Matias, V.: Submerged marine debris detection with autonomous underwater vehicles. In: 2016 International Conference on Robotics and Automation for Humanitarian Applications (2016)
9. Majchrowska, S., Mikolajczyk, A., Ferlin, M., et al.: Deep learning-based waste detection in natural and urban environments. Waste Manag. **138** (2022)
10. Xue, B., Huang, B.X., Wei, W.B., et al.: An efficient deep-sea debris detection method using deep neural networks. IEEE J. Selected Topics Appli. Earth Observat. Remote Sens. **14**, 12348–12360 (2021)
11. Watanabe, J., Shao, Y., Miura, N.: Underwater and airborne monitoring of marine ecosystems and debris. J. Appli. Remote Sens. **13**(4) (2019)
12. Politikos, D.V., Fakiris, E., Davvetas, A., et al.: Automatic detection of seafloor marine litter using towed camera images and deep learning. Mar. Pollut. Bull. **164**, 111974 (2021)
13. Singh, D., Matias, V.: The marine debris dataset for forward-looking sonar semantic segmentation. In: 2021 IEEE/CVF International Conference on Computer Vision Workshops (ICCVW) (2021)
14. Kikaki, K., Kakogeorgiou, I., Mikeli, P., et al.: MARIDA: a benchmark for marine debris detection from sentinel-2 Remote Sensing Data. PLOS ONE **1**(1) (2022)

15. Wolf, M., van der Berg, K., Garaba, S.P., et al.: Machine learning for aquatic plastic litter detection, classification and quantification (APLASTIC-Q). Environ. Res. Lett. **15**(11), 114042 (2020)
16. Hong, J.S., Fulton, M., Sattar, J.: Trashcan: A Semantically-Segmented Dataset Towards Visual Detection of Marine Debris". arXiv: 2007.08097 (2020)

# Forecasting Functional Time Series Using Federated Learning

Raúl Llasag Rosero[(✉)] [iD], Catarina Silva [iD], and Bernardete Ribeiro [iD]

University of Coimbra, Polo II - Pinhal de Marrocos, 3030-290 Coimbra, Portugal
{rosero,catarina,bribeiro}@dei.uc.pt

**Abstract.** The need for accurate time series forecasting has questioned the potential of Federated Learning (FL) in solving regression problems with privacy-preserving and collaborative prognosis requirements. While recent Machine Learning (ML) studies have shown accurate predictions in time series forecasting using functional principal component analysis, the potential of integrating this approach with FL has not been previously evaluated. This paper depicts the potential of combining functional time series regression with FL through the implementation of a Functional Multilayer Perceptron (FMLP). Experimental results on one of the most innovative industrial maintenance strategies, Predictive Maintenance (PM), demonstrate that the integration of FMLP with the well-known Federated Averaging (FedAvg) algorithm achieves accurate time series forecasting while preserving data privacy. These results, obtained using NASA C-MAPSS datasets, outperformed traditional ML and Deep Learning (DL) approaches in estimating the Remaining Useful Life (RUL) of aircraft components.

**Keywords:** Machine Learning · Federated Learning · Functional Multilayer Perceptron · Predictive Maintenance · Remaining Useful Life

## 1 Introduction

Time series forecasting analyses time series data to predict future states within a period or at a specific point in the future. Collecting this kind of data refers to measuring a particular process by recording observations over an equally spaced period [1]. The need for accurate forecasts has gained attention in decentralized data scenarios where data collection and analysis are conducted in multiple isolated silos [2]. This is particularly relevant in many industrial applications, where data may be distributed across different machinery, and maintaining data privacy and security is crucial [3]. In such scenarios, the application of the privacy-preserving and distributive Machine Learning (ML) named Federated Learning (FL) offers a promising solution [4] (Table 1).

Federated Learning enables local training of ML models while aggregating only their weights [5]. This ensures that sensitive data remains with its owners while allowing for improved model performance. However, regression problems

© The Author(s), under exclusive license to Springer Nature Switzerland AG 2023
L. Iliadis et al. (Eds.): EANN 2023, CCIS 1826, pp. 491–504, 2023.
https://doi.org/10.1007/978-3-031-34204-2_40

**Table 1.** Variables used to describe the FMLP model in Federated Learning

| Functional Multilayer Perceptron | | | |
|---|---|---|---|
| $D$ | Centralized dataset | $\beta_{k,m,p}$ | Learnable parameters |
| $N$ | Number of samples of $D$ | $W$ | Functional weight space |
| $M$ | Number of features | $W_{k,m}$ | $W$ for $k$ neurons and $m$ features |
| $X$ | Sample space of $D$ | $P$ | Meaningful curves |
| $Y$ | Label space of $D$ | $P_{FVE}$ | FVE hyperparameter of PCA |
| $T$ | Size of the time window | $\sigma$ | Activation function |
| $X_i$ | $i-$th input sample, s.t. $i = 1, \ldots, N$ | $\mu$ | Borel measurement $\in \mathbb{R}^T$ |
| $Y_i$ | Label of $X_i$ s.t. $i = 1, \ldots, N$ | $\phi_{m,p}$ | Eigenvectors |
| $X^{T \times M}$ | Shape of the $i$-th input sample | $\lambda_{m,p}$ | Eigenvalues |
| $b$ | Learnable parameters $\in \mathbb{R}$ | $\eta$ | Step-size of SGD algorithm |
| Federated Learning | | | |
| $J$ | Number of parties | $\kappa$ | $\kappa$-th global model computation |
| $j$ | $j$-th party | $\mathbf{w}_\kappa^j$ | Weights of $j$ at $\kappa$-th time |
| $D^j$ | Dataset of $j$ | $\mathbf{w}$ | Weights of global AI model |
| $N^j$ | Dataset size of the $j$ | $\mathbf{w}^*$ | Optimal weights of global model |
| $Y^j$ | Label space of $j$ | $F_\kappa^j(\mathbf{w}^j)$ | Loss function of $j$ at $\kappa$-th time |
| $E$ | Number of local training epochs | $F(\mathbf{w})$ | Global cost function |
| $K$ | Number of model aggregations | | |

using FL approaches have been limited to adopting traditional ML and Deep Learning (DL) approaches, whose final models often suffer notable performance losses in distributed scenarios compared with a centralized data scenario [2,3]. This has raised doubts about the potential of FL in regression problems. As a response, this paper adopts a time series forecasting approach that uses functional data as inputs of a neural network and evaluates its potential in the context of FL. Specifically, we draw on the promising results of functional data analysis in discovering and learning important sources of pattern and variation among data [7–9]. To evaluate this proposal, we implement a Functional Multilayer Perceptron (FMLP) algorithm in conjunction with the well-known Federated Averaging (FedAvg) algorithm [10].

The integration of FMLP with FL is evaluated through experiments on Predictive Maintenance (PM), one of the most innovative industrial maintenance strategies. The experiments were conducted using NASA C-MAPSS datasets and three popular metrics for Remaining Useful Life (RUL) estimation. The results demonstrated the competitiveness of the proposed approach, outperforming previous estimations using traditional ML and DL approaches developed in a centralized data scenario. Additionally, the proposed approach improved the lifetime predictions of an air fleet of aircraft engines collaboratively, thereby establishing its potential for industrial applications.

The contributions of this paper can be summarized as follows:

- The **combination** of functional time series forecasting using FMLP with FL in a horizontal data partitioning setting that refers to multiple parties analyzing the same input variables but different samples. The implementation of the well-known FedAvg algorithm of FL, which uses Stochastic Gradient Descent (SGD), is available in the following GitHub repository: https://github.com/rhllasag/FunctionalMultilayerPerceptronInFederatedLearning.
- Performance **improvements** in RUL estimation of aircraft engines compared with previous studies. These advances are achieved by conducting a hyperparameter grid search approach that includes the Fraction Variance Explained (FVE) $P_{FVE}$ of Principal Component Analysis (PCA) as a variable.

## 2   Literature Review

### 2.1   Functional Time Series Forecasting

The time series data analysis begins by performing statistics in time domains to find patterns and variations among stationary signals [12]. In the presence of smooth non-stationary signals, functional versions of these elementary statistics have been demonstrated to be a promising alternative, for example, functional means, variations, correlation and covariance [13]. The Functional Time Series (FTS) method is used to decompose smooth curves into a set of functional principal components and associated scores via Functional Principal Component Analysis (FPCA) [14].

At the beginning of the 21st century, studies have reached promising one-step-ahead and multi-step-ahead forecasts of functional time series using FPCA [7,8]. These studies have recently derived promising results in age-specific mortality rate prediction using ML-based FTS forecasting [9,11]. Mortality rate prediction data present features (e.g. geographic region or socioeconomic status) that usually contain heterogeneity and deteriorate the forecast results. Since decomposing functional time trends was helpful in this particular case to identify functional patterns, this research assumed that it is not the only case in which FTS can be applied.

In [7], Functional Multilayer Perceptron (FMLP), an extension of the classic Multilayer Perceptron (MLP) to functional inputs, was designed to learn the underlying structure of continuous and smooth curves by adding a functional hidden layer before numerical hidden layers. Since it is not possible to use directly functional data as input to a numerical MLP, mainly because evaluation points depend on the function, functions of a finite number of observations and variables are built [6]. While FMLP has shown promising results compared to traditional and DL (e.g. MLP [3], Convolutional Neural Network (CNN) [15], Long-Short Time Memory (LSTM) [16], and others) approaches by considering signal variability instead of directly mapping vectors, its potential in FL scenarios has yet to be fully explored.

## 2.2   Federated Learning

Federated Learning (FL) has emerged as a popular privacy-preserving and distributed Machine Learning (ML) technique for collaborative problem-solving in scenarios where $J$ parties face data scarcity issues [3,4]. This technique enables the training of ML models locally, allowing data owners to maintain their data privacy [2]. Furthermore, this approach improves the problem by repeatedly training, sharing and aggregating local models through a central server's intervention.

There are several FL algorithms in the literature to perform these standard loop steps until the problem convergence is achieved [5]. The adoption of a specific algorithm depends on various factors, such as the business topology (B2B, B2C), the type of problem (classification, regression or clustering), the data distribution setting (horizontal, vertical or hybrid), and the FL challenges (e.g. system heterogeneity). Given the importance of FL in horizontal data partitioning, this paper implements the FedAvg algorithm based on SGD [10].

## 3   Forecasting Functional Time Series Using Federated Learning

The functional time series forecasting problem considers functional inputs (vectors) from $\mathbb{R}^n$ to predict a target variable from $\mathbb{R}$. Functional Multilayer Perceptron (FMLP) is an extension of the standard Multilayer Perceptron (MLP), a model constructed by adding a functional hidden layer before hidden numerical layers [7]. The functional layer receives vectors and applies basis functions to extract relevant features. A visual representation of this process, along with the FMLP architecture, is depicted in Fig. 1.

Multiple curves are obtained by monitoring a certain process through multiple variables ($M$ features). To represent $M$ curves as a finite set of values functions, the $i$-th input sample of size $\mathbb{R}^{T \times M}$ is assumed to be composed of T-dimensional curves. Therefore, $X_i$ can be written as $[X_{i,1}(t); \ldots ; X_{i,M}(t)]$ s.t. $t = 1, \ldots, T$. Considering a target variable $Y_i$ for this sample, this problem aims

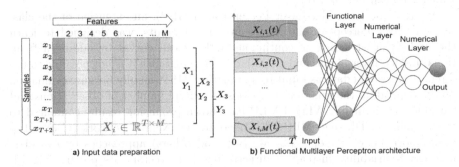

a) Input data preparation          b) Functional Multilayer Perceptron architecture

**Fig. 1.** Functional Multi-Layer Perceptron architecture and input data

to learn a mathematical mapping from $X_i$ to $Y_i$. This is essentially learning the following mapping from continuous observations.

$$Y_i = F(X_i). \tag{1}$$

### 3.1 Functional Neurons

A classical MLP neuron maps an input $x$ to the real output $\sigma(wx + b)$, where $\sigma$ is an activation function from $\mathbb{R}$ to $\mathbb{R}$, $w$ a vector from $\mathbb{R}^n$, and $b$ the bias term. In this expression, $wx$ is a linear expression in $\mathbb{R}^n$ space that restricts MLP to finite-dimensional inputs [7]. If it is considered a general vectorial input space $X$, a weight $W$ from $X_i$ can be used, for example, a set of continuous linear forms on $X$.

Literature generalizes to this neuron mapping as $\sigma(W(X)+b)$, where $W(X)$ is the generalization of $wx$ to arbitrary vectorial space. Because this manipulating linear forms on arbitrary vectorial space is simply impossible, the restriction to use functional inputs was proposed in [6–8,14,17].

The most common way to work with weight functions is configuring B-splines [7]. However, for the current experiments, $\mu$ is assumed a Borel measure $\in \mathbb{R}^T$ and $X_i$ a $L^p(\mu)$ space of measurable functions $f$ from $\mathbb{R}^T$ to $\mathbb{R}$ s.t. $\in |f|^p \delta\mu < \infty$. By assuming so, we can define a neuron that maps elements of $L^p(\mu)$ (where $q$ is the conjugate exponent of $p$) to $\mathbb{R}$. In consequence, the real output of the functional hidden layer $H(X_i)$ composed of $K$ neurons is given by:

$$H(X_i) = \sum_{k=1}^{K} \sigma(b_k + \int W_k X_i \delta\mu), \tag{2}$$

where $b_k$ are real numbers and $W_k$ are functions in $L^q(\mu)$.

### 3.2 Functional Multilayer Perceptron

Adding a hidden layer comprising $K$ functional neurons and its corresponding weight function $H(X_i, \beta)$ involves optimizing learnable parameters $\beta$ and associated biases $b$. This computation can be performed by assuming an observation measure $\mu$ and $M$ functional feature curves of the $i$-th sample denoted as $X_i = [X_{i,1}(t); \ldots; X_{i,M}(t)]$ s.t. $t = 1, \ldots, T$.

$$H(X_i, \beta) = \sum_{k=1}^{K} \sigma\left(b_i + \int_{t \in T} W_{k,p}(\beta_{k,m}, t) X_{i,m}(t) \delta t\right) \tag{3}$$

By conducting Functional Data Analysis (FDA), weight function $W_{k,p}(\beta_{k,m}, )$ enables the weight function $H$ to be easily computable by performing Principal Component Analysis (PCA). Furthermore, this approach allows the restriction of analysis to the $P$ most relevant components by defining a maximum Fraction Variance Explained (FVE) $P_{FVE}$. In practice, this $P_{FVE}$ hyperparameter prioritizes using the functional components $P$ that contain the most valuable information.

$$W_{k,p} = \sqrt{M} \sum_{p=1}^{P} \beta_{k,m} \phi_{m,p} \tag{4}$$

Considering a normalized input space $X_i \in [0,1]$, covariance function $Cov_m(c,d)$ is used to quantify the correlation between the $m$-th sensor measurements at any two time points $s$ and $t$ within the period $T$. Then, eigenvectors $\phi$ and eigenvalues $\lambda$ are calculated by performing PCA using the corresponding covariance matrix:

$$Cov_m(s,t) = \frac{1}{T-1} \sum_{i=1}^{T} \left[ X_{i,m}(s) - \bar{X}_m(s) \right] \left[ X_{i,m}(t) - \bar{X}_m(t) \right], \tag{5}$$

where $\bar{X}_m(s) = \frac{1}{T} \sum_{i=1}^{T} X_{i,m}(s)$. Then, eigenvalues are solutions from the following computation

$$\lambda_{m,p} \phi_{m,p}(t) = \int Cov_m(s,t) \phi_{m,p}(s) \delta s. \tag{6}$$

**Forward propagation step:** before any learning step, lets recall that covariance matrix $Cov_m$ that quantifies the correlation between two time points from $X_i \in \mathbb{R}^{T \times M}$ is square. This enables estimating the integral term of Eq. 3 using the approximator

$$\frac{1}{M} \sum_{m=1}^{M} W_{k,p}(\beta_{k,m}, t) X_i(t). \tag{7}$$

After all numerical hidden layers process the output of $H$, the output $\hat{Y}$ and the corresponding error can be computed using any statistics, for example, the Root Mean Squared Error (RMSE).

$$RMSE = \sqrt{\frac{1}{N} \sum_{i=1}^{N} (Y_i - \hat{Y}_i)^2} \tag{8}$$

**Backward propagation step:** assumes that there is a $\frac{\delta W_{k,m}(\beta_{k,m,p}, t)}{\delta \beta_{k,m,p}}$ exist almost everywhere for $t \in T$. However, there is still a problem with directly computing the second integral term of

$$\frac{\delta H(X_i, \beta)}{\delta \beta_{k,p}} = \sum_{k=1}^{K} \sigma' \left( b_i + \int_{t \in T} W_{k,p}(\beta_{k,m}, t) X_i(t) \delta t \right) \left( \int_{t \in T} \frac{\delta W_{k,m}(\delta \beta_{k,m}, t)}{\delta \beta_{k,m}} X_i(t) \delta t \right). \tag{9}$$

One way to resolve this concern is by approximating it using the below-mentioned expression.

$$\frac{\delta W_{k,p}(\beta_{k,m}, t)}{\delta \beta_{k,m}} = \sum_{p=1}^{P} \phi_{m,p}(t) \tag{10}$$

### 3.3   Federated Averaging: FedAvg

The Federation of FMLP models assumes that a centralized dataset $D$, composed of $N$ samples and $M$ features, can be distributed among $J$ parties. Because these experiments consider a horizontal data partition, parties share the same features but differ in sample space. In other words, the $j$-th party's dataset $D^j$ is composed of $N^j$ samples, s.t. $N = \sum_{j=1}^{J} N^j$. This implies that every party has its own input space $X^j$ label map $Y^j$ and local weights $\mathbf{w}^j$. Because the collaborative problem is solved by implementing the SDG-based algorithm FedAvg, the central computational server generates initial weights $\mathbf{w_0}$ at zero time and shares with parties. Federated Averaging (Algorithm 1) improves the solution of the problem by performing the following key steps: model download 2, local training (Line 4), model uploading (Line 5), and computing of the global model (Line 7). In this configuration, the local problem of party $j$ at $\kappa$ time refers to minimizing the local cost function $F_\kappa^j(\mathbf{w}^j)$ by measuring a loss function $f_i$ in the local sample space

$$\mathbf{w}^j \triangleq \arg\min F_\kappa^j(\mathbf{w}^j) = \frac{1}{N^j} \sum_{i=1}^{N^j} f_i(\mathbf{w}^j). \tag{11}$$

After computing the global model $K$ times (Line 7), optimal weights $\mathbf{w}^*$ are obtained by solving the global cost function $F(\mathbf{w})$, s.t.

$$\mathbf{w}^* \triangleq \arg\min F(\mathbf{w}). \tag{12}$$

---

**Algorithm 1.** Federated Averaging at $\kappa$ time

---

**Input:** Step-size $\eta$, Epochs $E$, Global weights $\mathbf{w}_\kappa$, Parties $J$, Local samples $N^j$
**Output:** Global weights $\mathbf{w}_{\kappa+1}$ at time $\kappa + 1$.
1: **for** $e = 1, 2, \ldots E$ **do**
2:     The server sends $\mathbf{w_k}$ to parties .
3:     **for** $j = 1, 2, \ldots J$ **do**
4:         Using $N^j$ samples, $j$ updates $\mathbf{w_k}$ on $F_\kappa^j(\mathbf{w}^j)$ with $\eta$ to obtain $\mathbf{w}^j_{\kappa+1}$.
5:         Each party sends $\mathbf{w}^j_{\kappa+1}$ back to server .
6:     **end for**
7:     The server aggregates weights as $\mathbf{w}_{\kappa+1} = \frac{\sum_{j=1}^{J} N^j \mathbf{w}^j_{\kappa+1}}{N}$. In the case of the functional hidden layer, $\beta^j$ and $b^j$ are considered instead of $\mathbf{w}^j$.
8: **end for**

---

## 4   Experimental Setup

The proposed approach has been evaluated within the context of a novel industrial maintenance strategy called Predictive Maintenance (PM), which relies on Condition Monitoring (CM) data to predict the Remaining Useful Life (RUL) of machinery. Accurate RUL prediction is essential to minimize unexpected maintenance and prevent accidents. However, data-driven methods for RUL prediction have been limited by a need for sufficient degradation data [18]. To address this gap, Federated Learning (FL) has emerged as a promising approach for privately aggregating knowledge from multiple data owners. Using Turbofan Engine Degradation Simulation datasets provided by NASA - Commercial Modular Aero-Propulsion System Simulation (C-MAPSS) [19], the RUL estimation accuracy of a centralized data scenario (Sect. 4.1) is compared with a horizontal federated scenario with a different number of parties (Sect. 4.2).

## 4.1    Remaining Useful Life Estimation of Aircraft Engines

C-MAPSS datasets are composed by observing multiple engines identified by a unique number id. Each engine is monitored by 21 sensors and three operating settings (Altitude, Mach number and Throttle Angle Resolver) along several operating cycles (flight hours), composing a single run-to-failure trajectory. Besides input sensor data, this group of four datasets provides values for the target vector RUL. For FMLP learning purposes, curves of sensors data are normalized as follows:

$$\mathbf{Curve}_m = \frac{\mathbf{Curve}_m - min\mathbf{Curve}_m}{max\mathbf{Curve}_m - min\mathbf{Curve}_m}, \tag{13}$$

limiting to $\sigma$ process values within $[0, 1]$. This implies a short consideration when computing the final estimation $R\hat{U}L$. Given a piece-wise degradation function $f(t)$ of two health degradation stages (imperceptible and abnormal)

$$f(t) = \begin{cases} Rc & if \quad 0 \le t \le t_{SoF} \\ t_{EoL} - t & if \quad t_{SoF} \le t_{EoL} \end{cases}, \tag{14}$$

$R\hat{U}L = \hat{Y} \times Rc$ and $RUL = Y \times Rc$. This is because an initial constant RUL value $Rc$ is considered. After crossing a start to failure $t_{SoF}$ point, the RUL linearly decreases until the $t_{EoL}$ last operational cycle. Considering that a single run-to-failure trajectory can be reshaped to multiple samples of size $X_i \in \mathbb{R}^{T \times M}$, and $h_i = R\hat{U}L_i - RUL_i$, the accuracy of FMLP can be evaluated by any cost function, for example, Root Mean Squared Error (RMSE), Mean Absolute Error (MAE), and Score.

$$MAE = \frac{1}{N} \sum_{i=1}^{N} |h_i| \tag{15}$$

$$Score = \begin{cases} \sum_{i=1}^{N^j} (e^{\frac{-h_i}{13}} - 1) & if \quad h_i < 0 \\ \sum_{i=1}^{N^j} (e^{\frac{h_i}{10}} - 1) & if \quad h_i \ge 0 \end{cases} \tag{16}$$

## 4.2    Horizontal Data Partitioning

Federated Learning evaluations are conducted on four FD00x datasets. Each dataset exhibits unique properties based on a combination $(x, op, fm)$ of operating conditions $oc$ and failure modes $fm$. The analysis of an array of multiple settings $[(1,1,1),(2,6,1),(3,1,2),(4,6,2)]$ allows for more robust conclusions to be drawn from the data. This analysis considers the differences among FD00x datasets outlined in Table 2, which are related to the number of run-to-failure trajectories available in the training and testing data sets. While the testing sets are used to make maintenance decisions and evaluate the precision of the RUL estimation, the training sets are used to train the FMLP model. In local training and evaluation procedures, 85% and 15% of the available data of the training set of each FD00x dataset are used.

The horizontal data partitioning is outlined in Table 2, where each FD00x dataset is divided at $J$ parties. Conducting a systematic sampling using the $Jn$ criterion, party $j$ gets run-to-failure trajectories of $D$ with a step of $J$ starting from the $j$-th and ending in $n$. Clearly, $n$ refers to the number of trajectories of training sets, while no systematic sampling refers to centralized data experiments.

**Table 2.** Number of run-to-failure trajectories per party at each FD00x dataset.

| Dataset | J | Systematic sampling | FD001 | FD002 | FD003 | FD004 |
|---------|---|---------------------|-------|-------|-------|-------|
| Training | 1 | None | 100 | 260 | 100 | 249 |
| | 2 | 2n | ≈50 | ≈134 | ≈50 | ≈124 |
| | 4 | 4n | ≈25 | ≈67 | ≈25 | ≈62 |
| | 8 | 8n | ≈12 | ≈33 | ≈12 | ≈31 |
| Testing | 1 | None | 100 | 259 | 100 | 248 |

## 5   Results and Analysis

This section describes the results of experiments conducted on a computer with AMD Ryzen 9 3900X 12-Core processor, 64 GB RAM, NVIDIA GeForce RTX 3080 GPU, Ubuntu 20.04 LTS 64-bit operating system and MATLAB R2021a.

### 5.1   Centralized Data Scenario

The development of accurate models for this scenario requires adjusting the time window dimension $T$. This is because the last operating cycle $t_{EoL}$ of each run-to-failure trajectory varies, and if $T > t_{EoL}$ is accomplished, there is the possibility of losing valuable information. This risk was accepted by setting $T = 31$ at every dataset.

Using all run-to-failure trajectories of each FD00x training set, 30 FMLPs were developed using different initial weights $\mathbf{w_0}$ to define baseline comparisons with standard deviation for FL scenarios. Particularly, those 30 models were trained using the hyperparameters in the blue colour of Table 3. Those hyperparameters, combined with sigmoid activation functions and early stopping criteria

**Table 3.** Hyperparameter tuning

| Hyperparameter | Search Range |
|---|---|
| Functional neurons | 4, 8, 16, 20 |
| Numerical layers | 1, 2, 3 |
| Neurons in the first numerical layer | 2, 4, 8, 16 |
| Neurons in the second numerical layer | 2, 4, 8, 16 |
| Step-size $\eta$ | 0.1, 0.01, 0.001, 0.0001 |
| $P_{FVE}$ Fraction Variance Explained | 80%, 85%, 90% |

waiting for performance losses during eight epochs, were defined after conducting a grid search method for a single FMLP construction.

Evaluating the RUL prediction on each FD00x testing set, RMSE values $15.68 \pm 0.75$, $16.27 \pm 1.55$, $12.93 \pm 0.67$ and $14.63 \pm 0.97$, and Scores $72.76 \pm 3.33$, $207.94 \pm 21.22$, $72.12 \pm 5.30$ and $210.44 \pm 17.99$, partially outperformed previous FMLP studies [6,7]. Indeed, those results, outlined in the centralized-data block of Table 4, also outperform previous studies using CNN [15] and LSTM [16].

## 5.2    Federated Scenarios

Federated scenarios consider multiple parties. Therefore, FMLP models for these scenarios, depending on the FD00x dataset adopted, were trained using the run-to-failure trajectories outlined in Table 2, where $J > 1$. To ensure an accurate evaluation, 30 global FMLPs were developed for each $J$ and FD00x combination, similar to the centralised data scenario. Blue values in Table 4 indicate that the RUL estimation of the global FMLP outperformed the evaluation metric of the centralized data scenario.

In our experiments, RUL estimation performance achieves the highest accuracy when $P_{FVE} = \%90$. Therefore, it is evident that parties find similar variation patterns by discarding a %10 of variance. This short variation percentage may be associated with pure noise because averaging model weights using FedAvg does not affect the RUL estimation accuracy of federated models. The non-blue values of the right block of Table 4 indicate the cases in which global FMLP models lost a bit of performance compared to centralized data scenarios. Given the similar results presented in [6] for these cases, the integration of FMLP and FL algorithms appears to be a promising approach.

Besides comparing models from centralized data and federated scenarios, experiments on FL also considered comparing models trained using local data of each party $j$ with models developed in a federated scenario. Results of these experiments, depicted in Table 5, show that parties presented performance improvements in at least two evaluation metrics using the FedAvg algorithm. It can be noticed by comparing the results of the left and right blocks of Table 5, where four nodes trained and tested 30 models using run-to-failure trajectories from training and testing sets of the FD004 dataset.

**Table 4.** Performance of RUL prediction by training 30 FMLPs with different $\mathbf{w}_0$.

| Parties $J$ | Centralized-data | | | Federated Averaging | | |
|---|---|---|---|---|---|---|
| FD001 | MAE | RMSE | Score | MAE | RMSE | Score |
| 2 | $10.98 \pm 0.64$ | $15.68 \pm 0.75$ | $72.76 \pm 3.33$ | $13.29 \pm 1.11$ | $18.22 \pm 0.38$ | $87.70 \pm 3.87$ |
| 4 | | | | $12.31 \pm 0.62$ | $18.18 \pm 0.48$ | $82.30 \pm 3.28$ |
| 8 | | | | $11.75 \pm 0.59$ | $18.12 \pm 0.59$ | $79.01 \pm 3.57$ |
| FD002 | MAE | RMSE | Score | MAE | RMSE | Score |
| 2 | $12.10 \pm 1.61$ | $16.27 \pm 1.55$ | $207.94 \pm 21.22$ | $11.83 \pm 0.85$ | $16.32 \pm 1.07$ | $202.40 \pm 13.41$ |
| 4 | | | | $11.71 \pm 0.67$ | $16.30 \pm 0.71$ | $197.61 \pm 8.76$ |
| 8 | | | | $11.63 \pm 0.73$ | $16.46 \pm 0.69$ | $196.44 \pm 10.23$ |
| FD003 | MAE | RMSE | Score | MAE | RMSE | Score |
| 2 | $8.00 \pm 0.69$ | $12.93 \pm 0.67$ | $72.12 \pm 5.30$ | $7.41 \pm 0.35$ | $13.89 \pm 0.36$ | $67.65 \pm 2.42$ |
| 4 | | | | $7.21 \pm 0.43$ | $14.10 \pm 0.48$ | $66.59 \pm 3.12$ |
| 8 | | | | $6.66 \pm 0.25$ | $14.02 \pm 0.28$ | $63.08 \pm 1.79$ |
| FD004 | MAE | RMSE | Score | MAE | RMSE | Score |
| 2 | $9.51 \pm 1.02$ | $14.63 \pm 0.97$ | $210.44 \pm 17.99$ | $13.52 \pm 1.36$ | $18.44 \pm 0.74$ | $89.03 \pm 7.96$ |
| 4 | | | | $12.48 \pm 0.59$ | $18.28 \pm 0.50$ | $83.23 \pm 2.99$ |
| 8 | | | | $11.69 \pm 0.58$ | $18.06 \pm 0.39$ | $79.18 \pm 2.97$ |

**Table 5.** Performance of FMLPs trained with local data $D^j$ and using FedAvg.

| Party $j$ | Local data $D^j$ | | | Federated Averaging | | |
|---|---|---|---|---|---|---|
| FD004 | MAE | RMSE | Score | MAE | RMSE | Score |
| 1 | $9.33 \pm 0.70$ | $14.96 \pm 0.73$ | $211.31 \pm 10.78$ | $12.51 \pm 0.60$ | $18.28 \pm 0.50$ | $83.23 \pm 3.02$ |
| 2 | $12.22 \pm 4.25$ | $17.31 \pm 3.30$ | $266.33 \pm 84.14$ | | | |
| 3 | $9.86 \pm 2.39$ | $15.77 \pm 1.79$ | $221.31 \pm 41.86$ | | | |
| 4 | $12.58 \pm 3.92$ | $17.44 \pm 3.15$ | $271.65 \pm 77.67$ | | | |

A visual representation of the potentiality of FMLPs in FL is depicted in Fig. 2, where blue curves refer to the ground truth $RUL$, and oranges curves refer to the estimated curve $R\hat{U}L$. In this figure, the most promising result refers to the 25th trajectory of the FD004 data split because predictions are close to the real RUL but allow to dispatch of early maintenance alerts.

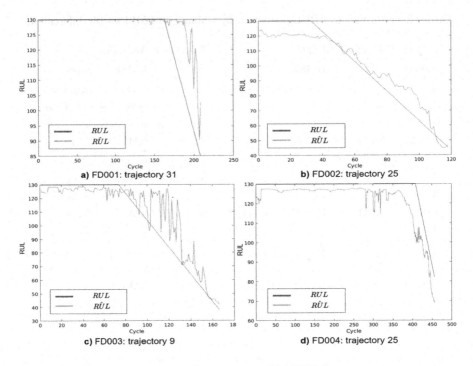

**Fig. 2.** RUL prediction using C-MAPSS dataset.

## 6    Conclusion and Future Works

Regardless of the Federated Learning (FL) context, functional time series forecasting has demonstrated superior performance to typical Machine Learning and Deep Learning approaches. Therefore, a Functional Multilayer Perceptron (FMLP) was implemented using Principal Component Data Analysis (PCA) and a grid search approach, which includes the Fraction Variance Explained (FVE) $P_{FVE}$ as a hyperparameter. The selection of $P_{FVE}$ has allowed prioritizing using functional components $P$ that contain the most valuable information, improving the FMLP model accuracy.

Our experiments on Remaining Useful Life estimation demonstrate the competitive performance of Functional Multilayer Perceptrons (FMLP) for time series forecasting in Federated Learning (FL) using horizontal data partitioning. Given the promising results obtained, collaborative time series forecasting using FMLP and FL seems promising in cases where features present contain heterogeneity.

Given the implementation of Federated Averaging, a basic FL algorithm based on Stochastic Gradient Descent (SGD) minimization, this research enables researchers to explore more advanced and potentially more accurate solutions. Despite our experiments being limited to a collaborative prognosis problem, integrating FMLP with FL enables exploring multiple research areas, mainly when features of time series datasets present heterogeneity and can deteriorate the forecast results.

Leveraging the capability of our approach in feature reduction and feature selection (selection of most influential functional components), we propose to evaluate the use of FMLP in FL scenarios in which datasets from multiple parties may differ in feature space. Particularly in FL literature, data distribution topologies considering parties varying in feature space are called vertical and hybrid data partitioning settings.

**Acknowledgements.** to (1) The Portuguese Foundation for Science and Technology (FCT) for supporting the project grant SFRH/BD/07344/2020, (2) The Center for Informatics and Systems of the University of Coimbra (CISUC), and (3) The European Union's Horizon 2020 research and innovation programme under the project No 769288 untitled "Real-Time Condition-based Maintenance for Adaptive Maintenance Planning-ReMAP"

# References

1. Liu, Z., Zhu, Z., Gao, J., Xu, C.: Forecast methods for time series data: a survey. IEEE Access **9**(1), 91896–91912 (2021). https://doi.org/10.1109/ACCESS.2021.3091162
2. Li, Y.: Federated learning for time series forecasting using hybrid model. Computer Science (2019)
3. Llasag Rosero, R., Silva, C., Ribeiro B.: Remaining useful life estimation in aircraft components with federated learning. Int. J. Prognostics Health Manage. **5**(1), 9–17 (2020). https://doi.org/10.36001/phme.2020.v5i1.1228
4. Dhada, M., Palau, A.S., Parlikad, A.K.: Federated learning for collaborative prognosis. In: International Conference on Precision, Meso, Micro, and Nano Engineering (COPEN 2019), vol. IIT, Indore (2019). https://doi.org/10.17863/CAM.50577
5. Zhang, X., Yin, W., Hong, H., Chen, T.: Hybrid federated learning: algorithms and implementation (2020). arXiv:2012.12420
6. Conan-Guez, B., Rossi, F.: Functional multi-layer perceptron: a nonlinear tool for functional data analysis (2017). arXiv:0709.3642
7. Rossi, F., Conan-Guez, B., Fleuret, F.: Functional data analysis with multi layer perceptrons. In: Proceedings of the 2002 International Joint Conference on Neural Networks, IJCNN 2002 (Cat. No.02CH37290), Honolulu, vol. 3, pp. 2843–2848 (2002). https://doi.org/10.1109/IJCNN.2002.1007599
8. Stinchcombe, M.B.: Neural network approximation of continuous functionals and continuous functions on compactifications. Neural Netw. **12**(3), 467–477 (1999). https://doi.org/10.1016/s0893-6080(98)00108-7
9. Tang, C., Shang, H.L., Yang, Y.: Clustering and forecasting multiple functional time series (2022). arXiv:2201.01024
10. McMahan, H.B., Moore, E., Ramage, D., Agüera y Arcas, B.: Federated learning of deep networks using model averaging (2016). arXiv:1602.05629
11. Beyaztas, U., Shang, H.: Forecasting functional time series using weighted likelihood methodology (2019). arXiv:1908.00336v1

12. Llasag, R.R., Silva, C., Ribeiro, B.: Remaining useful life estimation of cooling units via time-frequency health indicators with machine learning. Aerospace **9**(6), 309 (2022). https://doi.org/10.3390/aerospace9060309

13. Ramsay, J., Hooker, G., Graves, S.: Functional Data Analysis, 1st edn. Springer, New York (2009)

14. Beyaztas, U., Shang, H.: Machine-learning-based functional time series forecasting: application to age-specific mortality rates. Forecasting **4**, 394–408 (2002). https://doi.org/10.3390/forecast4010022

15. Sateesh Babu, G., Zhao, P., Li, X.-L.: Deep convolutional neural network based regression approach for estimation of remaining useful life. In: Navathe, S.B., Wu, W., Shekhar, S., Du, X., Wang, X.S., Xiong, H. (eds.) DASFAA 2016. LNCS, vol. 9642, pp. 214–228. Springer, Cham (2016). https://doi.org/10.1007/978-3-319-32025-0_14

16. Zheng, S., Ristovski, K.S., Farahat, A., Gupta, C.: Long short-term memory network for remaining useful life estimation. In: 2017 IEEE International Conference on Prognostics and Health Management (ICPHM), Dallas, pp. 88–95 (2017). https://doi.org/10.1109/ICPHM.2017.7998311

17. Conan-Guez, B., Rossi, F.: Multi-layer perceptrons for functional data analysis: a projection based approach. In: Dorronsoro, J.R. (ed.) ICANN 2002. LNCS, vol. 2415, pp. 667–672. Springer, Heidelberg (2002). https://doi.org/10.1007/3-540-46084-5_109

18. Lei, R., et al.: A data-driven auto-CNN-LSTM prediction model for lithium-ion battery remaining useful life. Trans. Ind. Inf. **17**(5), 3478–3487 (2021). https://doi.org/10.1109/TII.2020.3008223

19. Saxena, A., Goebel, K.: PHM08 challenge data set. (Vol. https://www.nasa.gov/content/prognostics-center-of-excellence-data-set-repository; Technical report). NASA Ames Prognostics Data Repository, NASA Ames Research Center, Moffett Field, CA (2008)

# Group-Personalized Federated Learning for Human Activity Recognition Through Cluster Eccentricity Analysis

Ahmed A. Al-Saedi[(✉)] and Veselka Boeva

Blekinge Institute of Technology, Karlskrona, Sweden
{ahmed.a.al-saedi,veselka.boeva}@bth.se

**Abstract.** Human Activity Recognition (HAR) plays a significant role in recent years due to its applications in various fields including health care and well-being. Traditional centralized methods reach very high recognition rates, but they incur privacy and scalability issues. Federated learning (FL) is a leading distributed machine learning (ML) paradigm, to train a global model collaboratively on distributed data in a privacy-preserving manner. However, for HAR scenarios, the existing action recognition system mainly focuses on a unified model, i.e. it does not provide users with personalized recognition of activities. Furthermore, the heterogeneity of data across user devices can lead to degraded performance of traditional FL models in the smart applications such as personalized health care. To this end, we propose a novel federated learning model that tries to cope with a statistically heterogeneous federated learning environment by introducing a group-personalized FL (GP-FL) solution. The proposed GP-FL algorithm builds several global ML models, each one trained iteratively on a dynamic group of clients with homogeneous class probability estimations. The performance of the proposed FL scheme is studied and evaluated on real-world HAR data. The evaluation results demonstrate that our approach has advantages in terms of model performance and convergence speed with respect to two baseline FL algorithms used for comparison.

**Keywords:** Federated Learning · Clustering · Eccentricity Analysis · Non-IID data · HAR

## 1 Introduction

With the recent development of edge devices, such as mobile phones, wearables, IoT devices etc., a massive amount of data can be generated. Such data can be utilized by training-based intelligent applications for human activity recognition (HAR). Traditional solutions require sending these data to a central server and training there in a centralized way. However, this introduces huge communication overhead, consumes network resources, and brings privacy concerns [1]. To solve this problem, Google proposes a decentralized approach called Federated Learning (FL), where model parameters instead of data are transferred between the central server and edge nodes (called workers hereafter) [2]. A central server

© The Author(s), under exclusive license to Springer Nature Switzerland AG 2023
L. Iliadis et al. (Eds.): EANN 2023, CCIS 1826, pp. 505–519, 2023.
https://doi.org/10.1007/978-3-031-34204-2_41

periodically sends the global model to a set of workers. These workers train the shared model without sharing their private data to generate updated local models, which are later submitted to the server [3]. Finally, the server aggregates the local models and generates a new global model. This process is repeated until a satisfactory global model is obtained. This approach is called naive FL, because the workers involved in training are usually randomly selected at each round, and the trained parameters are aggregated by averaging. This scheme works well for IID (independently identically distribution) data but has unsatisfactory performance for Non-IID data [2]. Practically, the assumption to consider that the local data of each edge device is always IID does not hold, often impacting overall model performance. However, compared with IID data, Non-IID datasets have significant variability in data class distribution and size [4].

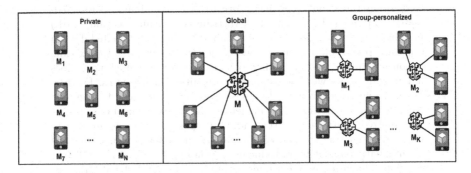

**Fig. 1.** Comparison of three different federated learning scenarios: (i) the left plot presents a setup in which each model is trained on the worker's private data; (ii) the middle plot is a scenario where a global model is built from the locally trained workers' models; (iii) the right plot illustrates a setting accounting for similarity among the workers and building a global model from the local models of each group of similar workers.

Figure 1 illustrates the different ways to model FL. The traditional FL setting, presented in the middle plot, assumes a federation of distributed workers, each with its own private data. These workers join the FL global training to achieve a better model performance. As a result, the global model is generated from local models with different characteristics, derived from different types of data. Thus, these different characteristics captured by the local models' parameters will be later mitigated when global aggregation occurs [5]. Furthermore, the traditional FL paradigm faces fundamental challenges, such as heterogeneous data across workers and a lack of solution personalization. In contrast to the traditional FL paradigm, Personalized Federated Learning (PFL) addresses the mentioned two fundamental challenges. PFL takes a completely local approach. In this context, each worker represents a different ML task with a different data distribution, and a private model for each task will be trained and used to deal with the specific nature of the data. Therefore, the output is a unique personal model for each worker, but no peer learning [6]. This scenario is illustrated in the left plot of Fig. 1. However, even though the tasks among workers are different, it is reasonable to assume that there is similarity across different tasks. On the other hand, in the traditional FL scenario (the middle plot of Fig. 1), in case of imbalanced data, where each worker only has one specific class of data, the results of averaging of the model parameters for producing an aggregated global model can lead in a significant accuracy decrease, e.g., up to 11% for MNIST and 51% for CIFAR-10 datasets, respectively are reported in [4].

Our proposed approach tries to tackle the discussed challenges and find a trade-off between the two extreme cases described above. Namely, we propose grouping workers based on their empirical probabilities, reflecting their current data class distribution. In particular, the workers with similar empirical probability vectors are placed in the same cluster. Later when updating the global model, we average the parameters from the same group. In that way, only local updates uploaded by the workers within the same group will be aggregated. Then in the next round, the aggregated group global model is sent to the same group to train, as it is illustrated in the right plot of Fig. 1. Evidently, our proposed Group-Personalized FL (GP-FL) algorithm is capable of training simultaneously several global models, one per each group of workers with similar activity patterns. At each training round, each worker's empirical probability vector is updated in order to reflect the information in its new data batch. In addition, cluster eccentricity analysis [7] is applied to the workers' current grouping. In that way, at the next round, some workers may change their cluster or even new singelton clusters may appear.

The GP-FL algorithm has been evaluated in a set of experiments, based on a well-defined evaluation setup in the HAR domain. The HAR problem is well suited to our FL scenarios, because various activities tend to have generic patterns while being highly idiosyncratic [8,9]. The performance of our GP-FL algorithm is benchmarked to that of two other FL algorithms, Federated Averaging (FedAvg) [2] and Clustered Federated Learning (CFL) [10]. GP-FL demonstrates its superiority over both algorithms in the conducted experiments with respect to the achieved performance.

## 2 Related Work

Recently we have witnessed a lot of attention on personalization in FL. Our proposed work is related to PFL in HAR and distributed multi-task learning. We explore some existing approaches related to those topics. For example, in [11] a random forest based personalized FL model is proposed for recognizing many human activities. In this work, the authors use local sensitivity hashing for calculating the similarity between different users. Based on this similarity, a subset of the top-$k$ most similar users is selected for training the federated forest model iteratively. In [12] a novel hybrid approach is suggested for HAR that combines semi-supervised and FL settings to build a global model for privacy awareness. Yu et al. [13] have developed a method that relies on a semi-supervised gradient aggregation strategy for activity detection using sensor data for online HAR tasks. In [14], the authors have proposed the FedStack framework, which supports ensemble heterogeneous architectural client models for mobile health sensor datasets. FedStack has been applied to mobile health sensor data to recognize 12 different activities. Presotto *et al.* [15] have proposed FedAR: a novel hybrid approach to unify federated learning with semi-supervised learning for activity recognition on mobile devices. It relies on active learning and label propagation to semi-automatically annotate the local streams of unlabeled sensor data. Tashakori *et al.* introduce in [16] a novel personalized semi-supervised learning (SemiPFL) approach focusing on edge intelligence. SemiPFL creates a personalized autoencoder to enable learning from user data representation. In [17], the authors have presented FedCLAR: a novel federated clustering framework according to the similarity of the local updates for HAR. FedCLAR combines federated clustering with transfer learning methods to reduce the non-IID issue. In [18], a method called SS-FedCLAR that combines federated clustering and semi-supervised learning in FL settings is introduced to reduce the non-IID and the data lack issues simultaneously. The authors in [19], have presented a federated transfer learning method for wearable healthcare to address security and personalization challenges. Lu *et al.* have proposed AdaFed: a weighted federated transfer learning framework to tackle domain shifts and to realize personalization for local clients in healthcare [20]. Ma *et al.* [21] have focused on label concept drift. They have presented a variational Bayes framework for PFL based on hierarchical Bayesian inference.

Similarly to our work, Sattler *et al.* [10] propose a hierarchical clustering FL scheme, forming client clusters, and those in the same cluster share the same model for training. This algorithm, called Clustering Federated Learning (CFL), is used as a baseline in the evaluation of our proposed GP-FL algorithm. Notice that most of the above mentioned works are aimed at the personalized training of deep learning models in a federated learning setup. Our work instead introduces a lightweight model based on logistic regression that is more suitable for modern resource-constrained wearable devices for HAR monitoring.

## 3   Preliminaries

In this section, we introduce the baseline FL algorithms used in the evaluation of our GP-FL algorithm. We also provide with a formal description of the FL setting, and motivate the methods and optimization procedures used in the proposed GP-FL algorithm.

### 3.1   Baselines

To assess the performance of our proposed method, we compare the GP-FL algorithm against two other FL methods, namely FedAvg [2] and CFL [10].

**Federated Averaging (FedAvg):** FedAvg is the predominant algorithm for federated learning [2], following a server-client setup with two repeating phases

(i) the clients train a shared global model locally on their data by making multiple local updates, and (ii) the server averages the locally updated models to obtain a new global model. In contrast to FedAvg method, GP-FL builds several global ML models, each one trained on a dynamic group of clients with homogeneous class probability estimations.

**Clustered Federated Learning (CFL):** A clustering framework to deal with federated multi-task learning have proposed in [10]. The CFL groups clients into clusters of similar clients according to their local data distribution. Thus, the goal is to train a single global model for each cluster. Similarly to the CFL method, our proposed GP-FL algorithm trains a set of global models, one per each cluster of workers. In our work, the workers are however, clustered into groups according to their local data distribution with respect to the classes. In that way, two workers are grouped together if they have similar local class probability distributions, i.e. evidently different groups of workers have different learning tasks. In addition, the clustering is adapted at each training round by accounting the evolving nature of data distribution with respect to the classes.

## 3.2   Problem Setting

As we stated in Sect. 1, our aim is to show how the fundamental idea behind our GP-FL approach can be exploited to design a group-personalized solution of FL problem. To do so, let us briefly describe the GP-FL setting. Given a set of workers in contrast to the traditional supervised federated learning setting, the goal in our GP-FL framework is not finding a global model that performs well for all the workers, but training a set of global-personalized models, one per a group of workers. Therefore in our GP-FL solution, we initially segment workers into groups based on the similarity of their class probability estimations.

We consider a typical setting of FL with a model $\mathcal{M}$ that is learned iteratively by using a randomly selected subset, denoted by $W_t$ ($W_t \subset W$), of the set $W$ of all available workers. The workers in $W_t$ participate at each round and compute the gradient of the loss over all the data held by them. Each worker $w \in W_t$ at round $t$ has its own row of data $D_t^w$ and a local model $\mathcal{M}_t^w$. At each round $t$, each worker trains its local model by iterating the local update multiple times of Stochastic Gradient Descent (SGD) before sending the next local model $\mathcal{M}_{t+1}^w$ to the server which holds the global model. The server, after collecting all the local models computed at round $t$, performs a synchronous update of the global model $\mathcal{M}_{t+1}$. The global model update can be computed using different criteria. In this paper, we assume it is calculated by means of federated averaging, that is the local model $\mathcal{M}_t^w$, $w \in W_t$ and global model $\mathcal{M}_t$ are updated by the following equations: [22]:

$$\mathcal{M}_{t+1}^w = \mathcal{M}_t^w - \eta g_t^w; \tag{1}$$

$$\mathcal{M}_{t+1} = \sum_{w \in W_t} \frac{n_w}{n} \mathcal{M}_{t+1}^w, \tag{2}$$

where $\mathcal{M}_{t+1}^w$ is the local update, $g_t^w$ are the updated weights on its local data in the current model $\mathcal{M}_t^w$, $\mathcal{M}_{t+1}$ is the global model, $\eta$ is a learning rate calculated by each worker, $W_t$ is the set of workers which participate in the training, $n$ is the total number of all data points and $n_w$ is the number of local data points of the worker $w \in W_t$.

In our GP-FL setup we compute a group global model for each cluster of workers $(C_{tj} \subset W_t)$, then Eq. 2 is changed to

$$\mathcal{M}_{t+1}^{C_{tj}} = \sum_{w \in C_{tj}} \frac{n_w}{n} \mathcal{M}_{t+1}^w, \tag{3}$$

where $\mathcal{M}_{t+1}^{C_{tj}}$ is the group global model built for each cluster $C_{tj}$ at round $t$. The server then distributes the group global model $\mathcal{M}_{t+1}^{C_{tj}}$ to its updated group of workers, i.e. for each $w_i \in C_{t+1j}$, where $C_{t+1j}$ is the updated version of $C_{tj}$, to perform another iteration of local training and model update.

### 3.3  Data Smoothing

In our proposed GP-FL solution each worker is modeled by its class probability estimations, i.e. an empirical probability vector, where each value represents the relative frequency of the corresponding class among the all training examples. For example, if we have a set $D$ of labelled examples, and the number of examples in $D$ of class $C_i$ is $n_i$ $(i = 1, 2, \ldots, k)$, then the empirical probability vector associated with $D$ is given by $\hat{p}(D) = (n_1/|D|, \ldots, n_k/|D|)$. Such empirical probability vector is initially calculated for each worker in our FL model and then update at each following round according to the current data batch at this worker.

In order to avoid issues with extreme values, such as 0 or 1, each empirical probability vector $\hat{p} = (\hat{p}_1, \hat{p}_2, \ldots, \hat{p}_k)$ can be smoothed by applying Laplace correlation which is expressed as:

$$\hat{p}_i(D) = \frac{n_i + 1}{|D| + k}, \tag{4}$$

where $D$ is set of labelled examples, $n_i$ is the number of examples in class $C_i$, and $k$ (the number of classes) is added to ensure that the posterior probabilities are never zero [23].

### 3.4  Markov Clustering Algorithm

Markov Cluster algorithm (MCL) is an unsupervised pattern recognition algorithm based on finding the optimal cluster of a connected graph, without any a priori knowledge of the cluster sizes. It is used to cluster sequence similarity or simple networks [24]. MCL can efficiently utilize 2000 compute nodes and cluster a network of about 70 million nodes with about 68 billion edges in approximately 2.4 h [25]. What really distinguishes MCL from other clustering techniques is that it does not require any input to form clusters, unlike $k$-means algorithm and other partitioning algorithms. This makes this algorithm crucial in network data, social network data, or even similarity detection.

### 3.5   Wasserstein Distance

The Wasserstein distance, which is a metric used to measure the distance between probability distributions, is induced by the optimal transport problems [26]. Methods based on the advantages of Wasserstein distance have been used successfully in several research areas, including statistics, machine learning, natural language processing, and computer vision [27]. In such applications, the distance is measured by comparing one probability distribution with another, which arises from the theory of optimal transport problems [26]. In the implemented version of our proposed FL model, we use Wasserstein distance to measure the similarity between class probability estimations of each pair of workers. In this way, the individuals who have similar activity patterns will be grouped together by applying the MCL algorithm discussed above.

### 3.6   Eccentricity Analysis

New eccentricity-based anomaly detection analysis principles have been introduced in [7]. An algorithm, called AutoCloud, based on the introduced principles is proposed in [28]. Similarly to the idea in AutoCloud, we use eccentricity analysis in our proposed FL solution to maintain a dynamic grouping of the workers. In this context, the eccentricity $\xi^j$ of a worker $w_i$ in relation to a cluster of workers $C_j$ can be calculated as [28]:

$$\xi^j(w_i) = \frac{1}{n_j} + \frac{(\mu_i^j - \hat{p}_i)^T (\mu_i^j - \hat{p}_i)}{\sigma_i^j n_j}, \tag{5}$$

where $n_j$ is the size of $C_j$, $\hat{p}_i$ is empirical probability vector associated with the worker $w_i$, and $\mu_i^j$ and $\sigma_i^j$ are the mean and variance, respectively, supposing $w_i \in C_j$.

Equation 6 presents how eccentricity can be applied to determine whether a worker belongs to a given cluster. Furthermore, the Chebyshev inequality has been utilized to apply a threshold to check whether a worker still belongs to an existing cluster [29]. A particular worker $w_i$ is considered to belong to a cluster $C_j$ if the following condition is satisfied

$$\xi^j(w_i) \leq v_j \text{ and } v_j = (m^2 + 1)/2n_j, \tag{6}$$

where $m$ ($m > 0$) is a user-defined parameter that directly affects the evaluation of clustering, and $v_j$ is the threshold associated with cluster $C_j$. Although it can be defined using multiple criteria, $m = 3$ is largely used as a standard value and leads to satisfactory results for different data sets and different configurations [30].

# 4   Proposed Approach

In this section, we formally present our proposed algorithm, namely group-personalized FL (GP-FL) to build a set of group global FL models. We propose to group the available workers according to their empirical class probability distributions. The workers with similar empirical probabilities are grouped together into the same cluster based on their similarity measured by Wasserstein distance. In addition, the built grouping is not static, but it is dynamically updated at each training round by applying cluster eccentricity analysis. This approach allows a global model at the cluster level to be built, overcoming the issue of personalization in traditional FL techniques.

The GP-FL algorithm foresees two distinctive phases: *initialization* and *iteration*. These phases are described in what follows. Let $W = \{w_1, w_2, \ldots, w_n\}$ be the set of all available workers, and $W_t$ is a subset of $W$ that contains the workers selected at round $t$.

**Initialization Phase:**

1. At time $t = 0$, the Server initializes the inputs for the GP-FL algorithm. These are model $\mathcal{M}_t$, set of workers $W_t$, and a number of iterations $T$.
2. The Server transmits the initial global model $\mathcal{M}_t$ to the set of workers $W_t$ ($W_t \subset W$).
3. Each worker $w_i \in W_t$ receives the global model $\mathcal{M}_t$ and optimizes its parameters locally, i.e. the $\mathcal{M}_t^i$ initial update is produced alongside with a vector $\hat{p}_t(w_i)$ that represents the empirical probabilities of the classes distribution and sent back to the Server.
4. The Server performs the following operations:
   (a) Laplace smoothing is applied to each vector $\hat{p}_t(w_i)$ of each worker $w_i \in W_t$.
   (b) The smoothed vectors $\hat{p}_t(w_i)$, for $w_i \in W_t$, are used to create a distance matrix. This matrix is then passed as an input parameter to the predicted function of a Markov clustering. As a result, groups of workers with similar empirical probability vectors are produced, i.e. an initial clustering $C_t = \{C_{t1}, C_{t2}, \ldots, C_{tk}\}$ of the workers is created.
   (c) For each cluster $C_{tj} \in C_t$, $(j = 1, 2, \ldots, k)$, a global group model $\mathcal{M}_t^j$, is built by averaging over the model parameters of the workers assigned to $C_{tj}$, i.e. a set of initial global group models is produced $\{\mathcal{M}_t^j \mid C_{tj} \in C_t\}$.
   (d) For each cluster $C_{tj} \in C_t$ mean data vector $\mu_i^j$ and aggregated variance $\sigma_i^j$ are calculated.
5. The Server aggregates the parameters $\{\mathcal{M}_t^i \mid w_i \in W_t\}$ uploaded by the selected workers $W_t$ to update the global model $\mathcal{M}_t$ through the FedAvg algorithm (Eq. 2).

**Iteration Phase:**

1. The Server sends each group global model $\mathcal{M}_t^j$, $(j = 1, 2, \ldots, k)$ to its group of workers $C_{tj}$.

2. Each worker $w_i \in C_{tj}$ receives the group global model $\mathcal{M}_t^j$ and optimizes its parameters locally, i.e. $\mathcal{M}_{t+1}^i$ local update and the empirical probability vector $\hat{p}_{t+1}(w_i)$ are produced.
3. The Server updates the existing empirical probability vector $\hat{p}_{t+1}(w_i)$ by taking the average of it with the information provided by the previous data batch, i.e. $\hat{p}_t(w_i)$.
4. The Server applies Laplace smoothing to each vector $\hat{p}_{t+1}(w_i)$, for $i = 1, 2, \ldots, |W_t|$.
5. The Server adapts the workers' grouping $C_t$ to the current empirical probability vectors $\hat{p}_{t+1}(w_i)$, for $i = 1, 2, \ldots, |W_t|$, by invoking eccentricity score $\xi^j(w_i)$ (see Eq. 5), $(j = 1, 2, \ldots, k)$ which assesses whether each worker $w_i \in C_{tj}$ is still adequately tight with its current cluster, the one it was assigned at the previous round $(t)$.
   (a) If $\xi^j(w_i)$ is below the threshold $v_j(t)$ (see Eq. 6) the worker does not change its cluster $C_{tj}$.
   (b) If $\xi^j(w_i) > v_j(t)$ then we calculate $\xi^l(w_i)$ for the other clusters, i.e. for each $C_{tl} \in C_t \setminus C_{tj}$, and will assign the worker $w_i$ to the cluster for each $\xi^l(w_i) < v_l(t)$. In case this is true for more than one cluster we will assign the worker to the cluster for which the score is lowest.
   (c) If $\xi^l(w_i) > v_l(t)$ for each cluster $C_{tl} \in C_t \setminus C_{tj}$ then this worker $w_i$ will give the start of a new singleton cluster, which means that this worker $w_i$ cannot be assigned to any existing cluster in $C_t$. Note that $k_{(t+1)} \geq k_t$, where $k_{(t+1)} = |C_{t+1}|$, since new singleton clusters may appear due to the updating operation.
6. For each cluster $C_{t+1j} \in C_{t+1}$, mean data vector $\mu_i^j$ and aggregated variance $\sigma_i^j$ are calculated, considering the current grouping of the workers and also using the current empirical probability vectors $\hat{p}_{t+1}(w_i)$, for $i = 1, 2, \ldots, |W_{t+1}|$. These values of $\mu_i^j$ and $\sigma_i^j$ will be needed at the next round to calculate the workers' eccentricity scores w.r.t. the current clusters.
7. The updated clustering $C_{t+1}$ is produced, and the clusters in $C_{t+1}$ may contain different workers from the clusters in $C_t$.

Steps 1–7 of the *iteration* phase are repeated until a certain number of training rounds $T$ is reached.

## 5   Experimental Design

### 5.1   HAR Datasets

Despite the UCI dataset [31] has been widely used as a benchmark in the HAR domain, this dataset is not realistic, since it is acquired in-lab following strict scenarios [8]. In our study, the experiments are conducted on two realistic, and publicly available datasets: REALWORLD, a large, diverse device positioning dataset [32], and HHAR, a HAR dataset [33].

Each dataset has its own set of activities, as shown in Table 1 with only some overlapping. These datasets deal with various activities: Sit (ST), Stand

**Table 1.** A summary of datasets' properties

| Dataset | Workers | No of data points | Activity | No of classes |
|---------|---------|-------------------|----------|---------------|
| REALWORLD | 15 | 356,427 | (ST,SD,W,U,D,J,L,R) | 8 |
| HHAR | 51 | 85,567 | (ST,SD,W,U,D,BK) | 6 |

(SD), Walk (W), Upstairs (U), Downstairs (D), Bike (BK), Jump (J), Lay (L), Run (R). The partitioning of the data has been performed as follows. For each dataset, 20% is left for testing at the central server, while the remaining 80% is used for training.

Note that the initial clustering of workers (individuals) has been produced by using the MCL algorithm, with parameters inflation 1.7 and threshold 2. The MCL algorithm is implemented in the MCL package in Python.

### 5.2 Evaluation Strategy

As previously explained, the aim of FL over classical learning is the ability to merge several worker models into a global one in order to improve model generalization without degrading specialization. To study and evaluate the performance of the proposed GP-FL algorithm, we have computed and compared three different evaluations calculated for each experiment for each worker's data:

- **Personal performance**: This is evaluated by computing the accuracy or F1 score achieved by the client's local model using its local data.
- **Global performance**: This is evaluated by calculating the accuracy or F1 score produced by the overall global model (aggregating all the clients' models) on each worker's local data.
- **Group performance**: This calculates the accuracy or F1 score achieved by each group global model on the local data of each worker from its group.

For each worker, the dataset is partitioned into a training set and a test set. The test set is used for the local evaluation of each worker's performance. These evaluation results are then aggregated to give the **personal performance** evaluation of each worker. The global model runs individually on each worker test set and then aggregates the obtained F1 scores, which is used to evaluate the **global performance**. Each group global model executes individually on the test set of each worker in the group associated with it to evaluate the **group performance**. In this way, three different models are evaluated on each worker test data, namely the worker locally trained model, the overall global model averaging over the parameters of all workers' local models and the group-personalized model based only on the local models of the workers having similar activity patterns, i.e. ones that are grouped together.

## 6    Experimental Results

We have initially compared the performance of workers' personal (local) models with that of both the traditionally built federated learning (global) model and global group models trained by our GP-FL algorithm. For each experiment, three evaluations have been performed. Namely, the three models (local, global, and group) associated with each worker are run on its test data at each round. The performance of each run is evaluated with respect to accuracy.

In order to illustrate the properties of the clustering scheme proposed in this study, we show in Table 2 the clustering updates in the first 10 global communication rounds of the GP-FL algorithm applied to the REALWORLD dataset. The performance in terms of accuracy of the three models (local (L), global (G), and group (Gr)) associated with each worker are compared in the table. As one can notice in the first round, the 15 workers have been clustered into 5 groups. Namely, "pink" cluster has two workers (1 and 12), "green" cluster has four workers (2, 3, 5, and 15), and the remaining three clusters (i.e. "yellow", "orange" and "blue") each one has three workers. It is interesting to notice that in round 10, worker 1 has moved to the "green" cluster, due to its eccentricity score being higher than the threshold of the "pink" cluster. Therefore, the eccentricity score of this worker has been calculated with respect to each one of the other clusters and as a result, it has been assigned to the "green" cluster.

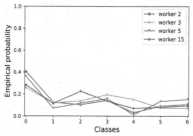 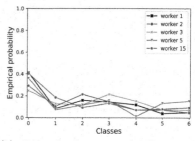

(a) "green" cluster workers' activity profiles at round 1

(b) "green" cluster workers' activity profiles at round 10

**Fig. 2.** Comparison of the workers' activity profiles (empirical probability vectors) distributed in the "green" cluster in the first and tenth rounds, respectively.

The workers' empirical probability vectors distributed in the "green" cluster in the first and tenth rounds, respectively are compared in Fig. 2. As one can see the worker 1 activity pattern in the tenth round is very similar to the other individuals distributed in this cluster, i.e. this is the reason to be moved to the "green" group. We can also observe that worker 8 has similar behavior of changing its cluster from "blue" to "orange". Notice that the clusters presented in Table 2 will continue to be optimized in the same fashion, discussed above, for the upcoming communication rounds. Overall, the group global models built by the GP-FL algorithm have produced accuracy scores that are higher or at least comparable with those generated by the global model as it can be noticed in the tenth round results in Table 2. The results generated on the experimental dataset of HHAR are similar.

**Table 2.** Comparison of the accuracy scores produced by the local (L), global (G), and group global (Gr) models on each worker's data for the conducted training rounds (only the results from the first two and the last two rounds are depicted) using REALWORLD dataset.

|  |  | Workers | | | | | | | | | | | | | | |
|---|---|---|---|---|---|---|---|---|---|---|---|---|---|---|---|---|
|  |  | 1 | 2 | 3 | 4 | 5 | 6 | 7 | 8 | 9 | 10 | 11 | 12 | 13 | 14 | 15 |
|  | L | 0.80 | 0.86 | 0.90 | 0.80 | 0.81 | 0.83 | 0.85 | 0.80 | 0.91 | 0.85 | 0.86 | 0.88 | 0.84 | 0.85 | 0.84 |
| 1 | G | 0.78 | 0.82 | 0.87 | 0.77 | 0.78 | 0.80 | 0.82 | 0.78 | 0.88 | 0.81 | 0.82 | 0.84 | 0.81 | 0.80 | 0.81 |
|  | Gr | 0.79 | 0.84 | 0.88 | 0.79 | 0.80 | 0.81 | 0.82 | 0.79 | 0.89 | 0.81 | 0.83 | 0.81 | 0.81 | 0.82 | 0.80 |
|  | L | 0.86 | 0.85 | 0.83 | 0.86 | 0.88 | 0.86 | 0.85 | 0.85 | 0.88 | 0.87 | 0.87 | 0.85 | 0.86 | 0.85 | 0.86 |
| 2 | G | 0.84 | 0.82 | 0.80 | 0.80 | 0.84 | 0.83 | 0.80 | 0.81 | 0.83 | 0.83 | 0.84 | 0.81 | 0.81 | 0.82 | 0.83 |
|  | Gr | 0.84 | 0.84 | 0.82 | 0.85 | 0.85 | 0.84 | 0.81 | 0.82 | 0.85 | 0.82 | 0.84 | 0.81 | 0.82 | 0.83 | 0.83 |
|  | L | 0.90 | 0.92 | 0.94 | 0.88 | 0.90 | 0.91 | 0.90 | 0.90 | 0.90 | 0.92 | 0.94 | 0.93 | 0.90 | 0.89 | 0.90 |
| 9 | G | 0.89 | 0.88 | 0.90 | 0.84 | 0.86 | 0.87 | 0.88 | 0.85 | 0.84 | 0.89 | 0.90 | 0.90 | 0.85 | 0.86 | 0.85 |
|  | Gr | 0.91 | 0.89 | 0.90 | 0.86 | 0.88 | 0.90 | 0.91 | 0.89 | 0.86 | 0.91 | 0.92 | 0.93 | 0.88 | 0.89 | 0.85 |
|  | L | 0.93 | 0.93 | 0.94 | 0.93 | 0.90 | 0.95 | 0.93 | 0.93 | 0.89 | 0.95 | 0.93 | 0.94 | 0.96 | 0.90 | 0.91 |
| 10 | G | 0.90 | 0.88 | 0.90 | 0.89 | 0.86 | 0.90 | 0.87 | 0.85 | 0.82 | 0.91 | 0.89 | 0.89 | 0.92 | 0.86 | 0.90 |
|  | Gr | 0.91 | 0.90 | 0.91 | 0.90 | 0.88 | 0.92 | 0.89 | 0.88 | 0.86 | 0.93 | 0.90 | 0.92 | 0.94 | 0.87 | 0.94 |

We also compare the performance of our GP-FL algorithm with that of FedAvg and CFL algorithms. The performance of the three compared algorithms has been evaluated by running 3-fold cross-validation on each experimental dataset of REALWORLD and HHAR for 20 communication rounds for Non-IID label skew data (30%). In Fig. 3a, we compare the F1-scores of the three FL approaches in case of the Non-IID data distribution scenario of REALWORLD data. Within 10 communication rounds, CFL and FedAvg reach 88%, and 87% F1-scores, respectively, while our GP-FL algorithm achieves an F1-score of 90% with the same number of communication rounds. Similar to the REALWORLD dataset, we can see in the case of HHAR Non-IID data (Fig. 3b), the GP-FL algorithm has obtained F1-score of 96% in 12 communication rounds, while CFL and FedAvg have reached 95% and 94%, respectively.

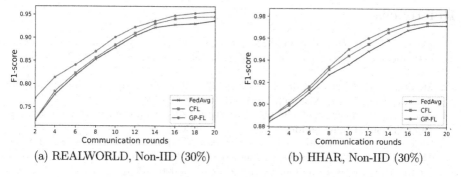

**Fig. 3.** Comparison of the achieved F1 scores versus the number of communication rounds for Non-IID data (30%) of the three FL algorithms: FedAvg, CFL, and GP-FL.

# 7   Conclusion

In this paper, we have proposed a new approach for building a set of group personalized models in case of Non-IID data in federated learning framework. Initially, Markov clustering algorithm is applied to divide the workers into groups according to the similarity between their empirical probability vectors reflecting the distribution of their training examples among the classes. This allows for building a private global model for each cluster of workers. The built global models, each one trained on a group of clients with homogeneous class probability estimations, are adapted at each training round with respect to the new data batches. The performance of the proposed GP-FL algorithm has been studied and evaluated on public HAR data. The obtained results have shown that the global models trained by the GP-FL algorithm can achieve better performance compared with that of the trained overall global model. The algorithm performance is also compared with that of two other baseline FL algorithms, namely FedAvg and CFL. The GP-FL has outperformed both algorithms in the conducted experiments with respect to the achieved performance and convergence speed.

Our future plans include the evaluation and further study of the properties and performance of the proposed GP-FL algorithm in other applied FL scenarios. In addition, we plan to research scenarios in which the recently arrived data batches have a higher importance on the trained group global models than the previous ones.

**Acknowledgements.** We appreciate and thank Emiliano Casalicchio for his support and involvement.

This research was funded partly by the Knowledge Foundation, Sweden, through the Human-Centered Intelligent Realities (HINTS) Profile Project (contract 20220068).

# References

1. Zheng, Q., et al.: Research on hierarchical response recovery method of distribution network fault based on topology analysis. Int. J. Crit. Infrastruct. **17**, 216–236 (2021)
2. McMahan, H.B., et al. Communication-efficient learning of deep networks from decentralized data. arXiv preprint arXiv:1602.05629 (2016)
3. Xia, Q., et al.: A survey of federated learning for edge computing: research problems and solutions. High-Confidence Comput. **1**, 100008 (2021)
4. Zhao, Y., et al.: Federated learning with non-IID data. arXiv:1806.00582 (2018)
5. Mei, C., et al.: C2s: Class-aware client selection for effective aggregation in federated learning. High-Confidence Comput. **2**(3), 100068 (2022)
6. Tan, A.Z., et al.: Towards personalized federated learning. IEEE Trans. Neural Netw. Learn. Syst. (2021)
7. Angelov, P.: Anomaly detection based on eccentricity analysis. In: 2014 IEEE Symposium on Evolving and Autonomous Learning Systems (EALS), pp. 1–8 (2014)
8. Sannara, E., et al.: Evaluation and comparison of federated learning algorithms for human activity recognition on smartphones. Pervasive Mob. Comput. **87**, 101714 (2022)
9. Sannara, E., et al.: Evaluation of federated learning aggregation algorithms: application to human activity recognition. In: ACM International Joint Conference on Pervasive and Ubiquitous Computing, UbiCompISWC 2020 (2020)
10. Sattler, F., et al.: Clustered federated learning: Model-agnostic distributed multitask optimization under privacy constraints. IEEE Trans. Neural Netw. Learn. Syst. **32**(8), 3710–3722 (2021)
11. Liu, S., et al.: Federated personalized random forest for human activity recognition. Math. Biosci. Eng. **19**(1), 953–971 (2022)
12. Bettini, C., et al.: Personalized semi-supervised federated learning for human activity recognition. arXiv:2104.08094 (2021)
13. Yu, H., et al.: FedHAR: semi-supervised online learning for personalized federated human activity recognition. IEEE Trans. Mob. Comput. **22**, 3318–3332 (2021)
14. Shaik, T.B., et al.: FedStack: personalized activity monitoring using stacked federated learning. Knowl. Based Syst. **257**, 109929 (2022)
15. Presotto, R., et al.: Semi-supervised and personalized federated activity recognition based on active learning and label propagation. Pers. Ubiquit. Comput. **26**, 1281–1298 (2022)
16. Tashakori, A., et al.: SemiPFL: personalized semi-supervised federated learning framework for edge intelligence. arXiv:2203.08176 (2022)
17. Presotto, R., et al.: FedCLAR: federated clustering for personalized sensor-based human activity recognition. In: 2022 IEEE International Conference on Pervasive Computing and Communications (PerCom), pp. 227–236 (2022)
18. Presotto, R., et al.: Federated clustering and semi-supervised learning: a new partnership for personalized human activity recognition. Pervasive Mob. Comput. **88**, 101726 (2022)
19. Chen, Y., et al.: FedHealth: a federated transfer learning framework for wearable healthcare. IEEE Intell. Syst. **35**, 83–93 (2019)
20. Lu, W., et al.: Personalized federated learning with adaptive batchnorm for healthcare. IEEE Trans. Big Data (2021)
21. Ma, X., et al.: Tackling personalized federated learning with label concept drift via hierarchical Bayesian modeling. In: Workshop on Federated Learning: Recent Advances and New Challenges (in Conjunction with NeurIPS 2022) (2022)

22. McMahan, H.B., et al.: Federated learning of deep networks using model averaging. arXiv preprint arXiv:1602.05629 (2016)
23. Flach, P.A.: Machine Learning - The Art and Science of Algorithms that Make Sense of Data (2012)
24. van Dongen, S.: Graph clustering by flow simulation (2000)
25. Azad, A., et al.: HipMCL: a high-performance parallel implementation of the Markov clustering algorithm for large-scale networks. Nucleic Acids Res. **46**, e33 (2018)
26. Kolouri, S., et al.: Optimal mass transport: signal processing and machine-learning applications. IEEE Sig. Process. Mag. **34**, 43–59 (2017)
27. Nguyen, V., Duy, L., Takeuchi, I.: Exact statistical inference for the Wasserstein distance by selective inference. Ann. Inst. Stat. Math. **75**, 127–157 (2021)
28. Bezerra, C.G., et al.: An evolving approach to data streams clustering based on typicality and eccentricity data analytics. Inf. Sci. **518**, 13–28 (2020)
29. Saw, J.G., et al.: Chebyshev inequality with estimated mean and variance. Am. Stat. **38**, 130–132 (1984)
30. Škrjanc, I., et al.: Evolving fuzzy and neuro-fuzzy approaches in clustering, regression, identification, and classification: a survey. Inf. Sci. **490**, 344–368 (2019)
31. Anguita, D., et al.: A public domain dataset for human activity recognition using smartphones. In: The European Symposium on Artificial Neural Networks (2013)
32. Sztyler, T., Stuckenschmidt, H.: On-body localization of wearable devices: an investigation of position-aware activity recognition. In: 2016 IEEE International Conference on Pervasive Computing and Communications (PerCom), pp. 1–9 (2016)
33. Stisen, A., et al.: Smart devices are different: assessing and mitigating mobile sensing heterogeneities for activity recognition. In: Proceedings of the 13th ACM Conference on Embedded Networked Sensor Systems (2015)

# Modeling Others as a Player in Non-cooperative Game for Multi-agent Coordination

Junjie Zhong$^{(\boxtimes)}$ and Toshiharu Sugawara

Waseda University, 3-4-1 Okubo, Shinjuku-ku, Tokyo 169-8555, Japan
`j.zhong@isl.cs.waseda.ac.jp`

**Abstract.** An *modeling other agents* (MOA) constructs a model of other agents in every agent. It enables the agents to predict the actions of other agents and achieve coordinated and effective interactions in multi-agent systems. However, the relationship between the executed and predicted actions of agents is vague and diverse. To clarify the relationship, we proposed a method by which an agent through communications constructs its MOA using the historical data of other agents and asymmetrically treats itself and its MOA in a non-cooperative game to obtain *Stackelberg equilibrium* (SE). Subsequently, the SE are used to choose actions. We experimentally demonstrated that, in a partially observable and mixed cooperative-competitive environment, agents using our method with reinforcement learning could establish better coordination and engage in behaviors that are more appropriate compared to conventional methods. We then analyzed the coordinated interaction structure generated in the trained network to clarify the relationship between individual agents.

**Keywords:** game theory · multi-agent reinforcement learning · modeling other agents

## 1 Introduction

Many real-world interaction problems such as vehicle movements on highways, can be considered as coordination problems between self-interested agents. However, achieving coordination between the agents is usually challenging owing to partial observation and limited information exchange [21]. Recent developments in deep learning have facilitated the investigation on using multi-agent deep reinforcement learning (MADRL) with deep neural networks (DNNs) [11] to generate effective coordinated behaviors. For example, a *multiagent bidirectionally-coordinated net* (BiCNet) [14] employs a bidirectional *recurrent neural networks* (RNN) [17] to process hidden states that contain the historical data of the agents to determine their actions. A *deep reinforcement opponent network* (DRON) [4] has a specific module for *modeling other agents* (MOA) to help the agents make decisions. However, these approaches remain open questions because a holistic analysis of their efficiencies is hindered by uninterpretable outputs from DNNs. Thus, there is a lack of sufficient insights into mutual modeling and the coordination/cooperative structure.

© The Author(s), under exclusive license to Springer Nature Switzerland AG 2023
L. Iliadis et al. (Eds.): EANN 2023, CCIS 1826, pp. 520–531, 2023.
https://doi.org/10.1007/978-3-031-34204-2_42

Identifying the complex relationships between agents is crucial for understanding interaction structures and establishing multi-agent coordination and competition in practical problems [7]. Game theory can be applied to derive *solution concepts* that describe the strategies that agents should adopt [24], such as the *Nash equilibrium* (NE) for non-cooperative settings [6] and the *Stackelberg equilibrium* (SE) [25], which provides potentially better solutions than NE. With MADRL networks, techniques such as *centralized training with decentralized execution* [13] and DNN-based *function approximations* can be employed to solve game-theoretic problems that model large-scale real-world problems. In identical-interest settings such as a *team game* [18], the Qmix algorithm [15] can be employed to learn Q-function factorization to enable agents to collaborate for their shared or non-conflicting goals. In StarCraft [23], a well-studied two-player zero-sum game, self-playing generates a sequence of strong opponents [10] that train an agent to reach the top level. However, in general, an agent's objectives may not remain consistent and vary within a broad spectrum between cooperative and competitive relationships. Moremore, considering the actions of other agents in the complex interaction structure entails the issues of combinatorial complexity, partial observability, and non-stationarity [21], leading the MADRL approach to rely on impractical assumptions such as perfect observation, including that on other agents' decisions [25].

To clarify an agents' action-generation process by considering the coordination structure between the agents' actions, we propose the method, *modeling others as a player* (MOP), which enables an agent to build through communications an MOA using the historical data of other agents. We assume that each agent treats itself and its MOA asymmetrically in a non-cooperative game to obtain its SEs. The SEs so obtained are fed to another network of the agent to choose the agent's actions. We evaluated the effectiveness of the proposed method in a *partially observable* and mixed cooperative-competitive environment [13]. We set a scenario involving non-cooperative but partially cooperative objectives between agents and their MOAs and investigated whether MOP could identify their relationships and mitigate non-stationarity to achieve better-coordinated behaviors. We also introduced a few reward schemes that reflected the internal coordination between the agent and its associated MOA. Our experimental results show that MOP outperforms state-of-the-art methods, namely single-agent reinforcement learning (RL) method, *proximal policy optimization* (PPO) [16] with/without communications and the most relevant MOA method *influential communication* (IC) [8]. Moreover, MOP can select more appropriate behaviors than those selected by the above methods. This provides us with a better insight into the estimated coordination structure and the executed actions.

## 2    Related Work

Many studies have attempted to mitigate the non-stationarity issue by enabling agents to learn in fully or partially observable environments through communication. For example, Sukhbaatar et al. [20] proposed a model based on full observations, the *communication neural net* (CommNet), consisting of agent networks that exchange messages to learn the way agents communicate to perform cooperative tasks. Some studies reported that exchanging the hidden states of an RNN [17] that contained an agents' historical information was effective for generating appropriate coordinated/competitive activities. For example, Jaques et al. [8] proposed a model based on *social influence*, in which every agent received messages from all other agents and fed the messages into a local RNN to generate subsequent messages. BiCNet [14] builds a communication channel using the hidden layer of a bi-directional RNN for taking appropriate decisions. However, their works assumed a centralized control wherein all agents must participate in shared communications to learn policies. This makes it difficult to sufficiently analyze a large amount of shared information and identify inter-agent relationships. To tackle such a scalability problem, we have designed MOP that processes historical information only from a limited number of agents.

MOA appears to be the primary means by which agents can predict the behaviors of other agents via models [1]. He et al. [4] proposed a new module, DRON, consisting of multiple networks for inferring the possible actions of other agents. Hong et al. proposed the *deep policy inference Q-network* [5] to learn suitable Q-functions using the feature representation of other agents' actions. These approaches require full observability because the actions of other agents must be inferred by observing the agents; therefore, the approaches cannot fully be employed in a partially observable environment. Albrecht et al. surveyed *policy reconstruction* [1] methods that leveraged machine learning techniques to compensate for missing information using the interaction of historical data. In our method, a part of the historical data only from the closest or surrounding agents is leveraged to construct an MOA in a partially observable environment.

MOA and the associated learning and communicating methods rely on the representational power of a DNN; however, the coordination and cooperative structures lack interpretability. Recently, game theory has provided solution concepts [24] for MADRL-based models and has yielded promising results in two-player zero-sum games or identical-interest games. In a study, *policy-space response oracles* [10] were leveraged to solve the zero-sum game StarCraft [23]. In an identical-interest setting, Rashid et al. [15] proposed an algorithm based on *Qmix* to learn Q-function factorization to solve team games. In contrast, general-sum games that partly contain cooperative and competitive relationships require strong assumptions. For example, *Nash-Q learning* [6] requires unique NEs in each stage of a *stochastic game* (SG). Using recently developed DNNs, some studies adopted the SE [22] as the solution concept and leveraged the use of leader-follower relationships. Zhang et al. proposed a MADRL-based *bi-level-actor-critic* [25] method and showed that an SE was likely to be Pareto superior to NE in general-sum games. However, their methods require treating homogeneous agents in different ways and allowing asynchronous decisions based on observations shared with all agents. In this study, we introduce an asymmetric SE-based leader-follower relationship between the agent and its internal MOA. SE is then used to decide the final actions in the game processes. We set different objectives to the agents and their MOAs to describe their various relationships and provide effective information for their decisions.

## 3   Background

### 3.1   Markov Game and MARL

An $N$-*player Markov game* (also known as an SG) [12] is a dynamic game played by $N$ ($> 0$) players (agents) in a finite set $\mathcal{A} = \{1, 2, \ldots, N\}$. The game involves multiple states traversed in discrete-time $t \geq 0$. It can be described by tuple $\langle \mathcal{A}, A, S, P, R, \gamma \rangle$, where $A = A_1 \times \cdots \times A_N$ is the joint action space consisting of $A_i$, the set of actions of $i \in \mathcal{A}$. $S$ is the possible state space shared by all agents. $P : S \times A \to S$ is a deterministic transition function in $S$, and $r_i : S \times A \to \mathbb{R}$ is $i$'s reward function. We focus on MADRL in the game, in which the objective of the $N$ agents is to find a joint policy $\pi = \pi_1 \times \cdots \times \pi_N$ that maximizes their individual discounted cumulative reward, $\sum_{t=0} \gamma^t r_i(s^t, a^t)$. Here, $\pi_i : S \to \mathcal{D}_{\mathcal{P}}(A_i)$ and $\mathcal{D}_{\mathcal{P}}(X)$ is the probability distribution space over discrete set $X$.

### 3.2   Bi-level Actor-Critic

A *bi-level actor-critic* [25] algorithm assumes that two agents, the leader ($L$) and follower ($F$) in a two-player Markov game, are asymmetric. That is, although they share the same observations $o_t \in \mathcal{O}$ at $t$, $F$ observes the actions of $L$, $a_t^L$, to determine its actions, $a_t^F$, as the response to $a_t^L$. However, $L$ must predict action $a_t^F$ using the learned policy $\pi_F$ of $F$ as follows.

$$a_t^L \leftarrow \underset{a \in A_L}{\arg\max} \, Q_L(o_t, (a, a^f|_{\sim \pi_F(o_t, a)})) \text{ and } a_t^F \sim \pi_F(o_t, a_t^L), \qquad (1)$$

where $a^f|_{\sim \pi_F(o_t, a)}$ indicates the sampled action $a^f$ that is selected according to $\pi_F(o_t, a_t^L) \in \mathcal{D}_{\mathcal{P}}(A_F)$, and $A_F$ and $A_L$ are the sets of actions of $F$ and $L$, respectively. The action of $L$, $a_t^L \in A_L$, is a part of states for policy function $\pi_F$ of $F$, while the leader $L$ is a Q-learner of the action-value function $Q_L$ over $\mathcal{O} \times A$ (where $A = A_L \times A_F$) and updated by a method such as *soft Q-learning* [3]. $Q_L$ evaluates the cumulative reward $r_{i,L} : S \times A \to \mathbb{R}$ by taking the joint action $(a, a^f|_{\sim \pi_F(o_t, a)})$ according to the observation $o_t$. Subsequently, $L$ chooses an action $a_t^L \in A_L$ whose $Q_L$ is the highest. Next, $a_f^F$ is sampled using $\pi_F(o_t, a_t^L)$. The bi-level actor-critic method was proposed to solve the bi-level optimization problem [19] in a Markov game, which is also known as a *Stackelberg game*. The upper-level and lower-level optimizers are the leader and follower agents, respectively, and its solution is an SE. This SE is the joint action $(a_t^L, a_t^F)$, where $F$ samples action $a_t^F$ according to $L$'s action $a_t^L$ and observation $o_t$.

### 3.3   Two-Player Non-cooperative Game with MOA

Although agents may have inconsistent objectives in a non-cooperative game, they attempt to maximize their own rewards independently without forming coalitions to make collective decisions [24]. Agent $\forall i \in \mathcal{A}$ uses the MOA to predict the actions of other agents in $\mathcal{A} \setminus \{i\}$. We regard an $N$-player non-cooperative game as a two-player non-cooperative game between $i$ and $i$'s MOA. Among the various solution concepts available for MADRL-based non-cooperative two-player games, such as NE, we adopted SE as our solution concept. SE considers an asymmetric relationship between a leader and follower by setting $i$ as the leader and $i$'s MOA as the follower as described in Sect. 4.2. SE often exhibits a better performance than NE in terms of Pareto superiority. Moreover, while multiple NEs often exist, SE is usually unique except under rare conditions [25].

## 4 Proposed Method

### 4.1 MOA with Historical Information

We describe the proposed method, which can be used in a partially observable environment for analyzing a non-cooperative game. Each agent has a leader and a follower networks. During an asymmetric game, its follower network generates the representative action of other agents according to the MOA. The action is then fed to its leader network to output the action. Jiang et al. claimed that information from various agents differ in importance and that the information from nearby agents was more useful in decision-making [9]. Therefore, in our proposed method, agent $i \in \mathcal{A}$ requests and receives the historical information of the *closest* agent $j \in \mathcal{A}$. We assume that the *historical information* of an agent is included in the hidden state of the RNN [17] of the agent and can be processed by all agents. The received historical information helps in constructing the MOA and thus deciding the next actions. In MOP, $i$'s follower network processes the hidden state of $j$'s leader network and then updates the MOA.

Figure 1 shows the proposed network architecture consisting of the leader and follower networks of agent $i$. At time $t$, $i$ feeds the partial observation $o_t^i$ and the hidden state $h_{t-1}^{j,L}$ of $j$'s leader network at $t-1$ to its follower network. The leader and follower networks contain *gated recurrent units* (GRU) [2], which is a type of RNN. The hidden state $h_{t-1}^{j,L}$ represents $j$'s history information at $t-1$ and is used to update the hidden state of $i$'s follower network, $h_{t-1}^{i,F}$. This hidden state indirectly includes the historical information of other (far-away) agents interacting with $i$ in the past, as well as $i$'s own information. Subsequently, $i$'s follower network updates the hidden state $h_t^{i,F}$ according to $h_{t-1}^{j,L}$ and $h_{t-1}^{i,F}$ and outputs the policy $\pi_F(o_t^i, a_t^i) \in \mathcal{D}_{\mathcal{P}}(A_F)$. Next, the action in $A_F$ is sampled using $\pi_F(o_t^i, a_t^i)$ and fed to $i$'s policy network.

This information-sharing pattern in which agents receive the information only from the closest agent reduces the effort required to understand far-away agents and can improve scalability and communication efficiency.

### 4.2 Markov Game with MOA

The agent and its MOA do not necessarily determine their actions simultaneously in a game round because only actions from the leader network are actually

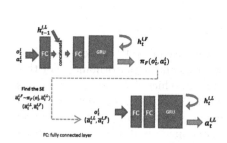

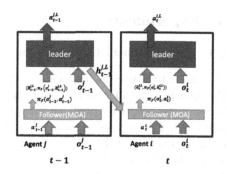

**Fig. 1.** Leader (down) and follower (up) networks in agent $i$.

**Fig. 2.** Information sharing within and among agent models.

considered to interact with other agents; therefore, the MOA is an auxiliary component for determining actions. In MOP, the follower network functions just as a collector and provider of information about other agents, and the SE of the game is treated as a high-dimensional input of the leader network. The follower network must also be optimized using a reward function although it does not proactively interact with other agents. Agents identify the relationships between leaders and other agents and engage in proper interactions by setting reward schemes for individual goals. The leader and follower networks process the reward functions to learn non-cooperative games.

Following the conventions adopted for bi-level actor-critic networks (Sect. 3.2), we denote the leader policy and follower policy of agent $i$ as $\pi_L^i$ and $\pi_F^i$, respectively. $\pi_L^i$ is trained using the action-value inferred by the leader's action-value function $Q_L^i$ and $\pi_F^i$ is trained using the follower's action-value function $Q_F^i$. The PPO [16], an actor-critic approach, is used to train stochastic policies and action-value functions in the proposed method. The flow of information within and among agent models is shown in Fig. 2; see also Fig. 1. The process of deciding $i$'s action $a_t^{i,L}$ is described as follows.

$$\overline{a}_t^{i,L} \leftarrow \underset{a_t^i \in A_L}{\arg\max}\, Q_L^i(o_t^i, (a_t^i, a_t^{i,F}|_{\pi_F(o_t^i, a_t^i)})), \quad a_t^{i,F} \sim \pi_F(o_t^i, a_t^i)$$

$$\overline{a}_t^{i,F} \sim \pi_F^i(o_t^i, \overline{a}_t^{i,L}) \text{ and } a_t^{i,L} \sim \pi_L^i(o_t^i, (\overline{a}_t^{i,L}, \overline{a}_t^{i,F})),$$

First, the partial observation $o_t^i$, the hidden state of the closest agent $j$'s leader network $h_{t-1}^{j,L}$, and the leader's action $\forall a_t^i \in A_L$ are fed to the follower's policy network at $t$, which outputs $\pi_F$ whose domain is $\mathcal{D}_\mathcal{P}(A_F)$. Next, using the leader's action-value function $Q_L^i$ and $\pi_F^i$, $i$ generates the SE, $(\overline{a}_t^{i,L}, \overline{a}_t^{i,F})$, which is the joint action corresponding to the highest value of $Q_L^i$ and the observation $o_t^i$. The SE is then fed into the leader network. Finally, agent $i$ takes the action $a_t^{i,L}$, which is sampled using $\pi_L(o_t^i, (\overline{a}_t^{i,L}, \overline{a}_t^{i,F}))$ by assuming that it is the probability distribution over $A_L$.

# 5  Experiments

## 5.1  Experimental Environment

We conducted experiments to assess the performance of MOP-based agents and the influence of leader and follower reward schemes on the performance. For this purpose, we adopted a predator-prey environment, which was used in a previous study [13]. It is a two-dimensional environment $\mathbb{R} \times \mathbb{R}$ in continuous space and discrete time. It consists of $N + 1$ agents (one prey and $N$ predator agents) and a few obstacles (see Fig. 4). The agents' action space is discrete, and at each time step, they decide to accelerate in one of the following directions: *up*, *down*, *left*, and *right*, or *null* (no acceleration). The prey and predators have maximum speeds of 1.3 and 1.0 unit distance per time step $(d/s)$ and constant accelerations of 4.0 and 3.0 d/s$^2$, respectively. The combinations of these values mean that the prey and predator always move with maximum speeds.

Let $\mathcal{A}$ assume the set of $N$ predators (agents). Agents can make only partial observations, including the relative positions of obstacles, the relative positions and velocities of the closest three agents and then decide their actions synchronously. If predator $i \in \mathcal{A}$ hits the prey at $t$, $i$ receives reward of $r_t^i = 1$, whereas the prey is penalized with $r_t^{prey} = -1$. Therefore, the predators have a non-cooperative relationship because they may collide with each other and impede their approach to the prey while competing to hit the prey first. However, they need to learn some degree of coordination to hit the prey, which is faster than they are.

As the prey is faster and can escape to infinity, we introduced another reward $r_t^{dist} \geq 0$ for every time step to the prey to restrain its movements to be near the origin of the environment while avoiding being hit; hence, the closer the prey is to the origin, the higher the $r_t^{dist}$ [13]. We defined $r_t^{dist} = -f(x) - f(y)$, where $(x, y)$ is the prey's coordinates; $f(a) = 0$ if $a \leq 0.9$ and $f(a) = a - 0.9$ if $0.9 \leq a \leq 1$. Otherwise, $f(a) = min(0.1 \times e^{2a-2}, 1)$. We then verified that different numbers of predators could exhibit coordinated behaviors in the environment using the proposed method.

In the experiment, the prey learns the policy $\pi_{prey}$ using PPO [16], which is a state-of-the-art RL algorithm. We compared the performances of the proposed model with those of the baseline methods for the predators, (1) PPO wherein no explicit communication existed between the predators and (2) *influential communication* (IC) [8], which is based on MOA and a centralized communication mechanism. To understand the effect of sharing *historical information* on the performance of agents, we also examined the performance under a PPO method that allowed communications, which is denoted by PPOwH. A predator $i \in \mathcal{A}$ under PPOwH has no follower network and only a leader network $\pi_{pred}^i$ whose architecture is identical to that shown in Fig. 1. In each time step, the predator obtains the hidden state from the GRU of the closet predator and feeds it to the leader network.

The leader network $\pi_L^i$ of predator $\forall i \in \mathcal{A}$ is trained using the reward $r_t^i$, as mentioned above. As described in Sect. 4.2, the relationship between the follower (the MOA) and leader networks represents the internal relationship with other predators. Therefore, we introduced three types of rewards for training the follower networks to learn the policy $\pi_F^i$ under different relationships. The rewards $r_t^{i,F_n}$, $r_t^{i,F_t}$, and $r_t^{i,F_s}$ are defined using equations Eqs. 2b, 2c, and 2d, respectively.

$$adv_t^L = Q_L(o_t, (a_t^{i,L}, a_t^{i,F})) - V_L(o_t), \tag{2a}$$

$$r_t^{i,F_n} = r_t^i - adv_t^L, \tag{2b}$$

$$r_t^{i,F_t} = \sum_{i=1}^{N} r_t^i, \text{ and} \tag{2c}$$

$$r_t^{i,F_s} = r_t^i \tag{2d}$$

where $adv_t^L$ is the *advantage* of $i$'s action $a_t^L$ inferred by $i$'s leader network for $\pi_L^i$; $V_L(o_t)$ is the *expected value of state* when $o_t$ is observed; $Q_L(o_t, (a_t^L, a_t^F))$ is the leader's *value of action*.

When the reward $r_t^{i,F_n}$ is used (hereafter denoted by MOP1), the follower network needs to maximize its own reward $r_t^i$ and minimize the advantage of the leader network $\pi_L^i$ to learn $\pi_F^i$. We assume that the proposed method adopts the rewards $r_t^{i,F_n}$ (MOP1) because of the balanced decisions between leader and follower networks for their activities. When predators use the reward $r_t^{i,F_t}$, which is denoted by MOP2, the follower networks learn $\pi_F^i$ to maximize the sum of rewards for all predator agents, $\sum_{i\in\mathcal{A}} r_t^i$, rather than considering only its own reward. Reward $r_t^{i,F_s}$ (denoted by MOP3) is inspired by team games [24] performed by cooperative agents. Hence, improving the individual rewards improves the overall performance via shared reward functions. These rewards may lead to competitive situations in our game setting.

We compared the performance under $N = 3$ and 6. The number of preys was fixed at one. The following section describes the average results obtained from 14 experimental runs until 5000 episodes, where one episode length consisted of 150 time steps.

## 5.2   Experimental Results

**Performance Analysis:** We first show the performance of predators, i.e., the total rewards that all predators received per episode, to understand the coordination capability. The results are plotted in Fig. 3a ($N = 3$) and Fig. 3b ($N = 6$).

As evident from the graphs, the predator agents using MOP1 outperform those using the baseline methods and those using MOP under other reward schemes (MOP2 and MOP3). In the simplest case ($N = 3$), agents using the PPOwH scheme obtained a higher total reward than the agents using the baseline methods (25 to 20 per episode). It implies that the historical data are important for achieving some degree of coordinated behaviors. However, sharing historical data alone cannot achieve excellent performance for the more complicated case under $N = 6$; the model performance was nearly the same as that observed

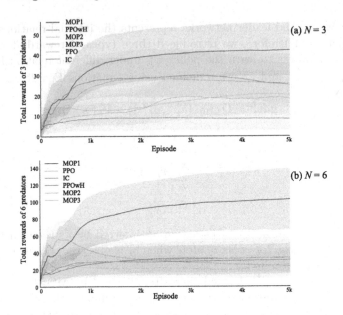

**Fig. 3.** Total reward per episode ($N = 3, 6$).

under PPO and IC because the volume of historical data increases rapidly with the increase in the number of agents. Therefore, the scalability problem resulted in ineffective learning.

Predator agents using MOP with the follower reward schemes MOP2 and MOP3 also exhibit a poor performance, especially at $N = 6$, because these reward schemes attempt to increase the own leader's rewards, which results in competitive situations that are partly inconsistent with the actual game structure. Figure 3a also shows that agents using the MOP3 scheme exhibit a better performance than those using the baseline methods, IC and PPO; however, the performance is poorer than that of agents using MOP2, probably due to more competitive behavior. In contrast, predators using the MOP1 scheme can coordinate behaviors by setting the reward to maximize its own reward $r_t^i$ while preventing the leader network from being selfish and choosing actions that minimize the advantage of the leader networks of all agents.

**Analysis of Behaviors:** To understand why the performance of predator agents using the MOP1, MOP2, and MOP3 schemes differed significantly, we examined the predator movements. Figure 4 shows the representative formation patterns of predators under the three reward schemes. First, as shown in Fig. 4a and 4b, predators using the MOP1 scheme always make tacit coordinated movements around the prey to respond to the prey's speed and yet follow the prey's escape movements. These predators require some cooperation to hit the prey, although the reward is exclusive. Figure 4a and 4b indicate that a balance of

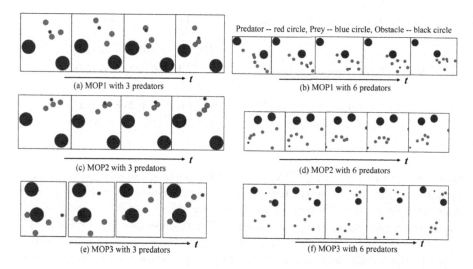

Predator -- red circle, Prey -- blue circle, Obstacle -- black circle

(a) MOP1 with 3 predators

(b) MOP1 with 6 predators

(c) MOP2 with 3 predators

(d) MOP2 with 6 predators

(e) MOP3 with 3 predators

(f) MOP3 with 6 predators

**Fig. 4.** Formation pattern of predators and prey in environment with obstacles.

cooperative and competitive behavior can be achieved using MOP under an appropriate reward scheme (MOP1), which result in high performance.

In contrast, as shown in Fig. 4e and 4f, predators under the MOP3 scheme exhibit insufficient learning because the predators cannot surround the prey and adequately follow the prey's faster movements. Figure 4c and 4d shows that almost all predators using MOP2 can follow the prey but cannot establish coordinated behaviors to surround the prey. Furthermore, Figs. 4d and 4f indicate that some predators ignore the prey and always move far away from it. These behaviors are learned because (1) predators using the MOP2 scheme can gain rewards without moving if others hit the prey and (2) only few predators using the MOP3 scheme can learn efficient behaviors and others do not have sufficient learning opportunities.

**Analysis of SE in MOP:** To investigate the relationship between SE and the chosen actions, and the performance with the trained MOP, we conducted 20 episodes for each of the two experiments after training and calculated the averages of the received rewards. Note that in the MOP method, SE, $(\overline{a}_t^{i,L}, \overline{a}_t^{i,F}) \in A$, is input to the leader network, which then outputs the action $a_t^{i,L}$ based on which agents interact. Therefore, we compared the total rewards when predators took $a_t^{i,L}$ with those when they took $\overline{a}_t^{i,L}$ from the SE. We also examined the rate at which action $\overline{a}_t^{i,L}$ was taken (i.e., $a_t^{i,L} = \overline{a}_t^{i,L}$). The results are listed in Table 1.

As shown in Table 1, in all cases, the total rewards when predators take the action $\overline{a}_t^{i,L}$ are much smaller than that when they take the final output $a_t^{i,L}$. Therefore, the rate at which the predators take the SE action ($a_t^{i,L} = \overline{a}_t^{i,L}$) is very small. Predators are awarded a higher reward when they take the SE action $\overline{a}_t^{i,L}$ under MOP1 compared to that observed under other reward schemes, indicating

**Table 1.** Comparison between SE $(\overline{a}_t^{i,L})$ and executed actions $(a_t^{i,L})$.

|  |  | MOP1 | MOP2 | MOP3 |
|---|---|---|---|---|
| $N = 3$ | Total rewards $(\overline{a}_t^{i,L}/a_t^{i,L})$ | 1.8/47.4 | 0.9/22.8 | 0.75/15.45 |
|  | Number of cases of $a_t^{i,L} = \overline{a}_t^{i,L}$ | 12.4% | 15.1% | 15.7% |
| $N = 6$ | Total rewards $(\overline{a}_t^{i,L}/a_t^{i,L})$ | 10.5/111.6 | 5.4/25.8 | 8.1/27.6 |
|  | Number of cases of $a_t^{i,L} = \overline{a}_t^{i,L}$ | 16.7% | 17.7% | 18.6% |

that the follower network (MOA) with MOP1 depicts the relationship among predator agents more closely than other models. Because the follower network does not interact directly with other agents, the SE action $\overline{a}_t^{i,L}$ is used only to choose the better response $a_t^{i,L}$ as shown in Fig. 1; subsequently, $i$ executes $a_t^{i,L}$. Therefore, the SE action $\overline{a}_t^{i,L}$ cannot be used to interact directly with others owing to the locally defined reward scheme but it carries useful information to decide better actions.

## 6    Conclusion

In this paper, we proposed the method of MOP, which uses historical data only from the closest agent and asymmetrically treats the owner agent as a leader network and the MOA as a follower network for a non-cooperative game. We conducted experiments in an environment with different number of agents. The proposed method identified the interaction structure between agents and exhibited a better performance than conventional methods with or without communications and the most relevant MOA method, IC. We also investigated the difference between SE actions and executed actions. In our future work, we aim to confirm the performance of our method in games of complicated structures.

## References

1. Albrecht, S.V., Stone, P.: Autonomous agents modelling other agents: a comprehensive survey and open problems. Artif. Intell. **258**, 66–95 (2018)
2. Cho, K., et al.: Learning phrase representations using RNN encoder-decoder for statistical machine translation. In: Proceedings of the 2014 Conference on Empirical Methods in Natural Language Processing (EMNLP), pp. 1724–1734 (2014)
3. Haarnoja, T., Tang, H., Abbeel, P., Levine, S.: Reinforcement learning with deep energy-based policies. In: International Conference on Machine Learning, pp. 1352–1361. PMLR (2017)
4. He, H., Boyd-Graber, J., Kwok, K., Daumé III, H.: Opponent modeling in deep reinforcement learning. In: International Conference on Machine Learning, pp. 1804–1813. PMLR (2016)
5. Hong, Z.W., Su, S.Y., Shann, T.Y., Chang, Y.H., Lee, C.Y.: A deep policy inference Q-network for multi-agent systems. arXiv preprint arXiv:1712.07893 (2017)

6. Hu, J., Wellman, M.P.: Nash Q-learning for general-sum stochastic games. J. Mach. Learn. Res. **4**, 1039–1069 (2003)
7. Huhns, M.N.: Distributed Artificial Intelligence: Volume I. Elsevier (1987)
8. Jaques, N., et al.: Social influence as intrinsic motivation for multi-agent deep reinforcement learning. In: International Conference on Machine Learning, pp. 3040–3049. PMLR (2019)
9. Jiang, J., Lu, Z.: Learning attentional communication for multi-agent cooperation. In: Advances in Neural Information Processing Systems, vol. 31 (2018)
10. Lanctot, M., et al.: A unified game-theoretic approach to multiagent reinforcement learning. In: Advances in Neural Information Processing Systems, vol. 30 (2017)
11. LeCun, Y., Bengio, Y., Hinton, G.: Deep learning. Nature **521**(7553), 436–444 (2015)
12. Littman, M.L.: Markov games as a framework for multi-agent reinforcement learning. In: Machine Learning Proceedings 1994, pp. 157–163. Elsevier (1994)
13. Lowe, R., Wu, Y.I., Tamar, A., Harb, J., Pieter Abbeel, O., Mordatch, I.: Multi-agent actor-critic for mixed cooperative-competitive environments. In: Advances in Neural Information Processing Systems, vol. 30 (2017)
14. Peng, P., et al.: Multiagent bidirectionally-coordinated nets: emergence of human-level coordination in learning to play StarCraft combat games. arXiv preprint arXiv:1703.10069 (2017)
15. Rashid, T., Samvelyan, M., De Witt, C.S., Farquhar, G., Foerster, J., Whiteson, S.: Monotonic value function factorisation for deep multi-agent reinforcement learning. J. Mach. Learn. Res. **21**(1), 1–51 (2020)
16. Schulman, J., Wolski, F., Dhariwal, P., Radford, A., Klimov, O.: Proximal policy optimization algorithms. arXiv preprint arXiv:1707.06347 (2017)
17. Schuster, M., Paliwal, K.K.: Bidirectional recurrent neural networks. IEEE Trans. Sig. Process. **45**(11), 2673–2681 (1997)
18. Semsar-Kazerooni, E., Khorasani, K.: Multi-agent team cooperation: a game theory approach. Automatica **45**(10), 2205–2213 (2009)
19. Sinha, A., Malo, P., Deb, K.: A review on bilevel optimization: from classical to evolutionary approaches and applications. IEEE Trans. Evol. Comput. **22**(2), 276–295 (2017)
20. Sukhbaatar, S., Fergus, R., et al.: Learning multiagent communication with backpropagation. In: Advances in Neural Information Processing Systems, vol. 29 (2016)
21. Tuyls, K., Weiss, G.: Multiagent learning: basics, challenges, and prospects. AI Mag. **33**(3), 41 (2012)
22. Von Stackelberg, H.: Market Structure and Equilibrium. Springer, Heidelberg (2010). https://doi.org/10.1007/978-3-642-12586-7
23. Wang, X., et al.: SCC: an efficient deep reinforcement learning agent mastering the game of StarCraft II. In: International Conference on Machine Learning, pp. 10905–10915. PMLR (2021)
24. Yang, Y., Wang, J.: An overview of multi-agent reinforcement learning from game theoretical perspective. arXiv preprint arXiv:2011.00583 (2020)
25. Zhang, H., et al.: Bi-level actor-critic for multi-agent coordination. In: The 34th AAAI Conference on Artificial Intelligence, pp. 7325–7332. AAAI Press (2020)

# Neural Network Bootstrap Forecast Distributions with Extreme Learning Machines

Michele La Rocca[iD] and Cira Perna[(✉)][iD]

Department of Economics and Statistics, University of Salerno, via Giovanni Paolo II, 132, 84084 Fisciano, SA, Italy
{larocca,perna}@unisa.it

**Abstract.** This paper proposes and discusses a new procedure to estimate the forecast distribution for nonlinear autoregressive time series. The approach employs a feed-forward neural network estimated using extreme learning machines (ELMs) to approximate the original nonlinear process and the pair bootstrap as a resampling device. Compared with conventional neural network algorithms, ELMs have substantial advantages such as fast learning speed and ease of implementation. Moreover, they are particularly useful in all cases which require real-time retraining of the network, significantly reducing the computational problems of the bootstrap procedure. The proposed approach is instrumental in all applications where time series should be longer to justify using complex neural network models, such as LSTM or other deep learning approaches. This is the case, for example, of economic time series, where it is rare to find time series longer than a few hundred-time points. The results of a Monte Carlo simulation experiment show that ELMs can significantly reduce the computational burden of the overall procedure while preserving the good accuracy of completely tuned neural networks.

**Keywords:** ELM · Bootstrap · Forecast densities · Nonlinear time series

## 1 Introduction

Forecasts of the future values of time series are widely used in decision-making. Recently, increasing emphasis has been given to estimating forecasting densities [1], defined as an estimate of the probability distribution of future values, which provides a complete description of the uncertainty associated with the point forecast. When a closed form does not exist for the predictive distribution or its parameters are a complex nonlinear function of the data, non-parametric techniques must be implemented (see [2] and the references therein).

Recently, a new approach has been proposed in [3] where feed-forward neural networks (NN), used to approximate the original nonlinear process and derive valid point forecasts, are combined with a resampling technique to estimate the forecast distribution. Neural network models show clear advantages over other nonparametric techniques, usually based on local polynomial regressions. Firstly,

L. Iliadis et al. (Eds.): EANN 2023, CCIS 1826, pp. 532–547, 2023.
https://doi.org/10.1007/978-3-031-34204-2_43

they are global non-parametric estimators of the data-generating process, providing an accurate approximation to almost any unknown target function of interest. Secondly, they show good forecasting performance with high accuracy. Thirdly, they can handle the curse of dimensionality that affects other nonparametric techniques. A standard neural network model should be preferred when dealing with short time series (usually available in economics or banking and insurance applications) where highly complex neural networks such as LSTM, CNN or other deep structures cannot be easily justified due to lack of information. Moreover, the forecasting distribution is estimated using a bootstrap resampling scheme which is distribution-independent and accounts for model estimation uncertainty. However, bootstrap requires thousands of replicates to estimate accurately the forecast densities, which in turn requires thousand of network training and meta parameters tuning, which makes the overall process soon unfeasible when deep learning is involved. The overall procedure delivers accurate and consistent results for pure autoregressive dependent structures. It is model-free within a general class of nonlinear autoregression processes. It avoids the specification of a finite-dimensional model for the data-generating process, a challenging task when dealing with nonlinearities of the unknown form [3]. However, despite the optimal theoretical properties of the procedure, bootstrapping NNs joins together two computer-intensive procedures. That leads to a computational burden that is too heavy in many applications.

In this paper, to overcome these computational problems, we propose and discuss the use of Extreme Learning Machines (for a survey on ELMs, see [4] and the references therein) to get a fast and accurate estimate of the bootstrap neural network forecast distributions. Unlike the other traditional learning algorithms, e.g., backpropagation-based neural networks, the parameters of hidden layers of the ELM are randomly generated and need not be tuned. Theoretically, the single hidden layer feedforward networks with randomly generated hidden neurons and the output weights tuned by regularised least square maintain its universal approximation capability [5,6], even without updating the parameters of hidden layers. In addition, solving the regularised least squares problem in ELM is faster than that of the quadratic programming problem in standard gradient methods in traditional back propagation-based NNs. Thus, ELM tends to achieve faster and better generalisation performance than NNs [7,8], reducing the computational burden of the overall procedure.

The paper is organised as follows. Section 2 briefly reviews NNs for approximating bootstrap forecast distributions in the context of nonlinear autoregressive time series. In Sect. 3, the extreme learning machine approach is presented and discussed, highlighting the advantages of its use for the neural network approach. In Sect. 4, a discussion of the advantages of using ELMs in terms of computational burden and algorithm scalability is reported. In Sect. 5, a simulation experiment is performed to evaluate the computational advantage of using an ELM-based procedure and assess the overall procedure's consistency based on ELMs. Finally, some remarks close the paper.

## 2   Bootstrap Forecast Densities with Neural Networks

Let $\{Y_t, t \in \mathbb{Z}\}$ a real-valued stationary stochastic process modelled as a Nonlinear Autoregressive process of order $p$,

$$Y_t = g(\mathbf{x}_{t-1}) + \varepsilon_t. \tag{1}$$

where $\mathbf{x}'_{t-1} = (Y_{t-1}, \ldots, Y_{t-p})$ is a $p$ dimensional vector of lagged values and $\{\varepsilon_t\}$ is an $iid$ zero mean White Noise process with positive variance $\sigma^2$ and continuous positive everywhere density function. Moreover, we assume that $\varepsilon_t$ is independent from $\{Y_s, s < t\}$ for all $t$. The function $g(\cdot)$ is an unknown (possibly) nonlinear regression function.

Given a time series $\{Y_1, \ldots, Y_T\}$, generated from the model NAR($p$), as specified in Eq. (1), the aim is to determine the forecast distribution $F_{T+1|T}(\cdot)$ of $Y$, at a given future time point $T+1$, conditioned on the set $\mathcal{I}_T$ including the information available up to time $T$. To solve this problem, we propose a strategy in which the unknown function $g(\cdot)$ is approximated using a feed-forward neural network estimator and the pair bootstrap approach is used to approximate the unknown forecasting distribution.

The function $g(\cdot)$ can be approximated by using a single input, single layer feedforward neural network model defined as

$$f_m(\mathbf{x}_{t-1}; \theta) = \sum_{k=1}^{m} c_k \psi(\mathbf{w}'_k \mathbf{x}_{t-1} + w_{k0}) \tag{2}$$

with $\theta' = (c_1, \ldots, c_m, \mathbf{w}'_1, \ldots, \mathbf{w}'_m, w_{10}, \ldots, w_{m0})$, parameter vector of dimension $m(p+2)$, where $m$ is the hidden layer size, $\{\mathbf{w}_k, k = 1, \ldots, m\}$ are the weight vectors of the connections between the input layer and the hidden layer; $\{c_k, k = 1, \ldots, m\}$ are the weights of the link between the hidden layer and the output neuron; $\{w_{k0}, k = 1, \ldots, m\}$ are the bias terms of the hidden neurons; $\psi(\cdot)$ is a proper chosen activation function for the hidden neurons. On the neural network, it is assumed that the activation function $\psi(\cdot)$ is a continuous squashing function with $\psi(\cdot) \in \mathcal{C}^2(\mathbb{R})$ and that the hidden layer size is such that $m = m(T) = O\left(\sqrt{T/\log T}\right)$, with $T$ the length of time series.

The problem is how to obtain the bootstrap distribution for the 1-step ahead forecast $F^*_{T+1|T}(y)$ of the unknown forecast density $F_{T+1|T}(\cdot)$. In this context, we use the neural network model:

$$Y_t = f_m(\mathbf{x}_{t-1}; \boldsymbol{\theta}) + \varepsilon_t. \tag{3}$$

whose parameter vector is estimated by using the set of tuples:

$$\mathcal{X} \equiv (Y_t, \mathbf{x}'_{t-1}) = (Y_t, Y_{t-1}, \ldots, Y_{t-p}), \ t = p+1, \ldots, T. \tag{4}$$

The overall procedure can be implemented as follows.

1. Fix the hidden layer size $m$ and the lag structure $p$. Estimate the weights of the network as:

$$\hat{\theta} = \arg\min_{\theta} \sum_{t=p+1}^{T} \mathcal{L}\left(Y_t, f_m\left(\mathbf{x}_{t-1}; \theta\right)\right) \tag{5}$$

where $\mathcal{L}$ is an appropriate loss function, such as the squared loss, and $f_m$ is a neural network model with $m$ neurons in the hidden layer used to predict $Y_{T+1}$.

Generally, the stability of the network solution can be improved by considering a regularized version of the optimization problem 5:

$$\arg\min_{\theta} \sum_{t=p+1}^{T} \mathcal{L}\left(Y_t, f_m\left(\mathbf{x}_{t-1}; \theta\right)\right) + \frac{\lambda}{2}\|\theta\|^2 \tag{6}$$

where $\|\cdot\|$ is the $L^2$-norm and $\lambda$ is called regularization parameter or weight decay as it forces the weights to decay towards zero. Larger weight values of the ANN will be more penalized if the value of $\lambda$ is large. Similarly, for a smaller value of $\lambda$, the regularization effect is smaller. This parameter is usually fixed by cross-validation.

2. Calculate the centered residuals from the estimated network (5) or (6) defined as:

$$\tilde{\varepsilon}_t = \hat{\varepsilon}_t - \frac{1}{T-p} \sum_{t=p+1}^{T} \hat{\varepsilon}_t. \tag{7}$$

where

$$\hat{\varepsilon}_t = Y_t - f_m\left(\mathbf{x}_{t-1}; \hat{\theta}\right) \tag{8}$$

3. Resample $\{(Y_t^*, \mathbf{x}_{t-1}'^*) = (Y_{t-1}^*, \ldots, Y_{t-p}^*), t = p+1, \ldots, T\}$, as an iid sample from the set of tuples $\mathcal{X}$.

4. Get the bootstrap estimate of the neural network weights:

$$\hat{\theta}^* = \arg\min_{\theta} \sum_{t=p+1}^{T} \mathcal{L}\left(Y_t^*, f_m\left(\mathbf{x}_{t-1}^*; \theta\right)\right). \tag{9}$$

5. Compute

$$\hat{Y}_{T+1}^* = f_m\left(Y_T, Y_{T-1}, \ldots, Y_{T-p}; \hat{\theta}^*\right) + \varepsilon_{T+1}^* \tag{10}$$

where $\varepsilon_{T+1}^*$ is a random sample from the centered residuals $\{\tilde{\varepsilon}_t\}$.

6. The bootstrap forecast distribution $F_{T+1|T}^*$ is given by the law of $\hat{Y}_{T+1}^*$ conditioned on $\mathcal{X}$.

The proposed procedure uses the pair bootstrap proposed in [9] as a resampling scheme which, when applied to autoregression models, delivers consistent results [10] also in the time-dependent context. This fully nonparametric procedure is robust to the misspecification of the functional form and/or the error distribution of the specified statistical model. That is particularly important when the bootstrap is applied to NNs that are intrinsically misspecified models.

Under general assumptions, concerning essentially the stationarity, the ergodicity and mixing conditions on the data generating process, the proposed bootstrap procedure is asymptotically justified for pure autoregressive dependent structures [3].

As usual, the bootstrap distribution can be approximated by Monte Carlo simulations. If steps 3–5 are repeated B times, the empirical cumulative distribution function (ECDF) can be obtained as:

$$\hat{F}^*_{T+1|T} = B^{-1} \sum_{b=1}^{B} \mathbb{I}\left(\hat{Y}^b_{T+1} \leq y\right)$$

where $\mathbb{I}(.)$ denotes the indicator function.

The introduced bootstrap can be also used to estimate the true distribution of a predictive root, which helps compare forecast densities and construct confidence intervals. Following [11], the 1-step ahead predictive root measures the error in the 1-step ahead prediction and is defined as:

$$Y_{T+1} - \hat{Y}_{T+1}. \tag{11}$$

where, as usual,

$$\hat{Y}_{T+1} = f_m\left(Y_T, Y_{T-1}, \ldots, Y_{T-p}; \hat{\theta}\right) \tag{12}$$

is the predictor of $Y_{T+1}$ based on the data $(Y_1, Y_2, \ldots, Y_T)$. Let $G_{T+1|T}$ be the law of the forecasting error defined in (11).

Given a bootstrap pseudo series $(Y_1^*, Y_2^*, \ldots, Y_T^*)$, the bootstrap counterpart of the prediction root is defined as:

$$Y^*_{T+1} - \hat{Y}^*_{T+1}. \tag{13}$$

where

$$Y^*_{T+1} = f_m\left(Y_T, Y_{T-1}, \ldots, Y_{T-p}; \hat{\theta}\right) + \varepsilon^*_{T+1} \tag{14}$$

$$\hat{Y}^*_{T+1} = f_m\left(Y_T, Y_{T-1}, \ldots, Y_{T-p}; \hat{\theta}^*\right). \tag{15}$$

The law of the bootstrap forecasting error defined in (13), namely $G^*_{T+1|T}$, can be used to approximate the unknown distribution $G_{T+1|T}$.

# 3    Extreme Learning Machines

Despite their optimal theoretical properties, NNs deal with challenging issues due to serious computational burdens related essentially to the possible complex nonlinear generating processes. First, a proper model selection procedure is needed to obtain a good approximation of the data-generating process. It requires the identification of the input layer and the hidden layer and choosing the activation function. Some proposals have been introduced in the specialised literature (see, for example, [12]), but the difficulty of finding a proper method capable of automatically identifying the optimal NN remains an open question.

Moreover, once a proper NN architecture has been identified, the parameter estimation problem has to be addressed. In this context, many algorithms have been proposed to improve the original backpropagation algorithm, which suffers from slow convergence and local minimum problems. Unfortunately, again, many of them still need help to guarantee global optimal solutions and fast convergence.

Extreme learning machine is a method for training NNs that has been proposed in the literature [13,14]) to overcome some problems other training techniques face. In the ELM context, the weights of the hidden nodes are randomly generated, and they do not need to be tuned. As a consequence, the algorithm analytically determines the output weights of NNs.

The ELM algorithm can be structured in two steps. In the first one, the hidden layer size is randomly initialised to map the input data into a feature space by some nonlinear functions such as the sigmoid or the hyperbolic functions. The hidden node parameters $\{(\mathbf{w}_k, w_{k0}), k = 1, \ldots, m\}$ are randomly generated according to any continuous probability distribution so that the matrix:

$$\mathbf{H} = \begin{bmatrix} \psi(\mathbf{w}_1'\mathbf{x}_p + w_{10}) & \cdots & \psi(\mathbf{w}_m'\mathbf{x}_p + w_{m0}) \\ \vdots & \ddots & \vdots \\ \psi(\mathbf{w}_1'\mathbf{x}_{T-1} + w_{10}) & \cdots & \psi(\mathbf{w}_m'\mathbf{x}_{T-1} + w_{m0}) \end{bmatrix} \tag{16}$$

is completely known. In the second step, the output weights $\mathbf{c}$ are estimated by solving the following minimization problem:

$$\hat{\mathbf{c}} = \arg \min_{\mathbf{c}} \|\mathbf{Hc} - \mathbf{y}\| \tag{17}$$

where $\mathbf{y} = (Y_{p+1}, \ldots, Y_T)$ is the training data target vector and $\|\cdot\|$ denotes the $L_2$-norm.

If $\mathbf{H}^\dagger$ denotes the Moore-Penrose generalized inverse of the matrix $\mathbf{H}$, the optimal solution to the previous optimization problem is:

$$\hat{\mathbf{c}} = \mathbf{H}^\dagger \mathbf{y} \tag{18}$$

The matrix $\mathbf{H}^\dagger$ can be calculated using one of the numerous methods proposed in the literature, including orthogonal projection, orthogonalisation method, iterative method and the single value decomposition, the last one being the most general.

Estimating the parameter vector $\mathbf{c}$ can also be obtained via regularised ELM [5]. If $\mathbf{H}$ has more rows than columns $(T - p > m)$, which is usually the case when the number of training data is larger than the number of hidden neurons, the following closed-form solution can be obtained:

$$\hat{\mathbf{c}} = \left(\mathbf{H}'\mathbf{H} + \frac{\mathbf{I}}{\eta}\right)^{-1} \mathbf{H}'\mathbf{y} \tag{19}$$

where $\mathbf{I}$ is an identity matrix of dimension $m$ and $\eta$ is a proper chosen constant.

If the number of training data is less than the number of hidden neurons $(T - p < m)$, an estimate for $\mathbf{c}$ can be obtained as:

$$\hat{\mathbf{c}} = \mathbf{H}'\left(\mathbf{H}\mathbf{H}' + \frac{\mathbf{I}}{\eta}\right)^{-1}\mathbf{y}$$

where $\mathbf{I}$ is an identity matrix of dimension $T - p$ this time.

It can be shown that Eq. 19 actually aims at minimising:

$$\hat{\mathbf{c}} = \arg\min_{\mathbf{c}} \|\mathbf{Hc} - \mathbf{y}\| + \frac{1}{\eta} \| \mathbf{c}\|$$

Compared to standard ELM, in which the target is to minimise $\|\mathbf{Hc} - \mathbf{y}\|$, an extra penalty term $\frac{1}{\eta}\|\mathbf{c}\|$ is added to the target of standard ELM. This is actually consistent with the theory that smaller output weights $\mathbf{c}$ play an essential role for ELM in achieving better generalisation ability.

The ELM approach has several advantages. It has good generalisation performance since it reaches the small training error and, contemporaneously, the smallest norm of output weights. Moreover, learning can be done without iteratively tuning the hidden nodes, independent of training data. Finally, ELMs, like NNs, enjoy the property of being universal approximators [15, 16].

In practice, being the hidden layer randomly generated, ELMs usually require more hidden neurons than NNs to obtain a given performance. However, this is a manageable problem due to the computational efficiency of ELMs. Moreover, ELMs are well-suited for extensive data processing. Even if a model selection process is implemented for optimal structure searching, the running time of ELMs is always lower than other competing strategies.

## 4   Computational Burden and Algorithm Scalability

In this section, we discuss the results of a simulation experiment performed to evaluate the computational advantage of ELMs with respect to NNs. A set of 5000 time series of different lengths, ranging from 250 to 1000, has been generated from an EXPAR(2) model, defined as:

$$Y_t = a_1\left(Y_{t-1}\right)Y_{t-1} + a_2\left(Y_{t-1}\right)Y_{t-2} + \varepsilon_t \tag{20}$$

where $a_1(u) = 0.5 + 0.9\exp(-u^2)$, $a_2(u) = -0.8 + 1.8\exp(-u^2)$ and $\varepsilon_t \sim \frac{T_6}{\sqrt{1.5}}$, being $T_6$ the Student $T$ distribution with 6 degrees of freedom.

For each time series, we have trained NNs and ELMs with input lags in the set $\{1, 2, 4\}$ and hidden layer size in the set $\{4, 8, 12, 16, 20\}$ to consider models with increasing complexity which requires increasing overall training time. Neural network models have been trained using a very efficient algorithm based on BFGS and implemented in the R package nnet in the language C. In contrast, ELMs have been implemented entirely in R by the authors.

In Fig. 1 we reported the ratio between the NNETs and ELMs training time, over 50 replicates. The results show a significant computational advantage in all cases in using neural networks trained without iterative tuning for fully iterated algorithms. Using backpropagation (a standard approach in neural computation) would make the overall training procedure even slower. For the simplest model (one input neuron and just two hidden neurons), training ELMs is about 20 times faster than training NNs. The computational advantage increases when the model complexity increases. When we consider neural networks with four input neurons and twenty hidden neurons, training ELMs is about 150 times faster than training classical NNs.

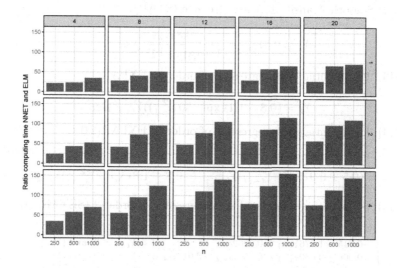

**Fig. 1.** Ratio mean training time for NNET and ELM for input neurons $p \in \{1, 2, 4\}$ and hidden neurons $m \in \{4, 8, 12, 16, 20\}$, with time series length $T \in \{250, 500, 1000\}$.

All neural networks have been estimated by restarting the training ten times to avoid being trapped in local minima (which is unnecessary when using ELMs). Also, note that the computational advantage can be further reduced when using ELMs with the regularisation learning process. The regularisation parameter has to be fixed on ad hoc choices, generally based on cross-validation. This makes the computational burden heavy and, in many applications, impracticable.

The computational problems of using NNs become even more considerable when used in computer-intensive resampling techniques, such as bootstrap or cross-validation, in which the training step must be repeated hundreds or thousands of times. When using ELMs, the whole bootstrap forecast distribution can be obtained at the same computational cost as training a single network.

## 5    Simulation Results

In this section, we present the results of a Monte Carlo experiment carried out to analyse the finite sample behaviour of the proposed bootstrap estimates based on ELMs of forecast densities for nonlinear processes. As data-generating processes, we consider the following models:

(M1): Nonlinear Autoregressive (NLAR)

$$Y_t = \frac{0.7|Y_{t-1}|}{2 + |Y_{t-1}|} + \varepsilon_t$$

(M2) Smooth Transition Autoregressive (STAR)

$$Y_t = 0.8Y_{t-1} - \frac{0.8Y_{t-1}}{1 + \exp(-10Y_{t-1})} + \varepsilon_t$$

(M3): Exponential Autoregressive of order 1 (EXPAR(1))

$$Y_t = (0.8 - 1.1\exp(-50Y_{t-1}^2))Y_{t-1} + \varepsilon_t$$

(M4): Exponential Autoregressive of order 1 (EXPAR(2))

$$Y_t = (0.5 + 0.9\exp(-Y_{t-1}^2))Y_{t-1} + (-0.8 + 1.8\exp(-Y_{t-1}^2))Y_{t-2} + \varepsilon_t$$

(M5): Self-exciting Threshold Autoregressive of order 2 (SETAR(2))

$$Y_t = \begin{cases} -0.015 - 1.076Y_{t-1} + 0.0062\varepsilon_t & \text{if } (Y_{t-1} < 0) \text{ and } (Y_{t-2} < Y_{t-1}) \\ -0.006 + 0.630Y_{t-1} - 0.756Y_{t-2} + 0.0132\varepsilon_t & \text{if } (Y_{t-2} \leq 0) \text{ and } (Y_{t-1} > Y_{t-2}) \\ -0.006 + 0.438Y_{t-1} + 0.0094\varepsilon_t & \text{if } (Y_{t-2} > 0) \text{ and } (Y_{t-1} \leq Y_{t-2}) \\ -0.004 + 0.443Y_{t-1} + 0.0082\varepsilon_t & \text{if } (Y_{t-2} > 0) \text{ and } (Y_{t-1} > Y_{t-2}) \end{cases}$$

Model M1 is a general Nonlinear Autoregressive (NLAR) model of order 1. Model M2 is a Smooth Transition Autoregressive (STAR) model of order 1; it is a natural extension of autoregressive models, allowing for a higher degree of flexibility in model dynamics through a smooth transition. Models M3 and M4 are Exponential Autoregressive (EXPAR) models of orders 1 and 2, respectively. Model M4 is the same model defined in Eq. 20. This family of models are particularly useful in explaining jump phenomena, amplitude-dependent frequency shifts and perturbed limit cycles. Model M5 is a Self-exiting Threshold Autoregressive (SETAR) model of order 2 in which flexibility in model dynamics is obtained through a regime-switching behaviour. These models have already been used in several other Monte Carlo studies [17–21].

For the simulation design, we have considered three different specifications for the error term: a standard Normal distribution, a standardised Student T distribution with degrees of freedom equal to 6, to simulate the case of heavy tails and a standard exponential distribution with a parameter equal to 1, to simulate asymmetric error terms. That is: (E1) $\varepsilon_t \sim N(0,1)$, (E2) $\varepsilon_t \sim T(6)/\sqrt{1.5}$ and (E3) $\varepsilon_t \sim Exp(1) - 1$. All simulations are based on $N = 500$ Monte Carlo runs with time series of length $T$ with $T \in \{250, 500, 1000\}$. We have also considered ELMs with different hidden layer sizes $m \in \{4, 8, 10, 12, 16, 20\}$ to verify the consistency of the implemented procedure and the stability of the results when changing the hidden layer size. The bootstrap forecast distributions have been estimated using $B = 1,000$ bootstrap replicates.

For the resampling step in NN training, we have used a local bootstrap scheme where, in each bootstrap, the network training is initialised by using the estimated values of the weights on the original sample. This strategy allows a more stable and efficient convergence to the solution in each bootstrap run.

The final experiment is based on design 270 points (five model specifications, three error specifications, three different time series lengths, and six hidden layer sizes for ELMs).

The Wasserstein distance of order one between the empirical cumulative distribution function (ECDF) of the true forecasting error distribution $(G(y))$ and the ECDF of bootstrap forecasting error distribution computed using the ELM $(G^*(y))$ defined as

$$W_1(G, G^*) = \int_{-\infty}^{\infty} |G(y) - G^*(y)| dy.$$

can be calculated as the area between the two ECDFs.

In Figs. 2 and 3 we have reported the kernel density estimation of the true forecasting error distribution estimated with NNs and ELMs for models STAR(1), NLAR(1), EXPAR(2) and SETAR (2), with time series lengths $\{250, 500, 1000\}$ and error distributions E1, E2 and E3. The distributions have been estimated with 10,000 Monte Carlo runs. In all cases, the estimated distributions obtained via ELMs are almost identical to the ones obtained via NNs. The same comments apply to the EXPAR(1), not reported here for space constraint.

Now, we focus on analysing the consistency of bootstrap forecast distributions estimated via ELMs. In Figs. 4 and 5 we have reported the Monte Carlo distribution of the Wasserstein distance of order one between the true forecast error distribution and the bootstrap forecasting error distribution for models STAR(1), NLAR(1), EXPAR(2) and SETAR (2), for different hidden layer sizes, error term distributions and time series lengths. In all cases, as the sample size increases, the distribution median tends towards zero, and its variability decreases, showing, for finite sample size, the convergence of the procedure and the good accuracy of the bootstrap distribution in approximating the true one.

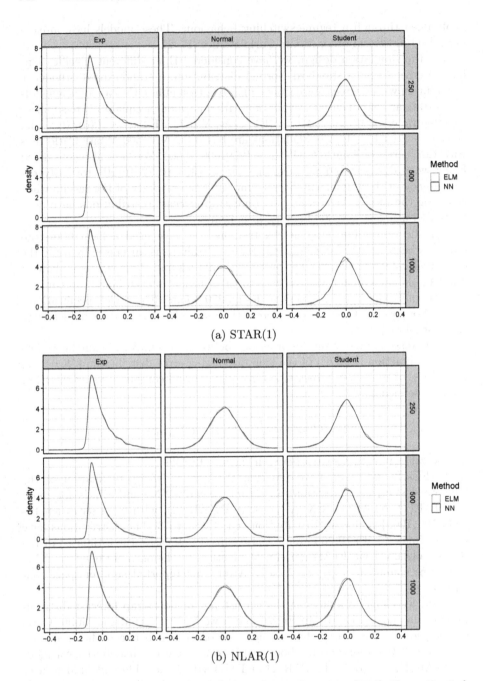

(a) STAR(1)

(b) NLAR(1)

**Fig. 2.** Kernel density estimation of the true forecasting error distribution estimated with NNs and ELMs for model model STAR(1) and NLAR(1) with different time series lengths and error distributions. The distributions have been estimated with 10, 000 MC runs.

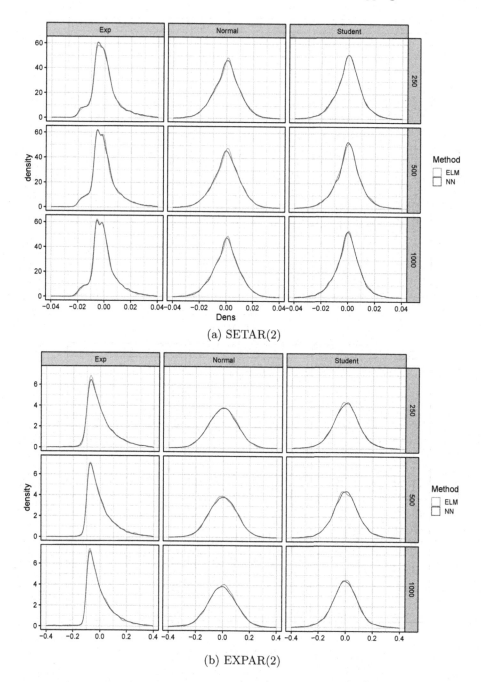

(a) SETAR(2)

(b) EXPAR(2)

**Fig. 3.** Kernel density estimation of the true forecasting error distribution estimated with NNs and ELMs for model model SETAR(2) and EXPAR(2) with different time series lengths and error distributions. The distributions have been estimated with 10,000 MC runs.

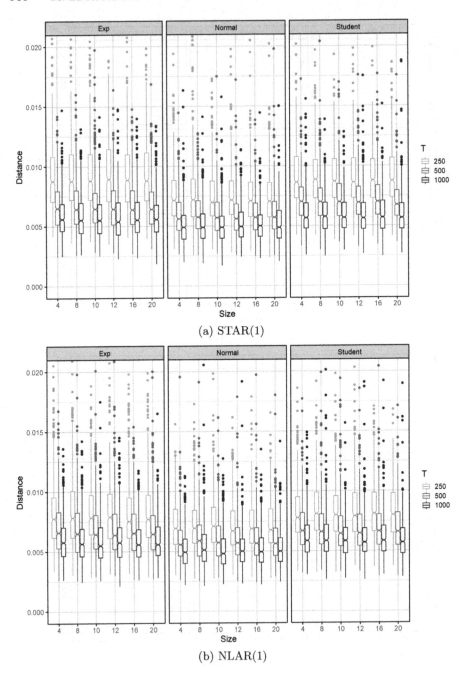

**Fig. 4.** Monte Carlo distribution of the Wasserstein distance of order 1 between the true forecasting error distribution and the bootstrap forecasting error distribution for different hidden layer sizes, error term distributions and time series lengths. The true distribution has been estimated with 10,000 MC runs, and the bootstrap distributions have been estimated with 1,000 MC runs STAR (1) and NLAR(1) Models.

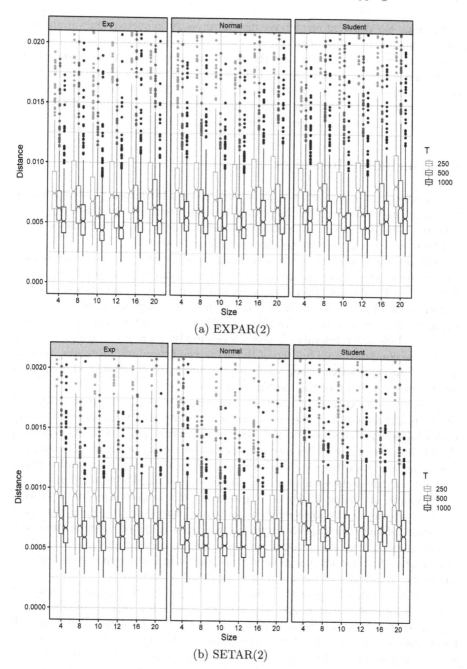

**Fig. 5.** Monte Carlo distribution of the Wasserstein distance of order 1 between the true forecasting error distribution and the bootstrap forecasting error distribution for different hidden layer sizes, error term distributions and time series lengths. The true distribution has been estimated with 10,000 MC runs, and the bootstrap distributions have been estimated with 1,000 MC runs EXPAR(2) and SETAR(2) Models.

Concerning the different error term distributions, as expected, the variability is slightly higher than that of the Normal case in the case of asymmetric distribution or heavy tails. Furthermore, the results remain stable when changing the hidden layer size $m$. Consequently, fixing $m$ does not appear as critical as fixing tuning parameters in other nonparametric approaches, as in the case of local kernel regressions or splines. The same comments apply to model the EXPAR(1), not reported here for space constraint.

## 6    Concluding Remarks

In this paper, a new bootstrap approach to estimate the forecast distribution for nonlinear time series has been presented and discussed. The proposed approach uses the pair bootstrap as a resampling device and employs extreme learning machines to approximate the original nonlinear process.

The overall procedure has a nice nonparametric property of being model-free within a general class of nonlinear processes, avoiding the specification of a finite-dimensional model for the data-generating process. Concerning competing conventional algorithms for single hidden layer feed-forward neural networks, ELMs have some advantages. In this algorithm, the input weights and the hidden layer bias are randomly chosen; consequently, their use can dramatically reduce the computational burden of the bootstrap procedure. Moreover, they do not need any restrictive assumptions on the activation function and are not so sensitive to the choice of the hidden layer size.

A simulation experiment has been carried out to verify the performance of the proposed approach. First of all, the results have shown the effectiveness of ELMs in reducing the computation time of the overall procedure. As expected, the advantage of using ELMs increases as the complexity of the model increases. The mean execution time for the learning process of a complete neural network is about 150 times slower for the learning process of ELM with regularisation.

Summing up, using ELMs to approximate the original non-linear process is advantageous in the implemented bootstrap procedure. It retains the good properties of the classical NN approach in a wide range of different nonlinear model specifications and error term distributions, considerably reducing computing times, making the use of bootstrap feasible in many application contexts where the complexity of the network is supposed to increase.

As a final remark, note that the proposed procedure can be extended to deal with forecast horizons greater than one in which a direct multistep forecasting approach can be used. Moreover, since the pair bootstrap can deal with heteroscedastic errors, a further extension in this direction might be straightforward. The suitability of ELMs in these contexts is still under investigation.

# References

1. Bassetti, F., Casarin, R., Ravazzolo, F.: Density forecasting. In: Fuleky, P. (ed.) Macroeconomic Forecasting in the Era of Big Data. ASTAE, vol. 52, pp. 465–494. Springer, Cham (2020). https://doi.org/10.1007/978-3-030-31150-6_15
2. Ng, J., Forbes, C.S., Martin, G.M., McCabe, B.P.: Non-parametric estimation of forecast distributions in non-Gaussian, nonlinear state space models. Int. J. Forecast. **29**, 411–430 (2013)
3. La Rocca, M., Giordano, F., Perna, C.: Clustering nonlinear time series with neural network bootstrap forecast distributions. Int. J. Approx. Reason. **137**, 1–15 (2021)
4. Huang, G.B., Wang, D.H., Lan, Y.: Extreme learning machines: a survey. Int. J. Mach. Learn. Cybern. **2**, 107–122 (2011)
5. Huang, G.B., Zhou, H., Ding, X., Zhang, R.: Extreme learning machine for regression and multiclass classification. IEEE Trans. Syst. Man Cybern., Part B **42**, 513–529 (2012)
6. Huang, G.B., Li, M.B., Chen, L., Siew, C.K.: Incremental extreme learning machine with fully complex hidden nodes. Neurocomputing **71**, 576–583 (2008)
7. Huang, G.B.: An insight into extreme learning machines: random neurons, random features and kernels. Cognit. Comput. **6**, 376–390 (2014)
8. La Rocca, M., Perna, C.: Nonlinear autoregressive sieve bootstrap based on extreme learning machines. Math. Biosci. Eng. **17**, 636–653 (2020)
9. Freedman, D.A.: Bootstrapping regression models. Ann. Stat. **9**, 1218–1228 (1981)
10. Gonçalves, S., Kilian, L.: Bootstrapping autoregressions with conditional heteroskedasticity of unknown form. J. Econom. **123**, 89–120 (2004)
11. Pan, L., Politis, D.N.: Bootstrap prediction intervals for linear, nonlinear and nonparametric autoregressions. J. Stat. Plan. Inference **177**, 1–27 (2016)
12. Wang, C., et al.: A fitting model for feature selection with fuzzy rough sets. IEEE Trans. Fuzzy Syst. **25**, 741–753 (2017)
13. Ding, S., Zhao, H., Zhang, Y., Xu, X., Nie, R.: Extreme learning machine: algorithm, theory and applications. Artif. Intell. Rev. **44**, 103–115 (2015)
14. Huang, G., Huang, G.B., Song, S., You, K.: Trends in extreme learning machines: a review. Neural Netw. **61**, 32–48 (2015)
15. Huang, G.B., Chen, L.: Convex incremental extreme learning machine. Neurocomputing **70**, 3056–3062 (2007)
16. Huang, G.B., Chen, L.: Enhanced random search based incremental extreme learning machine. Neurocomputing **71**, 3460–3468 (2008)
17. Zhang, G.P., Patuwo, B.E., Hu, M.Y.: A simulation study of artificial neural networks for nonlinear time-series forecasting. Comput. Oper. Res. **28**, 381–396 (2001)
18. Giordano, F., La Rocca, M., Perna, C.: Forecasting nonlinear time series with neural network sieve bootstrap. Comput. Stat. Data Anal. **51**, 3871–3884 (2007)
19. Vilar, J.A., Alonso, A.M., Vilar, J.M.: Nonlinear time series clustering based on non-parametric forecast densities. Comput. Stat. Data Anal. **54**, 2850–2865 (2010)
20. Bühlmann, P.: Bootstraps for time series. Stat. Sci. **17**, 52–72 (2002)
21. Tiao, G.C., Tsay, R.S.: Some advances in non-linear and adaptive modelling in time-series. J. Forecast. **13**, 109–131 (1994)

# Subsampled Dataset Challenges and Machine Learning Techniques in Table Tennis

Dimitrios Simopoulos[1] , Andreas Nikolakakis[2] ,
and George Anastassopoulos[1](✉)

[1] Medical Informatics Laboratory, Department of Medicine,
Democritus University of Thrace, Alexandroupolis 68100, Greece
{dsimopou,anasta}@med.duth.gr
[2] Department of Physical Education and Sport Sciences,
Democritus University of Thrace, Komotini 69100, Greece
andniko@phyed.duth.gr
http://www.phyed.duth.gr/, https://www.med.duth.gr/

**Abstract.** Artificial Intelligence has been widely used almost in every aspect of our lives, and sports activity is no exception. In that field, table tennis is a very demanding sport, in which predicting the winner of a point or a match can be quite challenging. This paper explores the application of several machine learning algorithms in subsampled table tennis data. Especially, the Multilayer Perceptrons, Random Forests, and Gradient Boosted Trees have been used in order to predict the result of individual points and matches. The algorithms were trained on real data from official First Division matches of the Hellenic Table Tennis Federation. The Gradient Boosted Trees achieved the highest level of accuracy (98.36%) in the prediction of each individual point and (74.92%) in the prediction of the winner of the match. The 98.36% accuracy is very high, while the 74.92% is affordable, because the match winner could have won even fewer points than its opponent. Also, Gradient Boosted Trees achieved the less computational time, making it suitable for use in real-time systems to assist tactical coaching in table tennis.

**Keywords:** Table Tennis · Random Forests · Gradient Boosted Trees · Artificial Intelligence · Machine Learning

## 1 Introduction

Table tennis is a complex sport involving a wide variety of strokes. These strokes when analysed can be useful inferences which in turn can lead to an improvement in the performance of a player. The strokes executed by a player are clearly visible to the opponent and hence, valuable inferences regarding the strokes can be easily made from the front view of the player [1].

A table tennis player considers various characteristics when it comes to hit the ball, such as their own and their opponent's position around the table, the

L. Iliadis et al. (Eds.): EANN 2023, CCIS 1826, pp. 548–557, 2023.
https://doi.org/10.1007/978-3-031-34204-2_44

hitting technique of the ball, and the area of the table where the ball will bounce. All these characteristics are being examined continuously and in parallel, playing a significant role in the result of each single point. For instance, if a player wants to win a match, they can adopt a strategy that involves the appliance of different tactics in a sequence of a few hits [2]. In the past, there have been many attempts to analyse sports games, primarily using historical data for statistical analysis. Therefore, it is interesting to examine the correlation between the hits and their success [3].

With the development of artificial intelligence, more and more smart technologies are being used in the sports industry, such as portable sensors, live video capture, technical and tactical analysis systems. However, in table tennis, the development of an intelligent real-time video capture system remains elusive because of the prominent tracking difficulties and challenges caused by the small size, light weight, fast speed and strong rotation of the table tennis ball [4]. In professional table tennis training, the trainer will carefully analyse the action features of the opponent before the video data. They also collect training, fitness and competition data from athletes and adjust training strategies over time based on attacking and defending weaknesses of opponents. For example, smart sensors such as portable devices or videos are common in teaching and training [5]. Researchers look at specific tactical details to see how each person performs. By studying the aforementioned information, it can be figured out how good an athlete is at their performance [6]. In bibliography, there are many studies concerning the data analysis of the game with the use of multiple sensors and cameras, especially during the services' process [7]. Also, in [8], the net of the table is monitored by force sensors and other electronic circuits. The ball's spin and speed can be monitored, using inertial sensors mounted on the racket [9], as well as the estimation of the trajectory of the racket [10]. In other studies, the detection of the stroke type [11] and the estimation of kinematic parameters [12] have been examined. Building upon the previous work, additional studies have been conducted to explore the application of Artificial Intelligence in predicting various table tennis factors [13].

Table tennis is a very demanding and technically complex sport. Athletes have to make quick decisions and plan tactics while under physical and emotional fatigue. Statistical analysis of matches or entire tournaments can help athletes and coaches learn a lot about their opponents and improve their skills [14].

The rest of this paper is organized as follows. After the description of the dataset and the fundamentals of the used machine learning algorithms presented in Sect. 2, Sect. 3 proposes our implemented model and depicts the experimental results, while the conclusions and future work are drawn in Sect. 4.

## 2 Methodology

### 2.1 Dataset Representation

There were 33 male athletes in the first 34 positions of the official Hellenic Table Tennis Federation male ranking. Furthermore, there were 18 female athletes in the first 26 positions of the respective female ranking.

These athletes competed in the men's and women's A1 league of the Hellenic Championship, during the 2019-2020 season. A total of 64 matches were recorded. In all of these matches 5.065 points were gained. The aforementioned matches were divided in 34 men matches with 2905 points and 30 women matches with 2160 points gained. Out of these men matches, twenty ended in a 3-0 sets, eight in a 3-1 sets, and six in a 3-2 sets. In the women's category, eighteen matches ended with a 3-0 sets, eight ended with a 3-1 sets, and four ended in a 3-2 sets victory. All athletes had an offensive style of play. All these matches were filmed by the official YouTube channel of the Hellenic Federation. The average age for men and women was 29.4 and 28.9 years old, respectively.

**Table 1.** Dataset input variables

| Variable Name | Discrete options | ID | Variable Name | Discrete options | ID |
|---|---|---|---|---|---|
| Category | Man | 1 | Shot used to receive | Forehand Push | 1 |
| | Woman | 2 | | Backhand Push | 2 |
| Service rank player | High rank | 1 | | Forehand Flick | 3 |
| | Low rank | 2 | | Backhand Flick | 4 |
| Receive rank player | High rank | 1 | | Forehand Topspin | 5 |
| | Low rank | 2 | | Backhand Topspin | 6 |
| Serve position | Forehand | 1 | | Forehand Drive | 7 |
| | Middle | 2 | | Backhand Drive | 8 |
| | Backhand | 3 | | False Receive | 0 |
| Service grip | Forehand Grip | 1 | Receive shot area | Forehand Short | 1 |
| | Backhand Grip | 2 | | Middle Short | 2 |
| Service area | Forehand Short | 1 | | Backhand Short | 3 |
| | Middle Short | 2 | | Forehand Inside/Out | 4 |
| | Backhand Short | 3 | | Middle Inside/Out | 5 |
| | Forehand Inside/Out | 4 | | Backhand Inside/Out | 6 |
| | Middle Inside/Out | 5 | | Forehand Long | 7 |
| | Backhand Inside/Out | 6 | | Middle Long | 8 |
| | Forehand Long | 7 | | Backhand Long | 9 |
| | Middle Long | 8 | | False Receive | 0 |
| | Backhand Long | 9 | Point analysis | Ace | 1 |
| Number of hits | Ace | 1 | | Point won on 3rd ball | 2 |
| | 2 Hits | 2 | | Point won after 3rd ball | 3 |
| | 3 Hits | 3 | | Point lost after service | 4 |
| | 4-5 Hits | 4 | | Point lost after 3rd ball | 5 |
| | 6 Hits | 6 | | | |

The input variables are presented in detail in Table 1. Furthermore, because of the dataset generation method, there are no missing values.

The table tennis service area is divided in three zones. From the left side is the backhand area, the middle of the table tennis table is the middle area and the right side is the forehand area (right-handed player). The table tennis serve is mainly done in two ways. The most common way is with Forehand Grip and the other is with Backhand Grip. The service from the right hand of the body and from inside hand of the racket is the Forehand service, and the service from the left hand of the body and from outside front of the racket is the Backhand service (right-handed).

The high rank players are the athletes that are in the first twelve positions on the official ranking list of Hellenic Table Tennis Federation and the low rank players are in the rest of the positions.

The area of the serve, depends on the second bounce of the ball. The short serve is the serve which the second bounce is near to the table net, the serve which the second bounce is in the middle from the net to baseline it's called inside/out service and the long service is the serve which the second bounce is near to the baseline. The serving area also it depends from the right or the left side on the table. The right side is the forehand side and the left side is the backhand side (right handed).

About the receive in table tennis, success receive is considered when the receiving athlete simply returns the ball to the opponent's area while fail receive is when the receive athlete can't return the ball into the opponent's area. The most used shot receive is the push, a not so aggressive shot with backspin and without speed, the topspin a very aggressive and powerful shot with a lot of spin and speed, the drive a "simple" shot with speed and without spin and the flick, a shot with spin and speed. Also, the serving result is very important in table tennis. When a serve player wins the point, that is called serve-won point. On the other hand, when a serve player lose the point, it is called serve-lost point.

Also, about the analysis of the point, an ace occurs when the point is won only by serving. When an athlete wins the point with a shot after the receive, that is called "won the point on the 3rd shot". Similarly, when an athlete wins the point later, this is called in the current study "won the point after the 3rd shot". On the other hand, when the service athlete loses the point immediately after the service this is called "lost the point after service", whereas when the athlete loses the point later that is called "lost the point after the 3rd shot".

## 2.2 Dataset Analysis

The dataset included in total 10 categorical variables, used as input for our prediction models. Indicatively, they included measurements such as the point analysis, length of service area, playing category and service grip of a table tennis player, as shown already in Table 1.

Analysing and combining the aforementioned variables allows us to capture the entirety of the information available about the players in the dataset and create a more robust model for predicting the winners of table tennis matches and their individual points. Furthermore, the use of categorical variables can be useful in modelling complex and non-linear relationships between input variables and the output variable, which can be important in sports like table tennis where specific factors can play a significant role in the outcome of a point or a match.

### 2.3   Implemented Machine Learning Algorithms

Multilayer Perceptrons (MLP), Random Forests, Random Trees, and Gradient Boosted Trees (GBT) are all different types of machine learning models that can be applied for a wide range of tasks and challenges belonging in the artificial intelligence sector. In order to make the most precise predictions, based on the type and nature of the given dataset, we carried out discrete comparisons on the aforementioned models.

A multilayer perceptron is a type of feed-forward artificial neural network that is composed of finite multiple layers of connected nodes, used to process and transform the input data by identifying the dominant characteristics and relationships of the given input variables [15]. MLPs are supervised learning models, which can successfully handle both classification and regression challenges. They are used in a wide range of sectors. Despite of that, they also deliver significant results in other fields. Among others, one of its advantages is the ability to model complex, non-linear relationships between inputs and outputs. Therefore, this model structure is often considered as an option for supervised learning tasks.

Random Forests and Random Trees are considered as extensions of the decision trees data structure, a predictive model that uses input feature values to make predictions [16]. These methods both involve training multiple decision trees on randomly selected subsets of data and either averaging or voting on their predictions. The difference is that Random Trees deliver a prediction each, while Random Forests average the aforementioned predictions from a variety of trees. Both methods have a tendency to overfitting minimisation and deliver efficient execution times, however Random Forests are generally considered to be more robust.

GBT is a also widely used and highly powerful machine learning model used for both classification and regression challenges and tasks, making it a versatile model that can be utilised with various types of data [17]. This is a learning method that combines predictions of multiple discrete models, such as the aforementioned decision trees, to form a highly efficient and accurate model. The algorithm trains decision trees on different subsets of data iteratively, combining their predictions and aiming to the overall prediction error reduction. GBT begins by training a simple decision tree, and then additional trees are added to the model, each of which tries to correct the mistakes made by previous trees, similar to back propagation. GBT can model complex relationships between discreet input features and the desired output variable, as it can combine the individual decision tree predictions. GBT has several advantages, such as being robust to possible outliers, missing values, and noise in data.

## 3   Implementation

### 3.1   Model Structures

The goal of the presented work was to make predictions about two different outcomes from the dataset we analysed. The first output was the winner identification for each individual point, while the second was the prediction of the overall match winner, based on the characteristics of each single point in the match. We adjusted and evaluated different models, aiming to find the less time and computation expensive way. In order to achieve this, we made use of TensorFlow [18] and Keras [19], which are two commonly known open-source libraries for machine learning. TensorFlow is a framework for custom defining different prediction model architectures and neural networks, while Keras is a high-level API which runs on top of the aforementioned framework and thus, it simplifies and speeds up the process of building and training models with TensorFlow. Together, these libraries provide a powerful toolset for our prediction models. The dataset employed in this study includes both numerical and categorical input variables.

First, we used 5-layer multilayer perceptrons (MLP) to predict if a player won the point or not. The model structure consisted of an input layer, four hidden layers, and an output layer. The input layer was designed to accept the numerical and categorical input variables from the dataset. The four hidden layers were used to extract and analyse complex patterns in the data, while the output layer was used to produce the final predictions by using the sigmoid activation function. However, the model training process took a significant amount of time compared to the other models due to its formation complexity and the dataset structure and size. To ensure optimal performance, we used techniques such as rectified linear unit and sigmoid activation functions, and regularisation to fine-tune the model. After thorough trials with different hyper-parameter values, we concluded that the epochs equal to 100 and batch size equal to 32 delivered the best results. In order to optimise the built model and its weights, we used the Adaptive Moment Estimation (Adam) [20] optimisation algorithm.

In an effort to improve the efficiency and time consumption of our model, we decided to try alternative models to the aforementioned model that we had previously used. One such model we explored was Random Forests. Random Forests is an ensemble method that builds multiple decision trees and combines them to produce a final prediction. The training time of this model was significantly faster compared to the MLP model, which made it a more attractive option. We observed the Random Forests model delivered higher accuracy and better metrics compared to the MLP model. This suggests that the Random Forests algorithm was able to capture the patterns and features of the dataset, making it a suitable model for our problem. Therefore, we conclude that Random Forests algorithm is a good alternative in terms of both performance and computation time when compared to MLP.

After evaluating several models, we concluded that the best model for predicting the winner of table tennis matches was Gradient Boosted Trees (GBT). To further improve the performance of the GBT model, we explored and tuned its hyper-parameters using techniques such as random search with a number of 100 trials. After experiment executions, we concluded the best predictions were delivered by the Classification and Regression Trees (CART) algorithm [21]. CART, a decision tree algorithm used for both classification and regression problems, stands for Classification and Regression Trees. It creates a binary tree that recursively splits the data into smaller subsets based on the value of the input features. The CART algorithm plays a significant role in creating decision trees, while it is easy to interpret the results. By using CART algorithm in the GBT model, we were able to extract the complex patterns and features of the data which improved the performance of the model. Overall, we found that GBT is the best overall model for the given dataset.

## 3.2  Results Comparison

In our research, we assessed the efficiency of the aforementioned machine learning models by means of several metrics for the two outputs. The results of our investigation provided us with insights into the relationship between the characteristics of each discrete point and the overall outcome of a match. Upon evaluating the results, we concluded that the model providing the most satisfactory performance for both cases was the Gradient Boosted Trees (GBT). The Random Forests model followed, while the Multi-layer Perceptron produced the lowest accuracy outcomes.

The first output, which was the prediction of each single point, was directly related to the input variables. As a result, the models were able to effectively identify the relationships between the given inputs and the point outcome. On the other hand, the second output was more complex as it required to predict the match winner based on the characteristics of each single point. This required a deeper understanding of the complex relationships present in the dataset and therefore the accuracy expectancy was lower.

For all validation purposes, the 10-fold cross-validation technique was used. That allowed us in the end of each model evaluation to determine their efficiency in unseen data. K-fold cross-validation can help to prevent overfitting in our built models by assessing their ability to generalise to new data and to fine-tune the respective hyper-parameters related to each model.

For the first output, we used first the typical 80–20% train-test split for the MLP. That allowed us to evaluate and micro-adjust the built MLP model. The model was tested with different hyper-parameters, i.e. epochs and batch size. The resulting point model metrics were a loss of 0.4119, accuracy of 0.5881, mean squared error of 0.4119, and mean absolute error of 0.4119. It is obvious that the delivered results were poor and therefore the model could not be considered as notable. Continuing with our research, we concluded that Random Forests and GBTs were the preferred ones, as they both demonstrated efficient time execution and high accuracy. Out of the two, Gradient Boosted Trees slightly outperformed in terms of overall accuracy. The Table 2 depicts the respective metrics for the developed MLP, RF and GBT models. In the implementation of the Gradient Boosted Trees (GBT) model, the selection of crucial hyper-parameters played a significant role in achieving the aforementioned results. The categorical algorithm utilised was 'CART', while the growing strategy adopted was 'LOCAL'. Additionally, the sparse oblique normalisation technique applied was Min-Max scaling. These hyper-parameter choices ultimately impacted the performance of the GBT model.

**Table 2.** Indicative point metrics comparison between MLP, RF and GBT

|          | Multilayer Perceptron | Random Forest | Gradient Boosted Tree |
|----------|----------------------|---------------|-----------------------|
| Accuracy | 58.81%               | 98.27%        | 98.36%                |
| MAE      | 0.4119               | 1.0688        | 1.0721                |
| RMSE     | 0.4119               | 1.2656        | 1.2662                |

Respectively, the same models were compared and used for the second output. That predicted the match winner based on the given characteristics of discrete points. This prediction required identifying more complex relationships between multiple inputs and points, and thus, we expected a lower accuracy compared to the first prediction. Additionally, it is also possible that the match winner could have won fewer points than their opponent, further complicating the prediction model. The results of the MLP model showed efficiency similar to the first prediction outcome, with a loss of 0.4983, accuracy of 0.5017, mean squared error of 0.4983, and mean absolute error of 0.4983. In contrast, the Random Forest and GBT models delivered significant improvement, with a noticeable increase in accuracy given the complexities and challenges associated with the second prediction. After conducting extensive experiments, we arrived at the conclusion that a slight modification of the hyper-parameters improved the performance of the prediction model. To be specific, we incorporated the use of standard deviation as a measure of the dispersion of data around its average, as a sparse oblique normalisation method. An overview of the aforementioned metrics is presented in Table 3.

**Table 3.** Indicative match metrics comparison between MLP, RF and GBT

|          | Multilayer Perceptron | Random Forest | Gradient Boosted Tree |
|----------|----------------------|---------------|-----------------------|
| Accuracy | 50.17%               | 73.93%        | 74.92%                |
| MAE      | 0.4983               | 1.1617        | 1.1815                |
| RMSE     | 0.4983               | 1.3199        | 1.3272                |

## 4   Conclusion

In table tennis there are many factors that affect the result of a point and the result of the whole match. In this study, data from matches of the official Hellenic Table Tennis Federation have been used, in order to predict the result of each single point and the result of the match, during the game, with various machine learning techniques. Gradient Boosted Trees achieved the best results, while it was also the quicker of the used techniques. The accuracy in prediction of each single point (98,36%) is very high, whereas the accuracy in prediction of the winner of the match (74,92%) is better than any other in bibliography. This can be affordable, because the match winner could have won even fewer or equal points than its opponent.

In the future, we will develop a real time system, which will extract the data from a camera and import them into a computational classification system to produce the factors that are going to be used from more machine learning techniques.

# References

1. Kulkarni, K., Shenoy, S.: Table tennis stroke recognition using two-dimensional human pose estimation. In: Proceedings Of The IEEE/CVF Conference On Computer Vision And Pattern Recognition, pp. 4576–4584 (2021)
2. Wu, J., Liu, D., Guo, Z., Xu, Q., Wu, Y.: TacticFlow: Visual analytics of ever-changing tactics in racket sports. IEEE Trans. Visual. Comput. Graph. **28**, 835–845 (2021)
3. Draschkowitz, L., Draschkowitz, C., Hlavacs, H.: Using video analysis and machine learning for predicting shot success in table tennis. EAI Endorsed Trans. Creative Technol. **2**, e2–e2 (2015)
4. Ji, Y., Zhang, J., Shi, Z., Liu, M., Ren, J.: Research on real-time tracking of table tennis ball based on machine learning with low-speed camera. Systems Sci. Control Eng. **6**, 71–79 (2018)
5. Zhang, H., et al.: Application of intelligent sensor network in the assessment of table tennis teaching and training intensity, training volume, and physical fitness. J. Sensors **2022** (2022)
6. Djokić, Z., Malagoli Lanzoni, I., Katsikadelis, M., Straub, G., et al.: Others Serve analyses of elite European table tennis matches, Universidad de Granada (2020)
7. Wong, P., Dooley, L.: Tracking table tennis balls in real match scenes for umpiring applications. British J. Math. Comput. Sci. **1**, 228–241 (2011)
8. Gastinger, R., Litzenberger, S., Sabo, A.: Design, development and construction of a monitoring table tennis net. Proc. Eng. **13**, 297–303 (2011)
9. Blank, P., Groh, B., Eskofier, B.: Ball speed and spin estimation in table tennis using a racket-mounted inertial sensor. In: Proceedings of the 2017 ACM International Symposium on Wearable Computers, pp. 2–9 (2017)
10. Nonaka, Y., Irie, K., Ando, S., Yamada, Y. Application of IMU-based motion measurement methods to table tennis coaching. In: Proceedings of the Symposium On Sports and Human Dynamics. Japan Society Of Mechanical Engineers, Tokyo, Japan (2018)
11. Blank, P., Hoßbach, J., Schuldhaus, D., Eskofier, B.: Sensor-based stroke detection and stroke type classification in table tennis. Proceedings of the 2015 ACM International Symposium on Wearable Computers, pp. 93–100 (2015)
12. Bańkosz, Z., Winiarski, S.: Using wearable inertial sensors to estimate kinematic parameters and variability in the table tennis topspin forehand stroke. Applied Bion. Biomech. (2020)

13. Li, H., et al.: Others Video-based table tennis tracking and trajectory prediction using convolutional neural networks. Fractals **30** (2022)
14. Malagoli Lanzoni, I., Di Michele, R., Merni, F.: A notational analysis of shot characteristics in top-level table tennis players. Europ. J. Sport Sci. **14**, 309–317 (2014)
15. Gardner, M., Dorling, S.: Artificial neural networks (the multilayer perceptron)-a review of applications in the atmospheric sciences. Atmos. Environ. **32**, 2627–2636 (1998)
16. Ali, J., Khan, R., Ahmad, N., Maqsood, I.: Random forests and decision trees. Int. J. Comput. Sci. Issues (IJCSI) **9**, 272 (2012)
17. Si, S., Zhang, H., Keerthi, S., Mahajan, D., Dhillon, I., Hsieh, C.: Gradient boosted decision trees for high dimensional sparse output. In: International Conference On Machine Learning, pp. 3182–3190 (2017)
18. Abadi, M., et al.: TensorFlow: Large-Scale Machine Learning on Heterogeneous Systems. (2015). https://www.tensorflow.org/, Software available from tensorflow.org
19. Chollet, F., et al.: Keras (2015). https://keras.io
20. Zhang, Z.: Improved adam optimizer for deep neural networks. In: 2018 IEEE/ACM 26th International Symposium on Quality of Service (IWQoS), pp. 1–2 (2018)
21. Denison, D., Mallick, B., Smith, A.: A bayesian cart algorithm. Biometrika **85**, 363–377 (1998)

# Towards Explaining Shortcut Learning Through Attention Visualization and Adversarial Attacks

Pedro Gonçalo Correia[(✉)] and Henrique Lopes Cardoso

Faculdade de Engenharia, Universidade do Porto, Rua Dr. Roberto Frias, 4200-465 Porto, Portugal
pedrogoncalocorreia@hotmail.com, hlc@fe.up.pt

**Abstract.** Since its introduction, the attention-based Transformer architecture has become the *de facto* standard for building models with state-of-the-art performance on many Natural Language Processing tasks. However, it seems that the success of these models might have to do with their exploitation of dataset artifacts, rendering them unable to generalize to other data and vulnerable to adversarial attacks. On the other hand, the attention mechanism present in all models based on the Transformer, such as BERT-based ones, has been seen by many as a potential way to explain these deep learning models: by visualizing attention weights, it might be possible to gain insights on the reasons behind these opaque models' decisions. This paper introduces Attentive-BERT, an interactive attention weights visualization tool for diagnosing BERT-based models, focusing on explaining the occurrence of shortcut learning. The distinctive feature of this tool is enabling the visual comparison of attention weights before and after a change to the model's input, in order to visually analyse adversarial attacks. Some illustrations of this use case are explored in this paper.

**Keywords:** Attention visualization tool · BERT · Shortcut learning · Adversarial attacks

## 1 Introduction

Over the past few years, the field of Natural Language Processing (NLP) has seen remarkable progress, with language representation models exhibiting ever-increasing gains on existing benchmarks. In fact, since its introduction, the Transformer architecture [37] has served as a base for many models that have achieved state-of-the-art performance on many NLP tasks [1,7,35].

This apparent success raises the question: are these models making progress towards being able to understand language like a human does? Unfortunately, studies have shown that these models often exploit biases in the dataset, leveraging spurious features in order to achieve the reported performances [12,14,27].

This research is supported by Calouste Gulbenkian Foundation and by Fundação para a Ciência e a Tecnologia, through LIACC (UIDB/00027/2020).

This phenomenon, known as shortcut learning, undermines the models' capability to generalize to data that does not present such spurious artifacts. This reveals not only that the model is unable to actually grasp the meaning of its inputs, but also that it is susceptible to unexpected failures, for example, in real world applications [12]. Thus, being able to diagnose a model to determine the occurrence of shortcut learning is desirable.

One way to assess whether the model is relying on undesired characteristics in the data is by testing it against adversarial attacks: small perturbations made to inputs intentionally designed to deceive a machine learning model into outputting an incorrect answer, without changing the semantics of the input [13]. If the model is changing its prediction based on differences that should be irrelevant to the meaning of the input and, by extension, the output result, then it is likely that the model is not learning to perform well in the task for the right reasons. In other words, successful adversarial attacks are a sign that shortcut learning may be occurring.

However, when an adversarial attack succeeds, the reason for the model's failure is not obvious. Deep learning algorithms are often labelled black box models [6,18,22] because their complexity and huge amount of parameters makes them extremely hard to interpret by humans. Despite that, many efforts have been made seeking to understand the language representation models' inner workings [8,15,19]. One topic of high interest for studying the explainability of these models is the visualization and interpretation of the attention mechanism [16,33,40], one of the core components of the Transformer and of the models that are based on it. As a high-level description, this mechanism consists of assigning non-negative weights to each input token, according to its relevance, and then doing the weighted sum of the tokens' representations based on those weights [10].

This paper presents AttentiveBERT[1], an interactive visualization tool of attention weights for diagnosing the Transformer-based model BERT [7] and its variants, with a focus on the analysis of adversarial attacks. This tool enables the visualization of attention weights for a single input, as well as comparing the attention weights of two inputs. It is possible to try to generate an adversarial attack for a given input or, for convenience, to include a pre-generated list of adversarial attacks to visualize. Additionally, this tool includes informative and didactic content to explain the main relevant concepts, such as the attention mechanism, shortcut learning and adversarial attacks.

The rest of the paper is structured as follows. In Sect. 2 we review relevant concepts for understanding the attention mechanism, shortcut learning, and related work concerning attention weights visualization. In Sect. 3 we describe in detail the AttentiveBERT tool, exposing several use cases. In Sect. 4 we show how to generate adversarial attacks in the tool and how differences can be observed. Section 5 concludes.

---

[1] Available on Github: https://github.com/Goncalerta/AttentiveBERT.

## 2   Background

### 2.1   Attention Mechanism

Just like humans don't tend to process the entirety of information received by their senses at once, the idea that machine learning models could focus their attention selectively on parts of their inputs first came from computer vision [10, 25]. Soon after that, this concept was introduced in the context of NLP for the task of machine translation [2], with the proposal of an encoder-decoder architecture that employed an *attention* mechanism in its decoder to decide which parts of the input state it should give more relevance to.

A prominent model largely based on attention mechanisms is the Transformer [37], an encoder-decoder architecture initially proposed for the task of machine translation that dispenses recurrence and convolutions (as used in recurrent and convolutional neural networks, the prior state-of-the-art architectures). Each encoder of the Transformer has six attention heads, which independently calculate the *self-attention* from the output of the previous encoder (or the word embeddings for the first encoder) so that the results are then combined. In short, in the *self-attention* mechanism, each input token becomes a weighted mean of all input tokens, where the weights given to each pair of tokens are known as *attention weights* and are calculated by the model.

Many recent models that have achieved state-of-the-art performance in NLP have been based on the Transformer architecture. One such example is the Bidirectional Encoder Representations from Transformers, best known as BERT [7]. As the name implies, this architecture only uses the stack of encoders from the Transformer architecture, discarding the decoders. BERT also adds special tokens to its input: $[CLS]$, whose corresponding output representation is to be fed into a classifier for classification tasks, $[SEP]$, to mark the end of a sentence, and $[MASK]$, to mark that a word has been masked for tasks such as masked language modeling.

### 2.2   Shortcut Learning

Given the impact shortcut learning may have on the usefulness of a model, it is important to study this phenomenon. Previous work has tried to explain and interpret the occurrence of shortcut learning in NLP.

Han *et al.* [15] develop a method to measure artifacts in the training data, such as lexical overlap, based on influence functions. This method is based on measuring how increasing the importance of a given training example would affect the model's prediction for the test input [18]. Intuitively, a positive influence score means that removing this training example would result in the model's confidence decreasing, while a negative influence means that it would result in the confidence increasing. If the model is exploiting a given data artifact then it is likely that it will be more influenced by training examples that also exhibit that artifact. Han *et al.* conclude that influence functions are consistent with gradient-based saliency maps in the task of sentiment analysis, but not on natural language inference. Their analysis of influence functions on natural language inference also revealed that their model might have relied on spurious artifacts such as lexical overlap between the premise and the hypothesis.

Other analyses have shown that the performance of BERT-based models for the natural language inference task could be explained by spurious artifacts such as the presence of the words "not", "do", "is", and bigrams such as "will not" [8,14,27]. Other found artifacts in natural language inference have to do with the sentence length, with shorter sentences being associated with entailment and longer sentences with the neutral relation [14].

Branco et al. [5] performed experiments to study whether language representation models are learning generalizable features in commonsense tasks, or simply exploiting shortcuts. In one experiment, they remove relevant parts of the input and retrain the task, finding that in some tasks the models retained their performance, suggesting that they are solving the tasks using shortcuts.

## 2.3 Visualizing Attention Weights

Other than the performance gains on the models in which they are applied, attention mechanisms also have the advantage of being an instrument to try to interpret models that employ them. In fact, by visualizing attention weights, studies have tried to explain these models' decisions.

Kovaleva et al. [19] manually inspected self-attention heatmaps of BERT models, identifying five types of patterns: *Vertical*, in which attention is given mainly to special tokens [CLS] and [SEP]; *Diagonal* in which attention is given mainly to the previous or next token in the input; *Vertical + Diagonal* which is a mix of the previous types; *Block*, in which the attention is mainly given to tokens in the same sentence; and *Heterogeneous* which is highly variable depending on the input, without a distinct structure. They noted that the first three types of patterns are less likely to capture interpretable linguistic features, because they only take into account adjacency of the tokens and special tokens.

Because of the potential that attention weights seem to offer to interpret language models, past work has already introduced interactive tools to visualize these weights. Lee et al. [21] introduced a tool to visualize and manipulate (manually and automatically) beam search trees and attention weights of neural machine translation models. Strobelt et al. [34] presented a tool to visually analyse each stage of the translation process of a trained sequence-to-sequence model, one of which was the attention stage. Vig [38] introduced an open-source visualization tool of Transformer-based models named BertViz. This tool provided three view modes: an attention head-view, to visualize a single attention head in a bipartite graph; a model view, which presents bipartite graphs of every head in every layer of the model in a tabular form; and a neuron view, which shows how the query and key learned parameters produce the attention weights. However, the tool only supports the visualization for a single input at a time, while in the context of adversarial attacks it is desirable to compare the difference in the attention patterns of two almost identical, yet different inputs.

# 3    AttentiveBERT

In order to study the attention patterns in adversarial attacks, we have developed a visualization tool named AttentiveBERT. This is an interactive tool designed to visualize the attention weights of BERT-based models, both for a single input and for comparing pairs of inputs. Although the tool is focused on the study of adversarial attacks, it can also be used for visualizing attention weights in other contexts.

## 3.1    Tasks

AttentiveBERT is designed to work with three different, but similar classification tasks. All three tasks deal with pairs of sentences as input, classifying their relation with one of three labels, depending on the relation between the sentences.

The first one is *Natural Language Inference* (NLI) [24], also known as *Recognizing Textual Entailment* (RTE). It consists of, given a premise and an hypothesis, determining whether the relation between them is of entailment, contradiction or neutral.

The second task is *Argumentative Relation Identification* (ARI) [28,31]. This is a subtask of *Argument Mining* that, given two Argumentative Discourse Units (ADU), aims at classifying whether the first (known as source ADU) supports, attacks or has no relation to the second (known as target ADU).

The third task is *Fact Verification* (FV), also known as *Claim Verification* (CV). This is a subtask of *Fact Extraction and VERification* (FEVER) [36]. It can be formulated as, given a claim and evidence, whether that evidence supports or refutes the claim, or rather if there is not enough information to determine the veracity of the claim [3,8].

## 3.2    Models and Configuration

The tool is designed to work with any BERT-based model available on HuggingFace Transformers [41]. For that, a JSON configuration file for each model must be included in the configuration folder before running the tool. This configuration includes the source for the model, the task, an array of pre-generated adversarial attacks, and optional metadata.

For illustration purposes, the tool includes by default the configuration for a case-sensitive DistilBERT [32] model that was fine-tuned to the NLI task with the Stanford Natural Language Inference (SNLI) dataset [4].[2] This is the model analysed in this paper.

## 3.3    Single Input Visualization

In AttentiveBERT, it is possible to select one of the available tasks and models and run the model for an inputted pair of sentences, observing the result.

---

[2] https://huggingface.co/boychaboy/SNLI_distilbert-base-cased.

The visualizer (see Fig. 1) is composed of three main components. The first is a *confidence bar* on the top, showing the model's predicted label and its confidence for each label, in percentage. The second component is an *attention weights heatmap* on the left, showing, for every pair of tokens in the input, how much weight is being attributed to that pair. The higher the intensity of blue, the more weight is being attributed, while the color white represents a weight of zero. The third component is an *attention head selector* on the right. This is a matrix of buttons to select the attention head to visualize. The x-axis exposes the heads and the y-axis the model's layers. Instead of visualizing a single head's attention weights, it is also possible to visualize average attention weights over multiple heads or layers. For that, the axis label itself may be selected. If the average attention weight over all heads and layers in the model is desired, the circular button in the bottom left of this component may be selected.

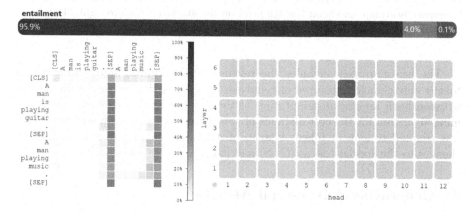

**Fig. 1.** Visualization of the attention weights of the 7th head on the 5th layer of a model for the premise "*A man is playing guitar.*" and hypothesis "*A man playing music.*".

### 3.4 Compare Inputs Visualization

In order to compare the attention weights before and after an adversarial attack, it is desirable to directly compare the attention weights of two inputs. For that, the tool offers the possibility of running the model with two different inputs, comparing the attention weights of both inputs in a single heatmap.

The resulting visualizer (see Fig. 2) is similar to the one described for single inputs. On top of the matrix of buttons, two new radio buttons are shown, to select the comparison mode. In "Compare heatmap" mode, each cell is divided in two, presenting the weight for the first input on its left side and the weight for the second input on its right side. In "Difference heatmap" mode, each cell presents the subtraction of the weights, with a green color for positive values and red for negative values, the intensity of the color denoting the absolute value.

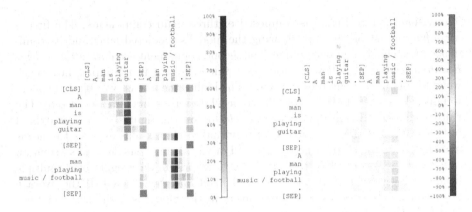

**Fig. 2.** Comparison of the attention weights for the premise "*A man is playing guitar.*" and hypotheses "*A man playing music.*" and "*A man playing football.*". On the left: "Compare heatmap" mode on the 4th head on the 4th layer. On the right: "Difference heatmap" mode for the average attention weights of the heads of the 6th layer.

The heatmap axes includes the tokens of both inputs, highlighting which tokens were changed, inserted or removed. In order to determine the differences between both inputs, an adaptation of the Wagner-Fischer dynamic programming algorithm for the edit distance of two strings [39] was used. The algorithm was adapted to look at tokens instead of individual characters and to disallow changes to the special tokens [CLS] and [SEP].

## 4   Generating Adversarial Attacks

AttentiveBERT can generate adversarial attacks for a given input using many techniques proposed in the literature, namely TextFooler [17], BERT-attack [23], BAE [11], the greedy algorithm proposed by Kuleshov *et al.* [20], PWWS [29], InputReduction [9], and Checklist [30]. The respective implementations offered by Textattack [26] were used. In the case of BERT-attack, the number of candidates was reduced to 8, given that the original value was unreasonably slow without significant gains. It is also possible to compose a list of pre-generated attacks, which AttentiveBERT can show in a tabular form.

By visually comparing the attention weights of the model given the input before and after the adversarial attacks, it is possible to notice interesting patterns.

For instance, in some cases where the model shifts prediction there is a shift in the average attention given to a token in favor of other tokens. This is the case with Fig. 3. On the left, a shift can be seen from the token "*summer*" to the token "*##arel*" and the prediction goes from contradiction (94%) to entailment (48%). Since the premise talks about a man in winter clothing, it is possible that having less attention in "*summer*" is responsible for the model changing the prediction. However, it is important to note that the the word "*apparel*" might not have appeared often in the training set, as suggested by its fragmented tokenization. On the right, the model changes the prediction from neutral (86.4%) to entailment (75%). A decrease in attention to the changed token can be seen, which might explain the change in the prediction. In fact, the tokens "*selling*"/"*gathering*" are the only ones in the hypothesis that are not implied by the premise, so they are the relevant tokens to conclude that the correct label is neutral.

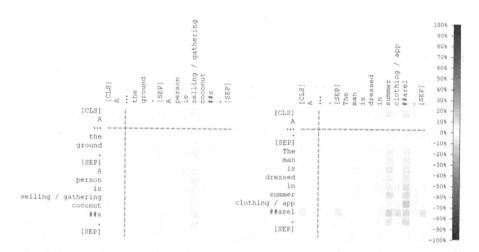

**Fig. 3.** On the left: Average attention weights difference over all heads for an example adversarial attack with premise "*A person wearing a straw hat, standing outside working a steel apparatus with a pile of coconuts on the ground.*" and hypotheses "*A person is selling coconuts.*" and "*A person is gathering coconuts.*". On the right: Comparison of the average attention weights difference over all heads for the pair of inputs with premise "*A person dressed in white and black winter clothing leaps a narrow, water-filled ditch from one frost-covered field to another, where a female dressed in black coat and pants awaits.*" and hypotheses "*The man is dressed in summer clothing.*" and "*The man is dressed in summer apparel.*", respectively. (some irrelevant tokens were omitted to reduce the size of the figure)

Another interesting finding is that, in this model, the 3rd head of the 2nd layer seemed to be specialized in, for each token, paying attention to tokens that appear later in the input and have a similar meaning. This may be relevant in explaining some adversarial attacks, as shown in Fig. 4, where the difference in predictions is, respectively: entailment (97.7%) to neutral (73.7%); entailment (97.2%) to contradiction (48.4%); neutral (97.3%) to contradiction (80.7%). In the first example, the words "*playground*" and "*play*" don't produce a strong connection as would be expected. The same happens in the second example, with the words "*river*" and "*wet*". In the third example, "*cup*" is much less associated with "*drinking*", "*alcoholic*" and "*beverage*" than "*beverage*" is. These weaker associations may be the cause of the model's wrong predictions.

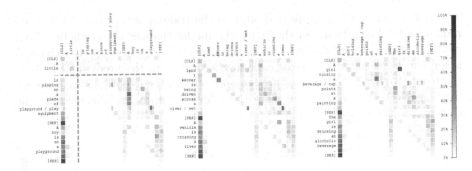

**Fig. 4.** Comparison of attention weights on the 3rd head of the 2nd layer of the model, before and after small changes to the inputs. From left to right: "*A little boy in a gray and white striped sweater and tan pants is playing on a piece of playground/play equipment. (Color figure online)*" and "*A boy is on a playground.*", "*A land rover is being driven across a river/wet.*" and "*A vehicle is crossing a river.*", "*A girl holding a beverage/cup points at a painting.*" and "*The girl is drinking an alcoholic beverage.*". (some irrelevant tokens were omitted to reduce the size of the figure)

## 5   Conclusion

In this work, a new tool was developed to visually analyse the attention weights of BERT-based models. This tool allows the visualization of those weights in different attention heads and even averages of heads for a single input or to compare the differences caused by changes in the input. This tool may prove useful in future studies of BERT-based models for interpreting the model behavior, particularly in the context of adversarial attacks. Some interesting use cases of this tool were explored, exposing patterns that may be further analysed in subsequent studies.

In future work, this tool may be extended to other NLP tasks and to other Transformer-based models. Another possibility is to implement alternative ways to visualize the weights, such as bipartite graphs or the total attention given to each token by all the others.

**Acknowledgements.** This research is supported by the Calouste Gulbenkian Foundation and by LIACC (FCT/UID/CEC/0027/2020), funded by Fundação para a Ciência e a Tecnologia (FCT).

## References

1. Chowdhery, A. et al.: PaLM: Scaling Language Modeling with Pathways. arXiv:2204.02311 (2022)
2. Bahdanau, D., Cho, K., Bengio, Y.: Neural Machine Translation by Jointly Learning to Align and Translate. In: Bengio, Y., LeCun, Y. (eds.) 3rd Int. Conf. on Learning Representations, ICLR 2015, San Diego, CA, USA, May 7–9, 2015, Conf. Track Proceedings (2015)

3. Bekoulis, G., Papagiannopoulou, C., Deligiannis, N.: A Review on Fact Extraction and Verification. ACM Comput. Surv. **55**(1) (nov 2021). https://doi.org/10.1145/3485127

4. Bowman, S.R., Angeli, G., Potts, C., Manning, C.D.: A large annotated corpus for learning natural language inference. In: Proceedings of 2015 Conference on Empirical Methods in Natural Language Processing, pp. 632–642. ACL, Lisbon, Portugal (Sep 2015). https://doi.org/10.18653/v1/D15-1075

5. Branco, R., Branco, A., António Rodrigues, J., Silva, J.R.: Shortcutted Commonsense: Data Spuriousness in Deep Learning of Commonsense Reasoning. In: Proceedings of 2021 Conference on Empirical Methods in Natural Language Processing, pp. 1504–1521. ACL (Nov 2021). https://doi.org/10.18653/v1/2021.emnlp-main.113

6. Buhrmester, V., Münch, D., Arens, M.: Analysis of Explainers of Black Box Deep Neural Networks for Computer Vision: a survey. Mach. Learn. Knowl. Extract. **3**(4), 966–989 (2021). https://doi.org/10.3390/make3040048

7. Devlin, J., Chang, M.W., Lee, K., Toutanova, K.: BERT: Pre-training of Deep Bidirectional Transformers for Language Understanding. In: Proc. 2019 Conf. of the North American Chapter of the Association for Computational Linguistics: Human Language Technologies, Volume 1 (Long and Short Papers), pp. 4171–4186. ACL, Minneapolis, Minnesota (Jun 2019). https://doi.org/10.18653/v1/N19-1423

8. Du, M., et al.: owards Interpreting and Mitigating Shortcut Learning Behavior of NLU models. In: Proc. 2021 Conf. of the North American Chapter of the Association for Computational Linguistics: Human Language Technologies, pp. 915–929. ACL (Jun 2021). https://doi.org/10.18653/v1/2021.naacl-main.71

9. Feng, S., Wallace, E., Grissom II, A., Iyyer, M., Rodriguez, P., Boyd-Graber, J.: Pathologies of Neural Models Make Interpretations Difficult. In: Proc. 2018 Conf. on Empirical Methods in Natural Language Processing, pp. 3719–3728. ACL, Brussels, Belgium (Oct-Nov 2018). https://doi.org/10.18653/v1/D18-1407

10. Galassi, A., Lippi, M., Torroni, P.: Attention in Natural Language Processing. IEEE Trans. Neural Netw. Learn. Syst. **32**(10), 4291–4308 (10 2021). https://doi.org/10.1109/tnnls.2020.3019893

11. Garg, S., Ramakrishnan, G.: BAE: BERT-based Adversarial Examples for Text Classification. In: Proc. 2020 Conf. on Empirical Methods in Natural Language Processing (EMNLP), pp. 6174–6181. ACL (Nov 2020). https://doi.org/10.18653/v1/2020.emnlp-main.498

12. Geirhos, R., et al.: Shortcut learning in deep neural networks. Nature Mach. Intell. **2**(11), 665–673 (11 2020). https://doi.org/10.1038/s42256-020-00257-z

13. Goodfellow, I.J., Shlens, J., Szegedy, C.: Explaining and Harnessing Adversarial Examples. In: Bengio, Y., LeCun, Y. (eds.) 3rd Int. Conf. on Learning Representations, ICLR 2015, San Diego, CA, USA, May 7–9, 2015, Conference Track Proceedings (2015)

14. Gururangan, S., Swayamdipta, S., Levy, O., Schwartz, R., Bowman, S., Smith, N.A.: Annotation Artifacts in Natural Language Inference Data. In: Proc. 2018 Conf. of the North American Chapter of the Association for Computational Linguistics: Human Language Technologies, Volume 2 (Short Papers), pp. 107–112. ACL, New Orleans, Louisiana (Jun 2018). https://doi.org/10.18653/v1/N18-2017

15. Han, X., Wallace, B.C., Tsvetkov, Y.: Explaining Black Box Predictions and Unveiling Data Artifacts through Influence Functions. In: Proceedings of the 58th Annual Meeting of the Association for Computational Linguistics, pp. 5553–5563. ACL (Jul 2020). 10.18653/v1/2020.acl-main.492

16. Jain, S., Wallace, B.C.: Attention is not Explanation. In: Proceedings 2019 Conf. of the North American Chapter of the Association for Computational Linguistics: Human Language Technologies, Volume 1 (Long and Short Papers), pp. 3543–3556. ACL, Minneapolis, Minnesota (Jun 2019). https://doi.org/10.18653/v1/N19-1357

17. Jin, D., Jin, Z., Zhou, J.T., Szolovits, P.: Is BERT Really Robust? A Strong Baseline for Natural Language Attack on Text Classification and Entailment. In: Proceedings of the AAAI Conference on Artificial Intelligence. vol. 34, pp. 8018–8025 (Apr 2020). https://doi.org/10.1609/aaai.v34i05.6311

18. Koh, P.W., Liang, P.: Understanding Black-Box Predictions via Influence Functions. In: Proceedings of the 34th International Conference on Machine Learning - Volume 70, pp. 1885–1894. JMLR.org (2017)

19. Kovaleva, O., Romanov, A., Rogers, A., Rumshisky, A.: Revealing the Dark Secrets of BERT. In: Proceedings of the 2019 Conference on Empirical Methods in Natural Language Processing and the 9th Int. J. Conf. on Natural Language Processing (EMNLP-IJCNLP), pp. 4365–4374. ACL, Hong Kong, China (Nov 2019). https://doi.org/10.18653/v1/D19-1445

20. Kuleshov, V., Thakoor, S., Lau, T., Ermon, S.: Adversarial Examples for Natural Language Classification Problems (2018). https://openreview.net/forum?id=r1QZ3zbAZ

21. Lee, J., Shin, J.H., Kim, J.S.: Interactive Visualization and Manipulation of Attention-based Neural Machine Translation. In: Proceedings of the 2017 Conference on Empirical Methods in Natural Language Processing: System Demonstrations, pp. 121–126. ACL, Copenhagen, Denmark (Sep 2017). https://doi.org/10.18653/v1/D17-2021

22. Lei, D., Chen, X., Zhao, J.: Opening the black box of deep learning. arXiv:1805.08355 (2018)

23. Li, L., Ma, R., Guo, Q., Xue, X., Qiu, X.: BERT-ATTACK: Adversarial Attack Against BERT Using BERT. In: Proceedings 2020 Conference on Empirical Methods in Natural Language Processing (EMNLP), pp. 6193–6202. ACL (Nov 2020). https://doi.org/10.18653/v1/2020.emnlp-main.500

24. MacCartney, B., Manning, C.D.: Modeling Semantic Containment and Exclusion in Natural Language Inference. In: Proceedings of the 22nd International Conference on Computational Linguistics (Coling 2008), pp. 521–528. Coling 2008 Organizing Committee, Manchester, UK (Aug 2008)

25. Mnih, V., Heess, N., Graves, A., Kavukcuoglu, K.: Recurrent Models of Visual Attention. In: Proceedings of the 27th International Conference on Neural Information Processing Systems - vol. 2, pp.. 2204–2212. NIPS'14, MIT Press, Cambridge, MA, USA (2014)

26. Morris, J., Lifland, E., Yoo, J.Y., Grigsby, J., Jin, D., Qi, Y.: TextAttack: A framework for adversarial attacks, data augmentation, and adversarial training in NLP. In: Proceedings 2020 Conference on Empirical Methods in Natural Language Processing: System Demonstrations, pp. 119–126. ACL (Oct 2020). https://doi.org/10.18653/v1/2020.emnlp-demos.16

27. Niven, T., Kao, H.Y.: Probing Neural Network Comprehension of Natural Language Arguments. In: Proceedings of the 57th Annual Meeting of the Association for Computational Linguistics, pp. 4658–4664. ACL, Florence, Italy (Jul 2019). https://doi.org/10.18653/v1/P19-1459

28. Peldszus, A., Stede, M.: Joint prediction in MST-style discourse parsing for argumentation mining. In: Proceedings of the 2015 Conference. on Empirical Methods in Natural Language Processing, pp. 938–948. ACL, Lisbon, Portugal (Sep 2015). https://doi.org/10.18653/v1/D15-1110

29. Ren, S., Deng, Y., He, K., Che, W.: Generating Natural Language Adversarial Examples through Probability Weighted Word Saliency. In: Proceedings of the 57th Annual Meeting of the Association for Computational Linguistics, pp. 1085–1097. ACL, Florence, Italy (Jul 2019). https://doi.org/10.18653/v1/P19-1103

30. Ribeiro, M.T., Wu, T., Guestrin, C., Singh, S.: Beyond accuracy: Behavioral testing of NLP models with CheckList. In: Proceedings of the 58th Annual Meeting of the Association for Computational Linguistics, pp. 4902–4912. ACL (Jul 2020). https://doi.org/10.18653/v1/2020.acl-main.442

31. Rocha, G., Stab, C., Lopes Cardoso, H., Gurevych, I.: Cross-lingual argumentative relation identification: from English to Portuguese. In: Proceedings of the 5th Workshop on Argument Mining, pp. 144–154. ACL, Brussels, Belgium (Nov 2018). https://doi.org/10.18653/v1/W18-5217

32. Sanh, V., Debut, L., Chaumond, J., Wolf, T.: Distilbert, a distilled version of bert: smaller, faster, cheaper and lighter. ArXiv abs/1910.01108 (2019)

33. Serrano, S., Smith, N.A.: Is Attention Interpretable? In: Proceedings of the 57th Annual Meeting of the Association for Computational Linguistics, pp. 2931–2951. ACL, Florence, Italy (Jul 2019). https://doi.org/10.18653/v1/P19-1282

34. Strobelt, H., Gehrmann, S., Behrisch, M., Perer, A., Pfister, H., Rush, A.M.: Seq2seq-Vis: a visual debugging tool for sequence-to-sequence models. IEEE Trans. Visual Comput. Graph. **25**(1), 353–363 (2019). https://doi.org/10.1109/TVCG.2018.2865044

35. Brown, T., et al.: Language Models are Few-Shot Learners. In: Larochelle, H., Ranzato, M., Hadsell, R., Balcan, M.F., Lin, H. (eds.) In: Advances in Neural Information Processing Systems. vol. 33, pp. 1877–1901. Curran Associates, Inc. (2020)

36. Thorne, J., Vlachos, A., Christodoulopoulos, C., Mittal, A.: FEVER: a Large-scale Dataset for Fact Extraction and VERification. In: Proceedings of the 2018 Conference of the North American Chapter of the Association for Computational Linguistics: Human Language Technologies, Volume 1 (Long Papers), pp. 809–819. ACL, New Orleans, Louisiana (Jun 2018). https://doi.org/10.18653/v1/N18-1074

37. Vaswani, A., et al.: Attention is All You Need. In: Proc. Int. Conf. on Neural Information Processing Systems, pp. 6000–6010. NIPS'17, Curran Associates Inc., Red Hook, NY, USA (2017)

38. Vig, J.: A Multiscale Visualization of Attention in the Transformer Model. In: Proceedings 57th Annual Meeting of the Association for Computational Linguistics: System Demonstrations, pp. 37–42. ACL, Florence, Italy (Jul 2019). https://doi.org/10.18653/v1/P19-3007

39. Wagner, R.A., Fischer, M.J.: The String-to-String Correction Problem. J. ACM **21**(1), 168–173 (1 1974). https://doi.org/10.1145/321796.321811

40. Wiegreffe, S., Pinter, Y.: Attention is not not Explanation. In: Proceedings of the 2019 Conference on Empirical Methods in Natural Language Processing and the 9th International Journal Conference on Natural Language Processing (EMNLP-IJCNLP), pp. 11–20. ACL, Hong Kong, China (Nov 2019). https://doi.org/10.18653/v1/D19-1002

41. Wolf, T., et al.: Transformers: State-of-the-Art Natural Language Processing. In: Proceedings of the 2020 Conference on Empirical Methods in Natural Language Processing: System Demonstrations, pp. 38–45. ACL (Oct 2020). https://doi.org/10.18653/v1/2020.emnlp-demos.6

# Natural Language - Recommendation Systems

# A Novel Neural Network-Based Recommender System for Drug Recommendation

Hadi Al Mubasher[1]([⊠]) [iD], Ziad Doughan[1] [iD], Layth Sliman[2] [iD],
and Ali Haidar[1] [iD]

[1] Faculty of Engineering, Beirut Arab Univeristy, Debbieh, Lebanon
{h.mubasher,z.doughan,ari}@bau.edu.lb
[2] École d'Ingénieurs Généraliste du Numérique, Paris, France
layth.sliman@efrei.fr

**Abstract.** With the advancement of Machine Learning, recommender systems have emerged with the aim of improving the user experience in a world where data and available alternatives are tremendously growing. Employing Natural Language Processing with such systems can provide them with a sense of empowerment, given that most of the users' opinions are reflected through reviews. Artificial Neural Networks, the core of Deep Learning, have sparked a lot of interest in many research fields, owing to the appealing property of learning feature representations out of nowhere. To that end, this paper presents a novel hybrid recommender system that is based on Natural Language Processing and Artificial Neural Networks. The proposed model is evaluated and compared with a similar model, where the advantages of the proposed model are clearly presented. The paper is concluded by highlighting research opportunities that can be done in the future.

**Keywords:** Machine Learning · Recommender Systems · Natural Language Processing · Deep Learning · Artificial Neural Networks · Drug Recommendation

## 1 Introduction

A recommender system is a class of Machine Learning that makes use of data to predict, narrow down, and find what users are looking for among a growing number of options. Personalization is an important strategy for improving user experience, given the exponential growth of information available on the web [30]. In general, recommendations are made based on item features and user preferences. This paper presents a hybrid recommender system that is based on Natural Language Processing (NLP) methods and Deep Learning models.

Recommender systems also make use of data related to previous user-item interactions to predict future user-item interactions. These systems can be based on demographic filtering, collaborative filtering, content-based filtering, or hybrid approaches [21]. Demographic Recommendation Systems (DRSs) are based on the demographic profile information of the user like location, age, gender, education, etc. Such recommender systems use clustering techniques to categorize the target users based on their demographic profile information. Collaborative Filtering Recommender Systems (CFRSs) are the mostly implemented recommender systems. Such systems recommend items for a certain user based on the preference information of other users; given the previous user-item interactions. CFRSs are based on the fact that if two or more users have common preferences, they are likely to share similar preferences in the future. For example, if two users have watched almost the same movies and the first user watched a certain movie that hasn't been watched by the second user, the second user might watch this movie in the future, so the system recommends this movie to the second user. Content-Based Recommender Systems (CBRSs) rely on item features or attributes. Such systems learn the attributes of the items chosen by a certain user and recommend similar items to the user. Hybrid recommender systems follow an approach that combines filtering methods used in CFRSs and CBRSs for the aim of improving the model accuracy.

NLP is a branch in Machine Learning that helps machines analyze and understand the human language [14]. NLP have played a significant role in the advancement of recommender systems, where users can express their opinions about a certain item through reviews. With the help of NLP, recommender systems can analyze user reviews [20]. NLP methods were used for building a customer loyalty improvement recommender system [23], and for developing an E-tourism recommender system [1].

Deep Learning is currently enjoying a lot of attention. Over the last few decades, this field has achieved tremendous success in many application domains like speech recognition and computer vision [30]. Artificial Neural Networks (ANNs), the core of Deep Learning, have the ability to model the non-linearity in data using non-linear activation functions. This property enables the capturing of intricate and complex user-item interaction patterns and therefore makes the recommender system more accurate. Also, ANNs were used in many applications like image recognition [9], pattern correction [8], and optimization of deformed images [10]. ANNs were also used in hardware design applications [11,12].

The following is a breakdown of the paper's structure. A literature survey with an emphasis on the weaknesses of existing similar works, in addition to the methodology of developing the proposed system, are presented in Sect. 2. Section 3 explains how the recommender system is implemented. The results and evaluation are discussed in Sect. 4. The paper is concluded and research opportunities and further investigations that can be done are highlighted in Sect. 5. A roadmap of the proposed model is presented in Fig. 1.

## 2    Related Work

To propose a novel recommender system, further investigations in the literature are required to highlight unsolved issues. The work presented in [25] aimed for developing a hybrid recommender system for movie recommendation with the use

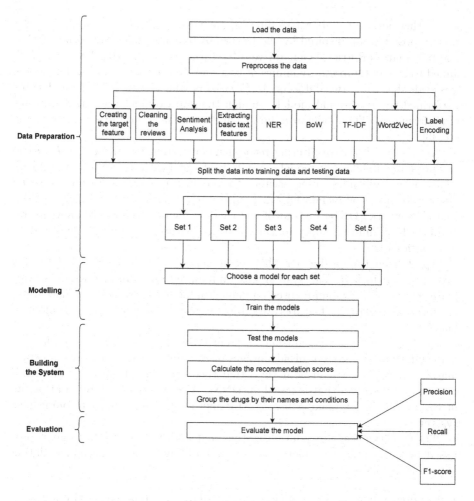

**Fig. 1.** Roadmap of the proposed model.

of an expert system. The system used the Singular Value Decomposition (SVD) algorithm, in addition to the Term Frequency-Inverse Document Frequency (TF-IDF) model and a linguistic Fuzzy logic controller. The system achieved better results than traditional systems, but the precision was still low (almost 80%).

In addition, a hotel content-based recommender system was proposed in [24]. The system was based on the similarity between users. The system had a low precision and a low accuracy [24].

Moreover, a content-based recommender system that uses Cosine Similarity and K-Nearest Neighbors (K-NN) Classification to recommend movies to users was presented in [22]. The model focused on minor features like the movie genre and movie popularity [22].

Furthermore, a collaborative filtering recommender system named *RecGAN* was proposed in [3], inspired by the Recurrent Recommender Networks (RRNs) and Information Retrieval Generative Adversarial Networks (IRGANs). *RecGAN* aimed to model temporal dynamics of user and item latent features. The model was evaluated using two datasets, *MyFitnessPal*, and *Netflix* [3]. The model outperformed the traditional models, though the improvement was slight in terms of performance. The model also didn't handle auxiliary data like texts, reviews, etc. [3].

Also, a collaborative filtering recommender system based on *AutoEncoders* was presented in [26]. The model was not able to deal with the cold-start problem, which occurs when the user or item has no history, so the system won't be able to do the recommendations [26]. Also, the authors suggested using a Deep Neural Network (DNN) instead of the shallow neural network. Shallow neural networks have limited ability to learn abstract features and model complex data distributions [26].

Apart from this, a demographic recommender system based on *Clustering* was proposed in [31]. The system was built based on a microblogging service platform [31]. The system focused on demographic features, which is inaccurate, given that demographic features are subject to change, and may cause popularity bias [18].

Consequently, the recommender system type, used approaches for the recommendation, and system disadvantages of the aforementioned works are summarized in Table 1. It can be noticed that there were no attempts to develop a recommender system that is based on DNNs. Also, there were limited attempts in the literature for making use of NLP methods in building a recommender system.

Thus, a drug recommendation system that addresses the limitations is proposed in this paper. The methodology for building the drug recommendation system is as follows:

1. Loading and preprocessing: Prepare the dataset, preprocess it by applying different NLP methods, and form different combinations of dataset features.
2. Model selection and training: Choose a DNN model for each combination and train the models.
3. Recommendation score determination: Use the trained models to calculate the recommendation score for each drug.

## 3   Designing the Recommender System

This section describes the steps of building our neural network based drug recommender system. First, a dataset is loaded and preprocessed using NLP methods. Second, different feature combinations were made and DNN models were trained. Finally, the trained models were used to determine the recommendation score for each drug.

**Table 1.** Summary of related works.

| Reference | Type | Used Approaches | Disadvantages |
|---|---|---|---|
| [25], 2020 | Hybrid | – SVD algorithm<br>– TF-IDF model<br>– Linguistic Fuzzy Logic Controller | Precision of the proposed model is low |
| [24], 2020 | Content-Based | Similarity | – The model achieved low accuracy and precision<br>– No Machine Learning model was used |
| [22], 2020 | Content-Based | – Cosine Similarity<br>– K-NN Classification | The model focused on minor features |
| [3], 2018 | Collaborative | – Recurrent Neural Networks<br>– Generative Adversarial Networks<br>– Gated Recurrent Units | – The improvement over traditional models is slight<br>– The model didn't handle auxiliary data |
| [26], 2016 | Collaborative | AutoEncoders | – The model couldn't handle the cold-start problem<br>– The used neural network is shallow |
| [31], 2014 | Demographic | Clustering | The model only depends on demographic information |

### 3.1 Loading and Preprocessing

The involved dataset is the drug review dataset [19]. The dataset was imported from the UCI Machine Learning Repository. The set contains 215,063 records and 7 features, the features are as follows:

1. UniqueID: The ID of the drug.
2. drugName: The name of the drug.
3. condition: The condition.
4. review: The patient review.
5. rating: A 10-point patient rating.
6. date: The date of review entry.
7. usefulCount: The number of users who found the review useful.

Records with missing features were discarded from the dataset, the number of records became 212,098 records. Records were split into training sets and testing sets.

**Creating the Target Feature.** The model target feature was created using the *rating*. For each record, the target feature value is 1 (positive rating) if its corresponding rating is above 5, or 0 otherwise (negative rating).

**Cleaning the Reviews.** Cleaning textual data is important in preprocessing. Such approach helps in the elimination of noises that are not used by machines [29]. The *reviews* were cleaned by removing digits, extra spaces, and stopwords, by stemming the words, and by converting the words to lowercase.

**Applying NLP Methods.** Various NLP methods were applied to the dataset features, which resulted in the generation of more features. Sentiment Analysis is an NLP approach that aims for analyzing the textual data and determining whether the textual data is positive, negative, or neutral [4]. When applying this approach, a numerical sentiment score is returned. The score is positive, negative, or zero, when the text is positive, negative, or neutral, respectively. The sentiment analysis approach was applied to the *reviews* and *cleaned reviews*.

Also, basic text features like word count, subjects count, objects count, etc. were extracted for the *cleaned reviews*.

In addition, Named Entity Recognition (NER), topic modeling, Bag of Words (BoW) model, TF-IDF model, and Word2Vec were applied to the *cleaned reviews*. NER is an NLP method that detects mentions of rigid designators from the text that belongs to predefined semantic types such as location, person, organization, etc. [16]. Topic modeling is to discover the topics that occur in a collection of documents [6]. The BoW model is an NLP approach that simplifies the representation of a certain text by turning it into fixed-length vectors by counting how many times each word appears [2]. It can be unigram, where the appearance of one word is counted for each vector element, or n-gram, where the appearance of n successive words is counted for each vector element. Both unigram and n-gram BoW models were applied to the *cleaned reviews*. The TF-IDF is a statistical value that intends to reflect the importance of a word in a collection of documents. The equation of the TF-IDF of the word $x$ within document $y$ is as follows:

$$TF - IDF_{x,y} = tf_{x,y} \times log(\frac{N}{df_x}) \tag{1}$$

where $tf_{x,y}$ is the term frequency of $x$ in $y$, $N$ is the total number of documents, and $df_x$ is the number of documents containing the word $x$.

Both unigram and n-gram TF-IDF models were applied to the *cleaned reviews*. Word2Vec is a vectorization method that is used to extract semantic relatedness, synonym detection, concept categorization, sectional preferences, and analogy across words or products [7].

As for the categorical features like *condition* and *year*, they were encoded using Label Encoder. Label Encoder is an encoding approach that converts labels to numbers so that they can be easily interpreted by machines [27].

**Forming Different Dataset Feature Combinations.** Different dataset feature combinations were made. Among the original features, features resulting from basic text feature extraction, NER, and topic modeling, important features were selected using the Random Forest Classifier. After that, combinations between important features and other features resulting from NLP methods were made. Five combinations were made. The feature combinations, in addition to the number of features for each combination, can be found in Table 2.

**Table 2.** Dataset feature combinations with their corresponding number of features.

| Set No. | Features | Number of features |
|---|---|---|
| 1 | Important features, sentiment scores, BoW model (unigram) | 7,340 |
| 2 | Important features, sentiment scores, TF-IDF model (unigram) | 7,340 |
| 3 | Important features, sentiment scores, BoW model (n-gram) | 2,314 |
| 4 | Important features, sentiment scores, TF-IDF model (n-gram) | 2,314 |
| 5 | Important features, sentiment scores, Word2Vec | 331 |

### 3.2 Model Selection and Training

With a large number of features, Convolutional Neural Network (CNN) models can be used. CNNs are designed to flexibly learn spatial feature hierarchies through backpropagation by utilizing multiple building blocks such as convolution layers, pooling layers, and fully connected layers [28].

For the first two sets, where the number of features is 7,340, *AlexNet* [15] was adopted. *AlexNet* is a CNN that is made up of eight layers [15]. The first five layers are convolutional layers, the remaining three are fully connected. The used activation function is the ReLU, except for the output layer, it's Sigmoid. Convolutional layers are followed by Maxpooling layers [15]. The model outperformed existing models [15]. The kernel sizes of the convolutional layers are 96, 256, 384, 384, and 256. The two fully connected layers are made up of 4096 neurons, and the output layer is made up of one neuron.

As for sets 3 and 4, a feed–forward DNN with 13 hidden layers was used. On the other hand, a feed–forward DNN with 7 hidden layers was used for set 5. For both models, neurons of the hidden layers are activated with the ReLU, and that of the output layer is activated with the Sigmoid.

### 3.3  Recommendation Score Determination

To determine the recommendation score for each drug, the labels generated by the trained models are summed up, and the sum is multiplied by the normalized *usefulCount* for each drug. The equations of the normalized *usefulcount* and that of the recommendation score for drug $d$ are shown in Eqs. 2 and 3, respectively.

$$u_d = \frac{U_d - m}{a - m} \tag{2}$$

where $U_d$ is the *usefulCount* of $d$, $m$ is the minimum *usefulCount*, and $a$ is the maximum *usefulCount*.

$$Rscore_d = \sum_{i=1}^{5} p_i \times u_d \tag{3}$$

where $p_i$ is the value predicted by model $i$.

## 4  Results and Evaluation

The adopted models were trained. The number of epochs, in addition to the training accuracy and testing accuracy for each model are shown in Table 3. The models achieved an average training accuracy of 97.22% and an average testing accuracy of 93.42%.

**Table 3.** Model training and testing accuracies for each set.

| Set No. | Model | Number of Epochs | Training Accuracy | Testing Accuracy |
|---------|-------|------------------|-------------------|------------------|
| 1 | *AlexNet* | 50 | 0.9939 | 0.9982 |
| 2 | *AlexNet* | 46 | 0.9931 | 0.9981 |
| 3 | *Feed–forward DNN* | 457 | 0.9506 | 0.9485 |
| 4 | *Feed–forward DNN* | 423 | 0.9400 | 0.9496 |
| 5 | *Feed–forward DNN* | 500 | 0.9837 | 0.7765 |

After training the models, the testing set was used to build the recommender system. The models were used to predict whether the review of each drug is positive or negative, then the recommendation score of each drug was calculated using Eq. 3. A sample is shown in Table 4.

After that, the drug names were grouped by condition, and the recommendation scores of drugs having the same condition for use were summed up. A sample is shown in Table 5. The model is used in a simple program that asks the user to enter a medical condition, the program uses the built model to return the top five drugs based on the highest recommendation scores under the given condition.

**Table 4.** Samples of the results.

| Drug Name | Condition | Useful Count | Model 1 | Model 2 | Model 3 | Model 4 | Model 5 | Recomm-endation Score |
|---|---|---|---|---|---|---|---|---|
| Prolia | Osteoporosis | 0.10767 | 0 | 0 | 0 | 0 | 0 | 0 |
| Fluoxetine | Obsessive Compulsive Disorder | 0.09915 | 1 | 1 | 1 | 1 | 1 | 0.495739737 |
| Remeron | Depression | 0.16421 | 1 | 1 | 1 | 1 | 1 | 0.821068939 |
| Mirena | Abnormal Uterine Bleeding | 0.00852 | 1 | 1 | 1 | 1 | 1 | 0.042602634 |
| Escitalopram | Depression | 0.01936 | 0 | 0 | 0 | 0 | 0 | 0 |

**Table 5.** Samples of the results after grouping by conditions.

| Condition | Drug Name | Recommendation Score |
|---|---|---|
| Anemia | Epoetin Alfa | 0.003098373 |
| | Ferralet 90 | 0.02788536 |
| | Oxymetholone | 0.00929512 |
| Anexiety | Alprazolam | 26.21688613 |
| | Atarax | 2.430673896 |
| | Bupropion | 3.206041828 |
| | Clorazepate | 1.402788536 |
| Asthma | Mepolizumab | 0.050348567 |
| | Prednisone | 1.7614252 |

### 4.1   Evaluation

The quality of a recommender system can be assessed using several metrics like precision, recall, and F1-score [13]. Precision is the proportion of recommended items that are actually applicable to the user, whereas recall is the proportion of applicable items that are also included in the set of recommended items [13]. As for the F1-score, it combines precision and recall by taking their harmonic means [13]. The equations of the aforementioned metrics are shown in Eqs. 4 through 6.

$$Precision = \frac{Correctly \quad Recommended \quad Items}{Total \quad Recommended \quad Items} \tag{4}$$

$$Recall = \frac{Correctly \quad Recommended \quad Items}{Total \quad Useful \quad Recommended \quad Items} \tag{5}$$

$$F1 - Score = 2 \times \frac{Precision \times Recall}{Precision + Recall} \tag{6}$$

The evaluation metrics were calculated for the recommender system. The model achieved a precision of 94.65%, which means that 94.65% of the items were correctly recommended. Also, the model achieved a recall of 95.56%, which means that among the useful recommendations, 95.56% of them are correct. In addition, the F1-score of the model is 95.103%, which means that the used models were able to make a high number of correct predictions. Therefore, the recommender system attains an excellent performance.

## 4.2   Comparison with an Existing Model

A similar drug recommendation system was developed in [17]. The system was based on the XGBOOST model. XGBOOST is a scalable gradient tree boosting algorithm [5]. Gradient boosting is a supervised learning algorithm, which aims to predict a target variable by combining the estimates of a set of simpler models [5].

The evaluation metrics of the existing model were determined. The values of the precision, recall, and F1-score of the existing model, in addition to those of the proposed model, are presented in Table 6. It can be noticed that the proposed model outperforms the existing model in terms of performance.

**Table 6.** Evaluation metrics of the existing model and proposed model.

| Evaluation Metric | XGBOOST Model [17] | Proposed Neural-Network Based Model |
|---|---|---|
| Precision | 94.53% | 94.65% |
| Recall | 95.14% | 95.56% |
| F1-Score | 94.83% | 95.103% |

The proposed model uses methods that are not traditionally used in recommender systems like CNNs and deep feed–forward neural networks. Also, the model solves the issues highlighted in the literature like the lack of using extensive NLP methods, focusing on minor features, etc. when it comes to recommender systems design.

## 5   Conclusion

This paper presents a hybrid recommender system that is based on CNNs and feed-forward DNNs. The model addresses the limitations of existing recommender systems. To the best of our knowledge, there are no recommender systems that utilize deep learning models with NLP methods in their recommendations. However, the model shows a slight improvement in terms of performance compared to an existing model. Future work can include using Long Short-Term Memory (LSTM) models for text classifications and sentiment analysis to improve the model performance. Also, the model can be transformed into a recurrent recommender system by allowing users to give their feedback upon recommendation.

## References

1. Artemenko, O., Pasichnyk, V.V., Kunanets, N., Shunevych, K.: Using sentiment text analysis of user reviews in social media for e-tourism mobile recommender systems. In: International Conference on Computational Linguistics and Intelligent Systems (2020)

2. Benamara, F., Taboada, M., Mathieu, Y.: Evaluative Language Beyond Bags of Words: Linguistic Insights and Computational Applications. Comput. Linguist. **43**(1), 201–264 (04 2017). https://doi.org/10.1162/COLI_a_00278

3. Bharadhwaj, H., Park, H., Lim, B.Y.: RecGAN: recurrent generative adversarial networks for recommendation systems. In: Proceedings of the 12th ACM Conference on Recommender Systems, pp. 372–376. RecSys 2018, Association for Computing Machinery, New York, USA (2018). https://doi.org/10.1145/3240323.3240383

4. Birjali, M., Kasri, M., Beni-Hssane, A.: A comprehensive survey on sentiment analysis: approaches, challenges and trends. Knowl. Based Syst. **226**, 107134 (2021). https://doi.org/10.1016/j.knosys.2021.107134

5. Chen, T., Guestrin, C.: XGBoost. In: Proceedings of the 22nd ACM SIGKDD International Conference on Knowledge Discovery and Data Mining. ACM (Aug 2016). https://doi.org/10.1145/2939672.2939785, https://doi.org/10.1145%2F2939672.2939785

6. Churchill, R., Singh, L.: The evolution of topic modeling. ACM Comput. Surv. **54**(10s), 0360–0300 (2022). https://doi.org/10.1145/3507900

7. Di Gennaro, G., Buonanno, A., Palmieri, F.A.: Considerations about learning word2vec. J. Supercomputing 1–16 (2021)

8. Doughan, Z., Al Mubasher, H., Kassem, R., El-Hajj, A.M., Haidar, A.M., Sliman, L.: Logic-based neural network for pattern correction. In: 2022 International Conference on Smart Systems and Power Management (IC2SPM), pp. 52–57 (2022). https://doi.org/10.1109/IC2SPM56638.2022.9988994

9. Doughan, Z., Kassem, R., El Hajj, A., Haidar, A.: Logic-based neural network for image compression applications, pp. 92–97 (12 2021). https://doi.org/10.1109/MENACOMM50742.2021.9678278

10. Doughan, Z., Kassem, R., El-Hajj, A.M., Haidar, A.M.: Novel preprocessors for convolution neural networks. IEEE Access **10**, 36834–36845 (2022). https://doi.org/10.1109/ACCESS.2022.3163405

11. Haidar, A., Hamdan, M., Backer, M., Hamieh, H., Issa, A., Kassem, A.: A novel neural network ternary arithmetic logic unit (Jan 2008)

12. Haidar, A.: A novel neural network half adder. In: Proceedings. 2004 International Conference on Information and Communication Technologies: From Theory to Applications, pp. 427–428 (2004). https://doi.org/10.1109/ICTTA.2004.1307814

13. Isinkaye, F., Folajimi, Y., Ojokoh, B.: Recommendation systems: principles, methods and evaluation. Egypt. Inform. J. **16**(3), 261–273 (2015). https://doi.org/10.1016/j.eij.2015.06.005

14. Kang, Y., Cai, Z., Tan, C.W., Huang, Q., Liu, H.: Natural language processing (NLP) in management research: a literature review. J. Manage. Analytics **7**(2), 139–172 (2020). https://doi.org/10.1080/23270012.2020.1756939

15. Krizhevsky, A., Sutskever, I., Hinton, G.E.: ImageNet classification with deep convolutional neural networks. In: Pereira, F., Burges, C., Bottou, L., Weinberger, K. (eds.) Advances in Neural Information Processing Systems. vol. 25. Curran Associates, Inc. (2012). https://proceedings.neurips.cc/paper/2012/file/c399862d3b9d6b76c8436e924a68c45b-Paper.pdf

16. Li, J., Sun, A., Han, J., Li, C.: A survey on deep learning for named entity recognition. IEEE Trans. Knowl. Data Eng. **34**(1), 50–70 (2022). https://doi.org/10.1109/TKDE.2020.2981314

17. Marshetty, R.: Drug recommendation system (Jun 2022). https://medium.com/@marshettyruthvik/drug-recommendation-system-1b32d1cda680

18. Neophytou, N., Mitra, B., Stinson, C.: Revisiting popularity and demographic biases in recommender evaluation and effectiveness. In: Hagen, M. (ed.) Advances in Information Retrieval, pp. 641–654. Springer International Publishing, Cham (2022)

19. Repository, U.I.M.L.: UCI machine learning repository: Drug review dataset (drugs.com) data set. https://archive.ics.uci.edu/ml/datasets/Drug+Review+Dataset+%28Drugs.com%29

20. Shalom, O.S., Roitman, H., Kouki, P.: Natural language processing for recommender systems. In: Ricci, F., Rokach, L., Shapira, B. (eds.) Recommender Systems Handbook. Springer, New York (2022). https://doi.org/10.1007/978-1-0716-2197-4_12

21. Singh, P., Dutta Pramanik, P., Dey, A., Choudhury, P.: Recommender systems: an overview, research trends, and future directions. Int. J. Bus. Syst. Res. **15**, 14–52 (2021). https://doi.org/10.1504/IJBSR.2021.10033303

22. Singh, R., Maurya, S., Tripathi, T., Narula, T., Srivastav, G.: Movie recommendation system using cosine similarity and kNN. Int. J. Eng. Adv. Technol. **9**, 2249–8958 (2020). https://doi.org/10.35940/ijeat.E9666.069520

23. Tarnowska, K.A., Ras, Z.: NLP-based customer loyalty improvement recommender system (CLIRS2). Big Data Cogn. Comput. **5**(1), 4 (2021). https://doi.org/10.3390/bdcc5010004

24. Wahyudi, K., Latupapua, J., Chandra, R., Girsang, A.S.: Hotel content-based recommendation system. J. Phys. Conf. Ser. **1485**(1), 012017 (2020). https://doi.org/10.1088/1742-6596/1485/1/012017

25. Walek, B., Fojtik, V.: A hybrid recommender system for recommending relevant movies using an expert system. Expert Syst. Appl. **158**, 113452 (2020). https://doi.org/10.1016/j.eswa.2020.113452

26. Wu, Y., DuBois, C., Zheng, A.X., Ester, M.: Collaborative denoising autoencoders for top-n recommender systems, pp. 153–162. WSDM 2016, Association for Computing Machinery, New York, USA (2016). https://doi.org/10.1145/2835776.2835837

27. Xie, Y.: Improve text classification accuracy with intent information (2022). https://doi.org/10.48550/ARXIV.2212.07649

28. Yamashita, R., Nishio, M., Do, R.K.G., Togashi, K.: Convolutional neural networks: an overview and application in radiology. Insights Imaging **9**(4), 611–629 (2018). https://doi.org/10.1007/s13244-018-0639-9

29. Zainol, Z., Jaymes, M.T., Nohuddin, P.N.: VisualURText: a text analytics tool for unstructured textual data. J. Phys. Conf. Ser. **1018**(1), 012011 (2018). https://doi.org/10.1088/1742-6596/1018/1/012011, https://dx.doi.org/10.1088/1742-6596/1018/1/012011

30. Zhang, S., Yao, L., Sun, A., Tay, Y.: Deep learning based recommender system: a survey and new perspectives. ACM Comput. Surv. **52**(1) (2019). https://doi.org/10.1145/3285029

31. Zhao, X.W., Guo, Y., He, Y., Jiang, H., Wu, Y., Li, X.: We know what you want to buy: a demographic-based system for product recommendation on microblogs. In: Proceedings of the 20th ACM SIGKDD International Conference on Knowledge Discovery and Data Mining, pp. 1935–1944. KDD 2014, Association for Computing Machinery, New York, USA (2014). https://doi.org/10.1145/2623330.2623351

# DACL: A Domain-Adapted Contrastive Learning Approach to Low Resource Language Representations for Document Clustering Tasks

Dimitrios Zaikis[✉][iD], Stylianos Kokkas[iD], and Ioannis Vlahavas[iD]

School of Informatics, Aristotle University of Thessaloniki, Thessaloniki, Greece
{dimitriz,kokkassk,vlahavas}@csd.auth.gr

**Abstract.** Clustering in Natural Language Processing (NLP) groups similar text phrases or documents together based on their semantic meaning or context into meaningful groups that can be useful in several information extraction tasks, such as topic modeling, document retrieval and text summarization. However, clustering documents in low-resource languages poses unique challenges due to limited linguistic resources and lack of carefully curated data. These challenges extend to the language modeling domain, where training Transformer-based Language Models (LM) requires large amounts of data in order to generate meaningful representations. To this end, we created two new corpora from Greek media sources and present a Transformer-based contrastive learning approach for document clustering tasks. We improve low-resource LMs using in-domain second phase pre-training (domain-adaption) and learn document representations by contrasting positive examples (i.e., similar documents) and negative examples (i.e., dissimilar documents). By maximizing the similarity between positive examples and minimizing the similarity between negative examples, our proposed approach learns meaningful representations that capture the underlying structure of the documents. Additionally, we demonstrate how combining language models that are optimized for different sequence lengths improve the performance and compare this approach against an unsupervised graph-based summarization method that generates concise and informative summaries for longer documents. By learning effective document representations, our proposed approach can significantly improve the accuracy of clustering tasks such as topic extraction, leading to an improved performance in downstream tasks.

**Keywords:** Representation Learning · Clustering · Low-Resource Language · Contrastive Learning · Domain Adaption · NLP

This research was carried out as part of the project KMP6-0096055 under the framework of the Action "Investment Plans of Innovation" of the Operational Program "Central Macedonia 2014–2020", that is co-funded by the European Regional Development Fund and Greece.

# 1    Introduction

Natural Language Processing (NLP) is a rapidly growing field of study that focuses on developing techniques and algorithms to enable computers to understand and interpret human language. With the increasing amount of unstructured data in the form of text, the ability to analyze and extract insights from such data has become increasingly important. In this context, document representation is a critical step in converting raw text data into numerical vectors that can be used for various text analysis tasks, such as document clustering [18]. This is especially important for low resource languages, where it becomes more challenging to develop effective NLP models due to the lack of available data and resources.

Document clustering aims to automatically organize documents into clusters based on their similarity to documents in other clusters. This approach traditionally required the use of a feature matrix, such as a tf-idf matrix, to describe the corpus, followed by a clustering algorithm applied to the matrix. However, more recent approaches using neural word embeddings have gained popularity due to their ability to yield dense semantic representations that significantly improve the models' performances [13].

Similarly, topic modeling is a document clustering-based task that involves discovering patterns of word usage in documents using various methodologies, where documents are modeled as a mixture of topics represented as a distribution of words. Similar to document clustering, it can be used for soft partition clustering, assigning a probability distribution over a set of topics to each document, and allowing for a probabilistic degree of affiliation with each cluster. Furthermore, the topic representation contains the word distribution for each topic, making it easier to interpret. [8].

While representation learning in English has become a very active study area in recent years, there has been relatively little published work for low-resource languages such as Greek [15]. Due to its rich morphological properties, written Greek is a particularly difficult language for NLP in general and for document clustering in particular (high inflection, stressing rules, etc.) This makes it challenging to create effective models for the various NLP tasks in Greek, and highlights the need for further research in this area to improve the accuracy and reliability of such systems.

In this paper, we propose a Domain-Adapted Contrastive Learning approach to Low Resource Language representations learning for document clustering tasks for the Greek language. To facilitate this research we also introduce and describe newly collected and manually annotated datasets for language model second-phase pre-training and clustering tasks representation learning. We investigate the effectiveness of combining domain-adapted Greek BERT and Greek Longformer models using contrastive learning with triplet-loss training across three source domains for document clustering tasks. Finally, we highlight the importance of adapting Language Models (LM) to specific domains and the importance of further training for improved representation generation.

The main contributions of our work are:

- A novel approach to representation learning using domain-adaption on pre-trained language models.
- Document-level clustering using a combination of a BERT-based LM with a Greek pre-trained Longformer LM.
- Release of the described datasets and the LMs to facilitate further research.
- A novel training approach that can be applied to other high and low resource languages.

## 2    Related Work

Semantic representations for documents are crucial in natural language processing (NLP). Recently, distributed document representations have gained importance due to their accuracy as semantic text representations. However, the context of a document differs significantly between different domains [2]. Deep neural networks are capable of learning transferable features, but recent research shows that the transferability of features decreases significantly in higher task-specific layers as the domain discrepancy increases. This means that the characteristics in deeper layers of the networks largely depend on specific datasets and tasks, which cannot be reliably transferred to new tasks [16]. To address this issue, adaptation approaches have become popular, which aim to reduce domain discrepancy via an adversarial objective with respect to a domain classifier. Ultimately, these approaches aim to improve the model's accuracy in different domains [17].

In some scenarios, learning tasks may vary across domains, requiring enough target-labeled examples to fine-tune the source network to the target task. However, in real-world scenarios, labeled data is often limited, making it challenging to apply the method directly to domain adaptation. To address this, Faralli et al. [10] proposed a domain-driven word sense disambiguation (WSD) method that constructs glossaries for multiple domains using a pattern-based bootstrapping technique. Although their work does not aim to learn word representations or their meanings in a domain, it highlights the importance of evaluating the domain-specificity of text senses. Neelakantan et al. [19] proposed a method that uses WSD and word embedding learning simultaneously, thereby learning several embeddings for each word type. However, their proposed methodologies are limited to a single domain and do not take into account how representations differ between domains.

Transformers have significantly enhanced document representation learning, achieving state-of-the-art results in various NLP tasks. This success can be attributed, in part, to their self-attention mechanism, which enables the network to capture contextual information throughout the entire sequence. Two self-attention methods have been explored. The first is a left-to-right approach that processes the sentence in left-to-right chunks that can be effective for autoregressive language modeling but is unsuitable for representation learning tasks that require bidirectional context [1]. BPTransformer [26] investigated machine translation (MT), but did not explore the pre-training and fine-tuning setting. Meanwhile, a more general approach involves defining sparse attention patterns that avoid computing the entire quadratic attention matrix multiplication. Sparse Transformer [4] is a paradigm that generates sparse representations using a dilated sliding window of blocks.

Since documents usually have a large body of text that contains thousands of tokens, several task-specific strategies have been devised to work around the 512 tokens limitation of pre-trained LMs. One straightforward approach is to abbreviate the documents [25]. Another option is to split the text into 512-byte chunks, and process each chunk individually before combining the results with a task-specific model [12]. For multi-hop and open domain QA tasks, a two-stage architecture is a popular solution, in which the first stage retrieves relevant documents that are then passed on to the second stage for response extraction [5]. However, all of these methods suffer from information loss or cascading errors, as a result of truncation or two-stage processing [3].

Recently, dense representation generation models have become more prevalent in document retrieval problems, outperforming traditional sparse vector space models. These models typically use a Bi-encoder structure to achieve high efficiency. For the document clustering task, recent approaches frequently utilize Bidirectional Encoder Representations from Transformers (BERT) based models [22]. Sentence BERT (SBERT) [20], which is a variation of the conventional BERT network, generates semantically meaningful phrase embeddings using siamese and triplet network architectures that can be compared using cosine-similarity. In the Greek document clustering domain, implementations rely on FastText, a Word2vec-like model, to create clusters from social media texts [23].

## 3    Materials and Methods

In this section we present a detailed description of the datasets, the LM domain adaption and the contrastive learning approach of our proposed methodology. Specifically, we created three datasets for second phase pre-training, contrastive representation learning and the clustering tasks, correspondingly and provide an overview of the data collection and annotation process. Furthermore, we provide an in-depth overview of our proposed approach to representation learning with domain-adapted contrastive learning for clustering tasks.

### 3.1    Datasets

Due to the lack of necessary resources, including datasets and tools, the Greek language is considered a Low Resource Language (LRL), emphasizing the necessity for large amounts of training data. To capture target-specific and period-specific characteristics in our representation learning approach, both unsupervised and supervised learning phases are necessary, requiring both unlabeled domain-specific data and labeled target-specific data. Our proposed approach utilizes Transformer-based LMs for domain adaptation (second phase pre-training) in the unsupervised phase and extends the training with contrastive learning in the supervised phase. To allow potential generalizability, we focused on collecting data from three distinct sources: Internet, Social Media, and Press. The Internet data consists of a collection of articles from blog posts, news sites, and news aggregators. The Social Media data is comprised of posts from Facebook, Twitter, and Instagram, while the Press data includes text clips from published newspapers and newsletters that are identical to the printed copies.

**Language Model Domain-Adaption Dataset.** The domain-adaption dataset was created to aid in the second phase pre-training of the Greek BERT model [14] and the pre-training of a randomly initialized Longformer [1] model. Pre-training language models on domain-specific data has proven to be effective in improving their performance on tasks within that domain, since even high-parameters models can struggle to capture the complexity of a single domain [11].

The dataset consists of sentence-level texts gathered from the aforementioned online sources and domains, but the sentences come from different contexts and are much larger in volume. In total, there are 1,590,409 instances, split into 25,118,855 sentences from all categories, with an average length of 24.2 tokens and a high variance of $\pm 28.5$. Table 1 provides detailed information about the source types and the instances in each category.

**Table 1.** Number of instances by category and domain in the LM Domain-Adaptation dataset.

| Domain | Category | Instances | Ratio (%) | Total |
|---|---|---|---|---|
| Internet | Blogs | 26,507 | 15.11 | 1,205,321 |
| | News sites/Aggregators | 1,178,814 | 74.02 | |
| Social Media | Facebook | 144,813 | 19.38 | 308,141 |
| | Twitter | 144,530 | 9.08 | |
| | Instagram | 18,798 | 1.18 | |
| Press | Free press | 5,212 | 3.85 | 76,947 |
| | Sports | 1,930 | 0.12 | |
| | Economics | 38,656 | 2.43 | |
| | Local | 31,149 | 1.96 | |

**Contrastive Learning Dataset.** We initially collected textual data using specific keywords (i.e. car brands, cosmetic brands, etc.) to create a pool with 13019 instances from internet sources, 12,391 instances from social media sources and 23,089 instances from press sources. The content was collected by randomly selecting articles, posts, and text to ensure a uniform distribution among each source, user, and topic. Additionally, the type of content such as 'news article', 'editorial', 'comment' and 'post' was automatically inferred and annotated. Non-Greek content was excluded, and the focus was on achieving diversity of content for each class.

Our aim was to gather representative samples of articles, posts, and text clips from each source, rather than selecting content based on any specific criteria. Finally, three expert annotators manually annotated the examples to determine whether the text was directly, indirectly or not related to the accompanying keyword (focus) based on a set of predetermined guidelines that were adjusted during the annotation process. The annotation was carried in batches and evaluated with Cohen's Kappa [7] and achieved a score of 0.84, indicating a very high agreement rate.

The contrastive learning dataset is comprised of sentence triplets, the anchor $(S^A)$, a positive $(S^+)$ and a negative $(S^-)$ sentence, inspired by the approach presented in [6]. Initially, a random sentence is selected as anchor. The positive example is selected based on the same keyword as the anchor in addition to having the same focus. Since the selection of the negative examples is crucial, we also considered two sets of negatives for each anchor and positive pair. The first negative instance is randomly chosen from the corpus but has a completely different keyword $(K)$, referred to as "easy negative $(S_E^-)$", while the second set, is selected based on the same keyword but different focus $(F)$, referred to as "hard negative $(S_H^-)$". Equations 1 and 2 describe the triplets selection process:

$$S_E^-(S^A, S^+) = s|s \notin \{S^A, S^+\} \wedge K_s \neq K_{S^A} \tag{1}$$

$$S_H^-(S^A, S^+) = s|s \notin \{S^A, S^+\} \wedge K_s = K_{S^A} \wedge F_s \neq F_{S^A} \tag{2}$$

where the symbols $|$, $\notin$ and $\wedge$ mean "such that", "not an element of" and "and" respectively and $s$ denotes the candidate sentence. For each anchor and positive pair $S^A, S^P$ we pick two $S_E^-$ and three $S_H^-$ instances.

The intuition behind using hard negatives is that the model should be able to distinguish between directly related instances and unrelated instances sampled randomly from the entire corpus when given a query sentence. However, randomly selected negative examples may be too easy for the model to distinguish from the positive examples.

The final datasets consists of 55,170 instances from internet sources, 99,875 instances from social media sources and 75,485 instances from press sources resulting in a total of 230,530 instances from all the sources combined.

**Clustering Dataset.** Similar to the previous datasets, the clustering dataset is comprised of texts from internet, social media and press sources collected using a wide variety of keywords with a total of 283,052 instances. Each instance has the related keyword, the text that can vary greatly in length and the title where applicable as social media posts usually do not have one. Finally, the total number of unique keywords used across all sources is 3,393 from multiple categories such as heavy industries, retail, government, contractors, pharmaceutics and much more.

## 3.2   Domain-Adapted Contrastive Representation Learning

Our proposed approach to contrastive representation learning utilizes two Transformer-based LMs, the BERT language model pre-trained on a large corpus of Greek texts, called Greek-BERT [14] and the Longformer language model [1], as the fundamental building blocks.

The Transformer architecture is composed of two main components: the encoder and the decoder. The encoder processes the input sequence and produces a sequence of contextualized embeddings, while the decoder uses those embeddings to generate an output sequence. In the case of BERT and Longformer, they only use the encoder part of the transformer. By using multiple stacked layers of the transformer encoder, both models can take advantage of the self-attention mechanism [24], which allows the model to attend to different parts of the input sequence and capture complex contextual relationships between tokens.

One key difference between them is in their ability to handle long sequences of text. BERT was designed to process relatively short input sequences of up to 512 tokens, which can be a limitation when working with longer texts such as long documents or articles, while Longformer is able to handle longer input sequences of up to several thousands of tokens. Longformer achieves this by introducing a new attention mechanism called "global attention", which allows the model to attend to tokens that are far apart in the input sequence without losing context. This global attention mechanism is more computationally efficient than attending to all input tokens, which is the approach used by BERT. Both models utilize the Masked Language Modeling (MLM) pre-training objective where random tokens in the input sequence are masked and the models are trained to predict the masked tokens.

**Domain-Adaption.** Domain adaptation is the process of adapting a pre-trained language model to a specific domain or topic by fine-tuning it on domain-specific data. This can be especially useful for low-resource LMs that do not perform well on text that is related to a specific topic or domain, such as medical texts, legal documents, or social media posts.

To perform the domain adaptation, also referred to as LM alignment, we fine-tuned the pre-trained Greek BERT LM on the domain-adaption dataset presented in Sect. 3.1 using the MLM training objective. This form of second phase pre-training involves re-training the model on the new data, while keeping the pre-trained weights from the original LM, effectively updating the model's parameters to better fit the new domain knowledge, allowing it to capture the specific language patterns and structures. However, due to the lack of a Greek pre-trained Longformer variant, we trained a randomly initialized model from scratch using the same domain-adaption dataset.

**Contrastive Learning.** By implementing contrastive learning with the use of triplet loss [21] as a type of contrastive loss function, we further train the

LMs while leveraging the label information more effectively. The aim is to pull instances that belong to the same class in the embedding space closer, while simultaneously pushing instances from different classes further apart.

Document-level contrastive learning aims to learn representations of documents that capture semantic and contextual information, while also capturing the differences between documents, effectively learning better representations that can be used for clustering-based downstream tasks. The LMs are trained to differentiate between the examples by maximizing the similarity between the representations of positive examples and minimizing the similarity between the representations of negative examples. By encoding the different documents and output embeddings for each document, which can be compared using a contrastive loss function.

### 3.3    Generating Representations

The Greek BERT and the domain-adapted Greek BERT models take a maximum input sequence of 512 tokens and generate word embeddings with a dimension of 768. Similarly, the Greek Longformer model generates word embeddings with the same dimension, with a maximum input sequence of 4,096 tokens. In order to generate document-level embeddings, a mean pooling layer is applied, to pool all the word embeddings into a single vector representation that is then normalized with L2 normalization. The resulting output constitutes the domain-adapted representations that include semantic information from contrastive learning.

## 4    Results and Discussion

This section describes the experimental setup and the experimental results of our proposed approach to domain-adapted contrastive representation learning for clustering tasks.

### 4.1    Experimental Setup

The Greek BERT domain-adaption is performed in a self-supervised manner using the MLM training objective, following the same setup as described in the published work where it was first presented [14]. The input sequences were tokenized and padded or truncated to a maximum of 512 tokens and the model was trained for a total of 3 epochs, achieving an accuracy of 76.16% on the evaluation set. Similarly, the Greek Longformer pre-training was carried out with randomly initialized weights (from scratch) using the same training objective and the proposed setup, with the input sequences having a maximum length of 4,096 tokens and achieved a relatively low accuracy of 37.05% on the evaluation set.

We extended the training of the LMs with contrastive learning using the triplet loss function and trained each pre-trained model on each source domain separately and combined, resulting in 4 models per LM. The models are evaluated using sentence triplets consisting of an anchor, a positive example, and a negative example. The evaluation considers the correct outcome to be when the distance between the anchor and positive example is smaller than the distance between the anchor and negative example. The distance metric can be either Manhattan, Euclidean or Cosine and the accuracy of each metric is calculated by dividing the correctly predicted triplets with the total number of triplets.

To handle large bodies of text in documents, we conducted experiments using summarization techniques that are used in place of feeding the larger documents to the Longformer-based models. Specifically, we explored the use of LexRank [9], an unsupervised graph-based method for text summarization that ranks the importance of sentences based on eigenvector centrality. This approach allows us to condense the potentially useful information in a document into a shorter, more manageable summary.

To evaluate the performance of our proposed approach, we conducted the experiments on the clustering dataset presented in Sect. 3.1 and used the Silhouette Coefficient (SC) as a goodness-of-fit metric, which measures the cohesion and separation of a data point by calculating its similarity to its own cluster compared to the other clusters, respectively. An SC of 1 indicates that the data points are very well matched to their own cluster, while a value of -1 indicates that they are more similar to points that belong to another cluster.

However, this metric can be sensitive to the choice of input parameters, such as the number of clusters, and may not always provide a reliable measure of model quality in cases where the number of clusters is not well-defined. To alleviate this issue, we evaluate the within-cluster variation of the data points for different numbers of clusters, and select the number of clusters that leads to the lowest Sum of Squared Errors.

The Domain-Adapted Greek BERT (DAGB) and Greek Longformer (GLF) training took approximately 11 and 4 d, respectively, on a computer with a 24-core Intel CPU and two Nvidia RTX A6000 graphics cards with 48GB memory each. The difference in training time can be attributed to the use of the more efficient global attention mechanism in the Longformer architecture compared to the attention mechanism used in the BERT-based models. The rest of the experiments were conducted on a single computer using a 16-core Intel CPU and a single Nvidia RTX 3090 graphics card.

## 4.2   Experimental Results

In Table 2, we present the training results of the contrastive training approach for each pre-trained language model using the triplet-loss evaluation. All LMs achieved high accuracy scores on each distance metric and dataset with our Triplet-Loss Domain-Adapted Greek BERT (TL-DAGB) and Triplet-Loss Greek Longformer (TL-GLF) outperforming the Triplet-Loss Greek BERT (TL-GB) model in all datasets and metrics. In comparing two models, the TL-DAGB model performed better than the Longformer-based model across all metrics. This highlights the significance of the first-phase pre-training process, which the DAGB model underwent by being initialized with Greek BERT weights. The results of the comparison provide further evidence for the importance of this

**Table 2.** Triple loss evaluation results of each LM trained using the contrastive learning approach.

| Model | Training Steps (approx.) | $Acc_{Cos}$ | $Acc_{Man}$ | $Acc_{Euc}$ |
|---|---|---|---|---|
| TL-GB | | | | |
| - internet | 6k | 90.78 | 90.76 | 90.77 |
| - press | 8k | 88.93 | 88.93 | 88.94 |
| - social | 10k | 91.48 | 91.94 | 91.74 |
| - combined | 22k | 90.32 | 90.33 | 90.34 |
| TL-DAGB | | | | |
| - internet | 6k | 97.87 | 97.86 | 97.93 |
| - press | 8k | 92.39 | 92.39 | 92.44 |
| - social | 10k | 98.44 | 98.49 | 98.47 |
| - combined | 22k | 96.23 | 96.24 | 96.25 |
| TL-GLF | | | | |
| - internet | 21k | 93.05 | 93.04 | 93.05 |
| - press | 56k | 90.15 | 90.18 | 90.13 |
| - social | 19k | 94.98 | 94.96 | 94.98 |
| - combined | 173k | 92.30 | 92.31 | 92.29 |

initial pre-training step in developing high-performing language models since our GLF model was pre-trained on a much smaller scale than Greek BERT.

To evaluate the effectiveness of our proposed approach and its impact on clustering tasks, we tested the generated representations with two clustering algorithms: Hierarchical Agglomerative Clustering (HAC) and K-means (KM). HAC is a bottom-up approach that merges document representations based on their similarity until a single cluster containing all the document representations is formed. On the other hand, KM is a top-down approach that assigns each document representation to the nearest centroid and updates the centroids until convergence to create non-overlapping clusters.

We evaluated each model using four variants of each dataset, each with different preprocessing steps. The full preprocessing (Full PP) variant included removal of users/links/email addresses, text cleanup, and lower-casing, while the Normalized variant only removed non-ASCII characters and converted the text to lowercase. The Raw variant refers to using the collected text without any preprocessing steps applied to it, while the Summary variant used summarized text instead of Longformer-based models to process longer sequences.

By testing each model with these different datasets and preprocessing steps, we assess the effectiveness of preprocessing in combination with our proposed approach on clustering tasks and present the results of each model on the text from the internet, social and press source domains in Tables 3, 4 and 5, respectively.

The results indicate that the combined use of BERT and Longformer-based models outperform the pure BERT-based variants in all three source domains

**Table 3.** Per model goodness-of-fit results based on the Silhouette Coefficient on the internet dataset.

| Internet | Raw | | Full PP | | Normalized | | Summary | |
|----------|-----|-----|---------|-----|-----------|-----|---------|-----|
| Models | HAC | KM | HAC | KM | HAC | KM | HAC | KM |
| GB | 0.33 | 0.31 | 0.33 | 0.34 | 0.34 | 0.31 | 0.33 | 0.33 |
| TL-GB | 0.33 | 0.30 | 0.32 | 0.35 | 0.33 | 0.31 | 0.01 | 0.01 |
| TL-GB-C | 0.33 | 0.31 | 0.30 | 0.31 | 0.33 | 0.33 | 0.01 | 0.01 |
| DAGB | 0.38 | 0.40 | 0.39 | 0.39 | 0.38 | 0.37 | 0.60 | 0.60 |
| TL-DAGB | 0.38 | 0.45 | 0.38 | 0.45 | 0.52 | 0.57 | 0.01 | 0.01 |
| TL-DAGB-C | 0.43 | 0.45 | 0.51 | 0.52 | 0.50 | 0.54 | 0.01 | 0.01 |
| GLF | 0.83 | 0.87 | **0.90** | **0.90** | 0.52 | 0.52 | - | - |
| TL-GLF | 0.52 | 0.56 | 0.56 | 0.59 | 0.57 | 0.57 | - | - |
| TL-GLF-C | 0.76 | 0.76 | 0.79 | 0.79 | 0.78 | 0.78 | - | - |

**Table 4.** Per model goodness-of-fit results based on the Silhouette Coefficient on the social dataset.

| Social | Raw | | Full PP | | Normalized | | Summary | |
|--------|-----|-----|---------|-----|-----------|-----|---------|-----|
| Models | HAC | KM | HAC | KM | HAC | KM | HAC | KM |
| GB | 0.34 | 0.12 | 0.36 | 0.38 | 0.32 | 0.34 | 0.11 | 0.13 |
| TL-GB | 0.33 | 0.34 | 0.35 | 0.36 | 0.34 | 0.31 | 0.01 | 0.01 |
| TL-GB-C | 0.36 | 0.37 | 0.38 | 0.38 | 0.36 | 0.35 | 0.01 | 0.01 |
| DAGB | 0.34 | 0.13 | 0.31 | 0.28 | 0.34 | 0.31 | 0.70 | 0.70 |
| TL-DAGB | 0.39 | 0.41 | 0.43 | 0.49 | 0.36 | 0.39 | 0.01 | 0.01 |
| TL-DAGB-C | 0.46 | 0.45 | 0.47 | 0.47 | 0.52 | 0.44 | 0.01 | 0.01 |
| GLF | 0.33 | 0.43 | 0.47 | 0.52 | 0.48 | 0.51 | - | - |
| TL-GLF | 0.78 | 0.80 | 0.84 | **0.86** | 0.83 | 0.84 | - | - |
| TL-GLF-C | 0.75 | 0.77 | 0.82 | 0.83 | 0.81 | 0.81 | - | - |

in the document clustering task. Our approach leverages the representation generation capabilities of the domain-adapted Greek BERT and the Greek Longformer by encoding the sequences that are up to 512 tokens with the former and sequences greater than 512 tokens with the latter. The GLF, TL-GLF and TL-GLF-C models are combined with the best performing DAGB-based models on each domain, where at least one variant always outperforms the best Greek BERT (GB) variant.

On the internet source dataset, the triplet-loss domain-adapted Greek BERT trained on all datasets (TL-DAGB-C) as presented in Sect. 3.2 in combination with the pre-trained Greek Longformer (GLF) on a fully preprocessed text, achieved the best results with an SC of 0.90, indicating a close to perfect goodness-of-fit. Similarly, on the social source dataset, the triplet-loss domain-

**Table 5.** Per model goodness-of-fit results based on the Silhouette Coefficient on the press dataset.

| Press | Raw | | Full PP | | Normalized | | Summary | |
|---|---|---|---|---|---|---|---|---|
| Models | HAC | KM | HAC | KM | HAC | KM | HAC | KM |
| GB | 0.34 | 0.13 | 0.42 | 0.44 | 0.39 | 0.42 | 0.34 | 0.13 |
| TL-GB | 0.33 | 0.31 | 0.34 | 0.34 | 0.33 | 0.34 | 0.01 | 0.01 |
| TL-GB-C | 0.33 | 0.31 | 0.40 | 0.40 | 0.38 | 0.40 | 0.01 | 0.01 |
| DAGB | 0.34 | 0.30 | 0.33 | 0.31 | 0.45 | 0.38 | 0.11 | 0.05 |
| TL-DAGB | 0.53 | 0.53 | 0.49 | 0.55 | 0.45 | 0.49 | 0.01 | 0.01 |
| TL-DAGB-C | 0.54 | 0.58 | 0.51 | 0.51 | 0.46 | 0.50 | 0.01 | 0.01 |
| GLF | 0.67 | 0.67 | 0.83 | **0.85** | 0.49 | 0.60 | - | - |
| TL-GLF | 0.61 | 0.61 | 0.63 | 0.62 | 0.61 | 0.59 | - | - |
| TL-GLF-C | 0.72 | 0.74 | 0.76 | 0.76 | 0.74 | 0.73 | - | - |

adapted Greek BERT (TL-DAGB) in combination with the triplet-loss Greek Longformer (TL-GLF), both trained on the domain-specific dataset, outperformed the rest with an SC of 0.86. A similar pattern can be observed in the press source domain, where the TL-DAGB model in combination with the Greek Longformer (GLF) model achieves the best score with an SC of 0.85.

The overall results show that both the domain-adaption as well as the contrastive learning approach to further train the Transformer-based language models improve the results over the representations gained from the models they are based on. While the use of the Greek Longformer with a triplet-loss BERT-based model performed better in two datasets, internet and press, the use of the triplet-loss Greek Longformer performed significantly better compared to the rest on the same social source dataset. This potentially can be attributed to the use of non-formal language where the communication norms are often ignored, and further training of the language model may be able to learn.

## 5    Conclusions

In this paper, we propose a Domain-Adapted Contrastive Learning approach to Low Resource Language representations for document clustering tasks. Our study investigated the effectiveness of combining domain-adapted Greek BERT and Greek Longformer models using contrastive learning across three source domains. Our findings demonstrated that both domain-adaptation and contrastive learning approaches using triplet-loss training improved the performance of Transformer-based language models for document clustering tasks. Overall, our study highlights the importance of adapting language models to specific domains and further training them using contrastive learning to improve the generated representations.

Future studies could explore the effectiveness of combining other pre-trained language models such as GPT-3 or RoBERTa and the impact of different preprocessing techniques on the performance. Finally, considering the performance that was achieved in our experimental setting, another direction for future work is to pre-train the Longformer model using a larger and more complete and diverse dataset.

# References

1. Beltagy, I., Peters, M.E., Cohan, A.: Longformer: The long-document transformer. arXiv preprint arXiv:2004.05150 (2020)
2. Bollegala, D., Maehara, T., Kawarabayashi, K.i.: Unsupervised cross-domain word representation learning 1 (05 2015). https://doi.org/10.3115/v1/P15-1071
3. Chen, D., Fisch, A., Weston, J., Bordes, A.: Reading Wikipedia to answer open-domain questions. In: Proceedings of the 55th Annual Meeting of the Association for Computational Linguistics (Volume 1: Long Papers), pp. 1870–1879. Association for Computational Linguistics, Vancouver, Canada (Jul 2017). https://doi.org/10.18653/v1/P17-1171, https://aclanthology.org/P17-1171
4. Child, R., Gray, S., Radford, A., Sutskever, I.: Generating long sequences with sparse transformers. CoRR abs/1904.10509 (2019), arxiv.org/abs/1904.10509
5. Clark, K., Khandelwal, U., Levy, O., Manning, C.D.: What does BERT look at? an analysis of BERT's attention. In: Proceedings of the 2019 ACL Workshop BlackboxNLP: Analyzing and Interpreting Neural Networks for NLP, pp. 276–286. Association for Computational Linguistics, Florence, Italy (Aug 2019). https://doi.org/10.18653/v1/W19-4828, https://aclanthology.org/W19-4828
6. Cohan, A., Feldman, S., Beltagy, I., Downey, D., Weld, D.S.: Specter: Document-level representation learning using citation-informed transformers (2020). https://doi.org/10.48550/ARXIV.2004.07180, https://arxiv.org/abs/2004.07180
7. Cohen, J.: A Coefficient of Agreement for Nominal Scales. Educ. Psychol. Measur. **20**(1), 37–46 (1960). https://doi.org/10.1177/001316446002000104
8. Curiskis, S.A., Drake, B., Osborn, T.R., Kennedy, P.J.: An evaluation of document clustering and topic modelling in two online social networks: Twitter and reddit. Inform. Process. Manage. **57**(2), 102034 (2020). https://doi.org/10.1016/j.ipm.2019.04.002
9. Erkan, G., Radev, D.R.: Lexrank: graph-based lexical centrality as salience in text summarization. J. Artif. Intell. Res. **22**(1), 457–479 (2004). https://arxiv.org/abs/1109.2128
10. Faralli, S., Navigli, R.: A new minimally-supervised framework for domain word sense disambiguation. In: Proceedings of the 2012 Joint Conference on Empirical Methods in Natural Language Processing and Computational Natural Language Learning, pp. 1411–1422. Association for Computational Linguistics, Jeju Island, Korea (Jul 2012), https://aclanthology.org/D12-1129
11. Gururangan, S., et al.: Don't Stop Pretraining: Adapt Language Models to Domains and Tasks (May 2020), https://arxiv.org/abs/2004.10964, arXiv:2004.10964 [cs]
12. Joshi, M., Levy, O., Weld, D.S., Zettlemoyer, L.: BERT for coreference resolution: Baselines and analysis. CoRR abs/1908.09091 (2019), https://arxiv.org/abs/1908.09091

13. Kokate, U., Deshpande, A., Mahalle, P., Patil, P.: Data stream clustering techniques, applications, and models: Comparative analysis and discussion. Big DataCogn. Comput. **2**(4) (2018). https://doi.org/10.3390/bdcc2040032, https://www.mdpi.com/2504-2289/2/4/32

14. Koutsikakis, J., Chalkidis, I., Malakasiotis, P., Androutsopoulos, I.: Greek-bert: The greeks visiting sesame street. In: 11th Hellenic Conference on Artificial Intelligence, pp. 110–117 (2020). https://doi.org/10.1145/3411408.3411440

15. Lekea, I., Karampelas, P.: Are we really that close together? tracing and discussing similarities and differences between greek terrorist groups using cluster analysis. In: 2017 European Intelligence and Security Informatics Conference (EISIC), pp. 159–162 (2017). https://doi.org/10.1109/EISIC.2017.33

16. Long, M., Cao, Y., Cao, Z., Wang, J., Jordan, M.I.: Transferable representation learning with deep adaptation networks. IEEE Trans. Pattern Anal. Mach. Intell. **41**(12), 3071–3085 (2019). https://doi.org/10.1109/TPAMI.2018.2868685

17. Long, M., Cao, Y., Wang, J., Jordan, M.I.: Learning transferable features with deep adaptation networks. In: Proceedings of the 32nd International Conference on International Conference on Machine Learning - Volume 37. pp. 97–105. ICML'15, JMLR.org (2015). https://arxiv.org/abs/1502.02791

18. M. Salih, N., Jacksi, K.: State of the art document clustering algorithms based on semantic similarity. Jurnal Informatika **14**, 58–75 (05 2020). https://doi.org/10.26555/jifo.v14i2.a17513

19. Neelakantan, A., Shankar, J., Passos, A., McCallum, A.: Efficient non-parametric estimation of multiple embeddings per word in vector space. In: Proceedings of the 2014 Conference on Empirical Methods in Natural Language Processing (EMNLP), pp. 1059–1069. Association for Computational Linguistics, Doha, Qatar (Oct 2014). https://doi.org/10.3115/v1/D14-1113, https://aclanthology.org/D14-1113

20. Reimers, N., Gurevych, I.: Sentence-BERT: Sentence embeddings using Siamese BERT-networks, pp. 3982–3992 (Nov 2019). https://doi.org/10.18653/v1/D19-1410, https://aclanthology.org/D19-1410

21. Schroff, F., Kalenichenko, D., Philbin, J.: FaceNet: A unified embedding for face recognition and clustering. In: 2015 IEEE Conference on Computer Vision and Pattern Recognition (CVPR). IEEE (jun 2015). https://doi.org/10.1109/cvpr.2015.7298682

22. Tang, H., Sun, X., Jin, B., Wang, J., Zhang, F., Wu, W.: Improving document representations by generating pseudo query embeddings for dense retrieval, pp. 5054–5064 (Aug 2021). https://doi.org/10.18653/v1/2021.acl-long.392, https://aclanthology.org/2021.acl-long.392

23. Tsirakis, N., Poulopoulos, V., Tsantilas, P., Varlamis, I.: Large scale opinion mining for social, news and blog data. J. Syst. Softw. **127**, 237–248 (2017). https://doi.org/10.1016/j.jss.2016.06.012

24. Vaswani, A., et al.: Attention is All you Need. In: Guyon, I., Luxburg, U.V., Bengio, S., Wallach, H., Fergus, R., Vishwanathan, S., Garnett, R. (eds.) Advances in Neural Information Processing Systems. vol. 30. Curran Associates, Inc. (2017). https://proceedings.neurips.cc/paper/2017/file/3f5ee243547dee91fbd053c1c4a845aa-Paper.pdf

25. Xie, Q., Dai, Z., Hovy, E.H., Luong, M., Le, Q.V.: Unsupervised data augmentation. CoRR abs/1904.12848 (2019). https://arxiv.org/abs/1904.12848

26. Ye, Z., Guo, Q., Gan, Q., Qiu, X., Zhang, Z.: Bp-transformer: Modelling long-range context via binary partitioning. CoRR abs/1911.04070 (2019). https://arxiv.org/abs/1911.04070

# Evaluating the Extraction of Toxicological Properties with Extractive Question Answering

Bruno Carlos Luís Ferreira[1]([✉]) [iD], Hugo Gonçalo Oliveira[1] [iD], Hugo Amaro[2],
Ângela Laranjeiro[3], and Catarina Silva[1] [iD]

[1] University of Coimbra, DEI, CISUC, Coimbra, Portugal
`{brunof,hroliv,catarina}@dei.uc.pt`
[2] Instituto Pedro Nunes, Coimbra, Portugal
`hamaro@ipn.pt`
[3] Cosmedesk, Coimbra, Portugal
`angela@cosmedesk.com`

**Abstract.** Preparing toxicological analysis of chemical substances is a time-consuming process that requires a safety advisor to search text documents from multiple sources for information on several properties and experiments. There has been a growing interest in using Machine Learning (ML) approaches, specifically Natural Language Processing (NLP) Techniques to improve Human-Machine integration in processes in different areas. In this paper we explore this integration in toxicological analysis. To minimise the effort of preparing toxicological analysis of chemical substances, we explore several available neural network models tuned for Extractive Question Answering (BERT, RoBERTa, BioBERT, ChemBERT) for retrieving toxicological properties from sections of the document sources. This formulation of Information Extraction as a targeted Question Answering task can be considered as a more flexible and scalable alternative to manually creating a set of (limited) extraction patterns or even training a model for chemical relation extraction. The proposed approach was tested for a set of eight properties, each containing multiple fields, in a sample of 33 reports for which golden answers were provided by a security advisor. Compared to the golden responses, the best model tested achieved a BLEU score of 0.55. When responses from different models are combined, BLEU increases to 0.59. Our results suggest that while this approach cannot yet be fully automated, it can be useful in supporting security advisor's decisions and reducing time and manual effort.

**Keywords:** Information Retrieval · Information Extraction · Question Answering · Transformers

## 1 Introduction

With the increasing amount of information available, organisations need to develop procedures for obtaining information that may be important to their business. Unfortunately, much of this information is not in structured databases,

L. Iliadis et al. (Eds.): EANN 2023, CCIS 1826, pp. 599–606, 2023.
https://doi.org/10.1007/978-3-031-34204-2_48

but in unstructured or semi-structured texts. Humans are capable of performing these processes of extracting and retrieving information from texts, but this can take a lot of time [4].

In the toxicological analysis process the problem arose from the need to optimise the time required to prepare a written report on a chemical substance. The process currently consists of a person searching for information about the chemical compound and preparing a report with all the relevant information. The search draws on various types of databases, including structured, *e.g.*, websites, and unstructured, *e.g.*, PDFs, articles. A chemical safety advisor is responsible for researching, comparing, and labelling information about chemical compounds. This process of "information extraction and retrieval" is done manually, and with a large number of documents and data sources, the time required can take weeks.

The security advisor accesses multiple data sources with different formats, *e.g.*, websites, xlsx files, PDF files, all of which are relevant to the security advisor, whether in terms of quantity or quality of information. The problem for the security advisor is that the documents in these sources contain a lot of information in an unstructured format, *i.e.*, natural language. In addition, it is often necessary to combine information from different sources for the preparation of toxicological reports.

In this paper, we elaborate on the approach presented in [6], which was developed to help the security advisor with the aforementioned challenges. The main goal of the approach is to find toxicological information in contexts, *i.e.*, text in PDF documents. We enter the desired contexts as input, and over a set of keywords defined as questions, we find the information using *Extractive Question Answering*(QA) models. Some advances and contributions since the original presentation of this approach in [6] are the implementation of this approach for the PDF documents of the *Australian Industrial Chemicals Introduction Scheme* (AICIS), the automatic *Combination Process*, and the extraction of golden answers from a set of 33 documents using the expertise of the security advisor. In the evaluation performed, we obtain a best BLEU score of 0.55 when using single models and an increase to 0.59 when combining models.

The remainder of the paper is organised as follows: in Sect. 2, we briefly present related work and inspirations that we used to propose our approach; in Sect. 3, we detail the approach and the developments carried out; in Sect. 4, we explain the experiments conducted, the acquisition of the golden answers, the evaluation and results; Sect. 5 concludes the paper and presents future lines of research.

## 2    Related Works

Since the introduction of transformers [13], several works have appeared with similar approaches to *Extractive Question Answering* (QA) for *Information Extraction and Retrieval*. For different domains, with different implementations and different levels of complexity, some works have preferred extractive QA models over other traditional methods because of: (1) limited data for domain-specific documents where information needs to be retrieved from [11]; (2) features such as shorter answers are harder to learn from other models [1], *e.g.*, *Named-entity recognition* (NER) models; and (3) generalization capability, as classification-based approaches cannot be generalized to new event types or argument roles without additional annotations [8]. In these different cases, the existing challenges for traditional approaches led to the application of *Extractive QA* models for information retrieval and extraction.

Nguyen et al. [11] proposed the use of a pre-trained *Bidirectional Encoder Representations from Transformers* (BERT) [5] model combined with a *Convolutional Neural Network* (CNN) to learn the localization of the context of each document. The proposed approach consists of three main components: the representations of the input vectors of the tokens, *BERT* to learn hidden vectors for each token from the input tag and document, a convolutional layer to capture the local context, and a *softmax layer* to predict the value location. The *Information Extraction* is reformulated as a *QA* task where the value is pulled from the document by querying the tag, *i.e.*, a list of required information is defined and represented as tags, *e.g.*, "Name of Institution" or "Deadline for Bidding" [11].

Arici et al. [1] used a *QA* approach to quantity extraction to solve a price-per-unit (PPU) problem. They first predict the type of *Unit of Measure* (UoM), *e.g.*, volume, weight, or count, to formulate the desired questions, *e.g.*, "What is the total volume?", and then use this question to find all relevant answers. The approach divides event extraction into three sub-tasks: Trigger Identification, Trigger Classification, and Argument Extraction. These sub-tasks are modeled by a set of *QA* templates based on *Machine Reading Comprehension* (MRC) [2].

Li et al. [8] formulate event extraction as a multi-turn *QA* approach. Typically, event extraction can be divided into two sub-tasks: trigger extraction and argument extraction. Event extraction approaches can be broadly classified into two groups: (1) pipeline approaches, in which the extraction of triggers and arguments is performed in separate steps, and (2) joint approaches, in which all sub-tasks are performed simultaneously in a joint learning fashion. Trigger identification is transformed into an extractive *MRC* problem where trigger words are identified from given sentences. Classification of triggers is formalized as a YES /NO *QA* problem, where it is judged whether a possible trigger belongs to a given event type or not. Argument extraction is also solved via extractive *MRC*, where questions are constructed iteratively by a target event type and the corresponding argument roles.

These approaches are also well suited for searching toxicological information, as some of the challenges encountered in related work are also present in the documents available for this task, such as, the presence of limited data for domain-specific documents and the variance in the nature and extent of expected responses.

# 3   Question Answering for Information Extraction

Considering the challenges and advantages of extractive QA models and the main goal of retrieving toxicological information in PDF documents, we propose an approach based on three phases (see Fig. 1): (1) preprocessing phase, (2) retrieval phase, and (3) verification phase [6].

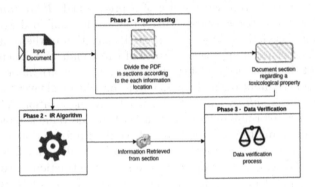

**Fig. 1.** General architecture of the proposed approach.

The preprocessing phase consists of dividing the input document into sections, each containing information about a specific property of the chemical substance. In this way we minimize the context given to the QA models and eliminate noise, *i.e.*, parts of the document that are not relevant to the individual properties. We use regular expressions to get the section identifiers, *i.e.*, section title and section number, in the documents of the *Scientific Committee on Consumer Safety* (SCCS)[1]. For *Australian Industrial Chemicals Introduction Scheme* (AICIS)[2] documents, we also use statistical methods to obtain the section identifiers, *i.e.*, the font size and font style of the mode.

In the retrieval phase, we use *Extractive QA* models to retrieve the values of the required properties. To this end, we identify the questions associated with each context and these properties. Together with the safety advisor, we identify the fields required for each toxicological property, *i.e.*, keywords, and we create a set of questions using these keywords as input to the *Extractive QA* models (see Table 1). QA models are fine-tuned in the *Stanford Question Answering Dataset* (SQuAD) using the six W's (Who, What, When, Where, Why, and How) in formulating the questions. Hence, we create this type of questions for each piece of information we want to extract. For example, in the sentence in one of the PDF documents, "The eye irritation potential of shampoo in rabbit eyes was not increased by the addition of ZPT" we want to know the species to which the

---

[1] https://health.ec.europa.eu/scientific-committees/scientific-committee-consumer-safety-sccs_en.

[2] https://www.industrialchemicals.gov.au/.

test applies, so we can formulate the question, "What is the species?". Given the sentence (as context) and the question, we hope to get the correct answer from the *Extractive QA* models, in this case "rabbit".

**Table 1.** Set of questions per property

| Substance Property | Questions |
|---|---|
| Repeated Dose Toxicity | What is the NOAEL value? What is the guideline?; What is the study? |
| Acute Toxicity | What is the guideline?; What is the study?; What is the species? What is the LD50?; What is the LC50? |
| Irritation | What is the guideline?; What is the study?; What is the species?; What is the concentration?; What is the conclusion? |
| Mutagenicity | What is the Guideline?; What is the study?; What is the conclusion? |
| Skin Sensitization | What is the Guideline?; What is the study?; What is the conclusion?; What is the concentration? |
| Carcinogenicity | What is the species?; What is the Guideline?; What is the study?; What is the conclusion? |
| Photo-induced Toxicity | What is the Guideline?; What is the study?; What is the conclusion?; What is the concentration? |
| Reproductive Toxicity | What is the Guideline?; What is the study?;What is the species?; What is the conclusion? |

In the verification Phase, we post-process the retrieved information, *i.e.*, we remove duplicates and implement a *Combination Process* with the goal of creating a method that achieves a certain level of acceptable confidence in the retrieved information. When comparing responses from different models, if the same information is returned from more than one model, this implies more confidence in the suitability of that response, which we could not otherwise guarantee with only one model. To this end, the implemented *Combination Process* consists of keeping the answers that are similar between the models used, *i.e.*, multiple fine-tuned models from the *Hugging Face* Hub[3], using *Recall-Oriented Understudy for Gisting Evaluation* (ROUGE) [9] as a similarity metric with a defined threshold. While ROUGE is not specifically designed as a similarity metric but as an evaluation metric for the task of automatic text summarization, it can also be used to evaluate the similarity between two texts, the candidate and the reference. We defined a threshold of 0.8 because we wanted to provided a high level of similarity between answers and we used ROUGE Unigram in the *Combination Process*, where the overlap of 1-grams between the candidate and reference answers are compared.

## 4 Experimentation and Results

### 4.1 Setup

Using the knowledge of the security advisor, we create a corpora of golden responses from a set of 33 reports, 15 reports from SCCS and 18 reports from

---
[3] https://huggingface.co/.

AICIS. From each report, we capture multiple fields from eight different toxicological properties. In total, we obtained a corpora of 1830 fields that we can use to evaluate our approach by using different individual models and different arrangements between them with the implemented *Combination Process.*

For the evaluation, we use the similarity metric *ROUGE* and the similarity metric *Bilingual Evaluation Understudy*(BLEU) [12] to compare the gold responses to the retrieved information. We chose to use both metrics because they complement each other, *i.e.,* BLEU measures precision and ROUGE measures recall. BLEU measures how many words occur in the retrieved information in the reference and ROUGE measures how many words occur in the reference in the retrieved information.

During our initial testing, we experimented with several models that were available at the *Hugging Face* library, but ultimately we continued our implementation and testing with four models: *BERT, BioBERT: a pre-trained biomedical language representation model for biomedical text mining* (BioBERT) [7], *ChemBERTa: Large-Scale Self-Supervised Pretraining for Molecular Property Prediction* (ChemBERTa) [3] and *Robustly Optimized BERT Pretraining Approach* (RoBERTa) [10]. We proceeded with those four models because, from the small experiments conducted, they were the models that achieved the best compromised between results and computational resources. We evaluated the models individually as well as the various combinations of them, excluding combinations of two.

## 4.2   Results and Discussion

Several discussion points emerge from the results of the evaluation, which can be found in Table 2. Compared to the individual models, RoBERTa provided the best results in all metrics, both ROUGE and BLEU. Also, the BERT and BioBERT models performed well compared to RoBERTa when comparing results from BLEU and ROUGE, respectively, implying that BERT generally achieved better precision and BioBERT better recall, but both fell short of the results achieved by RoBERTa. Although we anticipated that ChemBERTa could achieve good results, mainly due to the fact that the model was trained with texts closer to the domain of documents used in our test, in fact results show us the contrary, achieving the worst overall result in our evaluation.

Using the *Combination Process* and the different arrangements of the models, we can see the same pattern, *i.e.,* the combinations in which the ChemBERTa is present have worse results than the combinations without the ChemBERTa. Although better results were obtained when combining with all models, including ChemBERTa, they do not approach the results of the combination of RoBERTa, BioBERT, and BERT. This combination of RoBERTa, BioBERT, and BERT achieved the best performance in all our experiments and slightly improved the results of the individual RoBERTa models, especially in precision, *i.e.,* BLEU scores.

After evaluating the results, we should consider whether it is necessary to use a *Combination Process* to employ multiple models in the future. Even though

**Table 2.** Evaluation Results

|  | ROUGE | | BLEU |
|---|---|---|---|
|  | Unigram | LCS | Unigram |
| BERT | 0.57 | 0.56 | 0.52 |
| BioBERT | 0.59 | 0.58 | 0.51 |
| ChemBERTa | 0.41 | 0.41 | 0.39 |
| RoBERTa | 0.62 | 0.62 | 0.55 |
| RoBERTa + BioBERT + BERT | **0.63** | **0.63** | **0.59** |
| RoBERTa + BioBERT + ChemBERTa | 0.54 | 0.54 | 0.50 |
| RoBERTa +ChemBERTa + BERT | 0.55 | 0.55 | 0.51 |
| BioBERT + ChemBERTa + BERT | 0.52 | 0.51 | 0.47 |
| RoBERTa + BioBERT + BERT + ChemBERTa | 0.57 | 0.56 | 0.52 |

the RoBERTa model performed almost as well as the best combination, using multiple models may consume more time and computational resources. Thus, we must weigh the benefits and drawbacks of implementing a *Combination Process* having into consideration the different use cases and objectives that we may have. For example, a live service may prefer a faster processing time affording a worst performance by the models, meaning that implementing a certain level of acceptable confidence in the retrieved information may not be the highest priority. On the other hand, other use cases can benefit to a higher level of confidence, so such a implementation of a *Combination Process* is preferable.

## 5    Conclusion

This paper explores the use of *Question Answering* as an alternative to *Information Extraction* for analyzing toxicological properties which reduces the time and effort required in the early stages of the process. We tested this approach with SCCS and AICIS documents, evaluating the effectiveness of using multiple pre-trained *Language Models* for this task and demonstrating how they can be combined to achieve even better results.

Our approach using *Question Answering*, in combination with multiple models, was able to achieve a high ROUGE score of 0.63 and a BLEU score of 0.59, demonstrating its potential for accurately analyzing toxicological properties. These results are promising for reducing the time and effort required, and highlight the usefulness of machine learning in the field of toxicology.

The results demonstrated the effectiveness of the proposed approach, particularly in the early stages of the process, by reducing the time and effort required by safety advisors. Moving forward, we aim to expand this method to other sources of information on chemical substances beyond SCCS and AICIS. Furthermore, we plan to train new models by incorporating documents relevant to the target field during pre-training. Additionally, we hope to develop a more automated decision support system that includes online reinforcement to enhance the usability of the tool.

# References

1. Arici, T., Kumar, K., Çeker, H., Saladi, A.S., Tutar, I.: Solving price per unit problem around the world: Formulating fact extraction as question answering. arXiv preprint arXiv:2204.05555 (2022)
2. Baradaran, R., Ghiasi, R., Amirkhani, H.: A survey on machine reading comprehension systems. Nat. Lang. Eng. **28**(6), 683–732 (2022). https://doi.org/10.1017/S1351324921000395
3. Chithrananda, S., Grand, G., Ramsundar, B.: Chemberta: Large-scale self-supervised pretraining for molecular property prediction. CoRR abs/2010.09885 (2020), https://arxiv.org/abs/2010.09885
4. Cvitaš, A.: Information extraction in business intelligence systems. In: The 33rd International Convention MIPRO, pp. 1278–1282. IEEE (2010)
5. Devlin, J., Chang, M., Lee, K., Toutanova, K.: BERT: pre-training of deep bidirectional transformers for language understanding. CoRR abs/1810.04805 (2018). https://arxiv.org/abs/1810.04805
6. Ferreira, B.C.L., Gonçalo Oliveira, H., Amaro, H., Laranjeiro, A., Silva, C.: Question Answering For Toxicological Information Extraction. In: Cordeiro, J.a., Pereira, M.J.a., Rodrigues, N.F., Pais, S.a. (eds.) 11th Symposium on Languages, Applications and Technologies (SLATE 2022). Open Access Series in Informatics (OASIcs), vol. 104, pp. 3:1–3:10. Schloss Dagstuhl - Leibniz-Zentrum für Informatik, Dagstuhl, Germany (2022). https://doi.org/10.4230/OASIcs.SLATE.2022.3 ,https://drops.dagstuhl.de/opus/volltexte/2022/16749
7. Lee, J., et al.: Biobert: a pre-trained biomedical language representation model for biomedical text mining. CoRR abs/1901.08746 (2019). https://arxiv.org/abs/1901.08746
8. Li, F., et al.: Event extraction as multi-turn question answering. In: Findings of the Association for Computational Linguistics: EMNLP 2020, pp. 829–838 (2020)
9. Lin, C.Y.: ROUGE: A package for automatic evaluation of summaries. In: Text Summarization Branches Out, pp. 74–81. Association for Computational Linguistics, Barcelona, Spain (Jul 2004). https://aclanthology.org/W04-1013
10. Liu, Y., et al.: Roberta: a robustly optimized BERT pretraining approach. CoRR abs/1907.11692 (2019). https://arxiv.org/abs/1907.11692
11. Nguyen, M.T., Le, D.T., Le, L.: Transformers-based information extraction with limited data for domain-specific business documents. Eng. Appl. Artif. Intell. **97**, 104100 (2021)
12. Papineni, K., Roukos, S., Ward, T., Zhu, W.J.: Bleu: a method for automatic evaluation of machine translation. In: Proceedings of the 40th Annual Meeting of the Association for Computational Linguistics, pp. 311–318. Association for Computational Linguistics, Philadelphia, Pennsylvania, USA (Jul 2002). https://doi.org/10.3115/1073083.1073135 ,https://aclanthology.org/P02-1040
13. Vaswani, A., et al.: Attention is all you need. In: Advances in neural information processing systems, pp. 5998–6008 (2017)

# Semi-automated System for Pothole Detection and Location

Favell Nuñez(✉)[ID], Rodrigo Espinal[ID], Gerardo Zavala, and Josue Banegas

FI, Universidad Tecnológica Centroamericana (UNITEC), San Pedro Sula, Honduras
{favell.nunez,rodriespinal,gerardo.zavala,josue.banegas}@unitec.edu

**Abstract.** Imperfections in land transport infrastructure can be made up of various elements. As it will be seen in this report, these imperfections vary depending on the variables that make up their formation. However, one of the most damaging elements to cars is made up of large, deep blemishes also known as potholes, which present a constant threat to the integrity of cars. One of the problems with the process of recognizing potholes is that, in countries like Honduras, these routes are made on foot, which implies a great amount of time, effort and resources for those in charge of recognizing potholes. To solve this problem, a solution was proposed that would speed up the recognition process. This solution consists of an artificial intelligence model that was trained to recognize potholes, using a database made up of pothole images taken from the internet and pothole images captured in Tegucigalpa, which resulted in a model with a maximum precision value of 86.251% and a maximum sensitivity value of 80.035%. Along with this model, a VK-162 GPS module was used, which oversaw extracting the geographical location of each pothole after being detected. With these geographical points it was possible to map the coordinates corresponding to each pothole on a map to represent a pothole recognition route more easily and efficiently and thus creating a system that could identify and locating potholes in a semi-automated manner.

**Keywords:** Computer Vision · Machine Learning · Pothole · Pothole Detection

## 1 Introduction

The most frequent method of transportation in Honduras are vehicles, mainly particular vehicles and buses. In the capital, Tegucigalpa, most of the streets are paved with either asphalt pavement or hydraulic pavement. Asphalt pavement has an inherent property which is the formation of potholes. These potholes are formed mainly due to the weather conditions of the area and the amount of weight to which the material is exposed. An alternative to the problem of the formation of potholes that is not definitive, but if functional is the filling of

Supported by UNITEC.

potholes. Potholes generate discontent among the population in different ways, which is why repairing or covering potholes is essential. However, on many occasions there is a very slow response from the authorities due to the size of the city and this is why throughout this report we will seek to create a tool that facilitates the process of identification and location of potholes. This tool will have three fundamental stages; The first being the detection of potholes by means of an artificial intelligence and deep learning model so that the system can distinguish what is a pothole and what is not. This will be achieved by training the model fed with a database in which it will be shown what the potholes look like. The second part is based on assigning a geographic coordinate to each pothole that is detected, thus generating a list with all the potholes and their geographic locations. The final part will be the mapping of these points so that the user is able to see on a map where the potholes are located and then proceed to carry out the repair work. In this report, an introduction about artificial intelligence, computer vision, deep learning and how training and data capture work in an artificial intelligence system will first be presented. We will also proceed to talk about GPS systems and how you can obtain a coordinate through them. Finally, the proposed solution will be exposed and as it is, it will integrate everything previously proposed in order to carry out the detection and adequate mapping of potholes in the main streets of the city.

## 1.1 Objective

The intent of this project is to design and implement a semi-automated pothole detection and location system by means of artificial vision and geographic information systems on the main boulevards and the Peripheral Ring road in Tegucigalpa. To carry it out, it is necessary to separate the problem into different stages. The first stage will seek to build a database with images of potholes to be used as training for an artificial intelligence model. Artificial intelligence (AI) refers to systems or machines that mimic human intelligence to perform tasks and can iteratively improve based on the information they collect [6]. Once the database is created, it will help develop a system capable of recognizing potholes through video capture. This system will be in charge of making the detections and will be programmed in Python. In addition to this program, another system will be created capable of documenting the geographic coordinates corresponding to the potholes detected. This with the purpose of being able to store the coordinates to be able to use in the last stage which consists of using geographic positioning applications to map the points obtained on a map. Thus, finally, a map will be obtained in which the potholes in an area can be observed.

## 1.2    State of Art

There have been multiple research studies regarding the detection of potholes. These studies can be classified based on the technique used. According to [3], techniques used for pothole detection include manual techniques, vibration methods, 2D vision methods, 3D scene reconstruction, and learning methods.

In 2D vision methods, several authors have analyzed datasets of images to develop algorithms that can determine whether there is a pothole in the road. For example, PotSpot [15] developed an Android app that uses a convolutional neural network with an accuracy of 97.6% in detecting potholes. Other authors used a different approach for their learning models. Koch and Brilakis [10] used the geometric properties of a pothole in his implementation from 2011, analyzing images using morphological thinning and elliptic regression to extract the potential geometrical shape. His implementation achieved an 86% accuracy. [1] used image processing and spectral filtering and got an 81% accuracy. Ping Ping [16] tested four learning models and found that the Yolo V3 model with an accuracy of 82% worked best. [18] also used the Yolo V3 model and found that the Yolo V3 SPP model with an 88.93% accuracy was more accurate.

In a research from 2021, [9] used a convolutional neural network and an Inception V2 model were used to detect potholes with a mean average prediction of 86.41%. compared the Resnet 50, Inception V2, and VGG19 models and found that VGG19 delivered the best accuracy with 97% on highways and 98% on muddy roads.

Some other research studies used vibrations to detect potholes. In a paper by Mednis [12], an Android smartphone accelerometer was used, achieving a true positive rate of 90%.

In a review made by [3], several techniques for detecting potholes using 3D reconstruction were analyzed. For instance, [2,11] used 3D laser scanning, while [17] used stereo vision, and Jouber [8]and Moazzam [13] used a Kinect sensor.

## 2    Methodology

In this section, we will describe the methodology used to develop our pothole detection system, which consisted of three main components: an AI model capable of detecting potholes in real-time using a webcam, a GPS module to extract geographic coordinates of potholes, and a program to map the coordinates on the map. Additionally, we implemented a filtering program to eliminate false detections and ensure the accuracy of our system. In the following sections, we will provide a detailed description of each component and explain how they work together to create an effective pothole detection system.

### 2.1    AI Model

**Data Collection.** The AI model that was used in this system, was created using a dataset of 5,349 images. A portion of these images came from various datasets

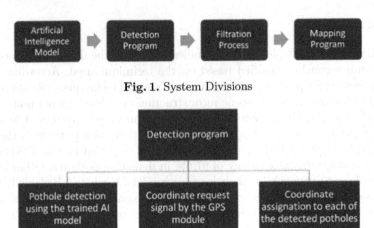

**Fig. 1.** System Divisions

**Fig. 2.** Screening Program Elements

found online. The other portion of these images was made up of pothole images that the authors captured on the streets of Tegucigalpa. Augmentation means is a series of techniques that are used to artificially increase the size of a dataset by creating new information from the information that is already available [4], and after applying the respective augmentations to these 5,349 images, the complete database happened to contain a total of 12,823 images.

**Training.** For this section we mainly used two programs to design and train the model: Roboflow and Google Colab as shown in Fig. 1. In this section we wanted to be able to obtain an AI model capable of distinguishing between what is and what is not a pothole (Fig. 2). These photos were separated into the three main data sets: validation, training, and test sets. Where the training set is used to train the model, the validation set is used to review or validate the training results and the test set consists of images totally foreign to the model to test the results of the training process [6]. Google Colab was then used to train our AI model. The technique used to train our AI model was adapted from a similar approach used in [7]. Here the images obtained from Roboflow were loaded along with the code with which the AI is trained and the model was trained until it reached a high confidence percentage. The AI model is evaluated according to its accuracy, sensitivity and mean average precision.

## 2.2 Filtration Program

Since each false detection would mean a wrong point on the map, it was considered necessary for the program to have a filtering system. In this way, an external user could be able to review each of the detections made by the system and eliminate false detections. Finally, a last program was executed which is responsible for generating the map with the filtered data.

## 2.3 Obtaining Geographical Coordinates

The aim of the second section of the project was to be able to obtain geographic coordinates. For this section, a "VK-162 G-Mouse USB GPS" module was necessary. This module connects via a USB cable to the computer. A code was used in Visual Studio Code which can send and storing the coordinates from the GPS periodically.

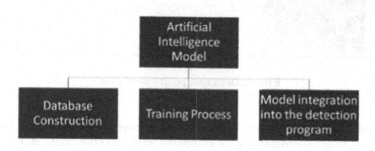

**Fig. 3.** Obtaining Geographical Coordinates

**Physical Assembly of Components and GPS Error.** The physical components are made up of a video camera, the GPS module and a laptop that would be where the data extracted by the previously mentioned instruments is collected and stored. In this case, both the video camera and the GPS module were placed on the hood of the car. This to provide the video camera with the best viewing conditions, so the model would be able to work in the best way possible. The GPS module was placed in front of the video camera, and the laptop was transported inside the car to be monitored by one of the authors.

Due to the position of the system components, there is another aspect that had to be considered. Due to the angle of the camera, it was possible to determine that the detection point of the camera was close to 2.36 m in front of the vehicle, as can be seen in Fig. 4. This calculation was possible by means of the following equation:

$$DetectionPoint = \frac{1\,m}{\tan 23} = 2.36\,m \tag{1}$$

This detection point would imply that at the time of detection the GPS is not exactly above the pothole being detected, which would imply an error value in the values extracted by the GPS. To corroborate the total error of the GPS, some potholes were chosen and the exact position of each one of them was

**Fig. 4.** Detection point calculation

confirmed. These potholes were selected for their easy identification and location. Then these exact coordinates were compared with the coordinate stored by the program, extracted by the GPS, and it was possible to determine that the total error of the GPS was a value close to 7.5 m.

### 2.4 Point Mapping

After analyzing all the options, it was concluded that a Python library would be used to map the points. We proceeded to create a code that was capable of mapping points on a city map to have a better view of the potholes using the data from an Excel file.

## 3    Results and Analysis

### 3.1    AI Model

To evaluate the model, several metrics were implemented. First accuracy, refering to the quality of the model's positive predictions, that is, the total number of true positives and true negatives divided by the total number of predictions [6].

Then, the mAP or mean average precision, takes the average of the precision averages for all the classes and is capable of presenting a single performance metric for the entire model [6]. The model was trained for a total of 200 epochs (Fig. 5) and it was able to reach a maximum mAP value of 85.867%, a maximum precision of 86.251% and a maximum sensitivity of 80.035%, below is the graph corresponding to the precision, the sensitivity and mAP during the training process.

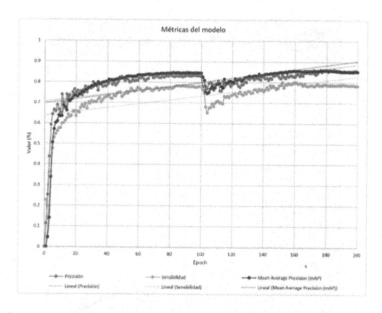

**Fig. 5.** Model metrics after 200 epochs

## 3.2 Data Generation

**Images.** After iterated testing, it was decided that the program should have a method to verify system detections. For this, the extraction of images by the system was implemented. The system was programmed so that the instant the model could make a detection and the program could count this detection, the program would take a snapshot and create an image of the object that the system was capable of counting. These images, after the program has been successfully executed, would be stored on the computer to be reviewed by the user to determine exactly what the system detected. Next, in Fig. 6 it is possible to appreciate the images captured at the time of detection.

**Video.** It was taken into account that it was necessary to take a video capture of the complete route during the tests in order to make the necessary corrections to the system. After the tests, it was decided to keep the video of the results in order to take control of the performance of the system and thus be able to analyze how the model behaved in real situations. This video, like the images, provides the user with a means to verify what the system has detected and thus confirm that the detections made are indeed potholes.

**Fig. 6.** Example of a successful detection

**Microsoft Excel Document.** After various tests, it was possible to determine that due to the way in which GPS works, it was not possible to run the detection program and the coordinates program within the same instance, so it was decided to separate them so that the program detection had more hardware freedom to work more efficiently. In this way, it was possible to extract the coordinates corresponding to each pothole detected and store them in an Excel document to later map the points.

### Limitations

1. GPS Operation: The operation of GPS depends on satellite devices around the earth. In order to deliver an exact coordinate, GPS uses a term called trilateration, which means that GPS modules work by measuring distances [5]. It was possible to determine that the GPS module has a latency equal to 1 s, which is the time window in which the GPS requests its current position and waits to receive this information. Due to this, the general program was subject to this latency, which limited the detection process, so it was decided to run the GPS program in a separate program and create a client-server type connection to be able to extract the coordinates of the potholes.

2. Erroneous Detections: Although the performance of the model was acceptable, it is not perfect. As noted in the model metrics, the accuracy value is not equivalent to 100%, which implies that the model incurs erroneous detections. One of the most common types of detections was the one corresponding to

asphalt patches. These erroneous detections accumulated to a considerable amount, which negatively affected the generated map, demonstrating erroneous information about the presence of potholes. Due to the repetition of these detections, it was necessary to create a manual filtering program, which eliminates the presence of patches on the map.

3. Hardware Limitations: The main hardware limitation found during the development of this project concerns the GPU included in the laptop used. Even though the laptop has a powerful enough GPU to run the program at an acceptable FPS value, it was concluded that with a more powerful GPU the model and the system as such could generate more detections and those of better quality. Another hardware limitation corresponds to the video camera to be used. Although the camera that was used is capable of recording at an adequate quality, it was possible to notice that the FPS at which the camera operates could limit the operation of the system.

### 3.3   Final Maps

The map was generated using a library included in Python called Folium. Figures 7 and 8 show the maps generated from the Los Hidalgos neighborhood to the ENEE headquarters in Tegucigalpa and along Fuerzas Armadas boulevard entering and exiting the peripherical ring road. This library allows the map to be automatically generated from the points provided after they have been filtered. It should be noted that the Excel document that is generated contains all the coordinates of all the detections that were counted and these same coordinates can be entered into other point mapping platforms, but in this case, it was decided to generate the maps automatically within from the same program. One of the most important aspects to highlight about the previous maps is the value they carry.

**Fig. 7.** Map generated from Los Hidalgos to the ENEE headquarters to In Tegucigalpa

As previously mentioned, there are other projects that have sought to develop a project similar to this one, with the difference that these projects have not been able to develop a map containing the position of these potholes. On this occasion it was possible not only to train a model capable of detecting potholes and making the respective count, but it was also possible to map each one of the potholes detected. In this way, the generated maps provide the necessary information to the authorities to make the appropriate decisions. In the same way, it is important to emphasize that the individual coordinates of each of the potholes are fully available for visualization within Excel for a deeper study with the possibility of mapping the points in third-party applications if the user wishes so.

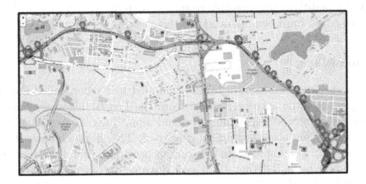

**Fig. 8.** Map Generated along the Boulevard Fuerzas Armadas

## 4    Conclusions

It was possible to carry out and implement a system that works through the use of artificial intelligence and deep learning which is capable of detecting nearby potholes and obtaining a geographic coordinate corresponding to each detected pothole so that unwanted data can be filtered later and generate a map where a representative point of each pothole has been observed. In addition to this, a database of 5,349 representative photos of potholes has been created, which was used to carry out training using Google Colab and from which, after 200 training epochs, a maximum mAP value of 85.867% has been obtained, a precision maximum of 86.251% and a maximum sensitivity of 80.035%. A program was developed which was able to read the training file in order to make real-time detections of potholes using a 720p video camera. The system worked using Python language, using Visual Studio Code as our compiler and Anaconda as our library manager. Using a GPS module, the coordinates of different detections along the route were extracted. These have been stored in an Excel file which has then been used as a basis for mapping the points. A special library has been used, called Folium, which works in Python language and allowed the mapping of the points. In addition to its potential applications in road maintenance and monitoring, this system could also be of great use in other contexts. For example, it could be used to validate road quality for vehicles in dry ports [19] or for mobile robots [14].

# References

1. Buza, E., Omanovic, S., Huseinovic, A.: Pothole detection with image processing and spectral clustering
2. Chang, K.T., Chang, J.R., Liu, J.K.: Detection of pavement distresses using 3D laser scanning technology, pp. 1–11. https://doi.org/10.1061/40794(179)103
3. Dhiman, A., Klette, R.: Pothole detection using computer vision and learning 21(8), 3536–3550. https://doi.org/10.1109/TITS.2019.2931297, Conference Name: IEEE Transactions on Intelligent Transportation Systems
4. van Dyk, D.A., Meng, X.L.: The art of data augmentation 10(1), 1–50. https://doi.org/10.1198/10618600152418584. Publisher: Taylor & Francis _eprint
5. El-Rabbany, A.: Introduction to GPS: the global positioning system. Artech House, google-Books-ID: U2JmghrrB8cC
6. Géron, A.: Hands-on machine learning with Scikit-Learn, Keras, and TensorFlow: concepts, tools, and techniques to build intelligent systems. O'Reilly Media Inc, second edition edn
7. Jimenez-Nixon, D.A., Corrales, J.F.M., Reyes-Duke, A.M.: Coral detection using artificial neural networks based on blurry images for reef protection in cayo blanco, honduras. In: 2022 IEEE International Conference on Machine Learning and Applied Network Technologies (ICMLANT), pp. 1–6. IEEE. https://doi.org/10.1109/ICMLANT56191.2022.9996481, https://ieeexplore.ieee.org/document/9996481/
8. Joubert, D., Tyatyantsi, A., Mphahlehle, J., Manchidi, V.: Pothole tagging system https://researchspace.csir.co.za/dspace/handle/10204/5384. Accepted: 2011-12-12T12:14:01Z
9. Gayathri, K., Thangavelu, S.: Novel deep learning model for vehicle and pothole detection 23(3), 1576. https://doi.org/10.11591/ijeecs.v23.i3.pp1576-1582, http://ijeecs.iaescore.com/index.php/IJEECS/article/view/25738
10. Koch, C., Brilakis, I.: Pothole detection in asphalt pavement images 25(3), 507–515. https://doi.org/10.1016/j.aei.2011.01.002, https://www.sciencedirect.com/science/article/pii/S1474034611000036
11. Li, Q., Yao, M., Yao, X., Xu, B.: A real-time 3D scanning system for pavement distortion inspection 21(1), 8, place: United Kingdom INIS Reference Number: 45005489
12. Mednis, A., Strazdins, G., Zviedris, R., Kanonirs, G., Selavo, L.: Real time pothole detection using android smartphones with accelerometers. In: 2011 International Conference on Distributed Computing in Sensor Systems and Workshops (DCOSS), pp. 1–6. https://doi.org/10.1109/DCOSS.2011.5982206, ISSN: 2325-2944
13. Moazzam, I., Kamal, K., Mathavan, S., Ahmed, S., Rahman, M.: Metrology and visualization of potholes using the Microsoft Kinect sensor. https://doi.org/10.1109/ITSC.2013.6728408

14. Ordonez-Avila, J.L., et al.: Study case: fabrication of a low-cost robotic mobile platform for logistic purposes. In: 2022 IEEE Central America and Panama Student Conference (CONESCAPAN), pp. 1–6. IEEE. https://doi.org/10.1109/CONESCAPAN56456.2022.9959686, https://ieeexplore.ieee.org/document/9959686/

15. Patra, S., Middya, A.I., Roy, S.: PotSpot: participatory sensing based monitoring system for pothole detection using deep learning. Multimedia Tools Appl. **80**(16), 25171–25195 (2021). https://doi.org/10.1007/s11042-021-10874-4

16. Ping, P., Yang, X., Gao, Z.: A deep learning approach for street pothole detection. In: 2020 IEEE Sixth International Conference on Big Data Computing Service and Applications (BigDataService), pp. 198–204. https://doi.org/10.1109/BigDataService49289.2020.00039

17. Staniek, M.: Stereo vision method application to road inspection **12**, 38–47. https://doi.org/10.3846/bjrbe.2017.05

18. Ukhwah, E.N., Yuniarno, E.M., Suprapto, Y.K.: Asphalt pavement pothole detection using deep learning method based on YOLO neural network. In: 2019 International Seminar on Intelligent Technology and Its Applications (ISITIA), pp. 35–40. https://doi.org/10.1109/ISITIA.2019.8937176

19. Vasquez, S., Perdomo, M.E., Dore, E.: Analysis of the installation of a dry port in Honduras, c.a. In: Proceedings of the 20th LACCEI International Multi-Conference for Engineering, Education and Technology: "Education, Research and Leadership in Post-pandemic Engineering: Resilient, Inclusive and Sustainable Actions". Latin American and Caribbean Consortium of Engineering Institutions. https://doi.org/10.18687/LACCEI2022.1.1.695, https://laccei.org/LACCEI2022-BocaRaton/meta/FP695.html

# Author Index

L. Iliadis et al. (Eds.): EANN 2023, CCIS 1826, pp. 619–621, 2023.
https://doi.org/10.1007/978-3-031-34204-2

Printed in the United States
by Baker & Taylor Publisher Services